T0211214

Expert Oracle
Application Express

■ ■ ■

John Scott, Nick Buytaert, Karen Cannell,
Martin D'Souza, Doug Gault, Dimitri Gielis,
Roel Hartman, Denes Kubicek, Raj Mattamal,
Dan McGhan, Francis Mignault, Tom Petrus,
Jorge Rimblas and Christoph Ruepprich

⟨IOUG⟩
Independent oracle users group

Apress®

Expert Oracle Application Express

Copyright © 2015 by John Scott, Nick Buytaert, Karen Cannell, Martin D'Souza, Doug Gault, Dimitri Gielis, Roel Hartman, Denes Kubicek, Raj Mattamal, Dan McGhan, Francis Mignault, Tom Petrus, Jorge Rimblas and Christoph Ruepprich

This work is subject to copyright. All rights are reserved by the Publisher, whether the whole or part of the material is concerned, specifically the rights of translation, reprinting, reuse of illustrations, recitation, broadcasting, reproduction on microfilms or in any other physical way, and transmission or information storage and retrieval, electronic adaptation, computer software, or by similar or dissimilar methodology now known or hereafter developed. Exempted from this legal reservation are brief excerpts in connection with reviews or scholarly analysis or material supplied specifically for the purpose of being entered and executed on a computer system, for exclusive use by the purchaser of the work. Duplication of this publication or parts thereof is permitted only under the provisions of the Copyright Law of the Publisher's location, in its current version, and permission for use must always be obtained from Springer. Permissions for use may be obtained through RightsLink at the Copyright Clearance Center. Violations are liable to prosecution under the respective Copyright Law.

ISBN-13 (pbk): 978-1-4842-0485-6

ISBN-13 (electronic): 978-1-4842-0484-9

Trademarked names, logos, and images may appear in this book. Rather than use a trademark symbol with every occurrence of a trademarked name, logo, or image we use the names, logos, and images only in an editorial fashion and to the benefit of the trademark owner, with no intention of infringement of the trademark.

The use in this publication of trade names, trademarks, service marks, and similar terms, even if they are not identified as such, is not to be taken as an expression of opinion as to whether or not they are subject to proprietary rights.

While the advice and information in this book are believed to be true and accurate at the date of publication, neither the authors nor the editors nor the publisher can accept any legal responsibility for any errors or omissions that may be made. The publisher makes no warranty, express or implied, with respect to the material contained herein.

Managing Director: Welmoed Spahr
Lead Editor: Jonathan Gennick
Development Editor: Douglas Pundick
Technical Reviewers: Patrick Cimolini, Vincent Morneau, and Alex Fatkulin
Editorial Board: Steve Anglin, Louise Corrigan, Jim DeWolf, Jonathan Gennick, Robert Hutchinson,
    Michelle Lowman, James Markham, Susan McDermott, Matthew Moodie, Jeffrey Pepper,
    Douglas Pundick, Ben Renow-Clarke, Gwenan Spearing, Steve Weiss
Coordinating Editor: Jill Balzano
Copy Editor: Kim Wimpsett
Compositor: SPi Global
Indexer: SPi Global
Artist: SPi Global
Cover Designer: Anna Ishchenko

Distributed to the book trade worldwide by Springer Science+Business Media New York, 233 Spring Street, 6th Floor, New York, NY 10013. Phone 1-800-SPRINGER, fax (201) 348-4505, e-mail orders-ny@springer-sbm.com, or visit www.springeronline.com. Apress Media, LLC is a California LLC and the sole member (owner) is Springer Science + Business Media Finance Inc (SSBM Finance Inc). SSBM Finance Inc is a Delaware corporation.

For information on translations, please e-mail rights@apress.com, or visit www.apress.com.

Apress and friends of ED books may be purchased in bulk for academic, corporate, or promotional use. eBook versions and licenses are also available for most titles. For more information, reference our Special Bulk Sales–eBook Licensing web page at www.apress.com/bulk-sales.

Any source code or other supplementary material referenced by the author in this text is available to readers at www.apress.com/9781484204856. For detailed information about how to locate your book's source code, go to www.apress.com/source-code/. Readers can also access source code at SpringerLink in the Supplementary Material section for each chapter.

This book is dedicated to Carl Backstrom and Scott Spadafore.
All author royalties will be donated equally to the charity trust funds of their respective families.

About IOUG Press

*IOUG Press is a joint effort by the **Independent Oracle Users Group (the IOUG)** and **Apress** to deliver some of the highest-quality content possible on Oracle Database and related topics. The IOUG is the world's leading, independent organization for professional users of Oracle products. Apress is a leading, independent technical publisher known for developing high-quality, no-fluff content for serious technology professionals. The IOUG and Apress have joined forces in IOUG Press to provide the best content and publishing opportunities to working professionals who use Oracle products.*

Our shared goals include:

- Developing content with excellence
- Helping working professionals to succeed
- Providing authoring and reviewing opportunities
- Networking and raising the profiles of authors and readers

To learn more about Apress, visit our website at **www.apress.com**. Follow the link for IOUG Press to see the great content that is now available on a wide range of topics that matter to those in Oracle's technology sphere.

Visit **www.ioug.org** to learn more about the Independent Oracle Users Group and its mission. Consider joining if you haven't already. Review the many benefits at www.ioug.org/join. Become a member. Get involved with peers. Boost your career.

www.ioug.org/join

Apress®

Contents at a Glance

Contents

Foreword

Over four years ago I had the idea for the first edition of this book, and the reason for the book was a deeply personal one: the Oracle APEX development team had sadly lost two members of the team, Carl Backstrom and Scott Spadafore. I knew both Carl and Scott and had met them a number of times at Oracle conferences over the years and corresponded with them frequently.

I was struck that both of these individuals had helped me over the years, and I wondered what I could do to help their families in some small way in return. I came up with the idea of writing a technical APEX book and donating all author royalties to their respective families.

To ensure the book was published and didn't just remain in my head as a "good idea," I came up with a plan. I approached a number of friends and fellow APEX experts and asked if they would consider writing a chapter. I have to say when I explained the purpose of the book to each of them, they all jumped at the chance.

Following the recent release of APEX 5, we once again decided it was time to update the book, again with all author royalties going to the same good causes. Once again I'm honored to know each of the chapter authors leapt at the opportunity. I thank each of them for agreeing to help update this book and continue helping, in our small way, the families of two people who helped us all over the years.

APEX 5 is the biggest release in the history of APEX, and the Oracle development team has done a tremendous job of making the APEX development environment a more productive, functional, and extensive development platform than ever before. We hope this book helps to show you why APEX 5 is second to none in terms of rapid web development backed by the security and functionality of the Oracle Database.

On a personal note, I would like to thank Jonathan Gennick and Jill Balzano of Apress for helping to shepherd us through the process of making the book a reality and supporting each of us in bringing our chapters to completion (which I can only imagine is like herding cats at times!).

—John Edward Scott

First-Edition Foreword

When I wrote my first book, *Pro Oracle Application Express*, in 2008 (with Scott Spendolini contributing a chapter on themes and templates), I found it an extremely rewarding experience. However, like a lot of first-time authors, I found it tough to fit writing into my regular day job and other commitments. *Pro Oracle Application Express* ended up taking a lot longer than originally anticipated and ran to almost twice as many pages as originally planned, mainly because of my passion for the subject matter—I kept wanting to give more and more information.

I was extremely happy to see that when *Pro Oracle Application Express* was released, it was a big success, at times ranking in the top 1,000 of all books sold on Amazon, which is quite an achievement for a technical book, let alone for a relatively niche area like Oracle Application Express. It was also the top-selling book at Oracle OpenWorld that year.

So I'd done it. I'd written my first book, something I always wanted to do, and it was (by relative standards) a great success. However, the questions soon started: "Hey, John, when are you writing another book?" Well, my reply was, "Never again!"

Are you surprised by that answer? Well, let me qualify it. I have such respect for people like Tom Kyte (who was kind enough to write the foreword to *Pro Oracle Application Express*) and my good friend, Steven Feuerstein, who write book after book, but I simply don't know how they manage to find the time to fit it into their schedules. Writing one book, while extremely rewarding once it was published, was at times one of the toughest things I've ever done. Sitting in front of a blank page at 4 a.m., trying to meet a publishing deadline, does not quite fit the glamorous image I had of being an author.

However, two events changed my opinion on writing another book. Those events were the deaths of my two good friends, Carl Backstrom and Scott Spadafore. Both Carl and Scott were longtime members of the Oracle Application Express development team, and I have lost count of the number of times both Carl and Scott have helped me in my time as a developer with Oracle Application Express. I also had the pleasure of meeting Carl and Scott in person many times during the various Oracle conferences we all attended over the years. One of my most vivid, happy memories during an Oracle conference was the day that Carl took Dimitri Gielis and myself for a tour around San Francisco during Oracle OpenWorld. One of my other vivid memories involves a deep discussion about the internals of APEX security with Scott Spadafore, sitting in a bar late in the evening, before Scott then turned the conversation to telling jokes.

With the sad and very unexpected passing of both Carl and Scott, I wanted to do something to help both families. Carl often spoke of his daughter, and I know that Scott was extremely proud of his family too. Following the success of my previous book, I felt that the best way I could do something to help would be to write another book where *all* of the author royalties were split between the charities of the two families.

Now since I already knew how much work is involved in writing a book, I came up with the idea of asking other people if they would be interested in writing a chapter. At the ODTUG Kaleidoscope event last year (2010), I approached my good friends, the authors whose names you see in this book, and asked each of them if they would be interested in writing a chapter. I asked every one of these people because they all knew Carl and Scott personally. I have the honor of saying that not one person hesitated to step up to the challenge of donating their time, experience, and knowledge to make this book happen. For that I am deeply grateful to all the authors (in alphabetical order): Anton, Dan, Denes, Dietmar, Dimitri, Doug, Francis, Martin, Mike, Raj, Roel, and Sharon. There were many times when it looked like this book might never make it to print; it was certainly a struggle to coordinate the book deadlines with the challenges of everyone's day jobs.

So, then, this book is dedicated to two people who were always so amazingly generous with their time and help, two people who were always held in the highest regard by the Oracle APEX community, and, most importantly, two people I had the honor calling friends.

—John Edward Scott
http://jes.blogs.shellprompt.net
www.apex-evangelists.com

I was fortunate enough to meet both Carl and Scott at the ODTUG Kaleidoscope conferences in 2008 and 2009, respectively. Carl was kind enough to spend some of his personal time answering all my questions and going through some of his examples with me. After writing about enhancing a security feature in APEX, Scott called me up right away to discuss it on a weekend. He was always very helpful, especially on the forums. Both Scott and Carl were great individuals who truly loved what they did and enjoyed passing along their wealth of knowledge to others. I'm honored to be able to contribute to this book in the same spirit that Scott and Carl engaged themselves within the Oracle community.

—Martin Giffy D'Souza
www.talkapex.com
www.clarifit.com

I had the distinct privilege of getting to know both Scott and Carl at many of the seminars and user groups they attended. Scott was scary smart with a dry and unforgiving sense of humor. His knowledge of the internal workings of APEX security was unmatched, and he shared the knowledge generously both in person and on the forums. Carl was quiet until you got to know him but a great guy and awesome JavaScript coder. In the early days, he personally helped me solve a few problems on how to integrate JavaScript into APEX, and his passion for APEX and JavaScript was apparent. When John Scott approached me with the idea of the book, I didn't hesitate and am honored to be able to be part of this tribute to two truly great men.

—Doug Gault

I first got in touch with Carl and Scott "virtually" on the Internet, through the APEX forum and the blogs. They were both extremely helpful to me and everybody in the APEX community.

I believe it was in 2007, at Oracle OpenWorld, that I met Carl and Scott personally for the first time. I guess my blog post (http://dgielis.blogspot.com/2007/11/oow07-day-1-sessions-apex-meetup.html) from that time says it all: "At the APEX demo grounds I met Scott Spadafore for the first time. 'He's the man!' some say, and I must confirm. Such a nice person, a great guy!"

I liked Scott very much, not only for his knowledge (especially in security) but even more for the person he was. And then Carl...I was truly shocked when I read about his car accident. Although we met in person only at the Oracle conferences, Carl became a real friend. I remember the many chats we had (in MSN). He was just a message away...I called him "Mister AJAX" because he was so strong in all the fancy web stuff. During conferences, we always met up.

When you were with Carl, there was always something happening. He had so many great stories. He liked to go out and have fun. I will never forget one Friday in San Francisco, just after OOW: Carl spent that day with John and me and showed us the coolest places in the city. He also took us to one of the best Chinese places in Chinatown and told us some great stories about his life. I remember Carl as an exceptional person—a great friend who was always willing to help others.

Scott, Carl, I feel honored to have known you both personally, and I am happy I could contribute to this book in your honor.

—Dimitri Gielis

The first time I met Carl in real life, it was during ODTUG's Kaleidoscope in New Orleans. I got the chance to show him a plan board with a drag-and-drop feature—all built in APEX, of course. He was truly impressed by what I'd done, saying "Did you truly build that in APEX?" He even convinced me to show it to the other APEX development team members.

One of the most striking things about Carl, apart from the fact he always did his utmost best to help everybody, was his fear of presenting. Although everybody recognized Carl as the leading expert, knowing way more than everyone else, he always was so nervous. But I guess that was one of his charms as well! I also remember, during that same event, Carl, John, and myself sitting at the bar, drinking some whiskey. And every glass poured contained a fly! So we talked about the never-ending fly whiskey for a long time (after a thorough inspection, the bottle itself appeared to contain a lot of flies).

Before I met Scott for real, we had some contact on the OTN Forum. All about security, of course, because that was Scott's main focus—but he also knew an awful lot of all other Oracle stuff! The thing I remember most is a night in Monterey during which the usual suspects of APEX people got together for some food and drinks. Scott was sitting next to Raj Mattamal, who is without any doubt the fastest speaker in the Oracle world. And with that they formed two opposites: Raj rambling on about whatever, and Scott just sitting there, most of the time silently. But every time Scott did say something it was either incredibly funny or so spot on, you couldn't imagine.

We owe a lot to these two great guys. APEX wouldn't be the great product it is today without them. They are missed a lot.

—Roel Hartman

As this book is an APEX one and nobody can deny Scott and Carl's unbelievable contributions to the community, I wanted to take this dedication moment to express that these guys were first and foremost amazing people. I had the pleasure of calling these guys my friends since the early APEX days (and before), and it's their unique personalities that I'll never forget. Not a week goes by that I'm not reminded of a joke from Scott (even the bad ones) or a story from Carl —and I'm forever grateful for that. That the community could come together to put such a book as this together in tribute to them is surely a testament to their impact, but it's critically important to me that people know what great guys they were as regular people.

—Raj Mattamal
http://nianticsystems.com

Unfortunately, I never had the opportunity to meet Scott, but a quick look at the APEX forum's "Top Users in Forum" list speaks volumes about the kind of guy he was—and his name will deservedly remain there for a long time to come. The number of people that Scott was able to help, myself included, is truly impressive and inspirational.

When it came to being helpful and inspirational, Carl was very much the same kind of guy that Scott was, and I'm very grateful to have met him. He was incredibly influential in my development career, having helped me along while I learned the basics of client-side development. He even introduced me to jQuery!

I find it especially rewarding to have been asked to write a chapter on plug-ins in APEX—a topic that often involves lots of JavaScript. To me it's proof positive that people like Carl and Scott live on in those they helped and mentored. I will always strive to have the same impact on others as they had on me.

—Dan McGhan

The first time I met Scott was at my first OpenWorld in 2007. In fact, he was the first member of the APEX development team that I've had the pleasure to meet. I remember that he introduced himself and that he recognized me from the forum. He seemed happy to see me, and I immediately felt part of the community. During the same conference, I also had the chance to meet Carl and the rest of the team. They both were always available to answer questions and propose solutions. They took notes of our suggestions, and the next thing we knew they were included in the next APEX release. I have been using Oracle products for more than 20 years, and have never seen a product team as close to their users. And that is in large part because of Scott and Carl. I am honored to contribute to this project in memory of two great colleagues and friends, and I would like to thank John for giving me the opportunity to pay tribute to them.

—Francis Mignault
http://insum-apex.blogspot.com
www.insum.ca

Pictured left-to-right: John Scott, Carl Backstrom, and Dimitri Gielis at IOUG Collaborate event 2007

Scott Spadafore (standing) deep in discussion with John Scott

About the Authors

John Scott has been using Oracle since version 7 (around 1993) and has used pretty much every release since then. He has had the good fortune to work on a wide range of projects for a varied group of clients. He was lucky enough to start working with Oracle Application Express when it was first publicly released and has worked with it nearly every day since (and loves it). John is an Oracle ACE Director and was named Application Express Developer of the Year in 2006 by Oracle Magazine. He is also the cofounder of ApexEvangelists (Apex-Evangelists.com), a company that specializes in providing training, development, and consulting specifically for the Oracle Application Express product. You can contact John at john.scott@apex-evangelists.com.

Nick Buytaert is an Oracle Certified Professional (OCP) with a bachelor's degree in applied computer science (2011). He works for a Belgian consulting firm called Contribute, which assists a wide variety of organizations in making the most of their Oracle technology stacks. Nick started his career working as an E-Business Suite consultant and then went on to specialize in APEX development. In April 2013, he became an Oracle Application Express Developer Certified Expert.

Nick furthermore participates actively in the APEX community by publishing technical articles on his blog APEXPLAINED (http://apexplained.wordpress.com). He also initiated and maintains several open source projects, such as the Oracle APEX Maven plugin and a series of APEX plugins. Nick occasionally engages in public speaking activities to share his ideas and experiences with the outside world. You can follow Nick on Twitter @nbuytaert1 to find out more about him.

Karen Cannell is president of TH Technology, a small consulting firm providing Oracle technology services, focusing on Application Express. A mechanical engineer by degree (one of them), she has analyzed, designed, developed, converted, upgraded, enhanced, and otherwise worked on legacy and commercial database applications for more than 25 years, concentrating on Oracle technologies since 1994. She has worked with Application Express since its Web DB and HTML DB beginnings and continues to leverage the Oracle suite of tools to build quality web applications for clients in government, medical, and engineering industries. Karen can be contacted at kcannell@thtechnology.com.

Martin D'Souza is cofounder and CTO at ClariFit, a consulting firm and custom solutions provider specializing in APEX and PL/SQL development. His experience in the technology industry has been focused on developing database-centric web applications using the Oracle APEX technology stack.

In addition to his day job, Martin is the author of the popular blog www.TalkApex.com. He is also a designated Oracle ACE Director and has coauthored and authored various APEX books. He has presented at numerous international conferences such as APEXposed, COUG, and ODTUG Kscope, for which he won the Presenter of the Year award in 2011.

Martin has a computer engineering degree from Queen's University in Kingston, Ontario, Canada. You can contact Martin at martin@clarifit.com.

Doug Gault is the APEX practice director at Enkitec, an Oracle Platinum partner founded in 2004, which provides consulting, education, and products based around Oracle technology. He has been working with Oracle since 1988, starting with version 5.1B, SQL*Forms 2.0, and RPT/RPF. He has focused his career on Oracle's development technologies, spending the majority of that time dedicated to web-based technologies including the OWA Web Toolkit, PL/SQL Server Pages, WebDB, Oracle Portal, and more recently HTML-DB and APEX. Doug's many years of Oracle experience have taken him all over the world to participate in some truly groundbreaking projects. Doug has presented at and participated in roundtable discussions at a number of conferences including Oracle OpenWorld, UKOUG, and ODTUG's APEXposed and Kaleidoscope conferences. He has an associate's degree in computer science and an honorary master's degree from The School of Hard Knocks, believing there is no replacement for hard-earned experience. Doug is an Oracle Ace and can be found on Twitter as @dgault_apex and on his blog at http://douggault.blogspot.com. You can contact Doug at doug.gault@enkitec.com.

Dimitri Gielis has been working with Oracle Database since he began his career in 2000 with Oracle in Belgium. Dimitri was an early adopter and supporter of HTML DB and later of Application Express. After many years of honing his expertise with Oracle Database and Application Express, Dimitri cofounded APEX Evangelists in 2007. In 2014 Dimitri set up APEX R&D (https://www.apexrnd.be), a company that focuses on web application development and creating innovative solutions with Oracle Application Express. The company also provides on-demand coaching and training in APEX. Dimitri is an active member of the Application Express community. He routinely posts insights into Application Express on his blog at http://dgielis.blogspot.com. He is a frequent presenter at the Oracle Benelux User Group (OBUG), IOUG collaborate, ODTUG Kaleidoscope, the UKOUG conference, and Oracle OpenWorld. Dimitri has been an Oracle ACE Director since 2008. He received the APEX Developer of the Year award from Oracle Magazine in 2009.

Roel Hartman has been using Oracle Database since version 5. At that time, he used Oracle Case*Designer, Oracle Forms 2.3, and other tools of the day. He has used all versions of those tools as they have evolved during the years since, giving him great depth of experience as an Oracle Database developer. Today he is a fierce advocate and user of Oracle Application Express. Roel has a master's degree in business informatics from the University of Twente in the Netherlands. He is an Oracle ACE Director. He works for Logica in the Netherlands as a lead technical architect. Roel has presented at all major Oracle conferences, such as ODTUG, Oracle OpenWorld, and UKOUG. He is a regular contributor to the OakTable Network APEX Forum.

Denes Kubicek is the chief executive officer and founder of bi-Cubes. He has been working with Oracle for more than 12 years. Denes is an Oracle ACE Director and was APEX Developer of the Year in 2008. Denes is also a coauthor of the first APEX book in German, *Oracle APEX und Oracle XE in der Praxis*. You can reach him at bi-Cubes.com.

Raj Mattamal is copresident of Niantic Systems, LLC (NianticSystems.com). He started developing web applications at Oracle in 1995 with the same people who came to create Oracle Application Express. In his more than ten years with the company, he helped customers in a wide range of industries to deliver web-based solutions on the Oracle Database. In addition to helping customers with their applications, Raj developed numerous web applications for use internally at Oracle. Outside of database application development, Raj spent much remaining time with Oracle evangelizing Oracle Application Express. This entailed teaching Oracle software development and APEX classes globally, writing articles for Oracle Magazine, writing Technotes for the Oracle Technology Network, and assisting with the development of training material and workshops.

Having earned a bachelor's degree in decision and information studies and another in marketing from the University of Maryland, Raj continues to apply his knowledge of and passion for technology and business to real-world issues. Since leaving Oracle in 2006, Raj offers his services and training to customers in a wide range of business lines to help them get the most out of their Oracle environments. In recent years, Raj has been recognized by his Oracle professional colleagues as an Oracle ACE Director, an honor, indeed, to be earned among so many knowledgeable colleagues.

Dan McGhan is a senior technical consultant with the Accenture Enkitec Group. He suffers from compulsive programing disorder, which is believed to be linked to his balding. Having started his development career in the land of MySQL and PHP, he was only too happy to have stumbled upon APEX. Since then he's dedicated his programming efforts to learning more about Oracle and web-based technologies in general. Dan is an Oracle Application Express Certified Expert, an Oracle PL/SQL Developer Certified Associate, and an Oracle

ACE. In addition to his "day job," he is one of the top contributors to the APEX forum, maintains his own Oracle and APEX blog (`www.danielmcghan.us`), and is a regular presenter at various events and user group meetings.

Francis Mignault is chief technology officer and cofounder of Insum Solutions. He has been working with Oracle Database for more than 23 years and is a certified Oracle database administrator. Francis began his work with APEX in 2004, when it was called HTML DB. He and his team have developed bilingual software as a service application that is now used by more than 60,000 active users. Francis is deeply involved in the APEX community. His first-rate PL/SQL and APEX expertise led to becoming the first APEX instructor in Quebec. He has presented at several APEX seminars and conferences in the United States and Canada, including Oracle OpenWorld, IOUG Collaborate, ODTUG Apexposed, ODTUG Kaleidoscope, and Ora*GEC.

Tom Petrus started out as an in-house Oracle Forms developer in 2007 and made the switch to Oracle Application Express in 2011 as a consultant. Since then he has had a wide range of projects and clients by which he has honed his knowledge on Apex. He has a preference for everything JavaScript related and is active on both StackOverflow and the OTN Apex forum, helping others solve problems and picking up new nuggets of knowledge in the process. He currently works as a consultant for iAdvise Belgium.

Jorge Rimblas is a senior technical consultant with the Accenture Enkitec Group and has been an Oracle Database professional since 1995. He started using APEX when it was known as HTML DB, starting with version 1.6. Since 2008, APEX is all he does. His areas of expertise include Oracle Application Express, Oracle e-Business Suite, Oracle Database, and related products. Jorge has helped several companies, in diverse industries, implement custom themes for their applications. His knowledge and experience with UI design, web technologies, and Adobe Photoshop uniquely position him to excel at this kind of work. He has taught APEX to dozens of people and has been a speaker at the RMOUG Training Days and ODTUG KScope conferences. Jorge is an Oracle ACE and can be found on Twitter as `@rimblas` and on his blog at `http://rimblas.com/blog`.

Christoph Ruepprich has worked as an Oracle DBA and developer since 1999. As a developer, he has worked with Oracle Forms and Reports and has extensive experience with Oracle Application Express. In his current role as senior technical consultant at Accenture Enkitec Group, he works on various APEX projects. He is also an active presenter on APEX topics at conferences and maintains an Oracle-related blog at `http://ruepprich.wordpress.com`.

About the Technical Reviewers

Patrick Cimolini specializes in project management, development, and training services for Oracle Application Express projects. Formal training in engineering, business administration, and project management is complemented by more than 30 years of experience that has evolved through mainframe, client-server, and web platforms. Patrick enjoys attending and presenting at Oracle-centric conferences such as Kscope, Collaborate, APEXposed, and Oracle OpenWorld, all of which have contributed significantly to his professional and personal growth. Patrick is currently working at Insum Solutions in Montréal, Québec.

Alex Fatkulin is a master of the full range of Oracle technologies. This mastery has been essential in addressing some of the greatest challenges his customers have met.

Alex draws on years of experience working with some of the world's largest companies, where he was involved with almost everything related to Oracle databases, from data modeling to architecting high-availability solutions to resolving performance issues of extremely large production sites.

Alex has a bachelor's of computer science degree from Far Eastern National University in Vladivostok, Russia. He is also an Oracle ACE and a proud OakTable member.

Vincent Morneau is a developer, blogger, and speaker. He has been working with APEX for more than five years in the world's largest APEX development team at Insum Solutions. His focus has recently shifted to the front-end aspect of development, where he shares his vision throughout Twitter at @vincentmorneau and his blog at `http://vmorneau.me`.

Vincent is also a big fan of open source coding, and he systematically shares any piece of code that he finds valuable on his GitHub account at `https://github.com/vincentmorneau`.

He is on his way to earning a bachelor's degree in software engineering by the end of 2015 and will finally be able to dedicate more time to the APEX community.

CHAPTER 1

■■■

Page Designer

by Denes Kubicek

The Page Designer in APEX 5.0 is one of the main new features and a major improvement for APEX developers. It changes the way you build your application pages and also the way you think about application development. It is also close to what you probably know from Oracle Forms. The Page Designer provides these new features:

- Drag-and-drop functionality
- Tree view and context menus
- Seamless adjustment of the Component View and Property Editor panels

Main Components

The Page Designer has four main components (Figure 1-1).

- Navigation toolbar
- Component View on the left side of the screen
- Grid Layout for drag-and-drop functionality in the middle
- Property Editor on the right side of the screen

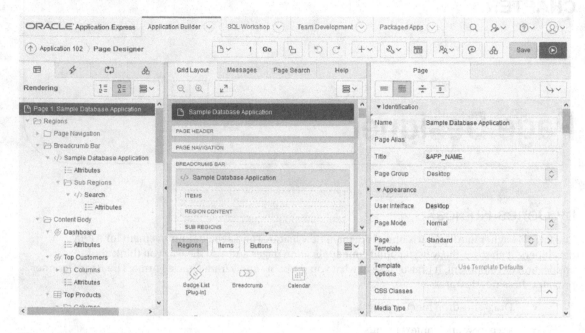

Figure 1-1. *Page Designer components*

Navigation

The navigation toolbar has lots of new options compared to previous versions of APEX. Some of them have been reworked, and their functionality is now different. Also, there are some new options that I will describe in detail.

Page Finder Icon

The Page Finder icon works differently compared to the old one. It will lead you to a page you type in directly or will open a modal window if you click the pop-up list of values (see Figure 1-2 and Figure 1-3).

Figure 1-2. *Page Finder icon*

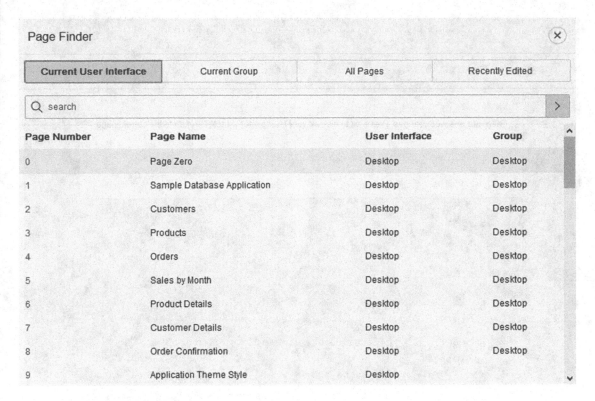

Figure 1-3. Page Finder list of pages

The Page Finder will also show a warning via a pop-up if you are leaving a page with unsaved changes (Figure 1-4).

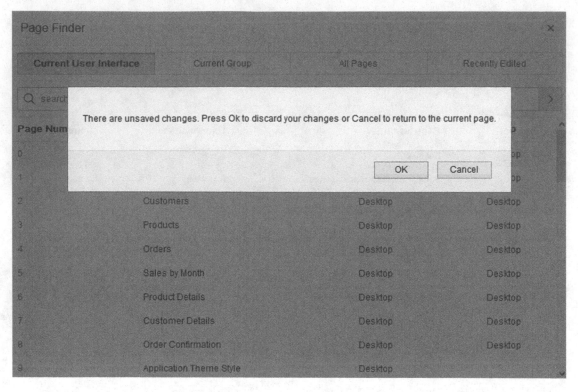

Figure 1-4. Page Finder unsaved changes prompt

One of the things missing in the navigation within the Page Finder is the old feature to go to the previous or next page. Even if you want to go to the previous or next page, you will be forced to do a couple of clicks to open the modal window and then search for the page number in the list.

Lock Pages and Undo and Redo Icons

The icon for locking pages (Figure 1-5) has the same functionality as it had before. The Redo and Undo icons allow you to undo and redo the unsaved changes similar to what you know from other programs (such as Microsoft Office). This feature is useful, but it works only for unsaved changes.

Figure 1-5. Icon for locking pages and the Undo and Redo icons

Create, Utilities, and Component View Icons

This section will cover the main set of icons in the Page Designer. You will use these icons frequently.

Create Icon

The icon for Create (Figure 1-6 and 1-7) offers a couple of options.

- Create a page
- Create a page as a copy of an existing page
- Wizards to create different complex page components such as forms and reports
- Access to the shared components
- Access to the page group
- Access to the Team Development features
- Add comments to the application

Figure 1-6. *Create, Utilities, and Component View icons*

Figure 1-7. *Create menu items*

When you click to create a Form or Report region, you will see the corresponding wizard as a modal dialog (Figure 1-8).

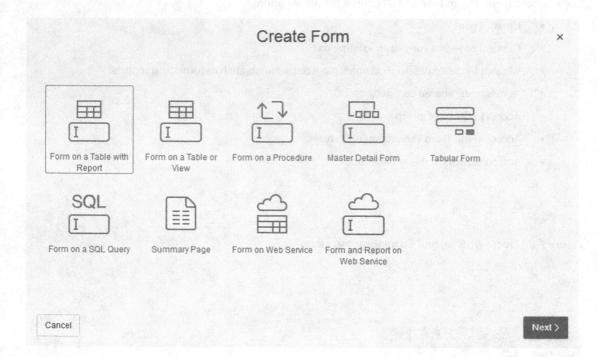

Figure 1-8. *Create Form Wizard*

Utilities Icon

The icon for Utilities (Figure 1-6 and 1-9) offers lots of options.

- Delete a page
- Create a page as a copy of an existing page
- Access the Caching, Attribute Dictionary, History, and Export options
- Access the Cross Page Utilities, Application Utilities, and Page Groups options
- Access the Upgrade Application option

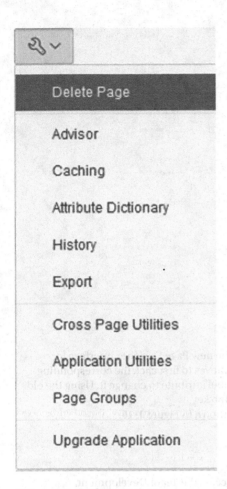

Figure 1-9. *Utilities options*

Component View Icon

The icon for the Component View (Figure 1-6 and Figure 1-10) shows the old HTML view of the Page Designer. This view option could be useful in these cases:

- When making mass changes of column names in a classic report
- When making mass changes of column names in an interactive report
- When making mass changes of item labels in a form region

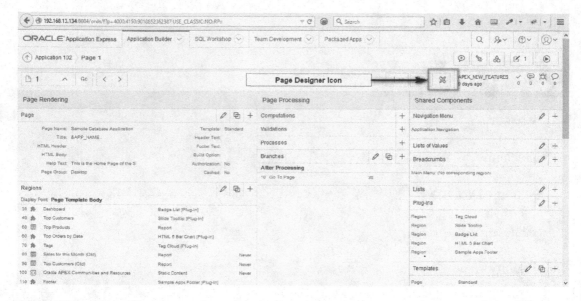

Figure 1-10. *Old HTML Page Designer layout*

The reason is for the old view's sefuleness is simple. If you use the new Page Designer interface for the purposes just listed, you will have to do lots of clicks and mouse moves to first click the corresponding column on the left side tree menu and then move the cursor to the label attribute to change it. Using the old view, it is possible to move faster from column to column using the Tab key.

You can always switch back to the new interface using the icon shown in Figure 1-10.

Other Navigation Bar Icons

The other icons on the navigation toolbar (Figure 1-11) are used to access the Team Development, Developer Comments, and Shared Components features.

Figure 1-11. *Other navigation toolbar icons*

Team Development Icon

Using this icon, you can access Team Development features.

Developer Comments Icon

Using this icon, you create a developer comment, add a bug, or add a to-do task.

Shared Components Icon

Using this icon, you can access application shared components.

Save and Save and Run Application Icons

The next set of icons is used to save the changes or save and run the application.

Save Icon

The Save icon will save the outstanding changes for the corresponding page.

Save and Run Icon

The Save icon will save the outstanding changes for the corresponding page and run the application in a new tab.

In earlier versions of APEX, you could run the application by right-clicking and opening the application in a new tab or in a new window. In APEX 5.0, this has changed; there is no right-click option anymore. The button is an image running JavaScript. The consequence is that the behavior will be different depending on the browser used and your browser settings. To see how to optimize the settings for Firefox, refer to this blog posting:

www.deneskubicek.blogspot.de/2015/06/apex-50-run-applications-in-new-tabs.html

Component View

The Component View has four tabs.

- Rendering
- Dynamic Actions
- Processing
- Page Shared Components

Rendering

The Rendering tab (Figure 1-12) lists all the components of the page grouped by either component type or processing order. Here, you can access all page regions, items, buttons, and processes (computations, processes, and branches) executed during page rendering. Also, the tree view will show all the dynamic actions or computations attached to one of the page components.

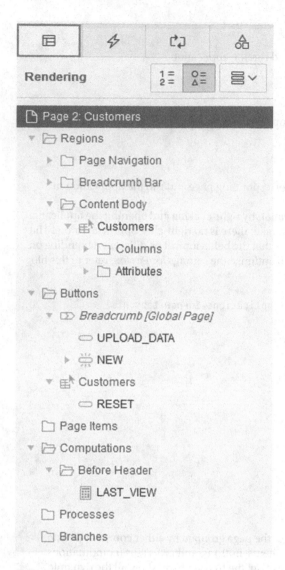

Figure 1-12. Component View: Rendering tab

Dynamic Actions

On the Dynamic Actions tab (Figure 1-13), you will find a list of all the dynamic actions used on that page. This is a useful new feature because of the growing number of dynamic actions. Now these components are shown and accessed separately, and this helps you keep an overview of it all.

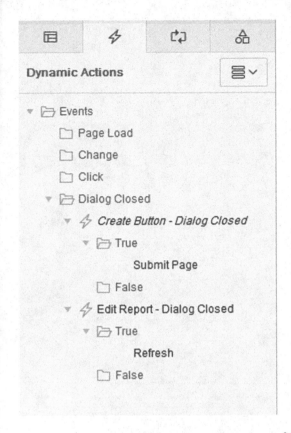

Figure 1-13. *Component View: Dynamic Actions tab*

Processing

The Processing tab (Figure 1-14) shows a list of the processes run on page submit. This includes the following:

- Validations
- Computations
- Page processes
- Branches

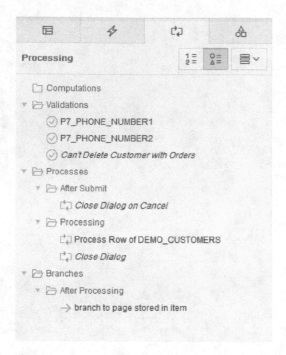

Figure 1-14. *Component View: Processing tab*

Page Shared Components

The Page Shared Components tab (Figure 1-15) shows a list of the shared components used on the corresponding page.

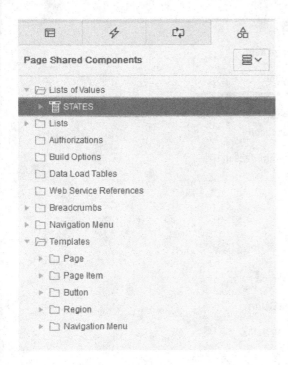

Figure 1-15. *Component View: Page Shared Components tab*

The Component View is a tree and provides a couple of useful features.

- Drag-and-drop functionality
- Context menu options

Using drag and drop, you can change the order sequence of the page elements and processes. Using the context menu options (Figure 1-16), you can easily access all the relevant component options.

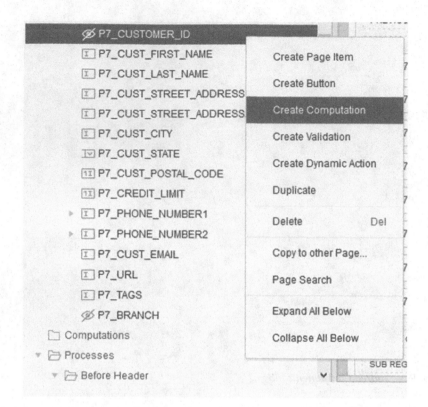

Figure 1-16. *Component View: context menu options*

Grid Layout

The Grid Layout also has different tabs.

- Grid Layout
- Messages
- Page Search
- Help

Grid Layout

Grid Layout (Figure 1-17) provides drag-and-drop functionality of components that can be selected from the Gallery menu and also allows you to reorder those components.

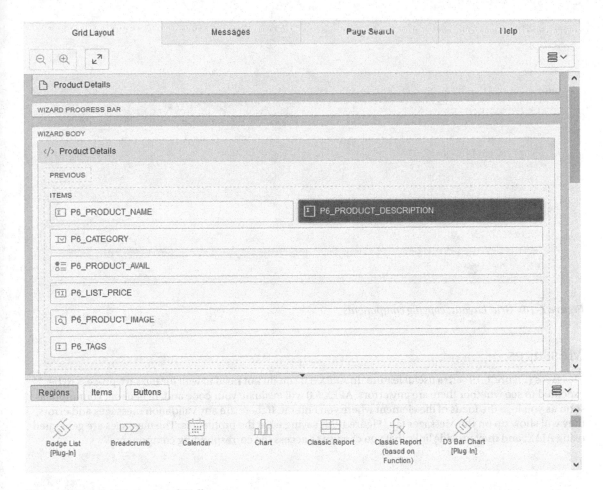

Figure 1-17. *Grid Layout and Gallery menu*

Using the Grid Layout tab, you can reorder all page elements in order to get a desired layout of the page. You can reorder the following elements:

- Items

- Regions

- Buttons

Using Grid Layout, you can also copy and move the copied elements. This can be achieved by selecting an element and pressing Ctrl on the keyboard (Figure 1-18). Once you get to the position where the copied element needs to be placed, you just release the Ctrl key and the mouse button. The element will be copied under a new name.

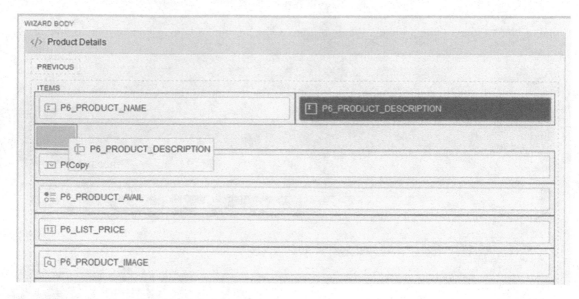

Figure 1-18. *Grid Layout: copying components*

Messages

Messages (Figure 1-19) are a useful feature. In APEX 5.0 you do not need to wait for the save process to be executed to see whether there are any errors. APEX 5.0 will evaluate your code and, in general, your input as soon as you lose the focus of the element where you enter it. If there are any validation messages and errors, they will show up on the Messages tab (Figure 1-20) saying what the problem is. The messages are generated using AJAX, and they provide links that you can use to access the corresponding component.

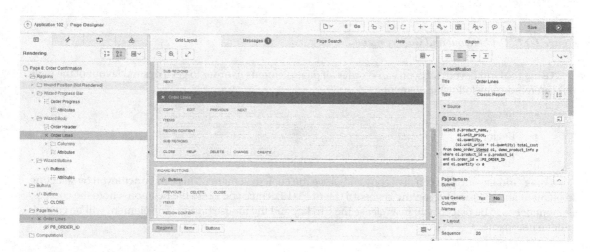

Figure 1-19. *Messages: highlighting*

Figure 1-20. *Messages: content*

If there are errors in your code or input, not only will the message show up, but all relevant parts of the page structure will be highlighted.

- Component View

- Grid Layout

- Element Properties

Clicking the message text will take you to the affected element property on the right side of the screen showing again the error in a separate widget (Figure 1-21).

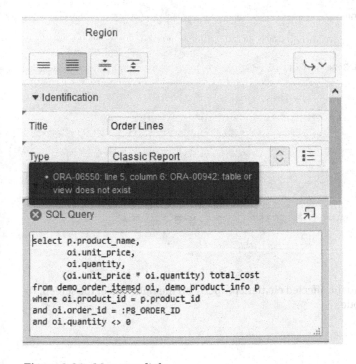

Figure 1-21. *Messages: link*

Page Search

The Page Search tab (Figure 1-22) works based on AJAX as well. You have two options and can search based on one of the following:

- Match case

- Regular expression

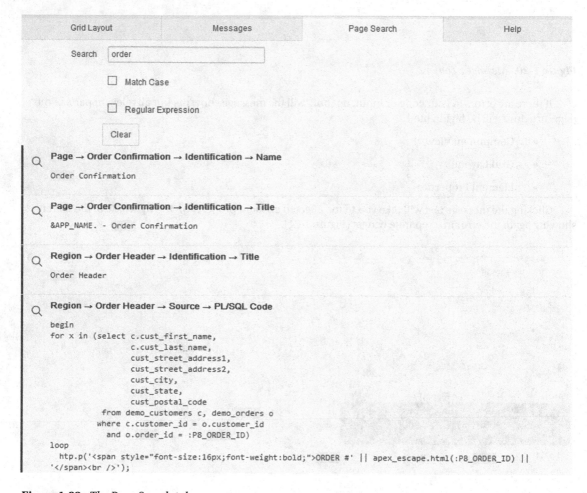

Figure 1-22. *The Page Search tab*

Clicking the search result will take you to the affected element property on the right side of the screen, and it will highlight the Component View node.

Help

The Help tab (Figure 1-23) provides instant help for the Property Editor on the right side of the screen. The help default says this:

> *"Select a component and then select an attribute in the Property Editor to display help on that attribute."*

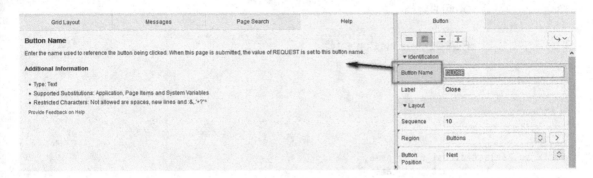

Figure 1-23. *Help*

Clicking any of the options available in the Property Editor will result in showing the corresponding help text.

Property Editor

The Property Editor in Figure 1-24 shows instantly the properties of a selected component. The Property Editor has four buttons for the view options.

- Show Common
- Show All
- Collapse All
- Expand All

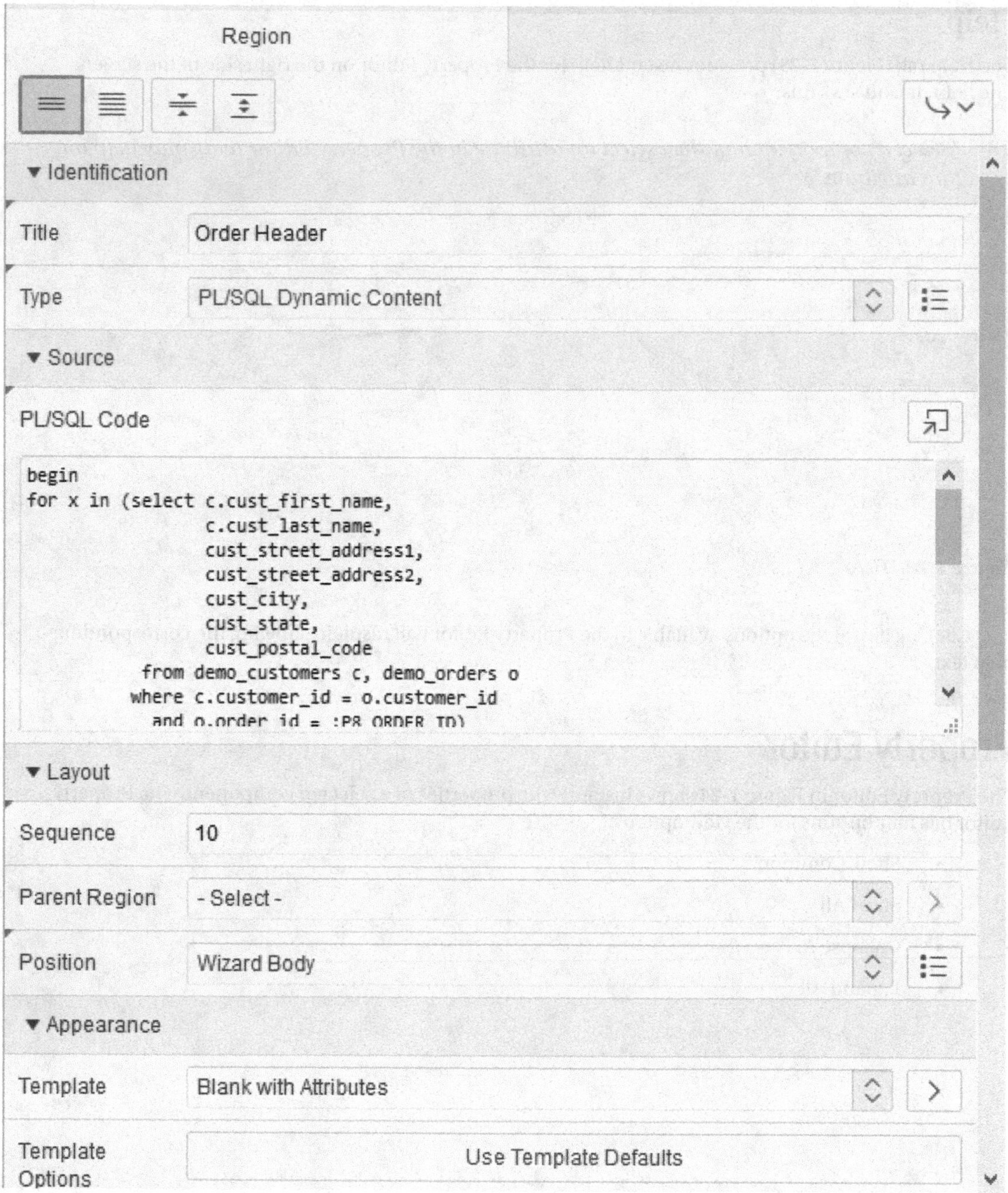

Figure 1-24. *Property Editor*

Show Common

Clicking the Show Common button (Figure 1-25) lists the most common component properties. Depending on the component you select, it will hide certain options.

Figure 1-25. *Show Common button*

Show All

Clicking the Show All button (Figure 1-26) lists all component properties. Depending on the component you select, it will hide or show certain options compared to the other types of component.

Figure 1-26. *Show All button*

Collapse All

Clicking the Collapse All button (Figure 1-27) collapses all Property Editor components and shows titles only. This feature is useful when the list of properties is long and you want to avoid scrolling.

Figure 1-27. *Collapse All button*

Show All

Clicking the Show All button (Figure 1-28) shows all available properties for the selected element.

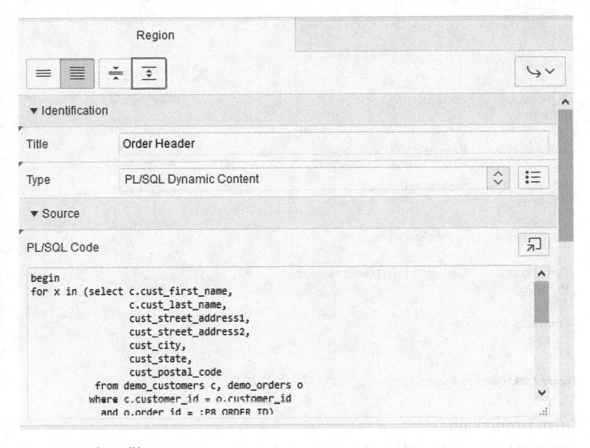

Figure 1-28. *Show All button*

Quick Pick, Go to Group, and Go to Component Icons

There are three new icons in the Property Editor:

- Quick Pick
- Go to Group
- Go to Component

Quick Pick Icon

Clicking the Quick Pick icon will show a list menu of the available options, as shown in Figure 1-29.

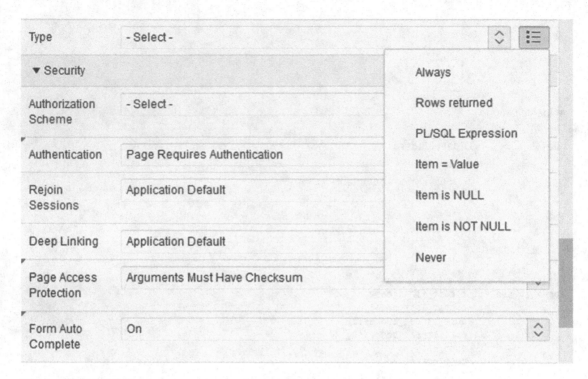

Figure 1-29. *Quick Pick icon*

Go to Group Icon

Clicking the Go to Group icon will have the same result as the Collapse All button; it lists the property titles for each property group. See Figure 1-30 for an example.

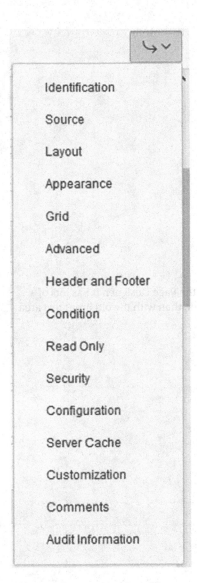

Figure 1-30. *Quick Pick icon*

Go to Component Icon

Clicking the Go to Component icon will lead you to the shared component used, as shown in Figure 1-31. Once you make a change to the selected shared component, you will be forwarded to the property you came from.

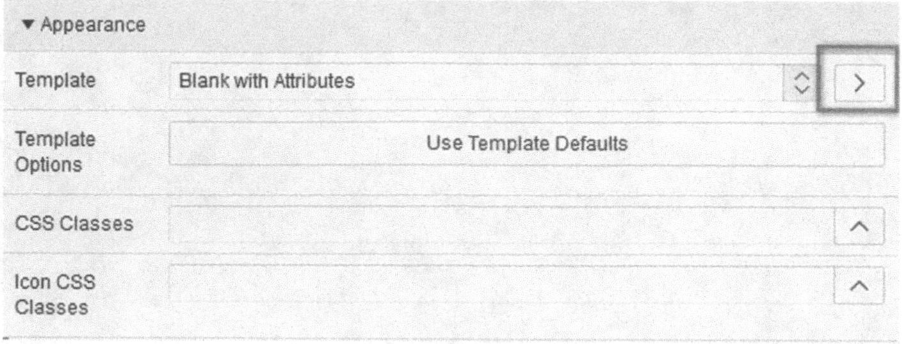

▼ Appearance

Template	Blank with Attributes
Template Options	Use Template Defaults
CSS Classes	
Icon CSS Classes	

Figure 1-31. *Go to Component icon*

Code Editor

The new Code Editor (Figure 1-32) in APEX 5.0 is one of the highlights of the Page Designer. It has lots of options for setting it up and provides a far better way to maintain your code than with the old input text area in older releases.

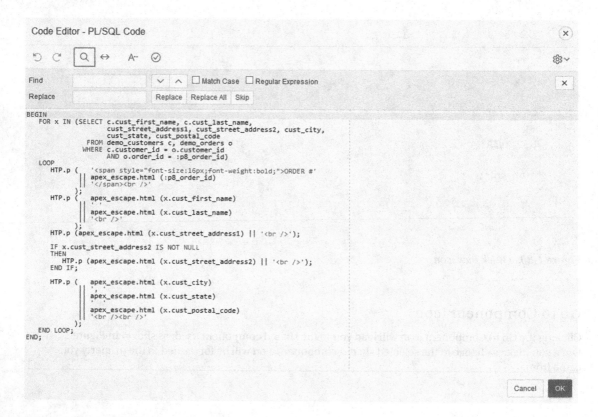

Figure 1-32. *Code Editor*

You can access the Code Editor by clicking the icon (Figure 1-33) for each property that has a code option.

Figure 1-33. *Code Editor icon*

The Code Editor has a few useful options that are shown in Figure 1-34:

- Code highlighting according to the code type of the particular property (PL/SQL, SQL, JavaScript, jQuery, CSS) and the selected template

- Tab-size option

- Indent option

- Selection of different themes for the Code Editor layout

- Line Numbers and Ruler options

- Search and Replace options

- Access to the Query Builder

- Autocomplete options

- Undo and Redo options

- Inline code validation

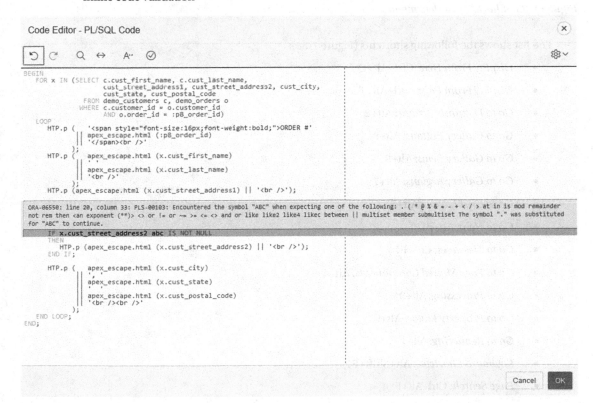

Figure 1-34. *Code Editor showing code and syntax highlighting*

27

Shortcuts

As of APEX 5.0, you can use shortcuts to move within the Page Designer. You can find the list of available shortcuts in the Page Designer's Help menu (Figure 1-35) or by pressing the keyboard combination Alt+Shift+F1.

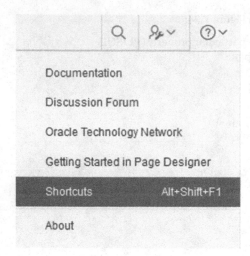

Figure 1-35. *Shortcuts in Help menu*

The list shows the following shortcuts (Figure 1-36):

- *Display From Here*: Ctrl+Alt+D

- *Display From Page*: Ctrl+Alt+T

- *Go to Dynamic Actions*: Alt+2

- *Go to Gallery Buttons*: Alt+9

- *Go to Gallery Items*: Alt+8

- *Go to Gallery Regions*: Alt+7

- *Go to Grid Layout*: Alt+5

- *Go to Help*: Alt+F1

- *Go to Messages*: Ctrl+F1

- *Go to Page Shared Components*: Alt+4

- *Go to Processing*: Alt+3

- *Go to Property Editor*: Alt+6

- *Go to Rendering*: Alt+1

- *Keyboard Shortcuts*: Alt+Shift+F1

- *Page Search*: Ctrl+Alt+F

- *Redo*: Ctrl+Y

- *Restore/Expand*: Alt+F11

- *Save*: Ctrl+Alt+S

- *Save and Run Page*: Ctrl+Alt+R

- *Toggle Hide Empty Positions*: Ctrl+Alt+E

- *Undo*: Ctrl+Z

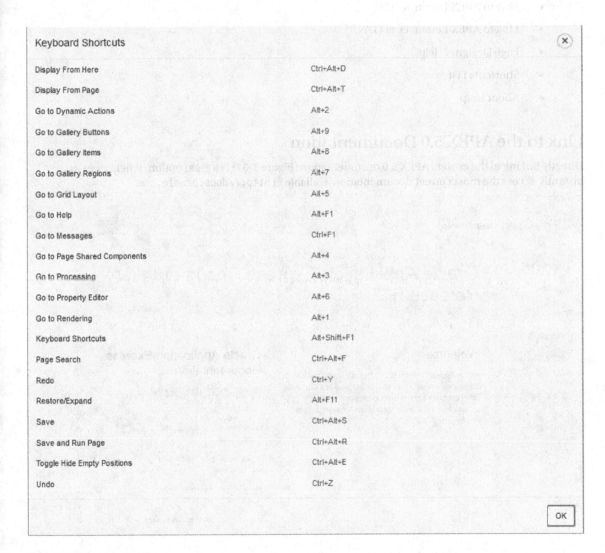

Keyboard Shortcuts	
Display From Here	Ctrl+Alt+D
Display From Page	Ctrl+Alt+T
Go to Dynamic Actions	Alt+2
Go to Gallery Buttons	Alt+9
Go to Gallery Items	Alt+8
Go to Gallery Regions	Alt+7
Go to Grid Layout	Alt+5
Go to Help	Alt+F1
Go to Messages	Ctrl+F1
Go to Page Shared Components	Alt+4
Go to Processing	Alt+3
Go to Property Editor	Alt+6
Go to Rendering	Alt+1
Keyboard Shortcuts	Alt+Shift+F1
Page Search	Ctrl+Alt+F
Redo	Ctrl+Y
Restore/Expand	Alt+F11
Save	Ctrl+Alt+S
Save and Run Page	Ctrl+Alt+R
Toggle Hide Empty Positions	Ctrl+Alt+E
Undo	Ctrl+Z

OK

Figure 1-36. *Shortcut list*

Unfortunately, you cannot define your own shortcut combinations. For sure, you will not need all the available shortcuts from the list, and it would be nice to have an option to define your own top-ten list. Maybe the next release will have this feature.

Help Functionalities

The Page Designer has a huge number of help options. Clicking the icon in Figure 1-35 will open a menu showing different possibilities to get help for the problems you may face during application development. The following help options are available:

- Link to the APEX 5.0 Documentation

- Link to APEX Forum at OTN

- Link to APEX Resources at OTN

- Page Designer Help

- Shortcuts List

- About Help

Link to the APEX 5.0 Documentation

Directly linking to the current APEX 5.0 documentation (Figure 1-37) is a great option. It helps you to instantly access the most current documentation available at http://docs.oracle.com.

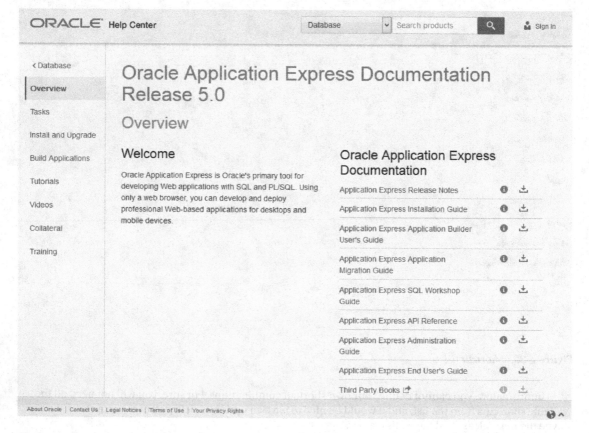

Figure 1-37. *APEX documentation*

Link to the APEX 5.0 Forum at OTN

The APEX 5.0 Page Designer is also connected to the APEX Forum at OTN (Figure 1-38), which is the best resource if you have a question on how to solve a problem. It should be used to post your questions and to help other developers to solve their problems.

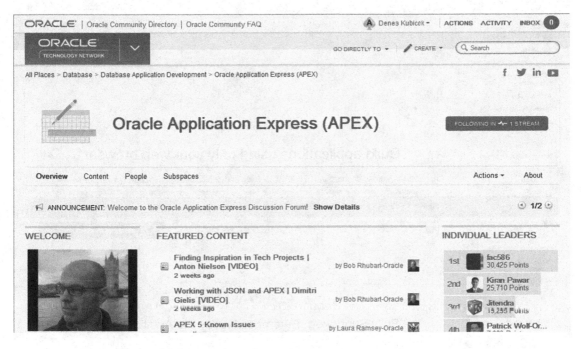

Figure 1-38. *APEX Forum at OTN*

Link to the APEX Resources at OTN

This link is important when you just start to learn APEX. This link provides you with the most recent resources related to APEX (see Figure 1-39), and those resources are an awesome source of knowledge. There is almost no topic related to APEX you can't find here.

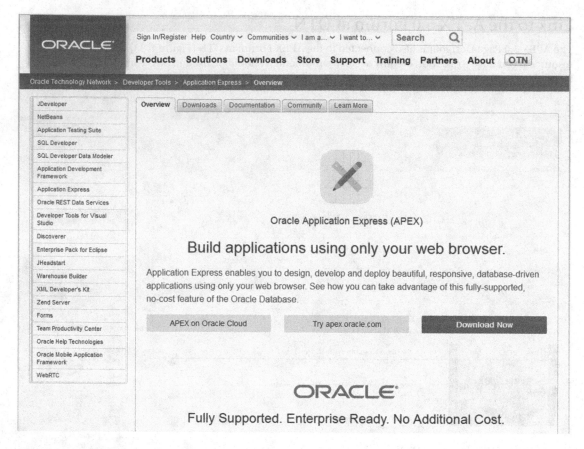

Figure 1-39. APEX resources at OTN

Page Designer Help: Getting Started in Page Designer

The Page Designer Help (Figure 1-40) is a short overview of Page Designer functionalities.

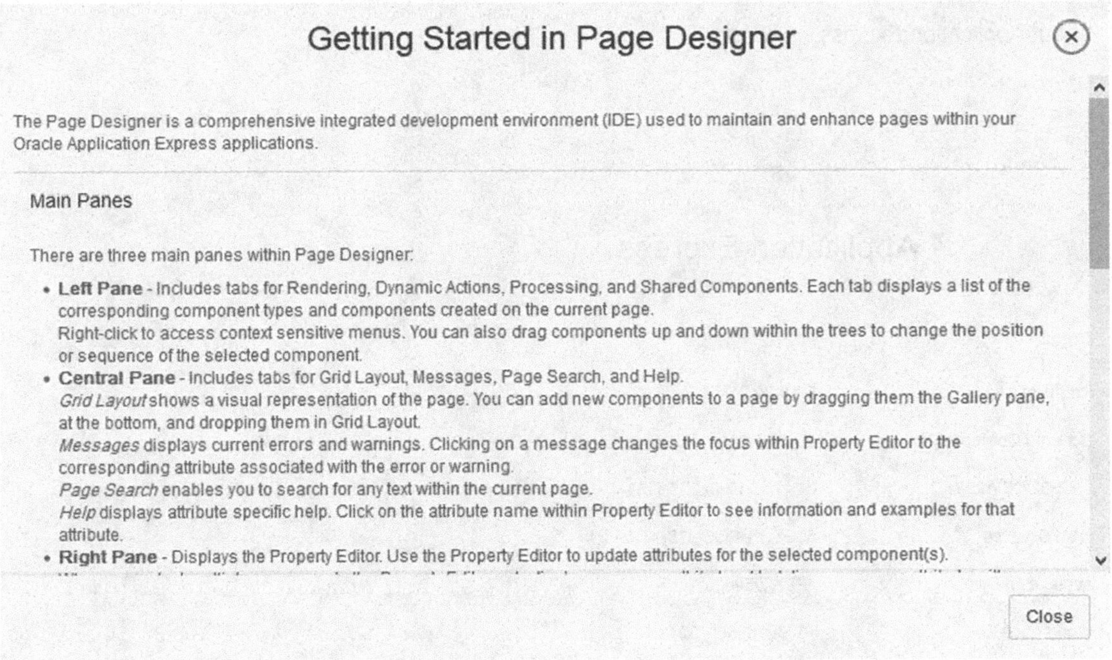

Getting Started in Page Designer ⊗

The Page Designer is a comprehensive integrated development environment (IDE) used to maintain and enhance pages within your Oracle Application Express applications.

Main Panes

There are three main panes within Page Designer:

- **Left Pane** - Includes tabs for Rendering, Dynamic Actions, Processing, and Shared Components. Each tab displays a list of the corresponding component types and components created on the current page.
Right-click to access context sensitive menus. You can also drag components up and down within the trees to change the position or sequence of the selected component.
- **Central Pane** - Includes tabs for Grid Layout, Messages, Page Search, and Help.
Grid Layout shows a visual representation of the page. You can add new components to a page by dragging them the Gallery pane, at the bottom, and dropping them in Grid Layout.
Messages displays current errors and warnings. Clicking on a message changes the focus within Property Editor to the corresponding attribute associated with the error or warning.
Page Search enables you to search for any text within the current page.
Help displays attribute specific help. Click on the attribute name within Property Editor to see information and examples for that attribute.
- **Right Pane** - Displays the Property Editor. Use the Property Editor to update attributes for the selected component(s).

Close

Figure 1-40. *Getting Started in Page Designer page*

About Page Designer

About Page Designer (Figure 1-41) gives you a short overview of the most important features such as Host Schema, Product Build, Last DDL time, and so on.

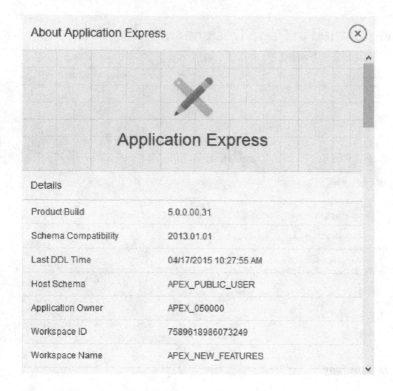

Figure 1-41. *About Page Designer*

Other Options

Page Designer has lots of other new features that need to be mentioned here.

- Multiple component selection
- Resizing areas
- Memory function
- Toolbar options

Multiple Component Selection

Using Page Designer Component View or Page Designer Grid Layout, you have a possibility to select multiple components of the same type at once and do the following:

- Modify them by setting the properties in the Property Editor (Figure 1-42)

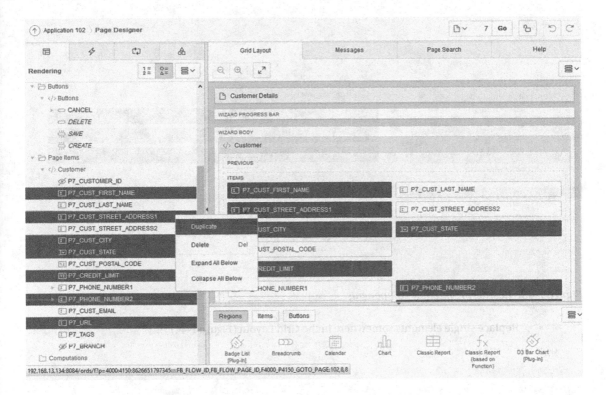

Figure 1-42. *Multiple component selection*

- Move them within the Component View (Figure 1-43)

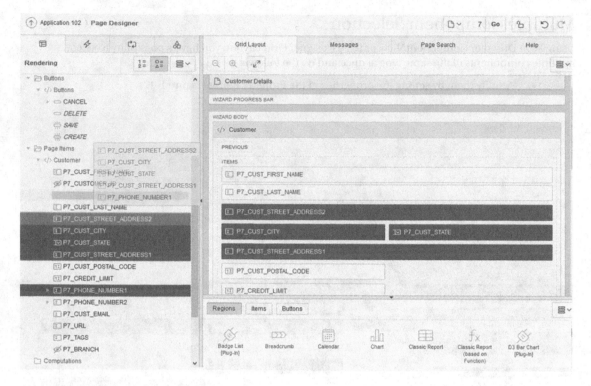

Figure 1-43. *Reordering multiple components*

- Replace single elements somewhere in the Grid Layout (Figure 1-44)

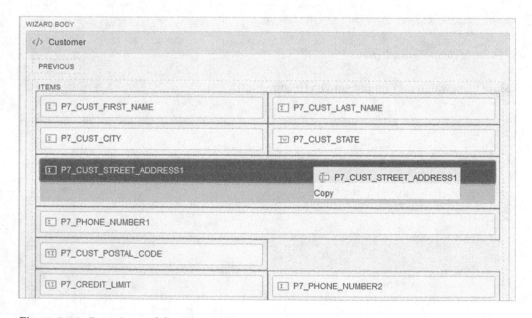

Figure 1-44. *Dragging and dropping single components in the Grid Layout*

Resizing Page Designer Areas

If one of the Page Designer sections and areas such as Component View, Grid Layout, and Property Editor are too small, you have the option to resize them and make them fit your needs (Figure 1-45).

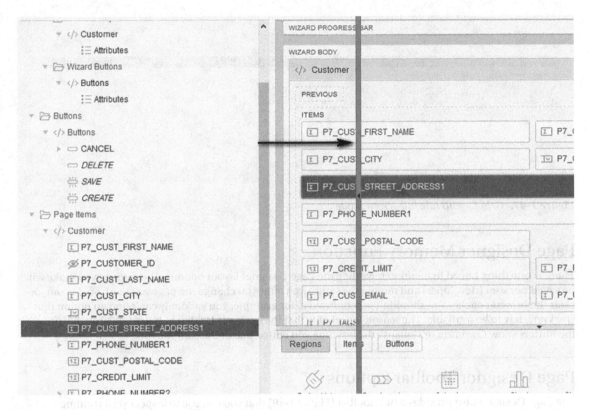

Figure 1-45. *Resizing Page Designer sections*

In addition, you can resize the entire Grid Layout by clicking the Expand icon on the Grid Layout tab (Figure 1-46 and Figure 1-47).

Figure 1-46. *Expand icon on Grid Layout tab*

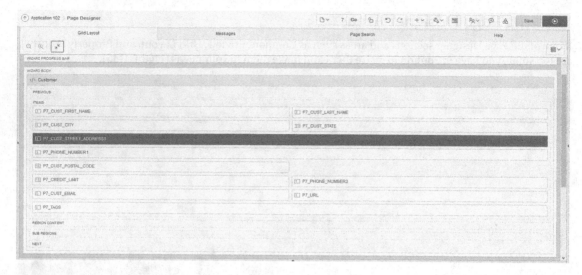

Figure 1-47. *Grid Layout tab: full-screen mode*

Page Designer Memory Function

There is one thing I need to mention regarding the Page Designer layout options. The settings you make will be saved per user (developer) and remain the same even after you change the page you work on, log out, or clear the browser cache. You shouldn't get confused if, for example, you suddenly can't find an option that you know has to be available. The reason is probably that the option is hidden because you probably used the button Show Common or Collapse the last time you edited one of the components.

Page Designer Toolbar Options

The Page Designer also provides a new toolbar (Figure 1-48) that you can use to inspect your runtime applications. Some of these options were available before, so I will mention only the new ones.

- Show Grid
- Quick Edit
- Theme Roller
- Toolbar options (the cog to the far right in Figure 1-48)

Figure 1-48. *Page Designer toolbar*

Show Grid

The Show Grid option (Figure 1-49) will show the page and region grids for your application pages. You can use it to improve the layout of your pages.

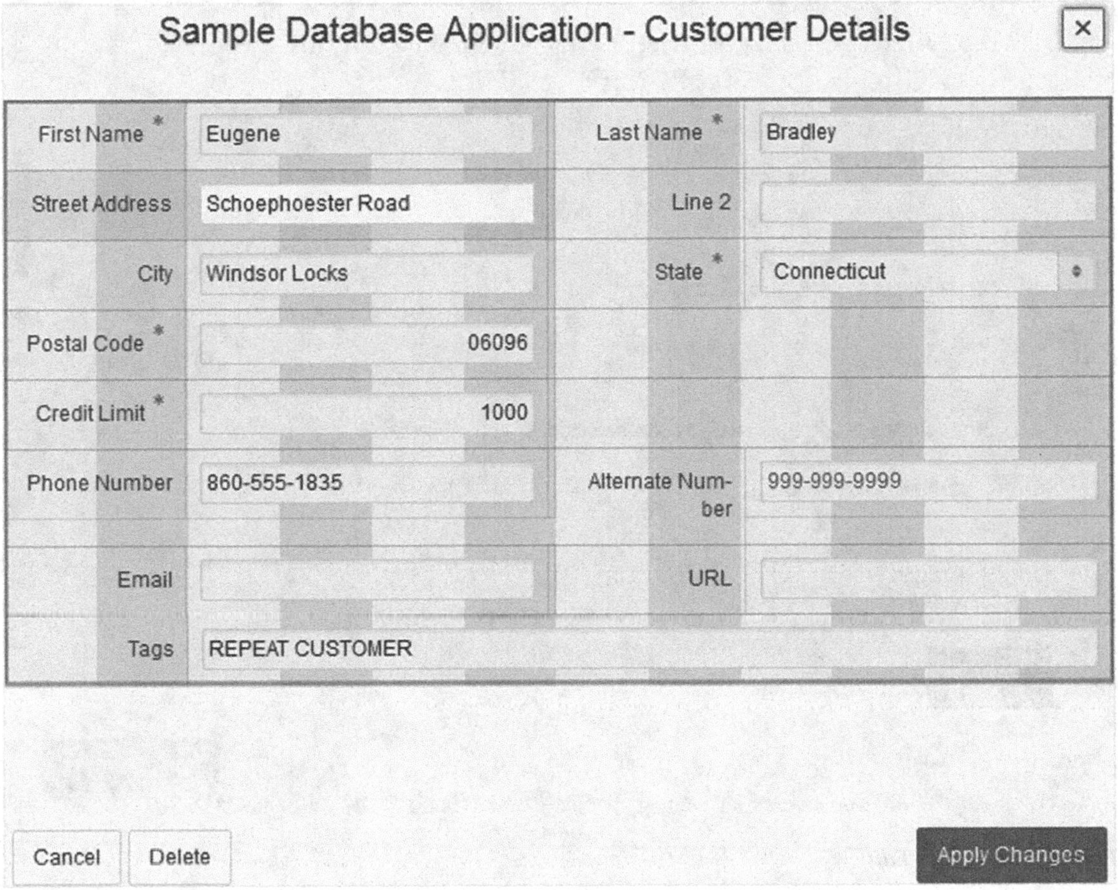

Figure 1-49. *Show Grid*

Quick Edit

Activating the Quick Edit (Figure 1-50), you can access a single component in your runtime application, and it will lead you to the properties of the selected element.

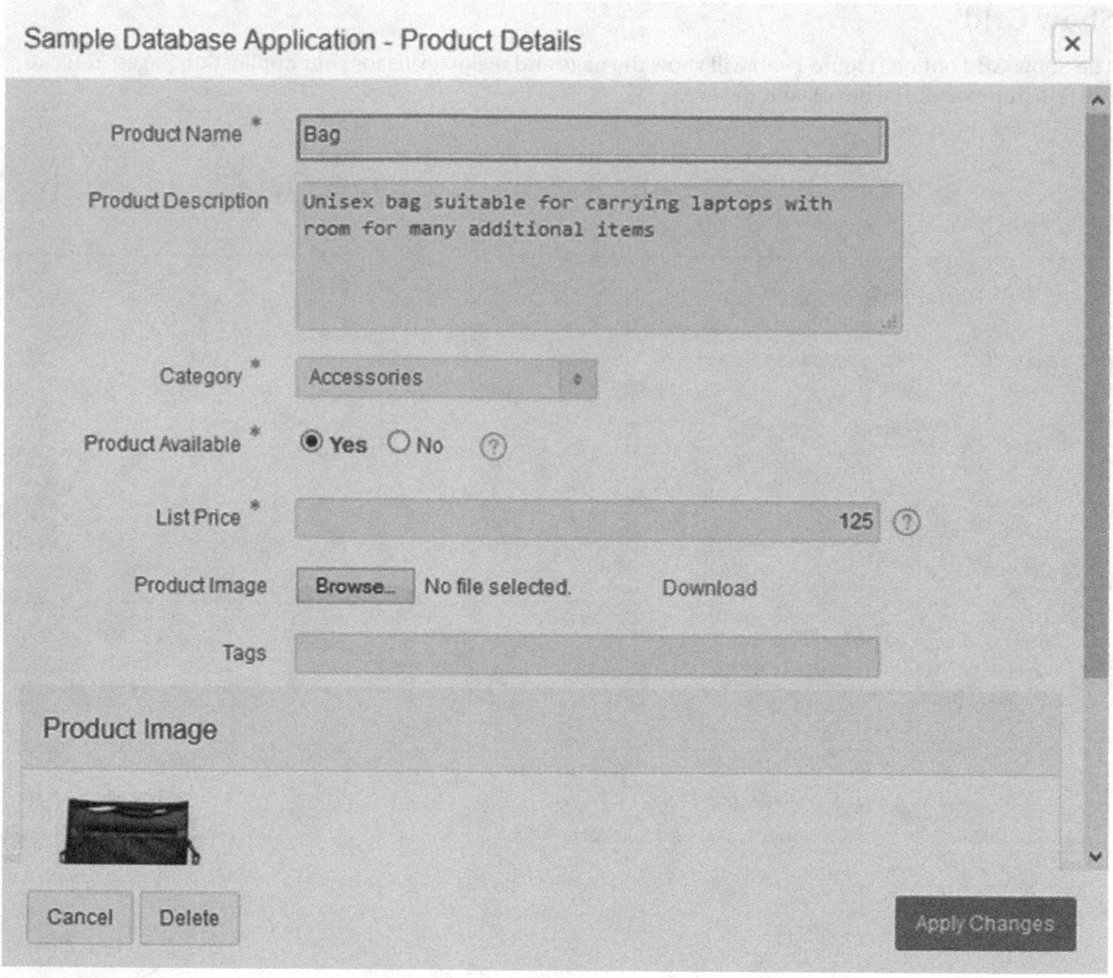

Figure 1-50. *Quick Edit*

Theme Roller

Selecting the Theme Roller will open the new Theme Roller panel in your runtime application. Figure 1-51 shows the panel for setting some of the Theme Roller options.

Figure 1-51. *Theme Roller*

Toolbar Options

Finally, there is a button in the Page Designer toolbar that you can use to change the toolbar settings. You can use it to change some basic settings like the following (Figure 1-52):

- Auto Hide
- Show Icons Only
- Display Position (left, right, top, or bottom)

Figure 1-52. *Toolbar settings*

Summary

The Page Designer interface is the most prominent new feature in APEX 5.0. It is different from the previous component or tree views, and it incorporates all application development options and features on a single screen.

The tree view was the beginning, and since version APEX 4.2, it has been reduced to the accordion on the left side of the screen. The rest of the screen is divided into a large Grid Layout area, allowing drag-and-drop page design, and a Property Editor area, which allows access to all the properties previously found on the edit screen.

This new interface allows for a much more efficient development of applications. Instead of editing individual screens and going back and forth, navigating away from the page you are looking at, you can now select components, change the attributes in the Property Editor, and save whenever you want to see what the application looks like. It is also possible to select multiple components of the same type and then change any common attributes in the Property Editor at once. You also have the possibility to redo and undo all changes in the Grid Layout or Property Editor as long as those changes are not saved (until the Save button is clicked and the application is run). The Page Designer adds a lot of other features such as instant error messages, AJAX page search, and the Code Editor, with native syntax highlighting, inline error highlighting, and autocomplete functionality.

The Page Designer also shows where the future development of APEX will go. In one of the next major releases, you can expect the same functionality you now have in the Page Designer for the applications you provide to your customers.

- AJAX forms

- AJAX trees with context menus and drag-and-drop functionality

- Drag-and-drop page content

CHAPTER 2

■ ■ ■

Oracle REST Data Services

by John Scott

Oracle REST Data Services (ORDS) is the current name for what once upon a time was termed the APEX Listener. Not only has Oracle changed the name, but it has changed a lot of the functionality as well. ORDS is notably different and broader in scope. For example, in ORDS 3 you'll find the following:

- Installation no longer requires APEX.

- ORDS provides Oracle NoSQL database support.

- ORDS autogenerates REST endpoints for tables and views.

One of the significant changes with ORDS 3.0 is that you no longer require APEX to be installed. When I first learned that, I wondered why you would want to use ORDS without APEX. Well, the simple answer is that Oracle has recognized that not everyone using the Oracle Database has APEX installed; however, they might want to REST enable tables or create manual REST endpoints.

While initially this might look like ORDS is trying to distance itself from APEX, this is actually a positive thing for APEX, since it might introduce a group of people who aren't already using APEX to the possibility of using APEX. If someone installs ORDS into a database that doesn't currently have APEX installed and then creates a bunch of REST-enabled services, then the next logical step is to install APEX to be able to provide added functionality (perhaps to manage those REST services, administer data, and so on).

So, don't worry about the name change. (Anecdotally, a couple of people contacted me around the time HTMLDB was renamed to Application Express and were worried that the name change signaled the end; I'm pleased to report that many years later APEX is stronger than ever.)

ORDS Defined

What is ORDS? Put simply, it's a Java EE alternative to the OHS or the EPG. In other words, it's a piece of infrastructure that either provides web server access to your APEX environment (and applications) or, if you're not using APEX, allows you to create and access your REST services in your database. With ORDS 3, you now have the following deployment options with ORDS:

- Stand-alone

- Oracle WebLogic Server (11g Release 1 [10.3.6] or newer)

- Glassfish Server (Release 3.1.2 or newer)

- Apache Tomcat (Release 7.0.56 or newer)

I could spend an entire book covering these various options, but what I want to concentrate on in this chapter is ORDS itself and not the deployment options (which are well documented in the Oracle documentation). So, in my examples, I will be using the stand-alone configuration, which is not recommended for production usage since it provides no capabilities for automatically restarting in the event of any issues.

What is my recommended production deployment option? Well, I'm afraid the simple answer is (as always!) "it depends." I think it depends on your current environment, your (company) skill set, and your budget. WebLogic Server is a powerful and configurable option; however, it is the most expensive option, so if you're not currently licensed for it, then be prepared for your licensing costs to increase (however, with that increased cost comes with increased support). Glassfish is a much cheaper option (or free if using the community edition). However, I think a great combination is ORDS embedded into Apache Tomcat with a reverse proxy Apache server (to help provide capabilities such as virtual hosts, compression, load balancing, intrusion detection, and so on).

ORDS Download and Setup

The ORDS home page is currently located at here:

`http://www.oracle.com/technetwork/developer-tools/rest-data-services/overview/index.html`

Figure 2-1 shows the download page.

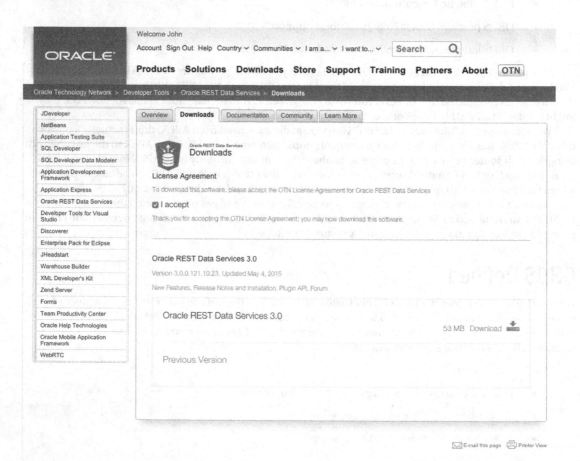

Figure 2-1. *Oracle REST Data Services download page*

The download is a self-contained ZIP file, which at around 50MB is quite a small download for Oracle software. When you unzip the file, you should end up with a directory structure like this:

```
[jes@AEMBP ords]$ ls -al
total 199192
drwxr-xr-x   9 jes  staff        306  5 May 10:53 .
drwxr-xr-x  10 jes  staff        340  5 May 10:52 ..
drwxr-xr-x@  3 jes  staff        102  1 May 10:23 docs
drwxr-xr-x@  6 jes  staff        204  1 May 10:28 examples
drwxr-xr-x@  2 jes  staff         68  1 May 10:28 logs
-rw-r-----@  1 jes  staff   55850624  5 May 10:46 ords.3.0.0.121.10.23.zip
-rw-r--r--@  1 jes  staff   46105869  1 May 10:28 ords.war
drwxr-xr-x@  3 jes  staff        102  1 May 10:28 params
-rw-r--r--@  1 jes  staff      23806  1 May 10:28 readme.html
```

Notice the ZIP file contains documentation and examples, but the main core of the download is the ords.war file (previously called apex.war). During the ORDS configuration you will need to specify the path to the APEX web server files (located in the images directory of the APEX download). These files are not bundled in the ORDS download, so you will need to download them separately.

Note in the following example I have already downloaded the APEX 5 web server files and copied them to a directory, which I will reference during the ORDS installation/configuration.

Running the Install

You can now begin the ORDS installation by running the following command:

```
java -jar ords.war
```

■ **Note**   You may need to give the full path to your Java binary, which requires Java JDK 1.7 or newer.

You should see the following output:

```
[jes@AEMBP ords]$ java -jar ords.war
This Oracle REST Data Services instance has not yet been configured.
Please complete the following prompts

Enter the location to store configuration data:
```

You need to specify the location where ORDS will store configuration files; this allows you to keep the configuration files in a different location than the main ords.war file so that when you upgrade you don't need to worry about overwriting the configuration (it also helps to make regressing easier in the case of a failed upgrade).

```
Enter the location to store configuration data:/u01/ords/ords-config
```

After entering the path to the configuration directory (which will be created for you), you will be prompted for a number of parameters. Notice that anything in square brackets will be used as a default value, so for example here you override the database server from localhost to aevm:

```
Enter the name of the database server [localhost]:aevm
```

If you want to accept the default, just press Enter/Return. In this case, you are using the default listener port of 1521, so you don't need to override it.

```
Enter the database listen port [1521]:
```

Now you specify the database service name or SID.

```
Enter 1 to specify the database service name, or 2 to specify the database SID [1]:
Enter the database service name:apex5.localdomain
```

Then you need to specify the password to be used for the ORDS_PUBLIC_USER account.

```
Enter the database password for ORDS_PUBLIC_USER:
Confirm password:
```

Note the username here: ORDS_PUBLIC_USER. This is the clue that ORDS can be used without APEX being installed since all the metadata for ORDS will now be located in the ORDS_PUBLIC_USER schema, and it does not rely on APEX in any way.

The next question can be misleading.

```
Enter 1 if you want to use PL/SQL Gateway or 2 to skip this step [1]:
```

When I first saw this, I thought it was referring to the Embedded PL/SQL Gateway; however, if you want to use ORDS to access APEX (rather than using it just for REST enabling your database), then you should choose option 1 here, and you will be prompted for the APEX_PUBLIC_USER passwords.

```
Enter 1 if you want to use PL/SQL Gateway or 2 to skip this step [1]:
Enter the database password for APEX_PUBLIC_USER:
Confirm password:
```

You will have set these passwords when installing APEX. Refer to the APEX documentation on how to reset them if you have forgotten your choices.

You will also be able to specify passwords for the APEX_LISTENER and APEX_REST_PUBLIC_USER users.

```
Enter 1 to specify passwords for Application Express RESTful Services database users
(APEX_LISTENER, APEX_REST_PUBLIC_USER) or 2 to skip this step [1]:
Enter the database password for APEX_LISTENER:
Confirm password:
Enter the database password for APEX_REST_PUBLIC_USER:
Confirm password:
May 5, 2015 11:31:33 AM oracle.dbtools.common.config.file.ConfigurationFilesBase update
INFO: Updated configurations: defaults, apex_pu, apex, apex_al, apex_rt
May 5, 2015 11:31:33 AM oracle.dbtools.rt.config.setup.SchemaSetup install
INFO: Oracle REST Data Services schema version 3.0.0.121.10.23
Enter 1 if you wish to start in standalone mode or 2 to exit [1]:
```

Finally, you need to tell ORDS where it can find the APEX static resources (the JavaScript and CSS files for APEX).

```
Enter the APEX static resources location:/u01/apex5
Enter the HTTP port [8080]:
```

Note the path I specified (/u01/apex5) is a directory that contains the images subdirectory from the APEX 5 file download. (In other words, it contains only the images, CSS, and JavaScript, not the SQL files used to install APEX.) Also, you can specify a port to listen on (with the default being 8080, so make sure nothing is already listening on this port if you accept the default).

All being well, you should now see the ORDS server start up.

```
May 5, 2015 11:31:24 PM oracle.dbtools.rt.config.setup.SchemaSetup install
INFO: Oracle REST Data Services schema version 3.0.0.121.10.23
2015-05-05 11:31:24.405:INFO::main: Logging initialized @13577ms
2015-05-05 11:31:27.528:INFO:oejs.Server:main: jetty-9.2.z-SNAPSHOT
2015-05-05 11:31:27.545:INFO:oejsh.ContextHandler:main: Started o.e.j.s.h.ContextHandler@13c
78c0b{/i,null,AVAILABLE}
2015-05-05 11:31:27.638:INFO:/ords:main: INFO: Using configuration folder: /home/oracle/
ords-config/ords
2015-05-05 11:31:27.639:INFO:/ords:main: FINEST: |ApplicationContext [configurationFolder=/
u01/ords/ords-config, services=Application Scope]|
May 5, 2015 11:31:27 PM oracle.dbtools.common.config.db.DatabasePools validatePool
INFO: Validating pool: apex
May 5, 2015 11:31:27 PM oracle.dbtools.common.config.db.DatabasePools validatePool
INFO: Pool: apex is correctly configured
May 5, 2015 11:31:27 PM oracle.dbtools.common.config.db.DatabasePools validatePool
INFO: Validating pool: apex_al
May 5, 2015 11:31:27 PM oracle.dbtools.common.config.db.DatabasePools validatePool
INFO: Pool: apex_al is correctly configured
May 5, 2015 11:31:27 PM oracle.dbtools.common.config.db.DatabasePools validatePool
INFO: Validating pool: apex_pu
May 5, 2015 11:31:27 PM oracle.dbtools.common.config.db.DatabasePools validatePool
INFO: Pool: apex_pu is correctly configured
May 5, 2015 11:31:27 PM oracle.dbtools.common.config.db.DatabasePools validatePool
INFO: Validating pool: apex_rt
May 5, 2015 11:31:28 PM oracle.dbtools.common.config.db.DatabasePools validatePool
INFO: Pool: apex_rt is correctly configured
2015-05-05 11:31:33.272:INFO:/ords:main: INFO: Oracle REST Data Services initialized|Oracle
REST Data Services version : 3.0.0.121.10.23|Oracle REST Data Services server info:
jetty/9.2.z-SNAPSHOT|
2015-05-05 11:31:33.274:INFO:oejsh.ContextHandler:main: Started o.e.j.s.ServletContextHandle
r@3dd3bcd{/ords,null,AVAILABLE}
2015-05-05 11:31:33.314:INFO:oejs.ServerConnector:main: Started ServerConnector@73846619{HT
TP/1.1}{0.0.0.0:8080}
2015-05-05 11:31:33.315:INFO:oejs.Server:main: Started @17492ms
```

By default ORDS will be listening on port 8080 (which you can see in the debug information output to the screen). If you want to stop the server, you can simply press Ctrl+C since you are running in stand-alone mode. If at any later point you want to change the configuration, you can do it from the command line, which also provides built-in help by typing the following:

```
[jes@AEMBP ords]$ java -jar ords.war help
```

This shows help for each specific option.

```
[jes@AEMBP ords]$ java -jar ords.war help
java -jar ords.war <COMMAND> [Options] [Arguments]
```

The following commands are available:

```
            configdir       Set the value of the web.xml
                            config.dir property

            help            Describe the usage of this
                            program or its commands

            install         Installs Oracle REST Data
                            Services

            map-url         Map a URL pattern to the
                            named database connection

            nosqladd        Add NoSQL store configuration

            nosqldel        Delete NoSQL store
                            configuration

            plugin          Package one or more plugin
                            jar files into ords.war

            set-properties  Edit the value of one or more
                            configuration settings via
                            the specified properties file

            set-property    Edit the value of a single
                            configuration setting

            setup           Configure database connection

            standalone      Launch Oracle REST Data
                            Services in standalone mode

            static          Generate a Web Application
                            Archive (WAR) to serve Oracle
                            Application Express static
                            resources

            uninstall       Uninstall ORDS_METADATA
                            schema, proxy user and
                            related database objects.
```

```
        user                    Create or update credentials
                                for a user
```

To see instructions on how to use each of these commands, type help
followed by the command name, for example

```
java -jar ords.war help configdir
```

If no command is provided Oracle REST Data Services is started in
standalone mode

If everything worked correctly (and assuming you didn't press Ctrl+C to exit ORDS, or if you did that, you restarted it again with java -jar ords.war), then you should be able to point your browser to point 8080 on whichever machine you installed ORDS on (in my example I installed it to my local machine). Assuming you already had APEX installed, then you should be greeted with the default APEX Application Builder login screen, as shown in Figure 2-2.

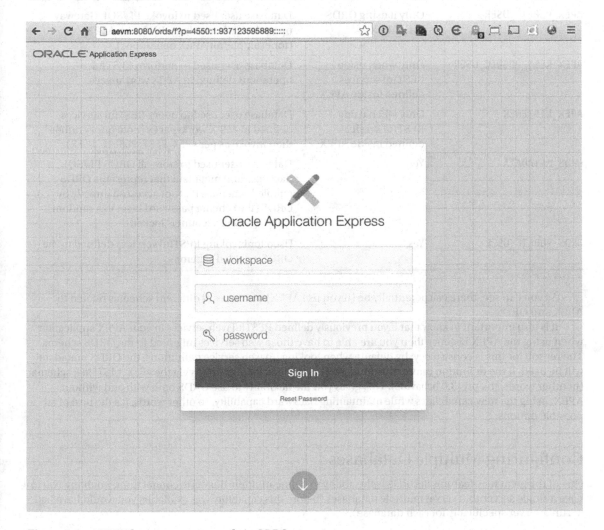

Figure 2-2. APEX 5 login screen accessed via ORDS

49

Notice the URL contains /ords rather than the /apex you are familiar with from the APEX Listener, or the /pls/apex you're familiar with from the mod_plsql handler via Apache OHS.

Success! You're now using ORDS to access APEX 5, so you're done right? Yes, if all you want to do is use ORDS as a basic web server, you'd done. But it's capable of much more than that. I'll cover some of those capabilities in the coming sections, but first I will give you some background on the various database users used by ORDS.

Database Users Used by ORDS

ORDS creates and uses a number of different database users, which can be confusing at first. Part of this complexity is because ORDS can be used without APEX and because APEX itself has a number of different functionalities that may or may not be utilized by ORDS. The following table attempts to give an overview of the types and purpose of each database user:

Username	Required	Description
APEX_PUBLIC_USER	Only if using ORDS with APEX	Database user used to invoke PL/SQL Gateway operations when using ORDS with APEX (for example, all APEX operations).
APEX_REST_PUBLIC_USER	Only when using RESTful services defined inside APEX	Database user used to perform RESTful operations defined in APEX workspaces.
APEX_LISTENER	Only when using RESTful services defined inside APEX	Database user used to query RESTful services defined in APEX workspaces (note query rather than invoke as per APEX_REST_PUBLIC_USER).
ORDS_METADATA	Yes	Database user used to store all ORDS PL/SQL packages and metadata that represents ORDS-enabled schemas. It is not accessed directly by ORDS (the schema password is set to a random value, and the account is locked).
ORDS_PUBLIC_USER	Yes	Used for invoking RESTful services defined in the ORDS-enabled schemas.

As you can see, there can potentially be (if you use APEX) a number of different schemas related to APEX and ORDS.

It is also important to know that if you previously defined RESTful web services in your APEX application when using the APEX Listener, then you are able to have those web services migrated to the ORDS schema. The reason for this is consistency; by default, when looking up web service definitions, the ORDS metadata will be used. If the definition cannot be found, then it will look for definitions via the APEX_LISTENER schema (in other words, the pre-3.0 behavior). This gives you the flexibility to use ORDS both with and without APEX, using the new capabilities while maintaining backward capability. In other words, it's the best of all possible options.

Configuring Multiple Databases

One of the great new features in ORDS is the ability to define multiple database connections, enabling you to have a single server that serves multiple databases (before this capability was available, you would have had to run a server specifically for each database).

When you installed ORDS, an initial database connection was created named apex. To create a new database connection, you can use the following command-line option:

```
java -jar ords.war setup --database <database name>
```

This will walk you through the same prompts you saw earlier.

```
[jes@AEMBP ords]$ java -jar ords.war setup --database demo2
Enter the name of the database server [aevm]:aevm2
Enter the database listen port [1521]:
Enter the database service name [apex5.localdomain]:
Enter 1 if you want to verify/install Oracle REST Data Services schema or 2 to skip this
step [1]:
Enter the database password for ORDS_PUBLIC_USER:
...<rest of code omitted>
```

Now that you have defined a second database, you will want to tell ORDS how it should decide to route traffic between the multiple connections.

Defining Request Path Routing

You can configure ORDS to route traffic depending on the request path in the URL, using the map-url configuration option, as shown here:

```
java -jar ords.war map-url --type base-path --workspace <workspace_name>
<path_prefix> <database_name>
```

where

- workspace is the name of the APEX workspace where the RESTful services are defined for this connection. If you are not using RESTful services, then you can omit this parameter.

- path_prefix is the prefix that must begin at the start of the request path.

- database_name is the name of the database connection you previously added.

So, for example, if you ran the following

```
java -jar ords.war map-url --type base-path --workspace uat /uat db2
```

and the ORDS server was running on the aevm hostname, then using the following URL

```
https://aevm:8080/ords/uat/
```

would allow you to access the uat workspace in the db2 database (note db2 is a database connection, not really a db2 database!).

Using this technique gives you great flexibility in defining your database connections (and to a certain degree allows some failover and load balancing across multiple ORDS servers).

Defining Request URL Prefix–Based Routing

Similarly to request path routing, you can define request URL prefix–based routing. For example, say you use the following command:

```
java -jar ords.war map-url --type base-url --workspace uat http://aevm:8080/ords/uat db2
```

This means that any URL that begins with

```
http://aevm:8080/ords/uat
```

will be routed to the db2 database. For example, all the following URLs would be processed by this routing:

```
http://aevm:8080/ords/uat/f?p=MYAPP
http://aevm:8080/ords/uat/generate_documents
http://aevm:8080/ords/uat/register?p_username=john
```

Configuration Files

As you have seen, ORDS is pretty straightforward to install and configure. However, what if you want to make a change after you have installed it? First, you will need to know where the configuration files are stored. You can check this by using the configdir command:

```
java -jar ords.war configdir
```

This should give you output similar to the following:

```
[jes@AEMBP ords]$ java -jar ords.war configdir
May 5, 2015 4:17:15 PM oracle.dbtools.cmdline.ModifyConfigDir execute
INFO: The config.dir value is /u01/ords/ords-config
```

Now you know the configuration files are stored in /u01/ords/ords-config.

Alternatively, if you want to change the location of the configuration files (perhaps you want to test a new configuration without modifying the existing configuration), you can specify a new location after the configdir command.

```
java -jar ords.war configdir </path/to/new/config>
```

Configuration File Structure

The configuration directory contains a number of different files contained within a specific structure.

```
[jes@AEMBP ords]$ pwd
/u01/ords/ords-config/ords
[jes@AEMBP ords]$ tree
.
```

```
├──./ords
│   ├── ./ords/conf
│   ├── ./ords/conf/apex.xml
│   │    ├── ./ords/conf/apex_al.xml
│   │    ├── ./ords/conf/apex_pu.xml
│   │    ├── ./ords/conf/apex_rt.xml
│   ├── ./ords/defaults.xml
│   ├── ./ords/standalone
│   │    ├── ./ords/standalone/standalone.properties
│   ├── ./ords/url-mapping.xml

3 directories, 7 files
```

The defaults.xml file contains settings that are inherited by all database connections (that is, global settings).

Database-specific configurations are stored in the files conf/<db-name>.xml, so for example in this case you have the conf/apex.xml file, which represents settings specific to the apex database connection.

If you are using APEX (and I'll assume you are since you bought this book!), then you will have additional configuration files including _al.xml, _rt.xml, and _pu.xml. These files store the configuration details for the APEX_LISTENER, APEX_REST_PUBLIC_USER, and ORDS_PUBLIC_USER.

Configuration File Format

The configuration files are text files in the Java XML properties format, which is fairly easy to read and understand. For example, my defaults.xml file contains the following:

```xml
<?xml version="1.0" encoding="UTF-8" standalone="no"?>
<!DOCTYPE properties SYSTEM "http://java.sun.com/dtd/properties.dtd">
<properties>
<comment>Saved on Mon Jun 29 11:33:55 BST 2015</comment>
<entry key="cache.caching">false</entry>
<entry key="cache.directory">/tmp/apex/cache</entry>
<entry key="cache.duration">days</entry>
<entry key="cache.expiration">7</entry>
<entry key="cache.maxEntries">500</entry>
<entry key="cache.monitorInterval">60</entry>
<entry key="cache.procedureNameList"/>
<entry key="cache.type">lru</entry>
<entry key="db.hostname">aevm</entry>
<entry key="db.port">1521</entry>
<entry key="db.servicename">apex5.localdomain</entry>
<entry key="debug.debugger">false</entry>
<entry key="debug.printDebugToScreen">false</entry>
<entry key="error.keepErrorMessages">true</entry>
<entry key="error.maxEntries">50</entry>
<entry key="jdbc.DriverType">thin</entry>
<entry key="jdbc.InactivityTimeout">1800</entry>
<entry key="jdbc.InitialLimit">3</entry>
<entry key="jdbc.MaxConnectionReuseCount">1000</entry>
<entry key="jdbc.MaxLimit">10</entry>
```

```
<entry key="jdbc.MaxStatementsLimit">10</entry>
<entry key="jdbc.MinLimit">1</entry>
<entry key="jdbc.statementTimeout">900</entry>
<entry key="log.logging">false</entry>
<entry key="log.maxEntries">50</entry>
<entry key="misc.compress"/>
<entry key="misc.defaultPage">apex</entry>
<entry key="security.crypto.enc.password">UL5dl18_fJOY8rNeQncA..</entry>
<entry key="security.crypto.mac.password">rPPOYi4KhOerYnV7HH3deQ..</entry>
<entry key="security.disableDefaultExclusionList">false</entry>
<entry key="security.maxEntries">2000</entry>
</properties>
```

(By the way, I have changed my encrypted password strings in there!)

You can see that it is relatively simple to change the configuration to point at a different hostname using the db.hostname parameter or, for example, turn on the debugger by changing debug.debugger from false to true. A side effect of these configuration files being text files is that it's easy to take a backup of a configuration file before making any changes and to revert to the old version if you hit any issues.

Configurable Parameters

You can configure pretty much all the parameters in both the defaults.xml file and the <database_name>.xml file. The official Oracle help, currently available at the following link, does a great job of listing each parameter:

http://docs.oracle.com/cd/E56351_01/doc.30/e56293/config_file.htm#AELIG7204

Administration via SQL Developer

If you were familiar with the APEX Listener, then you know that it provided a web-based configuration utility so you could fire up your web browser and configure it without having to resort to the command line. One of the downsides of this, however, was that frequently if the APEX Listener was misconfigured, you were unable to connect to the web front end in order to correct it.

One of the big enhancements with ORDS 3.0 is that you can configure it via SQL Developer 4.1. Do this from the View menu, as shown in Figure 2-3.

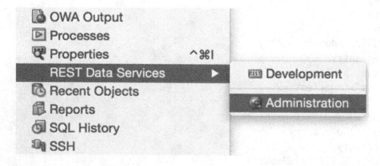

Figure 2-3. *Administering REST Data Services via SQL Developer 4.1*

You will need to create a new ORDS connection, as shown in Figure 2-4.

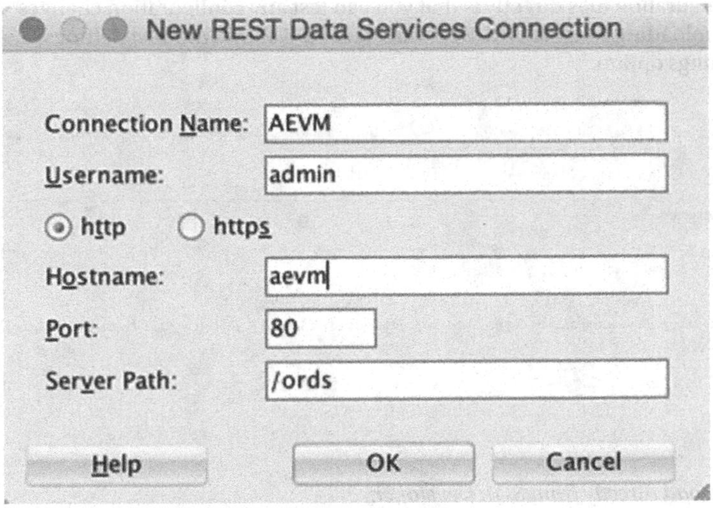

Figure 2-4. *Creating an ORDS connection in SQL Developer 4.1*

This is the piece that can catch you out. I must admit the first few times I attempted this either I missed a section in the documentation or I messed something up. The issue I had was that I didn't create the user (admin in my screenshot) that would enable me to connect via SQL Developer.

Create via two users via the command line.

```
java -jar ords.war user dev   "SQL Developer"
java -jar ords.war user admin  "Listener Administrator"
```

The first command will create a user for developing REST web services via SQL Developer; the second command will create a user that allows you to access (and modify) the ORDS configuration via SQL Developer 4.1.

The important piece here is the section in quotes (for example, SQL Developer and Listener Administrator); those are the roles that the user has. The first time I tried to set up these users, I mistyped the role name and was then frustrated when it did not work. The best advice I can give is to consult the documentation.

Once you have created these users, you should be able to connect via SQL Developer, as shown in Figure 2-5.

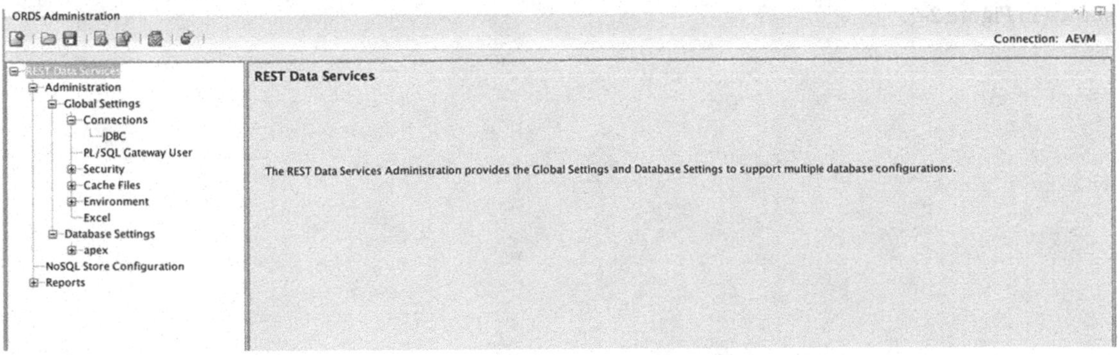

Figure 2-5. *ORDS administration via SQL Developer 4.1*

This GUI allows you to configure all the parameters that are available in the configuration files I discussed earlier, but obviously in a more user-friendly way. One nice feature of using the GUI as opposed to the command line or editing the configuration files directly is that you can test any configuration changes to ensure the values are correct before uploading them to ORDS server. Figure 2-6 shows the Test Settings menu option, as well as the Upload Settings option.

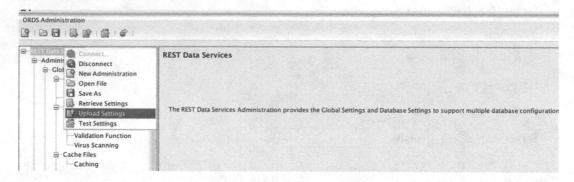

Figure 2-6. *You can test settings and upload directly from SQL Developer.*

I won't go into each setting here because they're the same as the parameters detailed earlier, but I encourage you to test administration via SQL Developer because it makes the configuration easier and less error prone than directly editing the configuration files.

ORDS Development via SQL Developer

So far you have configured ORDS to act as a regular web server, but you haven't exploited any of the interesting features in ORDS yet. Let's change that and dive into creating RESTful web services. You have a couple of options here. You can either REST enable the existing tables and views or create a new REST web service and have complete control over how it behaves.

REST Enabling an Existing Table

First, let's take a look at how easily you can REST enable an existing table using ORDS. In SQL Developer, you need to connect to the REST Development Wizard (I'm not quite sure if I should call this a wizard or tool, but I'll stick with wizard for now). Simply select View ➤ Rest Data Services ➤ Development in SQL Developer, as shown in Figure 2-7.

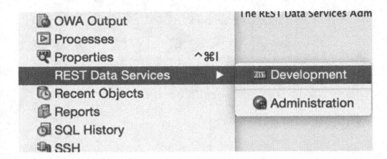

Figure 2-7. *Connecting to the Development Wizard via SQL Developer 4.1*

Once you have connected, you should see a window similar to Figure 2-8.

Figure 2-8. *REST Development Wizard via SQL Developer 4.1*

This is where you can easily create new REST endpoints; however, for a moment, let's try the simple REST enablement of tables. You might want to do this if you just need basic functionality and quickly want to allow your tables to be queried or modified via REST web service functionality (in practice, I find that I usually want a bit more control or fine-grained access).

First select one of your existing SQL Developer connections and right-click the top-level connection; you should now see a REST Services menu where you can choose to enable or disable at the schema level, as shown in Figure 2-9.

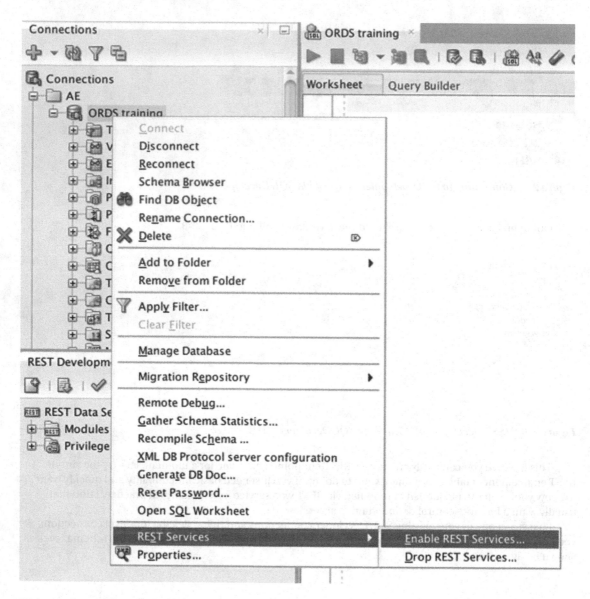

Figure 2-9. *Enabling REST services at the schema level*

You will be prompted to enter a schema alias (which allows you to hide the underlying schema name) and whether you want to enable authorization. In this example, I will alias my schema to ae and choose that authorization is not required. Once you have enabled REST services, you can right-click the table (or view) and select Enable REST Service, as shown in Figure 2-10.

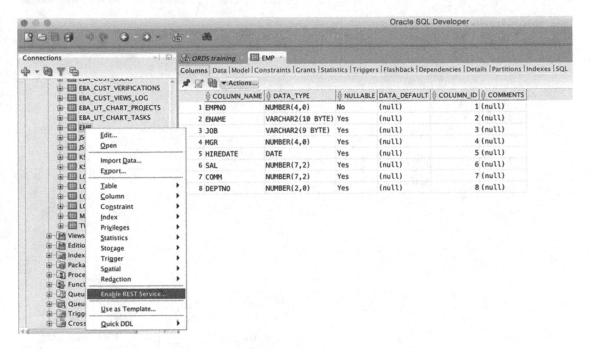

Figure 2-10. *Enabling the REST service on the EMP table*

You will now see a dialog (in Figure 2-11) that enables you to give the object an alias, which is useful if you want to hide the underlying object name, and to enable authorization if required.

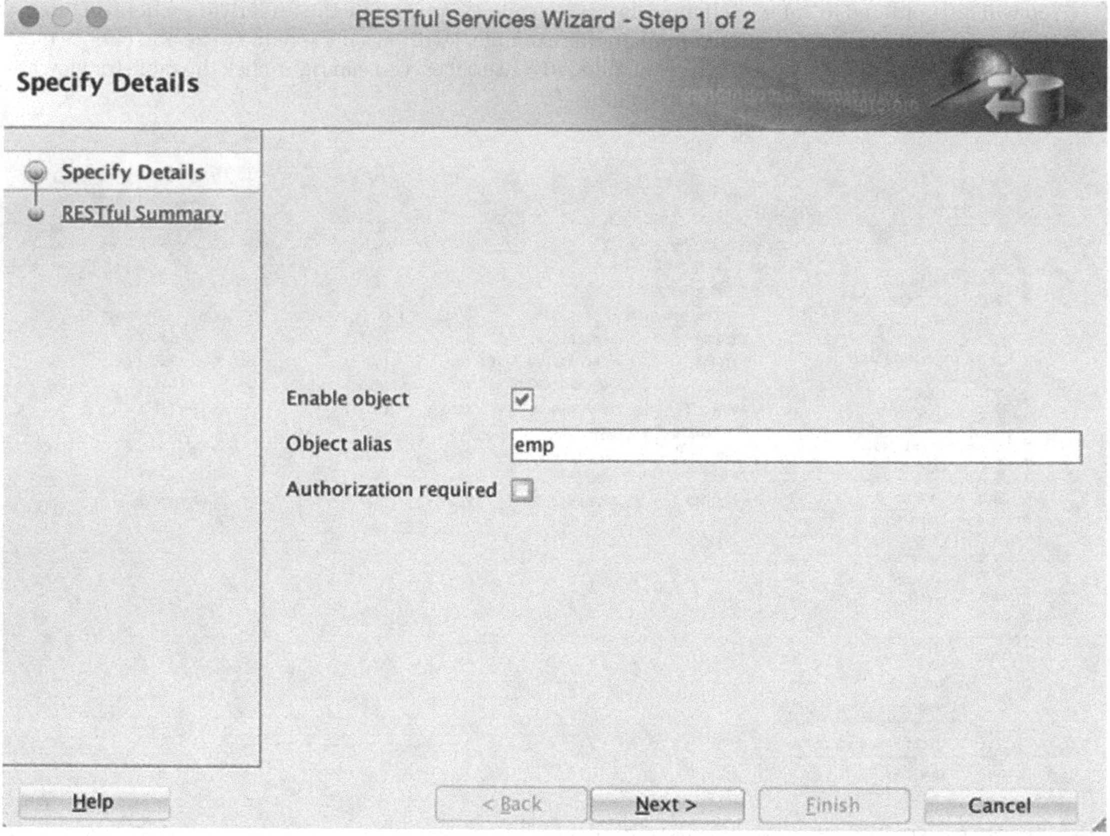

Figure 2-11. *Enabling REST services on the EMP table*

One of the nice features here is that the final step of the wizard actually shows you the DDL being executed, which in my example is as follows:

```
DECLARE
  PRAGMA AUTONOMOUS_TRANSACTION;
BEGIN

    ORDS.ENABLE_OBJECT(p_enabled => TRUE,
                       p_schema => 'TRAINING',
                       p_object => 'EMP',
                       p_object_type => 'TABLE',
                       p_object_alias => 'emp',
                       p_auto_rest_auth => FALSE);

    commit;

END;
```

So, you can easily enable objects for REST services using the ORDS.ENABLE_OBJECT procedure rather than using SQL Developer. (You might, for example, want to script the enabling and disabling or perhaps provide a front end to do this via an APEX application.)

Invoking the New REST Service

So, what did the previous section give you? Well, you should now be able to call your REST web service using the following uniform resource identifier (URI), where /ae/ represents the alias we used at the schema level and /emp/ represents the alias you used for the table:

http://aevm:8080/ords/ae/emp/

You can use any REST tool to perform a GET on this URI. For example, using the popular tool cURL, you should see the following:

```
[jes@AEMBP ~]$ curl http://aevm:8080/ords/ae/emp/
{"items":[{"empno":7839,"ename":"KING","job":"PRESIDENT","mgr":null,"hiredate":"1981-11-
17T00:00:00Z","sal":5000,"comm":null,"deptno":10,"links":[{"rel":"self","href":
"http://aevm:8080/ords/ae/emp/7839"}]},{"empno":7698,"ename":"BLAKE","job":"MANAGER","mgr":7
839,"hiredate":"1981-04-30T23:00:00Z","sal":90,"comm":null,"deptno":30,"links":[{"rel":
"self","href":"http://aevm:8080/ords/ae/emp/7698"}]},{"empno":7782,"ename":"CLARK","job":
"MANAGER","mgr":7839,"hiredate":"1981-06-08T23:00:00Z","sal":2450,"comm":null,"deptno":10,
"links":[{"rel":"self","href":"http://aevm:8080/ords/ae/emp/7782"}]},{"empno":7566,"ename":
"JONES","job":"MANAGER","mgr":7839,"hiredate":"1981-04-01T23:00:00Z","sal":2975,"comm":null,
"deptno":20,"links":[{"rel":"self","href":"http://aevm:8080/ords/ae/emp/7566
<..rest of output omitted..>
```

You can see that the output of the curl command is the response from the web service, which is a JSON representation of the EMP table. If you format the output, you can more easily see the way the data is returned.

```
{
  "items": [
    {
      "empno": 7839,
      "ename": "KING",
      "job": "PRESIDENT",
      "mgr": null,
      "hiredate": "1981-11-17T00:00:00Z",
      "sal": 5000,
      "comm": null,
      "deptno": 10,
      "links": [
        {
          "rel": "self",
          "href": "http://aevm:8080/ords/ae/emp/7839"
        }
      ]
    },
    <...other records omitted..>
    {
      "empno": 7934,
      "ename": "MILLER",
      "job": "CLERK",
      "mgr": 7782,
```

```
      "hiredate": "1982-01-23T00:00:00Z",
      "sal": 1300,
      "comm": null,
      "deptno": 10,
      "links": [
        {
          "rel": "self",
          "href": "http://aevm:8080/ords/ae/emp/7934"
        }
      ]
    }
  ],
  "hasMore": false,
  "limit": 25,
  "offset": 0,
  "count": 14,
  "links": [
    {
      "rel": "self",
      "href": "http://aevm:8080/ords/ae/emp/"
    },
    {
      "rel": "edit",
      "href": "http://aevm:8080/ords/ae/emp/"
    },
    {
      "rel": "describedby",
      "href": "http://aevm:8080/ords/ae/metadata-catalog/emp/"
    },
    {
      "rel": "first",
      "href": "http://aevm:8080/ords/ae/emp/"
    }
  ]
}
```

You get an items array containing each record as a JSON object together with some summary information to tell you how many rows were returned (the count property) and some standard REST attributes to represent links back to this object (which can in other cases be used to page through resultsets, and so on).

Now you may be thinking, "What use is this data in JSON format?" Well, the answer is that with either Oracle 12c or APEX 5 it has become much easier to parse and query JSON data than ever before. It's not the purpose of this chapter to go into detail on the new 12c or APEX 5 JSON functionality; however, using JSON is increasingly common among front-end web development. If you ever use third-party jQuery plugins, for example, or D3 visualizations, then the data typically needs to be provided in JSON format. Using ORDS to provide a REST web service in JSON format makes it incredibly simple to generate the data in the format you need.

Creating a REST Web Service

So, that was a simple REST-enabled table; let's take a look at creating a REST web service manually. Recall earlier you connected to the REST Development Wizard in SQL Developer. Now go back to that region and right-click the Modules link, which should allow you to select New Module, as shown in Figure 2-12.

Figure 2-12. *Selecting to create a new module*

You need to provide a module name as well as a URI prefix (note the trailing slash in the URI prefix), as shown in Figure 2-13.

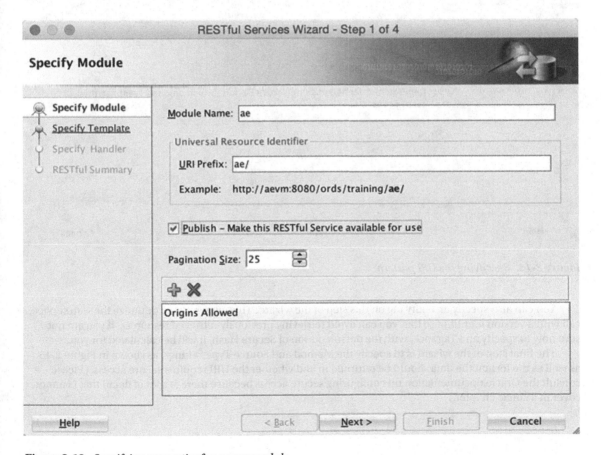

Figure 2-13. *Specifying properties for a new module*

I can't tell you how many times I forgot to select the Publish check box, only to be frustrated when my simple web service didn't work. So if you find yours doesn't work, edit your module and make sure you actually enabled it by selecting the Publish check box. (This provides a simple mechanism to configure your web services and to disable them without having to lose all the details.)

Now you need to provide the URI pattern that will be used to map to this web service. Notice in Figure 2-14 it shows the full URL combining the paths I used in step 1 and step 2 of the wizard so that you know how to call your web service after creation.

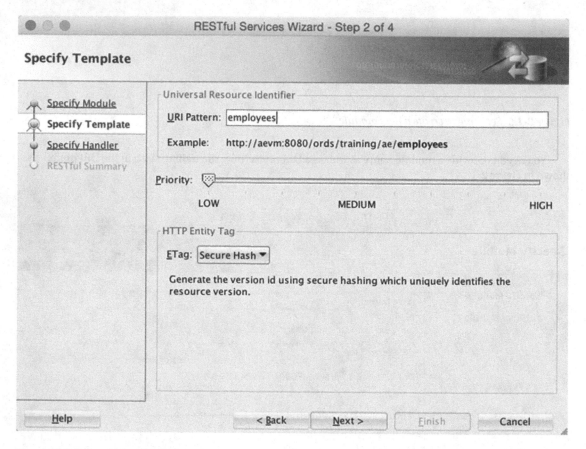

Figure 2-14. Specifying the URI pattern

You can also specify an entity tag on this step of the wizard. This allows you to optimize the web service call with a version identifier so that you can avoid retrieving previously retrieved resources. If you are not sure how to specify an ETag stick, with the default option of Secure Hash, it will be calculated for you.

The final step of the wizard is to specify the Method and Source Type settings, as shown in Figure 2-15, as well as the format the data should be returned in and whether the URI requires secure access. (Please consult the Oracle documentation on configuring secure access because there is a lot of detail that I cannot cover in a single chapter.)

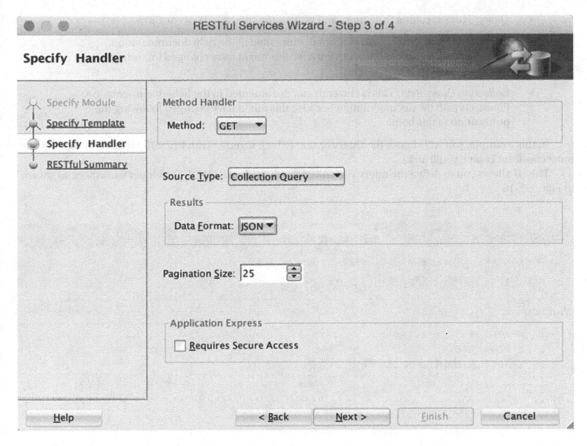

Figure 2-15. *Specifying the method handler and source type*

If you are unfamiliar with web services, there are the following method handlers:

- GET
- POST
- PUT
- DELETE

Think of the GET as analogous to a SQL INSERT statement, the POST as an INSERT statement, the PUT as a MERGE statement, and the DELETE as a—well you guessed it—a DELETE statement. In reality, you could handle these in any way you wanted, but that is a good general convention to think of these operations.

The Source Type field has the following options:

- *Feed*: This executes a SQL query and returns results in a JSON feed representation.

- *Media Resource*: This executes a SQL query and returns a binary representation with an HTTP Content-Type header to specify the type of the returned content (useful for downloading images or documents, and so on).

- *PL/SQL*: This executes an anonymous PL/SQL block with optional IN and IN/OUT parameters that accept and return a JSON representation.

- *Query*: This executes a SQL query and returns the results in JSON or CSV.

- *Collection Query*: This is currently not documented in the help documentation. Please consult the documentation because this might have changed following the publication of this book.

- *Collection Query Item*: This is currently not documented in the help documentation. Please consult the documentation because this might have changed following the publication of this book.

In this example, you will choose the Query option (which together with PL/SQL Method is probably the most common choice you'll pick).

The UI allows you to define the query you will use with the familiar SQL Developer worksheet, as shown in Figure 2-16.

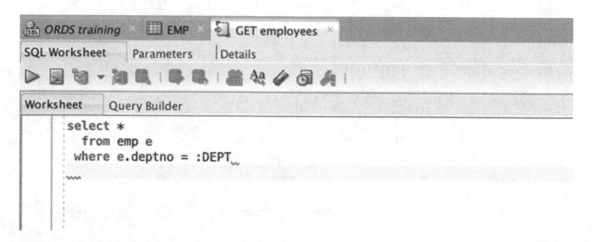

Figure 2-16. *Specifying the query for the web service*

Notice you have referenced a parameter here using the :BIND notation, so you need to specify how the parameter is passed, as shown in Figure 2-17.

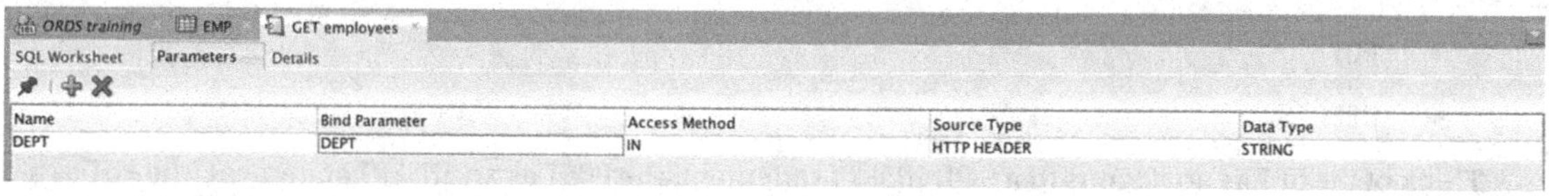

Name	Bind Parameter	Access Method	Source Type	Data Type
DEPT	DEPT	IN	HTTP HEADER	STRING

Figure 2-17. *Specifying parameters*

In this example, you will pass the parameters as HTTP headers. This screen allows you to map from an HTTP header variable to an internal parameter that you can use in the query or PL/SQL procedure, and so on.

Now you can test your new web service, but one important thing to remember is that whenever you create or modify a module or resource template in SQL Developer, you need to validate and re-upload it to ORDS.

■ **Tip**   If you have made changes to your resource template but it doesn't seem to work, check that you have uploaded it back to ORDS. I've lost count of the number of times I've changed something and seen the web service performing in the "old way," only to discover that I'd forgotten to upload the new definition back to ORDS.

Now if you rerun the `curl` command, you should see the following:

```
[jes@AEMBP ~]$ curl http://aevm:8080/ords/training/ae/employees
{"items":[]}
```

Note the empty return result (in other words, an `items` array with zero elements). This is because you added the following predicate to your query, but you have not passed a department to the web service:

```
where e.deptno = :DEPT
```

You can pass a department number in the HTTP header in cURL using the following command:

```
[jes@AEMBP ~]$ curl -H "DEPT:10" \ http://aevm:8080/ords/training/ae/employees
{
    "items": [
        {
            "deptno": 10,
            "empno": 7839,
            "ename": "KING",
            "hiredate": "1981-11-17T00:00:00Z",
            "job": "PRESIDENT",
            "sal": 5000
        },
        {
            "deptno": 10,
            "empno": 7782,
            "ename": "CLARK",
            "hiredate": "1981-06-08T23:00:00Z",
            "job": "MANAGER",
            "mgr": 7839,
            "sal": 2450
        },
        {
            "deptno": 10,
            "empno": 7934,
            "ename": "MILLER",
            "hiredate": "1982-01-23T00:00:00Z",
```

```
            "job": "CLERK",
            "mgr": 7782,
            "sal": 1300
        }
    ],
    "next": {
        "$ref": "http://aevm:8080/ords/training/ae/employees?page=1"
    }
}
```

You can see how easily you can now construct web services that can be called from any other systems to either pull data from your database or perhaps create or modify data.

Let's look at how you can create a web service that allows users to update the salary for an employee. First create a new handler called employee with a POST method (with a Source Type setting of PL/SQL), as shown in Figure 2-18.

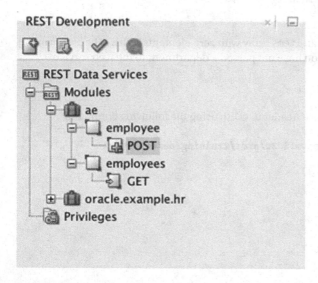

Figure 2-18. *Creating a new POST method to update an employee record*

Next you need to write the PL/SQL code for the web service (in the SQL worksheet like you did before).

```
begin
  update emp e
     set e.sal   = :SAL
   where e.empno = :EMPNO;
end;
```

Then you need to define the parameters, as shown in Figure 2-19.

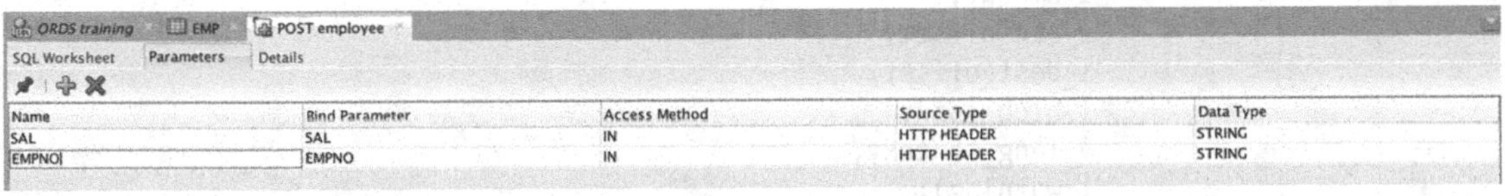
ORDS training
EMP
POST employee
SQL Worksheet
Parameters
Details
Name
Bind Parameter
Access Method
Source Type
Data Type
SAL
SAL
IN
HTTP HEADER
STRING
EMPNO
EMPNO
IN
HTTP HEADER
STRING

***Figure 2-19.** Parameters for the EMPLOYEE web service*

After uploading the changes back to ORDS, you can call the web service using cURL.

```
[jes@AEMBP ~]$ curl -X POST -H 'EMPNO:7839' -H 'SAL:30000'
http://aevm:8080/ords/training/ae/employee
[jes@AEMBP ~]$
```

You will notice you do not get any response (you could modify the PL/SQL routine to echo the updated employee record). However, if you query the emp table in your database, you should see that the employee with empno 7839 now has a salary of 30000.

If you wanted to retrieve an image of the employee from the database, then the Media Resource source type is a good option to choose. In this case, you need to provide a SQL query that returns exactly one record, and the query needs to return both the `content_type` and the `content_body`, similar to the following query:

```
select content_type,
       content_body
  from your_table
 where ...
```

Accessing Hidden Parameters

Depending on the type of URI you have defined, there may be some hidden parameters that are automatically defined for you so that you can use them inside your logic. For example, in a PL/SQL handler, you can access the `BODY` of the `POST`ed data using `:body`, so you could have a block of PL/SQL like this:

```
declare
  l_clob          clob;
  l_src_offset    number;
  l_dest_offset   number;
  l_blob_csid     number := dbms_lob.default_csid;
  v_lang_context number := dbms_lob.default_lang_ctx;
  l_warning       number;
  l_amount        number;
begin
  dbms_lob.createtemporary(l_clob, true);

  l_src_offset     := 1;
  l_dest_offset := 1;
  l_amount := dbms_lob.getlength(:body);
```

```
dbms_lob.converttoclob(l_clob,
                       :body,
                       l_amount,
                       l_src_offset,
                       l_dest_offset,
                       l_blob_csid,
                       v_lang_context,
                       l_warning);

    insert into mytable(
      id,
      data
    ) values (
      mytable_seq.nextval,
      l_clob
    );

end;
```

This block would convert the body of the POSTed data from a blob to a clob and store it in a table. Note that the purpose of this code is to show how you would reference the body rather than show a full end-to-end demonstration.

Accessing ORDS Web Services via APEX

Although this chapter is primarily about installing and configuring ORDS, I thought it would be useful to show just how easily you can access your ORDS web services from an APEX application. First, though, why would you want to do that? Well, recall that earlier I mentioned that most front-end web development requires that you will run into using JSON data at one point or another, typically if you are trying to integrate a jQuery plugin or perhaps a third-party visualization library such as D3.

Without getting into the specifics of an actual jQuery plugin, let's imagine two use cases.

- From APEX you want to access an ORDS web service via PL/SQL.

- From APEX you want to access an ORDS web service via jQuery.

In both cases the web service could be defined in the local ORDS server (that is, the one you're accessing APEX via) or in a remote web service.

In the PL/SQL method, you can use the APEX_WEB_SERVICE API and call the MAKE_REST_REQUEST procedure like this:

```
declare
    l_clob CLOB;
begin
    l_clob := apex_web_service.make_rest_request(
        p_url => 'http://aevm:8080/ords/training/ae/employees',
        p_http_method => 'GET');

    sys.htp.p(l_clob);
end;
```

Here you use the sys.htp.p command to output the response, but you could assign it to a variable, capture it in a table, and so on. If you wanted to pass some parameters to the web service, you could pass those via the p_parm_name and p_parm_value parameters. Here's an example:

```
declare
    l_clob        CLOB;
begin
    l_clob := apex_web_service.make_rest_request(
        p_url => 'http://aevm:8080/ords/training/ae/employees',
        p_http_method => 'GET',
        p_parm_name  => apex_util.string_to_table('param1:param2'),
        p_parm_value => apex_util.string_to_table('value1:value2')););

    sys.htp.p(l_clob);
end;
```

As you can see, it's pretty simple to call a web service via PL/SQL from APEX. If you want to do it via jQuery, there are a few different ways to do it, but typically I tend to use the $.ajax method. Here's an example:

```
$.ajax({
  method: "GET",
  url: "/ords/training/ae/employees"
})
  .done(function( data ) {
    console.log(data.items.count);
    for (var i = 0; i < data.items.length; i++) {
        emp = data.items[i];
        console.log(emp.ename);
    }
});
```

This will call the /ords/training/ae/employees URI on the same web server you are accessing APEX. When the web service response is returned, then you loop around the items (recall the array of items you saw earlier) and output the employee name.

Now with a web service and a few lines of code, your APEX application is able to query, create, and modify data easily in another Oracle Database using Oracle Rest Data Services as the interface.

There are so many more features available in ORDS (I've barely scratched the surface), I could spend an entire book on it; however, I have only a chapter. I do encourage you to look at the documentation that goes into far greater detail than I can here, as well as touching on some of the more specific features (for example, JSON query filters).

Summary

ORDS represents a new step in Oracle's evolution of the listener used with APEX. ORDS is more powerful than previous iterations and is more generally useful beyond merely for Application Express.

You learned in this chapter how to download ORDS and install it and then to configure it for your needs. You were also introduced to the administration interface that is now accessible via SQL Developer. Finally, you saw how to REST enable existing tables and how to create REST endpoints and service requests made to them.

CHAPTER 3

∎∎∎

Oracle APEX 5.0 Charts Inside Out

by Dimitri Gielis

This chapter will cover the charting possibilities in Oracle Application Express 5.0 and explain in great detail how APEX charts work behind the scenes.

In my experience, a lot of people who have been developing in APEX for years don't use charts much or haven't really invested time in reviewing all the options APEX provides. This is why, although this is an expert book, I will start this chapter by explaining what APEX charts are, how they work, and what types of charts you can create with the built-in functionality of APEX. In the second half of the chapter, I will go up a level and discuss how to produce more advanced charts.

The release of APEX 5.0 didn't bring a lot of changes in charting compared to APEX 4.2 (but it did compared to APEX 4.0). The built-in charts in APEX still rely on the AnyChart 6 engine.

By understanding the different components of a chart and how APEX handles them, you'll be able to visually display your data in almost any way you like. From combined charts to charts with thresholds to dashboards, this chapter will explain it all step-by-step. You'll also learn how to make charts more interactive and combine them with other elements on the page; for example, when you change your chart, a report on the same page changes automatically based on the change in your chart, and the other way around.

Finally, you will look both at the future of charts in APEX and at how you can already benefit from the latest and greatest technologies in the charting world. Charting in general has evolved over time, with more new charting engines becoming available; D3 charts are one of the more popular ones. Integrating these chart engines into APEX is surprisingly simple. There are even some APEX plugins available that do the integration for you. You'll find them in the Sample Charts packaged application.

APEX 5.0 includes two kinds of charts: HTML5 charts and Flash charts. The funny thing is that in APEX 4.0, HTML charts were limited, so we focused on Flash charts. Today it's the other way around: Flash charts are basically dead because the browser needs to have an up-to-date plugin to be able to show Flash content. If the plugin is outdated, many browsers will block the Flash content. Flash eats resources too and doesn't have the greatest performance. Making Flash content responsive isn't as straightforward, and Flash doesn't even run on many tablets (such as the iPad). When you create a Flash chart in APEX but run the chart on a device that doesn't have Flash installed, APEX will automatically show the chart in HTML5. As I don't really see any advantage to creating Flash charts, I decided to not spend too much time on Flash charts in this chapter.

There are different types of charts natively available in APEX, but you can categorize them into three big groups: charts, Gantts, and maps. This chapter will discuss charts in great detail and will combine them with other components such as reports later. Gantts and maps are not covered because they are still built using the Flash technology.

HTML5 Charts

Usually when you wanted to do serious charting in APEX 4.*x*, you used Flash charts. Flash charts offered many chart types, different animations, and different ways to adapt the look and feel. The AnyChart engine was used to render the charts, and initially only Flash charts were supported. Because the industry doesn't like Flash anymore (because of the reasons highlighted previously), AnyChart had to follow, so it made its charting engine available in HTML5 too. APEX 4.2 included the new AnyChart engine and introduced HTML5 charts at that time. The wizards in APEX stayed the same; you could switch your Flash chart to an HTML5 chart and AnyChart would take care of the rest. APEX 5.0 continues on this path; there's one chart wizard that offers you the different options for the chart type, and depending the rendering type, either Flash or HTML5, the chart is rendered in that technology.

Background

Flash charts were introduced with the release of APEX 3.0 in 2007. In addition to HTML and SVG charts, you could now create Flash-based charts. The Oracle APEX development team also made it clear that Flash-based charts would become the preferred charting engine and SVG wouldn't be developed further. The APEX development team didn't build the Flash charts from scratch and instead opted for a third-party solution. Oracle made an agreement with AnyChart (`www.anychart.com`) to license its Flash charts. What Oracle still needed to do was to create native Oracle APEX wizards to include these charts easily in an APEX project.

I believe Oracle made a great decision here in not trying to build a Flash chart engine because charting is a whole area in itself and evolves quickly. There were many charting engines around, but going with AnyChart was not a bad choice because the company was committed to evolving its product along with the rest of the charting world.

That AnyChart wouldn't stand still proved to be true over time. In Oracle APEX 3.0, version 3.3 of the AnyChart product was included, but a year later AnyChart 4 was already out, and soon after that, so was version 5. With the patch releases of APEX 3.*x*, Oracle included newer versions of AnyChart, but it was only in the interactive reports that AnyChart 4 and AnyChart 5 were used.

With the release of APEX 4.0, AnyChart 5 was completely supported in the wizards. In fact, all new charts you created would automatically use the AnyChart 5 engine. As Oracle wanted APEX to be compatible with older versions and needed to support existing applications using Flash charts, AnyChart 3.3 was also included in APEX 4.0. So if you ran your APEX 3.*x* application in APEX 4.0, it would still show AnyChart 3.3 charts. Also note that the version of AnyChart 5 was a special version compiled for Oracle and didn't include all the available chart types that the regular AnyChart 5 supported.

Over time, AnyChart developed other charting components. In addition to the AnyChart charting solution, it introduced AnyGantt, AnyMap, and AnyStock. In APEX 4.0, Oracle decided to also license AnyGantt Gantt charts and AnyMap interactive maps. The Oracle APEX development team built wizards around these engines, so you could create Gantt and Map types declaratively too.

With the release of APEX 4.2, AnyChart 6 was introduced, which replaced AnyChart 5. AnyChart 6 was backward compatible, and the main improvement of this version was the support of HTML5 charts. The same engine could render either in Flash charts or in HTML5 charts. The APEX wizards were changed, so more options became available (based on the AnyChart 6 engine), and you could just flip a switch to show your chart in HTML5 instead of Flash.

APEX 5.0 didn't introduce many new features compared to APEX 4.2 for charts; the latest release of AnyChart 6 and AnyGantt 4 were included, and some wizards were updated to make things easier to understand (especially with the Page Designer).

AnyChart already released version 7, but this version is not included in APEX because AnyChart hasn't made it backward compatible. AnyChart 7 is also a completely new code base, which means the APEX development team would need to spend a lot of effort in updating its code base to generate the correct settings for the chart.

Table 3-1 gives an overview of the versions of APEX and the evolution of the chart engines.

Table 3-1. *Versions of APEX and the Evolution of the Chart*

APEX < 3.0	APEX 3.0	APEX 3.2	APEX 4.0	APEX 4.2	APEX 5.0
HTML/SVG					
	AnyChart 3	AnyChart 4	AnyChart 5	AnyChart 6	AnyChart 6
	Flash	Flash	Flash	Flash/HTML5	Flash/HTML5
				Chart plugins: Flot Charts, and so on	Chart plugins: D3JS, Flot Charts, and so on

Creating a Chart

Let's say you want to create a page with a chart in your APEX application.

Hit the Create Page button in Application Builder and select as the page type Chart (Figure 3-1).

Figure 3-1. *Select Chart as the page type*

On the next page of the wizard, select HTML5 Chart for Chart Rendering and select the chart type you want to use (Figure 3-2).

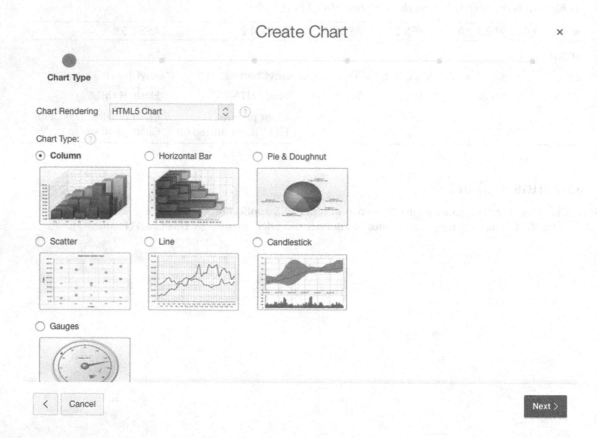

Figure 3-2. *Select a chart type*

The Create Chart Wizard categorizes the charts nicely. You first select the main chart type and then get the choice to select a subtype if that is available. For example, the Line chart type doesn't have any subtypes, whereas the Column chart type has seven subtypes (Figure 3-3).

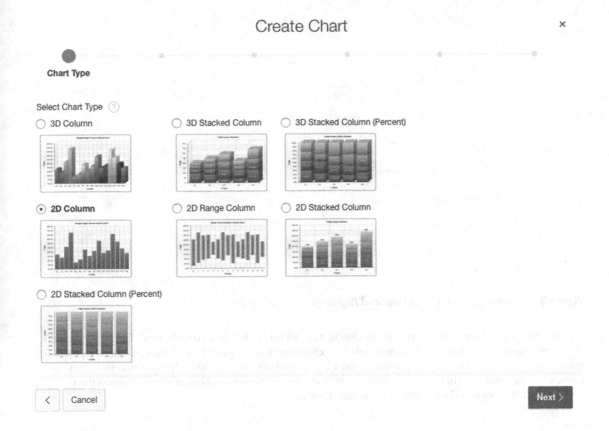

Figure 3-3. *Column subcharts*

Clicking the subtype brings you to the Page and Region Attributes page, which is not different from any other region screen in APEX (Figure 3-4). By default the region template is Standard, but you can choose any you like. Now give the region a title and click Next.

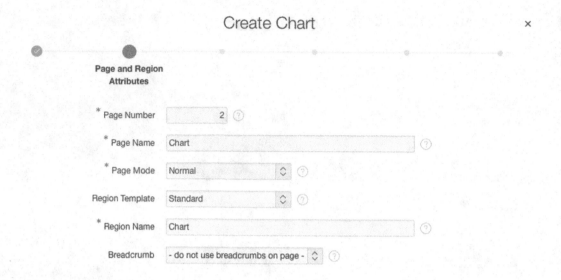

Figure 3-4. *Create Chart Wizard (Page and Region Attributes page)*

On the next screen, you can specify the Navigation Menu setting; just go with the default.

The next screen defines the look and feel of the chart and which options you want to include (Figure 3-5). You can go with the defaults during creation and adapt them later; or, if you already know exactly what you want, you can make the changes immediately. For example, if you want to include a legend, select the position where you'd like to see it (Left, Right, Top, Bottom, Float).

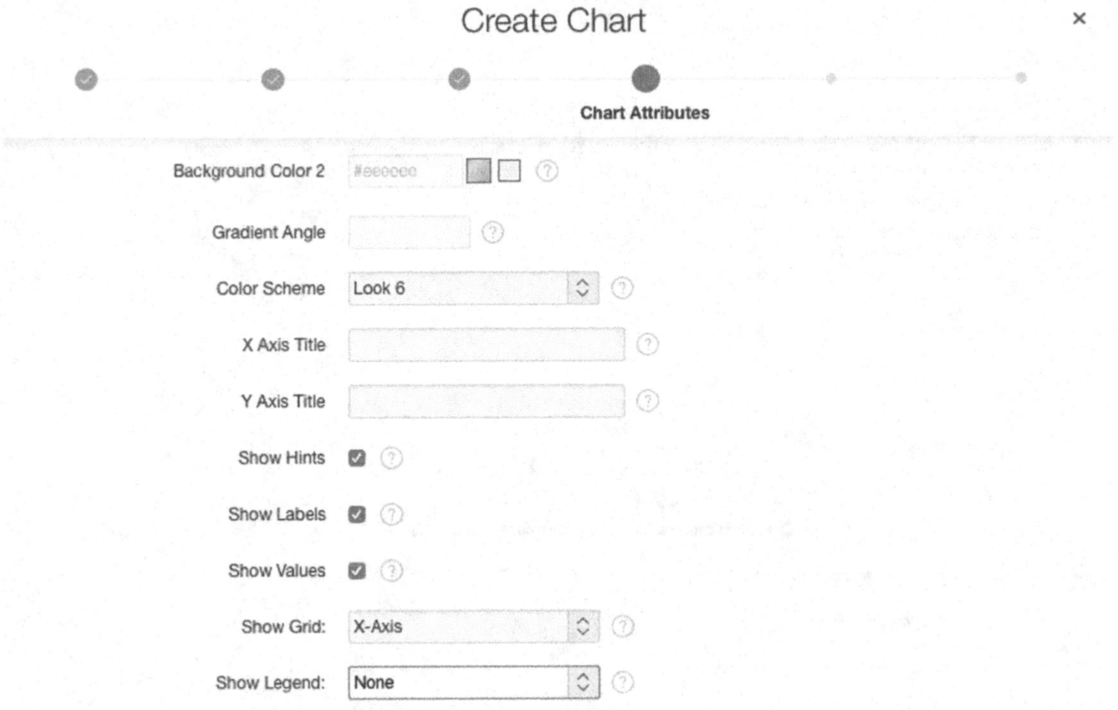

Create Chart

×

Chart Attributes

Background Color 2	#eeeeee ▣ ☐ ⑦
Gradient Angle	⑦
Color Scheme	Look 6 ⑦
X Axis Title	⑦
Y Axis Title	⑦
Show Hints	☑ ⑦
Show Labels	☑ ⑦
Show Values	☑ ⑦
Show Grid:	X-Axis ⑦
Show Legend:	None ⑦

Figure 3-5. *Define the chart attributes (if the screen is big, scroll down for more features, until you see the bottom part)*

Previously, you defined how the chart will look, but you didn't define the source of the chart yet. What data does the chart need to show? You'll need to add a SQL query that will be used to feed the chart with data (Figure 3-6). The SQL query syntax varies depending on the chart type you select.

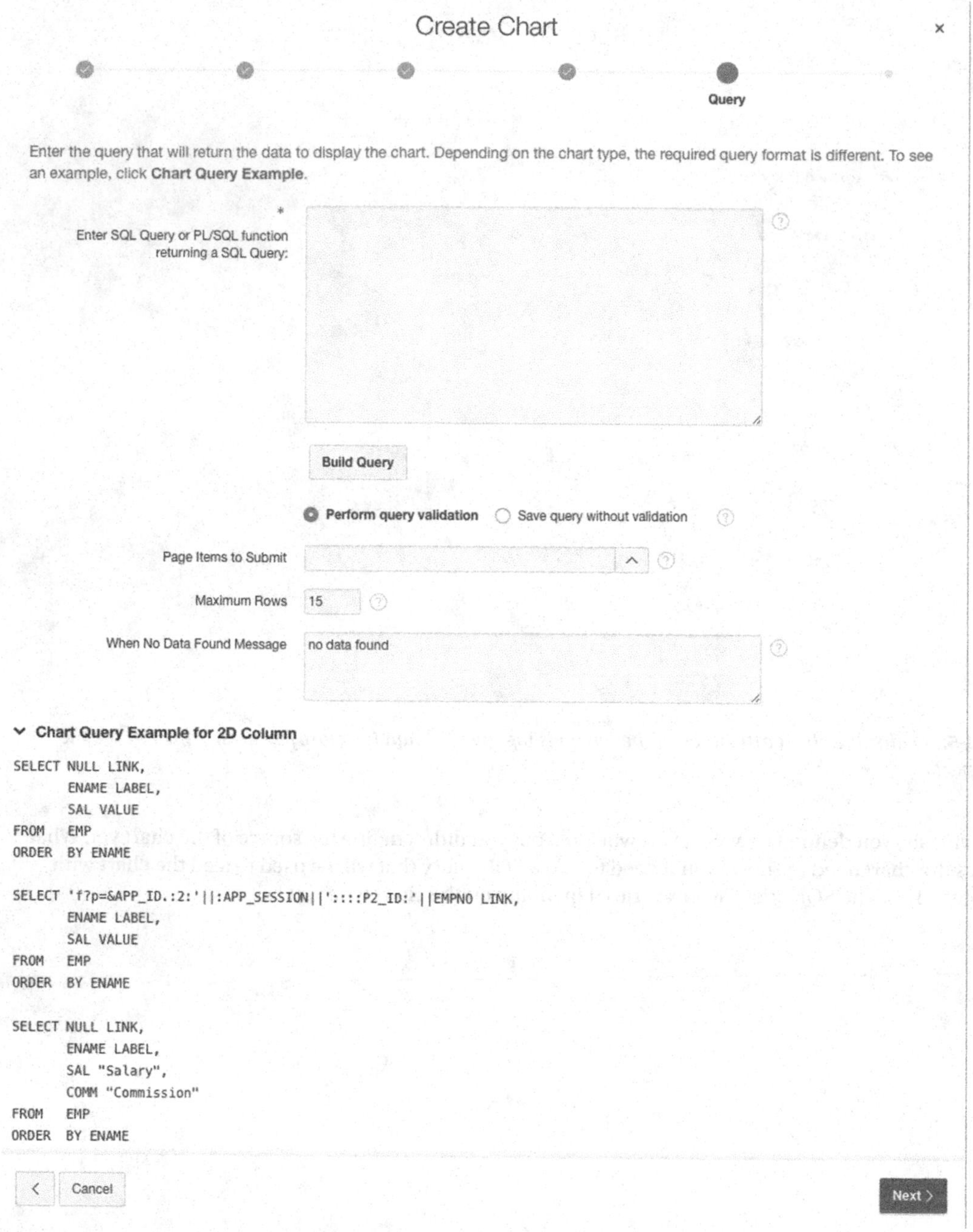

Create Chart   ×

Query

Enter the query that will return the data to display the chart. Depending on the chart type, the required query format is different. To see
an example, click **Chart Query Example**.

Enter SQL Query or PL/SQL function
returning a SQL Query:

Build Query

⦿ **Perform query validation**   ○ Save query without validation

Page Items to Submit

Maximum Rows   `15`

When No Data Found Message   `no data found`

∨ Chart Query Example for 2D Column

```
SELECT NULL LINK,
       ENAME LABEL,
       SAL VALUE
FROM   EMP
ORDER  BY ENAME

SELECT 'f?p=&APP_ID.:2:'||:APP_SESSION||'::::P2_ID:'||EMPNO LINK,
       ENAME LABEL,
       SAL VALUE
FROM   EMP
ORDER  BY ENAME

SELECT NULL LINK,
       ENAME LABEL,
       SAL "Salary",
       COMM "Commission"
FROM   EMP
ORDER  BY ENAME
```

< Cancel   Next >

Figure 3-6. *Define the SQL query of the chart*

Most of the charts have a query like this:

```
select link, label, value
from   table
order by label
```

where

- `link` is a URL.

- `label` is the text that displays in the chart.

- `value` is the numeric column that defines the size of the chart type.

As I said, the query of the chart depends on the type of chart you selected. At the bottom of the page you'll find some examples for the chart type you selected. This is handy to see the format of the `SELECT` statement. Alternatively, you can use the Build Query button to create the SQL statement with a wizard. I'll come back to the different select statements for the different chart types in the section "Understanding the Chart Attributes."

The Result

Once the page with the chart region is created, it will appear on the page with a chart icon in the Page Designer (Figure 3-7). Clicking the attributes shows the settings of the chart; clicking Series 1 shows the series, which contains the SQL statement to provide the chart with data.

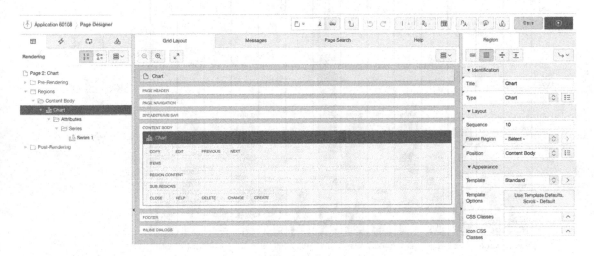

Figure 3-7. *Chart region selected in the Page Designer*

If you're using the Component View to develop, you will see the result in Figure 3-8.

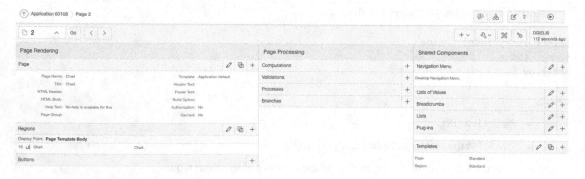

Figure 3-8. *Chart region in Component View*

Before you adapt the chart and look at what is happening behind the scenes, just run the page to see what it looks like (Figure 3-9).

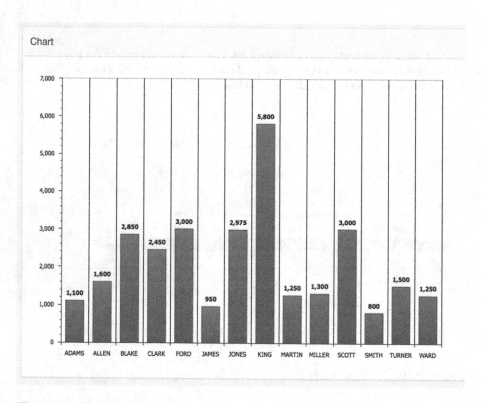

Figure 3-9. *The chart displayed on the page*

Page Designer vs. Component View

From APEX 5 onward, the Tree View of APEX 4.*x* is replaced by the Page Designer. The Page Designer allows you to access the different components (and make changes) a lot more quickly. Many features of the Tree View are incorporated in the tree on the left in the Page Designer. It takes a bit of time to get used to the Page Designer, and a large monitor is recommended, but I definitely recommend giving it a try.

The Component View has existed the longest, and some people still prefer that view to develop. When you're new to developing charts, the wizard kind of interface of the Component View might be a bit easier. When adding a chart region, you'll see the same wizard as when you add a new page with a chart (as shown previously). The wizard also contains examples for the queries, something that the Page Designer lacks when you add a chart region to an existing page.

With the Page Designer, you drag a chart region on your page and then customize the attributes. When you're more experienced with charts, the Page Designer allows you to add multiple charts more quickly, and adapting the attributes of the charts will be faster. All functionalities for the charts are the same regardless of which view you develop in, but some labels differ or are grouped a bit differently.

In the first half of this chapter, I will explain the different possibilities of the charts. I'll use the Component View to show the screenshots because that is a bit easier than with the Page Designer. When I create more advanced charts, I'll use the Page Designer.

Understanding the Chart Region

When editing the chart region (click the region name), you might be surprised at first because there is no Region Source setting (unlike with a report). You find the chart settings in the Chart Attributes section and the data part in the Series section. Behind the scenes, APEX will generate some HTML objects to render the chart (which is actually the region source), but because you can't change this rendering, I won't go much deeper into this.

Understanding the Chart Attributes

The previous section covered the region definition, but more importantly, if you want to change the appearance and behavior of a chart, you can do this via the chart attributes (just below the region name in the tree or the Chart Attributes tab in the Component View).

Depending on the chart type chosen, you have different sections in the chart attributes. As highlighted previously, the Component View (Figure 3-10) displays the options a bit differently than the Page Designer (Figure 3-11).

Figure 3-10. *The different sections of the chart attributes (for a bar chart) in the Component View*

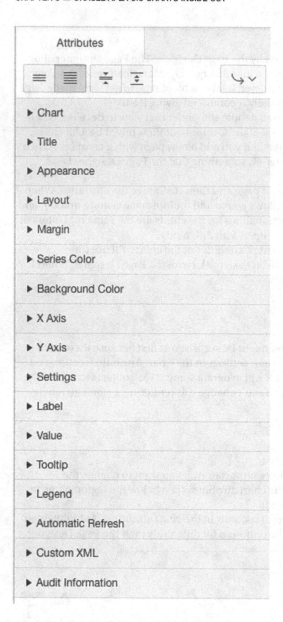

Figure 3-11. *The different sections of the chart attributes (for a bar chart) in the Page Designer*

Again, to discuss the different settings, I'll use the Component View screenshots, but all settings are also available in the Page Designer.

The Chart Settings options allow you to change the chart type, the title, the size of the chart, and the look and feel. Figure 3-12 shows the options, which you can set as follows:

- *Chart Rendering*: Flash or HTML5 Chart. Unless the chart type is not available as HTML5, I recommend going with HTML5 so that on every device the look and feel is the same.

■ **Note**   If Flash is selected but the device doesn't support Flash, it will be rendered as HTML5.

- *Chart Title*: Set a title on top of the chart.

- *Chart Type*: Change between chart types in a given family. For example, you can change between 3D Stacked Column, 3D Bar Chart, 3D Stacked Bar Chart, and so forth.

- *Chart Width and Height*: Specify the size of the region in which the chart is rendered (in pixels). Leave this blank for 100 percent.

- *Chart Margin*: Specify the amount of blank space surrounding the chart. Values are in pixels (Top, Bottom, Left, Right).

- *Color Scheme*: Select one of the built-in color schemes for your chart. Single-series charts use one color for each data point. Multiple-series charts use one color for each series. Look 7 will use the AnyChart default palette of colors, applying a different color to each data point in a single series. Select the Custom option to define your own color scheme.

- *Color Level: Series or Point*: Series will use one color per series (for example, all bars in the same series will use blue), while Point will use a different color for every point (for example, all bars will use a different color regardless of the series they are in). Look 7 will always use different colors for all points.

- *Hatch Pattern*: Toggle hatch patterns off and on. In a multiseries bar chart, for example, it will show one series as bars with lines in them, another series as bars with stripes, and so forth. You can change explicit control of which hatch pattern is used through adapting the XML code.

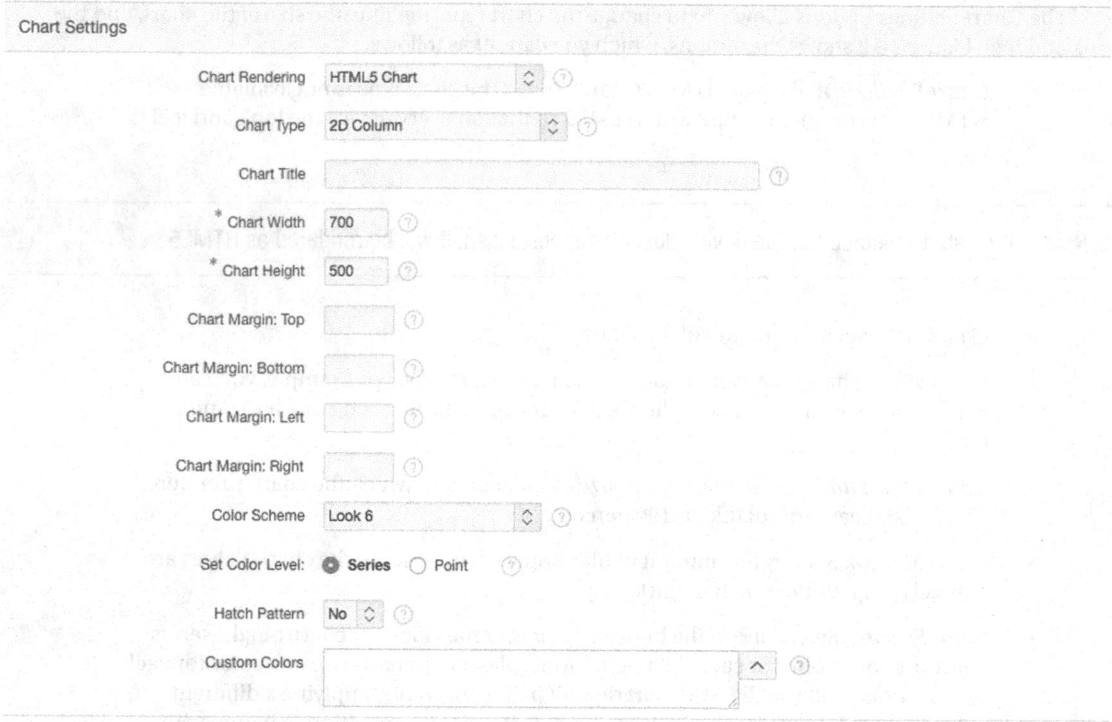

Chart Settings

Chart Rendering	HTML5 Chart
Chart Type	2D Column
Chart Title	
* Chart Width	700
* Chart Height	500
Chart Margin: Top	
Chart Margin: Bottom	
Chart Margin: Left	
Chart Margin: Right	
Color Scheme	Look 6
Set Color Level:	● Series ○ Point
Hatch Pattern	No
Custom Colors	

Figure 3-12. *The main settings of the chart in Chart Settings*

The Chart Series options hold the `select` queries that are used to feed the chart with data. You can have one or more series defined. To edit an existing series, you click the Edit icon, while to add a new series, you click the Add Series button (Figure 3-13). In the next section, "Adding Multiple Series and Combined Charts," I'll go into more detail about the series.

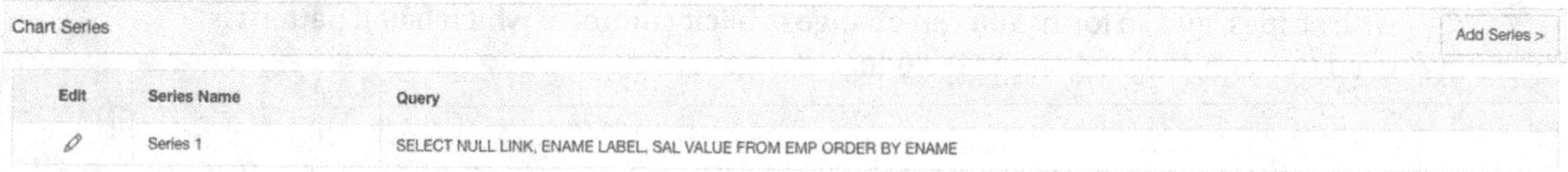

Chart Series   Add Series >

Edit	Series Name	Query
✎	Series 1	SELECT NULL LINK, ENAME LABEL, SAL VALUE FROM EMP ORDER BY ENAME

Figure 3-13. *One or more series per chart in the Chart Series settings*

In the Display Settings area, you define the main look and feel of the chart and the different features you want to enable. Figure 3-14 shows the following settings that you can control:

- *Animation* controls the initial appearance of this chart. There are 30 different types of animation available, such as Side from Left, Scale Y Top, and so on (this option is available only when Flash Chart is selected for Chart Rendering).

- *Style* defines the visual appearance of the data element, which is most apparent in 2D bar and column charts. There are four styles available in APEX 5.0: Default, Aqua Dark, Aqua Light, and Silver.

- *Background Type* has three choices. Transparent makes the chart background transparent. Solid Color uses the color specified in Background Color 1 for the background of the chart. Gradient uses Background Color 1 and 2 and fades between them depending the gradient angle specified lower down.

- *Include on Chart* allows you to select the options you want to display on your chart. Depending on the chart type, some options might not be available. The following are the options:

  - *Hints*: Select this box if you want to see the label and value when you hover your cursor over a data point on the chart.

  - *Values*: Select this box if you want to show the values next to the data points on the chart.

  - *Labels*: Select this box if you want to see the labels along the chart axis.

  - *Group by Series*: Select this box if you want to see your series split. Instead of seeing your data grouped by column (Allen: SAL, COMM – Blake: SAL, COMM – Clark: SAL, COMM), you will see it grouped by series first and then by column (SAL: Allen, Blake, Clark... – COMM: Allen, Blake, Clark...).

  - *Major Ticks*: Select this box if you want to see the big tick marks in a gauge or dial chart.

  - *Minor Ticks*: Select this box if you want to see the small tick marks between the big tick marks on your gauge (or dial) chart.

  - *Tick Labels*: Select this box if you want to see the values corresponding to the tick marks.

  - *Multiple Y-Axes*: Select the box if you want to see an extra y-axis positioned opposite to the existing y-axis on the chart. On a multiseries chart, the extra y-axis will be associated with the second series of the chart. If you customize the XML, you get even more choices. If you need more control than APEX gives you, check the AnyChart documentation for the XML you can use.

  - *Invert X-Axis Scale*: Select this box if you want the sorting to be reversed. For example, Adams – Ward becomes Ward – Adams.

  - *Invert Y-Axis Scale*: Select this box if you want the y-axis scale in an inverted mode. For example, selecting the box will cause a bar chart to go down instead of up.

  - *Invert Scale*: Select this box if you want the numbers to start from high to low on a Gauge (or Dial) chart.

  - *Overlay Y-Axis*: Select this box if you want bars shown one over another with multiple series (and same label). Depending on whether you use 2D or 3D charts, the behavior is different. You can experiment to see what looks best in your case.

  - *Sorted Overlay Y-Axis*: Select this box if you want series sorted and displayed with lower values in front of higher values.

  - *Smart Auto Calculation Mode*: Select this box if you want the y-axis to scale automatically based on the number of decimal digits and avoid duplicate items appearing on the axis scale.

- *Show Scrollbars* controls whether a scrollbar will be displayed on your chart. You can show a scrollbar on the x-axis, on the y-axis, or on both (available only in Flash rendering).

- *Show Grid* controls whether a value grid will be displayed on your chart. You can show the grid for the x-axis, for the y-axis, or for both.

- *Gradient Angle* defines the angle for the background type of Gradient. A value of 0 degrees results in a horizontal gradient with the first background color on the left and the second background color on the right. A value of 90 degrees results in a vertical gradient with the first background color at the top and the second background color at the bottom.

- *X-Axis Label*, *Y-Axis Label*, and *Values Rotation* define the amount of rotation, in degrees, for the chart labels. Positive values indicate clockwise rotation. Negative values indicate counterclockwise rotation. The Font Face setting for labels does not apply to rotated text. If the Y Axis Title setting contains non-ASCII characters, make sure you don't have a value specified in the Y-Axis Label Rotation setting.

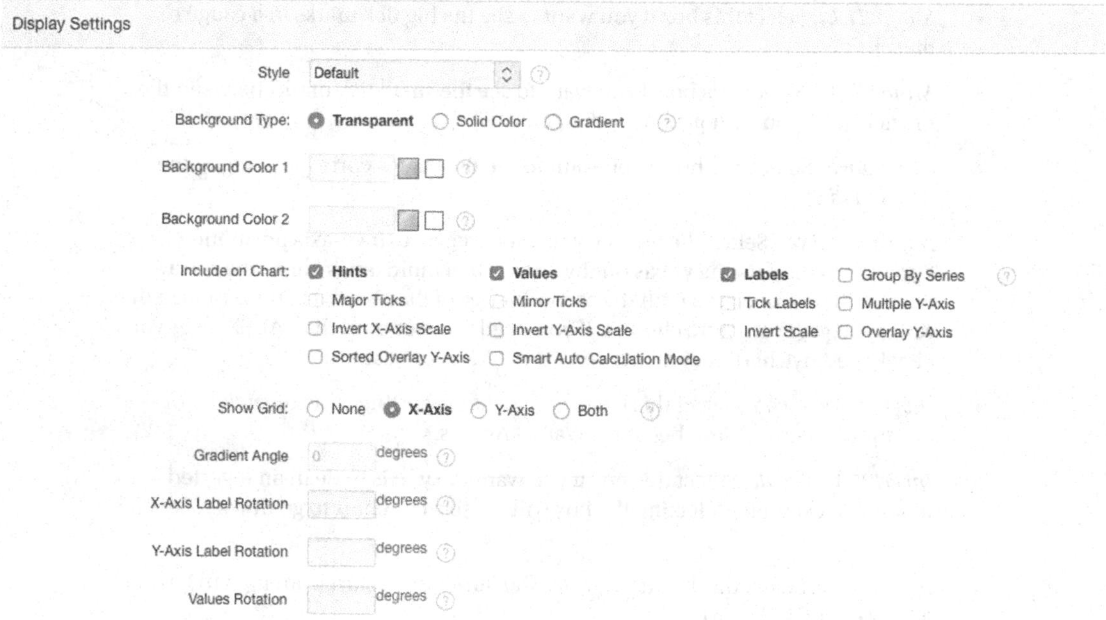

Figure 3-14. *Define the main look and feel of the chart in display settings*

In the Axes Settings area shown in Figure 3-15, you define the title of the axis, the interval, and the format of the values.

- *X Axis Title* and *Y Axis Title* are used to describe the labels along the horizontal and vertical axes of your chart.

- *X Axis Min/Max* and *Y-Axis Min/Max* define the smallest and largest data values you want to appear on the corresponding axis. You see these items depending on the chart type, such as a column chart.

- *X Axis Prefix* and *Y Axis Prefix* define text to display before values on the corresponding axes. This text prefix will appear before grid labels, value labels, and hint text. For example, you can enter a currency symbol as a prefix.

- *X Axis Postfix* and *Y Axis Postfix* define text to display *after* values on the corresponding axes. This text postfix will appear after grid labels, value labels, and hint text. For example, you can enter a percentage symbol as a postfix.

- *X-Axis Minor/Major Interval* and *Y-Axis Minor/Major Interval* settings control the minor and major scale steps used for the axis labels, the tick marks, and the grid on your chart. If these are not set, the steps are calculated automatically. Values entered must be positive. These settings will be used only when Show Grid in Display Settings is set.

- *Decimal Places* defines the number of decimal places to be used in the y-axis values.

■ **Note**   All these settings are static, so you can't use page items to dynamically set them. However, if you want to set, for example, the Y Axis Min value dynamically depending the data you return, you can set Custom XML to Yes on the Chart XML page and include your substitution strings there (for example, &PAGE_ITEM).

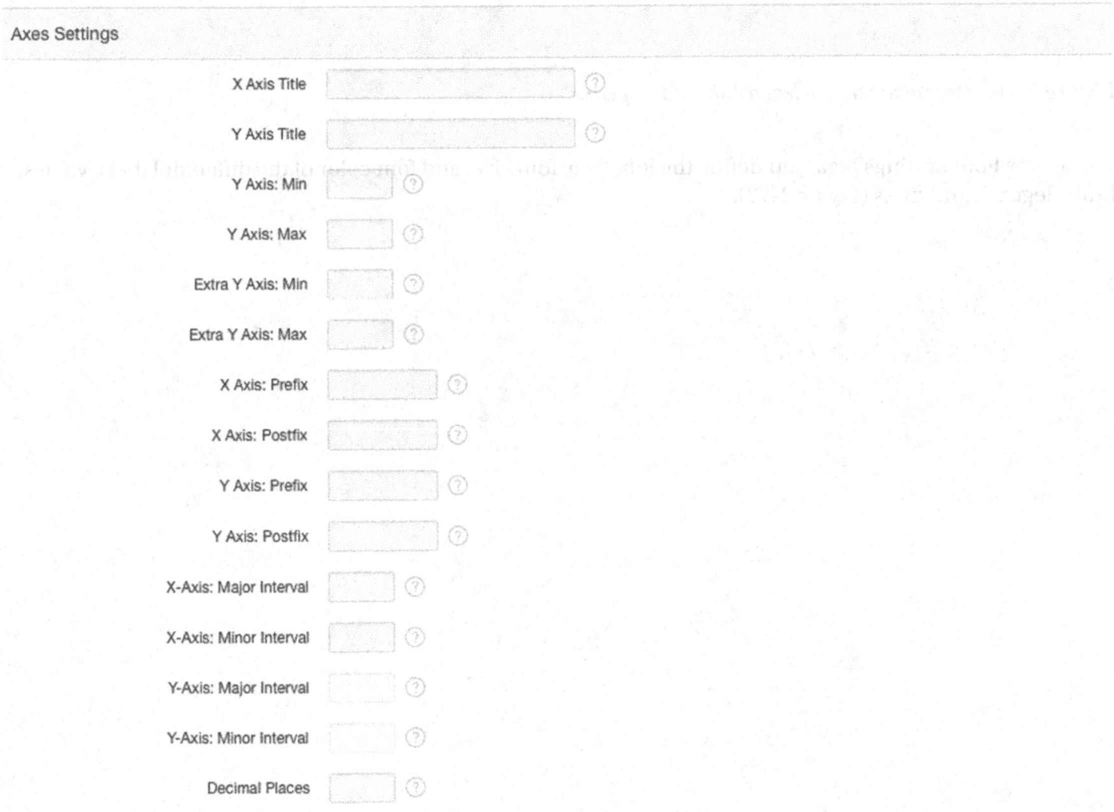

Figure 3-15. *The Axes Settings area*

In the Legend Settings area (see Figure 3-16) you specify whether you want a legend and where it should appear and what the look and feel of it is.

- *Show Legend* specifies whether a legend is displayed on your chart. Possible positions are Left, Right, Top, Bottom, and Float.

- The *Legend Title* is the title of the Legend. If no Legend Title is entered, the title will be empty.

- *Legend Element Layout* defines whether the items of the legend will appear next to each other or under each other. The Legend Element Layout is applicable only when Show Legend is set to Top or Bottom.

- *Show Legend Background* specifies whether the legend background (white) is visible on your chart or whether the legend is transparent.

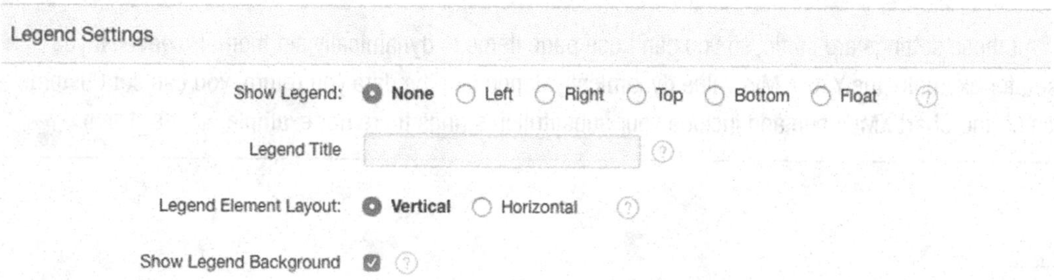

Figure 3-16. Define where the legend should appear

In the Font Settings area, you define the font face, font size, and font color of the different labels, values, hints, legend, and titles (Figure 3-17).

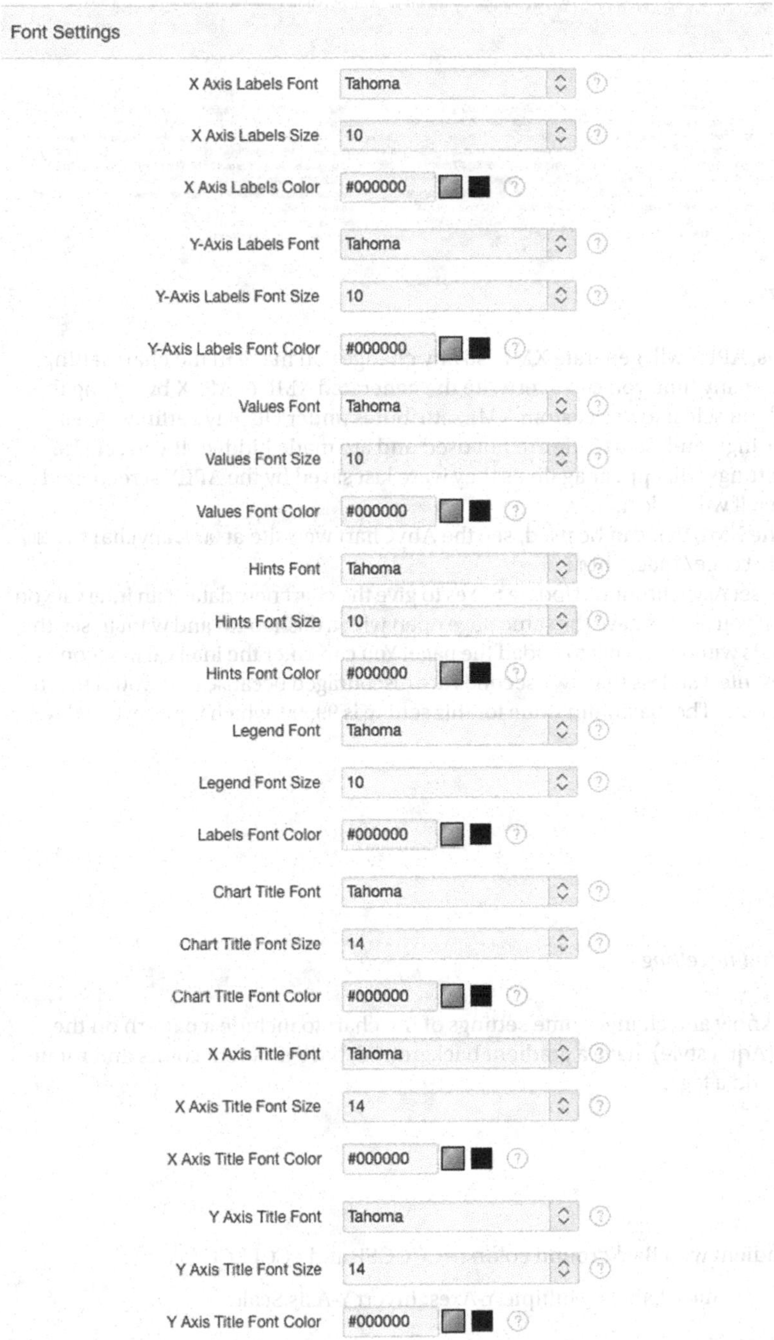

Font Settings

X Axis Labels Font	Tahoma
X Axis Labels Size	10
X Axis Labels Color	#000000
Y-Axis Labels Font	Tahoma
Y-Axis Labels Font Size	10
Y-Axis Labels Font Color	#000000
Values Font	Tahoma
Values Font Size	10
Values Font Color	#000000
Hints Font	Tahoma
Hints Font Size	10
Hints Font Color	#000000
Legend Font	Tahoma
Legend Font Size	10
Labels Font Color	#000000
Chart Title Font	Tahoma
Chart Title Font Size	14
Chart Title Font Color	#000000
X Axis Title Font	Tahoma
X Axis Title Font Size	14
X Axis Title Font Color	#000000
Y Axis Title Font	Tahoma
Y Axis Title Font Size	14
Y Axis Title Font Color	#000000

Figure 3-17. *The font settings of the different text on the chart*

The Chart XML page shows the XML that APEX will send to the AnyChart chart engine (more on that in the section "Behind the Scenes"). See Figure 3-18.

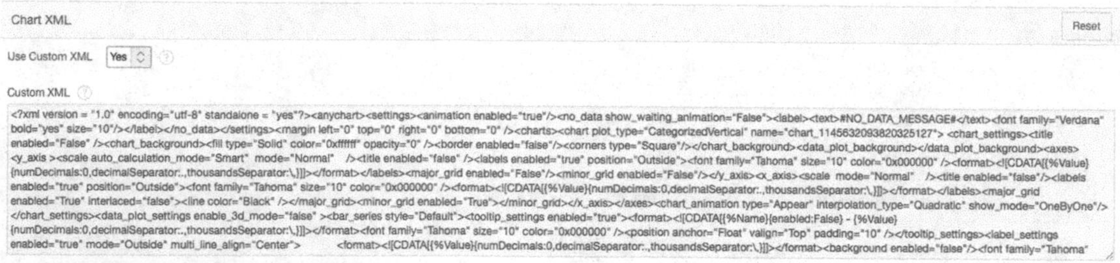

Figure 3-18. *The Chart XML area*

Based on the previous settings, APEX will generate XML, so any change you make in the chart settings will be translated into some XML. At any time you can overwrite the generated XML of APEX by setting the Use Custom XML setting to Yes. If you select to use custom XML, attributes under Display Settings, Axes Settings, Legend Settings, Font Settings, and Chart Title are not used and are made hidden. If you set Use Custom XML back to No, all the settings will appear again as they were last saved by the APEX screen, and your customizations in the XML itself will be lost.

For a complete reference of the XML that can be used, see the AnyChart web site at `www.anychart.com/products/anychart/docs/xmlReference/index.html`.

In the Refresh section, you can set Asynchronous Update to Yes to give the chart new data at an interval you specify (Figure 3-19). This is useful if you always have the same page open with a dashboard and want to see the latest data updated every few seconds without having to reload the page. You can enter the interval in seconds between chart updates, but updates intervals less than two seconds are discouraged because that would mean APEX has to constantly retrieve the data. The maximum value for this setting is 99999, which is just over a day.

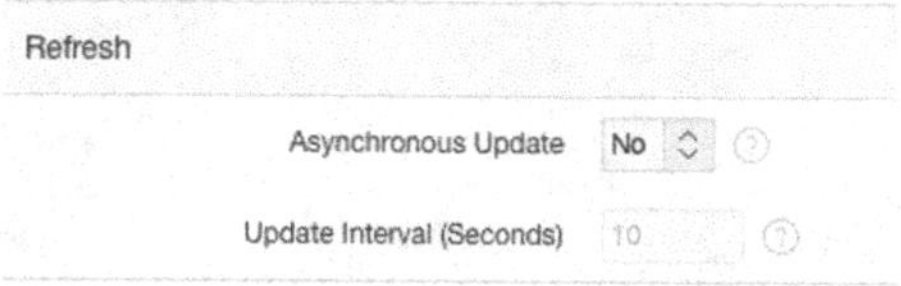

Figure 3-19. *The Asynchronous Update setting*

You can now apply what you know and change some settings of the chart to include a pattern on the bars (hatch), get a smoother look (Aqua style), have a gradient background, have different colors and rotate the labels, play with the axes, and add a legend.

- *Color Scheme*: Look 7

- *Hatch Pattern*: Yes

- *Style*: Aqua Light

- *Background Type*: Gradient with Background colors: #CCCCFF and #CCFFCC

- *Include on Chart*: Hints, Values, Labels, Multiple Y-Axes, Invert Y-Axis Scale

- *Show Grid* = Y-Axis

- *Gradient Angle*: 0 Degrees

- *X-Axis Label Rotation*: 45 Degrees

- *Values Rotation*: 90 Degrees

- *Y Axis*: Min: 200

- *Y Axis*: Prefix: $

- *Y-Axis Major Interval*: 400

- *Y-Axis Minor Interval*: 200

- *Decimal Places*: 2

- *Show Legend*: Left

- *Legend Title*: Legend

- *Legend Element Layout*: Vertical

- *Show Legend Background*: Selected

- *Font Settings*: Different colors starting with #000011 and ending with #000088 such as X Axis Labels Color = #000011, Y-Axis Labels Font Color = #000022, and so on

Figure 3-20 shows the result.

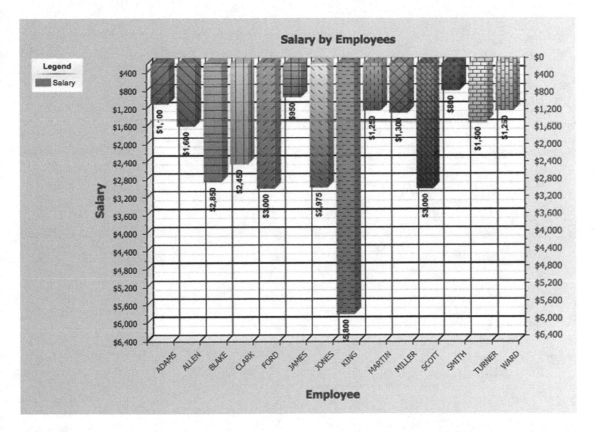

Figure 3-20. *An example of a modified chart*

Adding Multiple Series and Combined Charts

In Figure 3-13 in the previous section, you can see Series in the Chart Attributes. If you create a new series or edit an existing series, a new page will open called Chart Series (Figure 3-21).

Figure 3-21. *Chart Series page*

The Series Attributes section lets you define a name, type, and sequence for the series of that chart type. In Series Name, you enter a name for this series. For scatter marker and range charts, the Series Name setting is used to identify the series in hint and label text. Depending on the chart type chosen, you may able to change the series types. There are three options: Bar, Line, and Marker. For example, if you want to combine a line chart with a bar chart, you could have a main chart type setting of 2D Line and then define the Series Type setting for one of the chart series to be Bar. I will cover combined charts in the next section. Lastly, the sequence determines the order of evaluation.

The next section in Chart Series holds the series query. The Query Source Type setting can be of type SQL Query or Function Returning SQL Query. Most of the time Query Source Type will be SQL Query, but if you need to run a different query depending some values on the page, the Function Returning SQL Query type will probably be the one to pick in that case.

In SQL, you enter the SQL statement or function that will return the data to display this chart's series. Depending on the chart type you choose, a different query may be necessary. If you are unsure about which columns go first and which ones the chart type expects in the query, it's good to use the Build Query button because that will go through a wizard to define the query (Figure 3-22). The Build Query button is not available in the Page Designer view. But with the Page Designer, it's a lot quicker to add multiple series. Right-click Series in the left tree and click the Create Series link.

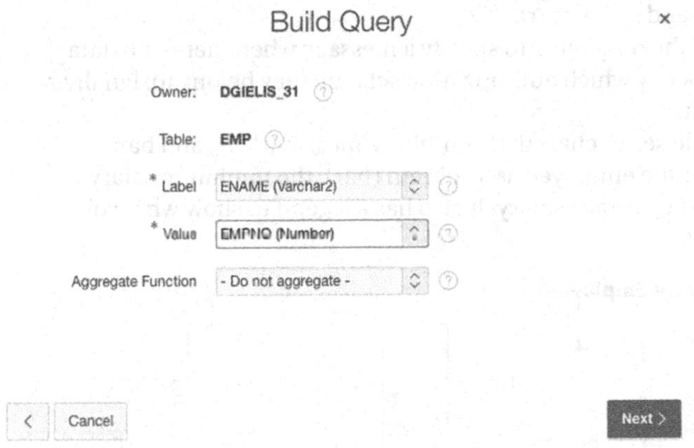

Figure 3-22. The Build Query Wizard

Once the query is defined, you can still adapt it to your needs.

For more experienced developers, it might be useful to create the SQL statement first in SQL Developer or a similar application. That allows you to see whether the query is returning the data you want and, in the case of a really complex statement, create a view or function first and base the SQL statement on that view or function.

The SQL query syntax for the various chart types is as follows:

- Most of the charts have a SQL query with the following syntax:

```
select link, label, value
from   ...
```

- In one query you can also define multiple values that will all be another series (also called multiple series syntax).

```
select link, label, series_1_value [, series_2_value [, ...]]
from   ...
```

- Dial charts have this syntax:

```
select value, maximum_value [ ,low_value [ ,high_value] ]
from  ...
```

- Range charts have this syntax:

```
select link, label, low_value, high_value
from  ...
```

- Scatter charts have this syntax:

```
select link, label, x_value, y_value
from  ...
```

- Candlestick charts have this syntax:

```
select link, label, open, low, high, close
from  ...
```

Maximum Rows contains the maximum number of rows you want to use to display the chart. For pie charts, you are restricted to displaying fewer than 50 rows; for the other charts, the number is unlimited, but the more rows you have, the longer it takes to render the chart.

Furthermore, in the series page, you have the possibility to specify a message when there's no data found; you can make series conditional and specify which authorization scheme they belong to. Finally, there's the possibility to add a build option to it.

Figure 3-23 shows an example of a multiple series chart that combines lines, markers, and bars. The chart shows the salary and commission for the employee as a column (bar), the minimum salary across employees as a marker, and a line with the average salary. It also has a legend to show what color corresponds with what value.

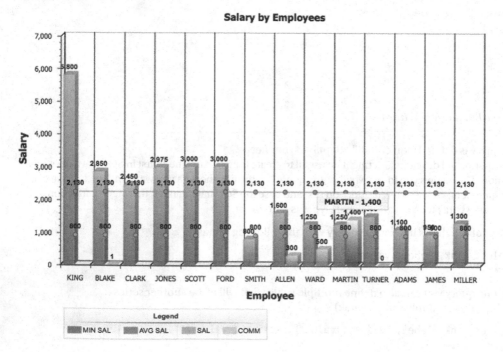

Figure 3-23. *Chart with multiple series*

Looking a bit closer at the series that are defined (Figure 3-24), the first series calculates the minimum salary, has a series type of Marker, and contains a SQL query. The second series calculates the average salary and has a series type of Line, and its Query Source Type setting is Function Returning SQL Query. Editing the series shows the content a bit better (Figure 3-25). The last series contains the salary and commission and uses the multiple series syntax, so one query actually contains two series: salary and commission. This series is of type Bar.

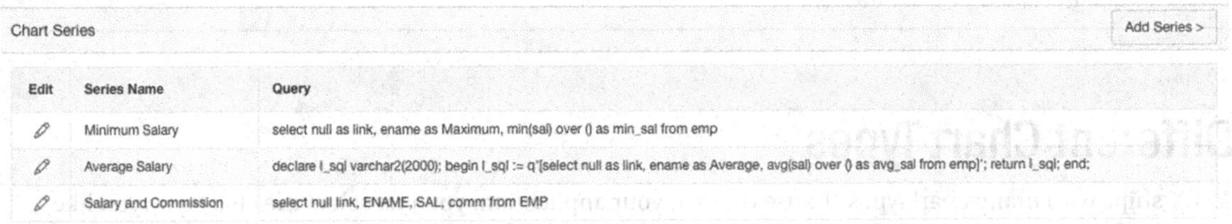

Chart Series		Add Series >

Edit	Series Name	Query
✎	Minimum Salary	select null as link, ename as Maximum, min(sal) over () as min_sal from emp
✎	Average Salary	declare l_sql varchar2(2000); begin l_sql := q'[select null as link, ename as Average, avg(sal) over () as avg_sal from emp]'; return l_sql; end;
✎	Salary and Commission	select null link, ENAME, SAL, comm from EMP

Figure 3-24. *Different Chart Series settings*

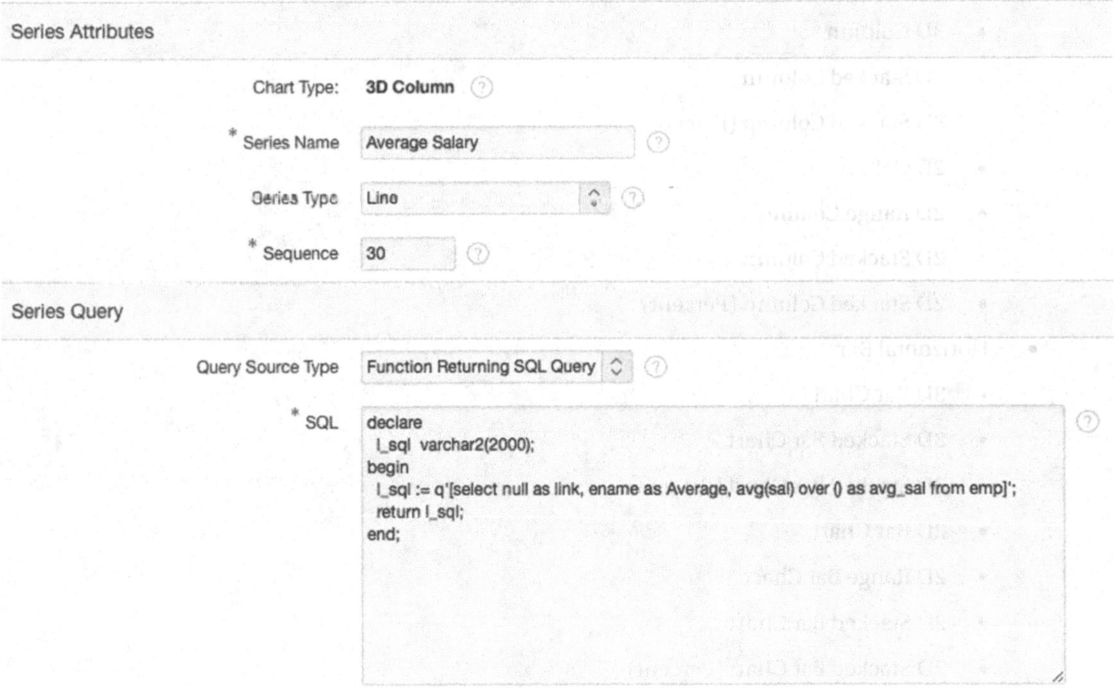

Series Attributes

Chart Type:	**3D Column** ⍰
* Series Name	Average Salary ⍰
Series Type	Line ⍰
* Sequence	30 ⍰

Series Query

Query Source Type	Function Returning SQL Query ⍰
| * SQL | ```
declare
  l_sql  varchar2(2000);
begin
  l_sql := q'[select null as link, ename as Average, avg(sal) over () as avg_sal from emp]';
  return l_sql;
end;
``` ⍰ |

Figure 3-25. *Query Source Type setting of Function Returning SQL Query*
```

■ **Caution** It is my recommendation that you suppress nulls because some chart types may show up differently than expected. For example, when you don't suppress null values in a line chart, the line will be interrupted where null values are, and empty spaces will appear in the line. If you put NVL around the column, in the case of a null value, it will draw the line correctly, but you will see the null values as the value 0. Putting a WHERE clause in the SQL statement to suppress the nulls, for example where comm is not null, will not show any value for that person.

Different Chart Types

APEX ships with many chart types. To use them in your application, you just select the chart type you like from the Create Chart Wizard. Oracle licenses these chart types from AnyChart, so you can use them freely anywhere in APEX. The following main and subchart types are natively available in APEX 5.0 by using the wizard:

- Column
  - 3D Column
  - 3D Stacked Column
  - 3D Stacked Column (Percent)
  - 2D Column
  - 2D Range Column
  - 2D Stacked Column
  - 2D Stacked Column (Percent)
- Horizontal Bar
  - 3D Bar Chart
  - 3D Stacked Bar Chart
  - 3D Stacked Bar Chart (Percent)
  - 2D Bar Chart
  - 2D Range Bar Chart
  - 2D Stacked Bar Chart
  - 2D Stacked Bar Chart (Percent)
- Pie and Doughnut
  - 3D Pie
  - 2D Pie
  - 2D Doughnut
- Scatter Marker
- Line

- Candlestick
- Gauges
  - Dial
    - Dial (Percent)
- Gantt (only Flash)
  - Project Gantt
  - Resource Gantt

If there is a chart type you want to use but you don't see it in the previous list (for example, a bubble chart), then you can get a separate license from AnyChart. Figure 3-26 gives an overview of the chart types that come with APEX (most of them are available in 2D and 3D) on the left side and shows the extra chart types that are available with the full version of AnyChart (version 6.2) on the right side.

To ease the integration of the other chart types, APEX R&D created an AnyChart plugin that you find at https://www.apexrnd.be.

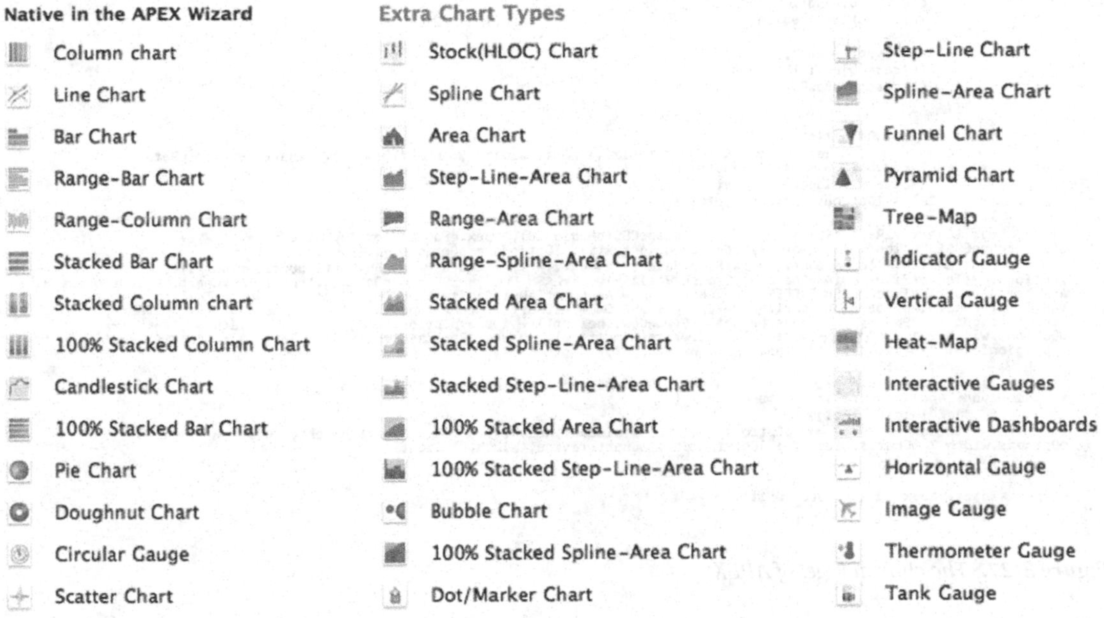

Native in the APEX Wizard	Extra Chart Types	
Column chart	Stock(HLOC) Chart	Step-Line Chart
Line Chart	Spline Chart	Spline-Area Chart
Bar Chart	Area Chart	Funnel Chart
Range-Bar Chart	Step-Line-Area Chart	Pyramid Chart
Range-Column Chart	Range-Area Chart	Tree-Map
Stacked Bar Chart	Range-Spline-Area Chart	Indicator Gauge
Stacked Column chart	Stacked Area Chart	Vertical Gauge
100% Stacked Column Chart	Stacked Spline-Area Chart	Heat-Map
Candlestick Chart	Stacked Step-Line-Area Chart	Interactive Gauges
100% Stacked Bar Chart	100% Stacked Area Chart	Interactive Dashboards
Pie Chart	100% Stacked Step-Line-Area Chart	Horizontal Gauge
Doughnut Chart	Bubble Chart	Image Gauge
Circular Gauge	100% Stacked Spline-Area Chart	Thermometer Gauge
Scatter Chart	Dot/Marker Chart	Tank Gauge

Figure 3-26. *Comparison of the out-of-the-box charts in APEX with all available AnyChart charts*

AnyChart also built an entire new engine, AnyChart 7.*x*, which is based entirely on JavaScript and HTML5, but at the time of this writing, it's not backward compatible, so APEX would need to recode a lot to be able to support the new version. It would also mean if people used Flash charts before, they would not work anymore, so for now in APEX 5.0 the latest version of AnyChart 6 is included.

Another alternative for other types of charts is to use other plugins. Later in this chapter you'll find some examples such as D3 chart plugins.

Behind the Scenes

To understand what's happening behind the scenes, you need to know how AnyChart works. The easiest way to understand AnyChart is to go to its web site and download a trial version. This is not related to APEX, but it shows the different components it needs to get a chart on an HTML page. It involves including the AnyChart JavaScript files, creating a div on your HTML page, and creating a small piece of JavaScript to create a new AnyChart chart and tell the engine to render the chart in the div.

This is exactly what the APEX engine is doing for you behind the scenes. The first thing it does is include the AnyChart libraries. AnyChart 6.2 comes with two libraries, AnyChart.js and AnyChartHTML5.js, which in APEX are located in /i/flashchart/anychart_6/js/. The next thing APEX is doing for you is creating a container for the chart, the div element. In APEX you'll find a div element called R<number>_chart. Finally, it includes some JavaScript to define the chart, the settings, and the data. APEX created a widget that you can find in /i/libraries/apex/minified/widget.chart.min.js (Figure 3-27).

```
< > | ⟨⟩ f ⟩ ▒ Scripts ⟩ 𝄞 widget.chart.min.js                                                    | {}
 1  !function(widget, $, util) {
 2      widget.chart = function(pRegionId, pOptions) {
 3          function _refresh() {
 4              apex.server.widget("chart5", {
 5                  pageItems: lOptions.pageItems,
 6                  x01: lOptions.regionId
 7              }, {
 8                  dataType: "text",
 9                  refreshObject: lRegion$,
10                  success: _showResult
11              })
12          }
13          function _showResult(pData) {
14              "100%" === pOptions.width && lChart.resize(lChart$.width(), lChart.height), lChart.setData(pData),
       lOptions.refreshInterval > 0 && setTimeout(function() {
15                  lRegion$.trigger("apexrefresh")
16              }, 1e3 * lOptions.refreshInterval)
17          }
18          var lChart, lRegion$ = $("#" + util.escapeCSS(pRegionId), apex.gPageContext$), lChart$ = $("#" +
       util.escapeCSS(pRegionId + "_chart"), apex.gPageContext$), lOptions = pOptions || {};
19          pOptions.swfFile && pOptions.swfFile.match(/anygantt.*/) ? lChart = new AnyGantt(pOptions.swfFile,
       pOptions.preloaderFile) : (AnyChart.useBrowserResize=!0, "FLASH_PREFERRED" === pOptions.type ? (AnyChart.renderingType =
       anychart.RenderingType.FLASH_PREFERRED, lChart = new AnyChart(pOptions.swfFile, pOptions.preloaderFile)) :
       (AnyChart.renderingType = anychart.RenderingType.SVG_ONLY, lChart = new AnyChart)), lChart.wMode = "transparent",
       lChart.height = "99%" === pOptions.height ? $(window).height() - 100 : pOptions.height, lChart.width = "100%" ===
       pOptions.width ? 1 : pOptions.width, lChart.write(lChart$[0]), 0 === lRegion$.length && (lRegion$ = lChart$.wrap('<div id="'
       + pRegionId + '"></div>')), lRegion$.on("apexrefresh", function() {
20              _refresh()
21          }).trigger("apexrefresh"), ("100%" === pOptions.width || "99%" === pOptions.height) &&
       $(window).on("apexwindowresized", function() {
22              var lWidth, lHeight;
23              lHeight = "99%" === pOptions.height ? $(window).height() - 100 : lChart.height, lWidth = "100%" ===
       pOptions.width ? lChart$.width() : lChart.width, lChart.resize(lWidth, lHeight)
24          })
25      }
26  }(apex.widget, apex.jQuery, apex.util);
27
```

Figure 3-27. *The chart widget of APEX*

When you call a page with a chart, the page is rendered, and the JavaScript to create the chart is executed. APEX gets data from the database (where the definition is of the chart), formats it in a way AnyChart understands it, and passes it to the AnyChart object, which in turn renders the chart.

More graphically presented, the flow is as shown in Figure 3-28.

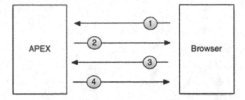

Figure 3-28. *Graphical representation of the flow to generate the chart*

The following are the steps shown in Figure 3-28:

1. The user requests a page with a chart, so the browser sends a request to APEX to retrieve the page.

2. APEX handles the request and sends back the HTML for that page, which includes a container div (region) and some JavaScript to create the chart.

3. The browser shows the HTML page and creates the chart object that will make a request back to APEX to get the data and settings for the chart.

4. APEX retrieves the request and sends back the XML for the data of the chart.

Looking at a real case when a user requests a page that holds a chart, the following happens:

5. The user clicks a tab that does a call with this URL: http://webserver/pls/apex/f?p=71450:3:103001531406712:::::.

6. APEX searches for Application 71450, Page 3 (and the session is 103001531406712). If you want more information about an Oracle APEX URL, click the Help in Oracle APEX and go to Home ➤ Application Builder Concepts ➤ Understanding URL Syntax. APEX will translate the source into HTML and some JavaScript to execute and then send it back to the browser (Figure 3-29).

```
<script type="text/javascript" src="/i/libraries/apex/minified/widget.chart.min.js?v=5.0.0.00.28"></script>
<script type="text/javascript" src="/i/flashchart/anychart_6/js/AnyChart.js?v=5.0.0.00.28"></script>
<script type="text/javascript" src="/i/flashchart/anychart_6/js/AnyChartHTML5.js?v=5.0.0.00.28"></script>
<script type="text/javascript" src="/i/apex_ui/js/minified/devToolbar.min.js?v=5.0.0.00.28"></script>
<script type="text/javascript">
  apex.jQuery( document ).ready( function() {
  (function(){apex.widget.chart("R154980299218541462 1",{"type":"SVG_ONLY","width":"700","height":"500","regionId":"154980299218541462 1"});})();
  (function(){apex.initDevToolbar([],"FOCUS",{"autoHide":"Auto Hide","iconsOnly":"Show Icons Only","noBuilderMessage":"This application was not run from
  the Application Express Application Builder or the Builder window cannot be found. The Builder will now replace the application in this
  window.","display":"Display Position","displayTop":"Top","displayLeft":"Left","displayBottom":"Bottom","displayRight":"Right"},42);})();
  apex.theme42.initializePage.noSideCol();

  });
</script>
```

Figure 3-29. *The HTML and JavaScript for the chart*

7. The page is shown in the browser, and the AnyChart object will request the data it needs to display. While it's getting the data, you will see a loading animation (Figure 3-30).

Waiting for data...

Figure 3-30. Rendered HTML and call for data of the chart object

8. To verify the request, it's best to use the developer tools of your browser or a developer extension for the browser such as Firebug for Firefox. When clicking the Network tab, you'll see the requests that are done by the browser.

The JavaScript will do an AJAX request (Figure 3-31). It will call the URL wwv_flow.show (as a POST request) and pass these parameters:

- p_request: APXWGT (the APEX widget)

- p_flow_id: 71450 (the application ID)

- p_flow_step_id: 3 (the page ID)

- p_instance: 8477258330126 (the session ID)

- x01: 1549802992185414621 (the region ID)

- p_widget_name: chart5 (so the APEX widget knows it's about an HTML5 chart)

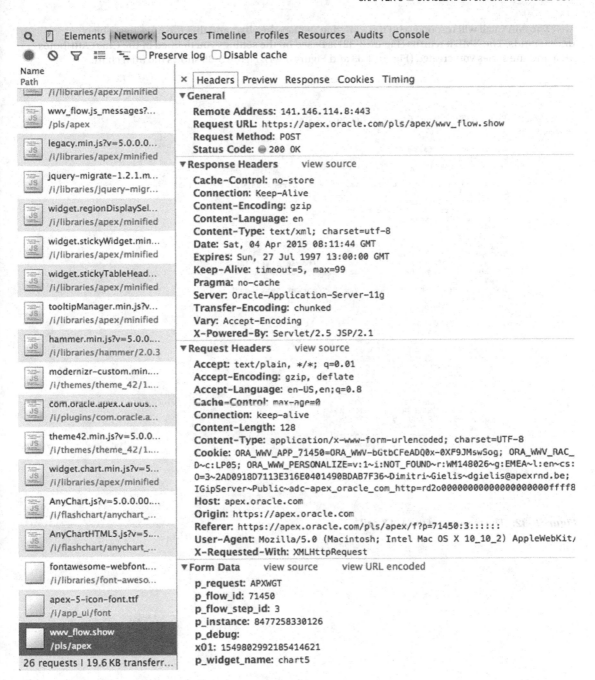

Figure 3-31. *AJAX request seen in the Developer Tools of the browser*

The AJAX call will respond with the XML that defines the chart and that the AnyChart object understands. The XML it returns (Figure 3-32) is based on the settings you defined in the Chart Attributes area and the series you created (Figure 3-33 and Figure 3-34). Figure 3-35 shows the final chart.

```xml
×  Headers │ Preview │ Response  Cookies  Timing
▼<anychart>
  ▼<settings>
      <animation enabled="false" />
    </settings>
    <margin left="0" top="0" right="0" bottom="0" />
  ▼<charts>
    ▼<chart plot_type="CategorizedVertical" name="chart_15498033323600414622">
      ▼<chart_settings>
          <title enabled="False" />
        ▶<chart_background>…</chart_background>
          <data_plot_background />
        ▶<axes>…</axes>
        </chart_settings>
      ▼<data_plot_settings enable_3d_mode="false">
        ▼<bar_series style="Default">
          ▶<tooltip_settings enabled="true">…</tooltip_settings>
          ▶<label_settings enabled="true" mode="Outside" multi_line_align="Center">…</label_settings>
            <bar_style />
          ▶<marker_settings enabled="True">…</marker_settings>
          </bar_series>
        </data_plot_settings>
      ▼<data>
        ▼<series name="VALUE" type="Bar" color="0x1D8BD1">
            <point name="ADAMS" y="1100" />
            <point name="ALLEN" y="1600" />
            <point name="BLAKE" y="2850" />
            <point name="CLARK" y="2450" />
            <point name="FORD" y="3000" />
            <point name="JAMES" y="950" />
            <point name="JONES" y="2975" />
            <point name="KING" y="5800" />
            <point name="MARTIN" y="1250" />
            <point name="MILLER" y="1300" />
            <point name="SCOTT" y="3000" />
            <point name="SMITH" y="800" />
            <point name="TURNER" y="1500" />
            <point name="WARD" y="1250" />
          </series>
        </data>
      </chart>
    </charts>
  </anychart>
```

Figure 3-32. *The response of the AJAX call*

Chart Settings

Chart Rendering	HTML5 Chart
Chart Type	3D Column
Chart Title	Salary by Employees
* Chart Width	700
* Chart Height	500
Chart Margin: Top	
Chart Margin: Bottom	
Chart Margin: Left	
Chart Margin: Right	
Color Scheme	Look 6
Set Color Level:	● Series ○ Point
Hatch Pattern	No
Custom Colors	

Chart Series

Edit	Series Name	Query
✎	Series 1	SELECT NULL LINK, ENAME LABEL, SAL VALUE FROM EMP ORDER BY ENAME

Figure 3-33. *First part of chart attributes*

Chart XML

Reset

Use Custom XML   No

Custom XML

```
<?xml version = "1.0" encoding="utf-8" standalone = "yes"?><anychart><settings><animation enabled="false"/><no_data show_waiting_animation="False">
<label><text>#NO_DATA_MESSAGE#</text><font family="Verdana" bold="yes" size="10"/></label></no_data></settings><margin left="0" top="0" right="0"
bottom="0" /><charts><chart plot_type="CategorizedVertical" name="chart_1535262734124867861"> <chart_settings><title text_align="Center" position="Top"
><text>Salary by Employees</text><font family="Tahoma" size="14" color="0x000000" /></title><chart_background><fill type="Solid" color="0xffffff"
opacity="0" /><border enabled="false"/><corners type="Square"/></chart_background><data_plot_background></data_plot_background><axes><y_axis >
<scale mode="Normal" /><title><text>Salary</text><font family="Tahoma" size="14" color="0x000000" /></title><labels enabled="true" position="Outside">
<font family="Tahoma" size="10" color="0x000000" /><format><![CDATA[{%Value}{numDecimals:0,decimalSeparator: .,thousandsSeparator:\,}]]></format>
</labels><major_grid enabled="False"/><minor_grid enabled="False"/></y_axis><x_axis><scale mode="Normal" /><title><text>Employee</text><font
family="Tahoma" size="14" color="0x000000" /></title><labels enabled="true" position="Outside"><font family="Tahoma" size="10" color="0x000000" />
<format><![CDATA[{%Value}{numDecimals:0,decimalSeparator: .,thousandsSeparator:\,}]]></format></labels><major_grid enabled="True" interlaced="false" >
```

Figure 3-34. *Last part of chart attributes, which shows the XML APEX will use*

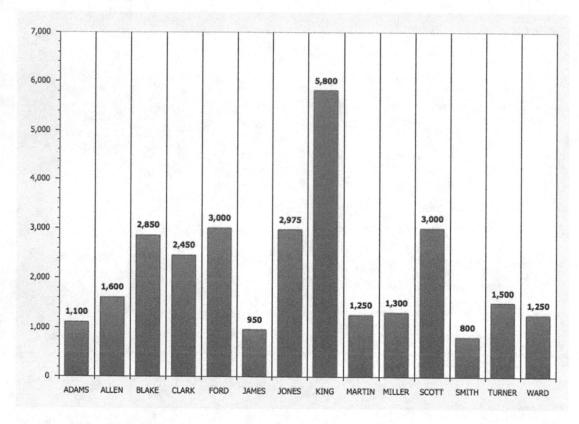

Figure 3-35. *Chart completely drawn when the XML is retrieved*

All the tokens (#...#) you see in the Chart XML area in APEX were replaced by values defined in the Chart Attributes area, and the #DATA# token was replaced by the output of the select statement defined in the series.

Debug and Performance

Debugging charts is done differently than debugging other components in APEX. After reading how these charts work behind the scenes, you know that there are different components and requests going on for a single chart. There is the HTML for the region of the chart, the JavaScript to include the AnyChart object, the call for the data (XML) for the chart, and the generation of the chart.

When you run your page in Debug Mode, you'll get two debug outputs (Figure 3-36). The first "show" (Path Info) is for the page, and the second "show APXWGT" (Path Info) is the AJAX request to get the settings and data for the chart.

View Identifier	Session Id	User	Application	Page	Path Info	Entries	Timestamp	Seconds
731129461	101365625597193	APEX_PUBLIC_USER	71450	2	show APXWGT	23	53 seconds ago	0.0560
731129447	101365625597193	APEX_PUBLIC_USER	71450	2	show	73	60 seconds ago	0.1990

Figure 3-36. *Debug output*

The first "show" gives you an idea of how long it took to generate the page with the chart region. Drilling into the details of the debug output shows how long it took to render the chart region (Figure 3-37). Note that only the container of the chart is counted here. The chart object still needs to be called by another process, and the XML still has to be generated. Most performance issues are based on the actual generation of the XML (based on the query that is in the series). How long it took to generate the XML for all the series is shown in the "show APXWGT" debug details (Figure 3-38).

| 0.15924 | 0.00004 | Render regions | 4 | |
| 0.15927 | 0.00018 | ...Region: 3D Column Chart | 4 | |

Figure 3-37. *Debug information for a page with the chart region (show)*

| 0.01556 | 0.01082 | Run APXWGT request | 4 | |
| 0.02638 | 0.00898 | ...Execute Statement: SELECT NULL LINK,
ENAME LABEL,
SAL VALUE
FROM   EMP
ORDER BY ENAME | 4 | |

Figure 3-38. *Debug information for the chart serie(s) (show APXWGT)*

Running the page in Debug Mode has another component that is valuable. In the page itself, underneath the chart, a Show XML link will appear, so you see exactly what the chart object receives (Figure 3-39).

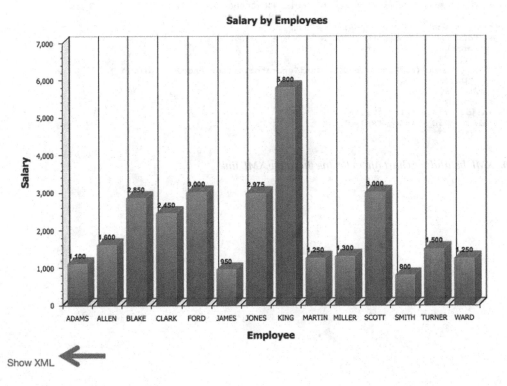

Figure 3-39. *Extra Show XML link when running the page in Debug Mode*

The Show XML link will show the XML output that was generated by APEX for the chart (Figure 3-40). Having this information is really important because the chart you see is defined by this XML. AnyChart has a complete XML reference in its documentation, which explains every node. You can find the URL to the AnyChart XML reference in the "Resources" section later in the chapter (Figure 3-41).

This XML file does not appear to have any style information associated with it. The document tree is shown below.

```
▼<anychart>
  ▼<settings>
     <animation enabled="false"/>
  </settings>
  <margin left="0" top="0" right="0" bottom="0"/>
  ▼<charts>
    ▼<chart plot_type="CategorizedVertical" name="chart_1535262734124867861">
      ▼<chart_settings>
        ▼<title text_align="Center" position="Top">
           <text>Salary by Employees</text>
           <font family="Tahoma" size="14" color="0x000000"/>
        </title>
        ▼<chart_background>
           <fill type="Solid" color="0xffffff" opacity="0"/>
           <border enabled="false"/>
           <corners type="Square"/>
        </chart_background>
        <data_plot_background/>
        ▼<axes>
         ▼<y_axis>
            <scale mode="Normal"/>
           ▼<title>
              <text>Salary</text>
              <font family="Tahoma" size="14" color="0x000000"/>
           </title>
           ▼<labels enabled="true" position="Outside">
              <font family="Tahoma" size="10" color="0x000000"/>
             ▼<format>
               ▼<![CDATA[
                  {%Value}{numDecimals:0,decimalSeparator:.,thousandsSeparator:\,}
                  ]]>
             </format>
           </labels>
           <major_grid enabled="False"/>
           <minor_grid enabled="False"/>
         </y_axis>
```

Figure 3-40. *XML behind the chart after clicking the Show XML link*

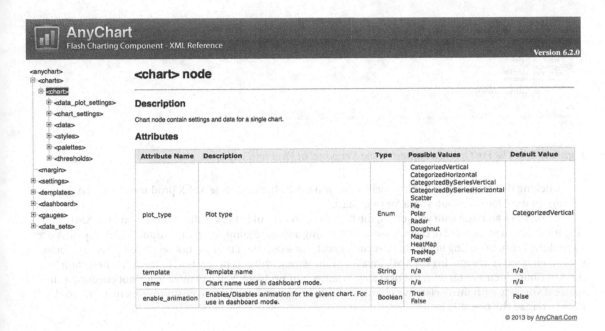

Figure 3-41. *XML reference by AnyChart*

To see exactly what is happening in the browser, you need to use an external tool, such as Firebug. Other browsers also have developer tools, which can do the same.

The Net panel in Firefox is most important for seeing what's going on behind the scenes (Figure 3-42). The main purpose of the Net panel is to monitor HTTP traffic initiated by a web page and simply present all collected and computed information to the user. Its content is composed of a list of entries where each entry represents one request/response round-trip made by the page. You can see the requests, the status, the size of what is returned, and the time it took.

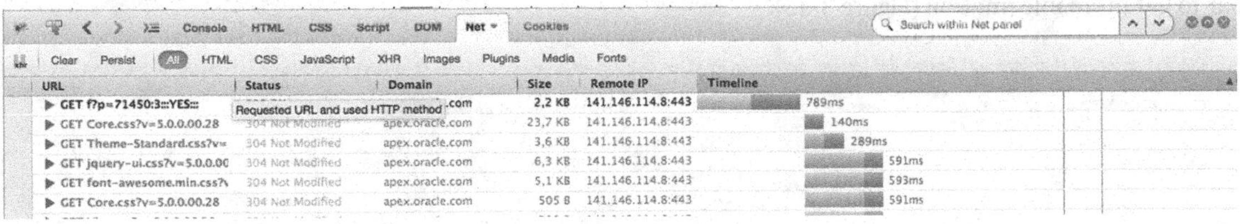

Figure 3-42. *The Net panel in Firebug/Firefox*

The first request is the request for the APEX page. The next requests are to get some CSS and JavaScript files. The last request is the call to wwv_flow.show to retrieve the data (xml). The XHR tab will show you the AJAX request for the chart data too.

Hovering over the request shows you the complete URL, and clicking it slides open other options, such as Params, Headers, Post, Response, XML, Cache, and Cookies. Depending on the call, you get different options to click. Just as in Figure 3-31 where you saw the developer tools, Firebug has this information too. Clicking the Post tab shows you more information about the call (Figure 3-43).

Figure 3-43. The Post tab of a request in the Net panel in Firebug/Firefox

Clicking the Response or XML tab will show you the XML that Oracle APEX produced based on the settings in the Chart Attributes area for that chart.

If you have an issue with your chart, the first thing you should check is the response and the XML (Figure 3-44). In 90 percent of cases, there is something awkward going on in the output, which explains why something is not behaving in the chart as you expect. For example, a tag may not be closed correctly, some special characters are making the XML invalid, or the wrong syntax is being used in the XML. Referring to the AnyChart documentation is the next step to solve your problem. You will most likely not encounter these issues if you stay with the declarative charts in APEX; however, if you start to customize them, come back here to reread the possible issues.

Figure 3-44. The XML tab of a request in the Net panel in Firebug/Firefox

If you find that some parts take a long time to load, you can investigate by hovering the cursor over the bar to get more information (Figure 3-45).

URL	Status	Domain	Size	Remote IP	Timeline		
▶ GET f?p=71450:3:::YES:::	200 OK	apex.oracle.com	2,2 KB	141.146.114.8:443		789ms	
▶ GET Core.css?v=5.0.0.00.28	304 Not Modified	apex.oracle.com	23,7 KB	141.146.114.8:443		140ms	
▶ GET Theme-Standard.css?v=	304 Not Modified	apex.oracle.com	3,6 KB	141.146.114.8:443		289ms	
▶ GET jquery-ui.css?v=5.0.0.0(	304 Not Modified	apex.oracle.com	6,3 KB	141.146.114.8:443		591ms	
▶ GET font-awesome.min.css?^	304 Not Modified	apex.oracle.com	5,1 KB	141.146.114.8:443		+867ms Request start time since the beginning	
▶ GET Core.css?v=5.0.0.00.28	304 Not Modified	apex.oracle.com	505 B	141.146.114.8:443		Request phases start and	
▶ GET Vita.css?v=5.0.0.00.28	304 Not Modified	apex.oracle.com	390 B	141.146.114.8:443		elapsed time relative to the request start:	
▶ GET jquery~2.1.3.js?v=5.0.0./	304 Not Modified	apex.oracle.com	75,5 KB	141.146.114.8:443		DNS Lookup 0ms	0ms
▶ GET core.js?v=5.0.0.00.28	304 Not Modified	apex.oracle.com	2,9 KB	141.146.114.8:443		Connecting 0ms	450ms
▶ GET debug.js?v=5.0.0.00.28	304 Not Modified	apex.oracle.com	2,3 KB	141.146.114.8:443		Sending +450ms	0ms
▶ GET util.js?v=5.0.0.00.28	304 Not Modified	apex.oracle.com	6,3 KB	141.146.114.8:443		Waiting +450ms	141ms
▶ GET locale.js?v=5.0.0.00.28	304 Not Modified	apex.oracle.com	646 B	141.146.114.8:443		Receiving +591ms	0ms
▶ GET lang.js?v=5.0.0.00.28	304 Not Modified	apex.oracle.com	1,5 KB	141.146.114.8:443			
▶ GET storage.js?v=5.0.0.00.2{	304 Not Modified	apex.oracle.com	2,6 KB	141.146.114.8:443		Event timing relative to the request start:	
▶ GET navigation.js?v=5.0.0.0(	304 Not Modified	apex.oracle.com	8,9 KB	141.146.114.8:443		+1,99s 'DOMContentLoaded' (event)	
▶ GET event.js?v=5.0.0.00.28	304 Not Modified	apex.oracle.com	610 B	141.146.114.8:443		+2,29s 'load' (event)	
▶ GET server.js?v=5.0.0.00.28	304 Not Modified	apex.oracle.com	7,7 KB	141.146.114.8:443			

Figure 3-45. Hovering over the timeline gives more information

If you encounter performance issues and your charts become slow, the first thing you need to look at is the debug output. Finally, you can also check the Net panel in Firebug and check the Timeline. That will tell you exactly where you are losing most of the time. Usually you will find that the last step (the generation of the XML) takes most of the time.

The more series you have, the longer it may take to see the data in the chart. If you can combine multiple series into one, you will gain performance. If you need multiple series, it's best to try them first in SQL Developer or SQL Workshop to see how fast the results arrive. If the query is slow in that environment, it will be slow in the chart too. You can then compare those results with the results shown in the debug output of the chart (show APXWGT details). (Tuning the SQL statements falls outside the boundaries of this chapter.)

Upgrading Oracle APEX 3.*x*/4.*x* Flash and SVG Charts

If you initially developed your application in an earlier version of APEX and you used SVG or Flash charts, you might want to upgrade them to the new charts in APEX 5.0. AnyChart 6 charts are integrated with APEX 5.0, which are nicer, are faster, and have more options than the earlier version of AnyChart charts that came with APEX 3.*x* and 4.*x*. The fastest way to upgrade all charts is to go to Utilities and then click Upgrade Application. This will show you which charts you can upgrade. Note that SVG charts can be upgraded with some restrictions.

■ **Note** Today I recommend migrating all types of charts to the HTML5 charts.

Follow these steps to upgrade all existing Flash and SVG charts to the latest AnyChart charts engine:

1. Go to the Application home page.

2. Click Utilities and then click Upgrade Application (Figure 3-46). The Upgrade Application Summary report appears (Figure 3-47).

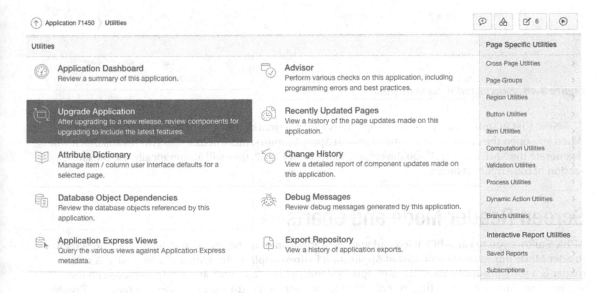

Figure 3-46. *Utilities section in APEX 5.0*

Figure 3-47. *Upgrade Application Summary page—Candidates of charts to upgrade to HTML5 charts*

3. Look for Upgrade SVG Charts to Flash Chart 5 and Upgrade Flash Charts to Flash Chart 5, or Upgrade Flash Charts to HTML5 Charts, and click the number of candidate objects.

4. Select the objects to upgrade and click Upgrade (Figure 3-48).

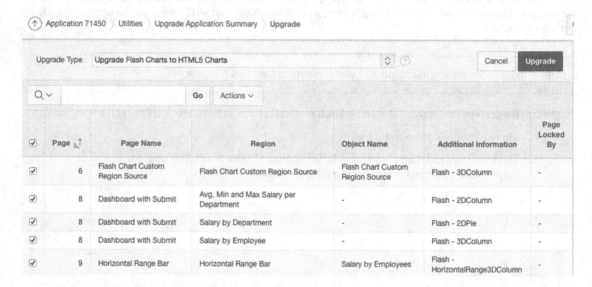

Figure 3-48. *Select candidates to upgrade*

Note that in some cases the charts might look a bit different or the label of the axis are not showing. When you open the chart attributes again and hit Apply Changes, this will fix itself. This means that it will regenerate the XML it needs. If you developed charts in APEX 4.2, they will automatically use the latest version of the AnyChart engine.

Screen Reader Mode and Charts

APEX 5 allows you to run APEX itself and your own application in the Screen Reader Mode. The Screen Reader Mode improves the usability of Application Express applications with a screen reader. A screen reader is a software application that attempts to identify and interpret what is being displayed on the screen. This interpretation is then re-presented to the user with text-to-speech, sound icons, or a Braille output device.

You can enable/disable the Screen Reader Mode in your own application in three ways.

- Add the #SCREEN_READER_TOGGLE# substitution string to the footer of your page template. Doing so results in a link on your pages that viewers can use to toggle the Screen Reader Mode on and off.

- Use the screen-reader APIs documented in the Oracle Application Express API Reference. Using the APIs is more work than adding the substitution string to your page footer, but they do provide you with more control.

- Create links that enable and disable the Screen Reader Mode by executing f?p session requests. Here's an example:

```
<a href="f?p=&APP_ID.:&APP_PAGE_ID.:&APP_SESSION.:SET_SESSION_SCREEN_
READER_ON">Reader Mode On</a>

<a href="f?p=&APP_ID.:&APP_PAGE_ID.:&APP_SESSION.:SET_SESSION_SCREEN_
READER_OFF">Reader Mode Off</a>
```

APEX charts are not currently accessible to screen readers; therefore, when running in the Screen Reader Mode, the user will get a report representation of the information conveyed in the chart. A separate report will be generated for each series of a multiple-series chart if the series were defined as separate series. If the multiple series were defined in a single query, only one report will be generated (Figure 3-49).

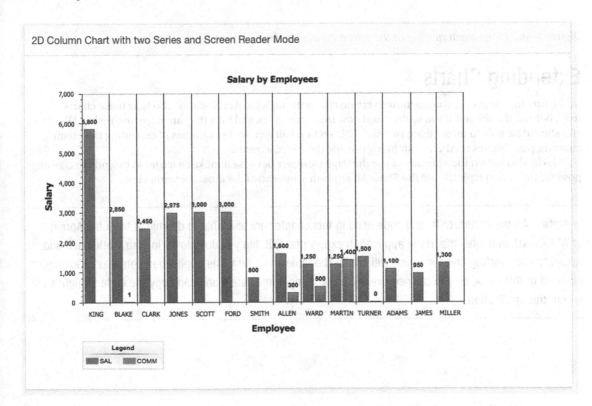

Figure 3-49. Chart when not in the Screen Reader Mode

When running in Screen Reader Mode (Figure 3-50), these data tables contain descriptive text, in the following format:

- *Summary Text*: In Application Builder, a combination of the chart title and chart series title is used.

- *Column Headers*: In Application Builder, the column name/alias in the chart series query is used to identify the columns in the report.

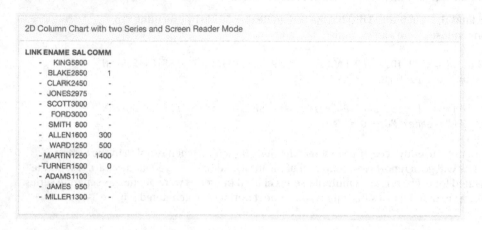

Figure 3-50. *Chart when running in the Screen Reader Mode*

Extending Charts

In the previous sections, you saw how to create charts through the APEX wizard and how these charts work behind the scenes. If you understand how the charts work and how they are implemented in APEX, you should be able to do anything you like. This section will give some examples of extending the existing charting possibilities of APEX by stepping outside the APEX wizards.

I will also switch the interface to use the Page Designer because it makes it easier to extend the charting possibilities. I also typically use the Show All attributes, instead of the most common view.

■ **Note**   All the tables, data, and code used in this chapter are available to download from the Apress or APEX R&D web site. Import the application export (the SQL file you download) in your workspace and install the supporting objects, which will create the tables and data. The application contains all examples covered in this book, so you can see everything working immediately and can copy the code straight from within the application.

Customizing Charts by Using Custom XML

A manager wants to see how sales are going based on her forecast and targets she previously set. Showing the budget can easily be done with a column chart, but showing the forecast and target lines is something that is not natively available (through the wizards) in APEX (unless you create another series for the line, but that is not quite the same). The following are the steps to add a 2D column chart and two trendlines, one for the forecast and one for the target:

1.   If you already have some experience with AnyChart XML and what each node is used for, go to the AnyChart reference documentation (you will find the URL in the "Resources" section).

2.   If you are less experienced, go to the AnyChart Gallery and click the 2D Column charts examples. Luckily there is something similar to the previous example in the gallery called Trendlines and Axis Ranges Demo. Click that example, and a pop-up will appear with an example chart in one tab (Figure 3-51) and the XML code that was used in the other tab (Figure 3-52).

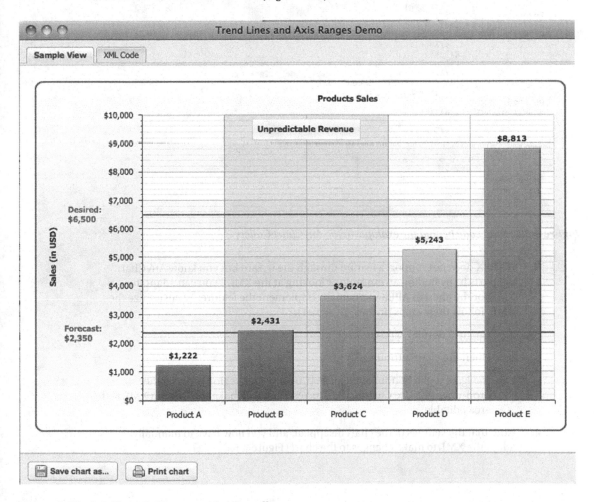

Figure 3-51. AnyChart Gallery example of trendlines

```
Sample View    XML Code                                                          <·> View Plain

13        <label_settings enabled="True">
14            <format><![CDATA[${%YValue}{numDecimals:0}]]></format>
15        </label_settings>
16      </bar_series>
17    </data_plot_settings>
18    <chart_settings>
19      <title enabled="true">
20        <text><![CDATA[Products Sales]]></text>
21      </title>
22      <axes>
23        <y_axis>
24          <title>
25            <text><![CDATA[Sales (in USD)]]></text>
26          </title>
27          <labels align="Inside">
28            <format><![CDATA[${%Value}{numDecimals:0}]]></format>
29          </labels>
30          <axis_markers>
31            <lines>
32              <line value="2350" thickness="2" color="Rgb(200,30,30)" caps="Square">
33                <label enabled="True" multi_line_align="Center">
34                  <font color="Rgb(200,30,30)" />
35                  <format><![CDATA[
36   Forecast:
37   ${%Value}{numDecimals:0}
38   ]]></format>
39                </label>
40              </line>
41              <line value="6500" thickness="2" color="Green" caps="Square">
42                <label enabled="True" multi_line_align="Center">
43                  <font color="Green" />
44                  <format><![CDATA[
45   Desired:
46   ${%Value}{numDecimals:0}
47   ]]></format>
48                </label>
49              </line>
50            </lines>
51          </axis_markers>
52        </y_axis>
```

Figure 3-52. XML code behind the example in the AnyChart Gallery

3. If APEX does not support a feature through the wizard but you know AnyChart supports it (by finding an example or looking at the XML), you can adapt the XML for the chart in APEX to manually implement the feature. To customize the XML, follow these steps (in Page Designer):

    a. Create a normal 2D column chart.

    b. Open the chart attributes.

    c. Navigate to the bottom of the page (Custom XML region) and set the drop-down for Use Custom XML to Yes. That will make the Custom XML text area editable.

4. Note that the settings of the chart disappear, and you now have to manually adapt the XML to make changes to the chart (Figure 3-53).

```
▼ Custom XML

Custom        Yes    No

XML                              ⅃

<?xml version = "1.0" encoding="utf-8"
standalone = "yes"?>
<anychart>
  <settings>
    <animation enabled="false"/>
    <no_data
show_waiting_animation="False">
      <label>
        <text></text>
        <font family="Verdana" bold="yes"
size="10"/>
```

Figure 3-53. Use Custom XML in Chart Attributes in the APEX Page Designer

a. Looking at the existing example of AnyChart or at the documentation, to
    add a trendline, you would add the Axis Markers node. As you want a line
    to go horizontally, add the marker to the y-axis. Locate the end of the y-axis
    node (<y_axis>), and just before that, add the following:

```
<axis markers>
 <lines>
    <line value="&P17_FORECAST." thickness="2" color="Rgb(200,30,30)" ↵
    caps="Square">
      <label enabled="True" multi_line_align="Center">
        <font color="Rgb(200,30,30)" />
        <format>Forecast: ${%Value}{numDecimals:0} </format>
      </label>
    </line>
    <line value="&P17_TARGET." thickness="2" color="Green" caps="Square">
      <label enabled="True" multi_line_align="Center">
        <font color="Green" />
        <format>Target: ${%Value}{numDecimals:0}</format>
      </label>
    </line>
 </lines>
</axis_markers>
```

b. In the code, you use &P17_TARGET. and &P17_FORECAST., which are
    substitution strings for the respective page items. You can dynamically set
    these items through, for example, a computation, so you can calculate the
    line from a SELECT statement or PL/SQL procedure. If the values are always
    fixed, you can just replace the substitution strings with a numeric value.

5. Saving the chart and running the APEX page gives the result shown in Figure 3-54.

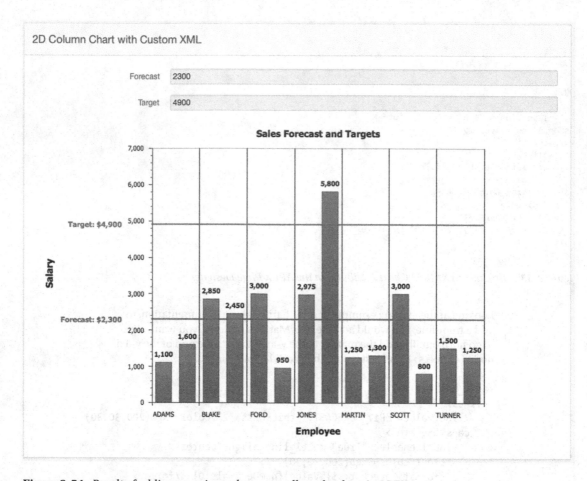

Figure 3-54. *Result of adding an axis marker manually to the chart in APEX*

This example shows how you can customize the XML of a chart to add features that APEX doesn't allow by using the wizard or chart attributes. It's useful to read the AnyChart documentation and review the XML reference to know what is possible. The principle is always the same: once you know what XML to include, you change the XML by setting Use Custom XML to Yes in the Chart Attributes area and, presto, you have extended your chart!

Customizing Charts by Using Custom XML, Dynamic Actions, and JavaScript

Customizing the XML is one way to get more out of charts, but sometimes even that is not enough and you need to take an extra step. To illustrate this, you will look at the use case where the manager of the previous example now wants to see which employees brought in a lot of sales, who performed well, and who did not. She could just look at the chart and do the math in her head, but giving colors to the columns (good = green, normal = yellow, bad = red) would make the job easier (Figure 3-55). This means you will define thresholds: sales numbers below a certain number (red), sales numbers between certain numbers (yellow), and sales numbers over a certain number (green).

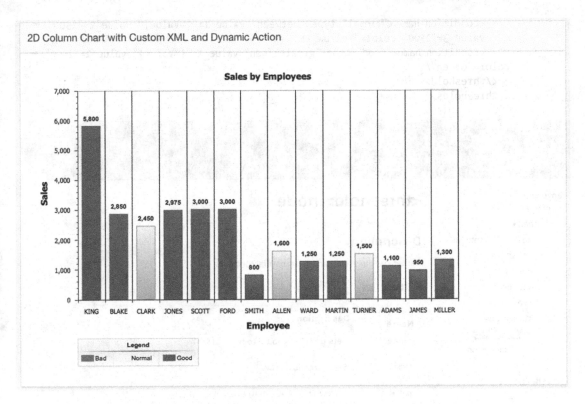

Figure 3-55. *Column chart with custom XML and dynamic action to show thresholds*

These are the steps to create a chart with thresholds:

1. Create a normal 2D column chart based on the following SQL statement:

```
SELECT NULL LINK,
       ENAME LABEL,
       SAL VALUE
FROM   EMP
ORDER  BY ENAME
```

2. Click the Attributes entry under the chart's region in the rendering side of the Page Designer.

3. Navigate to the bottom of the page (Custom XML region) and set the drop-down for Use Custom XML to Yes. That will make the Custom XML text area editable (Figure 3-53).

4. The AnyChart XML reference documentation (Figure 3-56) says you can use a threshold node (<threshold>). The following code needs to be added just after the </data_plot_settings> node (and before #DATA#):

```
<thresholds>
  <threshold name="sales_threshold">
    <condition name="Bad" type="lessThan" value_1="{%Value}" value_2="1500" ↵
    color="Red"/>
```

```
            <condition name="Normal" type="between" value_1="{%Value}" value_2="1500" ↵
            value_3="2500" color="Yellow"/>
            <condition name="Good" type="greaterThan" value_1="{%Value}" value_2="2500" ↵
    color="Green"/>
      </threshold>
    </thresholds>
```

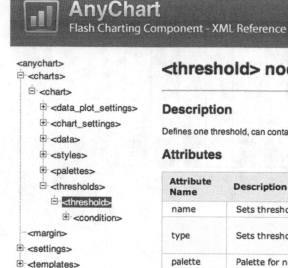

AnyChart
Flash Charting Component - XML Reference

<anychart>
├─ <charts>
│ └─ <chart>
│   ├─ <data_plot_settings>
│   ├─ <chart_settings>
│   ├─ <data>
│   ├─ <styles>
│   ├─ <palettes>
│   └─ <thresholds>
│   └─ <threshold>
│   └─ <condition>
│ ─ <margin>
├─ <settings>
├─ <templates>
├─ <dashboard>
├─ <gauges>
└─ <data_sets>

\<threshold\> node

Description

Defines one threshold, can contain several conditions.

Attributes

Attribute Name	Description
name	Sets threshold name to be used for binding it to data or series.
type	Sets threshold type.
palette	Palette for non-Custom thresholds only.
range_count	Number of ranges to be created by automatic thresholds.
auto_value	Changes thresholding value for automatic controls. Use keywords, for example {%BubbleSize} or {%CustomAttributeName}

Figure 3-56. *AnyChart XML reference documentation—<threshold> node*

5. If you run the page now with the custom XML, you don't see any difference, which is because the data node also needs to take the threshold into account. Now this isn't as straightforward as you might think. If you look at the XML, you will find a #DATA# token that gets replaced on the fly by Oracle APEX based on the series. The SQL statement of the series gets translated into the correct XML. APEX doesn't support the threshold tag out of the box, so you need to generate the correct XML so the thresholds are included manually.

6. Create a Hidden Item on the page (right-click the chart region by setting Create Page Item to Hidden) and call it P18_CHART_XML (because you are on page 18). You will use this item to store the data part of the chart.

7. In the Custom XML, replace #DATA# with &P18_CHART_XML. (note the . at the end), where P18_CHART_XML is the hidden page item. That item you will fill with the correct XML.

8. To fill P18_CHART_XML with the XML, add a computation to the page that generates the XML. Use the XMLDB feature of the database, which lets you create a SELECT statement that generates XML. The computation looks like this:

   • Type: SQL Query (return single value)

```
SELECT xmlelement("data", xmlattributes('sales_threshold' AS "threshold"), ↵
 xmlelement("series", xmlattributes('Series 1' AS "name"), xmlagg( ↵
 xmlelement("point",xmlattributes(ename AS "name", sal AS "y") ) ))) ↵
 .getClobVal() as data
FROM emp
```

9. If you want to add the legend of the thresholds, you have to make another small change to the XML in Use Custom XML. You have to tell the legend the source is now thresholds instead of the items. Search for *legend* (visible only when you defined Show Legend before you set Use Custom XML) and change it to the following code. If you don't find the legend node, add it after the </axes> node.

```
<legend enabled="true" position="Bottom" align="Near" ↵
elements_layout="Horizontal" ignore_auto_item="true" >
  <title enabled="true">
    <text>Legend</text>
    <font family="Arial" size="10" color="0x000000" />
  </title>
  <font family="Arial" size="10" color="0x000000" />
  <items><item source="thresholds"/></items>
</legend>
```

Saving the chart and running the APEX page should give you the result shown in Figure 3-55.

Note that if you have Asynchronous Update set to Yes, you will also need to refresh the hidden item with the correct data.

Creating Charts Manually

When you want full control over everything, you can choose to create a chart completely manually. AnyChart allows you to add events to the chart to control every step, from rendering to moving the mouse and clicking parts of the chart. In the following example, you will create a multiseries chart with multiple axes and different tooltips per series. You will also make the width and height of the chart depend on what the user defines on the page. I will also discuss having null values in the resultset (see item 6 in this list).

Follow these steps to create a chart manually:

Create a page with an HTML region (in this example, page 7) and name the region **Manual Chart**.

In the region source of the HTML region, add an empty div, which will be filled with the chart by using JavaScript:

```
<div id="chartDiv"></div>
```

You will also create three page items.

- One text item (text field) that defines the width of the chart: P7_CHART_WIDTH with a static value of 600 as the source

- One text item that defines the height of the chart: P7_CHART_HEIGHT with a static value of 400 as the source

- One hidden item where you store the XML data for the chart: P7_CHART_XML

Because you will load the entire chart with JavaScript, you need to add the JavaScript package that comes with AnyChart. Edit the page, and under JavaScript – File URLs, put the following:

```
#IMAGE_PREFIX#flashchart/anychart_6/js/AnyChart.js
#IMAGE_PREFIX#flashchart/anychart_6/js/AnyChartHTML5.js
```

Because you want to change the chart dynamically, you need to make sure that the chart variable in JavaScript is accessible in the entire page. That is why you add in the Page Definition in Function and Global Variable Declaration area the following variable declaration:

```
var chart;
```

You now need to initialize the chart by calling a specific AnyChart function, generate the data, and give the data to the chart.

■ **Note**   From APEX 4.0 onward, you should try to do as much JavaScript as possible through dynamic actions.

Create a new dynamic action to generate the XML. Set the following options:

- *Name*: Load Chart

- *Event*: Page Load

Make the action a true action, and specify the following:

- *Action*: Set Value

- *Fire On Page Load*: Yes

- *Set Type*: PL/SQL Function Body

- *PL/SQL Function Body*:

    ```
    declare
      l_chart varchar2(32767);
      l_xml   clob;
      l_data  varchar2(32767);
    begin
      l_chart := '<anychart>
      <settings>
        <animation enabled="True" />
      </settings>
      <charts>
    ```

```
    <chart plot_type="CategorizedVertical">
      <chart_settings>
        <title enabled="true">
          <text>Multi-Series: Multiple Y-Axes</text>
        </title>
        <axes>
          <x_axis tickmarks_placement="Center">
            <title enabled="true">
              <text>Arguments</text>
            </title>
          </x_axis>
          <y_axis>
            <title enabled="true">
              <text>Primary Y-Axis</text>
              <font color="#135D8C" />
            </title>
            <labels align="Inside">
              <font color="#135D8C" />
            </labels>
          </y_axis>
          <extra>
            <y_axis name="extra_y_axis_1" position="Right">
              <minor_grid enabled="false" />
              <major_grid enabled="false" />
              <title enabled="true">
                <text>Secondary Y-Axis</text>
                <font color="#A4300B" />
              </title>
              <labels align="Inside">
                <font color="#A4300B" />
              </labels>
            </y_axis>
          </extra>
        </axes>
      </chart_settings>
      <data_plot_settings default_series_type="Line">
        <line_series>
          <label_settings enabled="true">
            <background enabled="false" />
            <font color="Rgb(45,45,45)" bold="true" size="9">
              <effects enabled="true">
                <glow enabled="true" color="White" opacity="1" blur_x="1.5" blur_y="1.5"↵
strength="3" />
              </effects>
            </font>
            <format>{%YValue}{numDecimals:0}</format>
          </label_settings>
          <tooltip_settings enabled="true">
            <format>
Value: {%YValue}{numDecimals:2}
Argument: {%Name}
</format>
```

```
                <background>
                  <border type="Solid" color="DarkColor(%Color)" />
                </background>
                <font color="DarkColor(%Color)" />
              </tooltip_settings>
              <marker_settings enabled="true" />
              <line_style>
                <line thickness="3" />
              </line_style>
            </line_series>
        </data_plot_settings>
        <data>
        #DATA#
        </data>
      </chart>
   </charts>
</anychart>';
 SELECT xmlelement("series", xmlattributes('Series 1' AS "name"), xmlagg( xmlelement ↵
("point", xmlattributes(ename AS "name", sal AS "y") ) )).getClobVal()
 INTO l_xml
 FROM emp;

 l_data := l_data || wwv_flow_utilities.clob_to_varchar2(l_xml);

 SELECT xmlelement("series", xmlattributes('Series 2' AS "name", 'extra_y_axis_1' AS ↵
 "y_axis"), xmlagg( xmlelement("point", xmlattributes(ename AS "name", nvl(comm,0) AS "y") ↵
 ) )).getClobVal()
 INTO l_xml
 FROM emp;

 l_data := l_data || wwv_flow_utilities.clob_to_varchar2(l_xml);

 l_chart := replace(l_chart, '#DATA#', l_data);

 return l_chart;
end;
```

- Escape Special Characters: No

- Affected Elements – Selection Type: Item(s)

- Item(s): P7_CHART_XML

You use the same XML database features of the database to generate the data part. You also have a variable to store the XML definition of the chart. Note that the previous example works only with datasets that are less than 32KB because there is currently a limitation in APEX that you can assign a maximum of 32KB to a page item. If you need to work with big datasets, you need to slightly change the code. Later in this chapter, you will generate a dashboard and use the other technique, which supports XML bigger than 32KB. Also note that you used NVL(comm,0) for the value in the second series. If you don't use NVL, the line will be incomplete because the y value in the XML will contain an empty string and your result might not be correct. So, either you use NVL, which gives empty strings the value of 0 so every record will show up in the chart as a point, or you define a WHERE clause where you specify comm is not null; that means not every record will be shown, but your line will be complete.

Create a second true action to load the chart, with the following settings:

- *Action*: Execute JavaScript Code

- *Fire When Event Result Is*: True

- *Code*:

```
AnyChart.renderingType = anychart.RenderingType.SVG_ONLY;
chart = new AnyChart;
chart.width = $v('P7_CHART_WIDTH');
chart.height = $v('P7_CHART_HEIGHT');
chart.setData( $v('P7_CHART_XML') );
chart.write('chartDiv');
```

The chart JavaScript object you defined on the page level. The previous code initiates a new AnyChart HTML5 chart. The object can have different properties and events; in this case, I used the width and height to define that at runtime based on the value in the page item. The setdata event gives the XML it finds in P7_CHART_XML to the chart, and finally the write event will write the chart to the div.

■ **Caution** Make sure you adapt the code to use your item names. For example, if you are on page 1 in the dynamic action, you probably want to use P1_CHART_WIDTH.

Running the page gives the result shown in Figure 3-57.

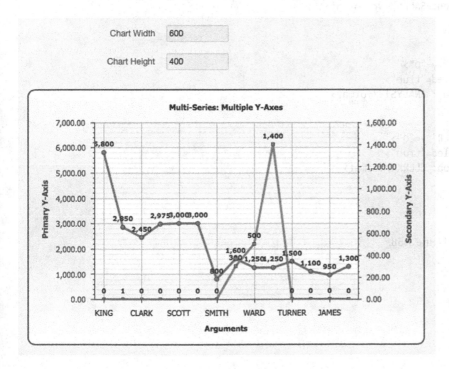

Figure 3-57. *A chart manually created with JavaScript*

You also want to change the tooltip of Series 2 to have a custom message. To achieve that, set the dynamic action Load Chart to Set Value in the true action. Then replace the existing SQL statement of Series 2 with the following code:

```
SELECT
  xmlelement("series",
    xmlattributes('Series 2' AS "name", 'extra_y_axis_1' AS "y_axis"),
    xmlagg( xmlelement("point",
      xmlattributes(ename AS "name", nvl(comm,0) AS "y"), ↵
      xmlelement("tooltip", xmlattributes('true' as "enabled"), xmlelement("format", ↵
'Job: ' || job)) ) )).getClobVal()
  INTO l_xml
  FROM emp;
```

The new SQL statement that you entered previously causes the APEX engine to add an XML tooltip to the generated XML (see that in the point node there's a tooltip node). The new generated XML code is as follows:

```
<series name="Series 2" y_axis="extra_y_axis_1">
    <point name="SMITH" y="0">
        <tooltip enabled="true">
            <format>Job: CLERK</format>
        </tooltip>
    </point>
    <point name="ALLEN" y="300">
        <tooltip enabled="true">
            <format>Job: SALESMAN</format>
        </tooltip>
    </point>
    ...
    <point name="FORD" y="0">
        <tooltip enabled="true">
            <format>Job: ANALYST</format>
        </tooltip>
    </point>
    <point name="MILLER" y="0">
        <tooltip enabled="true">
            <format>Job: CLERK</format>
        </tooltip>
    </point>
</series>
```

The result looks like Figure 3-58.

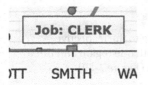

Figure 3-58. *The tooltip when hovering over a data point*

To let the user define the width and height of the chart, you need to add another dynamic action that fires when the user changes the width and height text items. Here are the steps to do this:

Add a new advanced dynamic action with the name **Change Chart Size** and the following settings:

- *Event*: Change

- *Selection Type*: Item(s)

- *Item(s)*: P7_CHART_WIDTH,P7_CHART_HEIGHT

Make the action a true action, and specify the following:

- *Affected Elements*: Selection Type = Region

- *Affected Elements*: Region = Manual Chart

- *Action*: Execute JavaScript Code

- *Fire When Event Result is*: True

- *Fire On Page Load*: No

- *Code*:

  ```
  chart.setSize($v('P7_CHART_WIDTH'),$v('P7_CHART_HEIGHT'));
  ```

  Now run the page and change the width and heights to see the results.

When you manually create a chart for the first time, it might be difficult to understand, but it comes down to going to the AnyChart Chart Gallery, finding an example you like, or looking into the documentation to know what XML and JavaScript you need to call. Next, you need to translate that logic into APEX components. Only by looking at the previous examples, trying things yourself, and gaining experience will this task become clear (if it is not already). After a while, the steps you have to take to create a chart completely manually will become trivial.

Drill-Down Charts, Dashboards, and Interactivity

In this section, you will look more at combining different charts on the same page and letting them work nicely together. You will create a page that will provide an instant snapshot of your business information, by combining different reports and charts on a dashboard. With drill-down capabilities, the charts on your dashboard can show different results based on the user interaction with the page. There are many different techniques to create dashboard pages in APEX, from simple examples using the built-in functionalities in APEX to complex dashboards using actions and events that come with the full license of AnyChart charts.

Simple Dashboard with Submit

In this first example, a manager wants to have an overview of the salaries he's giving to the respective departments and employees. To fulfil the manager's wish, you will create a page with one region and three subregions that hold the different charts so it looks like the charts are in one region (Figure 3-59).

- A pie chart with the salary by department

- A 2D column chart that shows the average, minimum, and maximum salaries by department

- Another 2D column with the salary by employee

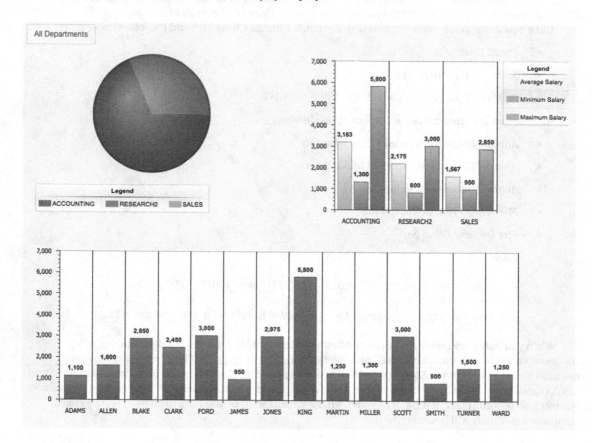

Figure 3-59. *A dashboard with three charts: one pie and two 2D column charts*

Next, you want to allow the manager to select a department in the pie chart and automatically update the other charts to show information only for the selected department (drill-down). Figure 3-60 represents the expected result when the manager clicks the Sales (green) slice of the pie chart.

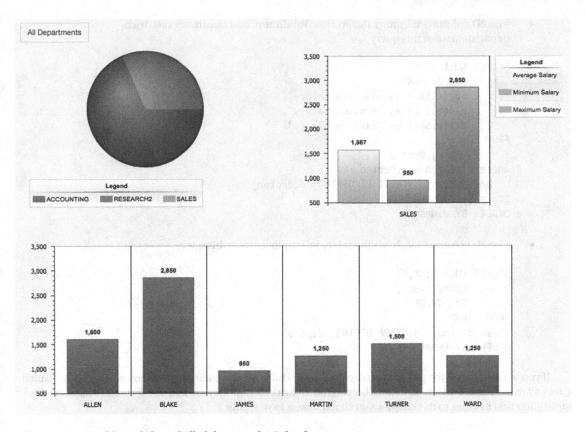

Figure 3-60. *Dashboard chart drilled down to the Sales department*

Behind the scenes, you used the wizard to create three different charts.

- The pie chart that shows the salary by department uses the following query:

```
SELECT 'f?p=&APP_ID.:&APP_PAGE_ID.:&APP_SESSION.:::::P8_DEPTNO:'||d.deptno LINK,
       d.dname LABEL,
       sum(e.SAL) sal
FROM   emp e, dept d
where e.deptno = d.deptno
group by 'f?p=&APP_ID.:&APP_PAGE_ID.:&APP_SESSION.:::::P8_DEPTNO:'||d.deptno, d.dname
ORDER  BY d.dname
```

- The 2D column that shows the average, minimum, and maximum salaries by department uses this query:

```
SELECT NULL LINK,
       d.dname LABEL,
       avg(e.SAL) as "Average Salary",
       min(e.SAL) as "Minimum Salary",
       max(e.SAL) as "Maximum Salary"
FROM
       emp e, dept d
where e.deptno = d.deptno
   and d.deptno = nvl(:P8_DEPTNO, d.deptno)
group by d.dname
ORDER  BY d.dname
```

- The 2D column that shows the salary by employee uses this query:

```
SELECT NULL LINK,
       ENAME LABEL,
       SAL VALUE
FROM   EMP
where deptno = nvl(:P8_DEPTNO, deptno)
ORDER  BY ENAME
```

If you want to create the previous example yourself while you are reading, take a look at Figure 3-61, which shows all the regions, buttons, and items behind the scenes and how they are laid out. If you downloaded the application that belongs to this chapter, you should take a look at page 8.

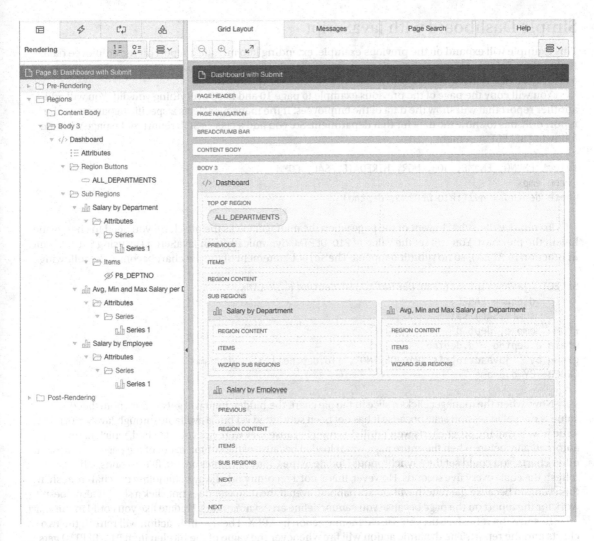

Figure 3-61. *Behind the scenes of the simple dashboard page with Submit*

Note that the pie chart has a link defined. That link will submit the page and set the item P8_DEPTNO, a hidden item you created in that region, with the value of the slice the user clicks.

You also use a button on the page called All Departments, which redirects to the same page and clears the cache. When creating the button for the action, select Redirect to Page in this Application (Page is 8 and Clear Cache is 8).

This example is the simplest dashboard you can create. It uses charts created by the wizard and provides interactivity and drill-down capabilities by using the link in the series SQL statement. To achieve the dashboard look and feel, I created a parent region with three subregions for the charts. That way the charts look like they are combined. The previous example has one big drawback: whenever the manager clicks a link, the entire page gets submitted, which isn't a nice effect and doesn't flow that well. You will fix the flow by adding a bit of JavaScript in the next section that will refresh the regions instead of submitting the entire page.

Simple Dashboard with JavaScript

This example will expand on the previous example, extending it to include a report on the employee data. Rather than doing a submit of the entire page, you will just refresh the necessary regions so the manager gets a nicer user experience.

You will copy the page of the previous example to page 10 and keep everything you did. You will add another report that will show the data of the employees. If the manager selects a specific department, the report only has to show the data for that department. So, you add a classic SQL report to the page with the following SELECT statement:

```
select EMPNO, ENAME, JOB, MGR, HIREDATE, SAL, COMM
  from emp
where deptno = nvl(:P10_DEPTNO, deptno)
```

To remove the submit event of the page when the manager clicks the pie chart, you need to change the link in the pie chart. You will set the value of P10_DEPTNO dynamically with JavaScript (by using $s(), a built-in function in APEX), so no submit happens. The select statement of the pie chart becomes the following:

```
SELECT 'javascript:$s("P10_DEPTNO",'||d.deptno||')' LINK,
       d.dname LABEL,
       sum(e.SAL) sal
FROM   emp e, dept d
where e.deptno = d.deptno
group by 'javascript:$s("P10_DEPTNO",'||d.deptno||')' , d.dname
ORDER  BY d.dname
```

Now, when the manager clicks a slice in the pie chart, the hidden item will get a value (note that this value is not yet in session state because it has not been submitted yet but is available through JavaScript). The issue now is that the other charts won't drill down yet because they were not yet refreshed, which happened automatically before when the entire page was reloaded because of the submit event of the page. To refresh the other charts, you could set the Asynchronous Update in the Chart Attributes area to five seconds, which will refresh the chart every five seconds. However, this is not a recommended way of handling the chart refresh in this scenario because the refresh will always happen, even if the manager does not click a slice. It also doesn't work for the report on the page because you cannot define an Asynchronous Update like you could in the chart.

To solve the refresh issue, you use a dynamic action in APEX. The dynamic action will refresh the two charts and the report. The dynamic action will fire whenever the value of the hidden item P10_DEPTNO gets changed. This is how the dynamic action is defined:

- *Event*: Change

- *Selection Type*: Item(s)

- *Item(s)*: P10_DEPTNO

- True Action 1
  - *Action*: Refresh
  - *Fire When Event Result is*: True
  - *Fire On Page Load*: No
  - *Selection Type*: Region
  - *Region*: Avg, Min and Max Salary per Department
- True Action 2
  - *Action*: Refresh
  - *Fire When Event Result is*: True
  - *Fire On Page Load*: No
  - *Selection Type*: Region
  - *Region*: Salary by Employees
- True Action 3
  - *Action*: Refresh
  - *Fire When Event Result is*: True
  - *Fire On Page Load*: No
  - *Selection Type*: Region
  - *Region*: Salary by Employees (Report)

In all the series that will get refreshed, make sure to add P10_DEPTNO in the Page Items to the Submit field so the value of P10_DEPTNO is set in session state before it's refreshed.

Finally, you can change the button for seeing all departments to Redirect to Url. Use the following for the URL: javascript:$s('P10_DEPTNO',''). This basically empties out the hidden item.

Figure 3-62 represents the result of the manager clicking a slice of the pie chart.

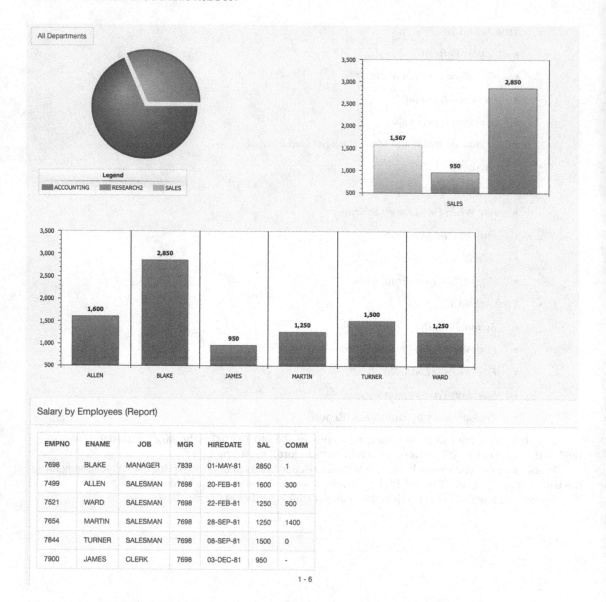

Figure 3-62. *Dashboard chart and report drilled down to Sales department (with JavaScript)*

As you can see, the Sales slice in the pie chart is moved out from the rest of the chart. This "explode" action is a feature of AnyChart when you click something in the chart, but you didn't see this in the first example because the entire page was submitted and rerendered.

Complex Dashboard with Actions

This example is completely different from previous examples and takes you beyond APEX. Oracle licensed only part of AnyChart charts, so for example if you want to create a real dashboard (one chart object with multiple charts inside it), you need to include the full AnyChart files. If you try to render the chart with Oracle's AnyChart version, you get an error (Figure 3-63).

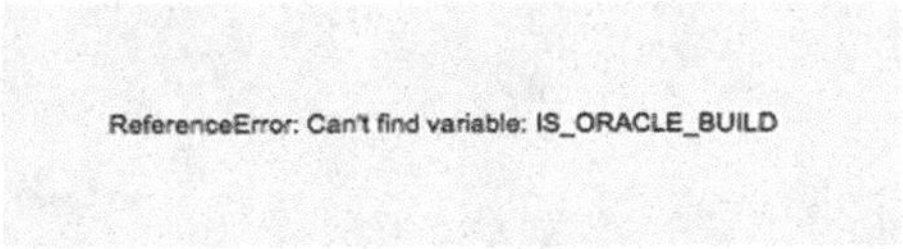

ReferenceError: Can't find variable: IS_ORACLE_BUILD

Figure 3-63. *The error when you try to run XML to generate a chart that is not licensed by Oracle*

This example (Figure 3-64) hardly uses any built-in features of APEX. The only thing you need is an HTML region where you define the `div` tag that holds the dashboard and a dynamic action to load the data for the dashboard. Unlike in the previous examples, this dashboard consists of only one AnyChart object, but inside that one object six different charts are defined. Column, bar, spline-area, spline, bubble, and range-area charts are inside one container.

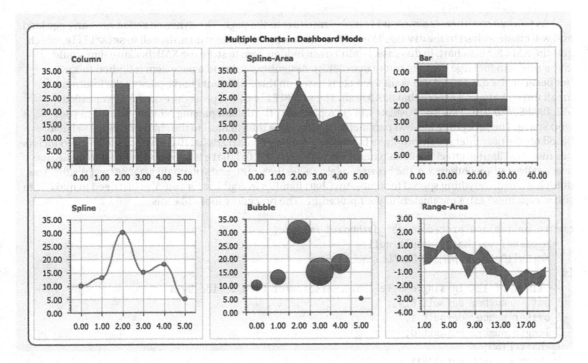

Figure 3-64. *A complex dashboard using the full AnyChart capabilities*

The definition of the HTML region is as follows:

```
<div id="chartDiv"></div>
```

And this is how the dynamic action is defined:

- *Event*: Page Load
- *True Actions*

- *Action 1*:

  - *Action*: Execute JavaScript Code

  - *Fire When Event Result is*: True

  - *Fire On Page Load*: No

  - *Code*:

```
AnyChart.renderingType = anychart.RenderingType.SVG_ONLY;
chart = new AnyChart;
chart.width = 800;
chart.height = 500;
chart.setXMLFile('#OWNER#.GET_DASHBOARD_XML_PRC?p_param1=Full');
chart.write('chartDiv');
```

As you can see, there is almost no complex structure to the page. The dynamic action runs on page load and will create a chart in the div tag. The only magic piece in the JavaScript is the call to setXMLFile, which gets the XML for the chart. In this case, I didn't use a hidden item to store the XML because that would give a problem for large datasets (more than 32KB). Assigning a value to a page item is limited to 32KB, but because the dashboard you want to create is based on three different charts, passing the information for all three charts will exceed that 32KB limit. The setXMLFile calls a procedure on the server called GET_DASHBOARD_XML_PRC. The #OWNER# will get replaced by the default parsing schema defined in your workspace. The procedure has two parameters to pass extra information to the chart or change behavior based on the user interaction, but there is another parameter called XMLCallDate, which you need to include because AnyChart is attaching extra parameters to the call. XMLCallDate is used by AnyChart to make sure every call is unique; otherwise, the browser might cache the result, and you might get incorrect results. You don't have to do anything special for that—AnyChart handles everything for you. You just need to make sure you accept these extra parameters in your procedure. The procedure looks like this:

```
create or replace procedure get_dashboard_xml:prc(
    p_param1 varchar2 default null,
    XMLCallDate IN NUMBER DEFAULT NULL)
is
  -- limit of 32K in single byte characterset, for UTF8 devide by 4 -1
  l_amt    number default 8191;
  l_offset number default 1;
  l_length number default 0;
  l_chart clob;
  l_chart_v varchar2(32767);
  l_chart_data clob;
begin
  dbms_lob.createtemporary( l_chart, FALSE, dbms_lob.session );
  dbms_lob.open( l_chart, dbms_lob.lob_readwrite );

    l_chart_v := '<?xml version="1.0" encoding="UTF-8"?>
<anychart>
  <dashboard>
    <view type="Dashboard">
      <title padding="0">
        <text>Multiple Charts in Dashboard Mode</text>
      </title>
```

```
      <background>
        <inside_margin all="3" top="10" />
      </background>
      <vbox width="100%" height="100%">
        <margin all="0" />
        <hbox width="100%" height="50%">
          <margin all="0" />
          <view type="Chart" source="Chart1" width="33.3%" height="100%" />
          <view type="Chart" source="Chart2" width="33.3%" height="100%" />
          <view type="Chart" source="Chart3" width="33.3%" height="100%" />
        </hbox>
        <hbox width="100%" height="50%">
          <margin all="0" />
          <view type="Chart" source="Chart4" width="33.3%" height="100%" />
          <view type="Chart" source="Chart5" width="33.3%" height="100%" />
          <view type="Chart" source="Chart6" width="33.3%" height="100%" />
        </hbox>
      </vbox>
    </view>
  </dashboard>
... /* TRUNCED FOR READABILITY */ ...';

  dbms_lob.writeappend( l_chart, length(l_chart_v), l_chart_v);
  dbms_lob.close( l_chart );
  --
  owa_util.mime_header('text/xml', FALSE, 'utf-8');
  owa_util.http_header_close;
  l_length := dbms_lob.getlength(l_chart);
  if l_length > 0 then
     while ( l_offset < l_length )
     loop
         sys.htp.prn(dbms_lob.substr(l_chart, l_amt, l_offset) );
         l_offset := l_offset + l_amt;
     end loop;
  end if;
  --
  if l_chart is not null then
     dbms_lob.freetemporary(l_chart);
  end if;
end;
```

When you look at this code for the first time, it might look challenging, but it comes down to generating the correct XML that AnyChart requires to render a dashboard. You would need to look into the AnyChart Gallery and Documentation to know what XML is expected.

In this case, you hard-code many things, but you can make this procedure as dynamic as you like by using more parameters or building more queries to retrieve the data. Because there is a limit in sys.htp.prn, you have to write a loop to pass the XML back in chunks. There are many ways to generate the data (XML), you could use AJAX (apex.ajax), a REST web service, an on-demand process, or a procedure. It's just what you feel most comfortable with what to use to generate the correct XML. I wanted to show how to do this manually, so you see the exact steps, but typically you would wrap the code in an APEX plugin. Further in this chapter, you'll see how much easier it is to use a plugin to build any chart you like.

There are many more options in AnyChart such as using specific events to refresh one particular view of the dashboard (setViewData in JavaScript) or letting the chart behave completely differently when the user is hovering over and clicking the chart.

The possibilities are endless, and you can't show every possible feature of AnyChart, but by understanding how AnyChart works behind the scenes and by looking at the different techniques used throughout this chapter, you should be able to build your dream chart.

Building Charts with the AnyChart Plugin

You saw before that Oracle licensed only part of AnyChart's charts. If you want to extend the existing charting capabilities, you'll need to include the full version (meaning, purchase a license) of the AnyChart engine (some JavaScript and other files) and create the correct XML for the chart. To ease that pain, APEX R&D developed an AnyChart plugin. By adding the region plugin to your page, it will include the full version of AnyChart and the ability to add the settings and data more easily. AnyChart is also moving more quickly than the releases of APEX, so the versions are out of sync. APEX 5.0 is based on AnyChart 6.2, but the latest release of AnyChart is at the time of writing already on version 7, which is actually a completely new code base and—so far—not backward compatible.

If you go to the AnyChart web site, all the new examples are based on the new engine, so using a plugin makes more sense than to manually include AnyChart. It's easier to upgrade the plugin with a new release of the AnyChart engine than to manually update your pages. For the latest release of the AnyChart plugin, check https://www.apexrnd.be.

To add a chart, drag the AnyChart plugin on your page in the Page Designer (Figure 3-65). You have different options to enter the source of the chart settings and data. To make it easy, you just copied an example JSON from the AnyChart Playground into the source of the region. You see the result in Figure 3-66.

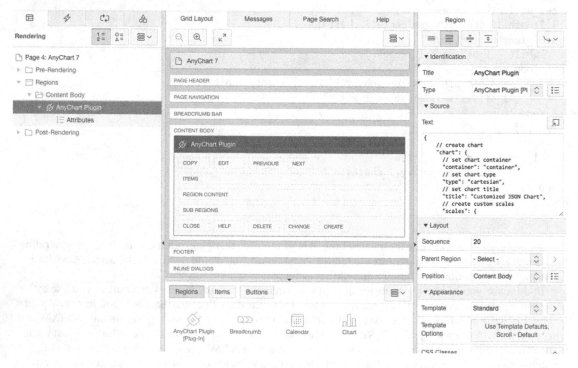

Figure 3-65. *AnyChart plugin in the Page Designer of APEX*

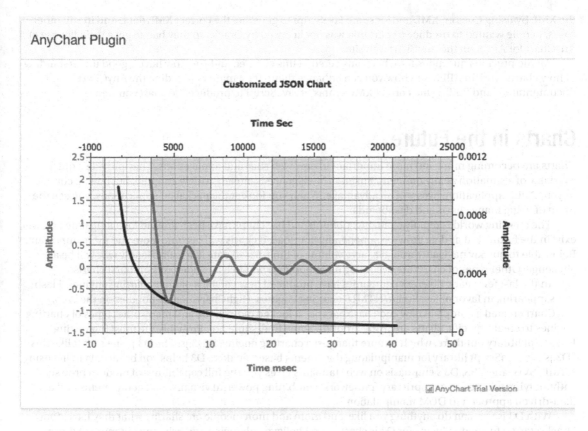

AnyChart Plugin

Figure 3-66. *The chart the AnyChart plugin rendered, based on AnyChart 7*

Most Common Issues

This section explains some issues people frequently seem to have and how they can be solved.

Chart Not Rendering Correctly

When upgrading the Flash charts to HTML5 charts, I noticed that sometimes my chart didn't look completely the same; for example, the labels were gone, or a title disappeared. It looks like some old syntax of AnyChart is not 100 percent compatible, but luckily there's an easy way to get around this issue. When you edit your chart attributes and series and save it again, APEX will regenerate the correct XML, which solved the issues in my case. If you use custom XML, you might want to set it first to not use custom XML, save it, and make the changes again when you set it back to use custom XML.

Search for a Specific Feature

Looking at the Oracle APEX Forum, most of the requests are about how to do a certain thing in a chart. In some cases, people don't know where to add a link or what every option in the APEX wizard means. In other cases, a feature wasn't supported by an option in the APEX screens, and a change had to be made in the XML by using Custom XML and/or some JavaScript to generate the correct XML data. And in still other cases, people wanted to produce a chart that was not licensed by Oracle, so they had to get a valid license of AnyChart for APEX on the AnyChart web site.

All the previous questions have been answered in this chapter, and you now have a good understanding of how charts work in APEX and how you can enhance them. It's a matter of reading the AnyChart documentation and finding the correct XML syntax or JavaScript to produce the chart you want.

Charts in the Future

Charts are becoming more and more important in new web sites and applications. They provide a quick overview of a situation at any moment. Business intelligence is already widely adopted, but having charts in your APEX application gives you an advantage. When you look at the packaged applications, you see the trend of using many charts and dashboards.

The charting world is rapidly changing. Column and bar charts have been around for a long time and will exist in the future, but as data grows exponentially, time-based charts will become more and more important. Being able to quickly navigate through a large volume of time-based data in a user-friendly way will be a challenge. Other types of charts are becoming more popular too, such as spider and sunburst charts.

In the last few years, different companies have produced new versions of their charting engines. Flash is disappearing in favor of JavaScript/HTML5 charting engines. HighCharts seems popular on the Web, AnyChart created a complete new code base because it looked old-school, and many other types of charting engines to create specific charts are flying around—some free, some not. Probably the most interesting JavaScript library out there, which is more than just a charting engine, is D3.js. The D3.js site says it like this: "D3.js is a JavaScript library for manipulating documents based on data. D3 helps you bring data to life using HTML, SVG, and CSS. D3's emphasis on web standards gives you the full capabilities of modern browsers without tying yourself to a proprietary framework, combining powerful visualization components and a data-driven approach to DOM manipulation."

With D3.js you can do anything you like, and more and more people are sharing what they have done. Oracle started to create plugins for D3.js charts, and I believe enhancing and bringing out more of those plugins will be the direction for the next couple of years.

Other elements of the future of charting solutions will include user interaction such as zooming, drag and drop, different information depending on user interaction, and the like. Allowing the user to do things in an innovative and intuitive way will become increasingly important and will decide whether your application is "wow" or just OK.

Chart Plugins

As the future of charts is in new (D3.js) plugins, I want to mention where you find those new types of charts in APEX 5.0 and highlight the most important features.

Sample Charts in Packaged Application

APEX 5.0 includes a new Sample Charts packaged application (Figure 3-67) that includes some interesting new chart engines.

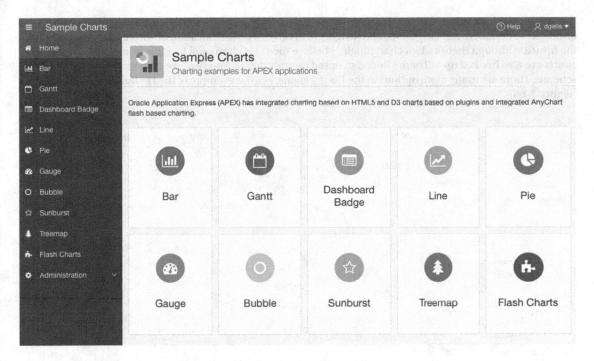

Figure 3-67. *Sample Charts packaged application*

The following plugins are available in the Sample Charts application:

- Badge List
- D3 Bar Chart
- D3 Bubble Chart
- D3 Line Chart
- D3 Pie Chart
- D3 Sunburst Chart
- D3 Treemap Chart
- Flot Line Chart
- Flot Pie Chart
- Gantt Chart
- HTML 5 Bar Chart
- JustGage Gauge

As you can see, many D3.js plugins are already available, which you can include in your own application too. You just export the plugin and import in your application and there you go. The different plugins have different settings and ways they work behind the scenes, but mostly it comes down to some JavaScript to define the chart, a way to generate the data in the correct format, and then the plugin to make it available natively in APEX.

When you look at the libraries that ship with APEX 5.0 (in the images folder), the following charting libraries are included: raphaeljs, d3js, and justgage. This gives a good indication of where Oracle is going in the future. Although there's a Flot chart plugin, I believe the D3.js charts will be most interesting. Those D3.js charts are also hooked up to Theme Roller, so based on your theme, you can give your charts the same color scheme. There are many more options in the D3.js plugins; see the example of the D3 Bubble Chart plugin (Figure 3-68).

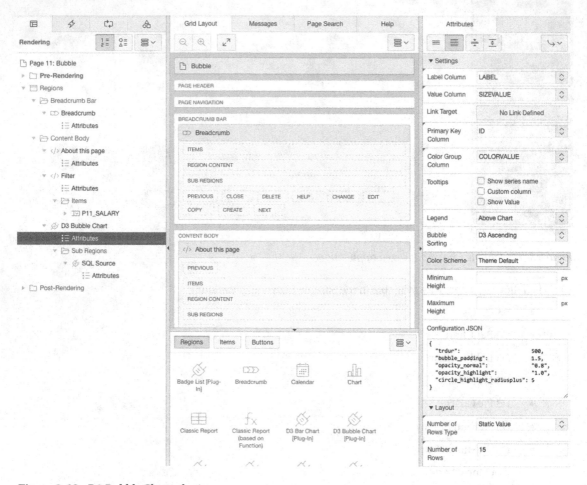

Figure 3-68. *D3 Bubble Chart plugin*

In the Source setting of the region, you define a SQL query. In the plugin attributes (Figure 3-68), you then define which column is used for the label, which one for the value, and so on. You can also define some custom JSON to extend and customize the chart even more.

Inline Charts in Report

Another interesting use of charts is in reports. It's actually easy to include a percentage bar in your own report. Go to a number column in your report (between 0 and 100) and set the type to Percent Graph. You can see the result in Figure 3-69.

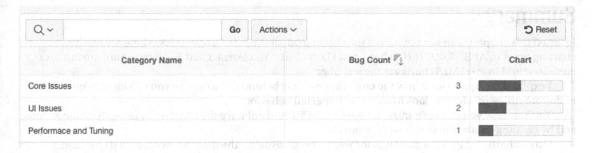

Figure 3-69. *Percent chart in an interactive report*

Other interesting use cases of charts are in lists or some custom regions. Looking at, for example, the Bug Tracker sample application or P-Track gives you some other ideas on how to incorporate badges, use inline charts, and combine different components in attractive dashboards.

Resources

These are the resources linked to using charts in a web environment and Oracle Application Express. You might find them useful if you need more information or examples:

- The APEX application used in this book:

  https://www.apexrnd.be/ords/f?p=APEX5_EXPERT_CHART

- APEX documentation, accessibility in Oracle Application Express:

  http://apex.oracle.com/doc50

- AnyChart 6.*x* resources:

  http://anychart.com/products/anychart/6.x/

- AnyChart XML reference:

  http://www.anychart.com/products/anychart/docs/xmlReference/index.html

- AnyChart plugin for APEX:

  https://www.apexrnd.be

- Hilary Farrell from the APEX Development Team also has a sample chart application with many demos and tips:

  http://apex.oracle.com/pls/apex/f?p=36648

- Firebug for Firefox:

  http://getfirebug.com

Summary

I started this chapter with an overview of the charting possibilities in Oracle APEX. There are two big charting types in APEX 5.0: HTML5 charts and Flash charts. You learned that Flash charts are not further enhanced and that HTML5 charts are the way to go.

I explained in great detail how the charts are working behind the scenes so you can identify quickly how to do something or where to look in case of unexpected behavior.

You saw how you can customize the AnyChart XML and enhance the charting by using dynamic actions and by creating charts and dashboards manually.

Using charts in APEX is a great way for your users to visualize the data they work with day-in and day-out. The native AnyChart charts combined with the newer charting plugins have everything on board to fulfill your charting dreams, and there is more to come in the future. If the current implementation of charting doesn't include a particular feature, there are already many extensions and plug-ins available that give you that functionality today.

Good luck with charting, and enjoy this wonderful technology!

■ ■ ■

Tabular Forms

by Denes Kubicek

A tabular form provides a way to display, create, edit, and delete multiple records using a grid. With tabular forms you can edit and change multiple records at once, without having to go back and forth like in a normal single record form.

How did tabular forms evolve? The feature has been part of APEX from the beginning. Until version 4.0, however, there were no major changes in the way tabular forms operated. A wizard was available to lead users through the creation of a tabular form. This wizard would create a simple editable report. In addition to the report, it would create some buttons required for saving or discarding changes and four processes for creating, updating, and deleting data. That was basically it. If you needed more, you had to create your own code.

Prior to starting work on this chapter, which was initially written for APEX 4.0, I was thinking about how to modify it to fit the new version 5.0, which was released in April 2015. However, tabular forms didn't change in 5.0. I decided to keep all the old parts of the chapter but present the changes between versions 4.0 and 5.0 (4.1 and 4.2). I added the major changes from releases 4.1 and 4.2 and removed the following topics:

- Simple autocomplete

- Autocomplete returning key value

- Clone rows

I added a new topic to the section "Interesting Techniques."

- Multiple tabular forms and modal pages

Changes in APEX 4.0

With APEX 4.0 came the first major changes to tabular forms since APEX was developed. These include the following:

- New item types (Single Checkbox, jQuery Date Picker, Radio Group, Popup Key LOV).

- The client-side Add Row capability.

- Validations for tabular form columns.

- Lost update protection. Finally it is possible to validate a tabular form and show the error message on the same screen without losing the updates.

- Fewer processes required for a tabular form (two instead of four).

- Some other features, which I will mention later in this chapter.

Changes in APEX 4.1/4.2

With APEX 4.1 and 4.2, a couple of significant changes were introduced. The following are the most important new features:

- Declarative validations using bind variable column syntax

- Declarative processing using :column syntax

- New variables available for the processing

- The ability to reference tabular form selectors in dynamic actions

The versions also fix numerous bugs related to tabular form validations and validation error message display.

Changes in APEX 5.0

Unfortunately, APEX 5.0 doesn't bring any significant changes to the previous versions. Only some layout modifications were made to match the new Universal theme, and the process of creating tabular forms has been changed in the Page Designer.

Constraints

APEX and its `wwv_flows` package provides 50 predefined PL/SQL arrays for tabular form operations. You can reference these arrays using the following syntax:

```
wwv_flow.g_f01 ... wwv_flow.g_f50
```

Or, you can use this:

```
apex_application.g_f01 ... apex_application.g_f50
```

Every updatable column in a tabular form will have a unique ID in a sequential order (the SQL statement) mapped to one of these arrays:

```
f01_0001, f02_0001 ... f50_0001
f01_0002, f02_0002 ... f50_0002
f01_0003, f02_0003 ... f50_0003
```

The limit of 50 arrays is a major constraint with tabular forms. Currently, a tabular form will allow users to update or create a maximum of 50 columns per page. The maximum number of columns an Oracle table can have is 1,024. Thus, you can find yourself in a position where a table has more columns than you can display on a page.

Depending on the PL/SQL you use, you will receive an error either in the Page Designer or while submitting the form when you exceed the 50-column limit, as shown in Figure 4-1.

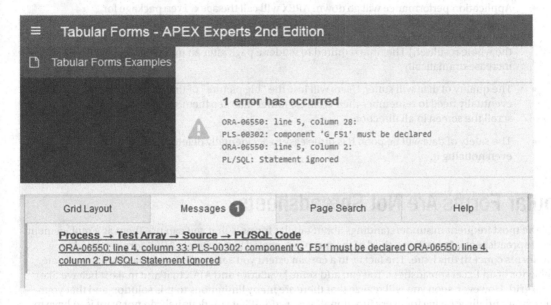

Figure 4-1. *Typical error message after referencing a nonexisting array*

■ **Caution**   Keep in mind that new item types available in APEX 4 (Simple Checkbox and Popup Key LOV) will require two of these IDs. Therefore, the limitation of 50 updatable columns per page may vary depending on how many of those elements you have.

Purpose of Tabular Forms

The main purpose of a tabular form can be described in two cases.

- To maintain smaller sets of data

- To maintain parent-child relations

A typical example of the first case would be a page in your application where you maintain lists of values. Normally a list of values will contain a couple of records (options), and you could display this set of data on one page. The reason for choosing this method is so that you can quickly edit and save records without having to drill down, paginate, or switch between the pages.

An example of the second case would be an application for order management. An order would be a parent record (master), and ordered items would be the child records (detail). In most cases, there is a limited (small) number of details for one master record. Normally you would want to maintain that relation between the master and the detail on one page. In that case, tabular forms are the way to go.

You can even use tabular forms to update thousands of records with up to 50 columns each. In that case, however, you will face several issues.

- Application performance will go down. APEX will call the apex_item package for each row and each column displayed on your page. (It will be even worse if you build tabular forms manually since this will happen not only for displayed rows but for the whole resultset.) The time required to render a page after an update process will increase dramatically.

- The quality of data will suffer. Users will lose the "big picture" of their data and will eventually need to remember their changes rather than see them since they need to scroll the screen in all directions.

- The safety of data will be poor. It is quite easy to accidentally delete records without even noticing it.

Tabular Forms Are Not Spreadsheets

One of the most frequent misunderstandings about tabular forms is that you can use them as a replacement for Excel spreadsheets. At least one-third of the questions posted in the Oracle APEX forum related to tabular forms concern this issue. The fact is, to a certain extent you can modify a tabular form to simulate the behavior of an Excel spreadsheet. You can add some JavaScript and AJAX to it and make it behave like an Excel grid. However, soon you will realize that there are many limitations to this solution and that your code is exponentially growing for every functionality you add. What you definitely do not want is to have to support and debug that code later. Tabular forms are not meant to replace Excel—they have a completely different purpose.

Features in APEX 4

As mentioned earlier, the first set of major changes to tabular forms happened in release 4 of APEX. Some important features were added and enhanced.

New Item Types

In prior releases of APEX, tabular forms were somewhat limited compared to single-row forms. A couple of important items were missing. Release 4 corrected that issue by introducing the following item types:

- Single Checkbox
- jQuery Date Picker
- Radio Group
- Popup Key LOV

Single Checkbox

In some cases, your tabular form will need to provide a column of type Checkbox to give your users the ability to "flag" a record. Usually it will be "Yes" or "Y" for an activated check box and "No" or "N" for the not-checked (empty) state. In earlier versions of APEX, such a requirement would cause a lot of coding just to create a workaround for a simple problem. The Checkbox item was different from the other items in APEX—its value was not submitted to the server for the empty state. This means that the array g_f01 would contain the values for checked items only; there was no really good way to get around this problem.

APEX 4 changed this for the better by introducing the Single Checkbox item. This item can be used like any other item and is capable of storing either a single value for checked (activated) or NULL for the empty state.

To demonstrate how this feature works, you will need to do a couple of preparation steps first.

1. Create a new workspace. (You need to make sure that your instance settings allow the creation of the demo application, so select Workspace: INTERNAL Home ➤ Manage Instance ➤ Feature Configuration. Set the option "Create demonstration objects in new workspaces" to Yes.)

    This will create the required tables you need for this demonstration (EMP and DEPT).

2. Change the EMP table by adding an additional column and changing one of the columns, as shown in Listing 4-1.

3. Create a new application.

4. Create a tabular form using a wizard based on the EMP table and include all the columns.

■ **Note**   Together, these steps provide a framework from which to experiment with the Simple Checkbox feature. Listing 4-1 shows the code to modify the EMP and DEPT tables. The valid column added to table EMP is the check box column.

Listing 4-1. Extending EMP and DEPT Tables

```
ALTER TABLE emp MODIFY (ename VARCHAR2(40) NOT NULL);

ALTER TABLE emp ADD (valid VARCHAR2(1));

CREATE TABLE emp_bkp AS SELECT * FROM emp;

CREATE TABLE dept_bkp AS SELECT * FROM dept;

CREATE SEQUENCE dept_seq START WITH 50 INCREMENT BY 10 NOCACHE;

CREATE SEQUENCE emp_seq START WITH 7950 INCREMENT BY 1 NOCACHE;

CREATE OR REPLACE TRIGGER dept_tr
   BEFORE INSERT
   ON dept
   FOR EACH ROW
BEGIN
   IF :NEW.deptno IS NULL
   THEN
      SELECT dept_seq.NEXTVAL
        INTO :NEW.deptno
```

```
        FROM DUAL;
    END IF;
END;
/
CREATE OR REPLACE TRIGGER emp_tr
    BEFORE INSERT
    ON emp
    FOR EACH ROW
BEGIN
    IF :NEW.empno IS NULL
    THEN
        SELECT emp_seq.NEXTVAL
          INTO :NEW.empno
          FROM DUAL;
    END IF;
END;
/
```

Now, editing the report attributes and the newly created column properties for the column VALID, you can change Type to Simple Checkbox, as shown in Figure 4-2.

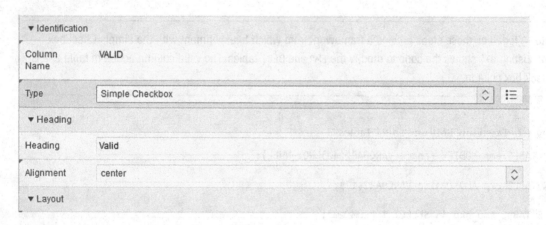

Figure 4-2. *Using the Simple Checkbox item type*

Using the List of Values section, you will need to enter the required static Checkbox Values for a simple check box (see Figure 4-3). If you require only one value, you will need to change the Checkbox Values definition to Y instead of Y,N.

Sequence	11
Column Alignment	center

▼ List of Values

Checkbox Values	Y,N

Figure 4-3. *Simple Checkbox LOV*

After saving the changes, running the application, and opening the page with the tabular form, you should see a result similar to Figure 4-4. Figure 4-5 shows the raw data from the EMP table that underlies the form.

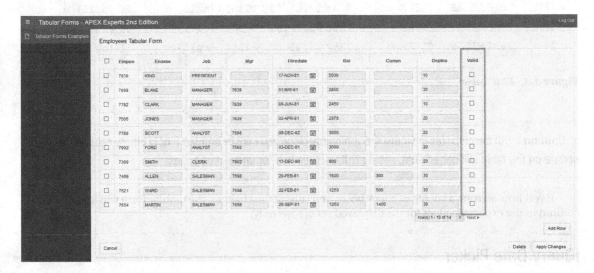

Figure 4-4. *Simple Checkbox in a tabular form*

	EMPNO	ENAME	JOB	MGR	HIREDATE	SAL	COMM	DEPTNO	VALID
1	7839	KING	PRESIDENT	(null)	17.11.81	5000	(null)	10	(null)
2	7698	BLAKE	MANAGER	7839	01.05.81	2850	(null)	30	(null)
3	7782	CLARK	MANAGER	7839	09.06.81	2450	(null)	10	(null)
4	7566	JONES	MANAGER	7839	02.04.81	2975	(null)	20	(null)
5	7788	SCOTT	ANALYST	7566	09.12.82	3000	(null)	20	(null)
6	7902	FORD	ANALYST	7566	03.12.81	3000	(null)	20	(null)
7	7369	SMITH	CLERK	7902	17.12.80	800	(null)	20	(null)
8	7499	ALLEN	SALESMAN	7698	20.02.81	1600	300	30	(null)
9	7521	WARD	SALESMAN	7698	22.02.81	1250	500	30	(null)
10	7654	MARTIN	SALESMAN	7698	28.09.81	1250	1400	30	(null)
11	7844	TURNER	SALESMAN	7698	08.09.81	1500	0	30	(null)
12	7876	ADAMS	CLERK	7788	12.01.83	1100	(null)	20	(null)
13	7900	JAMES	CLERK	7698	03.12.81	950	(null)	30	(null)
14	7934	MILLER	CLERK	7782	23.01.82	1300	(null)	10	(null)

Figure 4-5. EMP table

■ **Caution** All check boxes in Figure 4-5 are empty since you initially created a new empty column. The first update on the table will correct that, setting NULL values to N for unchecked boxes.

If you now activate a couple of check boxes and submit the changes, the tabular form will update the column to the expected values for the displayed set of rows only.

jQuery Date Picker

As of APEX 4, the wizard for creating tabular forms will do some additional work for you and save you some time. If you have columns of type DATE or TIMESTAMP in your table and include them in a tabular form, APEX will automatically set them up as Date Picker columns using the newest version of the jQuery calendar, as shown in Figure 4-6.

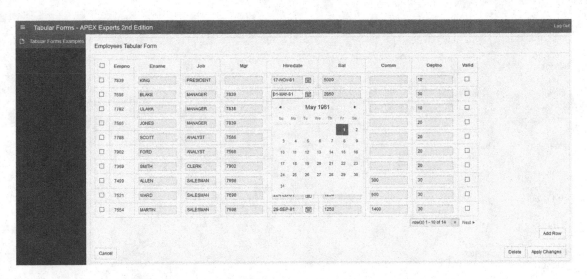

Figure 4-6. *jQuery Date Picker in a tabular form*

Unfortunately, you cannot extend the calendar feature the way you can in simple forms and specify the number of months or add a year range to it. Ideally that functionality will be included in one of the next releases.

Radio Group

The Radio Group type is the next tabular form item type that came with release 4 of APEX. In earlier versions, you were able to manually create that item type by using the `apex_item.radiogroup` packaged function. The disadvantage of doing so was that APEX would create one array per entry in the radio group and you needed to write your own code to handle that problem while inserting or updating the record.

To show how this feature works, you will now change the item type for the column VALID to Radio Group (with a Type value of Static Values), as shown in Figure 4-7. Change the Static Values field to the following:

```
STATIC:Yes;Y,No;N
```

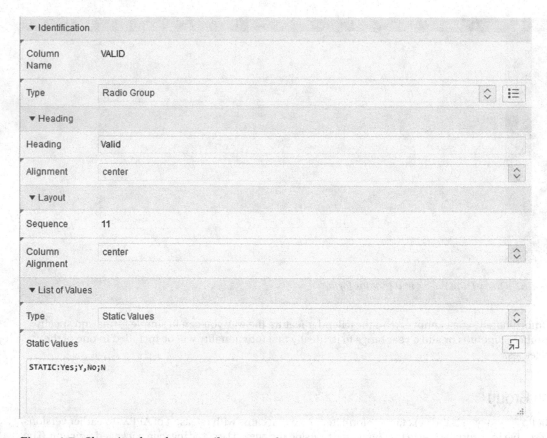

Figure 4-7. Changing the column attributes to Radio Group

After applying the changes, running the application, and opening the page with the tabular form, you should see a result similar to Figure 4-8.

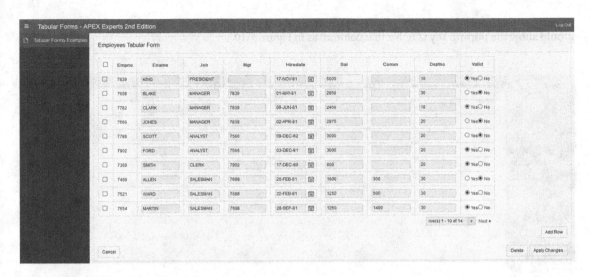

Figure 4-8. *Tabular form with Radio Group column*

Popup Key LOV

The limitation for the select list item type regarding the number of entries you could use was one of the biggest problems in earlier releases of APEX. As soon as the list grew over a certain size (a combination of the number and the size of the available options), you would receive an error saying the character string buffer was too small (see Figure 4-9).

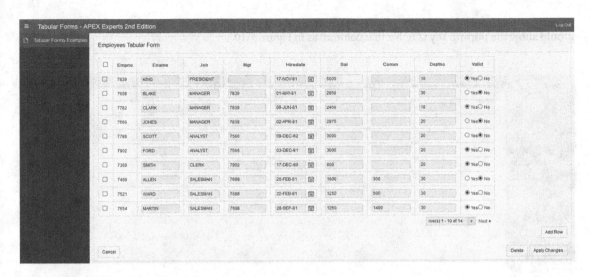

Figure 4-9. *Select list error*

For simple forms, the workaround was to use a pop-up LOV returning the key value, but for tabular forms this simply wasn't possible. APEX 4 changed this by including this item type for tabular forms.

To test this feature, you will need to modify your tabular form by editing the column DEPTNO and changing it to have a value of Popup LOV (SQL Query based LOV). Then add the following query to the list of values definition:

```
SELECT dname d, deptno r
  FROM dept
```

155

If you now apply the changes, run the application, and sort the tabular form using the DEPTNO column, it should show the pop-up key LOV for that column, as in Figure 4-10.

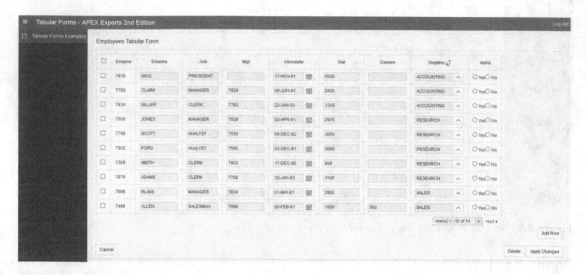

Figure 4-10. *Tabular form with a Popup Key LOV item*

One additional change was added to the select list item type in general. In earlier versions of APEX, the sorting on a column containing a select list would sort the values on the return value. Often this was not desirable. Since APEX 4, this behavior has changed, and the sorting is done on the displayed value, as you can see in Figure 4-10.

Declarative Validations

APEX 4 introduced declarative validations for tabular forms. This feature is quite important since it saves time while building your applications. Declarative validations can be created on a single column and are grouped as follows:

- NOT NULL validations
- Column string comparison validations

There are several column string comparison validations, and you can view them in Figure 4-11.

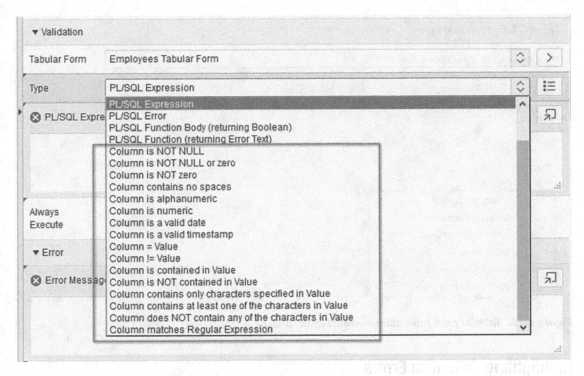

Figure 4-11. Tabular form validations—column string comparison validations

As of APEX 4.1/4.2, you can use declarative validations outside the scope of a single column. If you need such a validation, you will not have to write your own code anymore. I will show how to do that later in the chapter (see "Features in APEX 4.1/4.2" and "Custom Coding in Tabular Forms").

Validations Created by Tabular Form Wizard

After creating a tabular form, you will find a couple of validations created by the wizard. Figure 4-12 shows an example of these validations.

The APEX wizard that built the tabular form uses the table definition and sorts out the constraints you defined for your table. It will create a validation for each single column containing a NOT NULL definition (unless the column is a primary key used for the DML processes) or for columns of type Numeric and columns of type Date.

As you can see in Figure 4-12, the APEX tabular form Wizard created several validations automatically. If you remember the changes made in Listing 4-1, you will notice that this change resulted in a validation, checking the ENAME column (Validation with sequence 30 – ENAME not null. The other validations are related to the data type of all existing numeric and date columns included in the tabular form.

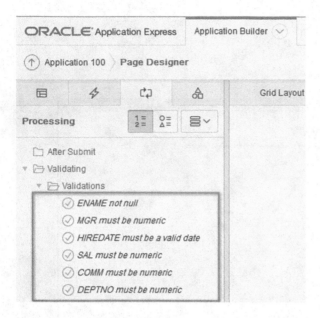

Figure 4-12. Tabular form validations—created by the wizard

Highlighting Validation Errors

If you want to test the validations created by the wizard, you can make a couple of changes in your table to see how they work, as shown in Figure 4-13.

Employees Tabular Form

	Empno	Ename	Job	Mgr	Hiredate	Sal
☐	7839		PRESIDENT		17-NOV-81 🗓	5000
☐	7782	CLARK	MANAGER	7839	09-JUN-81 🗓	2450
☐	7934	MILLER	CLERK	7782	23-JAN-82 🗓	1300
☐	7566	JONES	MANAGER	7839	02-APR-81 🗓	2975a

Figure 4-13. Tabular form validations

Change the entry for the column ENAME to NULL and modify the entry for the column SALARY to an alphanumeric character. If you try to save that, you should receive an error like the one shown in Figure 4-14.

⚠ **2 errors have occurred**
- Ename must have a value. (Row 1)
- Sal must be numeric. (Row 4)

Employees Tabular Form

	Empno	Ename	Job	Mgr	Hiredate	Sal
☐	7839		PRESIDENT		17-NOV-81 📅	5000
☐	7782	CLARK	MANAGER	7839	09-JUN-81 📅	2450
☐	7934	MILLER	CLERK	7782	23-JAN-82 📅	1300
☐	7566	JONES	MANAGER	7839	02-APR-81 📅	2975a

***Figure 4-14.** Tabular form validations, error highlighting*

If you remember how such validations worked before version 4, you will notice a few changes.

- APEX is now highlighting the cells where validation errors were found.

- APEX will tell you the name of the column affected by the error message.

- APEX will provide you with a direct link for setting the focus to the affected cell as a part of the error message.

- Most important, you didn't lose the changes you made.

In earlier versions of APEX, a lot of custom coding was required to get similar functionality. To avoid losing the changes you made after an unsuccessful validation, it was required that you display the validation errors on an error page and click the back button.

I need to mention one more important thing. If you edit one of the validations created by the wizard, you will notice that there is a new substitution string in the error message. You can use #COLUMN_HEADER# for the heading of the associated tabular form column in order to display the header name as part of the error message, as shown in Figure 4-15.

▼ Error

Error Message ↗

```
#COLUMN_HEADER# must have a value.
```

***Figure 4-15.** Tabular form validations—substitution string for column names*

Other Features

APEX 4 also introduced a couple of other neat features. One is protection against lost updates when you re-sort or paginate your data. Another is the ability to add new rows to a form without making a round-trip to the server for each row added. Finally, the overall number of processes has been reduced.

Lost Update Protection

APEX 4 will inform you about the changes you made and about the risk of losing your changes if you try to change the sorting of the tabular form or try to paginate the tabular form. Figure 4-16 shows this warning message.

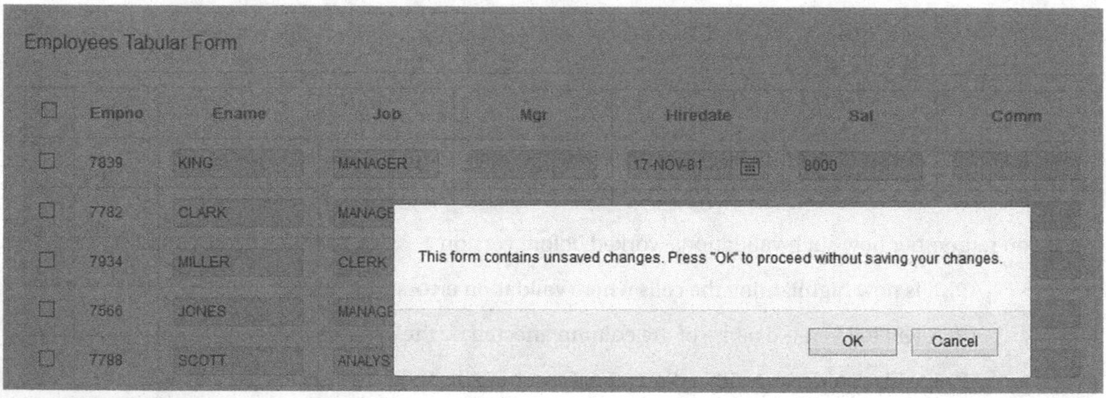

Figure 4-16. *Tabular form—lost update protection*

Client-Side Add Row Functionality

In earlier versions, the process for adding new rows to a tabular form required you to submit and load your page once per new row. This process had to validate and save changes each time you added a new row. The new Add Row functionality is done by using a new JavaScript function.

```
javascript:addRow();
```

You can find the function's invocation in the ADD button, as the URL target.

After the initial rendering of a tabular form, APEX will remove that new row from the DOM and put it in a JavaScript variable. After clicking the ADD button, JavaScript will replace some of the substitution strings in that variable (index, names, and so on) and add that row to the end of the table. If you want to add multiple rows to a tabular form, the only thing you need to do is to click the button again.

Reduced Number of Processes

The addition of functionality to add new rows using client-side code brings the additional benefit of reducing the number of processes required for DML. Earlier versions of APEX required four submit processes for DML.

- ApplyMRU process for saving data on submit

- ApplyMRU process for saving data after adding a new row

- ApplyMRD process for deleting of data

- AddRow process for adding one or multiple rows

APEX 4 requires only two of these processes. Only one MRU process is now needed because new rows are no longer added using server-side code. For the same reason, the Add Row process is redundant and has been removed.

Features in APEX 4.1/4.2

As mentioned earlier, APEX 4.1 and 4.2 introduced a couple of significant changes.

- Declarative validations using the :column syntax to reference single column values per row

- Declarative processing using the :column syntax to reference single column values per row

- New variables available for the processing

- Referencing tabular forms selectors in dynamic actions

- Removing numerous bugs related to tabular form validations and validation error message display

New Validation Types for Tabular Forms

As of APEX 4.1/4.2, you can use declarative validations and processes using the :column syntax, just as you do in normal PL/SQL processing.

- New validation types for tabular forms

- New process types for tabular forms

There are several new validation types for tabular forms, and you can view them in Figure 4-17.

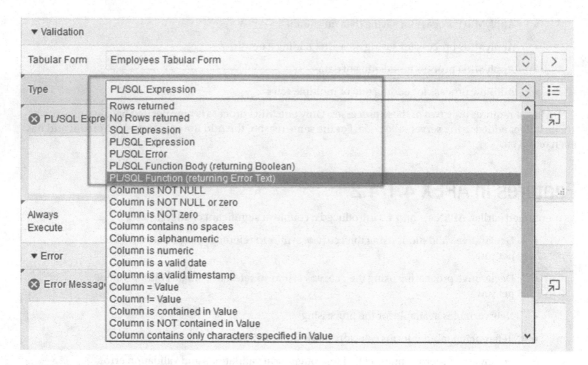

Figure 4-17. *Tabular form validations—column string comparison*

One of the most useful validations is PL/SQL Function (returning Error Text). I will use this one to demonstrate how the validation feature works.

Declarative Validations Using the :column Syntax New Process Type

Often it is necessary to compare different column values in the validation process of a tabular form prior to submitting the data and running into possible constraint errors. Prior to APEX 4.1/4.2, you had to write custom code. As of APEX 4.1/4.2, this is not required. You can handle the tabular forms the same way you handle a single-record form. In the following example, I will demonstrate how to validate the salary for a job role called CLERK, which shouldn't exceed 3,000.

In the Page Designer, switch to the Processes tab and create a validation using a right-click. Name the validation **Validate Clerk Salary** – Figure 4-18.

Figure 4-18. *Tabular form validations*

For the validation you will use a simple PL/SQL block, as shown in Listing 4-2.

Listing 4-2. Validation PL/SQL Block

```
DECLARE
    v_error    VARCHAR2 (4000);
BEGIN
    IF :job = 'CLERK' AND :sal > 3000
    THEN
        v_error := 'Salary may not exceed 3000 for the job CLERK.';
    END IF;

    RETURN v_error;
END;
```

This PL/SQL block is using column syntax for referencing tabular form columns as a bind variable, identical to the :P1_ITEM syntax.

You will also need to make a couple of other changes to set up the validation for the tabular form. Figure 4-19 shows how this needs to be done.

1. Select the tabular form.

2. Determine the button starting the validation.

3. Set the execution scope for the validation.

4. Reference the columns job and sal within the PL/SQL block, applying the bind variable syntax to it.

163

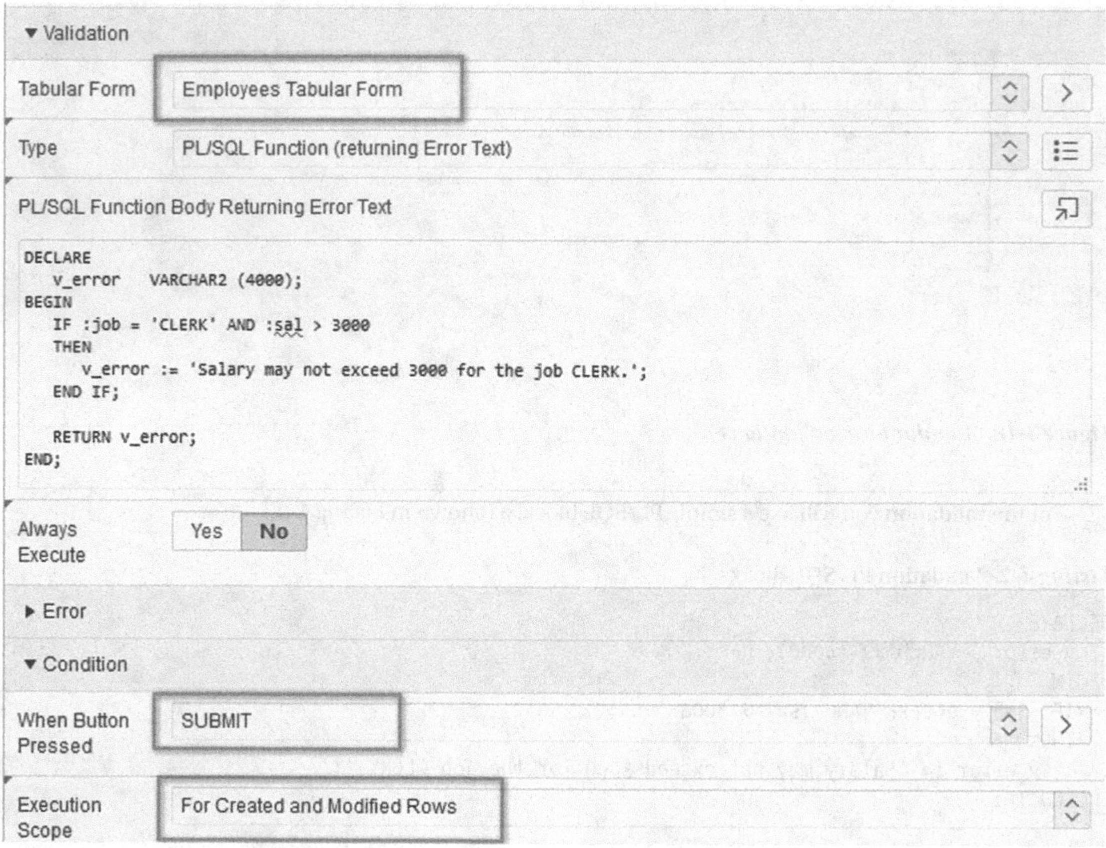

▼ Validation

| Tabular Form | Employees Tabular Form | ⌄ | > |

| Type | PL/SQL Function (returning Error Text) | ⌄ | ≡ |

PL/SQL Function Body Returning Error Text ⤢

```
DECLARE
   v_error   VARCHAR2 (4000);
BEGIN
   IF :job = 'CLERK' AND :sal > 3000
   THEN
      v_error := 'Salary may not exceed 3000 for the job CLERK.';
   END IF;

   RETURN v_error;
END;
```

Always
Execute   Yes   **No**

▶ Error

▼ Condition

| When Button Pressed | SUBMIT | ⌄ | > |

| Execution Scope | For Created and Modified Rows | ⌄ |

Figure 4-19. *Tabular form validations using the :column syntax*

■ **Caution**   The execution scope will be either for created and modified rows or for all submitted rows visible in the tabular form region.

If you save the changes, modify the salary for one of the records in the tabular form to exceed the limit, and try to save the changes, a validation error will be displayed, as shown in Figure 4-20.

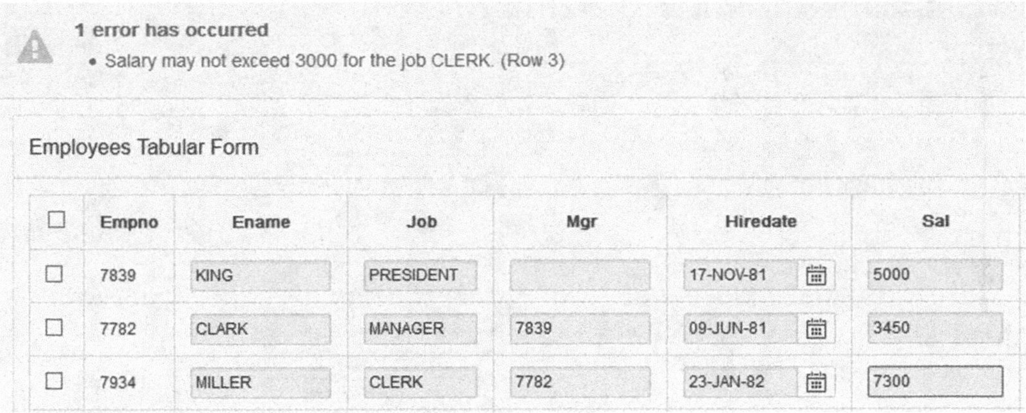

1 error has occurred

- Salary may not exceed 3000 for the job CLERK. (Row 3)

Employees Tabular Form

☐	Empno	Ename	Job	Mgr	Hiredate	Sal
☐	7839	KING	PRESIDENT		17-NOV-81 🗓	5000
☐	7782	CLARK	MANAGER	7839	09-JUN-81 🗓	3450
☐	7934	MILLER	CLERK	7782	23-JAN-82 🗓	7300

Figure 4-20. *Tabular form validation message*

Isn't that just great? Almost no custom coding is required using the `apex_application.g_fxx` syntax. The code validating tabular forms is now as transparent as for the rest of the application code. You don't need to understand the `apex_application` package logic anymore and count the column or be careful about the column order. This is simple and easy to debug.

Declarative Processing Using the :column Syntax New Process Type

It is logical to assume that if column syntax works for the validations, it should work for the processing as well. As you might notice for the validations, only the right assignment to the corresponding tabular form was required to make a PL/SQL function work. This is the same thing with the On Submit processes.

In the following example, I will demonstrate how to do some additional custom processing. You will write some code to extend the process success message.

In the Page Designer, switch to the Processes tab and create a new On Submit process using a right-click. Name the process **Show Process Details** – Figure 4-21. The sequence order of the process should be lower than the automated MRU/MRD process sequence. You will use an existing application item T_MESSAGE to store and display process messages.

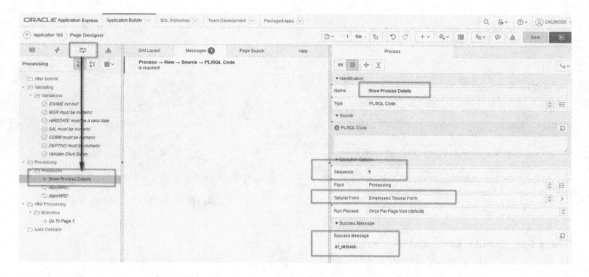

Figure 4-21. *Tabular form process—created by the wizard*

For the process you will use a simple PL/SQL block, as shown in Listing 4-3. The purpose of this block is to acquire information of the modified and added records.

Listing 4-3. On Submit Process PL/SQL Block

```
DECLARE
    v_message    VARCHAR2 (4000);
BEGIN
    IF :empno IS NOT NULL
    THEN
        v_message := 'Record ' || :empno || ' has been modified.' || '<br/>';
    ELSE
        v_message :=
                'New record for the Employee: '
            || :ename
            || ' and Job: '
            || :job
            || ' added.'
            || '<br/>';
    END IF;

    :t_message := v_message;
END;
```

You will also need to make a couple of other changes to set up the process for the tabular form. Figure 4-22 shows how this needs to be done.

1. Select the tabular form.

2. Determine the button starting validation.

3. Set the execution scope for the process.

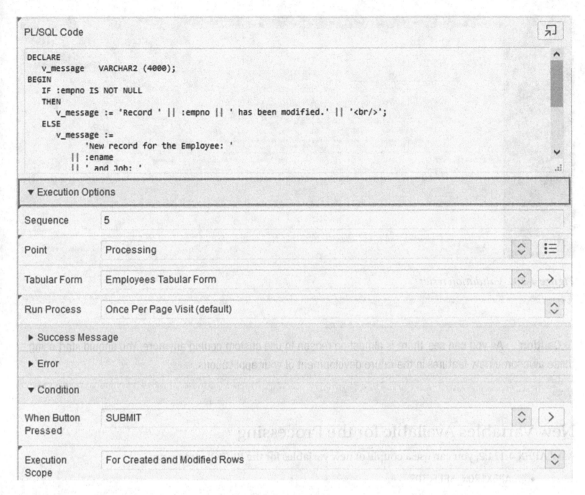

```
PL/SQL Code                                                                    ⤢

DECLARE
   v_message   VARCHAR2 (4000);
BEGIN
   IF :empno IS NOT NULL
   THEN
      v_message := 'Record ' || :empno || ' has been modified.' || '<br/>';
   ELSE
      v_message :=
         'New record for the Employee: '
      || :ename
      || ' and Job: '
```

▼ Execution Options

Sequence	5
Point	Processing
Tabular Form	Employees Tabular Form
Run Process	Once Per Page Visit (default)

▶ Success Message

▶ Error

▼ Condition

When Button Pressed	SUBMIT
Execution Scope	For Created and Modified Rows

Figure 4-22. *Tabular form validations using the :column syntax*

Once you are done, you can save the changes and modify and add a couple of records in the tabular form. After saving the changes, a success message, similar to the one in Figure 4-23, should be displayed.

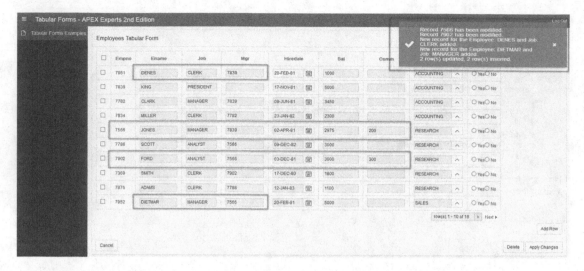

Figure 4-23. *Validation result*

■ **Caution**   As you can see, there is almost no reason to use custom coding anymore. You should start using these awesome new features in the future development of your applications.

New Variables Available for the Processing

As of APEX 4.1/4.2, you can use a couple of new variables for the PL/SQL processing.

- APEX$ROW_SELECTOR
- APEX$ROW_STATUS
- APEX$ROW_NUM

I will use the existing examples and extend them to demonstrate the possible usage of these variables.

Variable APEX$ROW_SELECTOR

APEX$ROW_SELECTOR is used for locating and fetching APEX delete check box item checked values. The value will be X for rows where the row selector has been checked.

Variable APEX$ROW_STATUS

APEX$ROW_STATUS is used for holding a value that indicates what is happening to the rows in question. The column holds U (update) for updating existing rows, D (delete) for the rows marked for deletion (including new rows that were added but not touched), and the value C (create) for rows to be inserted.

Variable APEX$ROW_NUM

APEX$ROW_NUM gives (as the name already says) the corresponding row number of the processed row.

I will modify the process for tabular forms slightly and show how these variables can be used in a PL/SQL on Submit process to acquire information about the modified and added records – Listing 4-4.

Listing 4-4. On Submit Process PL/SQL Block, Modified to Use the Variables

```
DECLARE
    v_message_update    VARCHAR2 (4000) := 'Update Process: ' || '<br/>';
    v_message_add       VARCHAR2 (4000) := 'Insert Process: ' || '<br/>';
    v_message_delete    VARCHAR2 (4000) := 'Delete Process: ' || '<br/>';
BEGIN
    IF :apex$row_selector = 'X'
    THEN
        v_message_delete :=
                'Record with EMPNO ' || :empno || ' has been deleted.'
                || '<br/>';
    ELSIF :apex$row_status = 'U'
    THEN
        v_message_update :=
                'Record with EMPNO ' || :empno || ' has been modified.'
                || '<br/>';
    ELSIF :apex$row_status = 'C'
    THEN
        v_message_add :=
                'New record for the Employee: '
            || :ename
            || ' and Job: '
            || :job
            || ' added.'
            || '<br/>';
    END IF;

    :t_message := v_message_update || v_message_add || v_message_delete;
END;
```

The goal is to find out the employee number of the records deleted from the form. Also, you want to distinguish between the records updated and the new created records and display this information in the success message.

After modifying the On Submit process's Show Process Details settings, you can test the process and modify/add/delete some records in the tabular form. The result will be displayed similar to Figure 4-24.

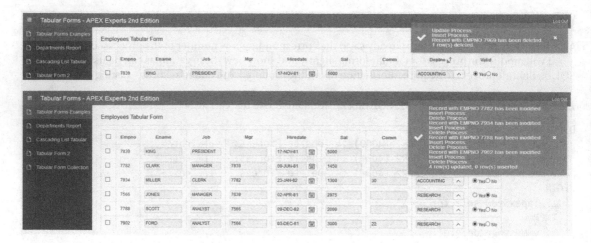

Figure 4-24. *Tabular form On Submit process using variables*

Tabular Forms and Dynamic Actions

As of APEX 4.1/4.2, you can reference tabular form selectors in dynamic actions. This gives you a couple of new options while creating user-friendly forms. I will explain two methods in the section "Interesting Techniques" and provide corresponding examples.

Using jQuery Selector

Every column in a tabular form can be considered an array, which is a set of items sharing the same name and having a unique ID. If you want to create user-friendly forms, you need to use dynamic actions. The dynamic actions will usually react on the following:

- Change of an element
- Region refresh
- Pagination
- Some other event

If working with tabular forms, you will need some help. The best thing is to use Firebug or a similar plugin for your browser. With this plugin, you can inspect the tabular form elements, as shown in Figure 4-25.

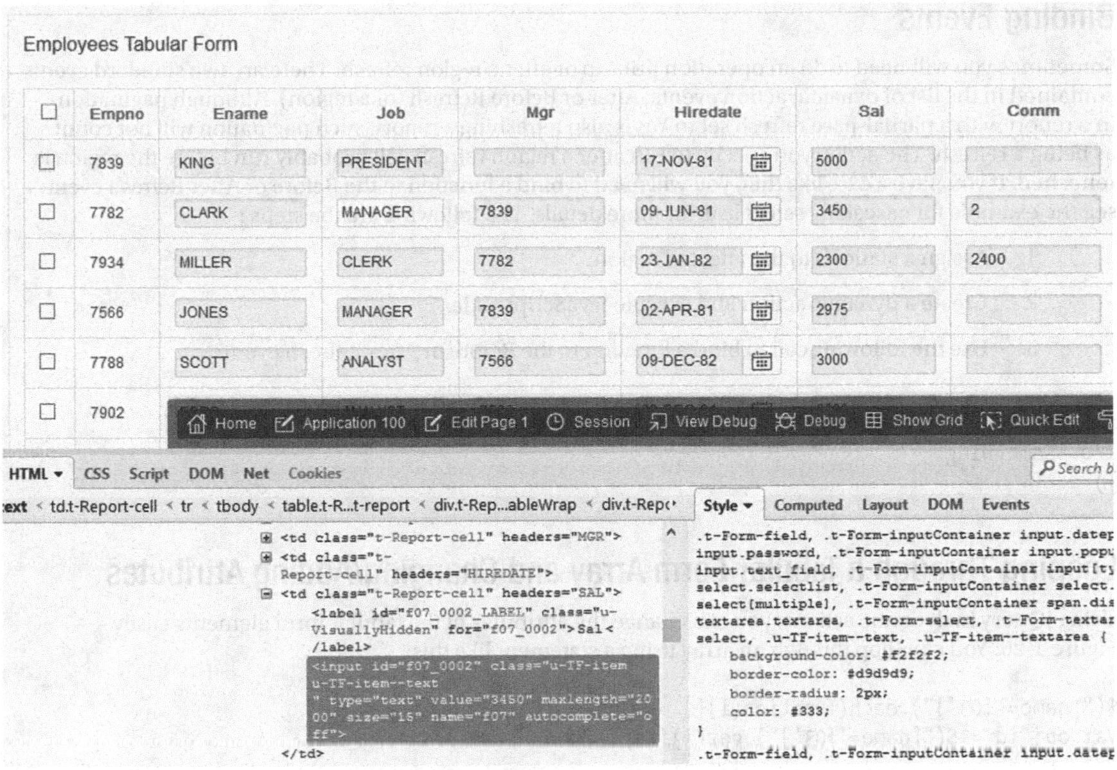

Figure 4-25. Firebug extension, inspecting column for salary called Sal

This way, you can find out the name or the ID of a column or for a particular item. For example, you can use the name of the column to start a dynamic action that could be triggered after changing a jQuery selector.

```
input[name="f07"],select[name="f08"]
```

That means if any of the elements (items) for the column Sal are changed, the dynamic action should fire.

In the Dynamic Action ➤ Action menu, you can reference that selector and get the other attribute values from it by using the following:

```
this.triggeringElement.id
```

or the following to do something in the further processing:

```
this.triggeringElement.value
```

If you need to reference any other column other than the triggering element column, you can use the following syntax to get the value of the column Ename:

```
$('#' + 'f03_' + this.triggeringElement.id.substring(4)).val()
```

Binding Events

Sometimes you will need to do an operation prior to or after a region refresh. There are two standard events contained in the list of dynamic action events: After or Before Refresh (of a region). Although pagination in a report with a partial-page refresh set to Yes is also refreshing a report, such pagination will not count as being a refresh. The action you specify to run after a region refresh will probably run before the region is refreshed. If you have a case like that, you will need to bind a function to the Before or After Refresh event; see the example for cascading select lists for more details. The following are the steps :

1. Assign a static ID to the affected region.

2. Create a dynamic action and execute JavaScript code.

3. Use the following call to bind a function to the Before or After Refresh event:

```
apex.jQuery('#EMP_TABULAR_FORM').bind("apexafterrefresh", function () {
//do something
})
```

Looping Through a Tabular Form Array and Changing/Adding Attributes

Using jQuery in dynamic actions, you can change the attributes of the tabular form elements easily – Figure 4-26. You can loop through an array using a statement like this:

```
$("[name='f03']").each(function(i){
var obj_id = $("[name='f03']").get(i).id;

//do something

});
```

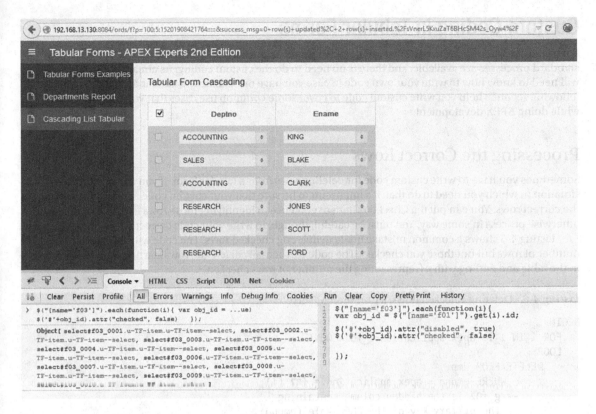

Figure 4-26. Looping through an array and changing attributes

Adding or changing element attributes is quite easy and can be done with a statement similar to these two statements (disabling and unchecking a check box column):

```
$('#'+obj_id).attr("disabled", true)
$('#'+obj_id).attr("checked", false)
```

So, the complete script that loops through a tabular form and disables and unchecks the check box column is as follows:

```
$("[name='f03']").each(function(i){
var obj_id = $("[name='f01']").get(i).id;

$('#'+obj_id).attr("disabled", true)
$('#'+obj_id).attr("checked", false)

});
```

Custom Coding in Tabular Forms

For a standard tabular form, custom coding isn't required anymore. As of APEX 4.1/4.2, all the necessary standard processes are available, and there is no need to do the custom coding. As already indicated, you will need to know how to write your own code in case you have more than one tabular form per page. The following sections help you write custom code to cover some common use cases that you will encounter while doing APEX development.

Processing the Correct Rows

Sometimes you have to write custom code for deleting rows from a tabular form. If you are faced with a situation in which you need to do that, it's important to be sure that your custom code actually does delete the correct rows. You can put the Checkbox item to good use in identifying those rows to delete or to otherwise process in some way. You must be careful, though, to write your code correctly.

Listing 4-5 shows a common mistake made in deleting checked rows. The code will delete the right number of rows but not those you checked. The code will actually delete the rows starting from the first row in the table and ending with *n* (representing the number of rows checked).

Listing 4-5. Deleting Checked Rows, a Common Mistake

```
BEGIN
   FOR i IN 1 .. apex_application.g_f01.COUNT
   LOOP
      DELETE FROM emp
             WHERE empno = apex_application.g_f02 (i);
          -- g_f02 is the hidden column containing
          -- the primary key of the EMP table (empno)
   END LOOP;
END;
```

Listing 4-6 shows how the correct code should look. Because several procedures are now used, they have been bundled together into a package. You can then simply call this package in your processes or validations.

The package in Listing 4-6 implements a couple of small procedures in order to make the overall processing easier. The goal is to avoid overloading the page and application with loose PL/SQL blocks.

Listing 4-6. Deleting Checked Rows, the Correct Procedure

```
CREATE OR REPLACE PACKAGE tab_form_emp_pkg
AS
  PROCEDURE disable_foreign_constraints;

  PROCEDURE enable_foreign_constraints;

  PROCEDURE restore_tables;

  PROCEDURE delete_emp_row (p_message OUT VARCHAR2);
END tab_form_emp_pkg;
/
```

```
CREATE OR REPLACE PACKAGE BODY tab_form_emp_pkg
AS
   PROCEDURE disable_foreign_constraints
   IS
   BEGIN
      FOR c IN (SELECT   constraint_name, table_name
                   FROM user_constraints
                  WHERE table_name IN ('EMP', 'DEPT')
                    AND constraint_type = 'R'
                ORDER BY table_name)
      LOOP
         EXECUTE IMMEDIATE    'ALTER TABLE '
                           || c.table_name
                           || ' DISABLE CONSTRAINT '
                           || c.constraint_name;
      END LOOP;
   END disable_foreign_constraints;

   PROCEDURE enable_foreign_constraints
   IS
   BEGIN
      FOR c IN (SELECT   constraint_name, table_name
                   FROM user_constraints
                  WHERE table_name IN ('EMP', 'DEPT')
                    AND constraint_type = 'R'
                ORDER BY table_name)
      LOOP
         EXECUTE IMMEDIATE    'ALTER TABLE '
                           || c.table_name
                           || ' ENABLE CONSTRAINT '
                           || c.constraint_name;
      END LOOP;
   END enable_foreign_constraints;

   PROCEDURE restore_tables
   IS
-- We will use this process to restore our date after testing.
   BEGIN
      FOR c IN (SELECT   constraint_name, table_name
                   FROM user_constraints
                  WHERE table_name IN ('EMP', 'DEPT')
                    AND constraint_type = 'R'
                ORDER BY table_name)
      LOOP
         EXECUTE IMMEDIATE    'ALTER TABLE '
                           || c.table_name
                           || ' DISABLE CONSTRAINT '
                           || c.constraint_name;
      END LOOP;
```

```
      EXECUTE IMMEDIATE 'TRUNCATE TABLE dept DROP STORAGE';

      EXECUTE IMMEDIATE 'TRUNCATE TABLE emp DROP STORAGE';

      INSERT INTO dept
         SELECT *
           FROM dept_bkp;

      INSERT INTO emp
         SELECT *
           FROM emp_bkp;

      COMMIT;

      FOR c IN (SELECT   constraint_name, table_name
                   FROM user_constraints
                  WHERE table_name IN ('EMP', 'DEPT')
                    AND constraint_type = 'R'
                ORDER BY table_name)
      LOOP
         EXECUTE IMMEDIATE    'ALTER TABLE '
                          || c.table_name
                          || ' ENABLE CONSTRAINT '
                          || c.constraint_name;
      END LOOP;
   END restore_tables;

   PROCEDURE delete_emp_row (p_message OUT VARCHAR2)
   IS
      v_row      INTEGER;
      v_count    INTEGER := 0;
   BEGIN
      FOR i IN 1 .. apex_application.g_f01.COUNT
      LOOP
         v_row := apex_application.g_f01 (i);

         DELETE FROM emp
               WHERE empno = apex_application.g_f02 (v_row);

         -- g_f02 is the hidden column containing
         -- the primary key of the EMP table (empno)
         v_count := v_count + 1;
      END LOOP;


      p_message := v_count || ' row(s) deleted.';
   END delete_emp_row;
END tab_form_emp_pkg;
/
```

Let's work through an explanation of Listing 4-6. You need to do the following preparations for a test:

- Create an application item T_MESSAGE and set the session state protection to Restricted; it may not be set from the browser. This application item will be used to display messages. In a case of an ApplyMRD process, you have the substitution strings like #MRD_COUNT# or #MRI_COUNT# or #MRU_COUNT#. For a custom process, you need a new variable.

- Set the existing ApplyMRD process to Conditional Never so it doesn't run.

- Create a new On Submit Process PL/SQL anonymous block. Name it ApplyMRD Manual and use the following code:

```
BEGIN
    tab_form_emp_pkg.disable_foreign_constraints;
    tab_form_emp_pkg.delete_emp_row (:t_message);
END;
```

- Use the substitution string for the success message.

```
&T_MESSAGE.
```

- Make the process conditional so it runs on condition type PL/SQL Expression.

```
:REQUEST IN ('MULTI_ROW_DELETE')
```

- Confirm and create a process.

■ **Caution** As you can see, some additional procedures to disable constraints for referential integrity were used. This is for testing purposes only because I am talking here about an isolated case. In the real world, you would create a validation to check whether such constraints exist.

You can now test this process and try to delete a couple of rows to see what you get. Figure 4-27 shows the selected rows to delete, and Figure 4-28 shows the result.

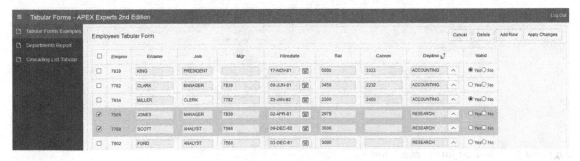

Figure 4-27. *Tabular form—deleting records using custom process*

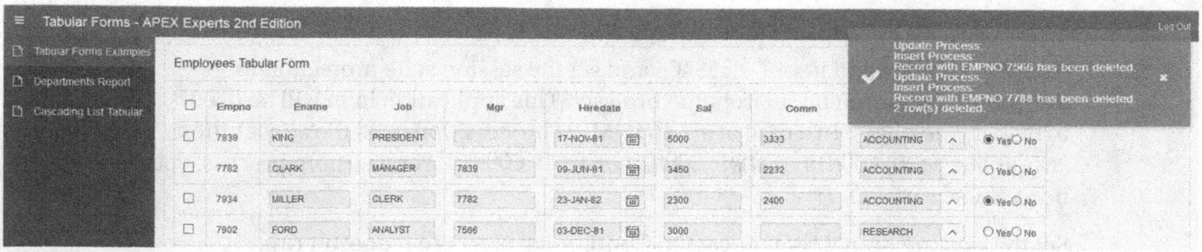

Figure 4-28. *Tabular form—the results*

Run the following block of code in SQL Workshop to restore the EMP table:

```
BEGIN
    tab_form_emp_pkg.restore_tables;
END;
```

Data Integrity

As already mentioned, there is much more work to do if you write your own custom processes. Automatic processes created using the Tabular Form Wizard ensure data integrity, and you would need to do the same kind of thing manually in your own code. Automatic processes may display confusing errors, but they are secure. It is not easy to write all of that code yourself since there are many details you need to think of. My goal now is to show you how to do that and make you aware of the most important things you should keep in mind.

Checksum

APEX 4's Tabular Form Wizard creates a hidden checksum item for every row in a tabular form. This checksum will be used for later automatic MRU and MRD processes. Using the Firebug extension of Firefox, you can see that hidden item if you investigate the generated HTML, as shown in Figure 4-29.

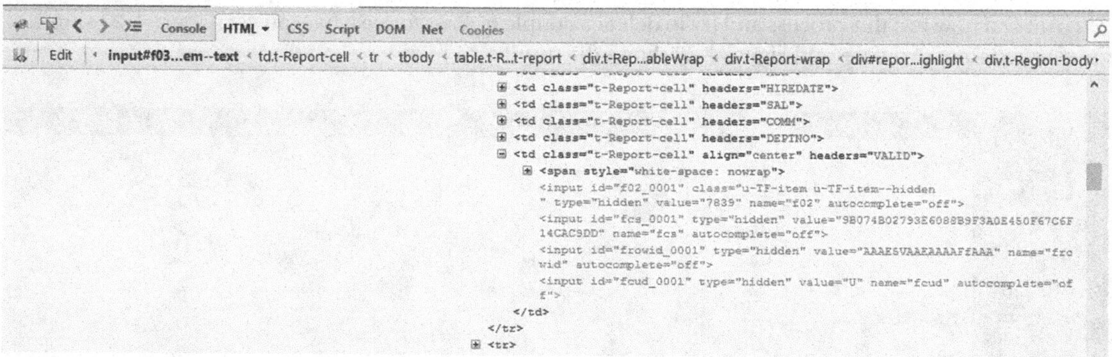

Figure 4-29. *Tabular form—checksum*

When talking about checksum and data integrity, you need to keep several issues in mind.

- If you want to run your custom code, you will need to do a check and find out whether the data in a row has changed. It doesn't make sense to do an update on a row that hasn't changed.

- If the data has changed, you will need to compare the checksum of the original data you loaded while rendering the page and the checksum of the current data in the table for each row.

- If a row has changed (if the old checksum in the g_fcs array is not the same as the new checksum of the tabular form rows you calculate), you will need to do an update.

- However, you should be able to update only if the original data in the table hasn't been changed since the last fetch (old checksum in the g_fcs array is not the same as the new checksum of the row in the table you need to calculate). Otherwise, there should be an error displayed, and you should stop the processing.

Validations

Following the rules outlined in the previous section, you can start extending your package by adding some new functions.

- The first function will compare the original checksum with the new generated checksum for each row in the tabular form. It will return a Boolean. (It will return FALSE when the data in the row has changed.)

- The second function will compare the original checksum with the checksum of the data in the table for each row where the first function returns FALSE. It will return a Boolean as well. (It will return FALSE when the data in the table has changed.)

- Finally, the third function will be a validation function returning an error message in case some of the rows you are trying to update have been changed by other users. The second function returns FALSE.

Let's extend the package tab_form_emp_pkg by adding the first function described, shown in Listing 4-7.

Listing 4-7. Checksum—Function 1

```
FUNCTION compare_checksum_change (p_array IN NUMBER)
  RETURN BOOLEAN;

FUNCTION compare_checksum_change (p_array IN NUMBER)
     RETURN BOOLEAN
  IS
  BEGIN
    IF apex_application.g_f02 (p_array) IS NOT NULL
    THEN
      IF apex_application.g_fcs (p_array) <>
      wwv_flow_item.md5 (apex_application.g_f02 (p_array),
                         apex_application.g_f03 (p_array),
                         apex_application.g_f04 (p_array),
                         apex_application.g_f05 (p_array),
                         apex_application.g_f06 (p_array),
                         apex_application.g_f07 (p_array),
```

```
                            apex_application.g_f08 (p_array),
                            apex_application.g_f09 (p_array),
                            apex_application.g_f11 (p_array)
                           )
        THEN
            RETURN FALSE;
        ELSE
            RETURN TRUE;
        END IF;
    ELSE
        RETURN TRUE;
    END IF;
END compare_checksum_change;
```

■ **Caution**   As already mentioned, the items of type Simple Checkbox and Popup Key LOV will reserve two arrays for one item. This is the reason for the gap between the g_f09 and g_f11 arrays.

After that, add the second function, shown in Listing 4-8.

Listing 4-8. Checksum—Function 2

```
FUNCTION compare_checksum_table (p_array IN NUMBER)
  RETURN BOOLEAN;

FUNCTION compare_checksum_table (p_array IN NUMBER)
     RETURN BOOLEAN
  IS
     v_empno          NUMBER;
     v_emp_checksum   VARCHAR2 (40);
  BEGIN
     IF apex_application.g_f02 (p_array) IS NOT NULL
     THEN
        v_empno := apex_application.g_f02 (p_array);

        SELECT wwv_flow_item.md5 (empno,
                                  ename,
                                  job,
                                  mgr,
                                  hiredate,
                                  sal,
                                  comm,
                                  deptno,
                                  valid
                                 )
          INTO v_emp_checksum
          FROM emp
         WHERE empno = v_empno;

        IF apex_application.g_fcs (p_array) <> v_emp_checksum
        THEN
```

```
            RETURN FALSE;
        ELSE
            RETURN TRUE;
        END IF;
    ELSE
        RETURN TRUE;
    END IF;
END compare_checksum_table;
```

As the last function, you can now create a validation function returning VARCHAR2, which you will then call on the page, as shown in Listing 4-9.

Listing 4-9. Checksum—Function 3

```
 FUNCTION validate_data_integrity
     RETURN VARCHAR2;

  FUNCTION validate_data_integrity
     RETURN VARCHAR2
  IS
     v_error    VARCHAR2 (4000);
  BEGIN
     FOR i IN 1 .. apex_application.g_f02.COUNT
     LOOP
        IF NOT compare_checksum_change (i)
            -- we changed the row
            AND NOT compare_checksum_table (i)
            -- however the table data has changed
        THEN
            v_error :=
                  v_error
               || '<br/>'
               || 'Row '
               || i
               || ': The version of the data in the '
               || 'table has been change since the last page '
               || 'rendering. Click <a href="f?p='
               || v ('APP_ID')
               || ':'
               || v ('APP_PAGE_ID')
               || ':'
               || v ('APP_SESSION')
               || '">here</a> to reload the page.';
        END IF;
     END LOOP;
     v_error := LTRIM(v_error, '<br/>');
     RETURN v_error;
  END validate_data_integrity;
```

You can test this code by creating a page validation of type PL/SQL Function (returning Error Text), using sequence 1 for the validation and naming the validation **Check Data Integrity**. Set the validation to Unconditional and enter the required call to the package procedure. Here is the PL/SQL code for the page validation:

```
BEGIN
    RETURN tab_form_emp_pkg.validate_data_integrity;
END;
```

Next, change one of the records using some other tool such as SQL Workshop and commit your changes. Go to the tabular form, change the same record, and submit the change. You should see an error message similar to that in Figure 4-30.

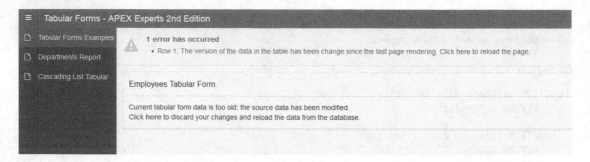

Figure 4-30. *Tabular form—data integrity validation error*

You don't need to use the technique described in this section in a standard tabular form. A similar message will be generated automatically in a standard form. You need the technique and code in this section only in a *manually generated* tabular form.

Manual Tabular Forms

As long as APEX doesn't allow the creation of multiple standard tabular forms per page, you will be faced with a requirement to create a workaround for those cases in which you need to manage one master table with multiple detail tables.

Let's look at how to write the code for a manual tabular form. You will use only the following item types:

- `apex_item.hidden`
- `apex_item.checkbox`
- `apex_item.text`

You will also use the `apex_item` package and parse parameters for the following:

- Column array
- Column value
- Column size
- Column max length

Create a second blank page (page 2) and call it tabular form 2. After that, create a Report region for your manual tabular form; it is a classic report based on a SQL statement. You will need to use a subquery in the region source. In the subquery you will create one empty row first to be able to enter new rows upon request. You will also need to generate a checksum for the rows that you will use later to check which rows have changed and run an update for them. Listing 4-10 shows the SELECT statement along with its subquery.

Listing 4-10. Manual Tabular Form—SQL

```
SELECT    apex_item.checkbox (1, '#ROWNUM#') empno,
          apex_item.hidden (2, empno)
      || apex_item.text (3, ename, 20, 20) ename,
          apex_item.text (4, job, 10, 10) job,
          apex_item.text (5, mgr, 5, 5) mgr,
          apex_item.text (6, hiredate, 12, 12) hiredate,
          apex_item.text (7, sal, 6, 6) sal,
          apex_item.text (8, comm, 6, 6) comm,
          apex_item.text (9, deptno, 4, 4)
      || apex_item.hidden (10, checksum) deptno
  FROM (SELECT NULL empno, NULL ename, NULL job,
               NULL mgr, NULL hiredate,
               NULL sal, NULL comm, NULL deptno,
               NULL checksum
        FROM DUAL
        WHERE :request IN ('ADD')
        UNION ALL
        SELECT empno, ename, job, mgr, hiredate,
               sal, comm, deptno,
               wwv_flow_item.md5 (empno,
                                  ename,
                                  job,
                                  mgr,
                                  hiredate,
                                  sal,
                                  comm,
                                  deptno
                                  ) checksum
        FROM emp)
```

The SELECT statement for the empty column will run only if REQUEST is set to the specified value.

■ **Caution**   Change the column type to Standard Report Column, or in the Page Designer, select Plain Text and set Escape special characters to "No". Otherwise, you will see HTML code in your report. The need to make this change is new in APEX 4 and has to do with security and cross-site scripting.

The next step is to create four buttons as follows:

- A SUBMIT button to submit the page.

- A MULTI_ROW_DELETE button to delete rows. The target of this button will be this URL:

  ```
  javascript:apex.confirm(htmldb_delete_message,'MULTI_ROW_DELETE');
  ```

- An ADD button to add new rows. This button will also submit the page.

- The following code needs to be added to the page's JavaScript.Function and Global Variable Declaration attributes.

  ```
  var htmldb_delete_message='"DELETE_CONFIRM_MSG"';
  ```

- A CANCEL button. This button will redirect to the same page. Each of these buttons will be positioned in the Report region. You will also need to create at least two branches.

The minimum two branches you need to create are the following:

- On Submit – After Processing

  - Condition: When Button Pressed "ADD"

  - Redirect to Page 2

  - include process success message is checked

  - Element Sequence should be set to 5

- On Submit – After Processing

  - This branch is Unconditional

  - Redirect to Page 2

  - include process success message is checked

  - Element Sequence should be set to 10

The first branch will submit the page and redirect to the same page.
You are now ready to write the code you will need for processing. You will create two processes:

- *ApplyMRU*: This process updates existing new rows. This process will be conditional using the PL/SQL expression :REQUEST IN ('ADD', 'SUBMIT').

- *delete_emp_row, from Listing* 4-6: This process and its associated package enable you to delete rows. Since you already know how to use a checksum to ensure data integrity, I will not repeat that part in this example. The process code will be as follows:

  ```
  BEGIN
      tab_form_emp_pkg.disable_foreign_constraints;
      tab_form_emp_pkg.delete_emp_row (:t_message);
  END;
  ```

Finally, you need to add a validation.

- *Validate Commission of type PL/SQL Function (returning Error Text)*: This is a page-level validation ensuring that you can enter a commission value only for the department SALES, which is department 30. This validation will be unconditional.

Listing 4-11 shows the procedure for updating and the validation in your package.

Listing 4-11. Manual Tabular Form—Update and Validation Processes

```
PROCEDURE save_emp_custom (p_message OUT VARCHAR2);

FUNCTION validate_emp_comm
  RETURN VARCHAR2;

PROCEDURE save_emp_custom (p_message OUT VARCHAR2)
IS
  v_ins_count    INTEGER := 0;
  v_upd_count    INTEGER := 0;
BEGIN
  FOR i IN 1 .. apex_application.g_f02.COUNT
  LOOP
    BEGIN
      IF apex_application.g_f02 (i) IS NOT NULL
      THEN
        IF apex_application.g_f10 (i) <>
            wwv_flow_item.md5 (apex_application.g_f02 (i),
                               apex_application.g_f03 (i),
                               apex_application.g_f04 (i),
                               apex_application.g_f05 (i),
                               apex_application.g_f06 (i),
                               apex_application.g_f07 (i),
                               apex_application.g_f08 (i),
                               apex_application.g_f09 (i)
                              )
        THEN
          UPDATE emp
            SET ename = apex_application.g_f03 (i),
                job = apex_application.g_f04 (i),
                mgr = apex_application.g_f05 (i),
                hiredate = apex_application.g_f06 (i),
                sal = apex_application.g_f07 (i),
                comm = apex_application.g_f08 (i),
                deptno = apex_application.g_f09 (i)
          WHERE empno = apex_application.g_f02 (i);

          v_upd_count := v_upd_count + 1;
        END IF;
      ELSE
        INSERT INTO emp
                   (ename,
                    job,
                    mgr,
```

```
                            hiredate,
                            sal,
                            comm,
                            deptno
                            )
                VALUES (apex_application.g_f03 (i),
                        apex_application.g_f04 (i),
                        apex_application.g_f05 (i),
                        apex_application.g_f06 (i),
                        apex_application.g_f07 (i),
                        apex_application.g_f08 (i),
                        apex_application.g_f09 (i)
                        );

        v_ins_count := v_ins_count + 1;
      END IF;
    EXCEPTION
      WHEN OTHERS
      THEN
          p_message := p_message || SQLERRM;
    END;
  END LOOP;

  IF v_ins_count > 0 OR v_upd_count > 0
  THEN
     p_message :=
            p_message
         || v_ins_count
         || ' row(s) inserted. '
         || v_upd_count
         || ' row(s) updated.';
  END IF;
EXCEPTION
  WHEN OTHERS
  THEN
     p_message := SQLERRM;
END save_emp_custom;

FUNCTION validate_emp_comm
   RETURN VARCHAR2
IS
   v_message    VARCHAR2 (4000);
BEGIN
   FOR i IN 1 .. apex_application.g_f02.COUNT
   LOOP
      IF    apex_application.g_f09 (i) <> 30
         AND apex_application.g_f08 (i) IS NOT NULL
      THEN
```

```
        v_message :=
                v_message
            || '<br/>'
            || 'Commission is allowed for the sales department only.'
            || ' (Row '
            || i
            || ')';
    END IF;
  END LOOP;

  v_message := LTRIM (v_message, '<br/>');
  RETURN v_message;
END validate_emp_comm;
```

The update/insert process will loop through the array of EMPNO (g_f02) and, for all rows containing the primary key, compare the original checksum with the new calculated checksum. If there is a difference, it will update the corresponding rows and update the counter. For the added rows where the array is NULL, it will insert a new row. You will use this PL/SQL block to start that process and put &T_MESSAGE. in the Process Success Message section:

```
BEGIN
  tab_form_emp_pkg.save_emp_custom (:t_message);
END;
```

The validation process is fairly simple. It will also loop through the array of EMPNO (g_f02) and check whether there is an entry for the COMM column (g_f08) where DEPTNO (g_f09) is different from SALES (value 30). You will use this PL/SQL block for the validation:

```
BEGIN
  RETURN tab_form_emp_pkg.validate_emp_comm;
END;
```

You can now test your form to confirm that it works as expected. Figures 4-31 through 4-34 will walk you through the steps in the test.

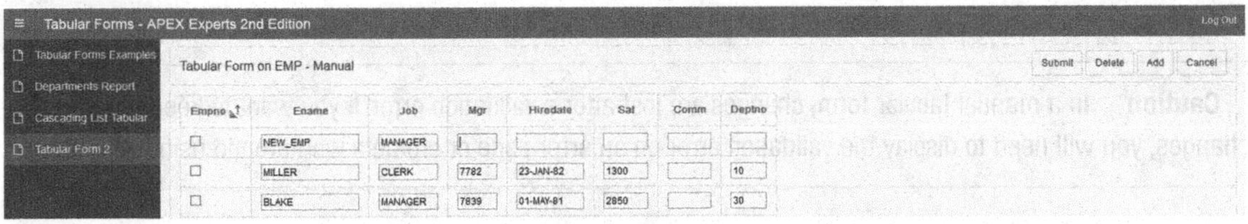

Figure 4-31. *Click the Add Row button to add a new row at the top of the form*

Figure 4-32. *Submit the form and notice the success message*

Figure 4-33. *Try entering an invalid commission value*

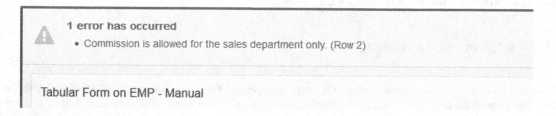

Figure 4-34. *Notice the error message from entering the invalid value*

■ **Caution**   In a manual tabular form, changes are lost after a validation error. If you want to keep the changes, you will need to display the validation error on an error page or create a workaround using collections.

Tabular Forms and Collections

Collections are one of the greatest features of APEX. An APEX collection is a set of tables, packaged procedures, and functions for maintaining session-related data. You can use a collection to create, modify, and delete your own datasets without having to touch the original source. Once the processing is done, you can decide either to save your changes to the source (insert, update, or delete) or to discard your changes. If you log off or somehow lose your session, you will not be able to retrieve that data again.

The need to use a collection often involves a small portion of data such as a snapshot or a window. For example, you might want to create a tabular form for modifying sales department records for only department 30. Figure 4-35 shows such a window.

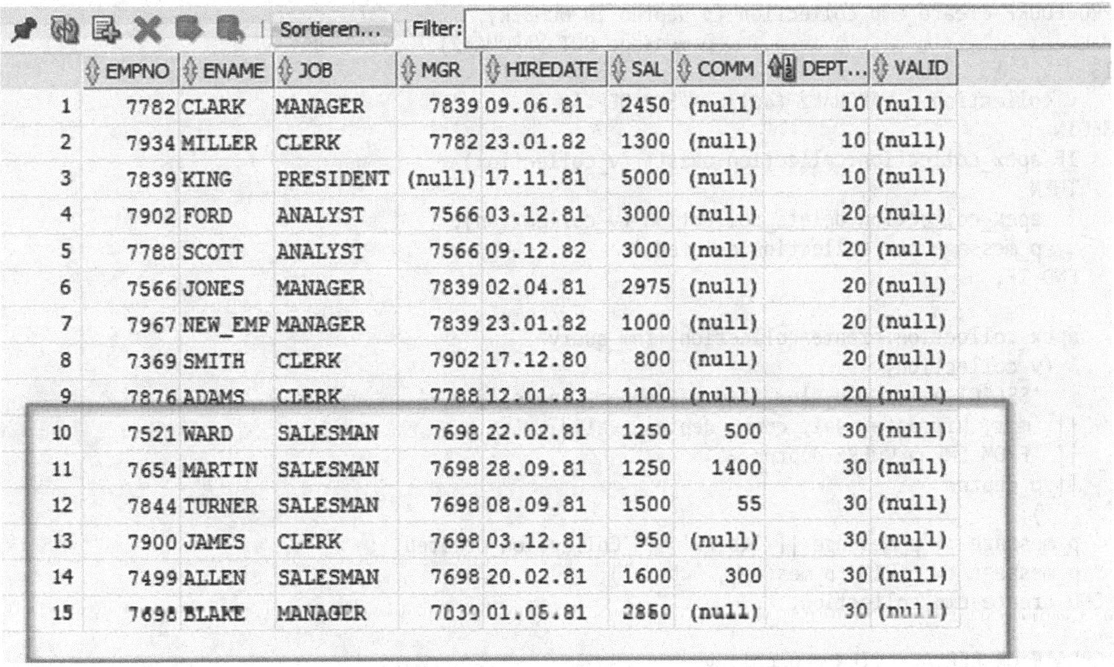

	EMPNO	ENAME	JOB	MGR	HIREDATE	SAL	COMM	DEPT...	VALID
1	7782	CLARK	MANAGER	7839	09.06.81	2450	(null)	10	(null)
2	7934	MILLER	CLERK	7782	23.01.82	1300	(null)	10	(null)
3	7839	KING	PRESIDENT	(null)	17.11.81	5000	(null)	10	(null)
4	7902	FORD	ANALYST	7566	03.12.81	3000	(null)	20	(null)
5	7788	SCOTT	ANALYST	7566	09.12.82	3000	(null)	20	(null)
6	7566	JONES	MANAGER	7839	02.04.81	2975	(null)	20	(null)
7	7967	NEW_EMP	MANAGER	7839	23.01.82	1000	(null)	20	(null)
8	7369	SMITH	CLERK	7902	17.12.80	800	(null)	20	(null)
9	7876	ADAMS	CLERK	7788	12.01.83	1100	(null)	20	(null)
10	7521	WARD	SALESMAN	7698	22.02.81	1250	500	30	(null)
11	7654	MARTIN	SALESMAN	7698	28.09.81	1250	1400	30	(null)
12	7844	TURNER	SALESMAN	7698	08.09.81	1500	55	30	(null)
13	7900	JAMES	CLERK	7698	03.12.81	950	(null)	30	(null)
14	7499	ALLEN	SALESMAN	7698	20.02.81	1600	300	30	(null)
15	7698	BLAKE	MANAGER	7039	01.05.81	2850	(null)	30	(null)

Figure 4-35. *A window of data for department 30*

Although a collection can accept almost an unlimited amount of data, it wouldn't make sense to use one for loading hundreds or even thousands of records. Collections are designed to serve smaller datasets.

Creating a Collection

The goal here is to show how to work with collections using tabular forms. This section will demonstrate a couple of possible ways and techniques to put collections to use. Specifically, you will do the following:

- Create a collection containing all employees of one department

- Create a couple of alternate processes you could use for updating collections from a tabular form

- Create a process for updating the original source using collection data

You will continue with the methods used earlier in this chapter and keep all your code in a package. You will use APEX regions and processes only to make calls into your package code.

First, create a procedure and a view. Listing 4-12 shows a procedure for creating a collection containing all employees of one department. Also in the listing is a view created upon that collection.

Listing 4-12. Procedure and View for a Tabular Form's Collection

```
PROCEDURE create_emp_collection (p_deptno IN NUMBER,
                                 p_message OUT VARCHAR2);

PROCEDURE create_emp_collection (p_deptno IN NUMBER,
                                 p_message OUT VARCHAR2)
IS
  v_collection    VARCHAR2 (40) := 'EMP_DEPT';
BEGIN
  IF apex_collection.collection_exists (v_collection)
  THEN
     apex_collection.delete_collection (v_collection);
     p_message := 'Collection deleted.';
  END IF;

  apex_collection.create_collection_from_query
    (v_collection,
     'SELECT a.*,  wwv_flow_item.md5(empno, ename, job, '
  || 'mgr, hiredate, sal, comm, deptno, valid)  '
  || 'FROM EMP a WHERE deptno = '
  || p_deptno
     );
  p_message := p_message || '<br/>' || 'Collection created.';
  p_message := LTRIM (p_message, '<br/>');
END create_emp_collection;

CREATE OR REPLACE VIEW emp_coll_v
AS
   SELECT seq_id, c001 empno, c002 ename,
          c003 job, c004 mgr, c005 hiredate,
          c006 sal, c007 comm, c008 deptno,
          c009 valid, c010 checksum, c011 delete_flag
     FROM apex_collections
    WHERE collection_name = 'EMP_DEPT';
```

The procedure will check whether the collection exists. If the collection does exist, the procedure will delete the existing collection and create a new one based on the input. Otherwise, the procedure creates a new collection.

The view will make it easier to deal with the collection. You will not need to remember the member number to insert, update, or delete a row. The view takes care of the member number for you.

You can now start creating a new page, which will be page 3. Use a standard tabular form based on the view emp_coll_v. Include all the columns. The primary key will be the combination of the SEQ_ID and EMPNO columns. Make all columns editable. Make the region title **Tabular Form Collection**. After creating the page, change the item type for the columns CHECKSUM and DELETE_FLAG to Hidden Column (Saves State).

You will also need to edit the generated SQL for the tabular form and add a condition as follows:

```
WHERE delete_flag IS NULL
```

This condition will exclude those records from the collection that are marked as deleted.

You will create a select list within the tabular form region: P3_DEPTNO. This select list will show a list of available departments based on the following SQL query:

```
SELECT dname, deptno
  FROM dept
```

You will also need a button displayed after the select list (create a button displayed among this region's items), which you will use to trigger the process. Name this button GO and select the action Submit Page.

Now you can start creating a page process (Create Collection) on submit for creating a collection. You will use the following PL/SQL block for this:

```
BEGIN
    tab_form_emp_pkg.create_emp_collection (:p3_deptno, :t_message);
END;
```

Make the block conditional to run based on the following PL/SQL expression:

```
:REQUEST IN ('GO')
```

Do not forget to code the following as the success message of the process:

```
&T_MESSAGE.
```

Finally, everything is set for testing what you have done. If you select the sales department from the list and click the GO button, you should get a result similar to the one shown in Figure 4-36.

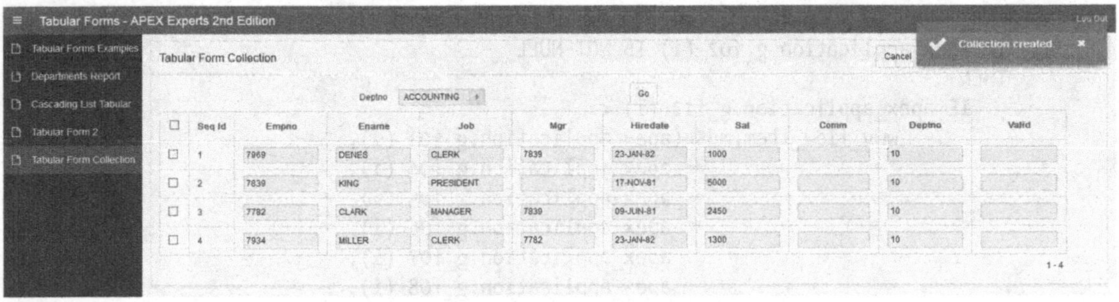

Figure 4-36. *Tabular form on APEX collection*

The question now is, how do you update your collection? The following are three possible methods for updating the collection:

- Instead of the trigger method
- Writing packaged procedures for updating collections
- Using the on-demand process and AJAX for collection updates

The sections that follow describe the second and third methods. The first method doesn't work even though in most of the cases it is the first choice.

Writing Packaged Update Procedures

Before you start writing packaged procedures, you should delete the automatic DML processes that the wizard created for you on page 3 of your application. You will need to create two procedures in your package. These procedures are similar to those you wrote for the manual tabular forms. Add the code shown in Listing 4-13 to the package.

Listing 4-13. Update and Delete Procedures for Tabular Form Collections

```
PROCEDURE save_emp_coll_custom (p_message OUT VARCHAR2);

PROCEDURE delete_emp_coll_custom (p_message OUT VARCHAR2);

PROCEDURE save_emp_coll_custom (p_message OUT VARCHAR2)
IS
    v_ins_count    INTEGER       := 0;
    v_upd_count    INTEGER       := 0;
    v_collection   VARCHAR2 (40) := 'EMP_DEPT';
BEGIN
    FOR i IN 1 .. apex_application.g_f02.COUNT
    LOOP
        BEGIN
            IF apex_application.g_f02 (i) IS NOT NULL
            THEN
                IF apex_application.g_f12 (i) <>
                        wwv_flow_item.md5 (apex_application.g_f03 (i),
                                           apex_application.g_f04 (i),
                                           apex_application.g_f05 (i),
                                           apex_application.g_f06 (i),
                                           apex_application.g_f07 (i),
                                           apex_application.g_f08 (i),
                                           apex_application.g_f09 (i),
                                           apex_application.g_f10 (i),
                                           apex_application.g_f11 (i)
                                          )
                THEN
                apex_collection.update_member
                (p_collection_name  => v_collection,
                 p_seq              => apex_application.g_f02(i),
                 p_c001             => apex_application.g_f03(i),
                 p_c002             => apex_application.g_f04(i),
```

```
  p_c003             => apex_application.g_f05(i),
  p_c004             => TO_NUMBER(apex_application.g_f06(i)),
  p_c005             => TO_DATE(apex_application.g_f07(i)),
  p_c006             => TO_NUMBER(apex_application.g_f08(i)),
  p_c007             => TO_NUMBER(apex_application.g_f09(i)),
  p_c008             => TO_NUMBER(apex_application.g_f10(i)),
  p_c009             => apex_application.g_f11(i),
  p_c010             => apex_application.g_f12(i),
  p_c011             => apex_application.g_f13(i));
            v_upd_count := v_upd_count + 1;
          END IF;
  ELSE
  apex_collection.add_member
  (p_collection_name  => v_collection,
  p_c001             => emp_seq.NEXTVAL,
  p_c002             => apex_application.g_f04(i),
  p_c003             => apex_application.g_f05(i),
  p_c004             => TO_NUMBER(apex_application.g_f06(i)),
  p_c005             => TO_DATE(apex_application.g_f07(i)),
  p_c006             => TO_NUMBER(apex_application.g_f08(i)),
  p_c007             => TO_NUMBER(apex_application.g_f09(i)),
  p_c008             => TO_NUMBER(apex_application.g_f10(i)),
  p_c009             => apex_application.g_f11(i)
                                );
            v_ins_count := v_ins_count + 1;
        END IF;
    EXCEPTION
      WHEN OTHERS
      THEN
        p_message :=    p_message
                     || '<br/>'
                     || 'Row: '
                     || i
                     || ' > '
                     || SQLERRM;
        p_message := LTRIM (p_message, '<br/>');
    END;
  END LOOP;

  IF v_ins_count > 0 OR v_upd_count > 0
  THEN
     p_message :=
          p_message || '<br/>'
      || v_ins_count
      || ' row(s) inserted. '
      || v_upd_count
      || ' row(s) updated.';
  END IF;
        p_message := LTRIM (p_message, '<br/>');
EXCEPTION
  WHEN OTHERS
```

```
   THEN p_message := SQLERRM;
END save_emp_coll_custom;

PROCEDURE delete_emp_coll_custom (p_message OUT VARCHAR2)
IS
   v_row          INTEGER;
   v_count        INTEGER        := 0;
   v_collection   VARCHAR2 (40) := 'EMP_DEPT';
BEGIN
   FOR i IN 1 .. apex_application.g_f01.COUNT
   LOOP
      v_row := apex_application.g_f01 (i);
      apex_collection.update_member
       (p_collection_name     => v_collection,
        p_seq                 => apex_application.g_f02(v_row),
        p_c011                => 'Y');
      v_count := v_count + 1;
   END LOOP;
   p_message := v_count || ' row(s) deleted.';
END delete_emp_coll_custom;
```

Before you can start testing this code, you will create two On Submit processes on application page 3:

- *Update Collection*: The process for updating existing and adding new rows. This process will be conditional using the following PL/SQL expression:

  ```
  :REQUEST IN ('ADD', 'SUBMIT')
  ```

- `Delete Collection Member`: The process for flagging deleted records to Y. This process will be conditional using this PL/SQL expression:

  ```
  :REQUEST IN ('MULTI_ROW_DELETE')
  ```

You are going to use the following PL/SQL blocks to run these processes. The first PL/SQL block is for the update process, and the second one is for the delete member process:

```
BEGIN
   tab_form_emp_pkg.save_emp_coll_custom (:t_message);
END;

BEGIN
   tab_form_emp_pkg.delete_emp_coll_custom (:t_message);
END;
```

And, of course, do not forget to put the following into the Process Success Message section:

```
&T_MESSAGE.
```

Now, you will test your new version of page 3 and change one of the records in your tabular form. Figure 4-37 shows a change being made.

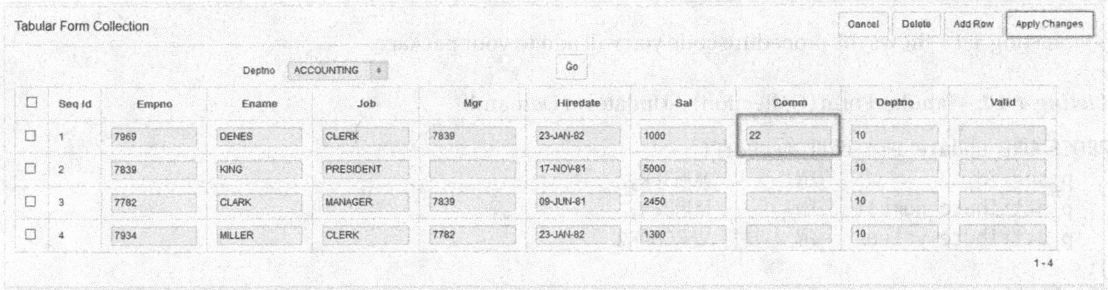

Figure 4-37. *Making a change to a tabular form built atop a collection*

You should get a similar result to the one shown in Figure 4-38.

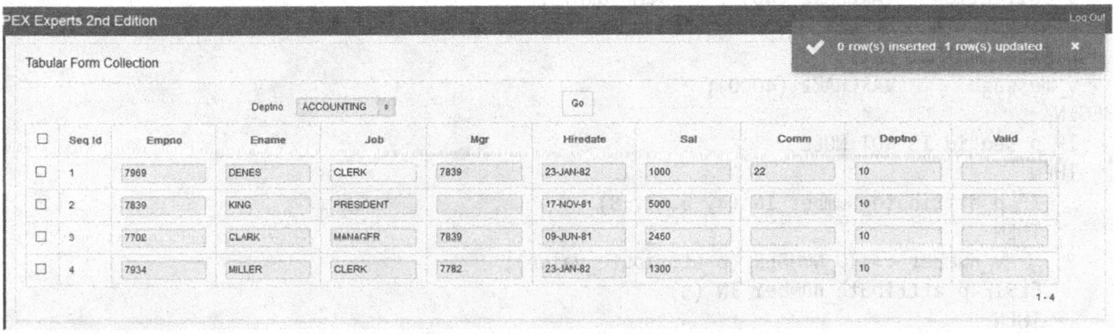

Figure 4-38. *A success message from making the change shown in Figure 4-37*

Updating a Collection via an AJAX-Callback Process

Since a collection is only a snapshot of the original data, you can use a different approach for an update. You can create some JavaScript code and combine that with an AJAX-callback process to update the collection when a single tabular form item changes. The validation of the collection values will be done only if you decide to save the collection to the source. You will include only some basic validations for numeric and date columns in this code.

The code you need to write for this demonstration consists of the following:

- One procedure for updating a collection member
- One dynamic action on the page
- One AJAX-callback process on the page

195

■ **Note** This example is showing how to update one column: Job. You can easily modify the code and apply the update on all the other columns.

Listing 4-14 shows the procedure code you will add to your package.

Listing 4-14. Tabular Form (Collection)—Update on Demand

```
PROCEDURE update_emp_coll_member (
    p_seq_id              IN        NUMBER,
    p_attribute_number    IN        NUMBER,
    p_attribute_value     IN        VARCHAR2
);
PROCEDURE update_emp_coll_member (
    p_seq_id              IN     NUMBER,
    p_attribute_number    IN     NUMBER,
    p_attribute_value     IN     VARCHAR2
)
IS
    v_collection    VARCHAR2 (40)    := 'EMP_DEPT';
    v_number        NUMBER;
    v_date          DATE;
    v_message       VARCHAR2 (4000);
BEGIN
    IF p_seq_id IS NOT NULL
    THEN
       IF p_attribute_number IN (4, 6, 7, 8)
       THEN
          v_number := TO_NUMBER (p_attribute_value);
       ELSIF p_attribute_number IN (5)
       THEN
          v_date := TO_DATE (p_attribute_value);
       END IF;

       apex_collection.update_member_attribute
          (p_collection_name       => v_collection,
           p_seq                   => p_seq_id,
           p_attr_number           => p_attribute_number,
           p_attr_value            => p_attribute_value
                                   );
    END IF;
EXCEPTION
    WHEN OTHERS
    THEN
       v_message := SQLERRM;
       HTP.p (v_message);
END update_emp_coll_member;
```

You will need to create an AJAX-callback process on the page and call it updateCollection. The code is a simple PL/SQL block.

```
BEGIN
    tab_form_emp_pkg.update_emp_coll_member
                                    (TO_NUMBER (apex_application.g_x01),
                                     TO_NUMBER (apex_application.g_x02),
                                     apex_application.g_x03
                                    );
END;
```

Finally, you will need a dynamic action on the page, and this dynamic action will react on a change of the column Job. You will use the jQuery selector input[name="f05"]. It will execute JavaScript code; Listing 4-15 shows the code.

Listing 4-15. JavaScript for Calling AJAX Process

```
var elem = '#' + this.triggeringElement.id;
var key = '#' + 'f02_' + this.triggeringElement.id.substring(4);
var key_val = $(key).val();
var elem_val = $(elem).val();

apex.server.process (
    "updateCollection",
    { x01: key_val,
      x02: 3,
      x03: elem_val},
      {success: function(data){
       alert (data);
       },
       dataType: "text"}
);
```

You are parsing three parameters here:

- The first one is the sequence number of the corresponding row.

- The second parameter is the attribute number of the column job in the collection.

- The third parameter is the actual value you changed.

Now run page 3 and try to update some of the rows in the tabular form, as shown in Figure 4-39.

	Seq Id	Empno	Ename	Job	Mgr	Hiredate	Sal	Comm	Deptno	Valid
☐	1	7969	DENES	PRESIDENT a.d]	7839	23-JAN-82	1000	22	10	
☐	2	7839	KING	PRESIDENT		17-NOV-81	5000		10	
☐	3	7782	CLARK	MANAGER	7839	09-JUN-81	2450		10	
☐	4	7934	MILLER	CLERK	7782	23-JAN-82	1300		10	

Figure 4-39. *Updating rows on the tabular form*

You can also activate Firebug and watch what happens at the browser level, as shown in Figure 4-40. Activate Firebug and switch to the Console tab. After updating a column, you should see the process running in Firebug. Opening that process will display more detail.

Figure 4-40. *Watching the on-demand process from Firebug*

Saving Collection Data to the Table

The final step in this exercise is to save the collection data to the table. For that you will create the following:

- One validation function that will take care of the data integrity

- One procedure that will save the data back to the table

Listing 4-16 shows the code for these procedures.

Listing 4-16. Tabular Form—Saving Collection Data to the Source

```
FUNCTION validate_collection_data
    RETURN VARCHAR2;

PROCEDURE update_table_from_collection (
    p_deptno      IN       NUMBER,
    p_message     OUT      VARCHAR2
);

FUNCTION validate_collection_data
    RETURN VARCHAR2
IS
    v_message     VARCHAR2 (4000);
    v_checksum    VARCHAR2 (400);
BEGIN
    FOR c IN (SELECT empno, ename, job, mgr, hiredate, sal, comm, deptno,
```

```
                    valid, checksum, delete_flag
             FROM emp_coll_v
             WHERE checksum IS NOT NULL)
   LOOP
      SELECT wwv_flow_item.md5 (empno,
                                ename,
                                job,
                                mgr,
                                hiredate,
                                sal,
                                comm,
                                deptno,
                                valid
                                )
        INTO v_checksum
        FROM emp
       WHERE empno = c.empno;

      IF c.checksum <> v_checksum
      THEN
         v_message :=
                v_message
            || '<br/>'
            || 'Empno: '
            || c.empno
            || ': Snapshot too old.';
      END IF;
   END LOOP;

   v_message := LTRIM (v_message, '<br/>');
   RETURN v_message;
END validate_collection_data;

PROCEDURE update_table_from_collection (
   p_deptno     IN         NUMBER,
   p_message    OUT        VARCHAR2
)
IS
   v_ins_count    INTEGER         := 0;
   v_upd_count    INTEGER         := 0;
   v_del_count    INTEGER         := 0;
   v_message      VARCHAR2 (4000);
BEGIN
   FOR c IN (SELECT empno, ename, job, mgr, hiredate,
                    sal, comm, deptno,
                    valid, checksum, delete_flag
             FROM emp_coll_v)
   LOOP
      IF c.delete_flag IS NULL AND c.checksum IS NOT NULL
      THEN
         IF c.checksum <>
```

```
                  wwv_flow_item.md5 (c.empno,
                                     c.ename,
                                     c.job,
                                     c.mgr,
                                     c.hiredate,
                                     c.sal,
                                     c.comm,
                                     c.deptno,
                                     c.valid
                                     )
        THEN
           UPDATE emp
              SET ename = c.ename,
                  job = c.job,
                  mgr = c.mgr,
                  hiredate = c.hiredate,
                  sal = c.sal,
                  comm = c.comm,
                  deptno = c.deptno
            WHERE empno = c.empno;

           v_upd_count := v_upd_count + 1;
        END IF;
     ELSIF c.delete_flag IS NULL AND c.checksum IS NULL
     THEN
        INSERT INTO emp
                     (empno, ename, job, mgr,
                      hiredate, sal,
                      comm, deptno, valid
                      )
              VALUES (c.empno, c.ename, c.job,
                      c.mgr, c.hiredate, c.sal,
                      c.comm, c.deptno, c.valid
                      );

        v_ins_count := v_ins_count + 1;
     ELSIF c.delete_flag IS NOT NULL AND c.checksum IS NOT NULL
     THEN
        DELETE FROM emp
             WHERE empno = c.empno;

        v_ins_count := v_ins_count + 1;
     END IF;
  END LOOP;

  p_message :=
       p_message
     || '<br/>'
     || v_ins_count
     || ' row(s) inserted. '
     || v_upd_count
```

```
        || ' row(s) updated. '
        || v_del_count
        || ' row(s) deleted.';

    create_emp_collection (p_deptno, v_message);
    p_message :=
            p_message
        || '<br/>' || v_message;
    p_message := LTRIM (p_message, '<br/>');
EXCEPTION
    WHEN OTHERS
    THEN
        p_message := SQLERRM;
END update_table_from_collection;
```

To be able to do an update of the table, you will need to create a button on your page 3 and name it as follows:

SAVE_DATA

You can now call the validation function and the update process on application page 3. You will create a page-level validation of type PL/SQL Function (returning Error Text) nd make it conditional upon the new button you created (SAVE_DATA).

```
BEGIN
    RETURN tab_form_emp_pkg.validate_collection_data;
END;
```

The process Save Collection to Table will be on submit, and it will be conditional when the button is clicked (SAVE_DATA). You will also enter the following in the Success Message of the process:

&T_MESSAGE.

It will look like this:

```
BEGIN
    tab_form_emp_pkg.update_table_from_collection
                            (:p3_deptno,:t_message);
END;
```

Now make a couple of changes in your collection and confirm that the code works as expected. Figure 4-41 shows some changes to be saved to the source table. Figure 4-42 shows the success message from saving those changes.

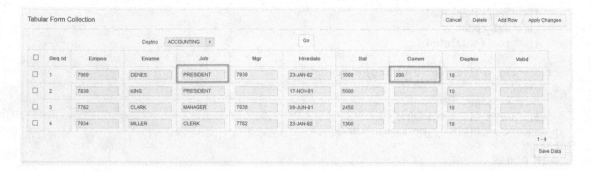

Figure 4-41. *Changes to be saved to the source table*

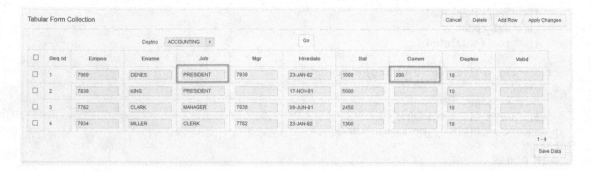

Figure 4-42. *The success message*

■ **Caution**   The examples shown here are not complete, and they focus on single functionalities. If you want to use the example code in your applications, you will need to complete the functionality that I've omitted to keep the examples simple. For example, you will need to take care of newly added rows when updating a collection using an on-demand process. The code shown here doesn't do that. However, that functionality should be fairly easy to add.

Interesting Techniques

This section will introduce two useful techniques for working with tabular forms. These techniques are possible with version 5.0.

- Multiple tabular forms and modal pages
- Cascading select list in a tabular form

Multiple Tabular Forms and Modal Pages

Multiple tabular forms per page are still a problem if you think about it the old way. You can create one standard per page and code the second one manually. That means you will need to take care of all the stuff APEX handles for you when you use the standard version, which could be hard. Also, it will be a pain to debug.

I used the following solution in the past:

1. Create a normal report instead of a tabular form.

2. Place the tabular form into a separate modal page, linked to the corresponding report.

This approach covered 99 percent of the requirements with multiple tabular forms and worked well. This solution was made possible after the modal page plugin was published. Now, with APEX 5.0, not even a plugin is required to make this work; a modal page is a standard page template in APEX 5.0. In the following example, I will show how you can easily make it work. In real life, it shouldn't take more than 30 minutes to get two tabular forms maintained through one parent page.

To make this example work, you will need to do a couple of steps:

1. Create a new page using the Page Designer and include an interactive report on table DEPT.

2. Create a new page and add a form for the DEPT detailed view.

3. Link those two pages.

4. On the form page, create a simple interactive report for employees of the selected department.

5. Finally, on the third page, create a standard employee tabular form using the same condition as for the report on the second page. Use Page Mode, and set it to "Modal Dialog for this page.

6. Link the report of employees on the second page with the tabular form on the third page using a normal button branch to the third page.

Figures 4-43, 4-44, and 4-45 show how it should look.

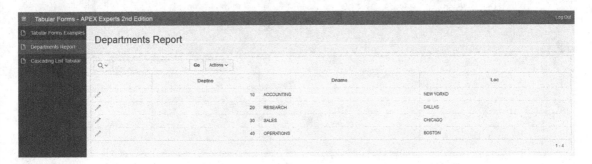

Figure 4-43. *Interactive report on DEPT table*

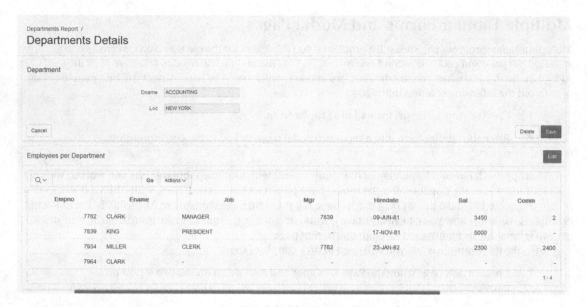

Figure 4-44. *Departments detailed view plus report on employees of each department*

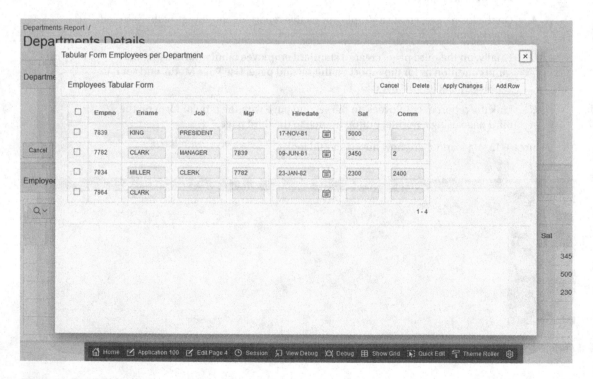

Figure 4-45. *Tabular form on employees as a modal page*

While doing the previous steps, you probably noticed the following:

- Creating a modal page in APEX 5.0 is equal to creating any other page type.

- Linking a button to a modal page is fairly simple; it is just like any other branch to any other page in your application.

- The modal page will create a process on submit for closing modal pages after a submit is successful and no validation errors are displayed.

- The success message will appear on the parent (calling) page.

- This may cause you to lose data on the parent page since a page refresh is triggered such as if you start entering data on the parent page and call the modal prior to saving the changes.

Now, there are just a couple of small things you need to do to make it better. You want to have the following things happen:

- After closing the modal dialog, you want to refresh only the corresponding report, not the whole page.

- You want to transfer the success message to the parent page and display it there.

To achieve that, do the following:

1. Create an item on the second page called P3_MODAL_PAGE_MESSAGE in the employee per department report region. This item will hold the success message to display.

2. On the modal page, you will create an additional PL/SQL process on submit, which will save the success message into the P3_MODAL_PAGE_MESSAGE item. Use the code in Listing 4-17. Please note that this process should fire prior to the Close Page process.

    Listing 4-17. Modal Dialog Page (Process on Submit), Unconditional

    ```
    BEGIN
        :p3_modal_page_message :=
                NVL (apex_application.g_print_success_message, 'Action processed.');
    END;
    ```

3. The last step you need to do is to create one dynamic action on the second page (parent page), which will do a couple of things.

    - Refresh the corresponding employee report to show the changes you did in the modal dialog

    - Return the submitted value for the P3_MODAL_PAGE_MESSAGE item

    - Display the corresponding success message on the calling (parent page)

4. After you created a dynamic action Close Modal, you can choose the Framework event Close Dialog to set the event it reacts upon.

5.　The following are the actions this dynamic action does:

- It will do a Region Refresh for the employees report.

- It will execute a PL/SQL block, as shown in Listing 4-18, and return the page item P3_MODAL_PAGE_MESSAGE.

Finally , it will execute a piece of JavaScript code, as shown in Listing 4-19, to display the success message.

Listing 4-18. Executing Pseudo PL/SQL to Return the Value for the P3_MODAL_PAGE_MESSAGE Item, Which Exists Only in the Session State

```
BEGIN
    NULL;
END;
```

Listing 4-19. JavaScript for Displaying the Success Message on the Parent Page

```
var message = '<div class="t-Body-alert">' +
'<div id="t_Alert_Success" class="t-Alert t-Alert--defaultIcons t-Alert--success t-Alert--
horizontal t-Alert--page t-Alert--colorBG is-visible" role="alert">'+
'<div class="t-Alert-wrap">' +
'<div class="t-Alert-icon">' +
'<span class="t-Icon"></span>' +
'</div>' +
'<div class="t-Alert-content">' +
'<div class="t-Alert-header">' +
'<h2 class="t-Alert-title">' +
$('#P3_MODAL_PAGE_MESSAGE').val() +
'</h2>' +
'</div>' +
'</div>' +
'<div class="t-Alert-buttons">' +
'<button class="t-Button t-Button--noUI t-Button--icon t-Button--closeAlert" title="Close
Notification" type="button" style="touch-action: pan-y;">' +
'<span class="t-Icon icon-close"></span>' +
'</button>' +
'</div>' +
'</div>' +
'</div>' +
'</div>';

$(message).appendTo("#t_Body_content");

$(function() {
  $('.t-Button--closeAlert').bind('click',function(){
    $(".t-Body-alert").remove();
  });
});
```

■ **Caution**   This JavaScript will use the same HTML code you have in your template for displaying a
success message. It will wrap the content of your success message in that code and present it on the page by
appending it to the body content. Finally, it will bind a function to the close button to remove the message after
a click. This function looks much bigger than it is.

At the end, the result will be as shown in Figure 4-46.

Figure 4-46. *Displaying the modal page success message on the parent page*

Adding Cascading Select Lists to a Tabular Form

There are a couple of solutions out there showing how cascading select lists in a tabular form can be done.
Usually these solutions contain some external code and will work until the next update of APEX appears.
I also created an implementation using the apex_item package in 2008. However, that solution is not easy
to understand and even harder to debug. Knowing the possibilities of APEX 4.2 and 5.0, I was thinking that
there must be an easy solution to this problem using standard functionalities only. In the following example,
I will show how indeed easy that is.

Let's create a simple page with a tabular form on employees using only three columns from the table
EMP; see Figure 4-47.

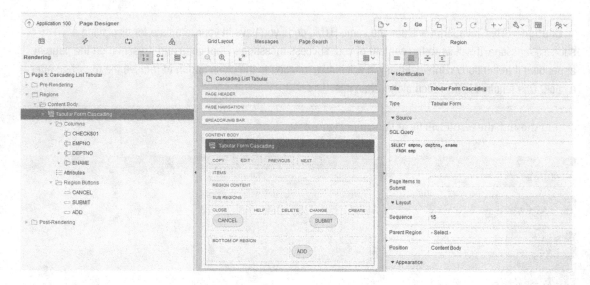

Figure 4-47. *Simple tabular form on employees with three columns: EMPNO, DEPTNO, ENAME*

You will add a static ID to the tabular form region, `EMP_TABULAR_FORM`, which you will use in the later processing. Both visible items on the page are select lists with a simple select on departments and employees; see Figure 4-48.

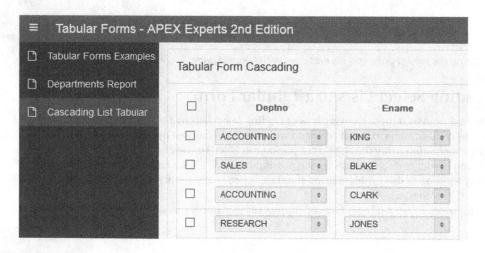

Figure 4-48. *Two items, both simple select lists*

Set the LOV definition of the select list as shown in the Figures 4-49 and 4-50.

Figure 4-49. *Select List LOV, departments*

Figure 4-50. *Select List LOV, employees*

The second select list of employees should be dependent on the selection you make in the first list. You can achieve that easily if you understand how this can be done and what you need for that. Basically, the following happens:

- You need a process that will get the dependent select list values based on the selection you do in the department's LOV; this will be an AJAX process returning a JSON string.

- You need a dynamic action, which will trigger that process and do something with the values returned. This dynamic action should fire on change of the department's LOV and on page load.

- Eventually, you will need a dynamic action to cover the additional actions you can do with a tabular form, such as a pagination event for a partial-page refresh.

Let's create those processes. The first process, getEmp, is the AJAX callback you create on the page. Listing 4-20 shows the code for that process.

Listing 4-20. Executing PL/SQL to Return the Value for the P3_MODAL_PAGE_MESSAGE Item, Which Exists Only in the Session State

```
DECLARE
    v_dept      NUMBER              := TO_NUMBER (apex_application.g_x01);
    v_empno     NUMBER              := TO_NUMBER (apex_application.g_x02);
    v_employee  VARCHAR2 (4000)
        := '{"KEY0": {"NAME":"- Select Employee -","VALUE":"","SELECTED":""},';
    v_count     NUMBER              := 1;
BEGIN
    FOR c IN (SELECT empno, ename
                FROM emp
               WHERE deptno = v_dept)
    LOOP
```

```
        v_employee :=
              v_employee
          || '"KEY'
          || v_count
          || '":{"NAME":"'
          || c.ename
          || '","VALUE":"'
          || c.ename
          || '","SELECTED":"'
          || CASE
                WHEN c.empno = v_empno
                    THEN c.ename
                ELSE NULL
             END
          || '"},';
      v_count := v_count + 1;
  END LOOP;

  v_employee := RTRIM (v_employee, ',');
  v_employee := v_employee || '}';
  HTP.p (v_employee);
END;
```

This AJAX callback is taking the values from both lists (departments and employees), and it is figuring out two things.

- Which employees belong to the selected department

- Which employee is the current selected employee for an already existing entry

This AJAX callback is then wrapping this information in a JSON sting and returning it to the calling function.

The second action you need is a dynamic action called Add Values, which reacts on a change of a jQuery selector, which is the department select list in this case: select[name="f03"]. Figure 4-51 shows how this dynamic action is set up.

Figure 4-51. *Dynamic action Add Values setup*

■ Caution   Use Firebug to inspect the form elements and find out the ID of the corresponding column. Please note that the dynamic action Event Scope is Dynamic.

The dynamic action called Action will be JavaScript code, as shown in Listing 4-21.

Listing 4-21. Executing Pseudo PL/SQL to Return the Value for the P3_MODAL_PAGE_MESSAGE Item, Which Exists Only in the Session State

```
var elem = '#' + this.triggeringElement.id;
var key = '#' + 'f02_' + this.triggeringElement.id.substring(4);
var set_list = '#' + 'f04_' + this.triggeringElement.id.substring(4);
var key_val = $(key).val();
var elem_val = $(elem).val();
var selected_val = '';

apex.server.process (
    "getEmp",
    { x01: elem_val,
      x02: key_val},
    { success: function( pData ) {
      $(set_list).find('option').remove();
      $.each(pData, function(key, innerjson) {
      $(set_list).append($('<option>', {
      value: innerjson.VALUE,
       text: innerjson.NAME
         }))
         if (innerjson.SELECTED != '') {selected_val = innerjson.SELECTED};
      });

      if (selected_val != '') {
        $('select' + set_list + ' option').each(function()
        {this.selected = (this.text == selected_val);});
      }},
    });
```

This code will do the following:

- It will call the AJAX process.
- It will take the JSON string.
- It will remove the existing LOV entries for the employee select list.
- Out of the JSON string, it will construct a new LOV and set the current value to whatever it is.

■ Caution   This action needs to fire on page load. Keep that option turned on.

If you now run the page, the dependent employee select list will be rendered according to your selection in the department select list; see Figure 4-52.

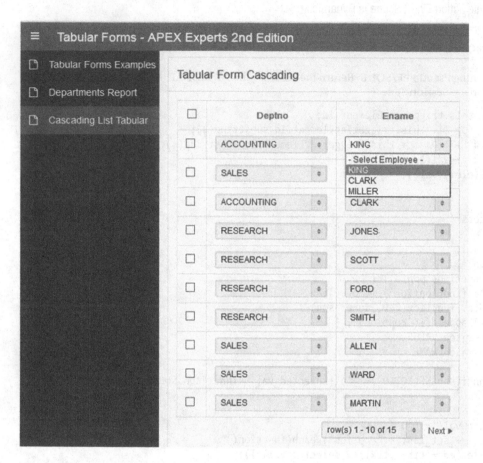

Figure 4-52. *Dynamic action Add Values setup*

The final step is to cover the additional event that may happen on the page. The pagination added to the tabular form will (if the option Partial Page Refresh turned on) refresh the report. You will add another dynamic action, After Refresh, as shown in Figure 4-53.

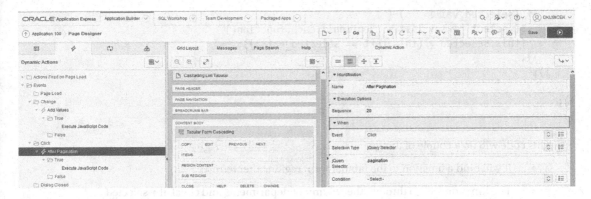

Figure 4-53. *Dynamic action After Pagination setup*

This dynamic action called Action will run basically the same JavaScript code as the first action. It will only bind the code to the tabular form and run it after the refresh is completed; see Listing 4-22.

Listing 4-22. Binding the Similar Code as in Listing 4-20 to the tabular form Partial Page Refresh (Pagination)

```
apex.jQuery('#EMP_TABULAR_FORM').bind("apexafterrefresh", function () {

$("[name='f03']").each(function(i){
var obj_id = $("[name='f03']").get(i).id;

var elem = '#' + obj_id;
var key = '#' + 'f02_' + obj_id.substring(4);
var set_list = '#' + 'f04_' + obj_id.substring(4);
var key_val = $(key).val();
var elem_val = $(elem).val();
var selected_val = '';

apex.server.process (
    "getEmp",
    { x01: elem_val,
      x02: key_val},
    { success: function( pData ) {
      $(set_list).find('option').remove();
      $.each(pData, function(key, innerjson) {
      $(set_list).append($('<option>', {
      value: innerjson.VALUE,
       text: innerjson.NAME
        }))
          if (innerjson.SELECTED != '') {selected_val = innerjson.SELECTED};
      });
```

```
      if (selected_val != '') {
        $('select' + set_list + ' option').each(function()
        {this.selected = (this.text == selected_val);});
      }},
    });


});
})
```

This code will do a couple of things.

- It will bind a function to the tabular form region, after refresh.

- The function will go through the column of departments and check the selected values.

- It will again trigger the AJAX callback function and return a JSON string.

- It will remove the existing LOV entries for the employee select list.

- Out of the JSON string, it will construct a new LOV and set the current value to whatever it is.

This is all you need to get it working.

■ **Caution**   This dynamic action doesn't need to fire on page load. Turn this option off. The first dynamic action will take care of setting the values on page load.

Summary

Tabular forms are one of the greatest features in APEX. Without this functionality, APEX simply wouldn't be as successful as it is. The next release of APEX 5.1 should introduce the jQuery Grid control as an alternative to tabular forms and finally remove all the current limitations.

- Multiple tabular forms per page

- Using dynamic actions for tabular form elements

- Unlimited number of arrays

- Options for adding/copying rows

This also means that tabular forms will be added to the list of deprecated features in APEX eventually (not in the next release but in APEX 6.0 at the latest).

In this chapter, you saw many techniques for using tabular forms and for implementing some of the functionality in the preceding list.

■ **Note**   For even more information about tabular forms, you can visit a demo application that I maintain at http://apex.oracle.com/pls/otn/f?p=31517:1. Look in Section VI of the demo for examples of tabular form usage.

CHAPTER 5

Team Development

by Roel Hartman

In this chapter, I will cover Team Development features. Team Development is an APEX application within the Application Express development environment and was introduced in version 4.0 of APEX. Figure 5-1 shows the Team Development main menu.

Milestones   Features   To Dos   Bugs   Feedback

Figure 5-1. Team Development main menu

Team Development can be used to track features, bugs, milestones, and other elements, but the most striking functionality is the feedback feature. Using the feedback feature, you can support the reporting and communication of bugs and enhancement requests from your business analysts, application testers, and end users; this can happen from a test or production environment to your development environment, and vice versa. This chapter will cover how to set up this built-in functionality and give some examples of how to use it. You'll also see how to use APEX views and packages to enhance Team Development's functionality to meet your specific needs.

The different parts of Team Development, pictured in Figure 5-1, are discussed in more detail in this chapter. Each section ends with some tips and tricks on how to extend the usability of the standard features. As an example, you'll use the development of an application you are familiar with: Oracle Application Express.

Milestones

Milestones being the first option in the menu shown in Figure 5-1 is not by accident. Defining the milestones is usually the first thing you want to do when you start with Team Development. A *milestone* is a project management term, marking the end of a stage, like the delivery of a work package. Milestones are used to determine whether a project is on schedule. For this reason, milestones are usually the first thing you'll define. The milestones in this example are the delivery of APEX Early Adopter Release 1, Release 2, and the final production versions of APEX 5.0 and 5.1.

The Basics

Figure 5-2 shows the high-level data model used to record milestones. Each milestone is categorized by a milestone type, is associated with a release, and is owned by an owner. The Milestone Type, Release, and Owner entities are not implemented as actual tables but as a list of used values, such as `select distinct milestone_type` of milestones.

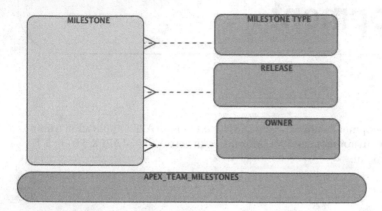

Figure 5-2. *Data model of milestones*

The advantage of the non-normalized implementation in Figure 5-2 is that you can create milestones quickly, without defining most related master data beforehand. All information regarding milestones is exposed through the `APEX_TEAM_MILESTONES` view.

To create a milestone, as shown in Figure 5-3, you have to set the milestone date and add some additional information. When entering this additional information, you might notice there is a feature in the user interface that differs from the other parts of APEX but is generally implemented in Team Development. For some fields you have the option to select a value from a select list or enter a new value. Be aware that the new value supersedes the value in the select list. So if you enter a new value, that one will be used, regardless of whatever you selected in the select list, even when the "new value" field is hidden when you select something from the select list!

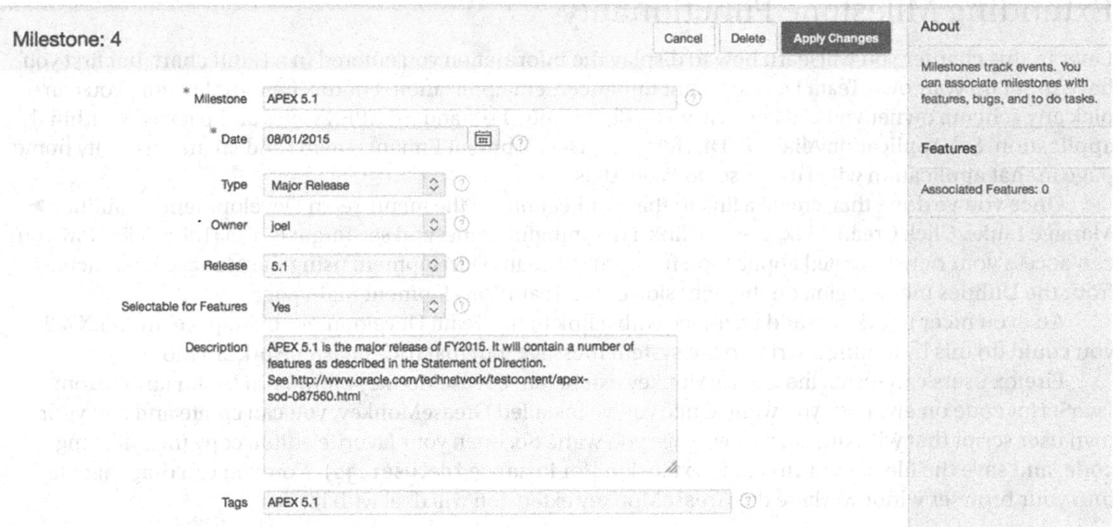

Figure 5-3. *Example of a milestone*

The following are some descriptions of the fields shown in Figure 5-3:

- The Type field can be used to differentiate the type of the milestone, such as Early Adopter, Major Release, or Patch Release.

- The Owner field indicates who is responsible for the milestone. The select list is populated from all fields within Team Development where you can enter names, such as assigned to, contributor, and others, so you are not restricted to previously entered milestone owners. Note that the names you enter will be converted to lowercase.

- The Release field defines the version of the software you set the milestone for. In this example, you can expect releases such as 5.0, 5.0.1, 5.0.2, and 5.1.

- The Selectable for Features field gives you the option to hide milestones when adding a feature. This can be used for milestones that are tentative and not yet ready for use. Note that switching this off for a milestone doesn't impact the features that are currently assigned to that milestone. Furthermore, you can add a full description of the milestone and add tags to it.

■ **Tip** From the Team Development dashboard you can create a milestone with one click by using the + icon in the upper-right corner of the milestone region on that page. Quick navigation to the Milestones dashboard can be done by clicking the > icon next to it.

Extending Milestone Functionality

Later in this chapter you will learn how to display the information you entered in a Gantt chart, but first you have to set up your own Team Development Enhancement application. For this new application, you can pick any schema owner you like because you will use only the standard APEX views and packages within this application. Set Application Alias to TDE (for Team Development Enhancement) and create an empty home page in that application with HOME set to Page Alias.

Once you've done that, create a link to that application via the menu Team Development ➤ Utilities ➤ Manage Links. Click Create Link, give the link a meaningful name, and set Target to f?p=TDE:HOME. Now you can access your newly created application from within Team Development using the Manage Links action from the Utilities menu region on the right side of the Team Development main page.

An even nicer tweak is to add an image with a link to the Team Development main page. In APEX 4.2 you could do this by adding a script to the system message, but that trick doesn't work anymore.

Firefox users can install the GreaseMonkey extension. GreaseMonkey allows you to run any custom JavaScript code on any page you want. Once you've installed GreaseMonkey, you can create and add your own user script that will run on any web page you want. So, open your favorite editor, copy the following code, and save the file using a .user.js extension (for instance tde.user.js). Now you can drag that file into your browser window where the GreaseMonkey extension will deal with it.

```
// ==UserScript==
// @name        Team Development Enhancements
// @namespace   apex
// @description Team Development Enhancements
// @include     http://oel6:8081/apex5/*    [The URL that points to your APEX environment]
// @version     1
// @grant       none
// ==/UserScript==
if ( $v('pFlowStepId')=='4000') {
  // Create Image + Link to Team Development Enhancement on this page"
  $('ul.a-ImageNav.team-dev')
  .append('
    <link rel="stylesheet" href="//maxcdn.bootstrapcdn.com/font-awesome/4.3.0/css/font-
awesome.min.css">
    <li class="a-ImageNav-item">
      <a title = "Team Development Enhancement"
         href  = "f?p=TDE:HOME::::::P_SESSION:' + $v('pInstance') +'"
         class = "a-ImageNav-link"
         target = "_blank" >
         <span class = "a-ImageNav-img fa fa-connectdevelop fa-4x"
               style = "padding-top:12px;"></span>
         <span class="a-ImageNav-label">Team Development Enhancement</span>
      </a>
    </li>
    ');
}
```

This code adds an image with a link to your application to the Team Development main page, just like the icon on the far right in Figure 5-4. You have to adapt the href and src attributes to your liking. Please note that all HTML text used as parameters to the append function should be on one line, without additional carriage returns. In the previous listing, the code is formatted just to improve readability. I'll explain the use of the P_SESSION parameter in a moment.

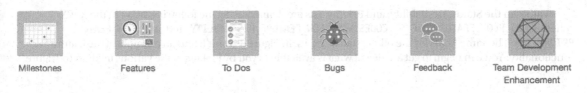

Figure 5-4. *Team Development menu with your own Enhancement*

Features

Using features, you describe the functionality you want to add to or change in your application. You can assign a feature to an owner, and a feature can have a contributor. You can also make a distinction based on focus areas, such as Charts, Interactive Reports, or Themes. Once you've decided when to implement a feature, you can assign it to a certain release and milestone. Earlier on you might have defined a milestone as set for a certain release and that relationship is now used in the feature functionality, unlike the previous releases. You can break down features into subfeatures, adding detail to your planning and making different people responsible for different subfeatures.

The Basics

In Figure 5-5 you can see how the data model used for the features functionality is implemented. In addition to the select lists for the Owner, Contributor, Focus Area, and Release fields, there are three other select lists you'll encounter when defining a feature: Status, Desirability, and Priority. Unlike the other select items, these last three contain predefined and fixed values and cannot be customized.

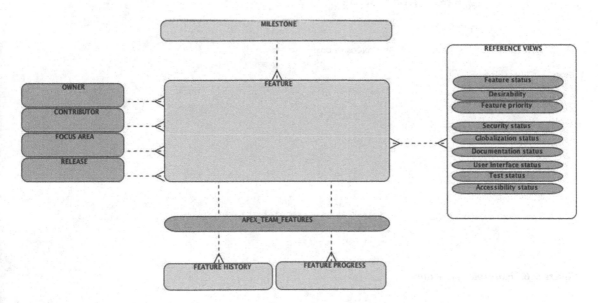

Figure 5-5. *Data model of features*

Values in the Status, Desirability, and Priority lists are defined using the following views in the APEX schema: `WWV_FLOW_FEATURE_DEF_ST_CODES`, `WWV_FLOW_FEATURE_DESIRABLITY`, and `WWV_FLOW_FEATURE_PRIORITIES`. The same holds for the other "status" views. In Figure 5-6 you'll find an example of the feature functionality. You can begin to get an idea of what is available to you by looking at the various fields in the figure.

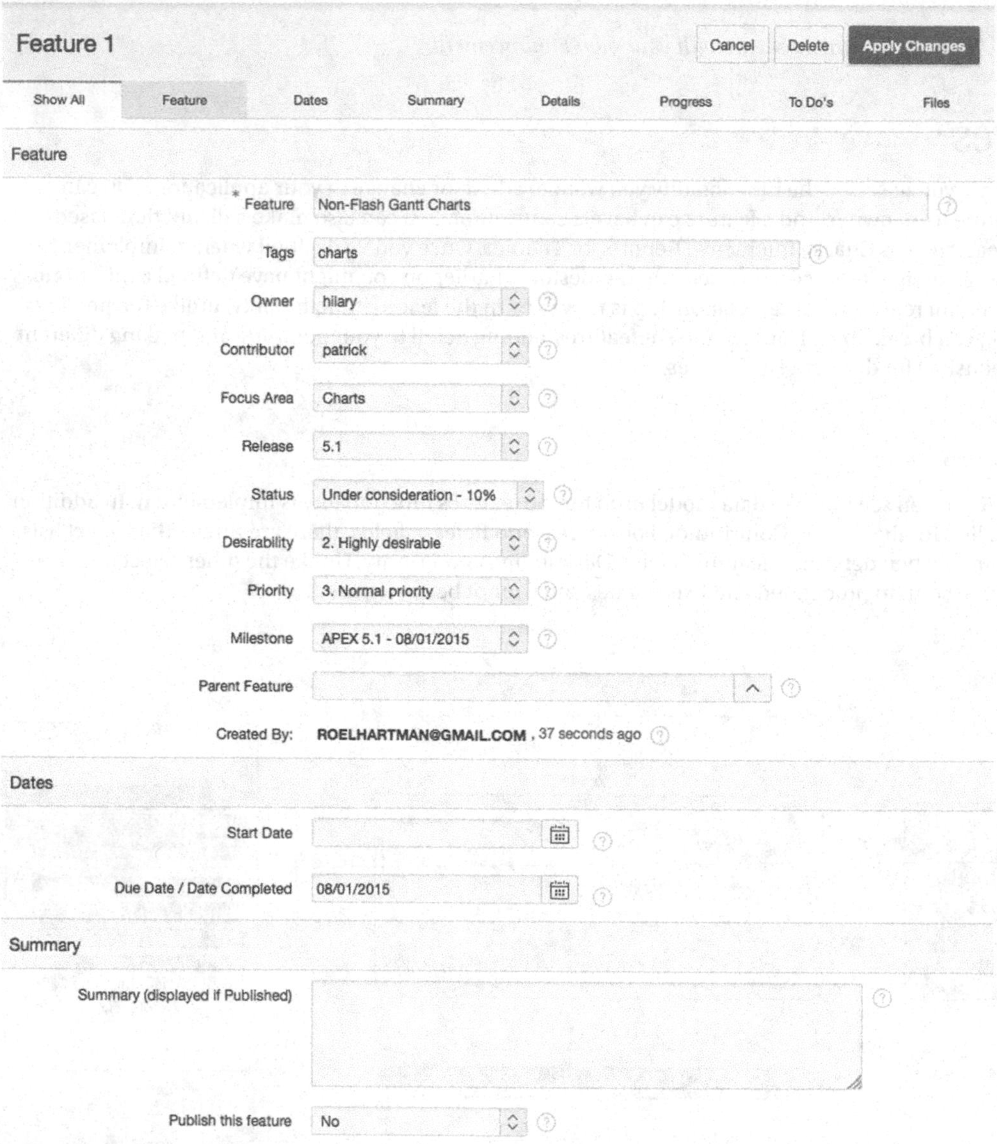

Figure 5-6. *Example of a feature*

There is some date information that you can add to a feature, such as start date and due date. The latter is defaulted to the date of the corresponding milestone. You can also add more details such as a description, a justification, and a progress log. You can use these fields to create your own reports.

Although the standard options already offer you a lot of functionality, you can even expand the amount of data you can enter. If you click Team Development Settings in the task list on the right side of the Team Development home page, you can enable the tracking of attributes for all aspects of application development, such as user interface, testing, security, and the like. Figure 5-7 shows the drop-down menu items to enable this level of tracking.

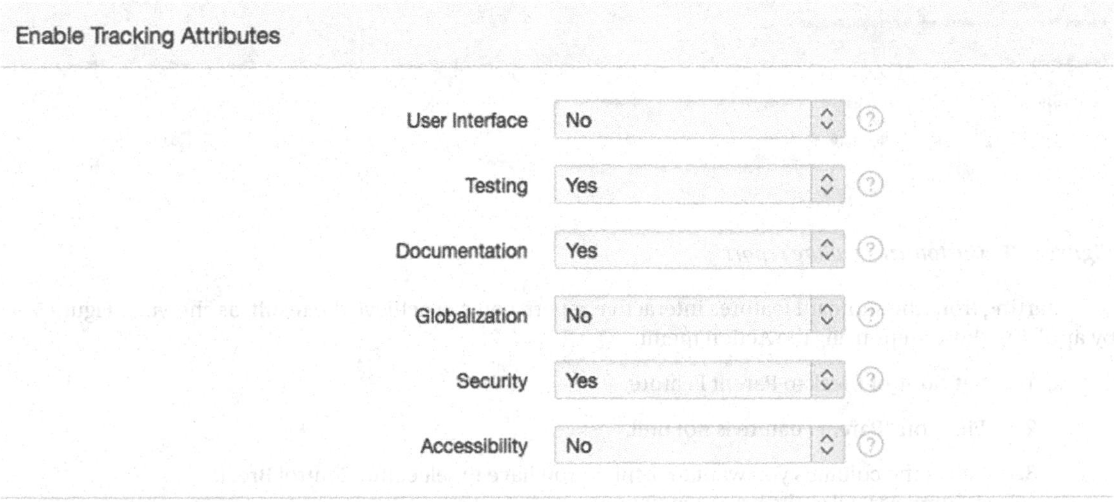

Enable Tracking Attributes

User Interface	No
Testing	Yes
Documentation	Yes
Globalization	No
Security	Yes
Accessibility	No

Figure 5-7. Dialog to enable tracking attributes

For each of the tracking attributes you enable, a new region within your features screen appears at the bottom, as shown in Figure 5-8.

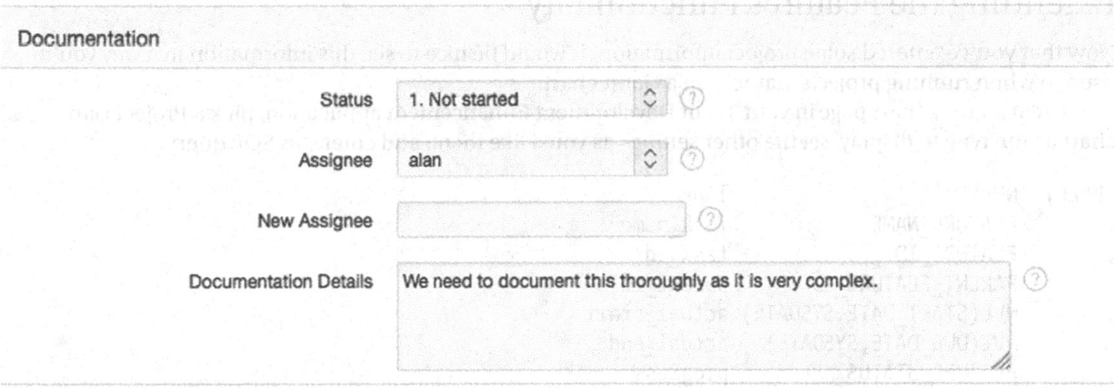

Documentation

Status	1. Not started
Assignee	alan
New Assignee	
Documentation Details	We need to document this thoroughly as it is very complex.

Figure 5-8. Additional documentation region

Now that you know what all these fields are for, you can use the standard functionality of APEX to customize the display of the feature's interactive report to fit—more or less—your specific needs. Figure 5-9 shows a customized report.

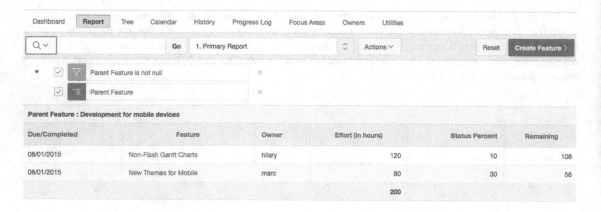

Figure 5-9. *Customized feature report*

Starting from the standard features interactive report, you can achieve the result, as shown in Figure 5-9, by applying these steps using the Action menu:

1. Set Control Break to Parent Feature.

2. Filter on "Parent Feature is not null."

3. Select the columns you want to display. You have to select the Control Break column as well or the break won't work.

4. Compute the Remaining field by entering a computation like BA * (100-BG)/100, where BA refers to the effort and BG to the status percent.

5. Aggregate the Effort field—and maybe the Remaining field as well.

Extending the Features Functionality

Now that you've entered some project information, it would be nice to see this information in a way you're used to when running projects, namely, in a Gantt chart.

Create a new chart page in your Team Development Enhancement application, pick a Project Gantt chart as the type to display, set the other settings as you'd like them, and enter this SQL query:

```
SELECT  NULL                      link
,       FEATURE_NAME              task_name
,       FEATURE_ID                task_id
,       PARENT_FEATURE_ID         parent_id
,       NVL(START_DATE,SYSDATE)   actual_start
,       NVL(DUE_DATE,SYSDATE)     actual_end
,       FEATURE_STATUS            progress
FROM APEX_TEAM_FEATURES
START WITH PARENT_FEATURE_ID IS NULL
CONNECT BY PRIOR FEATURE_ID = PARENT_FEATURE_ID
```

With data similar to the data presented in Figure 5-9 and a few additional features, you'll get a Gantt chart when you run the page. You'll notice that the start and end dates of the parent features don't match the dates of the subfeatures. You can solve that by including the calculation of those dates in the SQL code using analytic functions. Later in the chapter, when you generate the XML used by the chart by yourself, you'll learn how to let AnyChart do the calculation.

For now you can play with the settings until you get the desired result. Figure 5-10 shows the settings I used.

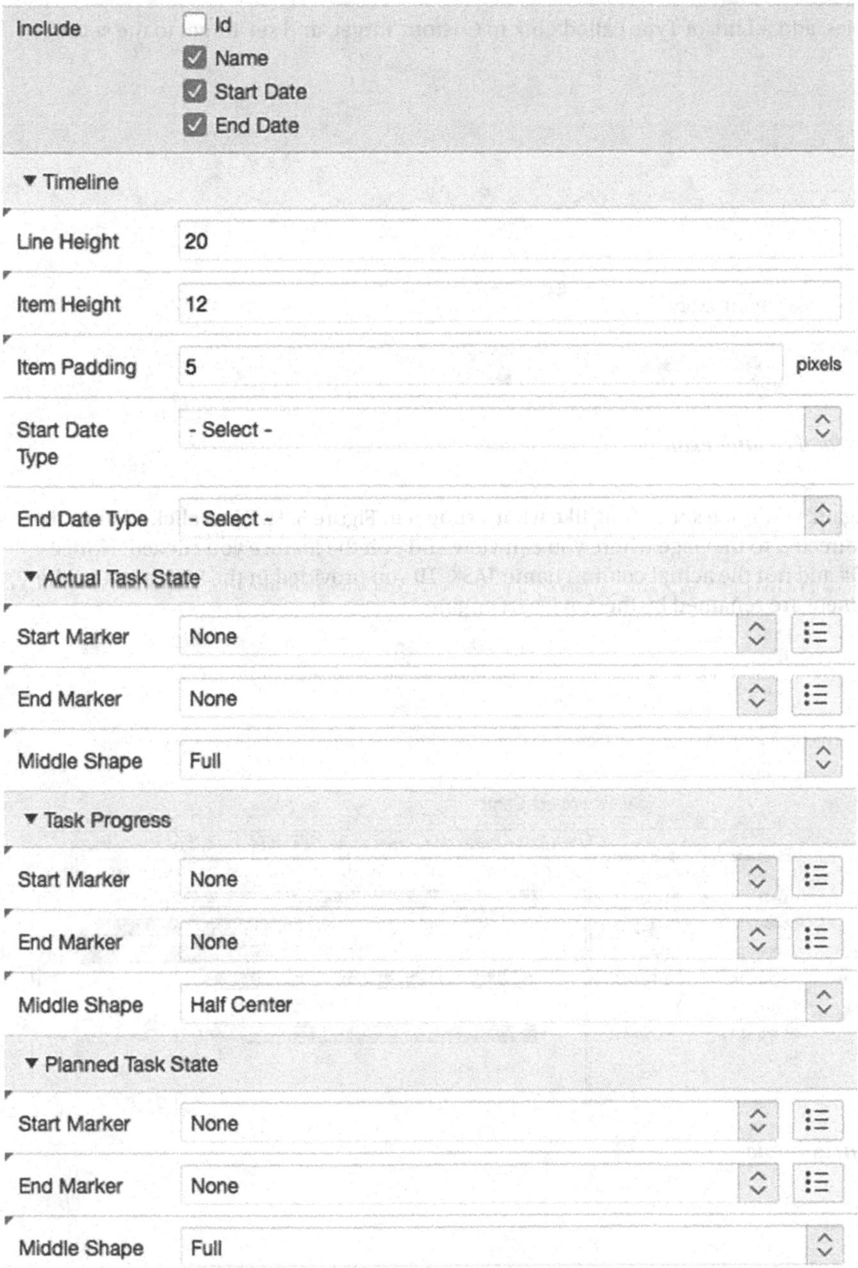

Include	☐ Id
	☑ Name
	☑ Start Date
	☑ End Date

▼ Timeline

Line Height	20	
Item Height	12	
Item Padding	5	pixels
Start Date Type	- Select -	
End Date Type	- Select -	

▼ Actual Task State

Start Marker	None	
End Marker	None	
Middle Shape	Full	

▼ Task Progress

Start Marker	None	
End Marker	None	
Middle Shape	Half Center	

▼ Planned Task State

Start Marker	None	
End Marker	None	
Middle Shape	Full	

Figure 5-10. Feature Gantt settings

Now, let's create a link from the Gantt chart back into Team Development. Notice I didn't include a link in the SQL query because that solution doesn't work anymore. Because APEX 5 automatically creates a new session when you run an application, you have to take care of the session ID of the originating session, such as the one that's running Application Builder. Therefore, you've already added a P_SESSION parameter in the GreaseMonkey script. To make use of that, add an application item named P_SESSION with Session State Protection set to Unrestricted.

Now, go to Chart Series, add a Link of Type called Link to Custom Target, and set Target to the settings shown in Figure 5-11.

Figure 5-11. *Link settings for the Gantt example*

If you run the page again, you'll see something like what's shown in Figure 5-12. Now click a bar in the charts, and you will be redirected to the page where you can view and edit the feature you clicked. Notice the parameter used is #ID# and not the actual column name TASK_ID you provided in the SQL because the columns in the SQL statement are renamed by the AnyChart engine.

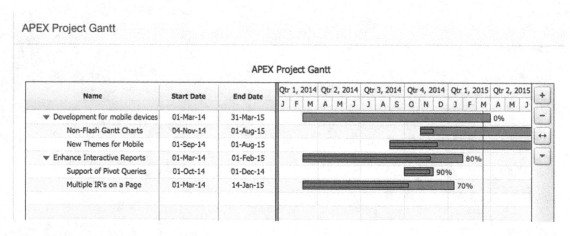

Figure 5-12. *Feature Gantt example*

To Do's

To-do items are small pieces of work, or tasks, you assign to your co-workers and want to track. As with features, you can create a multilevel breakdown of to-do items. But if you really want to keep track of things, creating a multilevel breakdown might not be the wisest thing to do, because if you have a lot of to-do items defined, it can be rather difficult to keep oversight of them all. Also, since Team Development is not a real planning tool (compared to Microsoft Project, for example), all the figures you enter, such as dates and estimated effort, are not accumulated to the higher level. So, you cannot simply rely on those figures; you'll need some additional reports to get closer to the real situation.

The Basics

Figure 5-13 shows the data model for a to-do item. This gives you an idea of how the tables and views are related and where the fields on the page in Figure 5-14 originate.

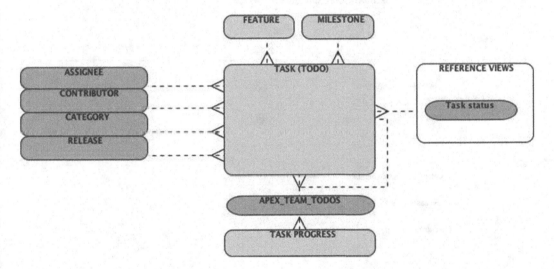

Figure 5-13. *Data model for to-do items*

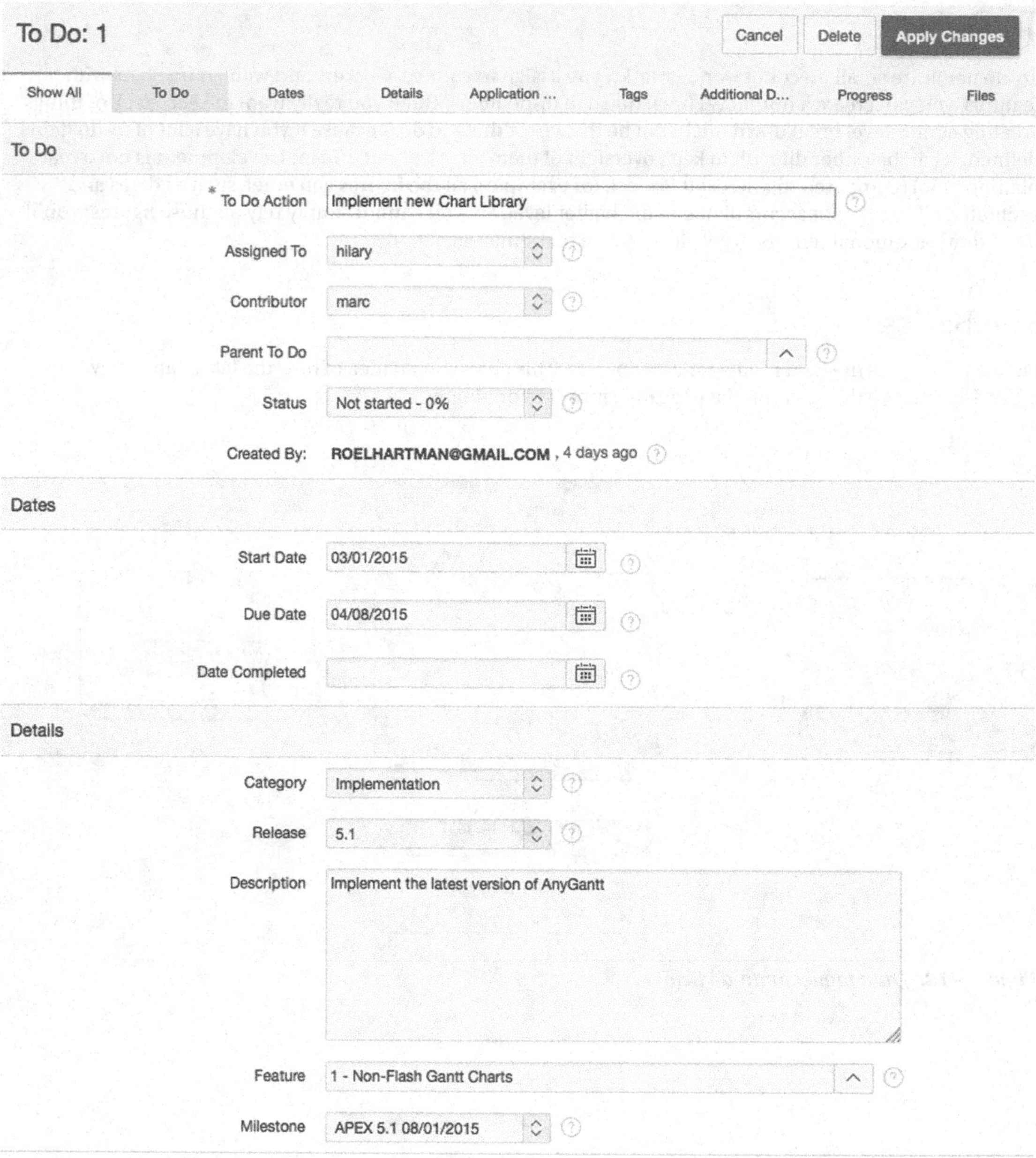

Figure 5-14. *Example of a to-do item*

A to-do item (also known as a *task*) is assigned to someone and can have a contributor or an additional contributor. A to-do item has a certain status. Similar to features, this status is hard-coded using a view: WWV_FLOW_TASK_DEF_STATUS_CODES. You can add more details to a to-do item by specifying a category, a release, a feature, and a milestone. Figure 5-13 shows an example of a to-do item.

All information regarding to-do items is exposed through the APEX_TEAM_TODOS view, which is mainly based on the WWV_FLOW_TASKS table. And, similar to feature progress, all information entered in the progress area is recorded as task progress and represented as a list of activities carried out.

Extending the To-Do Functionality

Now that you've explored the planning and activities aspects of Team Development, it would be nice to present milestones, features, and to-do items in one Gantt chart. The following are some of the details you'll need to attend to in order to accomplish that goal:

- The roll-up of start and end dates from lower-level features to higher-level features or from to-do items to features—defined as the parent feature of a feature or the feature of a to-do item

- Defining, and showing in the Gantt chart, a predecessor for a to-do item—defined as the parent to-do item of a to-do item

- Defining, and showing in the Gantt chart, what to-do item is the last step for a milestone—defined as the Milestone property of a to-do item

First create a new project Gantt chart. You can use the SQL query provided earlier in "Extending the Features Functionality," or any other valid query for the chart, because you won't use the results of that query anyway.

Now, create a (dummy) static content region before the Chart region with a hidden field, named P3_XML_PG. Next, edit the chart XML by providing this custom XML:

```xml
<?xml version = "1.0" encoding="utf-8" standalone = "yes"?>
<anygantt>
  <settings>
    <background enabled="false" />
    <navigation enabled="true" position="Top" size="30">
      <buttons collapse_expand_button="false" align="Far"/>
      <text>Project Gantt</text>
    </navigation>
  </settings>
  <datagrid enabled="true" width="400" />
  <styles>
    <task_styles>
      <task_style name="defaultStyle">
        <actual>
          <bar_style>
            <middle>
              <fill enabled="true" type="Gradient">
                <gradient angle="-90">
                  <key color="#689663" position="0"/>
                  <key color="#6B9866" position="0.38"/>
                  <key color="#B4FFAB" position="1"/>
                </gradient>
              </fill>
            </middle>
          </bar_style>
        </actual>
      </task_style>
    </task_styles>
  </styles>
&P3_XML_PG.
</anygantt>
```

See Figure 5-15 for where to put these lines of code.

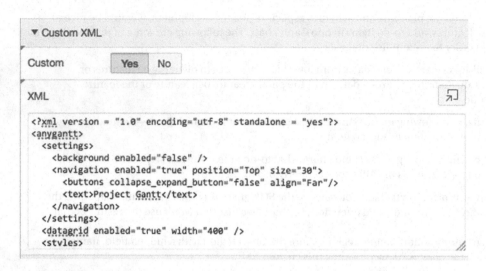

Figure 5-15. *Custom chart XML*

Instead of using the standard #DATA# replacement, the chart will use the contents of the P3_XML_PG field to generate the chart. So, define a Pre-Rendering – After Header page process to load data into that field using a function you will create shortly.

```
begin
    :P3_XML_PG := GenerateProjectXML;
end;
```

See Figure 5-16 for where to put this code. You might see a message that there is an error in your code, but you can save the change. You will fix that error in the next step.

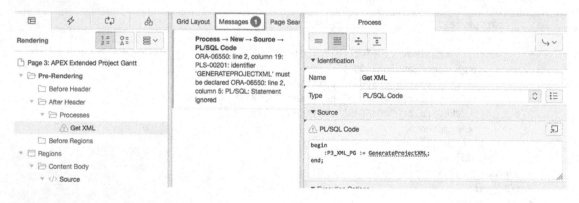

Figure 5-16. *On Load – After Header process*

Next switch to APEX's SQL Workshop and define that function.

```
create or replace function GenerateProjectXML
return varchar2
is
    l_chart_data_xml    varchar2(32767);
    l_task_xml          varchar2(32767);
    l_connector_xml     varchar2(32767);

    cursor tasks is
    select link
    ,      task_type
    ,      name
    ,      id
    ,      parent_id
    ,      predecessor
    ,      milestone_id
    ,      to_char(actual_start,'YYYY.MM.DD') start_date
    ,      to_char(actual_end,'YYYY.MM.DD')   end_date
    ,      progress
    from
    ( select null             link
    ,        'T'              task_type
    ,        todo_name        name
    ,        todo_id          id
    ,        feature_id       parent_id
    ,        parent_todo_id   predecessor
    ,        milestone_id     milestone_id
    ,        start_date       actual_start
    ,        due_date         actual_end
    ,        todo_status      progress
    from     apex_team_todos
    union
    select  null              link
    ,       'F'               task_type
    ,        feature_name     name
    ,        feature_id       id
    ,        parent_feature_id parent_id
    ,        null             predecessor
    ,        null             milestone_id
    ,        null             actual_start
    ,        null             actual_end
    ,        feature_status   progress
    from     apex_team_features
    union
    select  null              link
    ,        'M'              task_type
    ,        milestone        name
    ,        milestone_id     id
    ,        null             parent_id
    ,        null             predecessor
```

```
   ,         null              milestone_id
   ,         milestone_date    actual_start
   ,         null              actual_end
   ,         null              progress
  from apex_team_milestones
  order by 5
  )
  start with parent_id is null
  connect by prior id = parent_id
  ;
begin

  -- Project Chart Opening Tag
  -- Define "auto_summary" so Anycharts does the calculations
  l_chart_data_xml := '<project_chart>'||
                      '<auto_summary enabled="True" />'
                      ;

  -- Task & Connectors Opening Tags
  l_task_xml := '<tasks>';
  l_connector_xml := '<connectors>';

  -- Loop through series data
  for c1 in tasks
  loop
    if c1.task_type ='T' -- ToDo
    then
      -- Task Tag
      l_task_xml  := l_task_xml            ||
                     '<task id="'   ||c1.id          ||'" '||
                     'name="'       ||c1.name        ||'" '||
                     'parent="'     ||c1.parent_id   ||'" '||
                     'actual_start="'||c1.start_date ||'" '||
                     'actual_end="' ||c1.end_date    ||'" '||
                     'progress="'   ||c1.progress    ||'" '||
                     'style="Gantt" />'
                     ;
      l_connector_xml := l_connector_xml        ||
                     '<connector '              ||
                     'type="FinishStart" '      ||
                     'from="'||c1.predecessor ||'" '||
                     'to="'  ||c1.id           ||'" '||
                     ' />'
                     ;
      if c1.milestone_id is not null
      then
```

```
        l_connector_xml := l_connector_xml            ||
                        '<connector '                 ||
                        'type="FinishStart" '         ||
                        'from="'||c1.id               ||'" '||
                        'to="'  ||c1.milestone_id||'" '||
                        ' />'
                        ;
      end if;
   elsif c1.task_type = 'F' -- Feature
   then -- Start / End / Progress are auto-calculated
     l_task_xml   := l_task_xml                ||
                     '<task id="'        ||c1.id          ||'" '||
                     'name="'            ||c1.name        ||'" '||
                     'parent="'          ||c1.parent_id   ||'" '||
                     '/>'
                     ;

   elsif c1.task_type = 'M' -- Milestone
   then -- A Milestone has no End date
     l_task_xml   := l_task_xml                ||
                     '<task id="'        ||c1.id          ||'" '||
                     'name="'            ||c1.name        ||'" '||
                     'actual_start="'||c1.start_date||'" '||
                     '/>'
                     ;
   end it;
  end loop;

  -- Task Closing Tag
  l_task_xml := l_task_xml||'</tasks>';

  -- Periods Closing Tag
  l_connector_xml := l_connector_xml||'</connectors>';

  -- Project Chart Closing Tag
  l_chart_data_xml := l_chart_data_xml ||
                      l_task_xml         ||
                      l_connector_xml   ||
                      '</project_chart>';

  return l_chart_data_xml;
end;
```

If you run the page, you'll get a representation of your Team Development data in a Gantt chart. See Figure 5-17 for an example.

APEX Extended Project Gantt

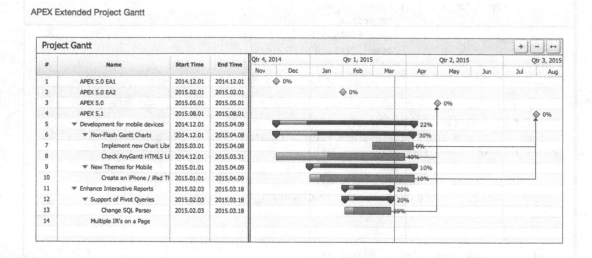

Figure 5-17. *Gantt chart with milestones, features, and to-do items*

Bugs

Bugs cover a functionality we are all familiar with. Bugs are deficiencies in the products we deliver, such as software or documentation. The model for bug tracking is built using a similar data structure as the other pieces of Team Development. Figure 5-18 shows the model. You'll see a few real tables, a few views with fixed values, and some dynamic lists of values.

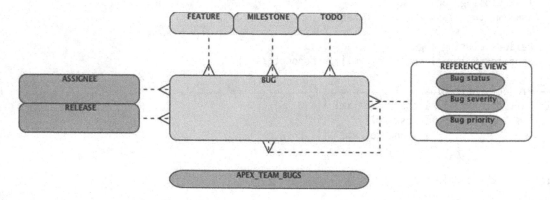

Figure 5-18. *Data model of bugs*

All information regarding to-do items is exposed through the APEX_TEAM_BUGS view, which is mainly based on the WWV_FLOW_BUGS table.

A bug has a status, a severity, and a priority. The values in these select lists are defined in the views WWV_FLOW_BUG_STATUS_CODES, WWV_FLOW_BUG_SEVERITY, and WWV_FLOW_BUG_PRIORITY. When resolving a bug, it's assigned to a person and planned to be fixed by some release, milestone, and/or date. Furthermore, you can add a lot more information on the bug itself, like the platform, browser, or operating system. Figure 5-19 shows an example of a filed bug.

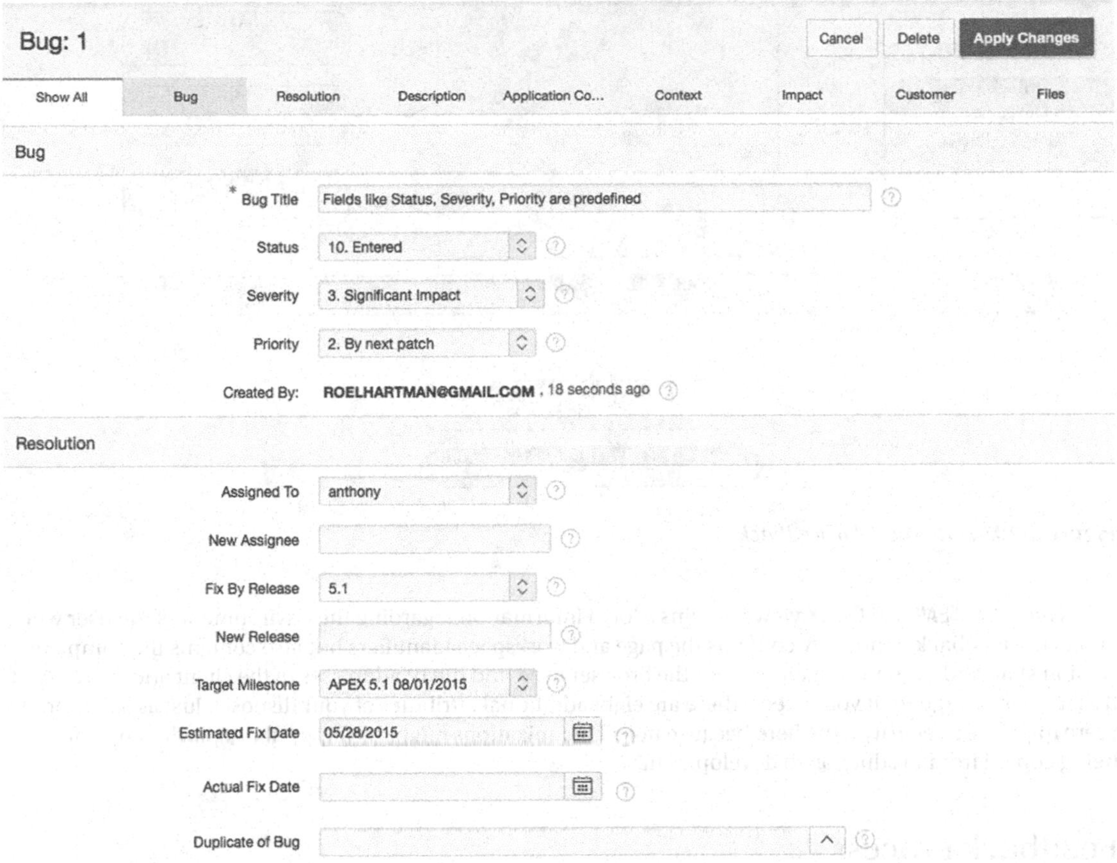

Figure 5-19. Example of a bug

Because a bug contains only a fix date—and no start date or effort—you have to link a bug to a to-do item in order to use a reported bug in your customized Gantt chart. The Bug section is intended for capturing issues that might be customer browser- or operating system–specific.

Feedback

Of all functionality in the Team Development application, feedback is without any doubt the most valuable. Feedback offers you a simple mechanism to communicate with your end users, fellow developers, and business analysts. And feedback can be installed in your application with just a few mouse clicks. Be careful, though: If your application has hundreds or thousands of users, you might want to reduce the number of people who are allowed to enter feedback. Otherwise, you might find yourself buried under hundreds of trivial feedback entries. All information regarding feedback is exposed through the APEX_TEAM_FEEDBACK view, which is mainly based on the WWV_FLOW_FEEDBACK table. Figure 5-20 shows the data model with all tables and views related to the feedback functionality.

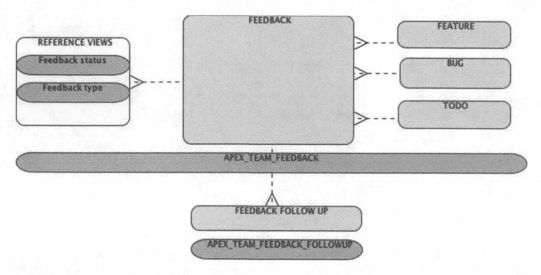

Figure 5-20. *Data model of feedback*

The APEX_TEAM_FEEDBACK view contains a lot of information regarding the environment of the user who enters the feedback. It not only contains the page and workspace identifiers but also contains the complete session state and even information about the browser used and the IP addresses of the client and server. And if that's not enough to fit your needs, there are eight additional attributes at your disposal. Just as a side note, there might be a security issue here because not all organizations might be happy about production data being copied from production to development.

Feedback Process

The feedback process as implemented in Team Development consists of a couple of steps that form a cycle together. The first step is creating a feedback entry by a user. Then the feedback is exported from the environment the user is working in and imported into the development environment. The business analyst or developer analyzes the feedback and responds to it. He can also log the feedback entry as a bug, a to-do item, or even a feature. The responses, which may contain questions for clarification, are exported from the development environment and imported into the user's environment. Then the user can follow up on the developer's question. That information can be exported again, and the cycle can go round and round, as Figure 5-21 indicates.

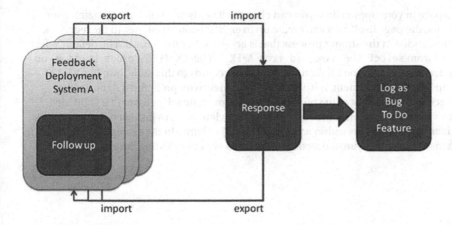

Figure 5-21. *Feedback process flow*

Within one development environment you can manage feedback from multiple sources—for instance, from a test and production environment or even multiple production environments running at different customer sites.

Enable Feedback

In your application, add a page of type Feedback Page. When you keep the default settings, the Feedback page itself is created, an entry is added to the navigation bar, and feedback is enabled. When you or the users of your application click the link in the navigation bar, a page pops up like in Figure 5-22.

Figure 5-22. *Feedback pop-up page*

Because this is just a page in your application, you can change all fields and behavior to match your requirements. When creating the page itself, you can create up to eight custom attributes to the feedback page. These attributes are included in the submit process that is generated by the wizard. The default select list feedback type is created from `select the_name, id from APEX_FEEDBACK_TYPES order by id`. If you needed more or different feedback types, you might think of adding records to this table, but, like a lot of these kinds of select lists in Team Development, it isn't a table but a view with predefined data. So, that wouldn't work. Also, replacing the select list with your own dynamic or static select list isn't a good idea because pages in Team Development rely on values that exist in that view. So, let's just keep that one as it is.

But you can add an item, as long as it fits within a `varchar2(4000)` column. In the example in Figure 5-23, I added two additional items to help qualifying the feedback when it comes in by letting the end user enter a severity and a priority.

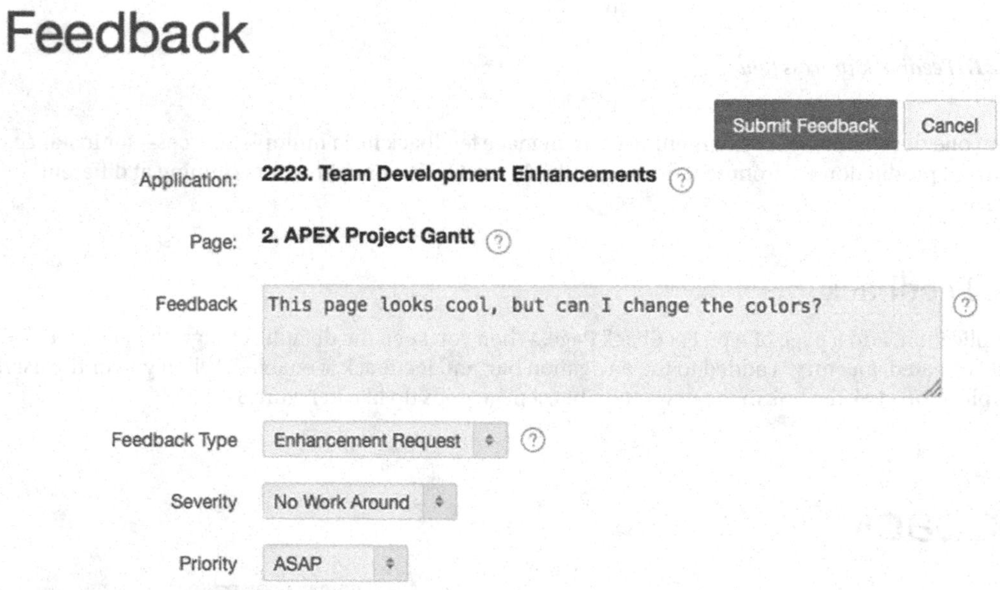

Feedback

	Submit Feedback	Cancel

Application:	**2223. Team Development Enhancements** ⑦
Page:	**2. APEX Project Gantt** ⑦
Feedback	This page looks cool, but can I change the colors? ⑦
Feedback Type	Enhancement Request ⑦
Severity	No Work Around
Priority	ASAP

Figure 5-23. *Customized feedback pop-up page*

If you've defined your own feedback items, you have to change the standard submit feedback page process a little. Here's an example:

```
apex_util.submit_feedback (
    p_comment         => :P102_FEEDBACK,
    p_type            => :P102_FEEDBACK_TYPE,
    p_application_id  => :P102_APPLICATION_ID,
    p_page_id         => :P102_PAGE_ID,
    p_email           => :P102_EMAIL,
    p_attribute_01    => :P102_SEVERITY,
    p_label_01        => 'Severity',
    p_attribute_02    => :P102_PRIORITY,
    p_label_02        => 'Priority');
```

You have to use your own items as values for the parameter p_attribute_01, and so on, and for easier interpretation of the values, it is a good idea to provide the parameter p_label_01 with a value that tells what attribute_01 actually is. These values show up in the Additional Attributes region of the feedback.

One of the other parameters is the user's e-mail address. This is automatically filled with the e-mail address of the user—but only if you use the APEX authentication. If you use another type of authentication, you should place your own function here to extract the e-mail address from the username. Or, if you use public pages with no authentication at all, you should add an e-mail address item on your feedback page.

Exporting Feedback to Development

If you develop your applications in the same workspace as your users are using, there is no need to export and import the feedback. But that's an unusual case. Mostly you develop in a development instance and your users are testing in a test environment—perhaps even more than one—and running production in another environment.

Exporting feedback starts from the Workspace Utilities main page. When you click the Export link there, you get a number of objects you can export. Just click the last one on the left, called Team Development Feedback (see Figure 5-24), or click the Feedback tab on the far right.

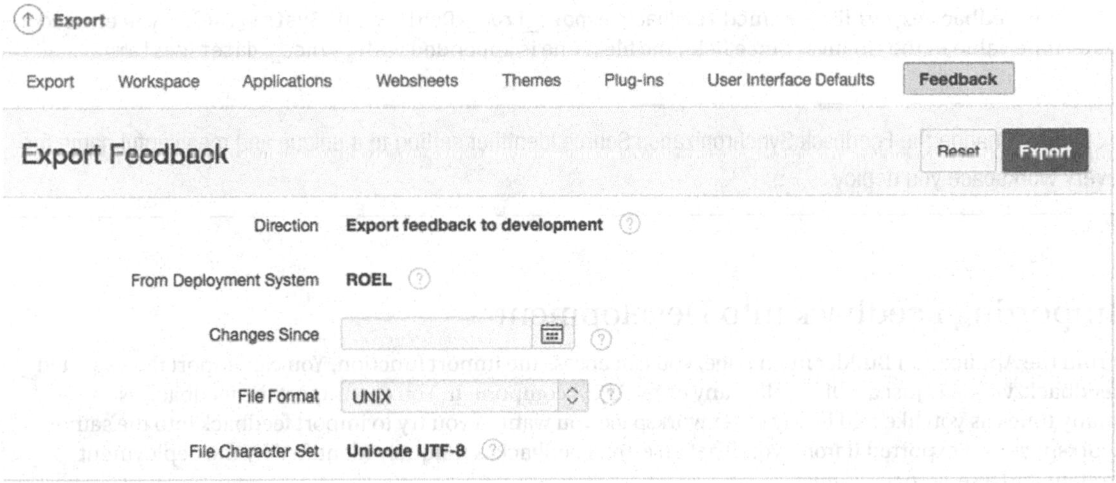

Figure 5-24. *Exporting feedback to development*

All feedback entered after the date you enter in the Changes Since field will be exported. Usually you'll set that to the date you last exported the feedback. Leave it empty for all feedback.

■ **Note** You can export feedback only for the whole workspace, which is to say for all applications that are contained within the workspace.

One other setting is Deployment System. This setting is used to distinguish feedback from one workspace and another. That's especially important if you have deployed your application in more than one workspace, like test and production, or in production at multiple customer sites. This way you can see where feedback originates from and where the responses on the feedback should be sent to. To make this distinction, you have to be sure that this value is different for each implementation. You can set this value in the APEX Administration utility, via Edit Workspace Information, as shown in Figure 5-25. There it is called Feedback Synchronization Source Identifier, and it's defaulted to the workspace name.

Edit Workspace Information

Workspace Identifier:	**1690400486946418** ⑦
Workspace Status:	**Assigned** ⑦
* Workspace Name	DEMO ⑦
First Schema Provisioned	**DEMO** ⑦
Feedback Synchronization Source Identifier	DEMO ⑦

Figure 5-25. *Changing Feedback Synchronization Source Identifier*

The feedback export file is named `feedback_export_from_<Deployment System>.sql`. If you entered a date/time value in the Changes Since field, the file name is appended with `_since_<datetimestamp>`.

■ **Note**   Change the Feedback Synchronization Source Identifier setting to a unique and meaningful name for every workspace you deploy.

Importing Feedback into Development

From the Application Builder main page, you can access the import function. You can import the exported feedback, which is just a SQL file, like any other APEX component. You can import the feedback as many times as you like and in any other workspace you want. If you try to import feedback into the same workspace you exported it from, you'll get an error. Feedback is uniquely identified by the deployment system and a sequence number.

Team Development Integration in the Page Designer

One of the really neat features of APEX 5 is a closer integration between Team Development and the Page Designer. This is because when you are working on a page, it would be nice if you could easily spot whether there are bugs or feedback entries reported on that page. In APEX 5, you are notified that there might be more to do on your page than you might think. The upper-right corner of the Team Development icon has a badge indicating the number of Team Development entries that are still open. You can open the drop-down and directly navigate to that relevant bug or feedback entry. See Figure 5-26 for an example.

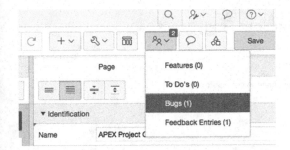

Figure 5-26. *Team Development notification in the Page Designer*

Processing Feedback

Once you've imported feedback, you can start processing it. Figure 5-27 shows the screen from which you begin doing that.

Figure 5-27. *Process feedback*

When you click the Log as Bug button on the page in Figure 5-27, the feedback is converted into a bug. During that conversion step you can change the title and add some additional information. Automatically some context is filled in, such as the application and the page affected by the bug. Figure 5-28 shows the resulting bug report.

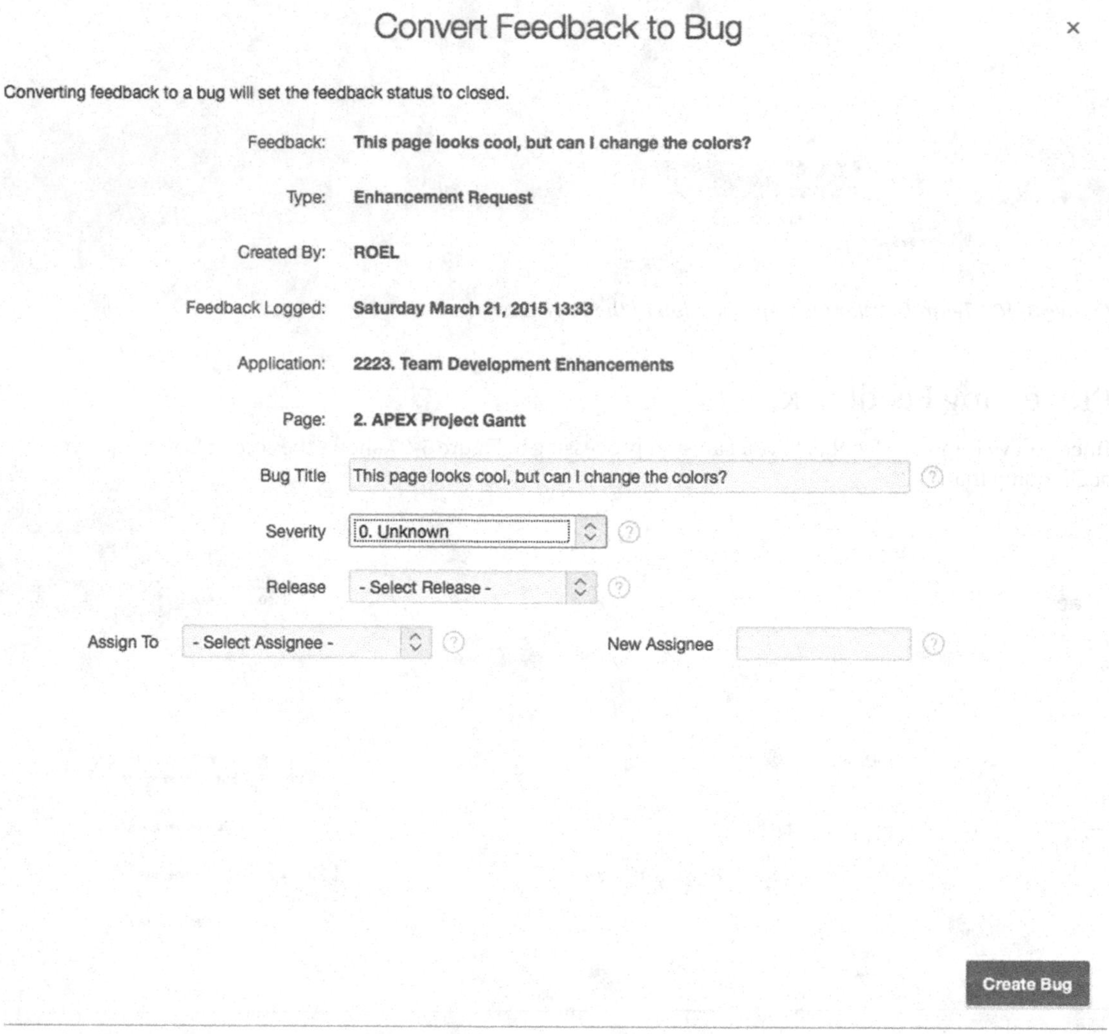

Convert Feedback to Bug   ×

Converting feedback to a bug will set the feedback status to closed.

Feedback:	**This page looks cool, but can I change the colors?**
Type:	**Enhancement Request**
Created By:	**ROEL**
Feedback Logged:	**Saturday March 21, 2015 13:33**
Application:	**2223. Team Development Enhancements**
Page:	**2. APEX Project Gantt**

Bug Title   `This page looks cool, but can I change the colors?` ⑦

Severity   `0. Unknown` ⑤ ⑦

Release   `- Select Release -` ⑤ ⑦

Assign To   `- Select Assignee -` ⑤ ⑦   New Assignee `           ` ⑦

Create Bug

Figure 5-28. *Bug report created from feedback*

Strangely, other information that is captured by using feedback isn't automatically added to the bug, such as the platform, browser, and operating system. And even more interesting stuff, such as the complete session state, is captured but not copied to the bug description. There is also no visible reference from the bug to the feedback to retrieve that information afterward.

Similar to creating a bug from a feedback entry, you can also create a to-do item from a feedback entry and even transform a feedback entry into a feature. Remarkably, only when transforming a feedback entry into a to-do item is there an option to delete the feedback entry. But deleting feedback before the issue is completely solved isn't a good idea because of all the information that's contained within the feedback that might be relevant for sorting out the issue.

Notice that Figure 5-28 mentions "Converting feedback to a bug will set the feedback status to closed." So, that saves you one step while processing your feedback items. Instead of—or in addition to—logging the feedback as a bug or a to-do item, you can also edit the feedback. Doing so, you can change the status and add comments. See the example in Figure 5-29.

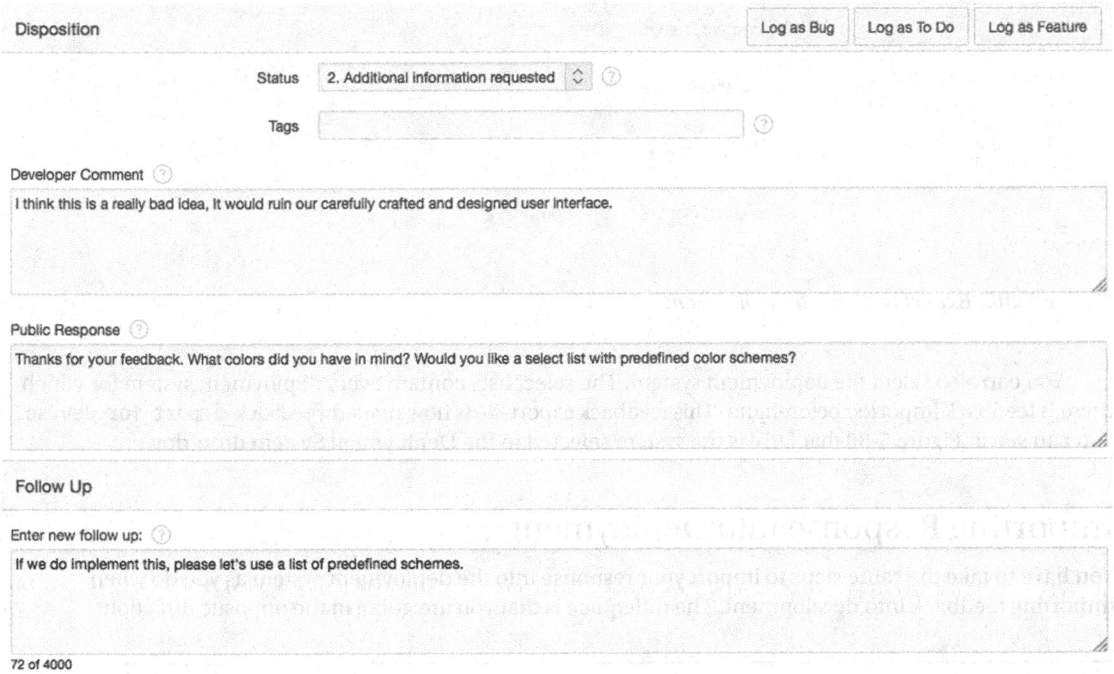

Figure 5-29. *Comment on feedback*

The next challenge is to get those comments back to the originating system. After all, it doesn't do much good to comment on feedback if the person originating that feedback never gets to see the comment. The next section shows how to meet this challenge.

Exporting Response to Deployment

For exporting your response back to deployment, you have to take the same steps as when exporting feedback from deployment into development. Notice the Direction setting in Figure 5-30 when exporting the feedback. It says "Export response to deployment" now.

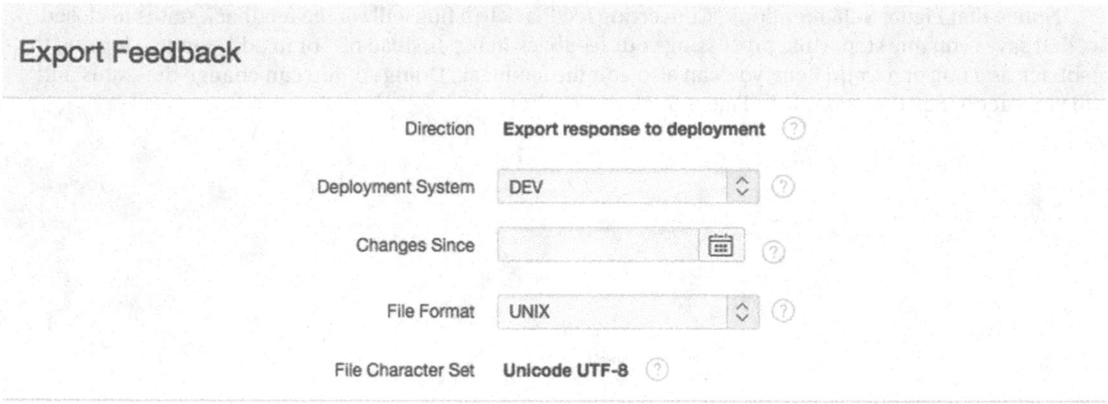

Export Feedback

Direction	**Export response to deployment** ⑦
Deployment System	DEV ◊ ⑦
Changes Since	📅 ⑦
File Format	UNIX ◊ ⑦
File Character Set	**Unicode UTF-8** ⑦

***Figure 5-30.** Export response to deployment*

You can also select the deployment system. The select lists contain every deployment system for which there is feedback imported beforehand. This feedback export file is now named `feedback_import_for_dev.sql`. You can see in Figure 5-30 that DEV is the system selected in the Deployment System drop-down.

Importing Response into Deployment

You have to take the same steps to import your response into the deployment system as you do when importing feedback into development. The difference is that you are going in the opposite direction.

■ **Note**   If you try to import a response into an environment it wasn't exported for, you'll get an error.

After importing, you will see that the changes you made in development are reflected in the feedback of the deployment system, as shown in Figure 5-31. And although the Developer comments you entered are exported, they are not imported.

Follow Up

Enter new follow up: ⑦

✎	Some SQL Tuning needed here. Tracing proves it is slow.	4 minutes ago	roel
✎	We could buy a faster machine.	47 hours ago	roel

***Figure 5-31.** Importing response into deployment*

Once you've imported the response, you have reached the end of the feedback life cycle. But sometimes you need some additional information to solve an issue, as in the previous example. Of course, you can call or e-mail the person who submitted the feedback, but there is an option within Team Development that supports this functionality as well. Unfortunately, it is not automatically implemented, but you can implement it yourself with some additional easy steps.

Extending Feedback: Creating a Report

The first thing to do is to create a report on the feedback, so the user not only can report feedback but also has insight on the status. To begin, create a report page, with page number 103 in this example, and make it accessible according to your standard application navigation style; it can be an entry in a list, a tab, or a link in the navigation bar. The following select statement selects the data from the apex_team_feedback view and should show only the feedback for the current application. You can also choose to narrow the selection down, so users can only see the feedback they entered themselves or feedback with a certain status. That's all up to you. If you use the wizard to create this report, you have to set Link to Single Row View to No in order to prevent an error from being raised.

```
SELECT feedback_number "Nr."
,       feedback_id     "Follow up"
,       feedback
,       CASE
        WHEN feedback_type = 1 THEN 'General Comment'
        WHEN feedback_type = 2 THEN 'Enhancement Requested'
        WHEN feedback_type = 3 THEN 'Bug'
        END             "Type"
,       CASE
        WHEN feedback_status = 0 THEN 'No Status'
        WHEN feedback_status = 1 THEN 'Acknowledged'
        WHEN feedback_status = 2 THEN 'Additional Info. Requested'
        WHEN feedback_status = 3 THEN 'Open'
        WHEN feedback_status = 4 THEN 'Closed'
        END             "Status"
,       page_name       "Page"
,       public_response "Response"
FROM    apex_team_feedback
WHERE   application_id = :APP_ID
ORDER BY updated_on DESC
```

Figure 5-32 shows what the report page you're trying to achieve will look like.

Nr.	Feedback	Type	Status	Page	Response	Follow Up
3	This page loads a little slow. Can you do something about that?	Bug	-	APEX Extended Project Gantt	-	✎
1	This page looks cool, but can I change the colors?	Enhancement Requested	Additional Info. Requested	APEX Project Gantt	Thanks for your feedback. What colors did you have in mind? Would you like a select list with predefined color schemes?	✎

1 - 2

Figure 5-32. *Feedback response report*

To get that result, you have to make some minor changes. First, the column Follow Up in Figure 5-32 is used as a link column. Set the link text to the image of your liking and set the URL target to `javascript:FollowUp( '#Follow up#')`;. The JavaScript function is defined in the Function and Global Variable Declaration section of the page as follows:

```
function FollowUp( pId ){
  $s('P103_FEEDBACK_ID', pId);
  $('#FollowUp').show();
}
```

Within the same page, create a new HTML region named FollowUp with two items: P103_FEEDBACK_ID as Hidden and Value Protected set to No and P103_FOLLOW_UP as a text area. Set the static ID of the region to FollowUp, and set Region Custom Attributes to `style="display:none; width:540px"`. So, the region will be hidden by default and shown when a user clicks the little edit image in the report. Also, create a Region Button there to submit the page.

Next, create an On Submit Page Process to save the follow-up on the feedback using the `apex_util.submit_feedback_followup` procedure, as shown in Figure 5-33.

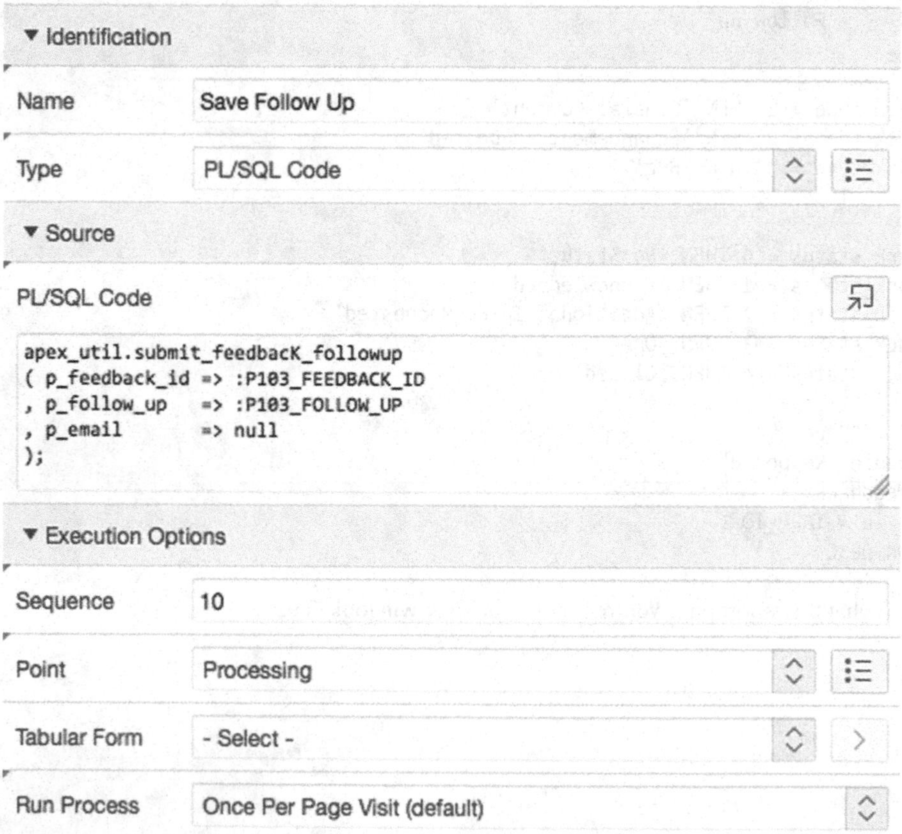

▼ Identification	
Name	Save Follow Up
Type	PL/SQL Code

▼ Source	
PL/SQL Code	

```
apex_util.submit_feedbacK_followup
( p_feedback_id => :P103_FEEDBACK_ID
, p_follow_up   => :P103_FOLLOW_UP
, p_email       => null
);
```

▼ Execution Options	
Sequence	10
Point	Processing
Tabular Form	- Select -
Run Process	Once Per Page Visit (default)

Figure 5-33. *Saving the follow-up process*

You can also show the follow-up on that page using the apex_util.get_feedback_follow_up function or querying the apex_team_feedback_followup view. Once the follow-up is entered by the end user, that information can be transferred back to the development system.

Extending Feedback: Feeding Back the Follow-Up

You execute the same steps to get follow-up back into the development system as you did to get the feedback from deployment to development. You export and import the feedback, and the follow-up is exported and imported as well.

■ **Note**   The Changes Since setting when exporting feedback applies only to the feedback itself and not to the follow-up. So, when using this setting, follow-up is exported only if the feedback is changed after the entered date. Exporting all feedback may be more appropriate.

Further Enhancements

Instead of waiting for the feedback to arrive in your development environment, you can also opt for sending the entered feedback by e-mail. This may be only for the more serious entries, but that's up to you. And of course that will work only if there is a mail server configured for sending e-mail from APEX.

Another enhancement you might think of is sending feedback automatically by e-mail on a regular basis. Obviously, you also need a mail server configured for this. You can create a procedure like the one listed next and use the apex_plsql_job.submit_process function to schedule the procedure.

```
create or replace procedure send_feedback
        ( p_workspace apex_workspaces.workspace%type
        , p_send_to   varchar2
        )
is
  l_mail_id      number;
  l_clob         clob;
  l_blob         blob;
  l_mail_blob    blob;
  l_dest_offset  number  := 1;
  l_src_offset   number  := 1;
  l_amount       integer := dbms_lob.lobmaxsize;
  l_blob_csid    number  := dbms_lob.default_csid;
  l_lang_ctx     integer := dbms_lob.default_lang_ctx;
  l_warning      integer;
  -- The name of the Workspace you want to export the Feedback from
  l_workspace_id apex_workspaces.workspace_id%type;
  -- Search string for removing all "trash". Real SQL starts from there
  l_search       varchar2(255) := 'set define off';
begin
  -- Get the ID of the Workspace and set the environment
  l_workspace_id := apex_util.find_security_group_id ( p_workspace );
  wwv_flow_api.set_security_group_id( l_workspace_id );
  -- Create the mail object
```

```
    l_mail_id    := apex_mail.send
                     ( p_to     => p_send_to
                     , p_from   => 'apex@oracle.com'
                     , p_subj   => 'Feedback Export from Deployment to Development'
                     , p_body   => 'See the attachment.'
                     );
    -- Create the CLOB
    -- Export the Feedback to Development for the Workspace provided
    l_clob :=
       wwv_flow_utilities.export_feedback_to_development ( l_workspace_id );
    -- Convert to BLOB
    dbms_lob.createtemporary ( lob_loc => l_blob
                             , cache   => true
                             );
    dbms_lob.converttoblob ( l_blob
                           , l_clob
                           , l_amount
                           , l_dest_offset
                           , l_src_offset
                           , l_blob_csid
                           , l_lang_ctx
                           , l_warning
                           );
    -- Remove all "trash", so only real SQL is left over
    dbms_lob.createtemporary ( lob_loc => l_mail_blob
                             , cache   => true
                             );
    dbms_lob.copy(  l_mail_blob
                 , l_blob
                 , dbms_lob.lobmaxsize
                 , 1
                 , dbms_lob.instr( lob_loc => l_blob
                                 , pattern => utl_raw.cast_to_raw(l_search)
                                 )
                 );
    -- Add the file as a BLOB attachment to the mail
    apex_mail.add_attachment
         ( p_mail_id    => l_mail_id
         , p_attachment => l_mail_blob
         , p_filename   => 'feedback_export_from_'||lower(p_workspace)||'.sql'
         , p_mime_type  => 'application/text'
         );
    commit;
end;
```

Summary

Now that you know about the functionality of Team Development, it may become clear that the planning capacity of Team Development doesn't beat a "real" project management tool, like Microsoft Project. Even if you add some nice Gantt charts, which are an absolute necessity for any planning tool, Team Development still lacks too much functionality. Here are a few things you can't do with Team Development:

- Add a capacity to a resource (like 40 hours per week)

- Plan using the given capacity

- Add a cost to a resource so you can plan how much money you have to spend

- Monitor how many hours a resource spends, using an interface with a time reporting application

- Add multiple predecessors to to-do items so you can plan and execute the actions in the right order and determine the critical path

Of course, you can build all this in your custom Team Development Enhancement application, but capacity planning and critical path determination are complex mathematical issues and not easy to solve. Still, for small projects (up to five people or so), Team Development might be a convenient—and inexpensive—tool to use. But when a project starts getting more complex, you have to spend some money and buy a specialized tool to support your business.

That said, the feedback feature of Team Development is in itself so powerful—especially when you add functionality like that shown in the examples—that for feedback alone you should consider using Team Development. When you're in the test phase of your project in particular, feedback will facilitate communication between users and developers. Your application can only benefit from that.

CHAPTER 6

■ ■ ■

Globalization

by Francis Mignault

As of its first release, APEX has supported globalized applications. Since, by definition, a web application can be accessed from anywhere, globalization is an important feature to consider. APEX and the Oracle Database provide the functionality to help you build applications that can display data based on the location of the end user.

In this chapter, I will cover two major aspects of globalization: translation and localization. *Translation* allows you to run applications in multiple languages without having to duplicate the logic. *Localization* is used to format and display the content in the application based on where the end user is located. Even if your applications are internal or intranet applications and do not need to be translated, the globalization parameters may still be useful for date and number formatting.

The first part of this chapter will be about translations. It will show you how to install the builder in different languages and how to translate an application, along with the configuration required to do so. Translation also covers how to implement the mechanism to switch from one language to another while executing an application. The second part of the chapter will cover localization, including time zones and date formats.

As you probably know by now, APEX is built with PL/SQL and runs directly in the database, allowing for the use of all language specifics available in the Oracle Database. For example, you could change the time zone or NLS_SORT using either an alter session or, in certain cases, built-in APEX utilities. Using the Oracle language capabilities allows you to build applications in 132 supported languages while the APEX builder is available in these 10 languages: English, German, Spanish, French, Italian, Japanese, Korean, Brazilian Portuguese, Simplified Chinese, and Traditional Chinese.

Using the Builder in Other Languages

When APEX is first installed, English is the default language. To be able to use the builder in other languages, you must install them. Note that uploading new languages for the builder will also translate action menus and error messages in interactive reports that will be used by the translated applications.

You can find the scripts required to load any of the nine other languages available for the builder in the APEX ZIP file within the builder folder, as shown in Figure 6-1. This directory contains one subdirectory for each of the available languages.

Figure 6-1. *Language directories of the APEX ZIP file*

■ **Note**   APEX is available in two different downloads, English Only and All Languages.

Within each directory, a language-loading script is identified by the language code (for example, `load_de.sql` or `load_ja.sql`).

To load the language, you must first set the `NLS_LANG` environment variable at the operating system level. Check the documentation for the proper command for your operating system (in this example I am running on Windows). Note that this setting is always the same for every language being loaded.

```
set NLS_LANG=AMERICAN_AMERICA.AL32UTF8
```

Then, run the appropriate `load_lang.sql` script in sqlplus using `sqlplus / as sysdba`, where `lang` is the specific language (for example, `load_de.sql` for German or `load_ja.sql` for Japanese).

```
ALTER SESSION SET CURRENT_SCHEMA = APEX_050000;
@load_lang.sql
```

Note that you will have to load the other languages every time you upgrade APEX.

You can remove a language by running the corresponding `unload_lang.sql` script.

Once the language is loaded, you can find the option to use this language at the bottom of the login region on the APEX login page, as shown in Figure 6-2.

Figure 6-2. *Available and loaded languages for the builder*

The option to change the language of the builder is also available at the bottom left of the APEX builder home page, as Figure 6-3 shows.

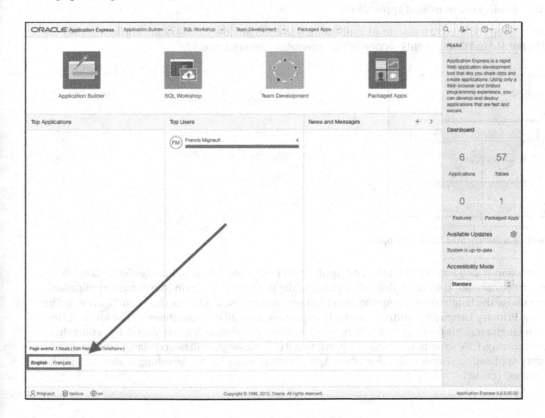

Figure 6-3. *Loaded languages for the builder and internal text*

There is a report available in the Administrative APEX workspace (internal) that shows which languages have been loaded for the builder. To view this report, log in as the administrator of the internal workspace and select the option Installed Translations under Manage Instance.

Translating Applications

Some systems are required to be bilingual or even multilingual, depending on where and how they are used. Applications are becoming more commonly available on the Internet, and users may prefer to access them in their own language. For example, Google, Hotmail, and even the iPhone are multilingual because the business market is literally worldwide.

The translation process has two parts: first the configuration of the parameters and then the application translation itself. Applications have to be translated and published every time changes are made to the primary application so that they can be applied to all the languages.

The following paragraphs will explain the different steps for translating your application. In short, they are as follows:

1. Configure the globalization attributes.

2. Map your primary application ID with the translated applications' IDs.

3. Seed the translated text to the APEX translation repository.

4. Translate your application.

5. Publish the translated applications.

The first step required to translate an application is to configure the globalization attributes. They are defined in the Shared Components section of the application (see Figure 6-4).

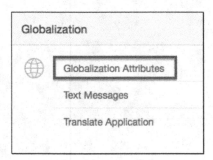

Figure 6-4. *Globalization Attributes option*

This section is also accessible via the Edit Application Properties dialog and the Globalization tab.

The first parameter to set is the default language of the primary application (the current application). To do so, choose the language in the Application Primary Language select list, as shown in Figure 6-5. The Application Primary Language setting is extremely important since all functionalities will be localized in the chosen language. This parameter should be set even when translation is not required. By setting this parameter, sorting, CSV exports, interactive reports, and APEX messages will be translated and localized for the primary application. The default value of the Application Primary Language setting is always English (United States) (en-us).

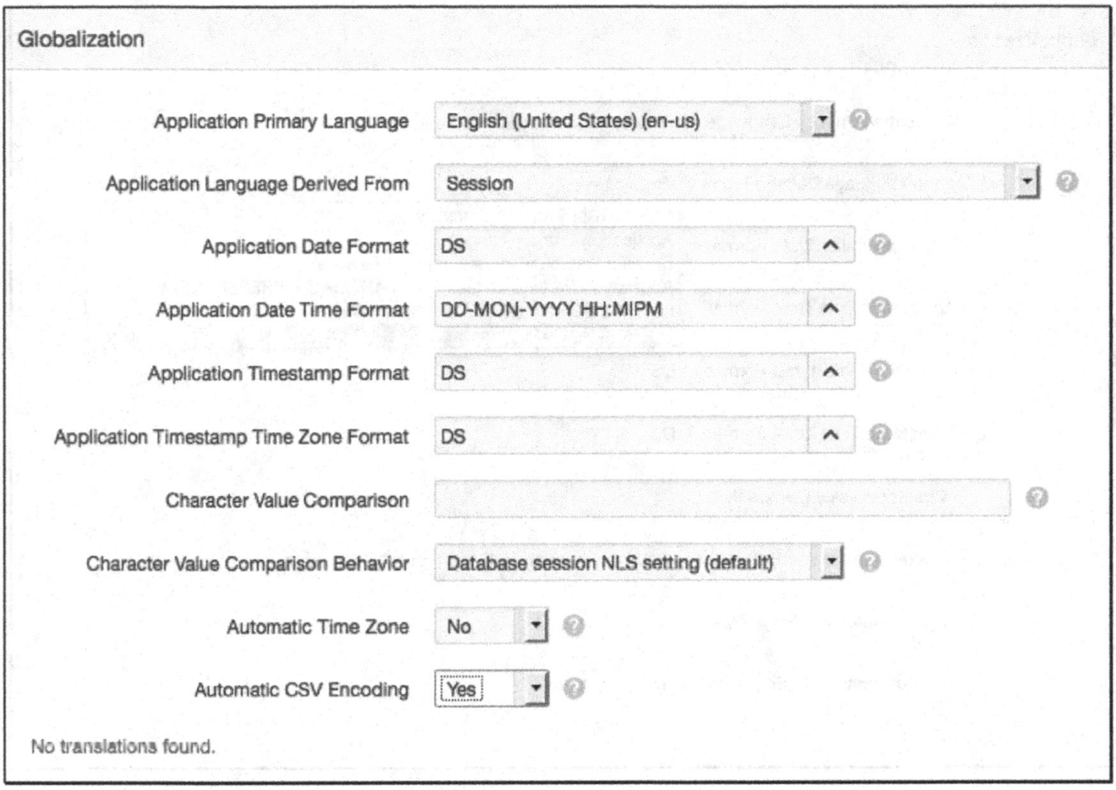

Figure 6-5. *Globalization attributes*

The way APEX supports multilingual applications is by creating a copy of the primary application for each translated version. At runtime, this is transparent to the end user. The developer makes changes to the primary application and then publishes these to the translated versions. This will be explained in more detail later in this chapter.

Application Language Derived From

Once the primary language is defined in the globalization attributes, the Application Language Derived From parameter must be set, as shown in Figure 6-6. This will determine how APEX decides which language will be used at runtime. Using this parameter, APEX will execute the corresponding translated application.

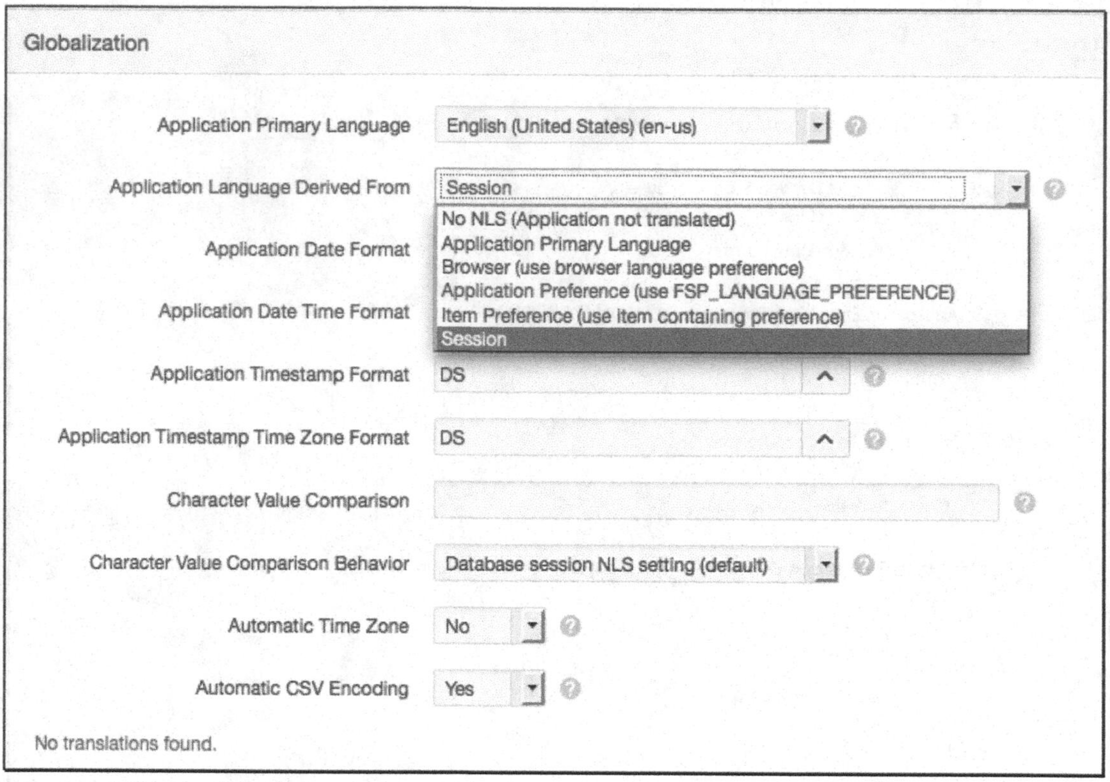

Figure 6-6. *List of choices for Application Language Derived From*

The different options to derive the language from are as follows:

- *NO NLS (Application not translated)*: Choose this if no translations are required for the application.

- *Application Primary Language*: This uses the primary language value as the application language. This is useful for developers to run tests in a specific language. For example, if the primary application is en-us (English US) and a fr-ca (French Canada) application is mapped, you could change the primary language to fr-ca and use an Application Language Derived From setting of Application Primary Language to run the fr-ca application. It is important not to forget to change the primary language back to its original setting once testing is complete. When the primary language is changed, the interactive report menus and the APEX error messages will both be displayed in that language. For this parameter, you can select any of the 132 available languages.

- *Browser (use browser language preference)*: When using this option, APEX will check the browser language and execute the mapped application in the same language code. For example, if the browser is set to fr-ca, APEX will run the translated fr-ca application if it exists. If, let's say, no fr-ca application exists, it will use the primary application language.

- *Application Preference (use FSP_LANGUAGE_PREFERENCE)*: This setting uses an APEX preference to determine which language to use. Preferences are programmatically set using the `APEX_UTIL.SET_PREFERENCE` procedure and are linked to an application user. To check the user preference, you can use the `APEX_UTIL.GET_PREFERENCE` API.

```
APEX_UTIL.GET_PREFERENCE (
p_preference   IN    VARCHAR2 DEFAULT NULL,
p_user         IN    VARCHAR2 DEFAULT V('USER'))
RETURN VARCHAR2;
```

- *Item Preference (use item containing preference)*: This setting can be confusing because of its use of an application item called `FSP_LANGUAGE_PREFERENCE` and *not* a preference. When you use this option, an application item called `FSP_LANGUAGE_PREFERENCE` has to be created in the Shared Components area. Afterward, to set the language of the application, a simple change of the value of `FSP_LANGUAGE_PREFERENCE` is needed. For example, in PL/SQL you could write the following:

```
:FSP_LANGUAGE_PREFERENCE := 'fr-ca' ;
```

- Once the value is changed, in the next page rendering, APEX will check that value and run the corresponding translated application with the corresponding language.

- Deriving the language using this method can sometimes be tricky when accessing a specific page in a specific language via a direct external URL.

- For example, if you wanted to access page 200 in fr-ca with a primary application in en-ca and while setting `FSP_LANGUAGE_PREFERENCE`, the URL would be as follows:

```
http://domain:port/pls/apex/f?p=999:200:::::FSP_LANGUAGE_PREFERENCE:fr-ca
```

- In that case, APEX will start to execute the application ID 999, page 200, in the default primary language en-ca. Then, it will set the application item `FSP_LANGUAGE_PREFERENCE` to fr-ca as defined in the URL.

- The en-ca application, which is the primary language, will be displayed, since the application item is set in the URL and will be processed during the page rendering. The problem here is that even if you want to see the fr-ca as specified in the URL, the first page view will still show the en-ca version. Only subsequent pages will be in fr-ca.

- One way to be able to see the fr-ca version on the first call would be to always go to a page that sets the application item and branches back. In this page, `FSP_LANGUAGE_PREFERENCE` would be set, followed by a redirection to page 200, in this example in order to then display the right application in fr-ca. The language switch will then be transparent to the end user.

- Another option to change the language via the URL is the `P_LANG` parameter. This can also be used to set the language when deriving the language with the `FSP_LANGUAGE_PREFERENCE` item, although this will not change the value of the `FSP_LANGUAGE_PREFERENCE` application item. Using `P_LANG` in the URL will make all subsequent page views in that language.

```
http://.../pls/apex/f?p=999 :1 :0 :::::&p_lang=fr-ca
```

- *Session*: The last option for Application Language Derived From is Session. When this option is selected, APEX will determine the application language from the session setting.

- The session is set by using the API APEX_UTIL.SET_SESSION_LANG or by using the P_LANG parameter in the URL. Here's an example:

  http://.../pls/apex/f?p=999 :1 :0 :::::&p_lang=fr-ca

- To get the session language value, use the API APEX_UTIL.GET_SESSION_LANG or use the variable BROWSER_LANGUAGE. To reset the session language value, use APEX_UTIL.RESET_SESSION_LANG. Those APIs can be used in application processes or in database packages and procedures.

Mapping

Once you have set the globalization attributes, the next step is to map your primary application to the application IDs that will be used by the translated applications.

Translations have to be mapped to an application ID. Those IDs will be used to generate the applications that APEX will run when a specific language is required. To do so, go to Translate Application under Globalization in the Shared Components area of the application, and select the first option: "Map primary language application to translated applications." Click Create. You will get to the application language mapping page, as shown in Figure 6-7.

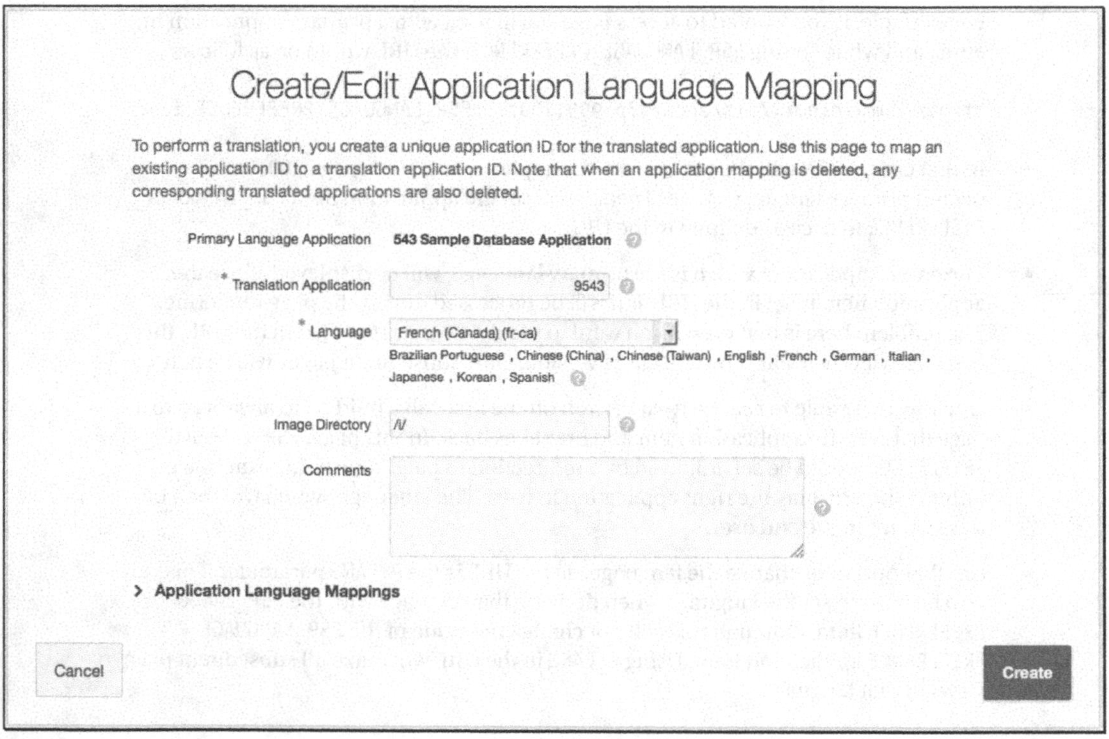

Figure 6-7. Application language mapping configuration

You can change the mapping when you import the primary application with translations. Also, if the application ID that is mapped to the translated application is already in use when you import, APEX will automatically assign another ID.

Enter the corresponding translated application ID. This ID must be available in the APEX installation. The translation will create a copy of the primary application using this translated application ID and assign it to the selected language.

One way of making sure that the translated application IDs are not already in use is to define a development standard and reserve a range of IDs. For example, all the translated applications could use ID 9001 and up. So, the primary application 543 would be mapped to the translated application 9543. This standard also makes it easier to see that two applications are related when exporting and importing them. Also note that translated application IDs cannot end with 0; an error message will be displayed if that is the case.

Once the application ID is defined, you can enter the language and the image logical directory defined in the web server configuration that the translated application will use. Using this option, all the images used by the translated application will have to be in that directory.

You can create as many mappings as required, one for each language that your primary application is going to be translated into.

CSV Encoding

When exporting the data in CSV format, it is important to make sure that the character set of the application running will be used. Setting Automatic CSV Encoding to Yes, as shown in Figure 6-8, will export the data in the character set of the language of the application that is currently running.

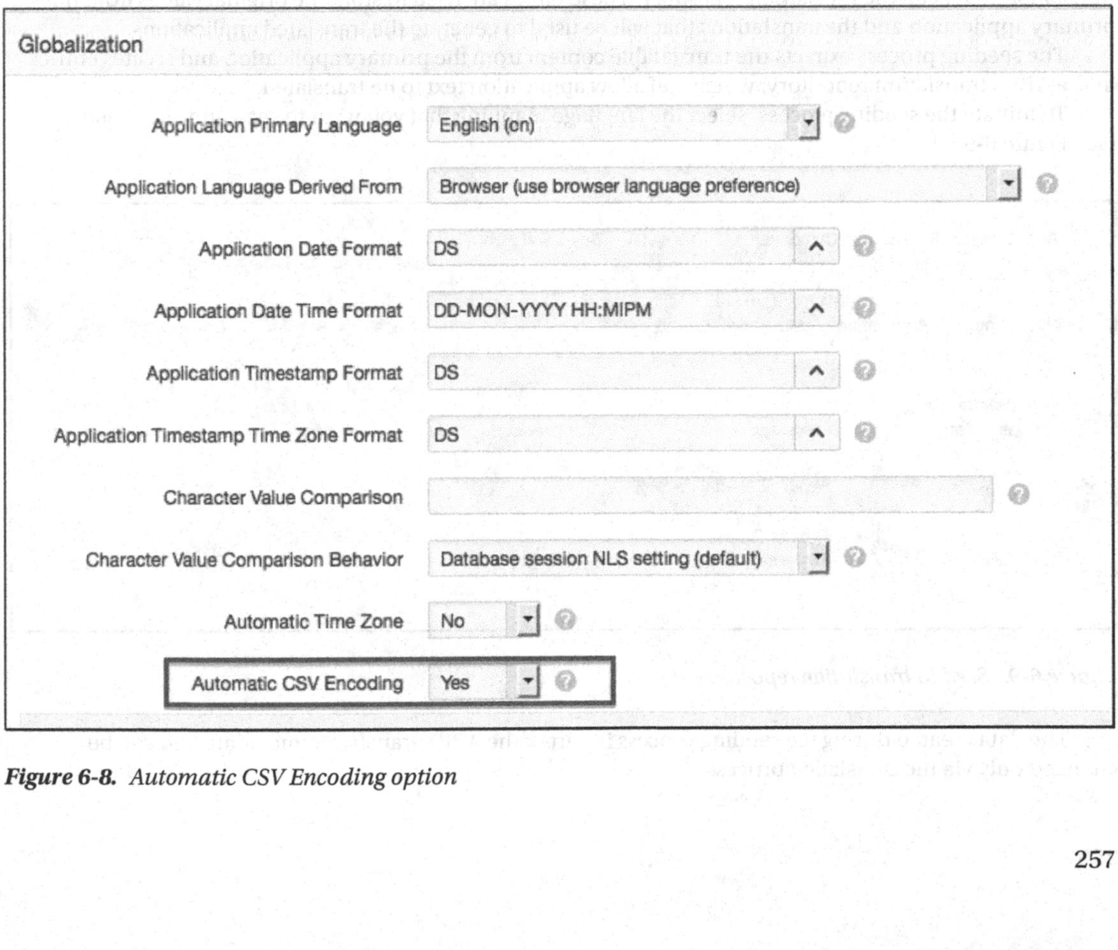

Figure 6-8. *Automatic CSV Encoding option*

To set Automatic CSV Encoding, go to Globalization Attributes in the primary application's Shared Components area.

If Automatic CSV Encoding is not set to Yes when running multilingual applications, Excel exports may not display special characters correctly. If it is enabled, the output will then be properly converted to match the localized applications.

Translating an Application

The translation process consists of the following:

- Seeding the translated application

- Translating text either manually or via an XLIFF file

- Publishing the translated application

This process must be done every time you make changes to the primary application, before they will appear in the translated applications. Translating a primary application creates a new translated application that is exportable/importable but not modifiable.

All the following steps are in the Shared Components area's Translate Application section.

Seed Translatable Text to Translation Repository

The APEX main database schema (APEX_050000 for APEX 5.0) contains a set of tables and views used for translation that I call the *translation repository*. These tables are used to store the original values from the primary application and the translations that will be used to generate the translated applications.

The seeding process extracts the translatable content from the primary application and creates entries in the APEX translation repository, which will allow application text to be translated.

To initiate the seeding process, select the language mapping that you want to seed and click Seed (see Figure 6-9).

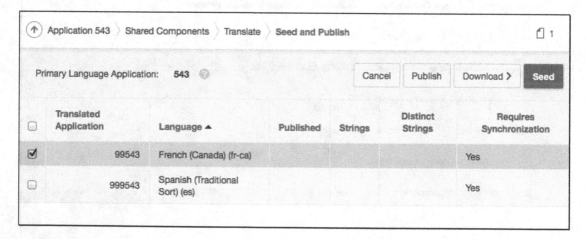

Figure 6-9. *Seed to translation repository*

The data created during the seeding process is part of the APEX translation metadata and can be changed only via the translation process.

To be able to publish the mapped applications, there must be values in the APEX translation repository.

Clicking the option to manually edit the translation repository will show a report containing the rows from the translation repository. The labels, region titles, and other translatable text will be in that report. I will come back to that option later.

Download Translatable Text from Repository to Translation File (XLIFF File)

This step extracts the data from the translation repository and creates an XML Localization Interchange File Format (XLIFF) file that you can save locally on your disk. This format is an official XML format for translations.

To download the XLIFF file on your client locally, select the language to extract and click the Export XLIFF File for Application option (see Figure 6-10). If desired, you can export only the elements requiring translation. This will extract only the text that is new in the translation repository or has been updated in the primary application but not translated in the repository. To be able to translate the text, the Include XLIFF Target Elements check box must be selected since it will be those values that will be updating the repository. It is also possible to download the XLIFF file for a specific page.

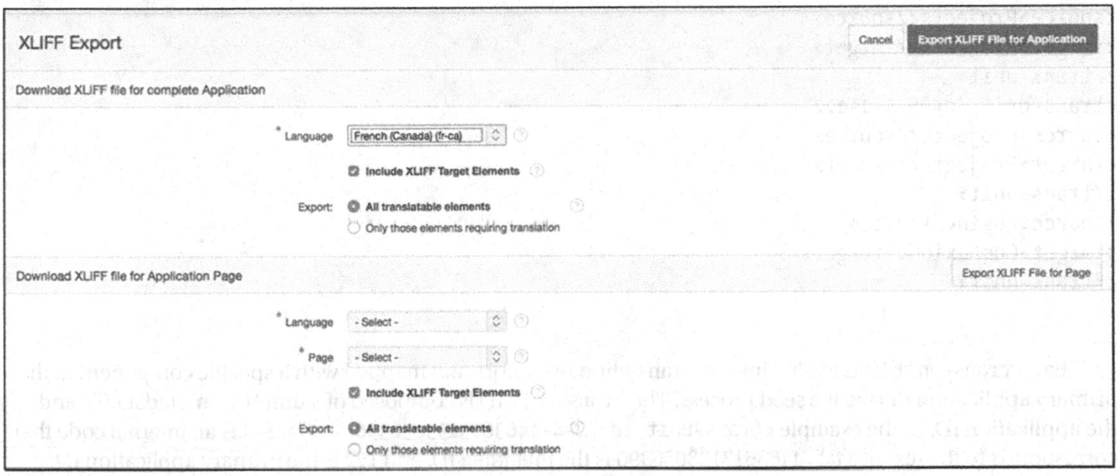

Figure 6-10. Download the XLIFF file

The download will generate an .xlf (XLIFF) file containing the source application ID, the target application ID, the source language, and the target language.

It is good practice to export the primary application with translations. This will keep the translation repository data in the export file. This way, you will always have the translations with your primary application. See the "Copying Translations to Other Environments" section.

The XLIFF file contains all translatable elements, including labels, region titles, button names, and more.

If you look at the header of the file, the source and target languages, as well as the generated XLIFF filename, are specified. When using source control software, this indicates when the file was generated.

```xml
<?xml version="1.0" encoding="UTF-8"?>
<!--
    ******************
    ** Source    :  122
    ** Source Lang: en-ca
    ** Target    :  9122
    ** Target Lang: fr-ca
    ** Filename:    f122_9122_en-ca_fr-ca.xlf
    ** Generated By: ADMIN
    ** Date:        07-FEB-2015 13:15:21
    ******************
  -->
<xliff version="1.0">
<file original="f122_9122_en-ca_fr-ca.xlf" source-language="en-ca" target-language="fr-ca"
datatype="html">
<header></header>
<body>
<trans-unit id="S-4-4463613133056390-122">
<source>Projects</source>
<target>Projects</target>
</trans-unit>
<trans-unit id="S-5-1-122">
<source>Projects</source>
<target>Projects</target>
</trans-unit>
<source>Login</source>
<target>Connexion</target>
</trans-unit>
```

Each trans-unit ID is loaded into the translation repository and mapped with a specific component in the primary application during the seed process. The trans-unit ID is composed of a unit ID, a metadata ID, and the application ID. In the example <trans-unit id="S-4-4463613133056390-122">, S-4 is an internal code that corresponds to the text of a tab, 4463613133056390 is the metadata ID, and 122 is the primary application ID.

■ **Warning**   If you change the primary application ID by exporting without translations and importing in another ID, you will not be able to reuse the same XLIFF file. See the section "Moving Translations to Other Environments" for more details.

Translate Text

In this step, you have to edit the XLIFF file and translate all the text extracted from the primary application.

Editing the XLIFF file is a relatively simple process. Since the XLIFF format is an official XML format for translations, translators will be able to use the XLIFF files with their specialized translation software. This way, the translation could also be done by a third party. But in the majority of cases, a simple text editor can be used to perform the translation as long as the text editor is UTF8 compatible.

To translate the text, you have to change the values of the text contained between the `<target>` tags. Only changes on the `<target>` tags will be taken into account when the file is applied to the translation repository.

```
<trans-unit id="S-5-101-122">
<source>Login</source>
<target>Connexion</target>
</trans-unit>
```

If the source tags are changed, these updates will not be applied to the primary application; in other words, you cannot use this process to change the original application.

In the translation process, sometimes there may be text in the application HTML templates that requires translation as well. To have the template text included in the XLIFF file, these templates have to be identified as translatable, as shown in Figure 6-11.

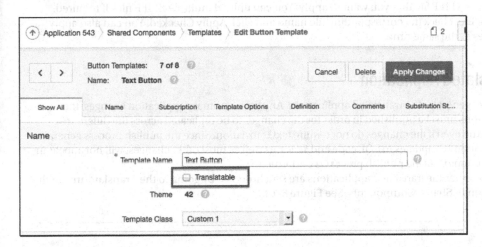

Figure 6-11. *Translatable option for templates*

Check the Translatable check box in the template properties. This tells APEX to include the content of the template in the translation repository and in the XLIFF file.

There is also a Translatable check box option for list entries that will make the Seed option extract the translatable text.

Apply XLIFF Translation File to Translation Repository

Once the translation of the XLIFF file is complete, it must be uploaded in APEX and applied to the translation repository. This will parse and insert the contents of the file in the APEX translation tables (see Figure 6-12).

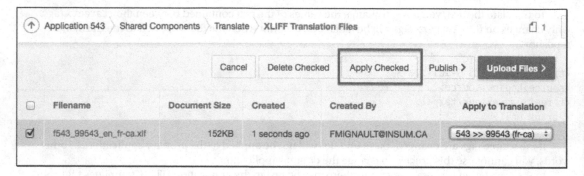

Figure 6-12. *Apply the XLIFF file*

First, upload the XLIFF file that you want to apply. You can upload multiple XLIFF files if required. To apply the XLIFF file, check the corresponding file name and click Apply Checked. You can also apply multiple XLIFF files at the same time.

Publish Translated Application

The publish process generates the translated applications. Any time a primary application changes, the translated applications must be published in order for the changes to be replicated across the different languages. This is true even if the changes do not require text translation. Since the publish process generates the mapped application ID, updates to SQL code and styles, as well as most other changes, will not appear in the mapped applications until the publish process is performed.

You can see whether the translated applications are synchronized by going to the Translate area in the globalization section in Shared Components. See Figure 6-13.

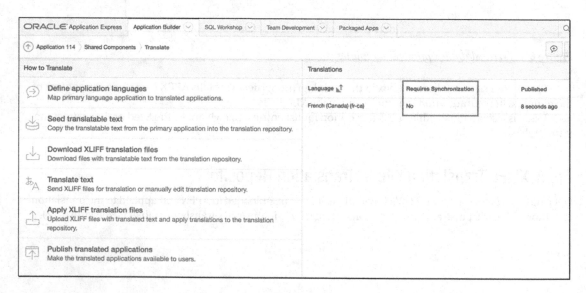

Figure 6-13. *See whether the translated applications are synchronized*

The mapped applications are not editable but can be exported. You will see them in the list of available applications in the export options and also in the list of applications in the administration of the workspace.

To execute the translated application, you have to first configure how to derive the translated application, as explained earlier. An easy way of quickly running the translated application would be to change the primary language of the primary application and use the "use primary language derived from" option. (Switching from one language to another is explained later in the chapter in the "Switching Languages" section.)

Manually Translate an Application

You can translate your application directly within APEX through the Shared Components ➤ Translate Application menu. This allows you to bypass the XLIFF file export and apply process. After you have manually translated your application, all you need to do is the publish process. You will find the option to manually edit the translation repository at the bottom of the page, in the Translation Utilities region, as shown in Figure 6-14.

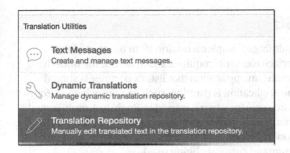

Figure 6-14. Option to manually edit the translation repository

This report, shown in Figure 6-15, shows the contents of the translation repository for the applications mapped to your primary application.

Edit	Translated Application	Page	Language	Translate From	Translate To	Column Description	Created	Created By	Updated	Updated By
✎	1114	1	fr-ca	Create	Créer	Page Button Text.	12 months ago	ADMIN	12 months ago	ADMIN
✎	1114	2	fr-ca	Create	Créer	Page Button Text.	12 months ago	ADMIN	12 months ago	ADMIN
✎	1114	2	fr-ca	Save	Sauvegarder	Page Button Text.	12 months ago	ADMIN	29 seconds ago	ADMIN
✎	1114	2	fr-ca	Delete	Détruire	Page Button Text.	12 months ago	ADMIN	9 seconds ago	ADMIN
✎	1114	2	fr-ca	Cancel	Canceller	Page Button Text.	12 months ago	ADMIN	Now	ADMIN

Figure 6-15. Manual translation in the translation repository

The application must first be *seeded* in order for the data to appear in the translation repository.

When making changes manually, the XLIFF file does not have to be exported and applied because the information was changed directly in the translation repository. All that must be done is to publish the translated application.

This report is useful for making quick changes without going through an XLIFF file. You could do the whole text translation with this option, but making a lot of changes for applications with lots of pages and text is much faster with the XLIFF file method explained earlier.

This report can also be used to visualize the component description related to the translation string. For example, to translate only the text buttons, you could use a filter on the Column Description for Page Button Text. Unfortunately, this information is not available in the XLIFF file.

■ **Note**   Another purpose of this report is to validate that the right XLIFF file was applied in the translation metadata. You can do this by simply validating whether the changes you made in the XLIFF file are in this report using the Search option. During the translation process, a lot of XLIFF files can be generated and applied and sometimes it gets confusing.

Translating Data in the Database

For multilingual applications, it is important to plan the multilingual implementation from the start of the project. It is important to remember that not only user interface elements require translation but the underlying data may as well. This will impact the data model. For example, an application that lists departments should display the department names in the language in which the application is running, such as a French name for when the user uses the application in French and an English name for when it is used in English. A multilingual application implies that the application will be used simultaneously in multiple languages.

For example, let's say you have a bilingual application in French and English. Descriptions must be displayed both in French and in English, based on the language currently being used.

In the database, you could use a table column to store the French description and another for the English description. When displaying the description to the end user, the application should show only the one that corresponds to the active language.

First, add a new column to the departments lookup table that will contain the French department name.

```
Alter table departments  add (DEPARTMENT_NAME_FR varchar2(30));
```

Then, to avoid having to check for the language in every single select throughout the application, you will create a view that will do just that. Notice the BROWSER_LANGUAGE variable. At any time, to know the language of the application running, you can check its value from the session state. Even if the name refers to the browser, it really contains the language of the application, not the browser. Also notice that you use the APEX V function. This function returns the values of the user session state.

```
CREATE OR REPLACE FORCE VIEW DEPARTMENTS_V
(DEPARTMENT_ID, DEPARTMENT_NAME, MANAGER_ID, LOCATION_ID) AS
select DEPARTMENT_ID
,decode(nvl(v('BROWSER_LANGUAGE'),'en-us'),'fr-ca',coalesce(DEPARTMENT_NAME_FR,↵
 DEPARTMENT_NAME),coalesce(DEPARTMENT_NAME, DEPARTMENT_NAME_FR)) DEPARTMENT_NAME
, MANAGER_ID, LOCATION_ID
from DEPARTMENTS;
```

Note that it is best to always display something as a description rather than nothing at all. This allows for the view to display the department name in the application language, but if it is null, it will display the department name in the other language. Therefore, if the application is run in French and no French department name is found, the English department name will be displayed.

Once the view is created, you can use it in all your lists of values, reports, and any other places that you have to display the department name in the appropriate language.

The advantage of such a view is that if you later want to add a new language or add other columns for translation to your tables, you will reduce the changes to your applications. Basically, adding a new language will require changing views.

Dynamic Translations

In some cases, lists of values or other strings used in queries may not be translatable using the XLIFF file.

The dynamic translations API (APEX_LANG.LANG) checks the language of the running application and returns the translation from an APEX table. The data in the dynamic translations table is populated by the developer of the primary application. The dynamic translations will be part of the application export file; therefore, they will be automatically imported.

To create dynamic translations, you must use the "Manage dynamic translation repository" option, as shown in Figure 6-16. You can find this section at the bottom of the page in Translate Application in the Shared Components area of the Globalization section.

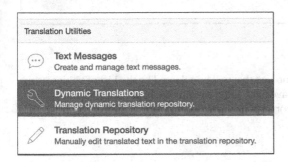

Figure 6-16. Dynamic Translations option

For example, you may decide to always translate Sales to Ventes, Accounting to Comptabilité, and Shipping to Livraison.

The steps are as follows (see Figure 6-17):

1. Select the language to translate to and that matches the mapped translated application language.

2. Enter **Sales** for Translate From Text.

3. Enter **Ventes** for Translate To Text.

Create/Edit Dynamic Translation

Dynamic translations are used by lists of values and by code you write in PL/SQL. You can call dynamic translations using the APEX_LANG package.

Application	**543 Sample Database Application**
* Language	French (Canada) (fr-ca)
Translate From Text	Sales
Translate To Text	Ventes

Cancel   Create

Figure 6-17. *Dynamic translation page*

The Translate From Text value must exactly match the text that will be selected by the List of Values using the APEX_LANG.LANG function. Once all the translations have been entered into the dynamic translations repository, the APEX_LANG.LANG function will return the corresponding translations in the lists of values.

```
Select APEX_LANG.LANG(Department), deptno
From departments;
```

Figure 6-18 shows the result of the LOV query in English (en-us).

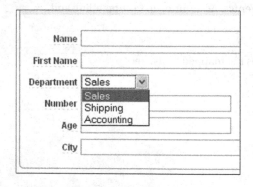

Figure 6-18. *Example of dynamic translation (en-us)*

Figure 6-19 shows the result of the same LOV query in French (fr-ca).

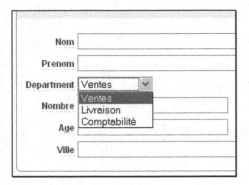

Figure 6-19. *Example of dynamic translation (fr-ca)*

Dynamic translations have to be entered manually through these pages. It would be nice to have the option of using an API to update these values programmatically, but none currently exists. There is a view called `APEX_APPLICATION_TRANS_DYNAMIC` that lists the content of dynamic translations.

Translating APEX Internal Text

As previously mentioned, when you apply the translations that come with APEX, every one of the internal APEX messages is translated. These messages include the interactive report menus, the help menus, and the report paginations.

If you want to translate into a language that is not part of the ten included APEX languages, you'll need to translate all the internal messages manually.

You can translate the internal messages by selecting Text Messages in the Shared Components area of the Globalization menu, shown in Figure 6-20. Other options exist in the Shared Components area that link to the same option. Text message translation is also accessible in the Translate Application section when selecting "Create and manage text messages," "Manage Messages Repository," "Create and Manage messages callable from PL/SQL," or "Optionally translate messages which are used by PL/SQL procedures and functions."

Figure 6-20. *Translating APEX internal text*

Table 6-1 lists the internal messages used for interactive reports.

Table 6-1. *Internal Messages for Interactive Reports*

APEXIR_ACTIONS	Actions
APEXIR_SELECT_COLUMNS	Select Columns
APEXIR_FILTER	Filter
APEXIR_ROWS_PER_PAGE	Rows Per Page
APEXIR_FLASHBACK	Flashback
APEXIR_SAVE_REPORT	Save Report
APEXIR_RESET	Reset
APEXIR_HELP	Help
APEXIR_DOWNLOAD	Download

As an example, consider a bilingual application with the primary language as English Canadian and a mapped Czech application. To translate the interactive report button Actions, the internal APEX messages must be translated using the APEX text messages. Create an entry in Shared Components ➤ Translate ➤ Text Messages for the APEXIR_ACTIONS message. The English text message is already defined in APEX; it was loaded at installation. If other languages have been loaded, the internal text messages in those languages are also already defined. They cannot be overridden.

Therefore, all that needs to be done is to create an entry for APEXIR_ACTIONS in cs (Czech), as shown in Figure 6-21.

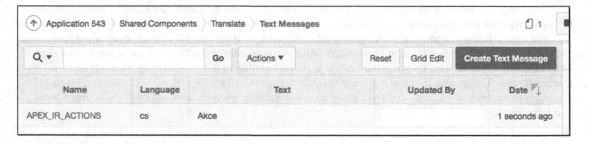

Figure 6-21. *Interactive report text translation*

When the application runs in Czech (cs)—for example, if I change Default Language to Czech (cs)—the correct translation will appear in every interactive report within the application, as Figure 6-22 shows.

Figure 6-22. *Interactive report Action button in Czech*

Keep in mind that these internal translations must be performed for every distinct primary application. If multiple applications must to be created and translated, a base application with internal messages translated could be created, and a copy can be used for new application developments. When exporting and importing an application, translated text messages and dynamic actions are also exported and imported.

Some of the internal messages use substitution variables, making it important to reuse them in the translated message text. For example, FLOW.VALIDATION_ERROR message text includes the number of errors that occurred; "%0 errors have occurred" could be translated to "%0 erreurs sur la page."

This feature of translatable messages can also be used for other strings used in applications generated from PL/SQL stored procedures, functions, triggers, packaged procedures, and functions. Simply define a new text message and use the APEX_LANG.MESSAGE function. This is the same function as the dynamic translation:

```
Ex : select APEX_LANG.MESSAGE('MY_MESSAGE')
```

This will display the text defined in the message text in the language in which the application is running for MY_MESSAGE.

There is a view called APEX_APPLICATION_TRANSLATIONS that lists all the text message translations.

The APEX_LANG API

Like many of the functionalities in APEX, there is an API that allows you to perform all the translation tasks programmatically. As explained earlier, you can use APEX_LANG.LANG to create dynamic translations and APEX_LANG.MESSAGE to translate the internal text used for interactive reports and other APEX functionalities. APEX_LANG can also be used for all the other translation functionalities such as creating mappings, seeding, publishing, and updating the translated strings. The APEX API documentation explains in great detail the APEX_LANG API and includes examples.

With the APEX_LANG API, you can use the following procedures to create or delete the language mapping for the translation of an application:

```
CREATE_LANGUAGE_MAPPING
DELETE_LANGUAGE_MAPPING
UPDATE_LANGUAGE_MAPPING
```

The LANG procedure is used for dynamic translations. See the "Dynamic Translations" section.

The MESSAGE and UPDATE_MESSAGE procedures are used for translatable text message and the APEX internal text (for example, the Interactive reports menu) for the specified application. See the "Translating APEX Internal Text" section.

The SEED_TRANSLATIONS procedure is used to see the translatable text from the specified application into the translation repository.

The UPDATE_TRANSLATED_STRING procedure allows you to change the translated strings in the translation repository.

The PUBLISH_APPLICATION procedure is used to publish the translated version of an applications. Perform a seed and publish process each time you want to update the translated version of your application and synchronize it with the primary application.

Copying Translations to Other Environments

In a standard configuration, you usually have multiple environments: one for development where developers have the flexibility to change almost anything and one for user testing that is usually more restricted and often used for testing the move to production, maybe a preproduction environment and a production environment that is completely secured and restricted. This section explains how you can move your applications and their translations from one environment to another.

Translating a primary application into multiple languages generates a separate translated application for each mapped language. When the seed is completed, the translation repository is populated, and this data is used to generate and publish the translated applications. The translated applications cannot be modified in the builder but can be exported and imported.

There are different ways to promote your applications and their translated versions from one environment to the other.

You can do the following:

- Export/import the primary application with the translation

- Export and import the primary application and the translated applications

- Export only the primary application and the XLIFF file

You should always use the first option of exporting the primary application with the translation. The other options, as explained later, can be used in specific cases.

A good practice is to use the same application IDs in all your environments. This makes it easier to maintain because you can relate and identify the same application everywhere. But, in certain cases, you may have to change the primary application ID or the translated application IDs. It could be because you are sending your application to the cloud or because you use the same database for dev and test.

The good news is that you can change the mapping of the translated application at import time. APEX will even automatically give you a new application ID for your mapped application if it is already used by another application.

Translation text messages and dynamic translations will always be included in the primary application export.

Export/Import the Primary Application with the Translations

To move your primary applications and their translation mappings from one environment to the other, you have to export the primary application with the translation. In the export preferences, there is an option called Export Translations (see Figure 6-23). This option is set to Yes by default.

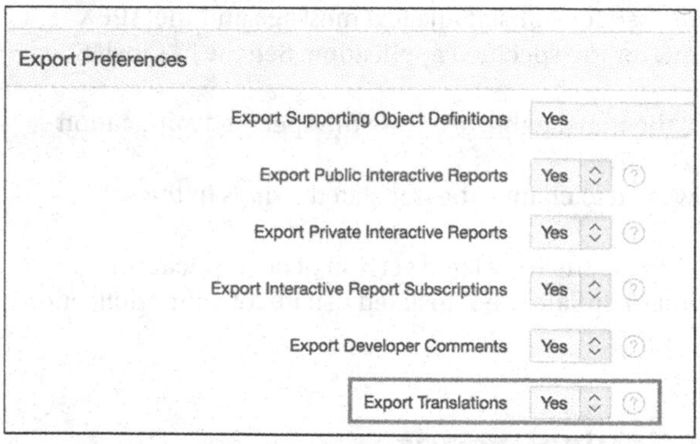

Figure 6-23. *Export translations*

Using this option will include the translation repository content of all your mapped translations in the export file.

After you import the primary application into the destination environment, the translation repository will be populated, and you will have to publish (synchronize) the translated applications. This is not done automatically.

If you want to change the primary application ID, this is the method you have to use. Importing an application that contains the translations will automatically map new application IDs.

Export/Import the Primary Application and the Translated Applications Separately

You can also export the primary application and the generated translated applications one by one separately. The translated applications cannot be modified but are accessible in the export process.

Be aware that if you import the translated application by itself, you will not be able to regenerate it without the content in the translation repository. If ever you import the primary application and the mapped applications separately and you want to regenerate the mapped applications at a later time, you will have to keep the mapping in the primary application and upload a valid XLIFF file that uses the same application IDs.

Export Only the Primary Application and the XLIFF

Another way of promoting your applications is to export the primary application without the translations and download the corresponding XLIFF files. This is the same as exporting the primary application with translations but doing so manually. The difference is that you will have to save the XLIFF file in your source versioning system and make sure that you apply it and publish in the destination environment.

This could be useful if ever you want to restart the translation from a backup or if you forgot to select the Export Translations preference during the export.

Localization

Localization refers to when data is displayed to the end user based on his location. It could be the time and date of a meeting or the number format used in the end user's region, for example. When localizing applications, special attention must be paid to the different formats used for dates and numbers. Date formats are different depending on the user's location.

Since APEX is a set of PL/SQL programs and runs in the Oracle Database, every database NLS setting can be changed using an alter session.

Oracle also provides locale-sensitive date formats, which, of course, can be used in APEX. For example, a Long Date format of DL can be used to show the date in different languages.

```
Alter session set NLS_TERRITORY='CANADA';
Alter session set NLS_LANGUAGE = 'FRENCH'
Select to_char(sysdate,'DL') from dual;

TO_CHAR(SYSDATE,'DL')
---------------------
lundi 21 février 2011

Alter session set NLS_TERRITORY='CANADA';
Alter session set NLS_LANGUAGE='ENGLISH'
Select to_char(sysdate,'DL') from dual;

TO_CHAR(SYSDATE,'DL')
---------------------
monday 21 february 2011
```

Developers should be careful in their choice of date formats that are used when developing global applications. Long Date format (DL) and Short Date format (DS) could be used to display dates in locale-sensitive formats.

Long Date format (DL):

- *en-us*: Monday, February 21, 2011

- *fr-ca*: lundi 21 février 2011

Short Date format (DS):

- *en-us mm/dd/yyyy*: 6/16/2008

- *de dd.mm.yyyy*: 16.06.2008

SINCE Format Mask

In APEX, you can use the SINCE format mask on date and timestamp columns. It has to be defined in the format mask of report columns or in the Automatic DML page items.

Values will be displayed in the format "x days ago," where x is the number of days before the current time, as shown in Figure 6-24. This format mask is also translated into the ten languages available for APEX builder (see "Loading Languages" at the beginning of this chapter).

Workspace	Application	Parsing Schema	Application Name	Updated By	Last Updated ▼	Pages	Language
INSUM	130	INSUM	SWITCH	ADMIN	3 days ago	4	en-ca
INSUM	9131	INSUM	SWITCH	ADMIN	3 days ago	4	fr-ca
INSUM	120	INSUM	globalization	ADMIN	2 weeks ago	5	en-ca
INSUM	121	INSUM	globalization	ADMIN	5 weeks ago	4	fr-ca
INSUM	116	INSUM	4.0 New Features	ADMIN	6 weeks ago	34	en-us
INSUM	117	INSUM	ADMIN 01	ADMIN	6 weeks ago	3	en
INSUM	114	INSUM	Example PLUG-IN	ADMIN	7 weeks ago	3	fr-ca
INSUM	10114	INSUM	Example PLUG-IN	ADMIN	8 months ago	3	fr-ca
INSUM	118	INSUM	New Features	ANONYMOUS	8 months ago	32	en-us
INSUM	112	INSUM	Customers1	ADMIN	1.3 years ago	3	en-us
INSUM	111	INSUM	Sample Application	ADMIN	1.3 years ago	20	en-us

Figure 6-24. *Example of SINCE date format*

Future dates and timestamps are also supported in APEX. It will display "x days from now," where x is the number of days after the current time. The SINCE format mask is supported against the columns of type TIMESTAMP, TIMESTAMP WITH TIME ZONE, and TIMESTAMP WITH LOCAL TIME ZONE.

The APEX_UTIL.GET_SINCE API can also be used to return the SINCE format for a DATE or a TIMESTAMP.

Numeric Formats

The same approach should be taken with numeric formats. If your application is going to be global, choose appropriate numeric formats. The important part of the format is the locale-neutral format G and D that defines the Group (G) separator and the Decimal (D) separator. The TO_CHAR function also accepts NLS parameters.

For example, to_char(123.45,'999D99','NLS_NUMERIC_CHARACTERS = '',''') will display the number 123.45 with the appropriate decimal notation depending on the territory defined in the APEX session. For the Currency format, the following should be used: FML999G999G999G990D00. The FML format will display the correct currency symbol depending on the territory of the session. Keep in mind that this formats only the number and that there are no automatic processes available to convert the amounts based on currencies and localization in APEX. To convert an amount to a different currency, a process has to be programmed in order to get the currency conversion rate and apply it to the amount.

The session NLS_DATE_FORMAT, NLS_TIMESTAMP_FORMAT, and NLS_TIMESTAMP_TZ_FORMAT are set in the Globalization attributes of the Shared Components of the application, as shown in Figure 6-25.

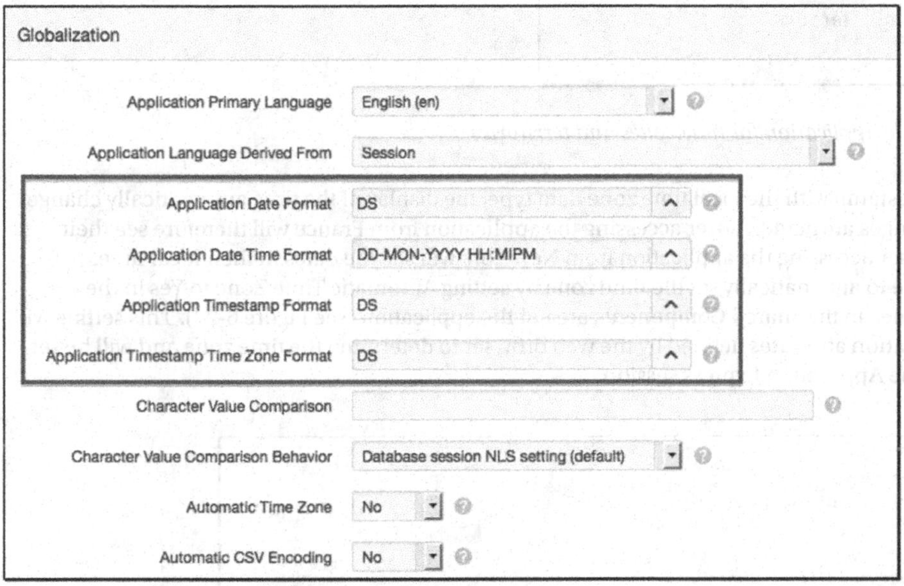

Figure 6-25. *Application date formats*

Time Zones and Territories

To demonstrate the time zone and territory localization features in APEX, I built a simple application. In the example shown in Figure 6-26, I am running the application in Canada, localized in Montreal. You can see that the time zone is Greenwich –5, the currency sign is $, and the decimals indicator is represented by a comma, which is the locale standard for that region.

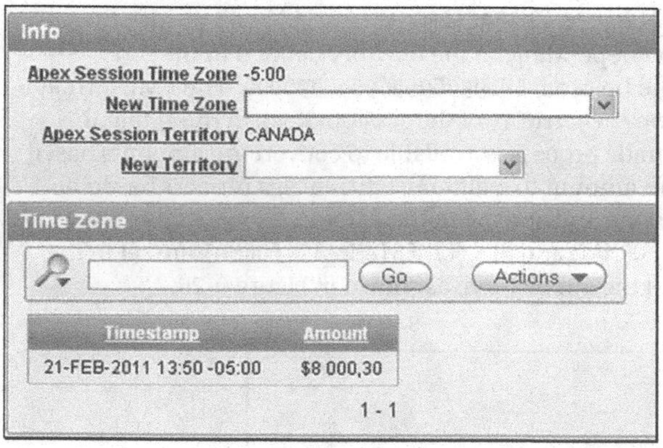

Figure 6-26. *Example application for time zones and territories*

If you use a timestamp with the local time zone data type, the display of the time automatically changes when time zone changes are made. A user accessing the application from France will therefore see their local time, while a user accessing the application from New York will see the dates in their local time.

It is also possible to automatically set the time zone by setting Automatic Time Zone to Yes in the Globalization attributes in the Shared Components area of the application (see Figure 6-27). This setting will use the client localization attributes defined by the web browser to determine the time zone and will be set for the duration of the Application Express session.

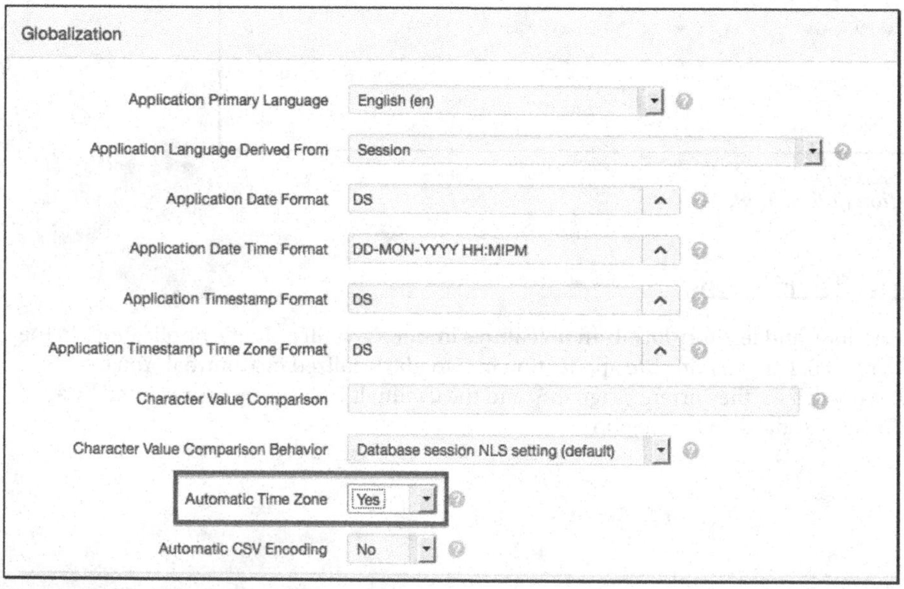

Figure 6-27. *Setting the time zone automatically*

When Automatic Time Zone is set to Yes, it is automatically set in the URL when the application is run for a new session. You can see the TZ parameter at the end of the URL. This setting can be overridden using `APEX_UTIL.SET_SESSION_TIME_ZONE` or reset using `APEX_UTIL.RESET_SESSION_TIME_ZONE`.

In this example, a select list is used to allow the user to select the time zone, as shown in Figure 6-28. Once selected, it is changed using the APEX_UTIL API as follows:

```
APEX_UTIL.SET_SESSION_TIME_ZONE(:P1_NEW_TZ);
```

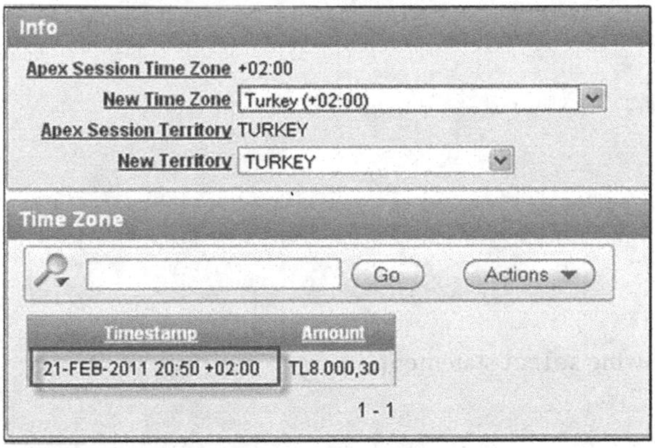

Figure 6-28. *Example of time zone change*

Because in this example you are using a data type timestamp with the local time zone, the query will automatically change the display of the time of the date value from the database to the corresponding time zone.

It is also possible to change the time zone directly in the URL; for example, you could add &tz=+2:00 for the Turkey time zone.

```
/pls/apex/f?p=115:1:0::::::&tz=+2:00
```

The territory is linked to the application language. When the language is derived using "session," the p_territory parameter can be changed in the URL without having to change the application language. There is also an API that can be used to change the territory programmatically.

This parameter also establishes the default date format, the default decimal character and group separator, the default International standard (ISO), and local currency symbols.

In this example, you added a select list to select the territory for the application, as shown in Figure 6-29. Changing the select list will call the APEX_UTIL API as follows: APEX_UTIL.SET_SESSION_TERRITORY (:P1_NEW_TERRITORY);.

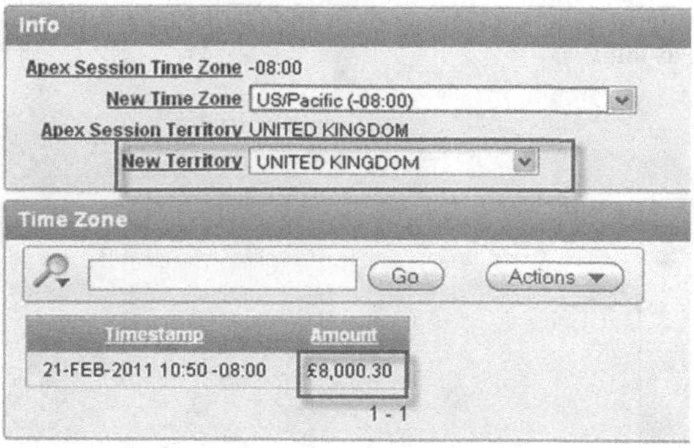

Figure 6-29. *Example of territory change*

For a list of valid territories, you can use the following select statement:

```
select value
from v$nls_valid_values
where parameter='TERRITORY'
order by 1
```

The number will then be localized based on the territory since you are using the number format FML999G999G999G990D00. The format changes only the display of the number; it does not convert the amount. To apply currency conversion, you need to get the current conversion rate, as explained earlier.

You can also change the territory in the URL by using the P_TERRITORY parameter with a valid Oracle territory name.

```
/pls/apex/f?p=115:1:0:::::&p_territory=AMERICA
```

Switching Languages

Using multiple languages in an application often means that the user can select which language he wants to access the application in.

A simple way to allow this is to add a link in the navigation bar to switch from one language to another. For example, let's assume that the language is derived using "session" as defined in the globalization attributes of the shared components of the primary application. What you want to do is change the Language value in the session and refresh the page.

One way of doing this is to use a dynamic action that changes the language in the session using the APEX_UTIL.GET_SESSION_LANG and SET_SESSION_LANG and JavaScript to reload the page.

For example, let's say that the language of the primary application is English and that the translated application is French. You want to display a link on the page to switch from one language to the other. So, in your English version, you want a link that says "Français" and in your French version you want a link that says "English."

Here are the steps to implement this:

1.   Add a link in all your pages to switch the language.

The first step consists of adding a link in your page to allow the user to switch to another language. One way of doing so is to add a link with a CSS id=switchlang. Using this ID you will be able to assign a dynamic action (see step 2) to this link.

You can use the navbar entries to have the link at the top of every page. For example, if you are using the APEX 5 universal theme, you can do the following:

a.   Edit the Navigation Bar list template in the User Interface section of the shared components.

•   Add the CSS id=#A03# to the list template in the Current and NonCurrent sections (see Figure 6-30).

```
1  <li class="t-NavigationBar-item is-active #A02#">
2    <a class="t-Button t-Button--icon t-Button--header t-Button--navBar" id=#A03#
3      href="#LINK#" role="button">
4      <span class="t-Icon #ICON_CSS_CLASSES#"></span>
5      <span class="t-Button-label">#TEXT_ESC_SC#</span>
6      <span class="t-Button-badge">#A01#</span>
7    </a>
8  </li>
```

Figure 6-30. *Modifying the list template in the Current and NonCurrent sections for id=#A03#*

•   At the bottom of the page, in the Attribute Descriptions section of the same template (see Figure 6-31), for the attribute #A03#, add a description like Switch Lang ID. This is the attribute you will use to set the link with CSS ID=switchlang.

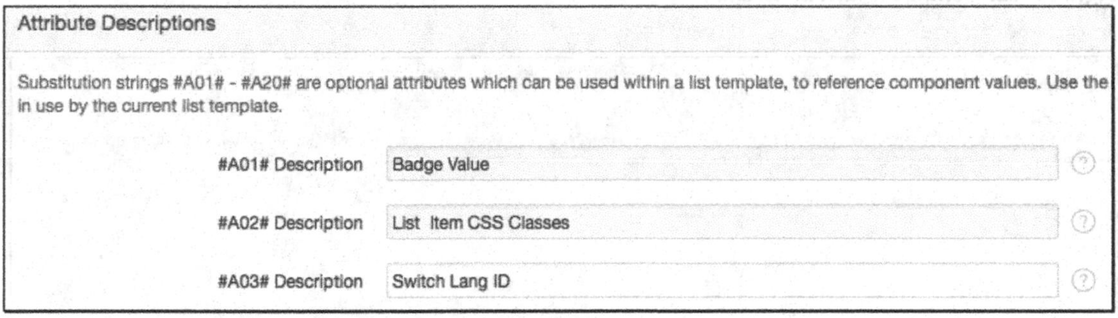

Figure 6-31. *Setting the #A03# attribute description*

b.   Edit the Navigation Bar List in the Navigation section of the shared components. Create a new entry in the Desktop Navigation Bar (see Figure 6-32) with the following:

•   *List Entry Label*: Français

•   *Target type*: URL

- *URL Target*: javascript:void()
- User Defined Attribute #3: switchlang (see Figure 6-33; this value will replace the #A03# that you added in the template in step 1a at runtime and set the id=switchlang)

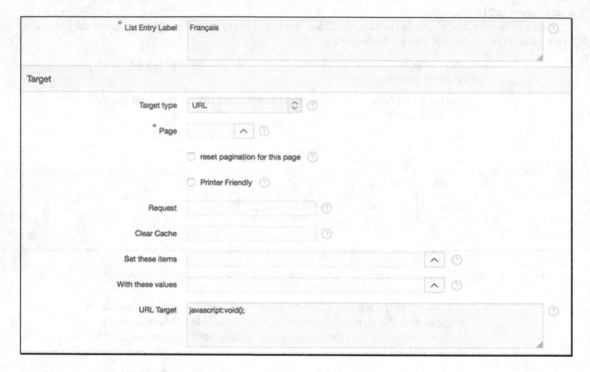

Figure 6-32. *Setting the navbar list entry*

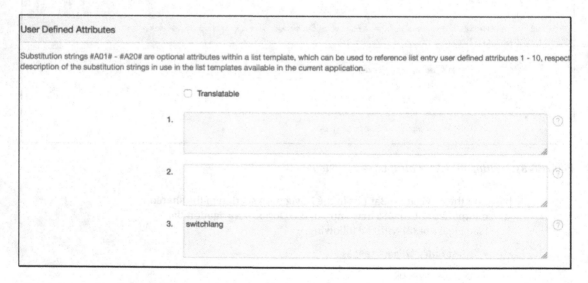

Figure 6-33. *Setting the navbar list entry user-defined attribute #3*

This will create a link on the top-right corner that says "Français" with the id=switchlang and a link that calls javascript:void();. Checking the Translatable check box indicates that this list entry will be extracted for translation.

2. In a page 0 global page, add a dynamic action on click, based on a JQuery selector of #switchlang with two true actions (see Figure 6-34).

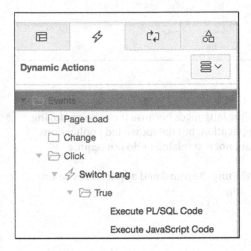

Figure 6-34. *Switch Lang dynamic action*

In the Execute PL/SQL Code area, do the following:

```
if nvl(apex_util.get_session_lang,'en-ca') = 'en-ca'
    then apex_util.set_session_lang('fr-ca');
    else apex_util.set_session_lang('en-ca');
end if;
```

In the Execute JavaScript Code area, do the following:

```
location.reload();
```

Make sure that both your actions are set to No for Fire on Page Load.

3. Seed, translate, and publish your application.

The last step is to translate the application so that the switch language link will be functional in both French and English.

Seed the application, translate List Item Display Text from "Français" to "English," and publish.

Voilà! (See Figure 6-35.) Using this example, the user will be able to switch languages on any pages within the application.

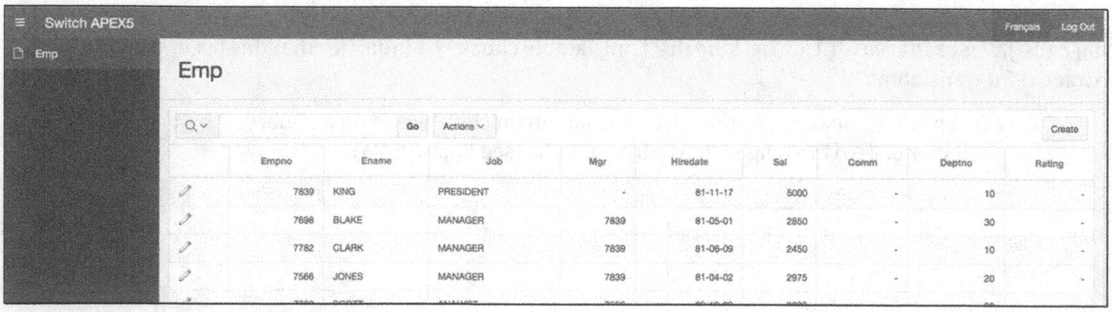

Figure 6-35. *Switch Lang dynamic action*

Care should be taken when running an application in multiple languages because it can be confusing. Development is always done in the default primary language application, but the translated applications must be resynchronized (published) even if the changes made are not text related or do not require translation in order for these to be included.

Testing an application in the default language first and publishing the translated applications before testing other languages is an essential part of debugging and testing.

Summary

In today's business market, globalization is an important aspect of application development. Companies often have offices all over the world, and customers can be located anywhere. Unfortunately, globalization is often a feature overlooked by many, but it is definitely worth looking at and may end up to be useful. The Internet allows you to create applications that can be used by multiple users in multiple locations at the same time. Oracle Application Express possesses all the required tools to support you in building globalized applications to help you better serve your customers.

As shown in this chapter, translation is relatively easy once you understand that an application must be seeded, translated, and published. Having all the information stored in a metadata makes it even easier. Another important aspect is that the translation process can be extended to third parties, because of its use of the standard XLIFF format, also used by translators.

Localization is the other aspect of globalization taken care of in APEX. Date formats, number formats, time zones, territories, and other NLS settings are easily customizable. There are even automatic settings available to developers for building fully localized applications. And even for U.S. English–only applications some of the globalization attributes can be useful.

All in all, APEX has been handling globalization from its first version, and this feature is well integrated. And I am sure that it will continue to improve in its next releases.

CHAPTER 7

■ ■ ■

Debugging

by Doug Gault

At some point during the process of writing or maintaining an APEX application you will need to step into the world of debugging. APEX 5 has quite extensive debugging capabilities compared to its predecessors. This chapter will introduce you to the nuances of debugging in APEX.

> ■ **Note**　This chapter specifically addresses the tools that APEX 5 provides for debugging and does not discuss external or third-party tools.

Principles of Code Instrumentation

While it may seem odd to start a chapter on APEX debugging with a discussion about what makes good code instrumentation, it's an important topic. In any development environment, the ability to quickly and easily see what your program is doing during execution is a critical component of debugging, especially when using a framework such as APEX where a large portion of the core code is beyond your capacity to change.

Proper code instrumentation has a set of precepts that should be followed. They include the following:

- *Exists in every environment*: Code instrumentation should be available in all environments, from development to production. Inserting instrumentation code in a development environment and then removing it before migrating to production not only takes away your ability to diagnose issues in production but also changes the core code, potentially introducing changes in functionality.

- *Easy to enable and disable*: The instrumentation should be easy for the programmer (and in certain cases, for the user) to enable and disable. Often code instrumentation is disabled by default and turned on only when there is a problem to diagnose.

- *Always available*: You should not need to recompile any code to turn on instrumentation. This is especially important in a production environment where on-the-fly code changes are often locked down tightly. Instead, instrumentation should be enabled by using a parameter or by adding a value to a table.

- *Lightweight*: The instrumentation should be "nonintrusive" in terms of the load it introduces to the process that it is measuring. The difference between timings when instrumentation is enabled and disabled should be minimal, if measurable at all.

- *Integrated*: Instrumentation should take advantage of any and all functionality that is built into its native environment, especially any functionality that will make problems easier to diagnose using other tools within the environment.

281

As you examine APEX 5's debugging features in greater depth, you'll see that APEX adheres to these precepts quite closely. I'll also discuss how you can extend instrumentation into your own code to provide even more granular coverage than what APEX provides by itself.

■ **Note** The remainder of the chapter discusses APEX debugging directly, but I challenge you to think about the aforementioned precepts and see how they are implemented in APEX and how they may be implemented in your own code.

Debugging Basics

To understand how debugging works, you need to take a quick tour of the core APEX engine. While this might seem like an unnecessary review for many people, it's important because of the way APEX 5 manages and logs debug information.

Page Processing and Rendering

An APEX application is basically a group of pages that are linked together via buttons, hyperlinks, tabs, and so on. When a user navigates through the application, submits data, or requests to view an APEX page, there are two phases that the APEX engine goes through to provide the correct information to the user.

- ACCEPT *(processing)*: This phase acts upon the request made by the user and, if appropriate, runs any defined validations, computations, processes, and branches. This includes setting session state and manipulating the underlying database tables.

- SHOW *(rendering)*: This phase executes all appropriate code to render the page that was identified by the branch taken in the processing phase. Page rendering may also contain computations, processes, and branches, as well as the visual components that make up the page to be rendered.

The reason these phases are important to debugging is that APEX breaks down the logging of debug information into these same component parts. When the application server tier connects to the Oracle database that contains the APEX installation, it grabs a connection from the database connection pool and uses that to service the user's APEX request. You can see this sequence in Figure 7-1.

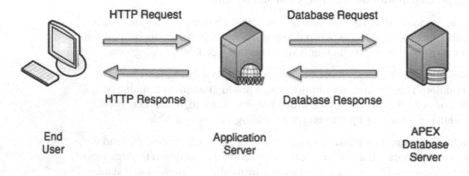

Figure 7-1. Simplified APEX request-response

The first phrase (ACCEPT) of servicing the user's requests is to process the current page and the user's input. Because the state of the connection from the pool cannot be guaranteed to match the requirements of the user's APEX session, the first thing that APEX does is to alter the session, setting the desired NLS parameters and session settings. Figure 7-2 shows this portion of the processing.

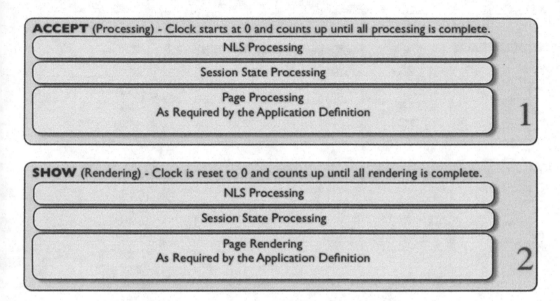

Figure 7-2. *APEX page phases*

Once the database session is in the proper state, APEX then begins checking to see whether the APEX session is still valid, checking to see whether the user has authorization to run the page, retrieving session state from the APEX data dictionary tables, setting session state that may have been altered by the user, and then running the page-processing components as defined in the metadata.

The last step of the processing is to decide which programmatic branch to take, which in turn decides which page will then be rendered and sent to the user. APEX always takes the first branch whose condition evaluates to true.

The second phase (SHOW) is to render the page identified by the branching section of the first phase. Because it is possible for page rendering to be called directly via a URL, this phase also walks through the process of altering the database session, retrieving the APEX session state from the metadata tables, and executing any required security checks. Figure 7-2 also shows the second phase of processing.

Once everything is set, APEX then walks through the process of rendering the page as defined in the APEX metadata and presenting that page to the user via the application server. Once the application server sees that the original request has been fully satisfied, it returns the Oracle database connection back to the connection pool to be reused.

The two phases can be mapped directly to the page editor, as shown in Figure 7-3. In the section on the left side of the page, the Rendering tab (1) equates to the SHOW phase, while the Processing tab (2) equates to the ACCEPT phase. Furthermore, each step is timed. Time is measured from the beginning of the current step to the beginning of the subsequent step. When debugging is turned on, these times are saved into the APEX dictionary along with the step detail.

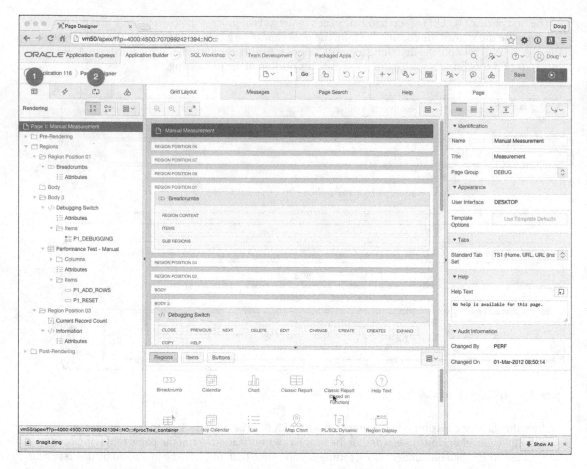

Figure 7-3. *Mapping the phases to the APEX page definition*

The two-phase process of ACCEPT and SHOW iterates as the user navigates through and uses an APEX application. At some point, you may run into issues in development where you want to see exactly what is happening during the execution of either one, or both, of these phases. This is where APEX debugging comes in.

APEX debugging indicates to APEX that it should emit information about exactly what it's doing during each of these phases. Unlike versions prior to 4.0, APEX does not emit the debug information into the page being processed or rendered but instead stores the full debug information in a set of tables in the APEX schema.

The newer approach is superior in that the debugging information persists beyond the lifetime of the rendered page so that you can view and analyze multiple runs of a single page, comparing and contrasting their debug output to see how changes you may have made might have affected the processing or performance.

Enabling Debug

Turning interactive debugging on is a straightforward process and can be done in one of two ways: via the Developer Toolbar or via the URL. The Developer Toolbar will be visible if you are running an application while you are also logged in to the application's parent workspace as a developer. Figure 7-4 shows the Developer Toolbar and highlights the Debug button, which toggles Debug mode on and off.

Figure 7-4. *APEX Developer Toolbar highlighting the Debug button*

You can also enable Debug mode by setting the DEBUG component of the APEX URL to either YES or LEVELn, where *n* is between 1 (most critical) and 9 (least critical). The following shows both the URL syntax and two examples of using the DEBUG component to enable Debug mode:

```
http://server/apex/f?p=App:Page:Session:Request:Debug:ClearCache:ItemNames:ItemValues

http://server/apex/f?p=100:1:23929384838429::YES:::
http://server/apex/f?p=100:1:23929384838429::LEVEL7:::
```

However, it is important to note that the ability to use either of these methods is controlled by an attribute in the application definition. Editing the application properties and navigating to the Properties region on the Definition tab will give you the ability to turn interactive debugging on or off. By default the attribute is set to disallow interactive debugging.

Even so, if you are running an application in development mode (that is to say, you are running the application while also logged in as a developer to the underlying workspace), debugging will always be available to you. While this may seem a bit odd, this fact will allow developers to interactively debug an application even if the application-level attribute is set to disallow debugging.

Figure 7-5 shows the Properties region and indicates the debugging attribute that should be changed to allow interactive debugging.

Properties	
Logging	Yes
Debugging	Yes ←
Allow Feedback	No
Compatibility Mode	Pre 4.1
Application Email From Address	
Proxy Server	

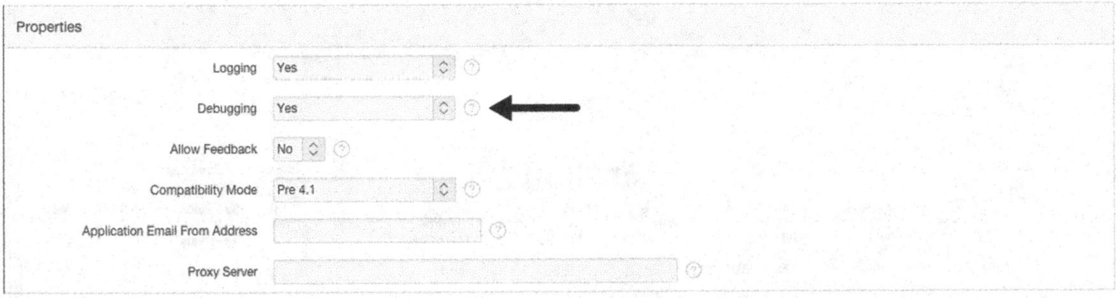

Figure 7-5. *The Properties region of the application definition where interactive debugging is enabled or disabled*

■ **Note** The debugging attribute enables and disables only *interactive* debugging. Programmatic debugging, discussed later in this chapter, is still possible even when the debugging attribute is set to NO.

While it may be slightly confusing, once debugging is enabled via either the Developer Toolbar or the URL, the page will refresh, but you will notice nothing externally different about the page per se. Just remember that APEX stores the debug information in its data dictionary tables and does not emit it into the page being debugged.

There are two visual clues that will help you recognize when debug mode is active. If the Developer Toolbar is visible, the text of the debug button will now be changed to No Debug, as shown in Figure 7-6. Even if the Developer Toolbar isn't visible, the URL will contain either YES or LEVEL*n* in the debug position.

Figure 7-6. Developer Toolbar with debugging enabled

Debug Information

Once Debug mode is turned on and you have executed the steps you want to debug, such as running a report or submitting a page, you will then want to view the debug information that was captured during your session. There are a couple of different places where you can do this.

Developer Toolbar

It's probably most common to want to view the debug information for the page you're currently running immediately after turning debugging on. To do this, you again use the Developer Toolbar and click the View Debug button. A pop-up window will appear that lists all the page views for the page you are currently running. Figure 7-7 shows an example. The pop-up screen presents a high-level overview of all the *views* (or debug sessions) that have been captured for the current page. This is actually an interactive report with a filter set to show only views for the current page in the current application. You can alter the filters to show whatever combination you want.

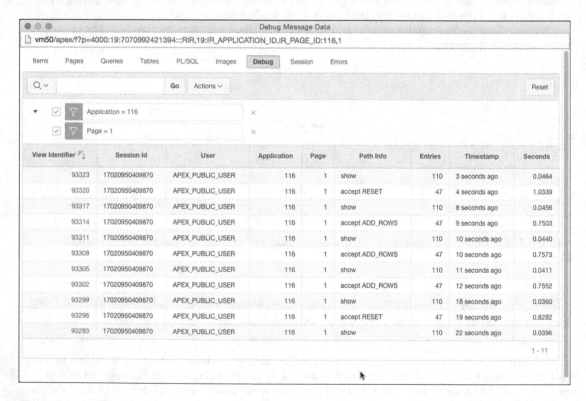

Figure 7-7. Pop-up window showing all debug views for page 1

From this screen you can click the View Identifier link to drill down into each view and see the detailed steps that APEX took to process and render the page. Figure 7-8 shows the detailed view for view ID 93320.

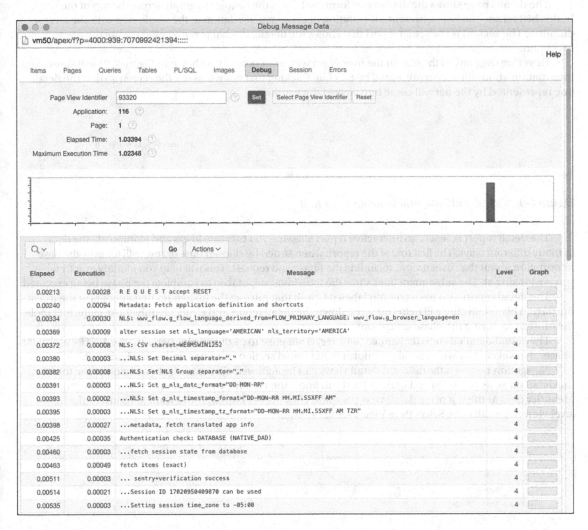

Figure 7-8. *Example detailed view of a debug session for page 1 in application 116, view ID 93323*

From the simple high-level view shown in Figure 7-7 you can actually see some interesting things. You can see the timeline of debug views that have been created for this page by looking at the Timestamp column, the action that was executed by looking at the Path Info column, the duration of each view by looking at the Seconds column, and the number of detailed debug entries for each view by looking at the Entries column.

Examining this particular example, you can see that one particular view (view ID 93320) took approximately around a second to complete while the others were less than one second.

Remember that there are two phases involved in processing a user request: ACCEPT and SHOW. The APEX debugging engine stores these two phases as separate "views" in the debug data. You can see from the overview report that the SHOW phases are all very fast, but the ACCEPT phases often take more time.

How much more time will depend upon how much "work" is being done in the processing of your page. The more work being done, the more likely it is that the page will take longer.

You can drill down into the individual views to see what the APEX engine was doing during each phase and identify the activities within the page that were taking the most time.

The details page shows the data in two formats. First is the histogram graph across the top of the page. In this histogram, the bars represent the duration of each step in relation to the single step with the largest duration. The second is the actual report that shows the details of what was executed during the phase execution.

Hovering over any of the bars in the histogram with your mouse (as shown in Figure 7-9) will show information about the step represented by that bar. Clicking that bar will scroll the screen so that the detail line represented by the bar will come into view in the window.

Figure 7-9. *View detail histogram showing hover hint*

The detail report is, again, an interactive report allowing you to create filters and manipulate the data in many different ways. The first row of the report, when sorted by elapsed time or row, will identify the base information about the current view, including the phase and request. This will help you identify exactly what you are looking at. The subsequent lines show the individual steps taken to complete the phase being executed.

The detail report also has a column labeled Graph that mirrors the histogram that appears at the top of the page. This visual clue will help you scroll down the detail report and easily identify those steps that took the most time during the phase execution.

The actual detailed steps that appear will vary from page to page and also between the ACCEPT and SHOW phases. However, they will generally conform to the broad sections outlined earlier in Figure 7-2.

Navigation between the different detail views can be achieved via the navigation region at the top of the detail page, as presented in Figure 7-10. If you know the view ID, you can simply type it in the Page View Identifier field at the top of the detail view page and click the Set button. If you want to return to the high-level view page, click the Select Page View Identifier button.

Page View Identifier	93320	⑦	Set	Select Page View Identifier	Reset
Application:	116 ⑦				
Page:	1 ⑦				
Elapsed Time:	1.03394 ⑦				
Maximum Execution Time	1.02348 ⑦				

Figure 7-10. *The Debug View Navigation region*

Clicking the Reset button will return the current report to its default settings, resetting any filters you may have implemented.

Application Utilities

Another place to view debug information is via the application utilities. You can reach these by clicking the large Utilities icon on the main application edit page (as shown in Figure 7-11) or by clicking the small Utilities icon in the menu at the top of the Page Designer and then selecting Application Utilities (as shown in Figure 7-12).

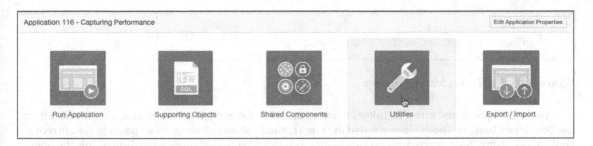

Figure 7-11. *Utilities icon on the Application edit page*

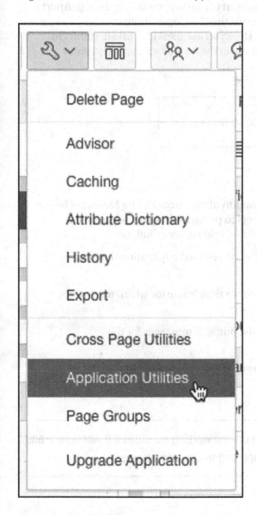

Figure 7-12. *Utilities icon on the Quick Links menu*

Selecting either option will take you to the Application Utilities page. From here, select the Debug Messages option (as indicated in Figure 7-13).

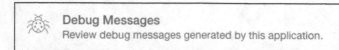

Figure 7-13. *The Debug Messages option*

You will be presented with a high-level report identical to the one you see when accessing the data from the Developer Toolbar. The difference is that the report initially shows all views for all pages in the current application. Using the interactive report capabilities, you can filter the debug views to display only the ones you're interested in.

Drilling down will take you to the detail report, this time without the histogram across the top. Apart from this small change, all the data is the same as you would see via the Developer Toolbar.

Navigation in this version of the report is slightly different. Here you use the APEX breadcrumbs to navigate between the Debug and Debug Message Data pages to select the desired views, as shown in Figure 7-14.

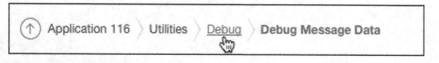

Figure 7-14. *Breadcrumbs for the Debug Messages utilities*

Another change to the utilities-based Debug view is the addition of the Purge Debug Messages button. This button allows both workspace administrators and developers to purge underlying debug data *for the currently selected application* based on certain criteria. The available criteria are as follows:

- *Purge all messages*: This option will purge all data for the selected application that currently resides in the underlying debug tables.

- *Purge messages by age*: This option allows you to select a time frame for which to purge, from 1 day to 4 weeks.

- *Purge current session messages*: This option allows the purge of messages for the currently active user session.

- *Purge by View Identifier*: This option allows the purge of messages related to a specific view ID.

■ **Caution**   When purging data, be aware of what other developers are working on within the workspace and application. It is possible to accidently purge data that may be important to other developers.

Benefits of Debug Mode

There are a few benefits to Debug mode that are worth mentioning because they help make debugging some of the more complex pieces of APEX a little easier. These benefits are particularly apparent when working with graphs and charts or when developing interactive reports.

Graphs and Charts

APEX 5 uses AnyChart 6 (www.anychart.com) as its main graphing and charting engine. While the APEX team has done a wonderful job of hiding the behind-the-scenes complexity of how charting works, sometimes you may need to dig into the details of how charts are being rendered.

As you learned in Chapter 3, everything you change on the Chart Attributes page of a given chart's definition ends up creating an XML document that determines how the chart will be drawn. You can, if you want, edit the XML manually to make changes that are not available via the Chart Attribute options.

Although you can get a good feel for the XML that will be generated, you cannot guarantee what the XML will look like until runtime. To be able to view the full runtime XML, prior versions of APEX required you to use third-party, browser-based debugging tools. APEX, however, has made things much easier.

When Debug mode is on, each chart will contain a link that will allow you to view the XML that was generated to drive it. Figure 7-15 shows a bar chart with the Show XML link visible in the lower-left corner.

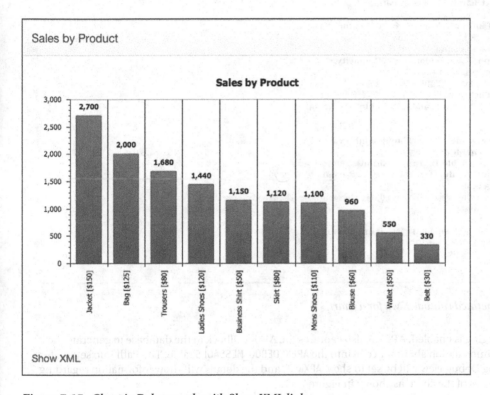

Figure 7-15. *Chart in Debug mode with Show XML link*

Clicking this link will display the full runtime XML that was generated to drive the chart. This is useful for debugging manual changes you may have made to chart XML or to view how the data has been emitted into the XML from the series queries you have defined. Figure 7-16 shows an example of the generated XML.

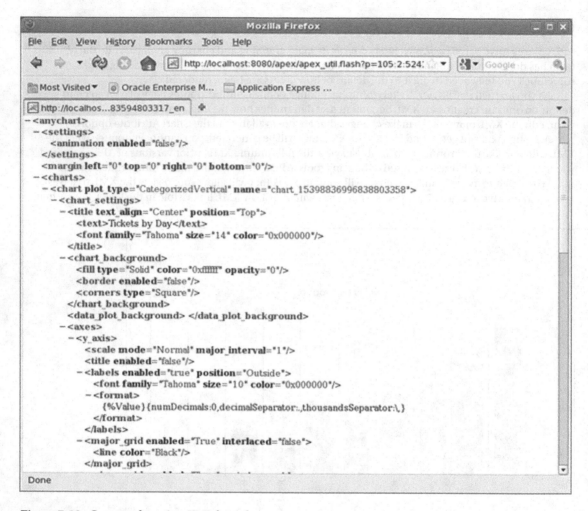

Figure 7-16. *Generated runtime XML for a chart*

When debugging is enabled, APEX 5 also captures the AJAX callback to the database to generate the XML and inserts information about that call into the APEX_DEBUG_MESSAGES table. The Path Info setting for the corresponding Debug view will be set to show APXWGT, and the details will show information regarding the underlying series of the chart, as shown in Figure 7-17.

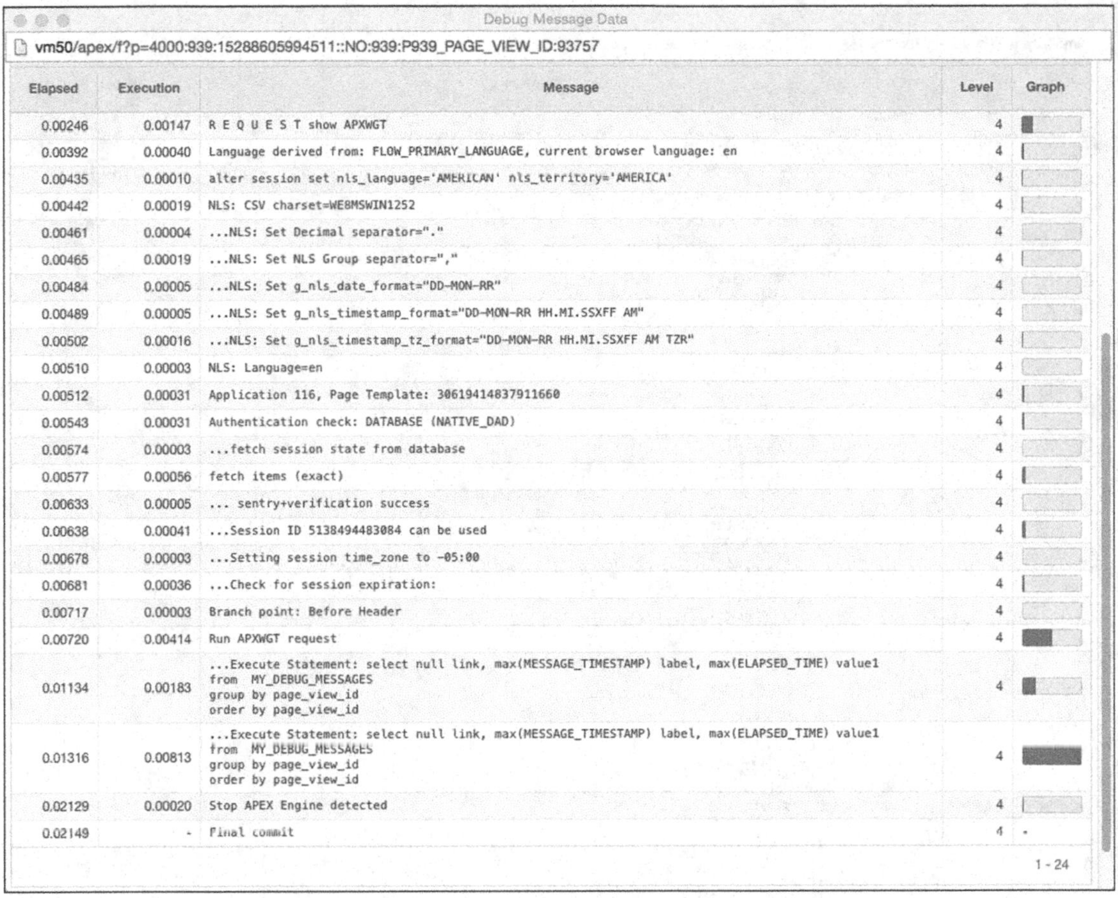

Debug Message Data

vm50/apex/f?p=4000:939:15288605994511::NO:939:P939_PAGE_VIEW_ID:93757

Elapsed	Execution	Message	Level	Graph
0.00246	0.00147	R E Q U E S T show APXWGT	4	
0.00392	0.00040	Language derived from: FLOW_PRIMARY_LANGUAGE, current browser language: en	4	
0.00435	0.00010	alter session set nls_language='AMERICAN' nls_territory='AMERICA'	4	
0.00442	0.00019	NLS: CSV charset=WE8MSWIN1252	4	
0.00461	0.00004	...NLS: Set Decimal separator="."	4	
0.00465	0.00019	...NLS: Set NLS Group separator=","	4	
0.00484	0.00005	...NLS: Set g_nls_date_format="DD-MON-RR"	4	
0.00489	0.00005	...NLS: Set g_nls_timestamp_format="DD-MON-RR HH.MI.SSXFF AM"	4	
0.00502	0.00016	...NLS: Set g_nls_timestamp_tz_format="DD-MON-RR HH.MI.SSXFF AM TZR"	4	
0.00510	0.00003	NLS: Language=en	4	
0.00512	0.00031	Application 116, Page Template: 30619414837911660	4	
0.00543	0.00031	Authentication check: DATABASE (NATIVE_DAD)	4	
0.00574	0.00003	...fetch session state from database	4	
0.00577	0.00056	fetch items (exact)	4	
0.00633	0.00005	... sentry+verification success	4	
0.00638	0.00041	...Session ID 5138494483084 can be used	4	
0.00678	0.00003	...Setting session time_zone to -05:00	4	
0.00681	0.00036	...Check for session expiration:	4	
0.00717	0.00003	Branch point: Before Header	4	
0.00720	0.00414	Run APXWGT request	4	
0.01134	0.00183	...Execute Statement: select null link, max(MESSAGE_TIMESTAMP) label, max(ELAPSED_TIME) value1 from MY_DEBUG_MESSAGES group by page_view_id order by page_view_id	4	
0.01316	0.00813	...Execute Statement: select null link, max(MESSAGE_TIMESTAMP) label, max(ELAPSED_TIME) value1 from MY_DEBUG_MESSAGES group by page_view_id order by page_view_id	4	
0.02129	0.00020	Stop APEX Engine detected	4	
0.02149	-	Final commit	4	-

1 - 24

Figure 7-17. *Debug detail for an XMLHttpRequest generated by an APEX chart*

Interactive Reports

While interactive reports give an amazing amount of power to the end user, debugging them can be a bit challenging because APEX basically rewrites the query behind the scenes based on the user's column selections, filters, and more. Enabling debugging on an Interactive Report page will emit the SQL that is generated for the current incarnation of the interactive report into the debug data.

Once an interactive report is rendered to the page, any changes made to the filters, sorting, column selection, and so on, are done via AJAX calls. If debugging is enabled, changes to the report will still be logged, but as an `ajax plugin` request for the page as opposed to a "show." In fact, APEX now logs any AJAX call having to do with the interactive report, including ones as simple as retrieving a distinct list of values when clicking a column heading. While this may seem like overkill, it is extremely useful to know what's going on as you click around the interactive report options.

Consider the three debug snippets shown in Figures 7-18, 7-19, and 7-20. All the snippets are from the same interactive report.

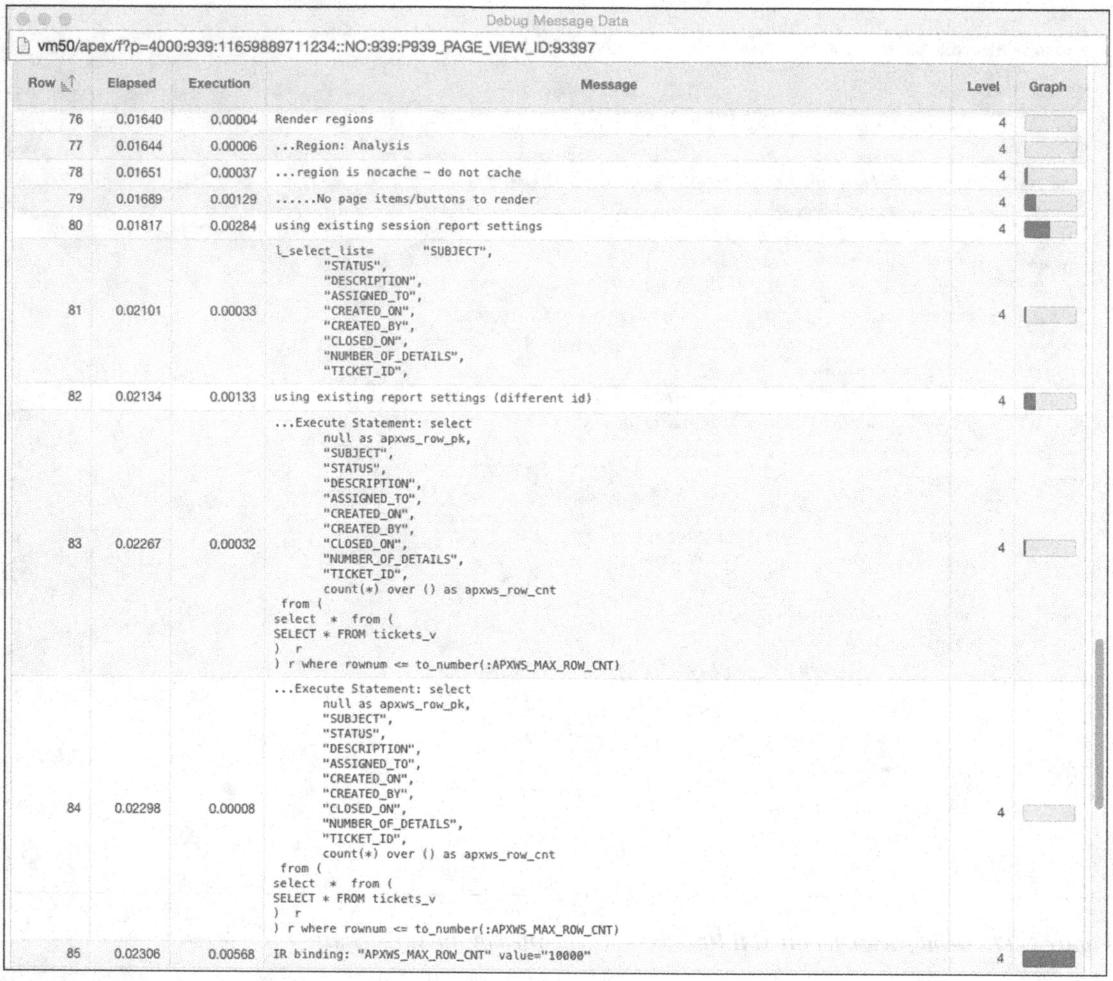

Row	Elapsed	Execution	Message	Level	Graph
76	0.01640	0.00004	Render regions	4	
77	0.01644	0.00006	...Region: Analysis	4	
78	0.01651	0.00037	...region is nocache – do not cache	4	
79	0.01689	0.00129	......No page items/buttons to render	4	
80	0.01817	0.00284	using existing session report settings	4	

81	0.02101	0.00033	l_select_list= "SUBJECT",
			          "STATUS",
			          "DESCRIPTION",
			          "ASSIGNED_TO",
			          "CREATED_ON",
			          "CREATED_BY",
			          "CLOSED_ON",
			          "NUMBER_OF_DETAILS",
			          "TICKET_ID",
				4	

82	0.02134	0.00133	using existing report settings (different id)	4	

83	0.02267	0.00032	...Execute Statement: select
			          null as apxws_row_pk,
			          "SUBJECT",
			          "STATUS",
			          "DESCRIPTION",
			          "ASSIGNED_TO",
			          "CREATED_ON",
			          "CREATED_BY",
			          "CLOSED_ON",
			          "NUMBER_OF_DETAILS",
			          "TICKET_ID",
			          count(*) over () as apxws_row_cnt
			 from (
			select * from (
			SELECT * FROM tickets_v
			) r
			) r where rownum <= to_number(:APXWS_MAX_ROW_CNT)
				4	

84	0.02298	0.00008	...Execute Statement: select
			          null as apxws_row_pk,
			          "SUBJECT",
			          "STATUS",
			          "DESCRIPTION",
			          "ASSIGNED_TO",
			          "CREATED_ON",
			          "CREATED_BY",
			          "CLOSED_ON",
			          "NUMBER_OF_DETAILS",
			          "TICKET_ID",
			          count(*) over () as apxws_row_cnt
			 from (
			select * from (
			SELECT * FROM tickets_v
			) r
			) r where rownum <= to_number(:APXWS_MAX_ROW_CNT)
				4	

85	0.02306	0.00568	IR binding: "APXWS_MAX_ROW_CNT" value="10000"	4	

Figure 7-18. Debug data for the default version of an interactive report

Figure 7-18 shows the detail debug data for an interactive report region *prior* to a user having made any changes to the report. The path info for this view would be SHOW. You can tell the following from the figure:

- Line 76 indicates the start of the region.

- Line 81 lists the columns that will be displayed.

- Line 83 shows the base SQL statement.

- Line 84 shows the value of the APXWS_MAX_ROW_CNT bind variable because it will be used in the SQL statement.

Figure 7-19 shows the AJAX plugin view that is associated with the user having clicked the Assigned To column in the report to get a distinct list of asignees. Here you can see the following:

- Line 25 indicates the request for a distinct list.

- Line 28 shows the SQL statement that is to be executed.

- Line 29 to 30 show the bind variables and their values.

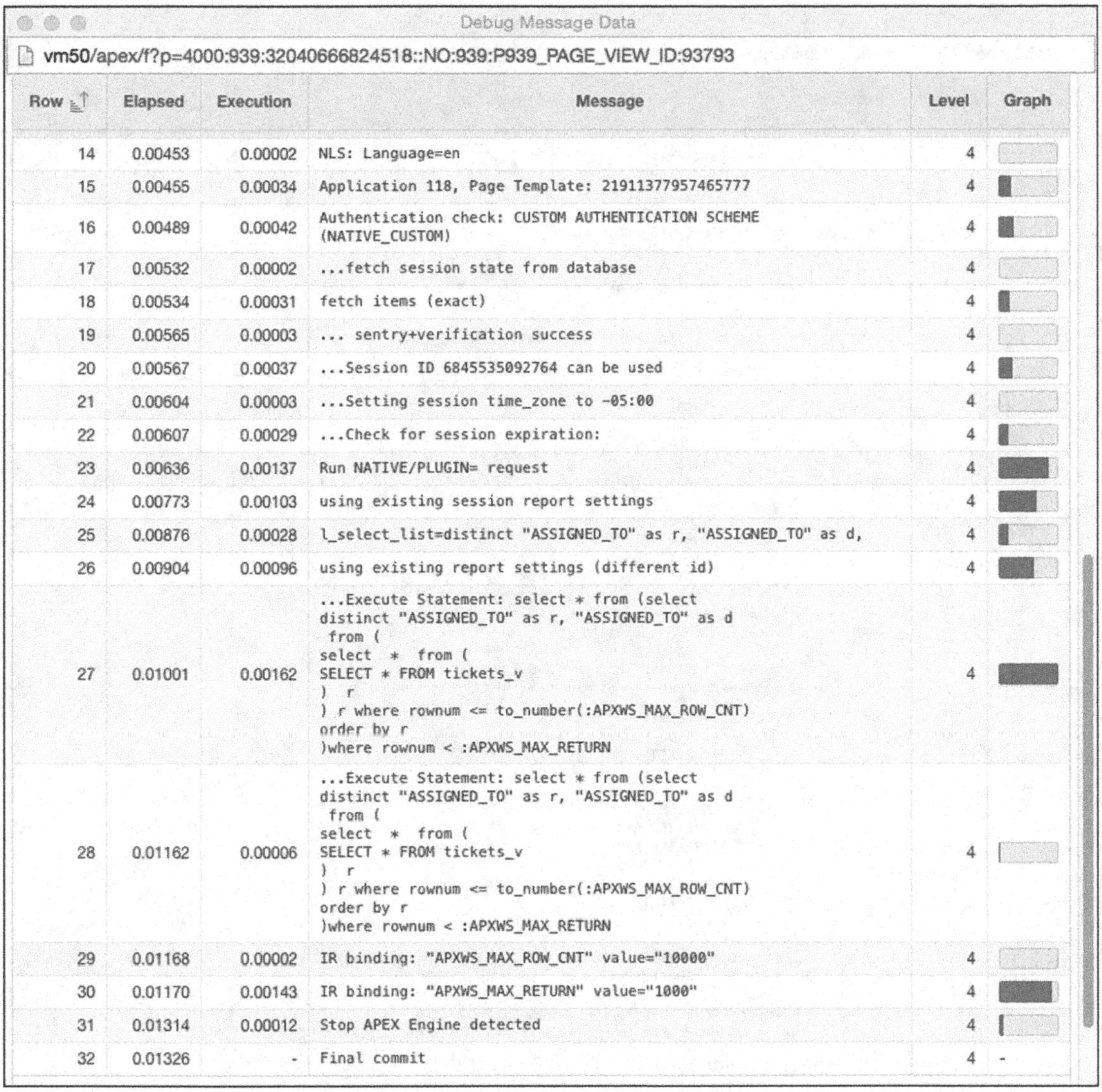

Row ↑	Elapsed	Execution	Message	Level	Graph
14	0.00453	0.00002	NLS: Language=en	4	
15	0.00455	0.00034	Application 118, Page Template: 21911377957465777	4	
16	0.00489	0.00042	Authentication check: CUSTOM AUTHENTICATION SCHEME (NATIVE_CUSTOM)	4	
17	0.00532	0.00002	...fetch session state from database	4	
18	0.00534	0.00031	fetch items (exact)	4	
19	0.00565	0.00003	... sentry+verification success	4	
20	0.00567	0.00037	...Session ID 6845535092764 can be used	4	
21	0.00604	0.00003	...Setting session time_zone to -05:00	4	
22	0.00607	0.00029	...Check for session expiration:	4	
23	0.00636	0.00137	Run NATIVE/PLUGIN= request	4	
24	0.00773	0.00103	using existing session report settings	4	
25	0.00876	0.00028	l_select_list=distinct "ASSIGNED_TO" as r, "ASSIGNED_TO" as d,	4	
26	0.00904	0.00096	using existing report settings (different id)	4	
27	0.01001	0.00162	...Execute Statement: select * from (select distinct "ASSIGNED_TO" as r, "ASSIGNED_TO" as d from (select * from (SELECT * FROM tickets_v) r) r where rownum <= to_number(:APXWS_MAX_ROW_CNT) order by r)where rownum < :APXWS_MAX_RETURN	4	
28	0.01162	0.00006	...Execute Statement: select * from (select distinct "ASSIGNED_TO" as r, "ASSIGNED_TO" as d from (select * from (SELECT * FROM tickets_v) r) r where rownum <= to_number(:APXWS_MAX_ROW_CNT) order by r)where rownum < :APXWS_MAX_RETURN	4	
29	0.01168	0.00002	IR binding: "APXWS_MAX_ROW_CNT" value="10000"	4	
30	0.01170	0.00143	IR binding: "APXWS_MAX_RETURN" value="1000"	4	
31	0.01314	0.00012	Stop APEX Engine detected	4	
32	0.01326	-	Final commit	4	-

Debug Message Data

vm50/apex/f?p=4000:939:32040666824518::NO:939:P939_PAGE_VIEW_ID:93793

Figure 7-19. *Debug data for the AJAX call to get the distinct list of asignees*

Figure 7-20 shows the detailed debug data for the same Interactive Report region *after* a user has made changes to the report, as indicated in Figure 7-21. The changes indicate that you are filtering on the ASSIGNED_TO value.

- Line 27 lists the columns that will be displayed.

- Line 30 shows the base SQL statement.

- Line 32 shows the value of the APXWS_EXPR_1 bind variable because it will be used in the SQL statement.

Row ⬍	Elapsed	Execution	Message	Level	Graph
~~26~~	~~0.01039~~	~~0.00230~~	~~using existing session report settings~~	~~4~~	

27	0.01278	0.00031	l_select_list= "SUBJECT",
			                "STATUS",
			                "DESCRIPTION",
			                "ASSIGNED_TO",
			                "CREATED_ON",
			                "CREATED_BY",
			                "CLOSED_ON",
			                "NUMBER_OF_DETAILS",
			                "TICKET_ID",
				4	

28	0.01308	0.00218	using existing report settings (different id)	4	

29	0.01527	0.00067	...Execute Statement: select
			                null as apxws_row_pk,
			                "SUBJECT",
			                "STATUS",
			                "DESCRIPTION",
			                "ASSIGNED_TO",
			                "CREATED_ON",
			                "CREATED_BY",
			                "CLOSED_ON",
			                "NUMBER_OF_DETAILS",
			                "TICKET_ID",
			                count(*) over () as apxws_row_cnt
			  from (
			select * from (
			SELECT * FROM tickets_v
			) r
			where ("ASSIGNED_TO" = :APXWS_EXPR_1)
			) r where rownum <= to_number(:APXWS_MAX_ROW_CNT)
				4	

30	0.01593	0.00008	...Execute Statement: select
			                null as apxws_row_pk,
			                "SUBJECT",
			                "STATUS",
			                "DESCRIPTION",
			                "ASSIGNED_TO",
			                "CREATED_ON",
			                "CREATED_BY",
			                "CLOSED_ON",
			                "NUMBER_OF_DETAILS",
			                "TICKET_ID",
			                count(*) over () as apxws_row_cnt
			  from (
			select * from (
			SELECT * FROM tickets_v
			) r
			where ("ASSIGNED_TO" = :APXWS_EXPR_1)
			) r where rownum <= to_number(:APXWS_MAX_ROW_CNT)
				4	

31	0.01601	0.00004	IR binding: "APXWS_EXPR_1" value="SCOTT"	4	

Debug Message Data

vm50/apex/f?p=4000:939:32040666824518::NO:939:P939_PAGE_VIEW_ID:93796

Figure 7-20. *Debug data for the altered version of an interactive report*

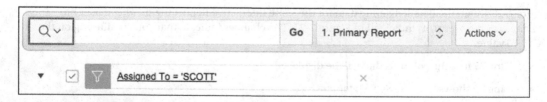

Figure 7-21. *The filters applied to the altered report*

With this debug data you have enough information to not only troubleshoot but also examine the potential performance of the query that was generated.

APEX Debugging API

Not only does APEX provide you with a method to interactively debug your application pages, it also provides a full API that allows you to instrument your own code and even turn on debugging programmatically. In this section, you'll examine the APIs and see how they can be put to use in an application context.

APEX_DEBUG

The core debugging API exists in the form of the APEX_DEBUG package. This package is now well documented in the Oracle Application Express API reference. The following sections are brief descriptions of what's available in the API and some usage notes. For full technical definitions, please refer to the official documentation. I'll discuss their usage further in later sections.

CONSTANTS

The package provides a number of constants used throughout the package itself as well as being available for developers to use.

```
subtype t_log_level is pls_integer;
c_log_level_error            constant t_log_level := 1; -- critical error
c_log_level_warn             constant t_log_level := 2; -- less critical error
c_log_level_info             constant t_log_level := 4; -- default debug level
c_log_level_app_enter        constant t_log_level := 5; -- APP: message when Procs/Funcs entered
c_log_level_app_trace        constant t_log_level := 6; -- APP: other messages within Procs/Funcs
c_log_level_engine_enter     constant t_log_level := 8; -- APEX: message when Procs/Funcs entered
c_log_level_engine_trace     constant t_log_level := 9; -- APEX: other messages within Procs/Funcs
```

DISABLE Procedure

This procedure allows the developer to programmatically disable debugging in the context of the current phase of page processing.

Usage Notes

DISABLE will turn off debugging no matter how it was enabled.

Disabling debugging in the middle of a phase will cause the actions that follow to be omitted from the debug information.

The latest points in an APEX page where debugging can be programmatically disabled are as follows:

- *Page rendering*: Occurs after the footer, making sure that the sequence number of the process is the *highest* in the set

- *Page processing*: Occurs on submit, after computations and validations, making sure that the sequence number of the process is the *highest* in the set

ENABLE Procedure

This procedure allows the developer to programmatically enable debugging in the context of the current phase of page processing.

Usage Notes

Level 1 is the most critical.

Level 9 is the least critical.

Setting p_level to 3 would log any message at levels 1, 2, and 3.

Enabling debugging programmatically is not limited by the application-level setting that disallows interactive debugging. Therefore, even if the application is set to disallow interactive debugging, programmatic debugging will still work as expected.

The earliest points in an APEX page where debugging can be programmatically enabled are as follows:

- *Page rendering*: You can create a branch of type Function Returning a Page (Show Only) with a processing point of Before Header, making sure that the sequence number of the process is the *lowest* in the set. Set the function body to simply return the current page number and use the condition to create a PL/SQL function body to use APEX_DEBUG to turn debugging on to the correct level. If the condition function always returns false, the branch will never be taken, but debugging can still be turned on.

- *Page processing*: You can create a process of type PL/SQL Code with a processing point of After Submit, making sure that the sequence number of the process is the *lowest* in the set.

When debugging is programmatically enabled via the API, APEX will not emit the debug message that indicates the phase (that is, SHOW or ACCEPT). Therefore, it is good practice to use the LOG_MESSAGE procedure to output a message immediately after debug that will help you to identify the phase. For example, the following code snippet could be placed in an On Load page process to programmatically enable debugging and immediately emit a message indicating the phase:

```
apex_debug.enable (p_level => 7);
apex_debug.log_message('S H O W --- Programmatically enabled');
```

Once turned on programmatically, debugging will remain on until it is either turned off programmatically or via the Developer Toolbar, if available.

ENTER Procedure

This procedure logs messages only when debugging is set to the level defined by the constant c_log_level_app_enter or higher.

Usage Notes

ENTER allows you to log the name of a routine being called and up to ten of its arguments and their values. You can also use the p_value_max_length to truncate the values passed to a finite length.

This procedure is useful when you need to understand what's being passed in to a procedure or function so you can debug what it will do with those particular values.

ERROR Procedure

This procedure logs messages only when debugging is set to the level defined by the constant c_log_level_error or higher.

Usage Notes

ERROR allows you to log errors into the DEBUG_MESSAGES table. This procedure will always log errors even if debugging is off.

The message passed to the ERROR procedure is reminiscent of the C language's sprintf routine and therefore can contain up to 20 occurrences of %s. Those occurrences will be replaced with the values of p0 to p19. Values passed via the p<n> variables can be truncated to a maximum length using the p_max_length parameter.

INFO Procedure

This procedure logs messages only when debugging is set to the level defined by the constant c_log_level_info or higher.

Usage Notes

INFO allows you to log errors into the DEBUG_MESSAGES table.

The message passed to the INFO procedure is reminiscent of the C language's sprintf routine and therefore can contain up to ten occurrences of %s. Those occurrences will be replaced with the values of p0 to p09. Values passed via the p<n> variables can be truncated to a maximum length using the p_max_length parameter.

LOG_DBMS_OUTPUT Procedure

This procedure uses dbms_output.get_lines to retrieve the current contents of the DBMS_OUTPUT buffer and write them to the DEBUG_MESSAGES table.

Usage Notes

Using this procedure, the messages emitted by legacy PL/SQL that contains calls to DBMS_OUTPUT can be captured and written to the debug log.

For these messages to be captured, debugging must be enabled.

LOG_MESSAGE Procedure

This procedure allows the developer to emit debug messages from within either APEX anonymous blocks or stored packages and procedures called from APEX.

Usage Notes

Level 1 is the most critical.

Level 9 is the least critical.

When using within stored PL/SQL program units that might be called outside of the context of APEX, always set P_ENABLED to FALSE. Failing to do so will result in an error because the APEX security group ID will not be set.

LOG_LONG_MESSAGE Procedure

This procedure allows the developer to emit debug messages larger than 4,000 characters from within either APEX anonymous blocks or stored packages and procedures called from APEX.

Usage Notes

Level 1 is the most critical.

Level 9 is the least critical.

Logging will be split into 4,000-byte chunks.

When using the LOG_LONG_MESSAGE procedure within stored PL/SQL program units that might be called outside of the context of APEX, always set P_ENABLED to FALSE. Failing to do so will result in an error because the APEX security group ID will not be set.

LOG_PAGE_SESSION_STATE Procedure

This procedure allows the developer to emit session state information into the debug messages table for a given page in the current application.

Usage Notes

Each item from the indicated page and its current value in session state will be emitted to the debug messages table.

MESSAGE Procedure

This procedure inserts a formatted debug message into the DEBUG_MESSAGES table.

Usage Notes

The message passed to the MESSAGE procedure is reminiscent of the C language's sprintf routine and therefore can contain up to 20 occurrences of %s. Those occurrences will be replaced with the values of p0 to p19. Values passed via the p<n> variables can be truncated to a maximum length using the p_max_length parameter.

If p_force is set to true, the message will be logged even if debugging is turned off or if the current debug level is smaller than that set using the p_level parameter.

REMOVE_DEBUG_BY_AGE Procedure

This procedure allows the developer to programmatically remove all debug messages for a specific application where the message timestamp is prior to *n* days before today.

REMOVE_DEBUG_BY_APP Procedure

This procedure allows the developer to programmatically remove any debug messages associated with a specific application.

REMOVE_DEBUG_BY_VIEW Procedure

This procedure allows the developer to programmatically remove any debug messages for a specific application that are identified as belonging to a specific debug view.

REMOVE_SESSION_MESSAGES Procedure

This procedure allows the developer to programmatically remove any debug messages associated with a specific user session.

TOCHAR Function

This function converts a Boolean true or false value to its VARCHAR2 equivalent.

TRACE Procedure

This procedure logs messages only when debugging is set to the level defined by the constant c_log_level_trace or higher.

Usage Notes

TRACE allows you to log messages into the DEBUG_MESSAGES table.

The message passed to the TRACE procedure is reminiscent of the C language's sprintf routine and therefore can contain up to ten occurrences of %s. Those occurrences will be replaced with the values of p0 to p10. Values passed via the p<n> variables can be truncated to a maximum length using the p_max_length parameter.

WARN Procedure

This procedure logs messages only when debugging is set to the level defined by the constant c_log_level_warn or higher.

Usage Notes

WARN allows you to log messages into the DEBUG_MESSAGES table.

The message passed to the WARN procedure is reminiscent of the C language's sprintf routine and therefore can contain up to ten occurrences of %s. Those occurrences will be replaced with the values of p0 to p10. Values passed via the p<n> variables can be truncated to a maximum length using the p_max_length parameter.

Programmatic Debugging

As you can see, the APEX_DEBUG_MESSAGE API provides the facilities necessary to enable and disable Debug mode programmatically. And as mentioned in the preceding documentation, the ability to use programmatic debugging is not affected by the application-level setting. This means that even if you have a standard that dictates that applications are deployed into production with debugging disabled, you still have the ability to capture debug information.

Figure 7-22 shows the capture of debug information for a single page in an application that displays a simple report. The debug information was captured interactively by using the Developer Toolbar.

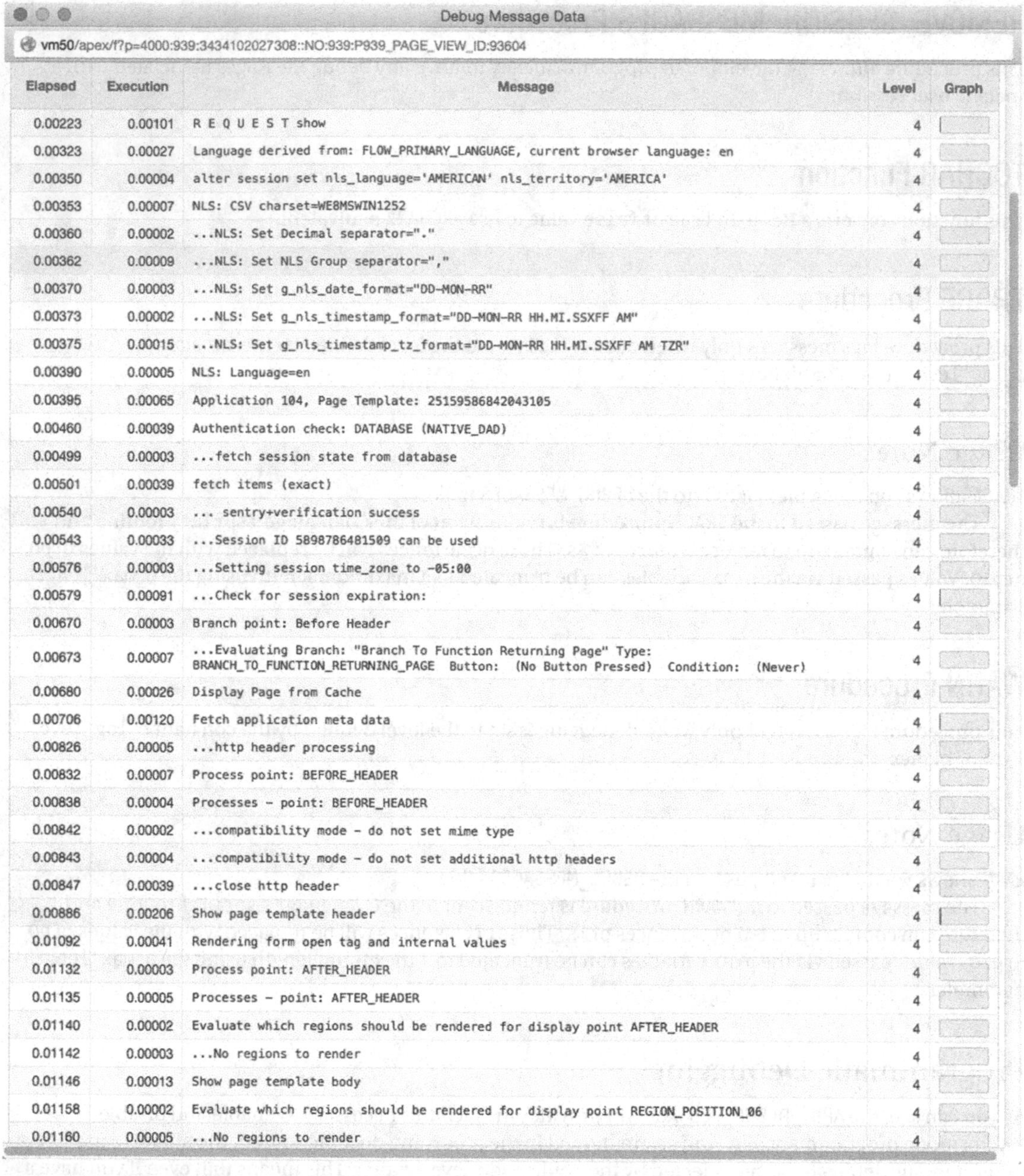

Elapsed	Execution	Message	Level	Graph
0.00223	0.00101	R E Q U E S T show	4	
0.00323	0.00027	Language derived from: FLOW_PRIMARY_LANGUAGE, current browser language: en	4	
0.00350	0.00004	alter session set nls_language='AMERICAN' nls_territory='AMERICA'	4	
0.00353	0.00007	NLS: CSV charset=WE8MSWIN1252	4	
0.00360	0.00002	...NLS: Set Decimal separator="."	4	
0.00362	0.00009	...NLS: Set NLS Group separator=","	4	
0.00370	0.00003	...NLS: Set g_nls_date_format="DD-MON-RR"	4	
0.00373	0.00002	...NLS: Set g_nls_timestamp_format="DD-MON-RR HH.MI.SSXFF AM"	4	
0.00375	0.00015	...NLS: Set g_nls_timestamp_tz_format="DD-MON-RR HH.MI.SSXFF AM TZR"	4	
0.00390	0.00005	NLS: Language=en	4	
0.00395	0.00065	Application 104, Page Template: 25159586842043105	4	
0.00460	0.00039	Authentication check: DATABASE (NATIVE_DAD)	4	
0.00499	0.00003	...fetch session state from database	4	
0.00501	0.00039	fetch items (exact)	4	
0.00540	0.00003	... sentry+verification success	4	
0.00543	0.00033	...Session ID 5898786481509 can be used	4	
0.00576	0.00003	...Setting session time_zone to -05:00	4	
0.00579	0.00091	...Check for session expiration:	4	
0.00670	0.00003	Branch point: Before Header	4	
0.00673	0.00007	...Evaluating Branch: "Branch To Function Returning Page" Type: BRANCH_TO_FUNCTION_RETURNING_PAGE Button: (No Button Pressed) Condition: (Never)	4	
0.00680	0.00026	Display Page from Cache	4	
0.00706	0.00120	Fetch application meta data	4	
0.00826	0.00005	...http header processing	4	
0.00832	0.00007	Process point: BEFORE_HEADER	4	
0.00838	0.00004	Processes - point: BEFORE_HEADER	4	
0.00842	0.00002	...compatibility mode - do not set mime type	4	
0.00843	0.00004	...compatibility mode - do not set additional http headers	4	
0.00847	0.00039	...close http header	4	
0.00886	0.00206	Show page template header	4	
0.01092	0.00041	Rendering form open tag and internal values	4	
0.01132	0.00003	Process point: AFTER_HEADER	4	
0.01135	0.00005	Processes - point: AFTER_HEADER	4	
0.01140	0.00002	Evaluate which regions should be rendered for display point AFTER_HEADER	4	
0.01142	0.00003	...No regions to render	4	
0.01146	0.00013	Show page template body	4	
0.01158	0.00002	Evaluate which regions should be rendered for display point REGION_POSITION_06	4	
0.01160	0.00005	...No regions to render	4	

Figure 7-22. *Debug data gathered interactively*

Figure 7-23 shows a branch created to gather debug information programmatically. The branch was created at the earliest possible point on the page. The branch does not in fact redirect to another page but instead simply enables debugging programmatically. Figure 7-24 shows the resulting debug data.

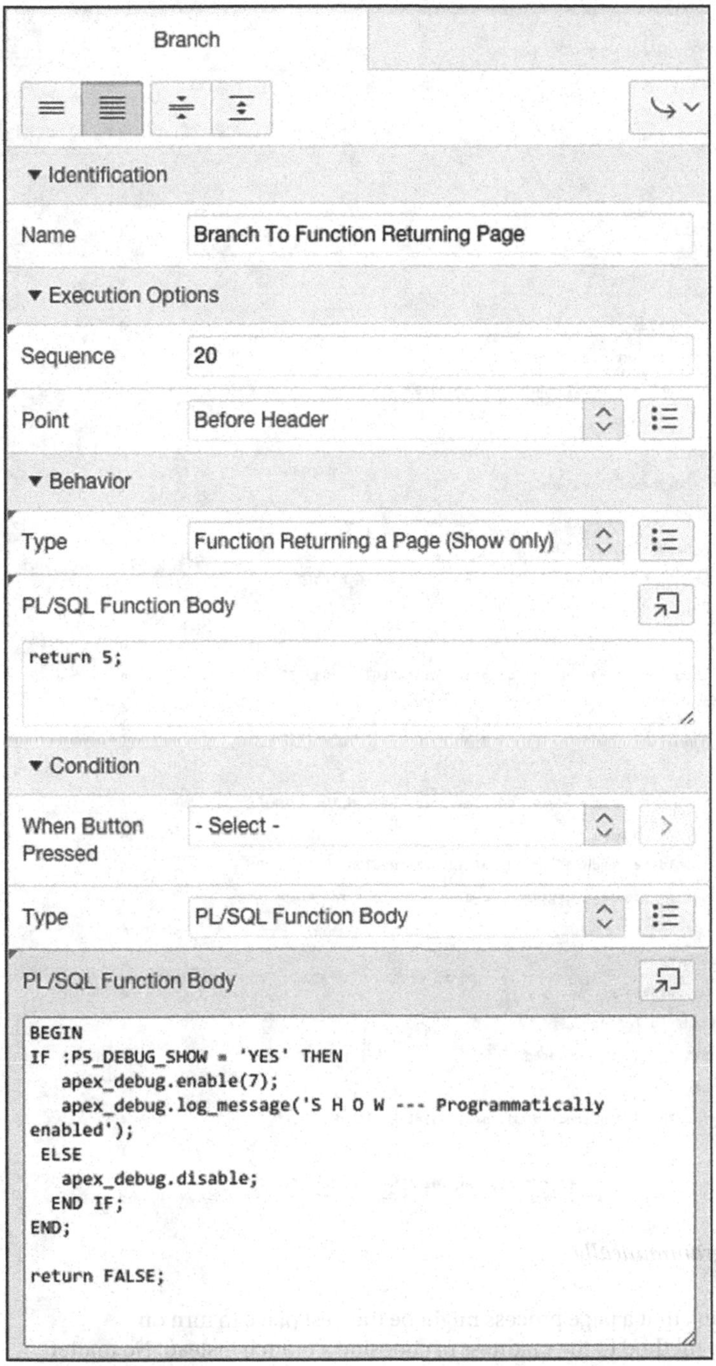

Branch

≡ ≣ ÷ ↑   ↳⌄

▼ Identification

Name	Branch To Function Returning Page

▼ Execution Options

Sequence	20

Point	Before Header	⌄	☰

▼ Behavior

Type	Function Returning a Page (Show only)	⌄	☰

PL/SQL Function Body	⤢

```
return 5;
```

▼ Condition

When Button Pressed	- Select -	⌄	>

Type	PL/SQL Function Body	⌄	☰

PL/SQL Function Body	⤢

```
BEGIN
IF :P5_DEBUG_SHOW = 'YES' THEN
   apex_debug.enable(7);
   apex_debug.log_message('S H O W --- Programmatically
enabled');
 ELSE
   apex_debug.disable;
  END IF;
END;

return FALSE;
```

Figure 7-23. Definition of a branch that programmatically enables debugging

Debug Message Data

vm50/apex/f?p=4000:939:3434102027308::NO:939:P939_PAGE_VIEW_ID:93607

Elapsed	Execution	Message	Level	Graph
0.00511	0.00009	S H O W ‑‑‑ Programatically Enabled	6	
0.00520	0.00005	......Result = false	4	
0.00526	0.00025	Display Page from Cache	4	
0.00551	0.00128	Fetch application meta data	4	
0.00679	0.00006	...http header processing	4	
0.00684	0.00011	Process point: BEFORE_HEADER	4	
0.00696	0.00004	Processes - point: BEFORE_HEADER	4	
0.00700	0.00002	...compatibility mode - do not set mime type	4	
0.00702	0.00001	...compatibility mode - do not set additional http headers	4	
0.00703	0.00037	...close http header	4	
0.00740	0.00236	Show page template header	4	
0.00976	0.00034	Rendering form open tag and internal values	4	
0.01010	0.00003	Process point: AFTER_HEADER	4	
0.01013	0.00005	Processes - point: AFTER_HEADER	4	
0.01017	0.00002	Evaluate which regions should be rendered for display point AFTER_HEADER	4	
0.01019	0.00002	...No regions to render	4	
0.01022	0.00018	Show page template body	4	
0.01040	0.00002	Evaluate which regions should be rendered for display point REGION_POSITION_06	4	
0.01042	0.00004	...No regions to render	4	
0.01047	0.00002	Evaluate which regions should be rendered for display point REGION_POSITION_07	4	
0.01049	0.00025	...No regions to render	4	
0.01073	0.00002	Evaluate which regions should be rendered for display point REGION_POSITION_08	4	
0.01076	0.00090	...No regions to render	4	
0.01166	0.00011	Evaluate which regions should be rendered for display point REGION_POSITION_01	4	
0.01177	0.00003	...No grid layout necessary, because everything is displayed in first column	4	
0.01180	0.00002	Render regions	4	
0.01182	0.00005	...Region: Automatic Measurement	4	
0.01187	0.00068	...region is nocache - do not cache	4	
0.01255	0.00010	......No page items/buttons to render	4	
0.01266	0.00002	Evaluate which sub regions should be rendered	4	
0.01268	0.00006	...No sub regions to render	4	
0.01274	0.00002	Evaluate which regions should be rendered for display point REGION_POSITION_04	4	
0.01276	0.00010	...No regions to render	4	
0.01286	0.00002	Evaluate which regions should be rendered for display point REGION POSITION 02	4	

Figure 7-24. *Debug data gathered programmatically*

While it may be more natural to think that a page process might be the best place to turn on programmatic debugging, there is some method to the madness of choosing a branch instead. No matter what its sequence number, page processes *always* execute after branches and computations. Therefore, if you want to capture information about branches and computations in your debug output, you must turn Debug mode on before these items are processed by APEX.

The ability to create a branch of type Function Returning a Page (Show Only) at a process point of Before Header that actually does not branch anywhere is perfect for these purposes. As long as its sequence number is lower than any other branch, programmatic debugging will capture all logged messages for any branch, computation, or process that follows it.

When debugging is turned on via the API, even at the earliest point possible, APEX will have already completed some of the steps involved in rendering or processing the page.

If you compare the interactive data to the data that was gathered programmatically, you'll notice there are a number of things that just don't get captured in the programmatic version. This shouldn't concern you too much because what is missing is directly related to core APEX code and not code for which you will likely be seeking to gather information.

However, one of the more important things that gets left out is the first line of debug information, which indicates the phase. This is easily remedied by following the ENABLE call with a call to LOG_MESSAGE, as shown earlier in Figure 7-23.

The same is true for the PROCESS phase as for the SHOW phase demonstrated earlier. When enabling debugging programmatically, there will be some things that get missed. In most circumstances, the missing data isn't significant enough to be concerned about; however, if you want to make sure you get *all* the data relating to a page, you're likely to want to enable debug as part of the page phase that is directly before the one you want to capture.

For example, if you want to capture all the details about page processing for a page, turn debugging on during that page's SHOW phase. Alternatively, if you want to capture all information regarding a page's SHOW phase, enable debugging as part of the processing phase of the page that branches to the page in question. If Debug mode is already enabled prior to reaching the desired phase, even if it was enabled programmatically, the entire phase's information will be captured.

Instrumenting Your Own Code

While having access to the debug information APEX emits by default is helpful, there will inevitably be times when you'll need deeper insight into what may be going on in the code that you have written.

The APEX Debugging API provides methods to expand the depth of information being gathered. This is especially useful when you're trying to understand what is happening within PL/SQL that might be part of a branch, computation, or process.

Logging Custom Messages

The LOG_MESSAGE and LOG_LONG_MESSAGE procedures are quite simple in signature; however, they provide an amazing amount of flexibility and functionality when it comes to gathering information about what's going on within your application.

The most straightforward use case would be one in which you might want to emit simple messages that mark the steps a piece of PL/SQL might be executing, such as marking the purpose of a simple code construct, like a loop, as in Listing 7-1.

Listing 7-1. Simple Code Demarcation Using LOG_MESSAGE

```
BEGIN
--
APEX_DEBUG.LOG_MESSAGE( P_MESSAGE =>'START - INSERTING 10000 RECORDS...');
--
FOR I IN 1..10000 LOOP
```

```
        INSERT INTO PERF_TEST (guid1, guid2, guid3, created_on)
        VALUES (SYS_GUID, SYS_GUID, SYS_GUID, SYSDATE);
END LOOP;
--
END;
```

Enabling Debug mode and running the page will produce the output shown in Figure 7-25.

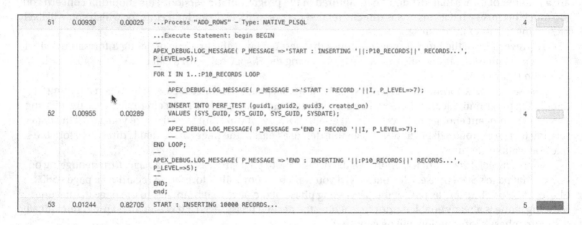

Figure 7-25. *Using LOG_MESSAGE to emit a line into the debug information*

However, to add *real* value, it behooves you to mark not only the beginning but also the end of each significant step, as in Listing 7-2.

Listing 7-2. Marking the Beginning and End of a Block of Code

```
BEGIN
--
APEX_DEBUG.LOG_MESSAGE( P_MESSAGE =>'START - INSERTING 10000 RECORDS...');
--
FOR I IN 1..10000 LOOP
        INSERT INTO PERF_TEST (guid1, guid2, guid3, created_on)
        VALUES (SYS_GUID, SYS_GUID, SYS_GUID, SYSDATE);
END LOOP;
--
APEX_DEBUG.LOG_MESSAGE( P_MESSAGE =>END - INSERTING 10000 RECORDS...');
--
END;
```

Remember that execution timing is measured from the beginning of the current step to the beginning of the subsequent step. These step boundaries coincide with the point at which a debug message is logged. Therefore, surrounding a code block with calls to LOG_MESSAGE provides the extra benefit of capturing an accurate timing of all the code that ran between those two messages, as shown in Figure 7-26.

51	0.00930	0.00025	...Process "ADD_ROWS" – Type: NATIVE_PLSQL		4	
			...Execute Statement: begin BEGIN			
			──			
			APEX_DEBUG.LOG_MESSAGE(P_MESSAGE =>'START : INSERTING '||:P10_RECORDS||' RECORDS...', P_LEVEL=>5);			
			FOR I IN 1..:P10_RECORDS LOOP			
			──			
			APEX_DEBUG.LOG_MESSAGE(P_MESSAGE =>'START : RECORD '||I, P_LEVEL=>7);			
			──			
52	0.00955	0.00289	INSERT INTO PERF_TEST (guid1, guid2, guid3, created_on) VALUES (SYS_GUID, SYS_GUID, SYS_GUID, SYSDATE);		4	
			APEX_DEBUG.LOG_MESSAGE(P_MESSAGE =>'END : RECORD '||I, P_LEVEL=>7);			
			──			
			END LOOP;			
			──			
			APEX_DEBUG.LOG_MESSAGE(P_MESSAGE =>'END : INSERTING '||:P10_RECORDS||' RECORDS...', P_LEVEL=>5);			
			──			
			END;			
			end;			
53	0.01244	0.82705	START : INSERTING 10000 RECORDS...		5	
54	0.83949	0.00020	END : INSERTING 10000 RECORDS...		5	

Figure 7-26. Surrounding code blocks with LOG_MESSAGE calls to capture an accurate timing

You have to be careful about your usage of the LOG_MESSAGE procedure, though. For instance, injecting a LOG_MESSAGE call in the middle of the loop would first create a huge number of log entries that you would be unlikely to want to wade through, and also it would potentially impact performance because you would be executing the full code path of the LOG_MESSAGE procedure 10,000 times.

That is where the p_level parameter comes in handy. Consider Listing 7-3. Here I've done exactly what I just warned against, but notice that the value for the level of the outer calls is at a higher level than that of the inner calls.

Listing 7-3. Using P_LEVEL to Designate the Message Level

```
BEGIN
--
APEX_DEBUG.LOG_MESSAGE( P_MESSAGE =>'START - INSERTING 10000 RECORDS...', P_LEVEL=>5);
--
FOR I IN 1..10000 LOOP
    --
    APEX_DEBUG.LOG_MESSAGE( P_MESSAGE =>'START RECORD '||I, P_LEVEL=>7);
    --
    INSERT INTO PERF_TEST (guid1, guid2, guid3, created_on)
    VALUES (SYS_GUID, SYS_GUID, SYS_GUID, SYSDATE);
    --
    APEX_DEBUG.LOG_MESSAGE( P_MESSAGE =>'END RECORD '||I, P_LEVEL=>7);
    --
END LOOP;
--
APEX_DEBUG.LOG_MESSAGE( P_MESSAGE =>'END - INSERTING 10000 RECORDS...', P_LEVEL=>5);
--
END;
```

Now when you choose to enable debugging programmatically, you can use the p_level parameter to decide to what level of message you want to log. Calling ENABLE with p_level set to 5 would log only the messages *outside* the loop. However, enabling debugging with a message level of 7 would log both outside and inside the loop. Using this mechanism, you can manage the level at which messages are logged and what level of log message you want to capture.

■ **Caution**   Using interactive debugging either by using the Developer Toolbar or by manipulating the URL and inserting YES in the debug position will *always* initiate logging to capture messages level 4 and above.

Lastly, using the p_enabled parameter of LOG_MESSAGE allows you to dictate that a message is important enough to *always* be logged, whether or not debugging has been enabled. Listing 7-4 shows the same code but injects a LOG_MESSAGE call in the top of the block that will always be written to the APEX dictionary, regardless of the state of debugging.

Listing 7-4. Using P_ENABLED to Always Log a Message

```
BEGIN
--
APEX_DEBUG.LOG_MESSAGE( P_MESSAGE =>'THIS MESSAGE IS ALWAYS LOGGED...', P_ENABLED=>TRUE,
P_LEVEL=>3);
--
APEX_DEBUG.LOG_MESSAGE( P_MESSAGE =>'START - INSERTING 10000 RECORDS...', P_LEVEL=>5);
--
FOR I IN 1..10000 LOOP
    --
    APEX_DEBUG.LOG_MESSAGE( P_MESSAGE =>'START RECORD '||I, P_LEVEL=>7);
    --
    INSERT INTO PERF_TEST (guid1, guid2, guid3, created_on)
    VALUES (SYS_GUID, SYS_GUID, SYS_GUID, SYSDATE);
    --
    APEX_DEBUG.LOG_MESSAGE( P_MESSAGE =>'END RECORD '||I, P_LEVEL=>7);
    --
END LOOP;
--
APEX_DEBUG.LOG_MESSAGE( P_MESSAGE =>'END - INSERTING 10000 RECORDS...', P_LEVEL=>5);
--
END;
```

Logging Session State

There are many instances when trying to debug a page where it would be beneficial to know specifically what was in session state. The LOG_PAGE_SESSION_STATE procedure will provide you with exactly that information.

The API will emit information into the DEBUG logs, which shows the session state for each item on the designated page. Like the LOG_MESSAGE procedure, the LOG_PAGE_SESSION_STATE procedure lets you dictate what log level will be associated with the emitted log records and allows you to decide whether to override the debug setting and always log the session state.

You can call the LOG_PAGE_SESSION_STATE procedure without passing any parameters, and it will log the session state for the currently processing page at debug message level 4, but it will do so only if debugging is enabled.

Figure 7-27 shows an example of the output of debug information that contains session state information. The session state information is specifically contained in rows 34 through 38 in the report.

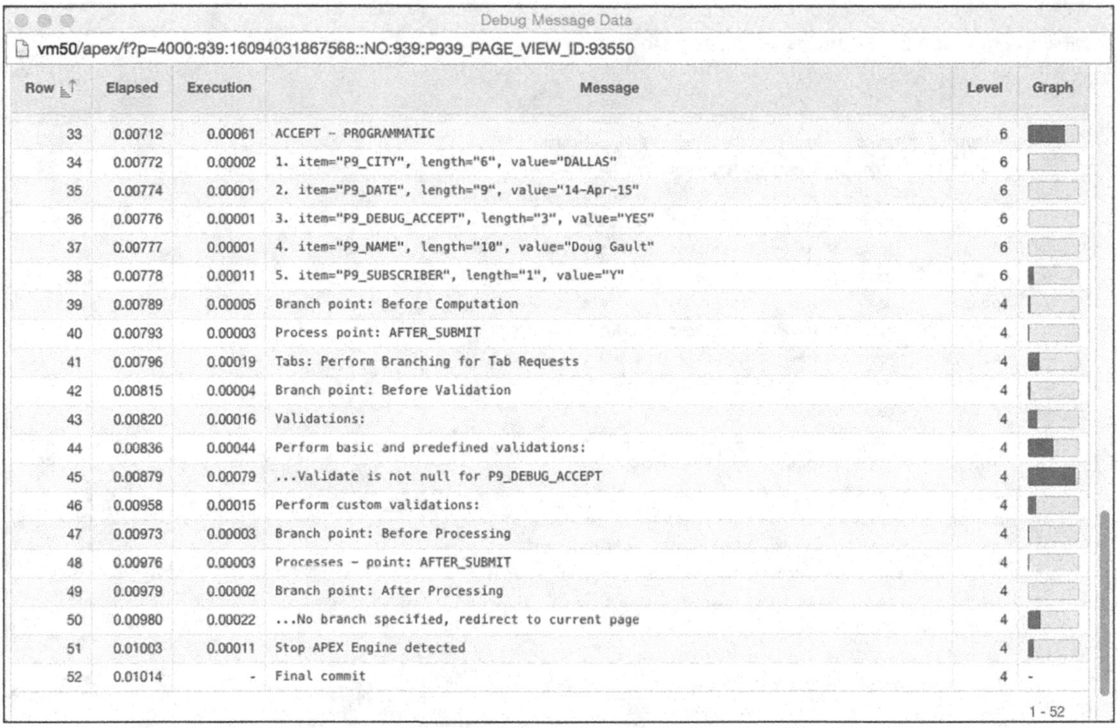

Row	Elapsed	Execution	Message	Level	Graph
			Debug Message Data		
			vm50/apex/f?p=4000:939:16094031867568::NO:939:P939_PAGE_VIEW_ID:93550		
33	0.00712	0.00061	ACCEPT - PROGRAMMATIC	6	
34	0.00772	0.00002	1. item="P9_CITY", length="6", value="DALLAS"	6	
35	0.00774	0.00001	2. item="P9_DATE", length="9", value="14-Apr-15"	6	
36	0.00776	0.00001	3. item="P9_DEBUG_ACCEPT", length="3", value="YES"	6	
37	0.00777	0.00001	4. item="P9_NAME", length="10", value="Doug Gault"	6	
38	0.00778	0.00011	5. item="P9_SUBSCRIBER", length="1", value="Y"	6	
39	0.00789	0.00005	Branch point: Before Computation	4	
40	0.00793	0.00003	Process point: AFTER_SUBMIT	4	
41	0.00796	0.00019	Tabs: Perform Branching for Tab Requests	4	
42	0.00815	0.00004	Branch point: Before Validation	4	
43	0.00820	0.00016	Validations:	4	
44	0.00836	0.00044	Perform basic and predefined validations:	4	
45	0.00879	0.00079	...Validate is not null for P9_DEBUG_ACCEPT	4	
46	0.00958	0.00015	Perform custom validations:	4	
47	0.00973	0.00003	Branch point: Before Processing	4	
48	0.00976	0.00003	Processes - point: AFTER_SUBMIT	4	
49	0.00979	0.00002	Branch point: After Processing	4	
50	0.00980	0.00022	...No branch specified, redirect to current page	4	
51	0.01003	0.00011	Stop APEX Engine detected	4	
52	0.01014	-	Final commit	4	-

1 - 52

Figure 7-27. Debug information containing session state information

The data contains a row for each item that appears on the page, whether visible to the user or not, and contains the item name, length, and value. While it may seem odd that the items are rendered not in the order that they appear on the screen, but in alphabetical order by item name, this is because many of the new APEX themes are div based and it is not necessarily possible to identify where they appear on the page.

You can also emit more than just the current page's session state, but to do this you will need to make an API call for each page you want to include. Figure 7-28 shows an example including session state for page 9 and page 7.

Row ↑	Elapsed	Execution	Message	Level	Graph
33	0.00827	0.00190	ACCEPT - PROGRAMMATIC	6	
34	0.01017	0.00003	1. item="P9_CITY", length="6", value="DALLAS"	6	
35	0.01019	0.00001	2. item="P9_DATE", length="9", value="14-Apr-15"	6	
36	0.01021	0.00001	3. item="P9_DEBUG_ACCEPT", length="3", value="YES"	6	
37	0.01022	0.00001	4. item="P9_NAME", length="10", value="Doug Gault"	6	
38	0.01024	0.00032	5. item="P9_SUBSCRIBER", length="1", value="Y"	6	
39	0.01057	0.00008	1. item="P7_DEBUGGING", length="7", value="Allowed"	6	
40	0.01064	0.00002	2. item="P7_DEBUG_ACCEPT", length="3", value="YES"	6	
41	0.01066	0.00002	3. item="P7_DEBUG_LEVEL", length="1", value="5"	6	
42	0.01067	0.00012	4. item="P7_DEBUG_SHOW", length="2", value="NO"	6	
43	0.01079	0.00005	Branch point: Before Computation	4	
44	0.01084	0.00003	Process point: AFTER_SUBMIT	4	
45	0.01087	0.00017	Tabs: Perform Branching for Tab Requests	4	
46	0.01104	0.00007	Branch point: Before Validation	4	
47	0.01111	0.00018	Validations:	4	
48	0.01129	0.00053	Perform basic and predefined validations:	4	
49	0.01182	0.00062	...Validate is not null for P9_DEBUG_ACCEPT	4	
50	0.01244	0.00012	Perform custom validations:	4	
51	0.01256	0.00004	Branch point: Before Processing	4	
52	0.01260	0.00003	Processes - point: AFTER_SUBMIT	4	
53	0.01263	0.00002	Branch point: After Processing	4	
54	0.01265	0.00036	...No branch specified, redirect to current page	4	
55	0.01301	0.00011	Stop APEX Engine detected	4	
56	0.01312	-	Final commit	4	-

Figure 7-28. Debug information including session state information for two separate pages

The Data Behind Debugging

As mentioned earlier, APEX debugging data is now kept in a set of data dictionary tables so that it can be examined and compared to other runs of the same page. In this section, you'll look at the underlying tables and view, the lifetime of the data in them, and how the data differs when captured interactively as opposed to when captured programmatically.

Tables and View

Debug data is stored as metadata in the core APEX schema and is split across two tables: WWV_FLOW_DEBUG_MESSAGES and WWV_FLOW_DEBUG_MESSAGES2. The data is exposed to the developer via a single APEX data dictionary view: APEX_DEBUG_MESSAGES.

■ **Caution** Don't try to query the tables directly. Focus on the view. You don't want to waste your time trying to sort out whether your debug data is contained in one table or spread across them both. Always query the view.

While it may seem odd that there are two underlying tables, APEX uses this two-table setup in a number of places to keep a finite duration of data around. The table into which data is actually inserted is switched, by default, every 14 days. When the switch occurs from one table to the other, APEX truncates the table that it's switching to. This means that at a minimum it will have no data (in other words, no debug information has been gathered) or, depending upon how APEX is configured, up to 360 days' worth of data. Figure 7-29 gives a visual depiction of this idea.

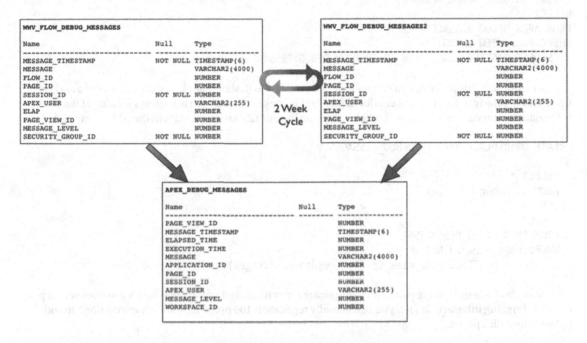

Figure 7-29. The view and underlying tables that hold APEX debug information

---

■ **Note**   The actual number of days in a cycle is defined at the APEX instance level by the APEX administrator and can be a maximum of 180 days between log switches.

You may think that having a finite amount of data available to you at any one time might be too limiting, and I would have to agree with you. If you want to keep more than that amount of data, you'll have to take matters into your own hands. Doing this is actually quite straightforward.

First, you'll need to create a local version of the debug data table that you control. The simplest way to do this is as follows:

```
CREATE TABLE MY_DEBUG_MESSAGES
AS
SELECT * FROM APEX_DEBUG_MESSAGES
WHERE 'X' = 'Y'
```

This will create the table without bringing any of the rows over. Then, you'll want to copy only the rows from the APEX_DEBUG_MESSAGES view to your new table, but to make this something that can be run over and over, you'll want to copy only the rows that don't already exist in the table. Luckily, the PAGE_VIEW_ID column gives you something unique to compare against. The following SQL statement will copy only the information that does not already exist in the table:

```
INSERT INTO MY_DEBUG_MESSAGES
SELECT *
FROM APEX_DEBUG_MESSAGES
WHERE PAGE_VIEW_ID NOT IN
  (SELECT DISTINCT PAGE_VIEW_ID FROM MY_DEBUG_MESSAGES);
```

To automate this process, you can include the previous SQL statement in a stored procedure and set it up to run regularly as a database-scheduled job. And to make sure that you are always looking at the latest information, you can create a view that joins the data in your table with the data in the APEX view, as follows:

```
CREATE OR REPLACE VIEW MY_DEBUG_MESSAGES_V
AS
  SELECT *
  FROM my_debug_messages
UNION
  SELECT *
  FROM APEX_DEBUG_MESSAGESS
  WHERE page_view_id NOT IN
    (SELECT DISTINCT page_view_id FROM my_debug_messages);
```

Now you have everything you need to duplicate the screens and reports that APEX provides you as part of the debugging interface. In fact, you can actually replicate it 100 percent by simply examining the code behind the APEX pages.

■ **Note**   If you're not already aware, you can load the APEX core applications into a workspace and examine the code and SQL statements that make them tick. Most of the core code of APEX is held in the wrapped packages in the APEX_050000 schema, but most of the APEX page magic is there for you to examine.

Examining the Debug Data

Now that you know where the debug data is kept, let's take a look at exactly what is being kept. Table 7-1 describes each column and the data it contains.

Table 7-1. *Columns of the APEX_DEBUGS View*

Column Name	Description
PAGE_VIEW_ID	Page view identifier that is a unique sequence generated for each page view recorded with debugging
MESSAGE_TIMESTAMP	Timestamp in GMT that the message was saved
ELAPSED_TIME	Elapsed time in seconds from the beginning of the page submission or page view
EXECUTION_TIME	Time elapsed between the current and the next debug message
MESSAGE	Text of the debug message
APPLICATION_ID	Application identifier, unique across all workspaces
PAGE_ID	Page identifier within the specified application
SESSION_ID	APEX session identifier
APEX_USER	Username of the user authenticated to the APEX application
MESSAGE_LEVEL	Level of debug message, ranging from 1 to 9
WORKSPACE_ID	APEX workspace identifier, unique within an instance

Most of the columns in the view are pretty self-explanatory, but the relationship between MESSAGE_ TIMESTAMP, ELAPSED_TIME, and EXECUTION_TIME merits some discussion.

The MESSAGE_TIMESTAMP column is straightforward; it's merely the accurate timestamp of when the debug message was entered into the underlying debug message tables. To get a clear picture of the order in which things happened during a page SHOW or ACCEPT, simply order the rows ascending by the MESSAGE_ TIMESTAMP.

The EXECUTION_TIME is calculated as the difference between the current timestamp and the timestamp from the subsequent record. So, in essence, it shows how much time has elapsed between the two records being inserted. You can see this calculation in the definition of the APEX_DEBUG view. The view uses the LEAD and PARTITION functions to calculate the difference between the two timestamps.

ELAPSED_TIME is something different entirely. This column is supposed to show the elapsed time since the beginning of the page submission or the page view. While logic might dictate that you should be able to perform some arithmetic using the timestamp and the calculated execution time to arrive at the elapsed time, you'd be wrong to do so. APEX actually uses yet another mechanism (a function call in this case) to calculate the elapsed time since the beginning of this phase. Because the function call actually takes some time (even if it's microseconds), the timing of the elapsed time is always just a little off from what you might expect. Don't get hung up on this. They are usually within such a small tolerance that it's fairly unmeasurable unless the task you are tracking is *huge*.

And in any account, what you really should be paying attention to is EXECUTION_TIME. If you want to find what you need to performance-tune within your page, pay attention to the thing with the largest execution time.

Using Debug Data for More Than Debugging

The fact that you have direct access to the data, and now know how to keep the data around for longer than the natural cycle that is built in to APEX, means that you can begin to use this data for more than just debugging. The overall information that is available makes this data perfect for performing longer-term analysis and performance tracking.

For instance, using programmatic debugging, you could choose to collect and keep performance information about your most important application pages. You may not want to keep information for every page view, but you could easily write logic that captures *n* percent of all page views. Then using the information contained in your long-term debug tables, you can track the performance over time. You could even begin to spot and map trends in performance, potentially identifying when a critical process might trend outside its window of acceptability.

Another potential use is to compare data before and after making a change to a page. If the main structure of the page hasn't changed, but instead the driving query behind it has changed, then you would be able to easily write code to compare, line for line, whether the new version of the page ran faster or slower than a previously captured version.

If a page calls stored PL/SQL code that is also instrumented using the APEX debugging API, you then have insight into the performance trends of the business logic that you've written in PL/SQL.

The bottom line is that you have this data for whatever purposes you want, and the better instrumented your code, the more detail you have at your disposal.

Debugging Dynamic Actions

Because the Dynamic Actions framework is actually implemented as JavaScript that is processed in the browser, debugging dynamic actions is approached a bit differently. APEX still uses Debug mode to determine whether the Dynamic Actions framework should emit data, and you can still enable debugging in all the same ways that have been discussed. However, instead of inserting data into the underlying debug messages tables, the Dynamic Actions framework emits message to the browser's JavaScript console.

The information that appears in the JavaScript console takes the following form:

```
Dynamic Action Fired: [Dynamic Action Name](Specific Action Fired)
```

Figure 7-30 shows an example of using Chrome's debug console to view the debug information.

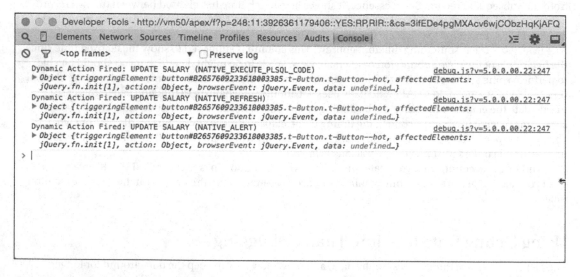

Figure 7-30. *The Chrome JavaScript console containing Dynamic Actions framework debug messages*

While this doesn't give you any detail about what the dynamic action code is doing, it does give you a visual indicator that the dynamic action code is firing. For a bit more information, you can edit the Chrome console's settings to include XMLHttpRequests, as shown in Figure 7-31.

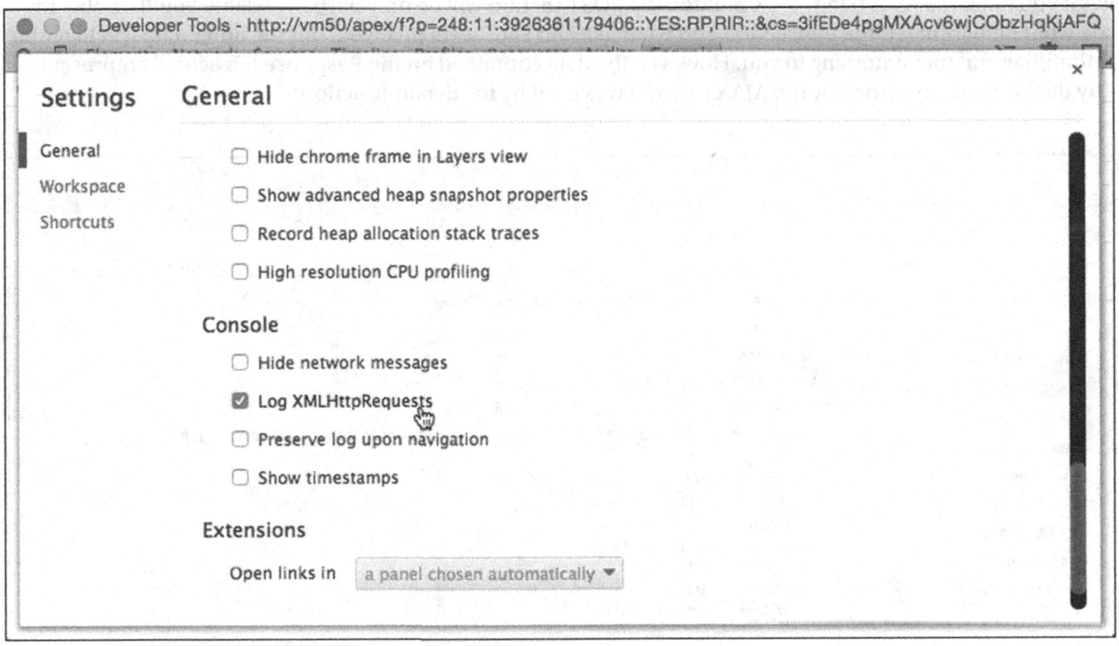

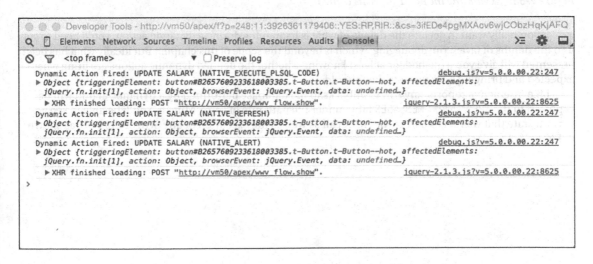

Figure 7-31. *Choosing to show XMLHttpRequests in the console*

After this is turned on, you'll not only see the dynamic actions that fire but also the calls to WWV_FLOW. SHOW that indicate XMLHttpRequests (or AJAX calls), as shown in Figure 7-32.

Figure 7-32. *Console containing XMLHttpRequests and dynamic action debug messages*

In Chrome, to view information about the XMLHttpRequest, click the link that contains the reference to wwv_flow.show. This will take you to the Network tab and briefly highlight the related row.

Clicking the indicated row will expand the detail of the AJAX call and will expose the header, post, response, and so on, as shown in Figure 7-33. Because the dynamic actions are generated code based on what you declared within the APEX builder, the POST section will be only partially useful. You'll be able to see what field initiated the transaction and what APP and PAGE were involved, but the other data will likely be unfamiliar and mean nothing to you. However, the data contained on the Response tab actually represents any data that was returned by the AJAX call and was used by the dynamic action.

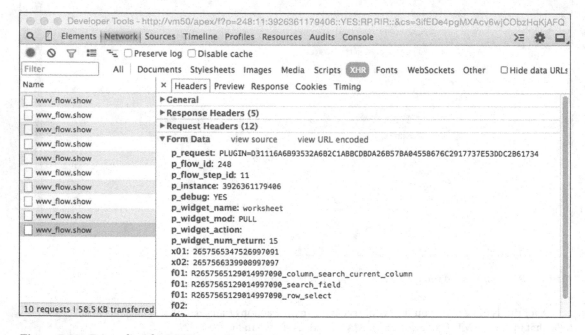

Figure 7-33. *Expanding the POST to see its content*

If you really want to get into the details of what is happening during a dynamic action, you'll need to get into the depths of JavaScript debugging, which is beyond the scope of this chapter. But ideally what has been presented will give you a method for at least knowing whether the defined dynamic actions are firing when expected and bringing back the data they should.

Like interactive reports, any AJAX callbacks to the database performed by a dynamic action will be captured in the APEX_DEBUG_MESSAGES table under the path info of ajax plugin. You'll be able to see any session state that was set as part of the AJAX call as well as the execution of any SQL or PL/SQL, as shown in Figure 7-34.

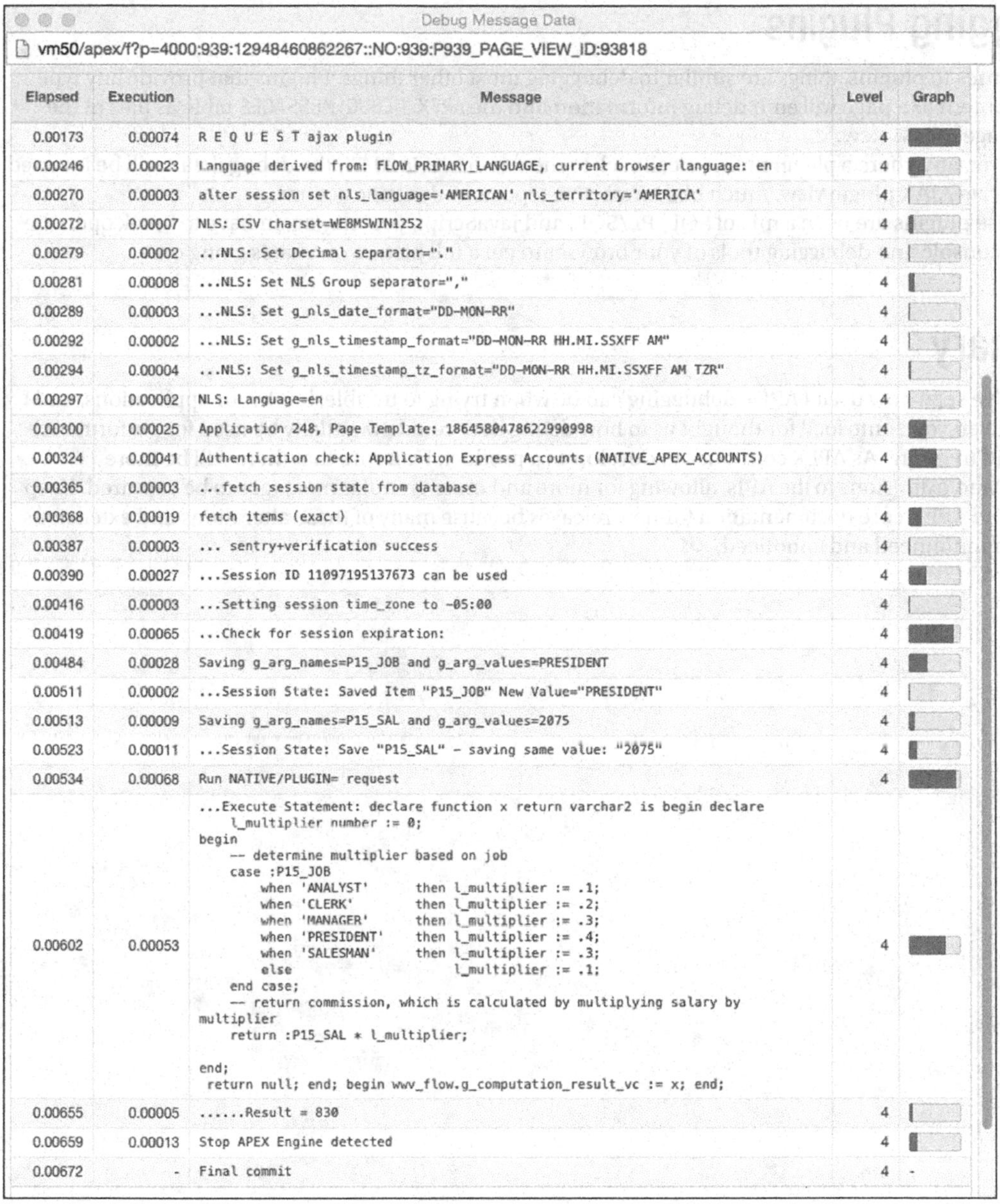

Debug Message Data

vm50/apex/f?p=4000:939:12948460862267::NO:939:P939_PAGE_VIEW_ID:93818

Elapsed	Execution	Message	Level	Graph
0.00173	0.00074	R E Q U E S T ajax plugin	4	
0.00246	0.00023	Language derived from: FLOW_PRIMARY_LANGUAGE, current browser language: en	4	
0.00270	0.00003	alter session set nls_language='AMERICAN' nls_territory='AMERICA'	4	
0.00272	0.00007	NLS: CSV charset=WE8MSWIN1252	4	
0.00279	0.00002	...NLS: Set Decimal separator="."	4	
0.00281	0.00008	...NLS: Set NLS Group separator=","	4	
0.00289	0.00003	...NLS: Set g_nls_date_format="DD-MON-RR"	4	
0.00292	0.00002	...NLS: Set g_nls_timestamp_format="DD-MON-RR HH.MI.SSXFF AM"	4	
0.00294	0.00004	...NLS: Set g_nls_timestamp_tz_format="DD-MON-RR HH.MI.SSXFF AM TZR"	4	
0.00297	0.00002	NLS: Language=en	4	
0.00300	0.00025	Application 248, Page Template: 1864580478622990998	4	
0.00324	0.00041	Authentication check: Application Express Accounts (NATIVE_APEX_ACCOUNTS)	4	
0.00365	0.00003	...fetch session state from database	4	
0.00368	0.00019	fetch items (exact)	4	
0.00387	0.00003	... sentry+verification success	4	
0.00390	0.00027	...Session ID 11097195137673 can be used	4	
0.00416	0.00003	...Setting session time_zone to -05:00	4	
0.00419	0.00065	...Check for session expiration:	4	
0.00484	0.00028	Saving g_arg_names=P15_JOB and g_arg_values=PRESIDENT	4	
0.00511	0.00002	...Session State: Saved Item "P15_JOB" New Value="PRESIDENT"	4	
0.00513	0.00009	Saving g_arg_names=P15_SAL and g_arg_values=2075	4	
0.00523	0.00011	...Session State: Save "P15_SAL" - saving same value: "2075"	4	
0.00534	0.00068	Run NATIVE/PLUGIN= request	4	

0.00602	0.00053	...Execute Statement: declare function x return varchar2 is begin declare
		l_multiplier number := 0;
		begin
		-- determine multiplier based on job
		case :P15_JOB
		when 'ANALYST' then l_multiplier := .1;
		when 'CLERK' then l_multiplier := .2;
		when 'MANAGER' then l_multiplier := .3;
		when 'PRESIDENT' then l_multiplier := .4;
		when 'SALESMAN' then l_multiplier := .3;
		else l_multiplier := .1;
		end case;
		-- return commission, which is calculated by multiplying salary by multiplier
		return :P15_SAL * l_multiplier;
		
		end;
		return null; end; begin wwv_flow.g_computation_result_vc := x; end;
			4	

0.00655	0.00005	......Result = 830	4	
0.00659	0.00013	Stop APEX Engine detected	4	
0.00672	-	Final commit	4	-

***Figure 7-34.** Detailed debug data for an AJAX call made by a dynamic action*

Debugging Plugins

When it comes to plugins, things are similar to debugging most other things. Plugins that provide any type of visual content to a page will emit debug information into the APEX_DEBUG_MESSAGES table as part of the standard page's SHOW view.

However, anywhere a plugin makes a callback to the database via AJAX, the debug detail will be inserted into a separate AJAX plugin view, much like interactive reports or dynamic actions.

Because plugins are often a mix of SQL, PL/SQL, and JavaScript, you may again have to break open the JavaScript console and debugging tools of your browser to get a full picture of what is going on.

Summary

I hope you've seen how useful APEX debugging can be when trying to troubleshoot your applications, and I hope I've given you some food for thought as to how debug data could potentially be used for performance analysis and trending. As APEX continues to develop as a product, I am sure that there will be more alterations and extensions to the APIs, allowing for more and more granular messages to be captured. Keep an eye on the APEX core documentation for new releases because many of these alterations and extensions often go unannounced and unnoticed.

CHAPTER 8

■■■

Dynamic Actions

by Martin Giffy D'Souza

Dynamic actions were first introduced in APEX 4.0. They allow developers to declaratively define actions based on browser events. This chapter will cover all aspects of dynamic actions including creating and modifying dynamic actions and how dynamic actions can interact with each other. This chapter is divided into three main sections. It will first compare the manual way of manipulating browser events using custom JavaScript to create a dynamic action. The second section will cover all the options and features available with dynamic actions. The last section will present a detailed example of using multiple dynamic actions.

This chapter assumes you are familiar with APEX and have a basic understanding of the following web technologies:

- JavaScript

- JQuery

- CSS

- HTML

If you are unfamiliar with any of these languages or need additional information, please go to www.w3schools.com. The JavaScript examples provided in this chapter will use jQuery, which is included as part of APEX 5.

■ **Note**   APEX 5 supports two development methods: Component View and Page Designer. Component view is the old (APEX 4 and older) developer page with the traditional Page Rendering, Page Processing, and Shared Components columns. The new Page Designer is a more modern IDE. It has a three-column development page that does not require wizards for each step. For the purpose of this chapter, all examples will use the new Page Designer view and refer to the three columns as the left, central, and right panes.

Custom JavaScript vs. Dynamic Actions

The best way to highlight dynamic actions is to compare them to the manual method using custom JavaScript. This section will examine a simple problem you may have faced when developing an APEX application and show how to resolve it first manually and then using a dynamic action. The purpose is to demonstrate the manual versus dynamic action way to handle browser-based events in APEX.

Suppose you have a select list for a department (P1_DEPTNO) and employees (P1_EMPNO) on page 1. If no department is selected, the list of employees should not be displayed, as shown in Figure 8-1. Once a department is selected, the list of employees should appear, as shown in Figure 8-2. The two subsections that follow compare the different ways to implement the functionality shown in the figures.

Figure 8-1. *No department selected*

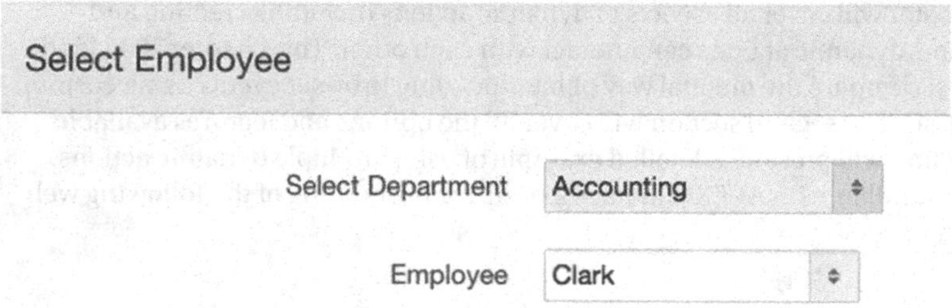

Figure 8-2. *Department selected*

Manual (Custom JavaScript) Method

Prior to APEX 4, if you wanted to perform an action based on a browser event, you needed to write custom JavaScript code. Writing custom JavaScript code poses several issues.

- The code can be stored in different locations such as an external file, HTML region, region header, as part of a page process, and so on. This can make it hard to find the exact location of the code if you need to debug or modify it.

- If developing in a team environment, each developer may use different techniques, and the code might not be reusable.

- Not all APEX developers understand JavaScript.

The following JavaScript example shows how to toggle a field based on a browser event prior to APEX 4. This code snippet needs to be included in your page. Since there are multiple ways to include it in your page, it can be hard for someone to track down where the code is stored.

```
/**
 * Toggle Empno based on P1_DEPTNO's value
 */
function showHideEmpno(){
  if ($v('P1_DEPTNO') == '')
    $x_HideItemRow('P1_EMPNO');
```

```
  else
    $x_ShowItemRow('P1_EMPNO');
}//showHideEmpno
//Wait for page to be ready
$(document).ready(function() {
  //Show/Hide Empno after page load
  showHideEmpno();

  //Register browser event (onChange)
  $('#P1_DEPTNO').on('change',function(){showHideEmpno();});
});
```

Dynamic Action Method

Starting in APEX 4, you can declaratively trigger actions based on browser events using dynamic actions. Dynamic actions are a preferred method over custom JavaScript functions because of the following reasons:

- They are declarative, which allows developers to easily identify where the code is stored.

- They have a built-in framework to maintain consistency across an application.

- They make it easy for non-JavaScript developers to apply browser event–based actions.

The following steps describe how to toggle the Employee field, as was done in the previous example, using a dynamic action. This example does not cover each step in detail since the goal is to quickly compare the manual method with the dynamic action. The next section of this chapter will describe each of the available options in detail.

1. In the Page Designer, click the Dynamic Actions icon at the top of the left pane, as shown in Figure 8-3.

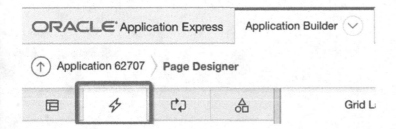

Figure 8-3. *Click the Dynamic Actions icon*

2. Right-click the Events folder and select the Create Dynamic Action option from the menu, as shown in Figure 8-4.

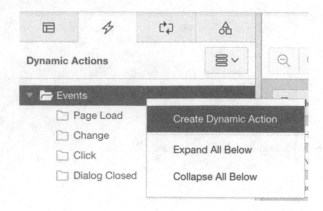

Figure 8-4. Create Dynamic Action menu item

3. The left pane shows the new (yet still unspecified) dynamic action, as shown in Figure 8-5. Some of the missing required information is highlighted in red. To see the complete list of missing components, click the Messages tab, as shown in Figure 8-6.

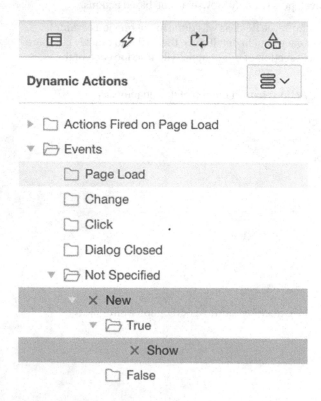

Figure 8-5. Newly created dynamic action

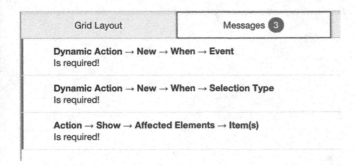

Figure 8-6. *Page Designer Messages notifications*

4. In the left pane, click the dynamic action currently labeled as X New and modify its properties in the right pane, as shown in Figure 8-7.

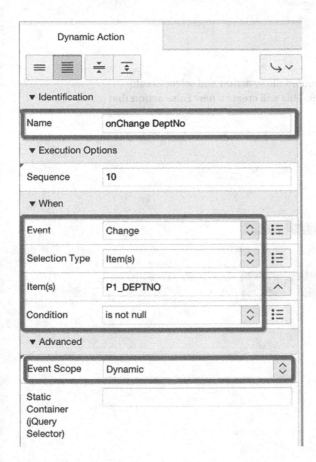

Figure 8-7. *Dynamic Action properties*

5. On the left pane, select X Show and edit its properties in the right pane, as shown in Figure 8-8.

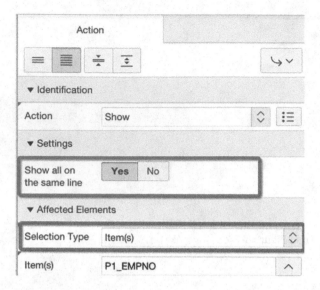

Figure 8-8. True Action properties

6. In the left pane, right-click the newly created Show action and select Create Opposite Action, as shown in Figure 8-9. This will create a new False action that will hide the employee row.

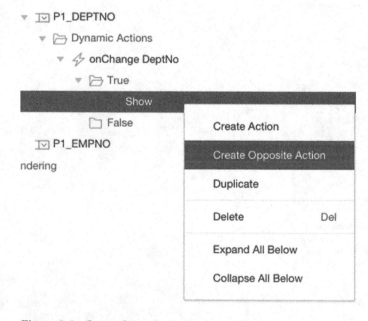

Figure 8-9. Create Opposite Action menu item

7. Click the Save button in the top-right corner of the page and run the page to test the new dynamic action. An employee should appear only when a department has been selected.

Dynamic actions have a lot of benefits; however, there are some situations where you may want use custom JavaScript, primarily for performance and control issues. For example, if you have a client-side action that needs to be performed as quickly as possible, then manually coding it using JavaScript may be a better approach. Dynamic actions add a minimal amount of overhead compared to certain manual techniques. In most situations, this additional overhead is not significant nor will it degrade the performance of your application.

Dynamic Actions in Detail

This section will cover all the options available for dynamic actions and will reference the OnChange DeptNo dynamic action that was created in the previous section.

An easy way to understand dynamic actions is to break down their components into two main parts: drivers and actions. The *driver* determines what causes a dynamic action to run and when an action is triggered. *Actions* contain the code to perform the tasks. In the previous example, the driver is when the P1_DEPTNO select list is changed. The actions is to either show or hide the P1_EMPNO select list. Figure 8-10 highlights the driver and actions concept as part of a flow chart. In Figure 8-10, DA stands for dynamic action.

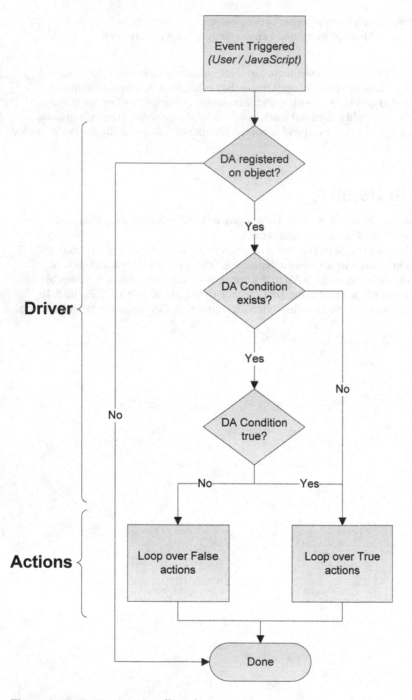

Figure 8-10. Dynamic action flow chart

When modifying a dynamic action, the When and Advanced sections allow you to define the driver. The True and False actions define the actions to perform based on a real-time condition.

To edit a dynamic action, simply click the Dynamic Actions icon (shown earlier in Figure 8-3) and click the desired dynamic action. Alternatively, you can select the rendering icon in the left pane, as shown in Figure 8-11. Then expand the P1_DEPTNO item and click its dynamic actions, as shown in Figure 8-12.

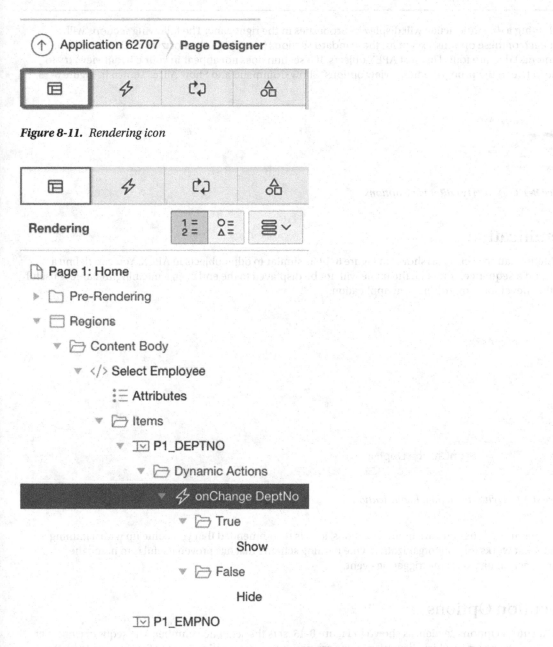

Figure 8-11. Rendering icon

Figure 8-12. Dynamic action under page item

■ **Note** When a dynamic action is linked to a region or an item, it will also appear in the region's or item's tree entry in the left pane.

Editing a dynamic action will display its properties in the right pane. The following sections will cover each of these options, except for the standard sections (Condition, Authorization, Configuration, Comments) that are found in most APEX objects. If a section does not appear in your current view, try to toggle between the property editor's view options, Show Command and Show All, as shown in Figure 8-13.

Figure 8-13. *Property editor view options*

Identification

The Identification section, as shown in Figure 8-14, is similar to other objects in APEX. You can define a name and a sequence. Although the name will not be displayed to the end user, a meaningful name is useful for other developers modifying your application.

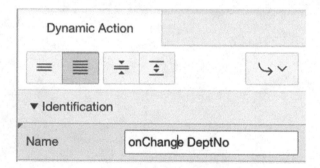

Figure 8-14. *Dynamic action: Identification*

Dynamic actions can have multiple actions, so it is recommended that you come up with a naming scheme that works for your organization. One naming scheme that has proven useful is to name the dynamic action based on the triggering event.

Execution Options

The Execution Options section, as shown in Figure 8-15, sets the sequence number. The sequence number determines the order in which dynamic actions are performed. If an action is set to fire on page load, the sequence number will determine the order of the actions, regardless of their triggering event, during the page load. After the page is loaded, the sequence is relevant only if you have multiple dynamic actions that are executed by the same event.

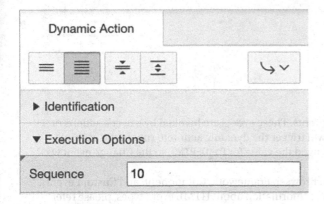

Figure 8-15. Dynamic action: Execution Options

When

APEX dynamic actions bind events to objects that you specify in the When section. When the defined event occurs on the objects, APEX will run the appropriate actions. Figure 8-16 shows the When section for the onChange Deptno dynamic action.

Figure 8-16. Dynamic action: When

There are three main components to the When section: Event, Selection Type, and Condition. If you click each of these labels, you'll get some excellent documentation about each of these components. You can find the documentation in the Help tab in the central pane, as shown in Figure 8-17.

| Grid Layout | Messages | Page Search | Help |

Figure 8-17. *Help tab*

Event

Dynamic actions are triggered by browser-based events. These events are invoked by a user's actions or by JavaScript. The event determines which event will trigger the dynamic action to run. In the example, the dynamic action is set to run when the user changed the value for P1_DEPTNO, so the Change event was selected.

Events are grouped into four main categories: Browser, Framework, Component, and Custom events. Browser events are standard HTML events (for more information about HTML event types, please refer to the jQuery event documentation: http://api.jquery.com/category/events). Framework events are triggered by APEX-specific events. For example, the After Refresh event is triggered after a report region is refreshed as part of report pagination. Component events are triggered by specific objects within APEX or by plug-ins. Custom events allow you to define a JavaScript event name to listen to. Use this option only if the required event is not available in the list of drop-down events. The following site covers custom events in detail: https://learn.jquery.com/events/introduction-to-custom-events.

Selection Type

The event option will determine which events APEX needs to "listen" for. The Selection Type option and its corresponding object determine the objects to listen on. In the example, Item(s) was selected. This means that APEX will wait for a change to occur on P1_DEPTNO. Once a user changes the P1_DEPTNO select list, the onChange DeptNo dynamic action will be triggered. There are five different selection types to choose from: Item(s), Button, Region, jQuery Selector, and JavaScript Expression.

If the selection type is set to Item(s), you need to specify a comma-delimited list of items in the Item(s) field. APEX will listen to all the specified items and apply the same actions, regardless of which item was selected. When the dynamic action is triggered, APEX passes the specific item that triggered it as part of a JavaScript object (more on this later).

Similar to Item(s), when specifying a selection type of Button, you need to select a button from the current page. This allows you to easily control what happens when a user clicks a button in the page without submitting the page.

The Region selection allows you to select a single region for APEX to listen on. A good example of this is if you wanted to display a custom wait message each time an interactive report is refreshed. In this case, you'd set the event to Before Refresh, set the selection type to Region, and select the region that contains your interactive report.

When using a region as the selection type, it is important to ensure that the region's template contains an ID. If the region's template is set to No Template, APEX will not be able to register its listener on the region since the region does not contain an ID. For more information, read the following blog post: www.talkapex.com/2011/01/missing-id-in-no-template-region.html. If using the new APEX 5 universal theme, this should not be an issue.

Instead of listening on APEX-specific objects such as items or a region, you can specify a jQuery selector or a JavaScript expression. In most cases, the jQuery selector should be sufficient; however, they are cases when you want to use JavaScript expressions for more complex selections.

For example, if you wanted APEX to perform a dynamic action each time someone moved their mouse over an HTML element with a class of highlight-me, you would select jQuery Selector and enter .highlight-me, as shown in Figure 8-18. The jQuery Selector option uses jQuery notation. You can find detailed information about the jQuery selector notation on the jQuery API site: http://api.jquery.com/category/selectors.

Figure 8-18. When selection type: jQuery Selector

If JavaScript Expression is selected, it expects a DOM object, an array of DOM objects, or a jQuery object. Examples of a DOM object are objects such as document and window. The jQuery object can be any jQuery object such as a tree traversal. An example of this is using `$('p').children()` to select all the children of paragraph (p) elements. You can find more information about jQuery tree traversals here: `http://api.jquery.com/category/traversing/tree-traversal/`.

Condition

Dynamic actions allow you to perform different actions based on a condition. This condition is not the same as a standard APEX object condition. It is evaluated in real time against the triggering element each time the event occurs. If the condition is true or not defined, then the True actions are executed. If the condition is false, the False actions are performed.

In the example, the condition (previously shown in Figure 8-16) is set to "is not null." This means that each time the triggering element P1_DEPTNO is changed, APEX will evaluate it to see whether it is null. If it is null, then it will hide the list of employees (False action). If a department is selected, it will show the list of employees (True action).

Figure 8-19 shows a list of conditions. All conditions, except for "is not null" and "is null," require that you enter some additional information in the Value(s) field.

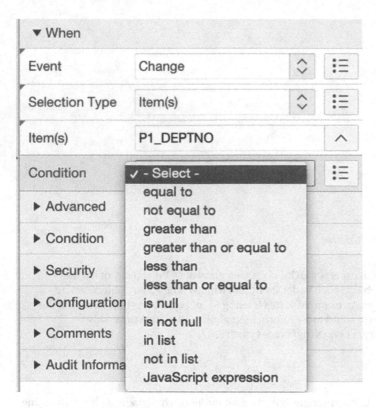

Figure 8-19. List of conditions

The value required for the first six comparison conditions is a static value. You can reference an item value, but you must use the substitution string &PX_ITEM_NAME. notation. If you use a substitution string, it will use the value of the item when the page is loaded, which may not be the same value that is currently on the page when the condition is evaluated.

The two list conditions compare static comma-delimited lists. If referencing a substitution string, the value of the item at the time the page is loaded will be used.

The last condition, "JavaScript expression," allows you to compare values in real time when the condition is evaluated. All the other conditions are evaluated against the triggering element. If you use a JavaScript expression, you can compare any set of values. In most cases, part of the expression will include the triggering element.

The JavaScript expression condition type contains several objects.

- `this.triggeringElement`: The DOM object that triggered the dynamic action. `this.triggeringElement.value` will give you the value of the triggering element. If you defined multiple objects for Selection Type, this will let you know which one was triggered.

- `this.browserEvent`: The event object that caused the dynamic action to run. `this.browserEvent.type` will give you a string value of the type of event that occurred. If this were used in the example, `this.browserEvent.type` would have been "change."

- `this.data`: Additional data that can be passed from the event. In most cases, this value will be null. Dynamic action plug-ins may populate this field to pass additional data.

If you want to quickly see all the additional information that is available in each of the attributes listed previously, set the condition to "JavaScript expression" and in the Value field enter `console.log(this);`, as shown in Figure 8-20. Refresh the page and trigger the event. If you look at the console, you will see the output of the `this` object, as shown in Figure 8-21.

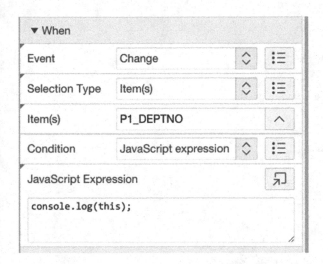

Figure 8-20. *Configuring condition to display this object*

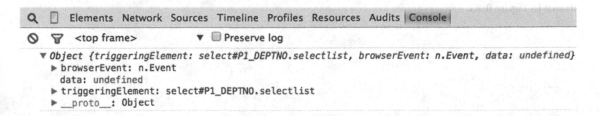

Figure 8-21. *Console output of condition of this object*

■ **Note** The console is available in most browsers (except for Internet Explorer 8 and older). The following list describes how to view the console output in each of the major browsers:

- *Firefox*: Install FireBug (`http://getfirebug.com`), F12
- *Google Chrome*: Ctrl+Shift+J
- *Safari*: Ctrl+Alt+C
- *Internet Explorer 9*: F12

To demonstrate a condition that uses a JavaScript expression, add an additional Number Field item on page 1 called P1_X. Change the condition in the OnChange DeptNo dynamic action from "is not null" to JavaScript Expression. In the JavaScript Expression text area, enter `this.triggeringElement.value > apex.item('P1_X').getValue()`, as shown in Figure 8-22. Refresh the page and enter 20 in the P1_X field.

When you change the department, the list of employees will appear only when you select Operations (40) and Sales (30). You'll notice that if you change the value of P1_X, the condition will evaluate without having to submit the page or set the value in session state.

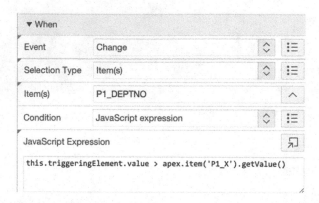

Figure 8-22. *JavaScript condition*

Advanced

The When section defines the events and objects that APEX should listen to. The Advanced section defines how the events are bound to the objects. There are three different ways to attach an event to an object, as shown in Figure 8-23.

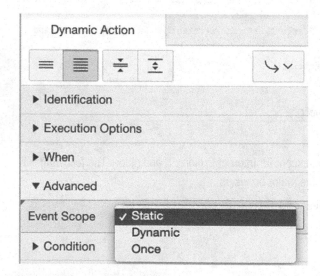

Figure 8-23. *Event scopes*

- *Static*: The default method that APEX attaches events to objects with is the bind method. *Static* means that the dynamic action will be run each time the event occurs on the object. If the object is replaced, the event is no longer attached to the object (it's considered a new object), and the dynamic action will not be triggered. An object can be replaced during a partial-page refresh on a report or interactive report.

- *Dynamic*: Dynamic is similar to the bind option except that the event will be attached to the object for the lifetime of the page or any new objects of that type are added to the page. If a dynamic action is attached to a row in an interactive report, then this option will ensure that the dynamic action will be triggered each time the interactive report is refreshed.

- *Once*: If you want a dynamic action to fire only once, select this option. For example, you would use this option if you wanted to display a warning message the first time the user selected a department. Otherwise, it may get annoying to the user to consistently see the same warning message. If the action dynamic action is set to trigger on page load and is executed during the page load, it will still run one more time when its event is triggered.

For more information about attaching events, please refer to the following documentation: http://api.jquery.com/category/events/event-handler-attachment. The jQuery API contains additional event handler attachment options that are currently not available in APEX.

Actions

Prior to APEX 5, the True and False actions used were modifiable on the Dynamic Action edit page. Starting with APEX 5, they are now visible in the left pane under each dynamic action, as shown in Figure 8-24. They contain actions to perform based on the dynamic action's condition. If multiple actions exist in each section, they will be synchronously executed in order (unless specified), determined by their sequence number.

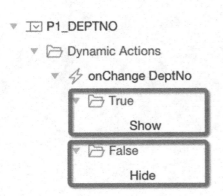

Figure 8-24. *True and False actions*

Earlier in this chapter, you created the OnChange DeptNo dynamic action. The True/False Actions steps allowed you to define True and False actions (see Figure 8-8).

To help describe the options available when editing an action on the right pane, edit the True (Show) action by clicking it in the left pane, as shown in Figure 8-25. The action's properties are now available in the right pane, as shown in Figure 8-26. The following subsections will describe all the options available when modifying an action.

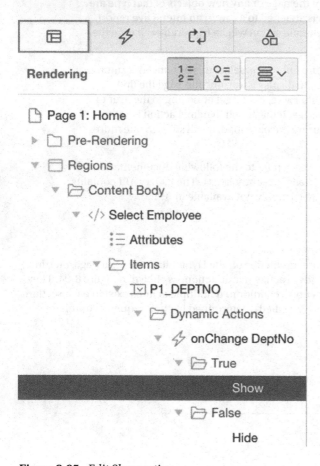

Figure 8-25. Edit Show action

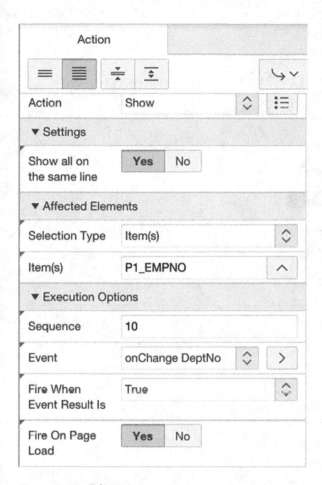

Figure 8-26. Edit action

Identification

The Identification section allows you to select the action that the action will perform. The options in the Action select list are broken up into six categories, as shown in Figure 8-27. The categories have no impact on the system and are there to help organize the list of available actions. This list also includes plugin dynamic actions that are suffixed with [Plug-in]. When the Action option selected, click the Help tab in the central pane to get a brief description for each of the built-in actions. Some actions require additional configuration, which is covered in the "Settings" and "Affected Elements" sections.

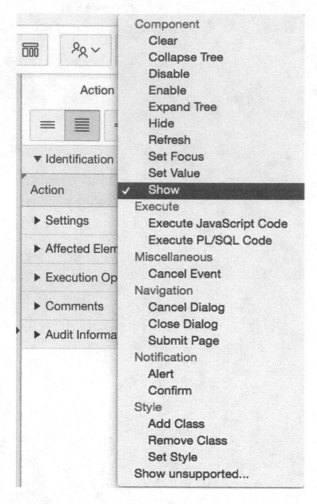

Figure 8-27. Action select list

Settings

The Settings section is available only for certain actions. Each Settings section is different depending on the action selected. In the example, the only available option is to show all page items on the same line. This section will cover the settings options for two different action types: Execute JavaScript Code and Execute PL/SQL Code.

Execute JavaScript Code: When the action is set to Execute JavaScript Code, the Settings section contains a text box where you can enter some JavaScript code to run. To help, APEX provides the this object that contains five different elements. this.triggeringElement, this.browserEvent, and this.data were already covered in the "Dynamic Actions Condition" section.

- `this.action`: This contains information about the action along with some additional information such as action attributes. Action attributes are useful in plug-in development. Please refer to Chapter 12 for more information about plug-ins.

- `this.affectedElements`: This is a jQuery object array of all the elements that should be affected as part of this action. If your JavaScript code needs to modify anything on the page, you should reference this object to find out which elements to modify. The affected elements are defined in the Affected Elements section that will be covered in the next subsection.

You can get an overview of these objects by clicking the Code label and clicking the Help tab in the central pane. To explore all the options available, enter `console.log(this);` in the Code section, refresh your page, trigger the dynamic action, and then look at the console window.

Execute PL/SQL Code: When the action is set to Execute PL/SQL Code, APEX will send an AJAX request to the database to execute the block of PL/SQL code. You can reference page and application items using bind variables in this block of code. It's important to remember that the page and application items are the values in session state, which may not be the same as the values currently displayed on the page.

To submit page items as part of the AJAX request, enter them as a comma-delimited list in the Page Items to Submit field. If any of the items submitted as part of the action have session state protection enabled, the action will fail since the item requires a checksum, which is not provided in AJAX requests. This is done for security reasons to prevent malicious users from tampering with data.

Values from session state (page and application items) can be returned by the PL/SQL code by entering the item names in the Page Items to Return field. When doing so, the item's value on the page will automatically be updated with the value in session state at the end of the action.

Affected Elements

The Affected Elements section allows you to define which elements on the page are impacted by the dynamic action. This section will show up only for actions that can affect an object on the page. In the example, the affected element type was Item(s) on `P1_EMPNO` since it needed to be shown and hidden. The different types of affected elements are as follows:

- *Item(s)*: This is the comma-delimited list of items that will be affected by the action.

- *Button*: Select a button that will be affected by the action.

- *Region*: Select a region from the drop-down list. The list of regions will include both the current page regions and regions on page 0 (in other words, the global page).

- *jQuery selector*: This is a jQuery selector that can select multiple elements on the page. Read `http://api.jquery.com/category/selectors` for more information and examples.

- *JavaScript expression*: This is a DOM object, an array of DOM objects, or a jQuery object. Examples of a DOM object are objects such as document and window. The jQuery object can be any jQuery object such as a tree traversal. An example of this is using `$('p').children()` to select all the children of paragraph (p) elements. You can find more information about jQuery tree traversals at `http://api.jquery.com/category/traversing/tree-traversal`.

- *Triggering element*: The triggering element is the element that was defined in the When section for the dynamic action. In the example, it is P1_DEPTNO.

- *Event source*: The event source is the specific element that triggered the dynamic action to fire. This may be the triggering element or a child of the triggering element. For example, suppose that you created a dynamic action for a click event on the Select Employee region. If you click a blank part of the region, the event source will be the region itself, which is the same as the triggering element. If you click one of the select list items, the event source will be the select list (P1_EMPNO or P1_DEPTNO) since that is the element that caused the dynamic action to run.

Not all actions require or allow for affected elements to be defined. For example, it doesn't make sense for the Alert action type, which triggers a pop-up notification, to have any affected elements.

Execution Options

The Execution Options section (as shown in Figure 8-28) determines when to run the action based on the dynamic action's condition. An action can be run when the condition is either true or false. Setting the value to True or False will determine which section the action is listed in, as shown in Figure 8-25.

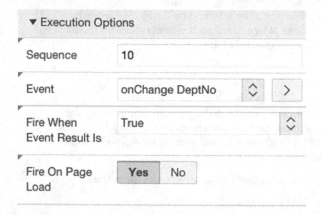

Figure 8-28. Execution Options

You can choose whether to fire the action once the page is loaded. For the option to be run on page load, this option needs to be selected, and the dynamic action's condition result must match the True/False setting during the page load. For example, both of the actions in the OnChange DeptNo dynamic action are set to fire on page load. Only one of these will actually be run during the page load based on the value of P1_DEPTNO at the time the dynamic action is executed. Some actions, such as Execute PL/SQL Code and Set Value, allow you to select additional attributes: Stop Execution On Error and Wait for Result, as shown in Figure 8-29.

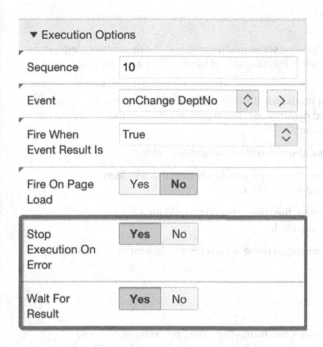

Figure 8-29. *Execution Options additional attributes*

- *Stop Execution On Error*: If the action causes an error and this option is set, any other actions that are part of the same dynamic action will not run.
- *Wait for Result*: This determines whether this action should be run asynchronously. If no other dynamic action is dependent on this action being run, set to Yes.
  - Future versions of APEX will use asynchronous AJAX requests, and this attribute will be deprecated. See http://docs.oracle.com/cd/E59726_01/doc.50/e39143/toc.htm#HTMRN313 for more information.

Dynamic Actions in Action

The example that was used in the previous sections was a basic Show/Hide dynamic action. This section will cover how to create more complex dynamic actions. All the available actions won't be covered in this chapter; however, this example will make you familiar with some of them and how they can interact with one another. A final copy of this example is included in the book's files as an application. The file is 08_example-2_finished_application.sql.

■ **Note**   The following example will leverage some features available only in recent web browsers. If you are using Internet Explorer, please ensure that it is version 8 or newer.

Business Case

After showing users the previous example, they requested some modifications to the department/employee behavior. Instead of selecting an employee from a select list, they would like to select an employee from a report. The full list of requirements is as follows:

- When a user selects the department, a modal window is displayed with a report listing all the employees in the selected department. The report will include the employee's name, job, hire date, and salary.

- When the user hovers over a report row, the row will be highlighted yellow.

- If the user clicks a row in the report, the employee's number is stored in a hidden field, and the employee name is selected for P1_EMPNO.

- Immediately after an employee is selected, the name should be bold for a few seconds to emphasize that it has been selected.

Using dynamic actions, you'll be able to implement all these requirements. To simplify the solution, it has been broken up into small sections.

Setup

Before working on this example, you'll need to modify a few things from the first example. You will find an application that was configured with the following modifications in the Source Code/Download area of the Apress web site at www.apress.com. You can skip this section if you import the application 08_example-2_base_application.sql.

1. Change the P1_EMPNO type to Text Field. Leaving it as a text field will help debug any issues with the dynamic action, and later in this example it will be set to hidden.

2. Create a new field called P1_ENAME and set its properties as the same as in Figure 8-30. This field will be used to display the selected employee's name.

Figure 8-30. P1_ENAME properties

3. Remove the existing dynamic action, which is onChange DeptNo, that is currently attached to the P1_DEPTNO item.

Create Department Employees Report

To meet the first requirement, create a Classic Report region that lists the employees in the selected department. To create this report, follow these steps:

4. Create a standard report region called Department Employees using the following query:

```
select e.empno,
       initcap(e.ename) ename,
       initcap(e.job) job,
       e.hiredate,
       e.sal
from emp e
where e.deptno = :p1_deptno
```

5. Modify the region's attributes and set Page Items to Submit as P1_DEPTNO, as shown in Figure 8-31.

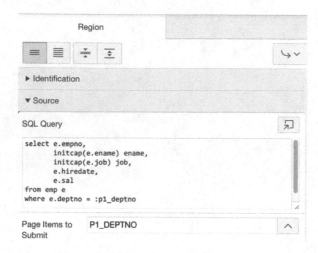

Figure 8-31. Region's Source

6. Modify the report column attributes so that EMPNO is not displayed by setting its column type to Hidden Column.

7. Some additional attributes need to be added to the ENAME column that will be used to send data to P1_EMPNO and P1_ENAME when the user clicks a row in the report. To edit the ENAME column, click the column name in the left pane, and its properties will be in the right pane. In the Column Formatting section, enter `<span data-empno="#EMPNO#" data-ename="#ENAME#">#ENAME#</span>` in the HTML Expression field, as shown in Figure 8-32. The HTML Expression field allows you to customize the appearance of each column.

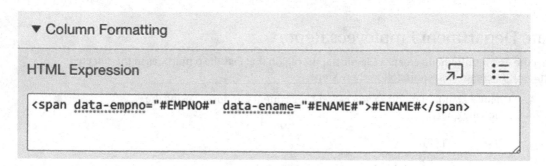

Figure 8-32. Column formatting/HTML expression

■ **Note** The two custom attributes, data-empno and data-ename, are HTML 5–compliant custom attributes. HTML 5 supports custom attributes by prefixing the attribute name with data-. The following blog contains a brief overview of HTML 5 custom data attributes: http://ejohn.org/blog/html-5-data-attributes.

If you refresh page 1, it will look like Figure 8-33. If you change the department, nothing happens, since you haven't applied any dynamic actions.

Figure 8-33. *Department Employees report added*

Refresh Department Employees Report

The first dynamic action to create is to refresh the Department Employees report when the P1_DEPTNO select list changes. The following steps will create the dynamic action when the department is changed:

1. In the left pane, right-click the P1_DEPTNO page item and select Create dynamic action from the content menu.

2. Modify the dynamic actions properties as follows:

    • *Name*: onChange DeptNo

3. Modify the True Action (currently set to Show by default) properties to the same configuration in Figure 8-34. The items to change are highlighted.

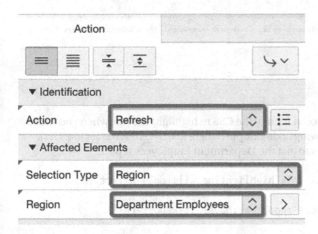

Figure 8-34. *OnChange True Action properties*

If you refresh the page and change the department, the report should be updated. Figure 8-35 shows the page when Accounting is selected as the department.

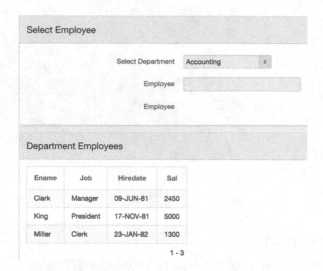

Figure 8-35. *Department Employees report updated by dynamic action*

Highlight Row

Now that the Department Employees report refreshes when the department is changed, the next step is to add the ability to highlight each row when a user hovers over it. If you inspect the CSS styles for a column in the department employee's table when you hover over it, the style changes to Figure 8-36.

```
Style ▼    Computed    Layout    DOM    Events

.t-Report--rowHighlight .t-Report-report tr:hover .t-Report-cell, .t-Report--rowHighlight .t-Report-report tr:nth-
child(2n+1):hover .t-Report-cell {
    background-color: #fafafa !important;
}
```

Figure 8-36. *Table row hover CSS*

Using the CSS definition from Figure 8-36, you can modify the CSS to highlight the row when you move it to yellow. The new CSS should look like the following code sample (where REGION_ID is the region's ID). Adding #REGION_ID restricts the new highlight rules to just the Department Employees report.

```
/* Using the DEPT_EMP_REPORT id ensures that this highlighting will only affect the
 Department Employees report */
#<REGION_ID> .t-Report--rowHighlight .t-Report-report tr:hover .t-Report-cell{
  background-color: yellow !important;
}
```

Normally you would include the CSS in the page's inline CSS area by selecting Page 1 in the left pane and then modifying its properties in the right pane. Figure 8-37 shows where to include the custom CSS. If you want to make the CSS available to the entire application, you can modify the custom CSS option in the Theme Roller, as shown in Figure 8-38.

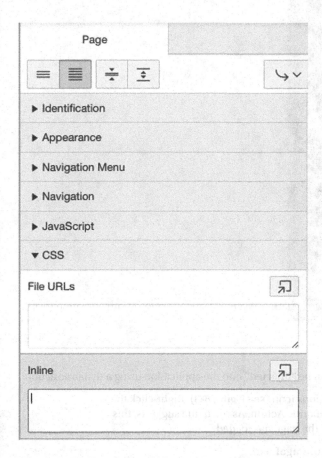

Figure 8-37. *Page inline CSS*

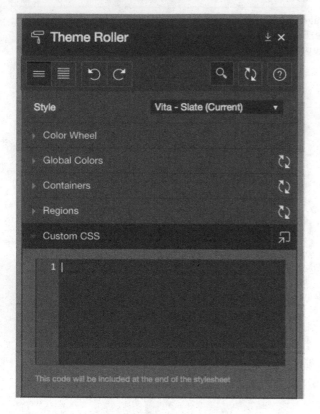

Figure 8-38. *Theme Roller custom CSS*

For the purpose of this example, inline CSS will be "injected" into the application using a dynamic action.

1. In the left pane, click the Dynamic Actions icon (see Figure 8-3). Right-click the Page Load folder and select Create Dynamic Action. As the name suggests, this dynamic action will be executed once the page has loaded.

2. Change the dynamic actions name to **onPageLoad**.

3. Modify the True action (currently set to Show). Set the Action and Affected Elements properties, as shown in Figure 8-39.

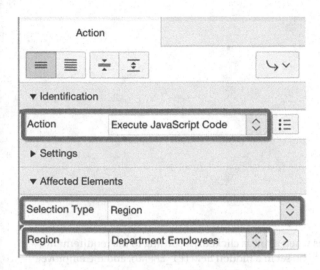

Figure 8-39. *onPageLoad Action configuration*

4. Use the following code snippet and put it in the action's Settings ➤ Code text area. Note that the code does not reference the Department Employees region at all; rather, it references the `this.affectedElements` jQuery object. By doing so, this leverages APEX's declarative dynamic action functionality. Referring to the region also means that only the Department Employees region will be affected with the yellow highlighting.

```
var regionId = this.affectedElements.attr('id');

var css = '#REGION_ID .t-Report--rowHighlight .t-Report-report tr:hover
.t-Report-cell{ background-color: yellow !important; }';

css = css.replace('REGION_ID', regionId);

$(this.affectedElements).prepend('<style type="text/css">' + css + ' </style>' );
```

If you refresh the page and hover over each row, you should notice that the current row is highlighted in yellow, as shown in Figure 8-40. You can change the color by modifying the value in the dynamic action's JavaScript code.

Department Employees

Ename	Job	Hiredate	Sal
Clark	Manager	09-JUN-81	2450
King	President	17-NOV-81	5000
Miller	Clerk	23-JAN-82	1300

1 - 3

Figure 8-40. *Highlighted row*

Row Click

The next dynamic action will handle what happens when a row is clicked. According to the requirements, when a row is clicked, the employee number should be set in a hidden field (P1_EMPNO), and the employee name should be displayed.

To meet this requirement, the additional custom data attributes that were added to the ENAME column in the report will be leveraged. If you inspect the HTML of an employee name in the report column, you'll notice the additional attributes, data-ename and data-empno, as shown in Figure 8-41.

```
▼ <table class="t-Report-report" summary="Department Employees">
  ▶ <thead>
  ▼ <tbody>
    ▶ <tr>
    ▶ <tr>
    ▼ <tr>
      ▼ <td class="t-Report-cell" headers="ENAME">
          <span data-ename="Martin" data-empno="7654">Martin</span>
        </td>
        <td class="t-Report-cell" headers="JOB">Salesman</td>
        <td class="t-Report-cell" headers="HIREDATE">28-SEP-81</td>
        <td class="t-Report-cell" headers="SAL">1250</td>
      </tr>
```

Figure 8-41. *HTML 5 custom data attributes*

The following steps will create the dynamic action that will handle the row click event:

1. Create a dynamic action on the Department Employees region.
2. Make the changes highlighted in Figure 8-42 to the newly added dynamic action. The event scope was changed to Dynamic since the report will be refreshed after each change in department. If the dynamic action were to remain static, it would not work after the first report refresh.

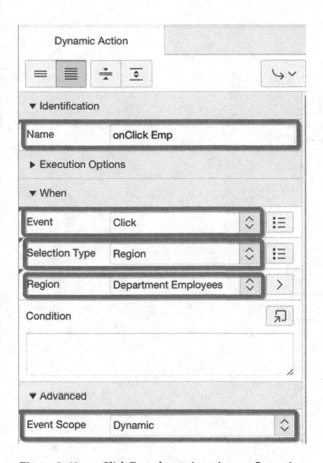

Figure 8-42. onClick Emp dynamic action configuration

3. Set the dynamic action's Condition field to the following code. Without this condition, the dynamic action will fire on any click event in the entire region (not just in the visible employees table). Adding this condition ensures that only clicks in a row containing an employee will trigger the actions.

```
$(this.browserEvent.target).closest('tbody', this.browserEvent.
currentTarget).length > 0
```

4. Modify the True action to the settings highlighted in Figure 8-43.

Figure 8-43. onClick Emp True action

5. Add the following code to the Settings ➤ Code field, and it will set P1_EMPNO and P1_ENAME. In this example, the values are being set with JavaScript. Alternatively, two actions to set the values could have been used.

```
//dataSpan will represent the span tag that was created earlier
//which contains the custom data attributes
var dataSpan = $(this.browserEvent.target).closest('tr').
find('[data-empno]');

//Set the EMPNO and its display values using the data attributes
apex.item('P1_EMPNO').setValue(dataSpan.data('empno'));
apex.item('P1_ENAME').setValue(dataSpan.data('ename'));
```

If you refresh the page and click a row in the Department Employees region, the associated employee's name should be displayed beside the Employee label, and P1_EMPNO will be populated accordingly, as shown in Figure 8-44.

Figure 8-44. *Select Employee, row click*

Once you confirm that everything is working, change P1_EMPNO to a hidden field. Since you're modifying its value in JavaScript, change the Value Protected option on the item to No.

Emphasize Employee Change

The displayed employee name needs to be emphasized after the employee has been selected. To emphasize the name, immediately hide the employee name, make it red, and then have it fade in. Once the fade-in is complete, remove the highlighted red color.

There are various ways to do this in dynamic actions. You could modify the existing dynamic action and append some additional JavaScript. The following steps will help highlight another type of action and how multiple actions work within a dynamic action:

1. Create a new action in the onChange Emp dynamic action and set its properties to Figure 8-45.

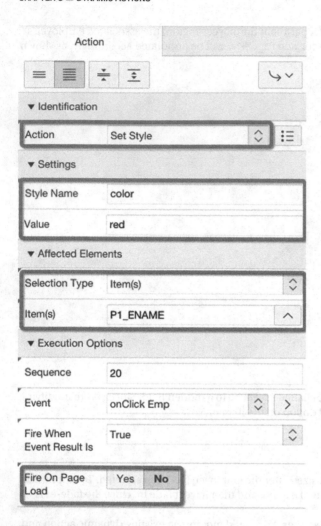

Figure 8-45. *Set Style action*

2. In the left pane, drag the newly created action above the existing Execute
   JavaScript Code action so that it runs first. Figure 8-46 shows the new order.

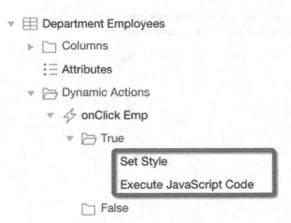

Figure 8-46. Updated dynamic action execute order

3. Add an additional JavaScript action at the end of the current actions with the following configurations:

   - Action: *Execute JavaScript Code*
   - Affected Elements > Selection Type: *Item(s)*
   - Affected Elements > Item(s): *P1_ENAME*
   - Fire On Page Load: *No*

4. Set the Settings ➤ Code field to the following:

```
this.affectedElements.hide().fadeIn(2000, function(){
  //The second parameter in the fadeIn function allows you to define a
  //function to be run once the fadeIn is completed.
  //This function will be used to reset the color
  $(this).css('color', '');
});
```

Refresh Page 1, select a department, and then click an employee in the Department Employees report. When the name appears in the Employee field, it should fade in and be red. Once the fade-in is complete, it should return to its original color (black in this example).

Modal Window

So far all the requirements have been met except for the modal window. Because it is easier to develop, debug, and demonstrate the example without the extra complexities of a modal window, I saved this for last.

Similar to other requirements in this example, there are several ways to implement this solution. One option would be to use the new APEX 5 modal page feature; however, it would add unnecessary complexity to the application.

Instead, this solution will take advantage of some of the features found in the new APEX 5 Universal theme. This solution will leverage the jQuery UI Dialog widget (https://jqueryui.com/dialog/), which is already included in APEX 5. This solution will use a simple command to open and close the dialog window. You can find more options in the jQuery UI Dialog API documentation: http://api.jqueryui.com/dialog/.

1. In the left pane, click the Department Employees region. In the right pane, edit the Template to Inline Dialog, as shown in Figure 8-47. This built-in template uses the jQuery UI Dialog widget.

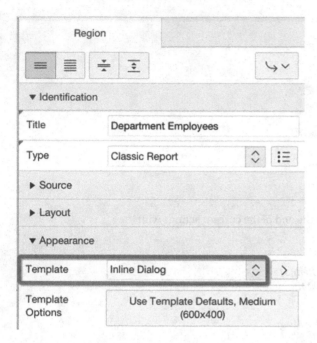

Figure 8-47. *Modify region's template*

2. Click the button Use Template Defaults, Medium (600x400), as shown in Figure 8-47. This will display a new modal window to edit the Inline Dialog template's properties. Change Dialog Size to Small, as shown in Figure 8-48.

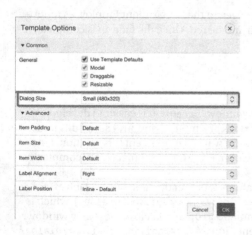

Figure 8-48. *Template Options*

3. Refresh Page 1, and you'll notice that the Department Employees region is no longer visible on the page. That is because it is a jQuery UI Dialog window, which needs to be opened and closed using JavaScript.

4. To open the dialog window, add another True action to the onChange DeptNo dynamic action. Modify the new action's properties to look like Figure 8-49.

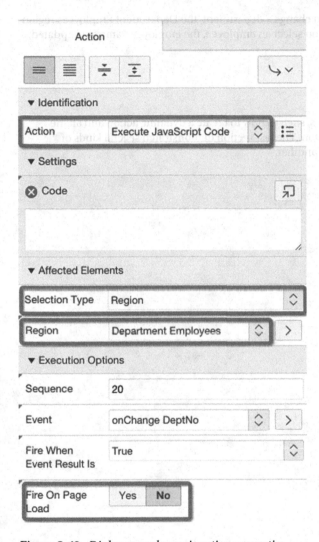

Figure 8-49. *Dialog open dynamic action properties*

5. Use the following for the Code property:

```
this.affectedElements.dialog('open');
```

6. To close the dialog window, add another True action to the onClick Emp dynamic action. Modify the new action's properties to look like Figure 8-49.

7. Use the following for the Code property:

```
this.affectedElements.dialog('close');
```

Refresh Page 1 to view the changes. When you change a department, the Department Employees region should appear as a modal dialog window. When you select an employee, the employee name gets updated, and the Department Employees region closes.

Summary

This chapter covered all aspects of dynamic actions, such as how to create a dynamic action and all the options available when configuring a dynamic action. The last section demonstrated several kinds of dynamic actions and how they can work with one another.

CHAPTER 9

■ ■ ■

Lifecycle Management

by Nick Buytaert

The practice of software development these days includes much more than just writing lines of code. To successfully deliver high-quality applications on time and within budget, modern development teams rely on areas in the field of application lifecycle management (ALM). ALM encompasses the coordination of a software product from its initial planning through retirement and includes all sorts of practices and techniques, such as the following:

- Project and requirements management

- Software development

- Test management and quality assurance

- Build automation and deployment

- Release management

- Operations

ALM is thus a broad term that spans the full range of activities occurring throughout a project's life. The idea for a new application forms the starting point in the ALM process, while the lifecycle ends once the application loses its business value and is no longer used. ALM is therefore a continuous process, which can be divided into three distinct aspects. You typically maximize the business value of your software by performing well in all three aspects.

- *Governance*: Make decisions about the project and ensure maximum business value realization.

- *Development*: Create the software product and maintain it further.

- *Operations*: Run, manage, and monitor the application.

I will not cover the entire ALM stack because that would take us too far afield. This chapter will mainly focus on technical topics with the intention to facilitate the overall APEX development and deployment process. I will introduce, for example, several build automation techniques that can significantly improve the quality and efficiency of your day-to-day development activities. The main part of this chapter guides you through the steps of incorporating a set of powerful tools and practices that take APEX development to the next level.

Challenges

Oracle Application Express is an easy-to-use development framework intended to rapidly create database-centric web applications on top of the Oracle Database. Developing applications with APEX is no rocket science, but that does not mean there are no challenges associated with it. The following subsections describe the typical challenges faced by a team of developers working on an APEX project. It might be interesting to note that some of these challenges even apply when working on a single-person project.

Deploying Database Changes

Oracle APEX development is tightly coupled to database development since you typically work with the concept of a thick database. The thick database approach is considered a general best practice and refers to putting as much code as possible in the database layer. You should treat APEX as the front-end or presentation layer, meaning that it should not contain any form of business logic.

As a result of the thick database approach, many different database objects are created and manipulated during the development phase: tables, views, packages, triggers, sequences, indexes, and so on. The difficulty, however, arises when a new version of the application has to be deployed. This inevitable and critical moment requires you to collect all database object changes since the previous release.

The task of collecting these changes is often laborious and error-prone, especially when you did not explicitly track any of your database changes during development. This sort of manual operation as part of the deployment process should be avoided at all times. Fortunately, there are ways to drastically minimize the risk of deploying database changes, which you will read about later in this chapter.

Collaborative Development

It is common for a development team to run into concurrency issues when working in a shared development environment, which happens to be the most widely used strategy in APEX projects. In a shared setup, developers work simultaneously on the same application and source code. A classic example of the concurrency problematic in APEX occurs when one of the developers unintentionally invalidates a widely used PL/SQL package. As a result of this action, all database objects and APEX pages that depend on that package will be invalidated too. It is therefore likely that fellow team members will suffer consequences from this situation, resulting in unnecessary frustrating moments and a loss of time. Another example is accidentally overwriting someone else's changes when working on the same piece of code in the database.

The use of local development environments overcomes the shortcomings of the shared development strategy. In a local development setup, each developer has its own separated work area, rendering it impossible to run into concurrency issues. This is a common practice in most mainstream development technologies. Oracle APEX, however, is a different story since it is designed to behave better in a shared setup than in a local one. The main reason for this argument is the incapability of the APEX application export file to be easily merged in version control systems.

As you probably know, an application export file is nothing more than a series of black-box PL/SQL calls that rebuild all pieces of the exported application in a target workspace. In a local development setup, developers would have to include the large application export file with almost every commit to source control in order to share their individual changes to the APEX application with the rest of the team. With this approach, you will quickly find yourself having to manually merge changes from other developers in the export file. The task of resolving these so-called merge conflicts is time-consuming and error-prone, simply because APEX export files are not supposed to be edited manually. Given this restriction, most development teams settled on using a shared setup, taking into account the attached downsides.

Another argument in favor of using a shared development environment is the APEX application builder, which includes several helpful features that facilitate team development. You can, for example, lock pages to restrict other developers from modifying the pages you are currently working on. The application builder also applies optimistic locking to prevent developers from overwriting each other's changes. Figure 9-1 shows an example error message generated by the application builder when running into concurrency issues.

Figure 9-1. *Optimistic locking error message*

Parallel Development

In the early stages of a project, the development team typically follows a linear progression in which each new version of the application is based on the prior one. Parallel development occurs as soon as you branch off the main development line for an extra development path. Such an extra path might be necessary, for example, when having to fix critical bugs in the production environment while the rest of the team has already started working on the next release.

Fixing these bugs directly in production is definitely not a good idea because there is a chance you make things even worse with a direct impact on the end users. The far more appropriate solution consists of checking out the tagged production version from source control, fixing the bugs in a separate development environment, and finally propagating the changes to production.

Unfortunately, you will run into trouble when trying to merge the changes made on your branch back into the master branch. In other words, something is preventing you from easily incorporating the production bug fixes into your main line of development. Again, as you might have guessed, it is the application export file that spoils the merge process between the two branches. APEX projects therefore typically follow a linear approach, in which parallel development is avoided as much as possible.

An underutilized feature in the area of parallel development is build options, which is part of your application's shared components. Build options allow you to enable or disable various application components at runtime or during application export. The APEX development itself uses build options extensively, especially when building early-adopter releases where certain components may not be ready for release yet. Build options have two possible values: include or exclude. If you specify a component as being included, then the APEX engine considers it part of the application definition. Conversely, if you specify a component as being excluded, then the APEX engine treats it as if it did not exist.

The drawback of build options is the level of granularity. Not all components, let alone attributes, in the application builder can have a build option assigned. This shortcoming is probably a reason why build options is not the most commonly used feature. However, build options can come in handy when dealing with new separate features that you want to exclude in an upcoming release.

Enterprise APEX Development

Creating applications with APEX is by no means affiliated with enterprise web development. Oracle itself positions Application Express as a so-called Rapid Application Development (RAD) tool but recommends other technologies as soon as project complexity and size increases. There are limitations, of course, but I do believe that the RAD concept can be taken a step further in a way that APEX is capable of dealing with more complex projects.

However, enterprise-level development with APEX requires you to use a more sophisticated development approach and tool set. This chapter covers a solution that has proven to be effective in real-world APEX projects. The solution combines APEX with a set of powerful third-party tools, resulting in a robust and agile development technique. The main part of this chapter will focus on how one can take advantage of these tools to turn the APEX development and delivery process into a well-oiled machine.

The Demo Project

I have set up a demo project on GitHub, which I will use for reference in the upcoming sections. It is publicly available at the following URL:

```
https://github.com/nbuytaert1/orclapex-maven-demo
```

The demo project includes a simple APEX 5.0 application built on top of two tables you should be familiar with: EMP and DEPT. The project has been configured with several third-party tools, which make it possible to deploy all the application's components simply by executing a single command.

Make sure you have access to an Oracle Database running APEX 5.0 or higher, if you want to try the technique from the demo project yourself. It is perfectly possible, however, to apply the same techniques to older versions of Application Express. Just keep in mind that you cannot import an APEX 5.0 application export into an APEX 4.x instance. Figure 9-2 shows the demo project's data model.

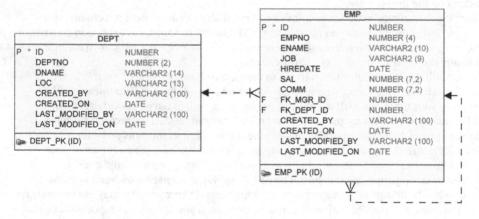

Figure 9-2. *The demo application's data model*

■ **Note**   Please be aware that it is not possible to use Oracle's apex.oracle.com evaluation service in combination with the techniques described in this chapter.

Extending the APEX Development and Deployment Process

The objective of this section of the chapter is to set up and configure an automated build system for APEX applications that empowers both the development and deployment processes. This approach will allow you to receive instant feedback on the stability of the project's code base, and it makes application deployment a breeze. However, before getting to that point, it is important to start with the basics and think of what a standard APEX application consists of. The best way to identify the main building blocks is by going through the APEX packaging process.

APEX Application Packaging

Packaging an application in APEX is mainly taken care of in the Supporting Objects section. This utility makes it possible to easily define the steps required to successfully deploy an application. Prior to APEX 5.0, the Supporting Objects section could be used for the deployment of two different types of objects.

- Database scripts (DDL and DML)

- Static files (CSS, images, JavaScript, and so on)

Starting from APEX 5.0, the Supporting Objects section has been limited to database scripts only. Static files are now automatically part of the application export file, something that was not the case in previous versions of Application Express. During the application export wizard, there is an option that determines whether you want to export the Supporting Objects as well. Figure 9-3 shows this setting on the Export Application page.

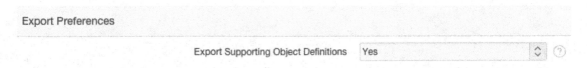

Figure 9-3. *The preference that determines whether to export supporting object definitions with your application*

Setting this option to Yes or Yes and Install on Import Automatically results in a single export file containing all required application components and database code for deployment. The Supporting Objects can then be imported during the application import wizard or at a later time. This deployment technique, where everything is packaged into a single SQL file, is what APEX defines as a custom packaged application.

Database Scripts

Deploying an APEX application involves nearly always the execution of database scripts to manage schema objects on which the APEX application is built. Data Definition Language (DDL) statements allow you to define the structure of database objects. Data Manipulation Language (DML) statements, on the other hand, control the data within objects.

APEX 5.0 introduces an interesting new feature to simplify DDL script management. When creating an installation script in Supporting Objects, you have the ability to associate a script with one or more database objects, as shown in Figure 9-4.

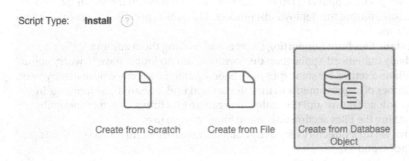

Figure 9-4. *The Create from Database Object installation script method*

The install script will then automatically contain the DDL statements for all associated database objects. Furthermore, the script remembers the database objects to which it has been linked, making it possible to synchronize the script's content at a later time. This can be achieved by checking the appropriate scripts in the Installation Scripts overview, followed by clicking the Refresh Checked button, as shown in Figure 9-5. Please note that other script types cannot be refreshed this way.

Figure 9-5. *Refresh checked scripts*

This feature has certainly improved the ease of use and maintainability of the database scripts in Supporting Objects. Dealing with the project's database changes through the Supporting Objects mechanism is therefore a valid solution, on the condition that the number of database objects is not too large. As soon as you start working with the thick database approach, I recommend you manage the database changes through a database migration tool. Liquibase (www.liquibase.org) is my personal favorite in this area and will be discussed later in the chapter.

Static Files

Prior to APEX 5.0, the Supporting Objects section was also capable of including static files in the form of installation scripts. Static files are defined in the Files section under Shared Components. The tricky thing about these files was that they were not automatically part of the application export file, not even if you explicitly associated the file with the application you were exporting. Only the static files included in Supporting Objects were part of the export file.

You also had to keep in mind that there was no actual relation between the file in Shared Components and its associated script in Supporting Objects. Any changes made to the files were not reflected in the scripts. Forgetting to update the scripts in Supporting Objects, after making changes to the files in Shared Components, was a common mistake during the deployment process. This was especially the case when you had to deal with a fair number of files.

The decision to disconnect static files from Supporting Objects and making them automatically part of the application export has positively influenced application deployment. You no longer have to worry about the question of whether all installation scripts for static files have been updated correctly before deployment. There have also been made a number of improvements to the Files section under Shared Components in APEX 5.0. The zip upload and download feature and the ability to organize files into a directory hierarchy have been valuable additions, making the Files section only more interesting to use.

As shown in Figure 9-6, I have set up a directory hierarchy containing five different folders: css, images, images/contribute, images/oracle, and js.

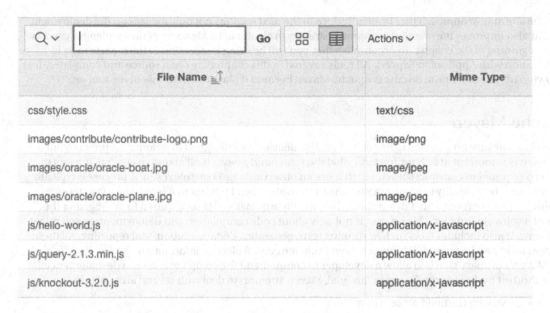

Figure 9-6. *An example directory hierarchy in the Files section*

One culprit in the past for static files in Shared Components was browser caching. Prior to APEX 5.0, any static file you referenced in your APEX application had to be downloaded to the client's browser by calling the get_file database procedure. This approach made browser caching unreliable, leading to slower-loading pages and unnecessary extra load on the database. It was therefore a common practice to store the application's static files on the web server, making them easier to cache. In APEX 5.0, however, web browsers can seamlessly cache files uploaded into Shared Components.

As you can see in Listing 9-1, there is a clear difference in file referencing between APEX 4.2 and APEX 5.0. Version 4.2 uses the get_file procedure, while 5.0 takes advantage of relative file URLs.

Listing 9-1. The File Referencing Difference Between APEX 4.2 and 5.0

```
<img src="wwv_flow_file_mgr.get_file?p_security_group_id=5569195&p_fname=oracle-plane.jpg">

<img src="nbuytaert1/r/9714/files/static/v34/images/oracle/oracle-plane.jpg">
```

Applicability

I have found that the packaged application concept works well for simple and small-sized applications, but it can become difficult for mid- to large-scale applications that require many different scripts to be managed. Also, keep in mind that small applications can quickly evolve into larger ones over time. Taking into account these considerations, I prefer to leave aside the Supporting Objects section whenever I can.

Not using the Supporting Objects section requires you to look for an alternative approach that simplifies and, while at it, enhances application deployment. You are in need of a solution that is able to manage all parts of a packaged APEX application. After going through the Supporting Objects mechanism, you can conclude that a packaged application consists of the following three main parts:

- The APEX application itself (in the form of a SQL export file)

- Database scripts

- Static files (part of the application export since APEX 5.0)

The alternative approach that I will introduce in the next sections not only focuses on the deployment part but also improves the overall development strategy in an aim to tackle some of the challenges you saw at the beginning of the chapter. To accomplish this, you will be using a collection of third-party tools in combination with Application Express. All tools covered in this chapter are open source and completely free to download. The first one to discuss is Apache Maven because it plays a central role in the tool set.

Apache Maven

Maven is a software project management and comprehension tool designed to automate a project's build process. It is important to fully understand what the term *build process* is all about. In general, it refers to the steps required to construct something that has an observable and tangible result. A process is typically characterized by its ability to be automated. In other words, when I talk about a build process in terms of software development, I am talking about the—ideally automated—tasks required to put together the parts of a software product. This process is not only about code compilation and deployment, as you might think now. It also includes tasks such as running tests, generating documentation, and reporting. All these different tasks can be managed through Maven from one central piece of information.

Maven's primary goal is to allow a developer to comprehend the complete state of a development effort in the shortest period of time. To attain this goal, Maven attempts to deal with several areas of concern.

- Making the build process easy
- Providing a uniform build system
- Providing quality project information
- Providing guidelines for best-practices development

The best way to think of the build process in the context of an APEX application is by going through the parts of a packaged application, as you did in the previous section. Thus, the basic build process will consist of importing the APEX application export file into a target workspace, executing all appropriate database scripts, and optionally uploading static files to the web server in case you are not using the Files section under Shared Components.

Maven is primarily used in the Java world, but nothing stops you from using it in APEX projects. You will use only a subset of Maven's features because some of them are applicable only to Java-based projects. The primary task of Maven in this case is the automation of the APEX application build process. First, let's take a look at the Maven installation procedure.

Installation

Maven requires the Java Development Kit (JDK) to be installed on your machine.

1. Download the latest JDK release from the Oracle web site.

2. Run the JDK installer and follow the instructions.

3. Create the JAVA_HOME environment variable by pointing to the JDK folder.

   ```
   usr/jdk/jdk1.7.0
   ```

4. Update the PATH environment variable by pointing to the JDK's bin folder.

    ```
    $JAVA_HOME/bin:$PATH
    ```

- Validate the JDK installation.

    ```
    $ java -version
    java version "1.7.0_07"
    Java(TM) SE Runtime Environment (build 1.7.0_07-b10)
    Java HotSpot(TM) 64-Bit Server VM (build 23.3-b01, mixed mode)
    ```

Now install the latest version of Apache Maven.

1. Download the latest version of Maven at http://maven.apache.org.

2. Extract the downloaded archive file into the directory where you want to install
    Maven. I have put mine in the /Users/Nick folder.

3. Set the MAVEN_HOME environment variable.

    ```
    /Users/Nick/apache-maven-3.1.1
    ```

- Update the PATH environment variable.

    ```
    $MAVEN_HOME/bin:$PATH
    ```

- Validate the Maven installation.

    ```
    $ mvn --version
    Apache Maven 3.1.1 (0728685237757ffbf44136acec0402957f723d9a; 2013-09-17
    17:22:22+0200)
    Maven home: /Users/Nick/apache-maven-3.1.1
    Java version: 1.7.0_07, vendor: Oracle Corporation
    Java home: /Library/Java/JavaVirtualMachines/jdk1.7.0_07.jdk/Contents/Home/jre
    Default locale: en_US, platform encoding: UTF-8
    OS name: "mac os x", version: "10.10.1", arch: "x86_64", family: "mac"
    ```

Project Directory Layout

One of the ideas behind Maven is to provide guidelines for best-practices development in Java-based
projects. It is not possible for APEX projects to comply with these conventions, simply because there are
practically no similarities between Java and APEX development. Luckily, Maven leaves enough room for
deviations from these conventions.

Maven allows you to define your own best practices on how to manage an APEX project. Having
these rules and uniformly applying them allows developers to freely move between different projects that
use Maven and follow the same or similar best practices. By understanding how one project works, they
will understand how all of them worked. This approach can save developers a lot of time when switching
between projects.

An important aspect in Maven's guidelines for best-practices development is the project directory
layout. It determines how the project-related files should be organized on the file system. This is actually
how you will get to the point of creating the project's code repository. All files required to build the project
must be present in the code repository. This is an absolute necessity since you want Maven to be able

to build all parts of the application to a target environment. Another important aspect of having a code repository is the ability to apply version control on it. The use of a version control system is a topic that I will discuss later in this chapter.

Listing 9-2 shows an overview of the most important top-level directories that I am using in the demo project's code repository. I will discuss each one of the directories in more detail later. You can of course implement your own preferred project directory layout.

Listing 9-2. The Demo Project's Directory Layout

```
my-project
    -- pom.xml
    -- src
        -- main
            -- apex
            -- database
            -- web-files
    -- util
```

■ **Note**   The src and main directories are part of Maven's common directory layout. The src directory contains all source code for building the project. Its subdirectory main includes the source code for building the main build artifact. The src/test directory, for example, would contain only test sources.

The Project Object Model (POM) File

The POM file is the fundamental unit of work in Maven. It is a configuration file in XML format that contains the majority of information required to build the project. In other words, this is the place where the project's build process is being automated. The standard name for the POM file is pom.xml, and it is always located under the project's root directory. Listing 9-3 shows how the demo project's POM file is organized.

Listing 9-3.   pom.xml

```xml
<?xml version="1.0" encoding="UTF-8"?>
<project xmlns="http://maven.apache.org/POM/4.0.0"
        xmlns:xsi="http://www.w3.org/2001/XMLSchema-instance"
        xsi:schemaLocation="http://maven.apache.org/POM/4.0.0
                            http://maven.apache.org/xsd/maven-4.0.0.xsd">
  <modelVersion>4.0.0</modelVersion>

  <groupId>com.contribute.apex</groupId>
  <artifactId>orclapex-maven-demo</artifactId>
  <version>1.0</version>

  <build>
    <plugins>
      ...
    </plugins>
  </build>
</project>
```

The project element is the root node in the POM file and declares several attributes to which the document can be validated. The modelVersion value is 4.0.0, which is currently the only supported POM version for both Maven 2 and 3.

A Maven project is uniquely identified by its coordinate elements: groupId, artifactId, and version. All three items are required fields. These coordinate elements, however, have a useful meaning only in the context of Java-based projects. For you, it does not really matter what you fill in here.

The plugins element, under the build element, contains the tasks that must be executed to successfully build the project. Defining these tasks is achieved by adding plugin elements, which contain configuration details to fulfill a certain build task. In the next section, you will take a closer look into the plugin element definition for each task that is required to successfully deploy an APEX application. The first task or plugin you will execute during the build process is Liquibase.

Liquibase

The thick database approach that I talked about earlier, in combination with the code repository concept, introduces an extra challenge: all database scripts that are part of the APEX application must be stored in the code repository in the form of SQL files. Storing these files in the code repository makes it possible for Maven's automated build to execute all appropriate database scripts to successfully migrate a database schema to a specific version. This stage of the build process is where most things can go wrong because of the inherent complexity of deploying database changes. That is why you will take advantage of Liquibase, a powerful database migration tool that will effectively help you in organizing and executing database scripts.

Organizing Database Scripts

You are completely free in how you organize the directory structure for your project's database scripts. However, I recommend you to come up with a well-thought-out and unambiguous approach, which leaves little or no room for interpretation. Make sure you can immediately identify the appropriate folder to locate a specific database script. Having a logical and organized directory structure will save you a lot of time in the long run, and it makes life just a little easier.

The directory structure that I typically use is the one I have applied in the demo project. It is based on the different types of database objects that exist in the Oracle Database. Listing 9-4 shows you what the directory structure looks like under the src/main/database directory.

Listing 9-4. The src/main/database Directory Layout

```
my-project
   -- src
      -- main
         -- database
            -- changelog
               -- data
               -- install
               -- latest
               -- master.xml
               -- post-build
            -- data
            -- install
               -- sequence
               -- table
```

```
            -- latest
                -- function
                -- package
                -- procedure
                -- trigger
                -- view
        -- model
        -- post-build
        -- technical-docs
```

As illustrated in Figure 9-7, I first differentiate between DML and DDL scripts: DML scripts always go into the data folder, while DDL scripts get a place in either the install folder or the latest folder. In the case of DDL, you need to ask yourself the question of whether the script contains a replaceable or nonreplaceable database object. The following is an explanation of these two database object categories:

- A replaceable object is characterized by its ability to override an already existing object definition with a new one. Objects that can be compiled using the or replace clause fall in this category. Executing a replaceable script constitutes a change that completely replaces the previous version of the object, if it already existed. These sorts of scripts should go into one of the subdirectories of the latest folder. The name of the latest folder simply refers to the fact that the scripts in the subdirectories always contain the latest version of a database object. Examples are packages, triggers, views, and so on.

- A nonreplaceable object cannot be created with the or replace clause. Modifying the definition of a nonreplaceable object requires you to write an alter statement. These sorts of scripts, also known as *incremental scripts*, should go into one of the subdirectories of the install folder. It is important to realize that scripts in the install folder can be executed only once, whereas replaceable scripts can be executed over and over again. An example of a nonreplaceable object is a table. Suppose you want to add an extra column to an already existing table. It would not be possible to replace the previous version of the table with a new one because this would imply dropping and re-creating the table, resulting in the loss of data.

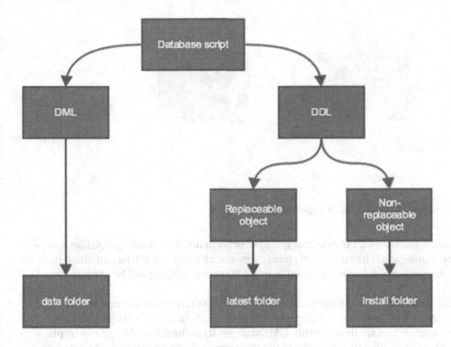

Figure 9-7. *Database script file organization*

The actual content of the files includes nothing more than plain SQL or PL/SQL code. There are three different kinds of database statements that can be executed through these files.

- DML statements in the data folder

- DDL statements in the install and latest folders

- PL/SQL anonymous blocks in all folders

You should think of each SQL file as an atomic change to the database schema. Atomicity is part of the ACID model (Atomicity, Consistency, Isolation, and Durability) and states that database transactions must follow an all-or-nothing rule, meaning that all statements within a transaction are either executed successfully or not executed at all. Liquibase treats each SQL file in the code repository as a single transaction.

That last sentence is actually not entirely true since transaction control is not defined at the file level. Liquibase executes the SQL files as part of so-called changeSets, which are part of changeLog files. Each changeSet gets executed in a separate transaction that is committed at the end, or rolled back if an error occurred. Figure 9-8 shows a visual representation of where transaction control is applied in Liquibase.

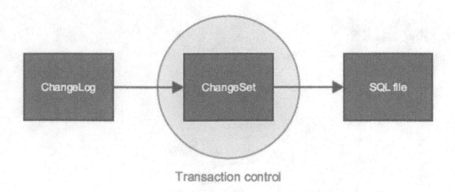

Transaction control

Figure 9-8. *The relation between changeLogs, changeSets, and SQL files*

It is possible to reference multiple files in one changeSet, which implies that multiple SQL files can be executed within the same transaction. The concept of changeSets and changeLogs will be explained in more detail in the next two subsections. But for now, just keep in mind that every SQL file will be executed in a separate transaction.

It is important to fully understand the transaction control behavior in Liquibase because it helps to answer the question of whether it is advisable to group multiple statements in a single file. The answer depends on the sort of statements you are dealing with. DML statements in the data folder, for example, are typically grouped in one file to guarantee the atomicity of the transaction. As an illustration, the data script insert_dept_demo_data.sql in Listing 9-5 contains insert statements for the DEPT table.

Listing 9-5. src/main/database/data/insert_dept_demo_data.sql

```
insert into dept (id, deptno, dname, loc)
values (1, 10, 'ACCOUNTING', 'NEW YORK');
insert into dept (id, deptno, dname, loc)
values (2, 20, 'RESEARCH', 'DALLAS');
insert into dept (id, deptno, dname, loc)
values (3, 30, 'SALES', 'CHICAGO');
insert into dept (id, deptno, dname, loc)
values (4, 40, 'OPERATIONS', 'BOSTON');
```

There is no need to include a commit statement at the end of the file because Liquibase will automatically commit the database transaction after the corresponding changeSet terminates successfully. A rollback statement will be performed if the script produces an error during its execution, leaving the database in a consistent state.

DDL statements in the install and latest folders are preferably limited to one per file. Imagine a situation wherein you include multiple CREATE TABLE statements in one file and let it execute through Liquibase. If for some reason the second statement fails, Liquibase would not be able to roll back the first statement because the Oracle Database automatically commits DDL statements. Running Liquibase a second time will now undoubtedly fail because the first statement in the file will be executed again, resulting in the following error message: ORA-00955: name is already used by an existing object. The only way to get past this error is to manually drop the table from the first statement and fix the problem with the second statement. Manually dropping one table is not a big deal, but what if you try to execute a SQL file that includes ten DDL statements and the last one fails?

Therefore, always remember that DDL statements get automatically committed and that it is better to prevent transaction mismatches between Liquibase and the Oracle Database. Restricting DDL statements to one per file also greatly improves the maintainability of the code repository. The script create_dept.sql in the src/main/database/install/table folder, for example, contains the nonreplaceable DDL code to create the table DEPT. Listing 9-6 shows the content of the create_dept.sql file.

Listing 9-6. src/main/database/install/table/create_dept.sql

```
create table dept(
  id number not null,
  deptno number(2),
  dname varchar2(14),
  loc varchar2(13),
  created_by varchar2(100),
  created_on date,
  last_modified_by varchar2(100),
  last_modified_on date,
  constraint dept_pk primary key (id)
);
```

On a side note, it might be interesting to outline the steps needed to alter the DEPT table from the previous code fragment. A common mistake when starting with Liquibase in a situation like this is to modify the previous CREATE TABLE statement in order to alter the structure of the DEPT table. However, this is not how Liquibase works. It is not allowed to modify the content of the create_dept.sql script, if the file has already been executed through Liquibase. The following actions should be taken to correctly alter the DEPT table:

1. Create a new SQL file, alter_dept_add_col.sql for example, and save it to the following location: src/main/database/install/table.

2. Add the ALTER TABLE statement to the SQL file from step 1.

3. Open the src/main/database/changelog/install/1.0.xml changeLog file and append a changeSet that references the alter_dept_add_col.sql file.

Another example script is the br_iu_dept.sql file in the src/main/database/latest/trigger directory. As you can see in Listing 9-7, the file contains the replaceable DDL code to create or alter the BR_IU_DEPT trigger.

Listing 9-7. src/main/database/latest/trigger/br_iu_dept.sql

```
create or replace trigger br_iu_dept
before insert or update on dept
for each row
declare
  l_user varchar2(100) := nvl(v('APP_USER'), user);
begin
  if inserting then
    :new.id := nvl(:new.id, seq_dept.nextval);
    :new.created_by := l_user;
    :new.created_on := sysdate;
  end if;
```

```
if updating then
  :new.last_modified_by := l_user;
  :new.last_modified_on := sysdate;
end if;
end br_iu_dept;
```

Making a change to a replaceable database object is much easier since you can simply overwrite the existing DDL code in the SQL file. Liquibase will pick up the changes made to the content of the file and will reexecute the script on the next Liquibase run. More in-depth information on this behavior will be given in the following subsection.

The following are other folders under the src/main/database directory I have not yet discussed:

- changelog

- model

- post-build

- technical-docs

The changelog folder contains the Liquibase changeLog XML files. These files describe what, when, and how database scripts should be executed during the database migration process. More information on changeLogs and changeSets will be given in the following subsection.

The model folder simply contains the entity-relationship model (ERD) for the database schema. Oracle SQL Developer Data Modeler has been used to create the demo project's ERD.

The post-build directory includes scripts that will be executed at the end of the database migration. The compile_schema.sql script is unarguably the most essential post-build script. It is the last script to be executed by Liquibase, and its task is to scan the schema for invalid database objects. The script throws an error if one or more invalid objects are found. The names of all invalid objects are printed out in the build log, and the build itself terminates with a "build failed" message. The compile_schema.sql script, shown in Listing 9-8, plays an important role during the build process because it gives the project team invaluable feedback on the stability of the database code.

Listing 9-8. src/main/database/post-build/compile_schema.sql

```
declare
  l_compilation_errors varchar2(32767);

  cursor lcu_invalid_objects is
    select object_type, object_name
    from user_objects
    where status = 'INVALID'
    group by object_type, object_name
    order by object_type, object_name;
begin
  dbms_utility.compile_schema(user);

  for rec_invalid_object in lcu_invalid_objects loop
    l_compilation_errors := l_compilation_errors || chr(10) || ' ' || rpad(rec_invalid_
object.object_type, 20) || rec_invalid_object.object_name;
  end loop;
```

```
if l_compilation_errors is not null then
   l_compilation_errors := chr(10) || chr(10) || 'Invalid objects in schema ' || user ||
':' || l_compilation_errors;
   raise_application_error(-20000, l_compilation_errors || chr(10));
   end if;
end;
```

The last folder under the src/main/database directory is technical-docs. In here, you will automatically generate technical documentation based on comments in your SQL scripts.

ChangeLog Files

Liquibase uses changeLog files to describe what database scripts should be executed to successfully migrate a target database schema to a desired version. ChangeLog files also define the order of script execution and include other relevant meta-information. Let's first take a look at how the master changeLog file looks because it defines the main order of execution for your different types of scripts. Listing 9-9 shows the content of the master.xml file.

Listing 9-9. src/main/database/changelog/master.xml

```xml
<?xml version="1.0" encoding="UTF-8"?>
<databaseChangeLog xmlns="http://www.liquibase.org/xml/ns/dbchangelog"
                   xmlns:xsi="http://www.w3.org/2001/XMLSchema-instance"
                   xsi:schemaLocation="http://www.liquibase.org/xml/ns/dbchangelog
                                       http://www.liquibase.org/xml/ns/dbchangelog/
                                       dbchangelog-3.0.xsd">

   <include file="src/main/database/changelog/install/1.0.xml" />
   <include file="src/main/database/changelog/latest/1.0.xml" />
   <include file="src/main/database/changelog/data/1.0.xml" />
   <include file="src/main/database/changelog/post-build/1.0.xml" />

</databaseChangeLog>
```

The master changeLog file is merely a collection of other changeLog files that in their turn include so-called changeSets. Before explaining what changeSets are, let me clarify the order of execution. It is actually all common sense.

1. The first scripts to be executed through Liquibase are those in the install folder. That is because other types of scripts typically depend on objects in the install folder. As an illustration, you cannot run a data script that inserts rows in the DEPT table before the DEPT table actually exists.

2. Scripts in the latest folder are executed afterward. These replaceable objects also depend on objects in the install folder, but that is not the main reason why they are being executed at this moment. Unlike nonreplaceable objects, Liquibase does not halt the build when it compiles invalid replaceable objects. The reason behind this is caused by the behavior of the underlying OJDBC driver, which Liquibase uses to compile the database scripts to the Oracle Database. However, it is possible that data scripts depend on objects in the latest folder. Take, for instance, a series of insert statements that depend on a before row insert trigger to assign a sequence generated primary key value.

3. After compiling all database objects, run the DML scripts in the data folder.

4. Finally, run any post-build scripts. This is where the compile_schema.sql script is being executed to validate whether the schema contains invalid objects. If it does, halt the build and print out the names of all invalid objects.

The most common way to organize your changeLogs is by major release and database script type. As you can see in the demo project, the src/main/database/changelog folder includes a subfolder for every type of database script: install, latest, data, and post-build. Each of the four subfolders contains a 1.0.xml changeLog file in which the database scripts of the corresponding type are grouped together. Please note that you are completely free in how you organize the changeLog files for your project. You can, for example, use a single changeLog for all the different types of database scripts. This, however, quickly results in a large and unorganized changeLog file, especially when your project counts many database objects. Listing 9-10 shows the contents of the changelog folder.

Listing 9-10. The src/main/database/changelog Directory Layout

```
my-project
    -- src
        -- main
            -- database
                -- changelog
                    -- data
                        -- 1.0.xml
                    -- install
                        -- 1.0.xml
                    -- latest
                        -- 1.0.xml
                    -- post-build
                        -- 1.0.xml
                    -- master.xml
```

ChangeLog files are composed of changeSet elements, which represent isolated transactions through which database statements can be executed. In the demo project, you will quickly notice that each changeSet points to a SQL script in one of subdirectories of the src/main/database directory. Listing 9-11 shows the content of the changeLog file for nonreplaceable objects.

Listing 9-11. src/main/database/changelog/install/1.0.xml

```xml
<?xml version="1.0" encoding="UTF-8"?>
<databaseChangeLog xmlns="http://www.liquibase.org/xml/ns/dbchangelog"
                   xmlns:xsi="http://www.w3.org/2001/XMLSchema-instance"
                   xsi:schemaLocation="http://www.liquibase.org/xml/ns/dbchangelog
                                       http://www.liquibase.org/xml/ns/dbchangelog/
                                       dbchangelog-3.0.xsd">

  <!-- tables -->

  <changeSet id="create_dept" author="nick.buytaert">
    <sqlFile path="src/main/database/install/table/create_dept.sql" />
  </changeSet>
```

```
<changeSet id="create_emp" author="nick.buytaert">
  <sqlFile path="src/main/database/install/table/create_emp.sql" />
</changeSet>

<!-- sequences -->

<changeSet id="create_seq_dept" author="nick.buytaert">
  <sqlFile path="src/main/database/install/sequence/create_seq_dept.sql" />
</changeSet>

<changeSet id="create_seq_emp" author="nick.buytaert">
  <sqlFile path="src/main/database/install/sequence/create_seq_emp.sql" />
</changeSet>

</databaseChangeLog>
```

As you can clearly see, a changeLog file is yet another XML file filled with changeSet elements. Liquibase sequentially reads out the changeLog files, starting from the master changeLog, and determines what changeSets must be executed to successfully migrate a target database schema to the desired version. The decision of whether to execute a changeSet is based on two aspects.

First, you should be aware that Liquibase keeps track of all previously executed changeSets within a given schema. On its first execution in a schema, Liquibase creates the DATABASECHANGELOG and DATABASECHANGELOGLOCK tables. The latter is a simple single-row table that prevents multiple Liquibase executions from running at the same time. The other table contains all changeSets that have already been run against the given database schema. The DATABASECHANGELOG table even calculates an MD5 checksum for each entry, based on the content of the changeSet's SQL script or scripts. This checksum allows Liquibase to detect differences between the changeSets you are trying to execute and what was actually ran against the database. This stateful concept is essential when having to decide whether a script should or should not be executed during a database migration in a target schema.

Second, changeSet attributes are used to define script execution behavior. These attributes allow you to easily differentiate between replaceable and nonreplaceable scripts. Table 9-1 gives an overview of the most important changeSet attributes.

Table 9-1. Most Frequently Used changeSet Attributes

Attribute	Description	Default Value	Required
id	Uniquely identifies a changeSet within a changeLog file	-	Yes
author	The name of the person who created the changeSet	-	Yes
runAlways	Indicates whether the changeSet should be executed on every run, even if it has been executed before	False	No
runOnChange	Execute the changeSet only the first time and each time the content of the changeSet changes	False	No

The runAlways and runOnChange attributes accept a Boolean value and determine whether a script should be executed once or repeatedly. Omitting these two attributes results in false values, indicating that a changeSet may be executed only once per schema. Thus, both changeSet definitions in Listing 9-12 are identical.

Listing 9-12. ChangeSet Default Values

```
<changeSet id="create_dept" author="nick.buytaert">
  <sqlFile path="src/main/database/install/table/create_dept.sql" />
</changeSet>

<changeSet id="create_dept" author="nick.buytaert" runAlways="false" runOnChange="false">
  <sqlFile path="src/main/database/install/table/create_dept.sql" />
</changeSet>
```

This changeSet definition is typically used for nonreplaceable objects in the install folder and for data scripts in the data folder. Setting both attribute values to true causes a changeSet to always execute when Liquibase runs. This execution behavior is ideal for replaceable objects in the latest folder. The src/main/database/changelog/latest/1.0.xml file contains the changeSets for the replaceable objects. Listing 9-13 includes an example of a changeSet definition that compiles the BR_IU_DEPT trigger.

Listing 9-13. ChangeSet for Compiling a Replaceable Object

```
<changeSet id="br_iu_dept" author="nick.buytaert" runAlways="true" runOnChange="true">
  <sqlFile splitStatements="false" path="src/main/database/latest/trigger/br_iu_dept.sql" />
</changeSet>
```

It is also possible to only set the runOnChange attribute to true, resulting in a changeSet that executes only when the content of the referenced script was changed since its last execution. Also notice the splitStatements attribute on the sqlFile element, which has been given the Boolean value false. The default value for this attribute is true, meaning that Liquibase splits multiple statements on the semicolon character. This is the desired behavior for most nonreplaceable and data scripts. Replaceable scripts, on the other hand, should not interpret a semicolon as a statement separator.

The changeSet for a database package typically includes two sqlFile elements. As you might have guessed, you need one for the package specification and one for the package body. Remember that a changeSet demarks one database transaction in Liquibase. The changeSet for the database package will be executed in two transactions, though. The reason is that both the package specification and body scripts contain DDL, which gets automatically committed by the Oracle Database. Listing 9-14 shows an example changeSet that compiles the DAO_DEPT package.

Listing 9-14. ChangeSet for Compiling a Database Package

```
<changeSet id="dao_dept" author="nick.buytaert" runAlways="true" runOnChange="true">
  <sqlFile splitStatements="false" path="src/main/database/latest/package/dao_dept.pks.sql" />
  <sqlFile splitStatements="false" path="src/main/database/latest/package/dao_dept.pkb.sql" />
</changeSet>
```

The Liquibase Maven Plugin

It is possible to use Liquibase in a stand-alone fashion, but what you will actually do is execute it as part of your Maven build. Integrating Liquibase with Maven is easily accomplished by adding the Liquibase Maven plugin to the pom.xml file. Simply append the plugin element from Listing 9-15 as a child to the plugins element.

Listing 9-15. Liquibase Maven Plugin Definition

```xml
<plugin>
  <groupId>org.liquibase</groupId>
  <artifactId>liquibase-maven-plugin</artifactId>
  <version>3.2.0</version>

  <dependencies>
    <dependency>
      <groupId>com.oracle</groupId>
      <artifactId>ojdbc7</artifactId>
      <version>12.1.0.2.0</version>
    </dependency>
  </dependencies>

  <executions>
    <execution>
      <id>liquibase-update</id>
      <phase>compile</phase>
      <goals>
        <goal>update</goal>
      </goals>

      <configuration>
        <driver>oracle.jdbc.driver.OracleDriver</driver>
        <url>jdbc:oracle:thin:@localhost:8202/pdbdb01</url>
        <username>tst_apex_maven_demo</username>
        <password>secret</password>
        <changeLogFile>src/main/database/changelog/master.xml</changeLogFile>
        <promptOnNonLocalDatabase>false</promptOnNonLocalDatabase>
        <verbose>false</verbose>
      </configuration>
    </execution>
  </executions>
</plugin>
```

The plugin element contains all configuration details for the Liquibase Maven plugin. The groupId, artifactId, and version tags uniquely identify the Maven plugin that should be executed as part of the build. It is also required to define the Oracle JDBC driver as a plugin dependency because Liquibase depends on it to execute the SQL scripts.

The executions element configures the execution details of a plugin's goal. Every execution gets a unique ID assigned and is linked to a phase in Maven's build lifecycle. Without getting into too much detail here, think of the Maven build lifecycle as a series of stages to which you can link a plugin's execution. In the demo project, all plugin executions are linked to the compile phase. The goal element contains the name of the goal you want the plugin to execute. Every plugin defines its own goals. In case of the Liquibase Maven plugin, you will execute the update goal, whose task is to apply a changeLog file to a target database schema.

The configuration element allows you to specify goal specific properties. The update goal requires you to provide several database connection parameters to successfully log on as the parsing schema of the APEX application you are deploying. You must also reference the path to the master changeLog file so that Liquibase can determine what subchangeLog files must be read out. The following is an overview of the specified properties:

- *driver*: The fully qualified name of the driver class that is used when connecting to the database. The value for this property will always be oracle.jdbc.driver. OracleDriver in combination with an Oracle Database.

- *url*: The JDBC connection URL of the target database where Liquibase will be executed.

- *username*: The parsing schema of the APEX application.

- *password*: The database password of the parsing schema.

- *changeLogFile*: The path to the changeLog file that must be applied to the database schema.

- *promptOnNonLocalDatabase*: Controls the prompting of users as to whether they really want to run the changes on a database that is not local to the machine that the user is current executing the plugin on.

- *verbose*: Controls the verbosity of the output.

A great thing about the Liquibase Maven plugin is that it is available from a public Maven repository. Maven itself will download and install the required library files into the local Maven repository to get Liquibase up and running. There is just one catch, and that is the Oracle JDBC driver, which you will have to manually download and install because of Oracle license restrictions. Follow these steps:

1. Download the appropriate OJDBC driver from the Oracle web site. Make sure to select the driver that is compatible with your specific Oracle Database version.

2. Open a command-line window and change the directory to the location where you downloaded the OJDBC driver.

3. Run the Maven install command.

```
mvn install:install-file -Dfile=ojdbc7.jar -DgroupId=com.oracle
-DartifactId=ojdbc7 -Dversion=12.1.0.2.0 -Dpackaging=jar
```

■ **Note** The version numbers in the previous install command may vary depending on the version you have downloaded.

After adding the Liquibase plugin to the pom.xml file and installing the appropriate OJDBC driver, you are ready to run Maven for the first time. Simply open a command-line window and change the directory to the root of the project. Execute the mvn compile command to start the build. Maven will automatically look for the pom.xml file in the current directory and will try to run all plugin executions that are part of the compile phase. Listing 9-16 shows the build log produced by Maven.

Listing 9-16. A Successful Maven Execution

```
$ mvn compile
[INFO] Scanning for projects...
[INFO]
[INFO] ------------------------------------------------------------------------
[INFO] Building orclapex-maven-demo 1.0
[INFO] ------------------------------------------------------------------------
[INFO]
[INFO] --- maven-resources-plugin:2.6:resources (default-resources) @ orclapex-maven-
demo ---
[WARNING] Using platform encoding (UTF-8 actually) to copy filtered resources, i.e. build is
platform dependent!
[INFO] skip non existing resourceDirectory /Users/Nick/Documents/github/orclapex-maven-demo/
src/main/resources
[INFO]
[INFO] --- maven-compiler-plugin:2.5.1:compile (default-compile) @ orclapex-maven-demo ---
[INFO] No sources to compile
[INFO]
[INFO] --- liquibase-maven-plugin:3.2.0:update (liquibase-update) @ orclapex-maven-demo ---
[INFO] ------------------------------------------------------------------------
[INFO] there are no resolved artifacts for the Maven project.
[INFO] Executing on Database: jdbc:oracle:thin:@localhost:8202/pdbdb01
INFO 2/20/15 8:37 PM: liquibase: Successfully acquired change log lock
INFO 2/20/15 8:37 PM: liquibase: Creating database history table with name: DATABASECHANGELOG
INFO 2/20/15 8:37 PM: liquibase: Reading from DATABASECHANGELOG
INFO 2/20/15 8:37 PM: liquibase: src/main/database/changelog/master.xml: src/main/database/
changelog/install/1.0.xml::create_dept::nick.buytaert: SQL in file src/main/database/
install/table/create_dept.sql executed
INFO 2/20/15 8:37 PM: liquibase: src/main/database/changelog/master.xml: src/main/database/
changelog/install/1.0.xml::create_dept::nick.buytaert: ChangeSet src/main/database/
changelog/install/1.0.xml::create_dept::nick.buytaert ran successfully in 166ms
INFO 2/20/15 8:37 PM: liquibase: src/main/database/changelog/master.xml: src/main/database/
changelog/install/1.0.xml::create_emp::nick.buytaert: SQL in file src/main/database/install/
table/create_emp.sql executed
INFO 2/20/15 8:37 PM: liquibase: src/main/database/changelog/master.xml: src/main/database/
changelog/install/1.0.xml::create_emp::nick.buytaert: ChangeSet src/main/database/changelog/
install/1.0.xml::create_emp::nick.buytaert ran successfully in 176ms
...
INFO 2/20/15 8:37 PM: liquibase: src/main/database/changelog/master.xml: src/main/database/
changelog/data/1.0.xml::insert_emp_demo_data::nick.buytaert: SQL in file src/main/database/
data/insert_emp_demo_data.sql executed
INFO 2/20/15 8:37 PM: liquibase: src/main/database/changelog/master.xml: src/main/database/
changelog/data/1.0.xml::insert_emp_demo_data::nick.buytaert: ChangeSet src/main/database/
changelog/data/1.0.xml::insert_emp_demo_data::nick.buytaert ran successfully in 784ms
INFO 2/20/15 8:37 PM: liquibase: src/main/database/changelog/master.xml: src/main/database/
changelog/post-build/1.0.xml::compile_schema::nick.buytaert: SQL in file src/main/database/
post-build/compile_schema.sql executed
INFO 2/20/15 8:37 PM: liquibase: src/main/database/changelog/master.xml: src/main/database/
changelog/post-build/1.0.xml::compile_schema::nick.buytaert: ChangeSet src/main/database/
changelog/post-build/1.0.xml::compile_schema::nick.buytaert ran successfully in 6571ms
INFO 2/20/15 8:37 PM: liquibase: Successfully released change log lock
```

```
[INFO] ---------------------------------------------------------------------
[INFO]
[INFO] ---------------------------------------------------------------------
[INFO] BUILD SUCCESS
[INFO] ---------------------------------------------------------------------
[INFO] Total time: 23.956s
[INFO] Finished at: Fri Feb 20 20:37:56 CET 2015
[INFO] Final Memory: 11M/26M
[INFO] ---------------------------------------------------------------------
```

I have removed some of the lines in this build log to make the output not too overwhelming. The "build success" message at the end of the log indicates that all build actions have been executed without errors. In this case, it means that the update goal of the Liquibase plugin successfully executed all appropriate SQL scripts in the target database schema.

Running Maven a second time with the same mvn compile command will start the build again but produce a different build log. That is perfectly normal since Liquibase will reexecute only the changeSets that have been assigned the value true for the runAlways attribute. The nonreplaceable objects from the first Liquibase run will not be executed anymore.

The last changeSet executed by Liquibase is the compile_schema.sql script. Its job was to look for invalid objects within the currently connected database schema. The script has executed successfully in the previous example, which means that all database objects are valid. This approach greatly benefits the overall stability of the project because it feeds the development team with constant feedback on the source code's health.

Let's take a look at how the build reacts when you introduce an invalid object in the code repository. As an example, I have deliberately invalidated the bl_user_registration package body. Firing up the Maven build with the same mvn compile command will now result in an unsuccessful execution, as shown in Listing 9-17.

Listing 9-17. An Unsuccessful Maven Execution

```
$ mvn compile
[INFO] Scanning for projects...
[INFO]
[INFO] ---------------------------------------------------------------------
[INFO] Building orclapex-maven-demo 1.0
[INFO] ---------------------------------------------------------------------
[INFO]
[INFO] --- maven-resources-plugin:2.6:resources (default-resources) @ orclapex-maven-
demo ---
[WARNING] Using platform encoding (UTF-8 actually) to copy filtered resources, i.e. build is
platform dependent!
[INFO] skip non existing resourceDirectory /Users/Nick/Documents/github/orclapex-maven-demo/
src/main/resources
[INFO]
[INFO] --- maven-compiler-plugin:2.5.1:compile (default-compile) @ orclapex-maven-demo ---
[INFO] No sources to compile
[INFO]
[INFO] --- liquibase-maven-plugin:3.2.0:update (liquibase-update) @ orclapex-maven-demo ---
[INFO] ---------------------------------------------------------------------
[INFO] there are no resolved artifacts for the Maven project.
[INFO] Executing on Database: jdbc:oracle:thin:@localhost:8202/pdbdb01
INFO 2/21/15 12:44 PM: liquibase: Successfully acquired change log lock
```

```
INFO 2/21/15 12:44 PM: liquibase: Reading from DATABASECHANGELOG
...
INFO 2/21/15 12:44 PM: liquibase: src/main/database/changelog/master.xml: src/main/database/
changelog/latest/1.0.xml::bl_user_registration::nick.buytaert: SQL in file src/main/
database/latest/package/bl_user_registration.pks.sql executed
INFO 2/21/15 12:44 PM: liquibase: src/main/database/changelog/master.xml: src/main/database/
changelog/latest/1.0.xml::bl_user_registration::nick.buytaert: SQL in file src/main/
database/latest/package/bl_user_registration.pkb.sql executed
INFO 2/21/15 12:44 PM: liquibase: src/main/database/changelog/master.xml: src/main/database/
changelog/latest/1.0.xml::bl_user_registration::nick.buytaert: ChangeSet src/main/database/
changelog/latest/1.0.xml::bl_user_registration::nick.buytaert ran successfully in 343ms
...
SEVERE 2/21/15 12:44 PM: liquibase: src/main/database/changelog/master.xml: src/main/
database/changelog/post-build/1.0.xml::compile_schema::nick.buytaert: Change Set src/main/
database/changelog/post-build/1.0.xml::compile_schema::nick.buytaert failed.  Error: Error
executing SQL
...
Invalid objects in schema TST_APEX_MAVEN_DEMO:
  PACKAGE BODY        BL_USER_REGISTRATION
ORA-06512: at line 19
...
INFO 2/21/15 12:44 PM: liquibase: src/main/database/changelog/post-build/1.0.xml::compile_
schema::nick.buytaert: Successfully released change log lock
[INFO] ------------------------------------------------------------------------
[INFO] BUILD FAILURE
[INFO] ------------------------------------------------------------------------
[INFO] Total time: 14.307s
[INFO] Finished at: Sat Feb 21 12:44:37 CET 2015
[INFO] Final Memory: 11M/26M
[INFO] ------------------------------------------------------------------------
...
```

This time, the compile_schema.sql script execution fails, resulting in the "build failure" message. A list of invalid objects in the schema is printed out in the build log. This makes it easy for the development team to quickly identify and fix the database objects that cause the build to fail. Note that the changeSet for the bl_user_registration package executed successfully, even though the package body includes a compilation error. The reason for this behavior is the underlying OJDBC driver, which does not return an error when it compiles an invalid replaceable object. Nonreplaceable scripts that return an error during their execution will immediately halt the build. Executing the ALTER TABLE script from Listing 9-18 as part of the alter_emp_add_birthdate changeSet, for example, will result in an output as in Listing 9-19.

Listing 9-18. An ALTER TABLE Script

```
alter table emp
add birthdate date not null;
```

Listing 9-19. An Unsuccessful Maven Execution Caused by an Error in a SQL Script

```
$ mvn compile
[INFO] Scanning for projects...
[INFO]
[INFO] ------------------------------------------------------------------------
[INFO] Building orclapex-maven-demo 1.0
```

```
[INFO] -------------------------------------------------------------------------
[INFO]
[INFO] --- maven-resources-plugin:2.6:resources (default-resources) @ orclapex-maven-demo
---
[WARNING] Using platform encoding (UTF-8 actually) to copy filtered resources, i.e. build is
platform dependent!
[INFO] skip non existing resourceDirectory /Users/Nick/Documents/github/orclapex-maven-demo/
src/main/resources
[INFO]
[INFO] --- maven-compiler-plugin:2.5.1:compile (default-compile) @ orclapex-maven-demo ---
[INFO] No sources to compile
[INFO]
[INFO] --- liquibase-maven-plugin:3.2.0:update (liquibase-update) @ orclapex-maven-demo ---
[INFO] -------------------------------------------------------------------------
[INFO] there are no resolved artifacts for the Maven project.
[INFO] Executing on Database: jdbc:oracle:thin:@localhost:8202/pdbdb01
INFO 2/28/15 4:24 PM: liquibase: Successfully acquired change log lock
INFO 2/28/15 4:24 PM: liquibase: Reading from DATABASECHANGELOG
SEVERE 2/28/15 4:24 PM: liquibase: src/main/database/changelog/master.xml: src/main/
database/changelog/install/1.0.xml::alter_emp_add_birthdate::nick.buytaert: Change Set src/
main/database/changelog/install/1.0.xml::alter_emp_add_birthdate::nick.buytaert failed.
Error: Error executing SQL alter table emp
add birthdate date not null: ORA-01758: table must be empty to add mandatory (NOT NULL)
column
...
INFO 2/28/15 4:24 PM: liquibase: src/main/database/changelog/install/1.0.xml::alter_emp_add_
birthdate::nick.buytaert: Successfully released change log lock
[INFO] -------------------------------------------------------------------------
[INFO] BUILD FAILURE
[INFO] -------------------------------------------------------------------------
[INFO] Total time: 11.520s
[INFO] Finished at: Sat Feb 28 16:24:19 CET 2015
[INFO] Final Memory: 12M/28M
[INFO] -------------------------------------------------------------------------
[ERROR] Failed to execute goal org.liquibase:liquibase-maven-plugin:3.2.0:update (liquibase-
update) on project orclapex-maven-demo: Error setting up or running Liquibase: Migration
failed for change set src/main/database/changelog/install/1.0.xml::alter_emp_add_
birthdate::nick.buytaert:
[ERROR] Reason: liquibase.exception.DatabaseException: Error executing SQL alter table emp
[ERROR] add birthdate date not null: ORA-01758: table must be empty to add mandatory (NOT
NULL) column
[ERROR] -> [Help 1]
[ERROR]
[ERROR] To see the full stack trace of the errors, re-run Maven with the -e switch.
[ERROR] Re-run Maven using the -X switch to enable full debug logging.
[ERROR]
[ERROR] For more information about the errors and possible solutions, please read the
following articles:
[ERROR] [Help 1] http://cwiki.apache.org/confluence/display/MAVEN/MojoExecutionException
```

The `alter_emp_add_birthdate` changeSet executes with an Oracle error code and automatically terminates the build. As a result of the error in the `ALTER TABLE` script execution, the changeSet will not be written to the `DATABASECHANGELOG` table and will therefore be executed again on the next Liquibase run.

Other Features

With the adoption of Liquibase in your project's workflow, a continuous connection is made between database development and deployment. Each change to the database should be captured immediately as a Liquibase changeSet to define and control its execution through the build process. Database changes can also be tested more often and in smaller parts, resulting in faster problem detection and resolution.

So far in this chapter, I have given a detailed explanation on the core features of Liquibase. However, it is certainly worth mentioning that there are still many features left undiscussed. Next up is a listing of some of these features, without getting into too much detail.

ChangeSets can accept `rollback` elements to undo database changes. A `rollback` element typically performs the opposite action of the changeSet it is attached to. A changeSet that creates the `EMP` table, for example, will drop that same table in its `rollback` element, as shown in Listing 9-20.

Listing 9-20. A changeSet with a Rollback Element Defined

```
<changeSet id="create_emp" author="nick.buytaert">
  <sqlFile path="src/main/database/install/table/create_emp.sql" />
  <rollback>
    drop table emp;
  </rollback>
</changeSet>
```

You can specify what changes to roll back in three ways.

- *Tag*: A changeSet has the ability to tag the database. Such a tag can then be specified to roll back all changeSets that were executed after the given tag was applied.

- *Number of changeSets*: Specify the total number of changeSets to roll back.

- *Date*: Choose a specific date to roll back to. The following is an example that undoes all changeSets that were executed after January 1, 2015.

  ```
  mvn liquibase:rollback -Dliquibase.rollbackDate="JAN 1, 2015"
  ```

Another powerful Liquibase feature is the concept of *preconditions,* which can be used to conditionally execute a changeLog or changeSet based on the state of the database. Suppose you want to insert demo data in the `EMP` table only when the table is empty. The changeSet definition in this case would look like the one in Listing 9-21.

Listing 9-21. A changeSet with a preCondition Element Defined

```
<changeSet id="insert_emp_demo_data" author="nick.buytaert">
  <preConditions onFail="WARN">
    <sqlCheck expectedResult="0">
      select count(*)
      from emp;
    </sqlCheck>
  </preConditions>
  <sqlFile path="src/main/database/data/insert_emp_demo_data.sql" />
</changeSet>
```

Yet another technique to conditionally execute changeSets is the *context* mechanism. It is possible to associate a changeSet with one or more contexts, while the update goal of the Liquibase Maven plugin lets you set one or more contexts as part of the execution. Only changeSets marked with the passed contexts will be executed. This is extremely helpful when having to run scripts that are environment dependent. It is highly unlikely, for example, to write demo data into production tables. Thus, only the development and test environment should execute the insert_emp_demo_data changeSet.

The insert_emp_demo_data changeSet from Listing 9-22 will be executed only when the context DEV or TST is included in the Liquibase Maven plugin configuration section. If the PRD context is passed, for example, the changeSet will be skipped. Listing 9-23 shows how to include the contexts parameter.

Listing 9-22. A changeSet with a Context Element Defined

```
<changeSet id="insert_emp_demo_data" author="nick.buytaert" context="DEV,TST">
  <sqlFile path="src/main/database/data/insert_emp_demo_data.sql" />
</changeSet>
```

Listing 9-23. The Liquibase Configuration Section with contexts Element

```
<configuration>
  <driver>oracle.jdbc.driver.OracleDriver</driver>
  <url>jdbc:oracle:thin:@localhost:8202/pdbdb01</url>
  <username>tst_apex_maven_demo</username>
  <password>secret</password>
  <changeLogFile>src/main/database/changelog/master.xml</changeLogFile>
  <contexts>TST</contexts>
  <promptOnNonLocalDatabase>false</promptOnNonLocalDatabase>
  <verbose>false</verbose>
</configuration>
```

You can find more information on these and other Liquibase features at Liquibase's official documentation guide:

www.liquibase.org/documentation/

The Oracle APEX Maven Plugin

Plugins are essential when it comes to defining a project's build process in Maven. A plugin is merely a collection of goals with a general common purpose. The purpose of the Oracle APEX Maven plugin is to facilitate the APEX development and deployment process. Each plugin goal is responsible for performing a specific action. The Liquibase Maven plugin, for example, included the update goal, which allowed you to apply a changeLog to a target database schema.

Unlike the Liquibase plugin, the Oracle APEX Maven plugin is not publicly available in the Maven repository. This means you will have to manually download and install the plugin yourself.

1. Go to https://github.com/nbuytaert1/orclapex-maven-plugin and download the latest stable release.

2. Unzip the downloaded archive file.

3. Open a terminal window and change directory to the unzipped orclapex-maven-plugin folder.

4. Install the plugin in your local Maven repository with the following command:

```
mvn install:install-file -Dfile=orclapex-maven-plugin-1.0.jar
-DpomFile=orclapex-maven-plugin-1.0-pom.xml
```

■ **Note** The version numbers in the previous install command may vary depending on the version you have downloaded.

The import Goal

The most essential goal of the Oracle APEX Maven plugin is the import goal, whose task is fairly simple: import the SQL application export files into a target APEX workspace. The technical implementation and complexity of a plugin's goal is hidden for the developer in the form of a Maven old Java object (MOJO). A MOJO is a Java class that specifies metadata about its goal, such as the goal name and the parameters it is expecting.

The import goal requires one extra piece of software on your machine to successfully execute its task: SQL*Plus. That is because an APEX application export file is filled with SQL*Plus commands. This means that the import goal has no other option than executing the export file with SQL*Plus. OJDBC would have been an alternative if the export files were just plain SQL. But since that is not the case, make sure you have SQL*Plus installed on your machine.

Adding the Oracle APEX Maven plugin and the import goal to the POM file is pretty straightforward. Simply append the plugin element from Listing 9-24 to the plugins tag, after the Liquibase Maven plugin. That way, database code gets compiled first, followed by the APEX application import.

Listing 9-24. The Oracle APEX Maven Plugin Definition

```
<plugin>
  <groupId>com.contribute</groupId>
  <artifactId>orclapex-maven-plugin</artifactId>
  <version>1.0</version>

  <executions>
    <execution>
      <id>app-import</id>
      <phase>compile</phase>
      <goals>
        <goal>import</goal>
      </goals>

      <configuration>
        <connectionString>localhost:8202/pdbdb01</connectionString>
        <username>tst_apex_maven_demo</username>
        <password>secret</password>
        <appExportLocation>src/main/apex</appExportLocation>
        <workspaceName>tst_apex_maven_demo</workspaceName>
        <appId>1010</appId>
      </configuration>
```

```
    </execution>
  </executions>
</plugin>
```

In this example, the import goal is tied to the compile phase, just like the update goal of the Liquibase Maven plugin. Goals tied to the same phase in the POM are executed in order of occurrence. The configuration element contains the import goal parameters. These parameters allow you to specify how SQL*Plus should execute the SQL export file into a target workspace. Here is a short explanation on the used parameters:

- connectionString: The database connection string used in the SQL*Plus login argument.

- username: The database username used to log in with SQL*Plus.

- password: The database user's password.

- sqlplusCmd: The command to start the SQL*Plus executable. The default value is sqlplus if omitted.

- appExportLocation: The relative path to the folder containing the application export files.

- workspaceName: The APEX workspace in which you want to import the application.

- appId: The ID for the application to be imported. Omit this parameter to import the application with its original ID.

The import goal allows you to set the same application attributes as the APEX_APPLICATION_INSTALL API package. The appId parameter, for example, uses the set_application_id procedure in the background to set the ID of the application to be imported. The following application attributes can be set through the import goal parameters:

- appId: The application ID

- appAlias: The application alias

- appName: The application name

- appParsingSchema: The application parsing schema

- appImagePrefix: The application image prefix

- appProxy: The proxy server attributes

- appOffset: The offset value for the application import

■ **Note**   More information on these application attributes is available at the official documentation page of the APEX_APPLICATION_INSTALL API package.

After adding the Oracle APEX Maven plugin to the pom.xml file, you should be able to import the application export as part of the Maven build. The command to run the Maven build is still mvn compile. Maven will first run Liquibase, followed by the application import. If something goes wrong with the update goal of Liquibase, the application import will not take place. This is the desired behavior since you do not want to import an application that would work on a previous version of the database schema. Listing 9-25 shows the Maven build log after executing the mvn compile command.

Listing 9-25. Part of the Maven Build Log

```
...
[INFO] --- orclapex-maven-plugin:1.0:import (app-import) @ orclapex-maven-demo ---
[INFO]
[INFO] SQL*Plus: Release 11.2.0.3.0 Production on Sat Jan 31 16:56:06 2015
[INFO]
[INFO] Copyright (c) 1982, 2012, Oracle.  All rights reserved.
[INFO]
[INFO]
[INFO] Connected to:
[INFO] Oracle Database 12c Enterprise Edition Release 12.1.0.2.0 - 64bit Production
[INFO] With the Partitioning, OLAP, Advanced Analytics and Real Application Testing options
[INFO]
[INFO] workspace ID set: 25290313466775650 (TST_APEX_MAVEN_DEMO)
[INFO] application ID set: 1010
[INFO]
[INFO] PL/SQL procedure successfully completed.
[INFO]
[INFO] APPLICATION 1000 - APEX Maven Demo
[INFO] Set Credentials...
[INFO] Check Compatibility...
[INFO] Set Application ID...
[INFO] ...ui types
[INFO] ...user interfaces
[INFO] ...plug-in settings
[INFO] ...authorization schemes
[INFO] ...navigation bar entries
[INFO] ...application processes
...
```

The SQL*Plus prompt commands from the application export file are printed out in the Maven build log. The output also informs you on the configuration parameters that have been set through the plugin's configuration properties. As you can see in the previous example, the application has been imported in the TST_APEX_MAVEN_DEMO workspace with application ID 1010.

The run-natural-docs Goal

It is also worth mentioning that the Oracle APEX Maven plugin includes the run-natural-docs goal. Natural Docs is an open source technical documentation generator. It scans the source code for Javadoc-like comments and builds high-quality HTML documentation from it. All package specifications in the demo project have been documented with these comments. Take, for example, the bl_user_registration package specification, shown in Listing 9-26, which contains the validate_password_strength function.

Listing 9-26. src/main/database/latest/package/bl_user_registration.pks.sql

```
/*
  package: bl_user_registration
  Contains the business logic for the user registration process.
*/
create or replace
package bl_user_registration is

  /*
    function: validate_password_strength
    Determine whether a given password is strong enough.

    parameters:
      in_password - the password entered by the user

    returns:
      A boolean value. True means OK. False means that the password is not strong enough.
  */
  function validate_password_strength(
    in_password in varchar2
  ) return boolean;

end bl_user_registration;
```

Adding these comments to the source code is sufficient for Natural Docs to start generating technical documentation. All you have to do is add another execution element to the Oracle APEX Maven plugin in the pom.xml file, as shown in Listing 9-27. Please refer to the demo project on GitHub to see the entire content of the pom.xml file.

Listing 9-27. The run-natural-docs Execution Element in pom.xml

```
<execution>
  <id>generate-natural-docs</id>
  <phase>compile</phase>
  <goals>
    <goal>run-natural-docs</goal>
  </goals>

  <configuration>
    <naturalDocsHome>util/naturaldocs</naturalDocsHome>
    <inputSourceDirectories>
      <inputSourceDirectory>src/main/database</inputSourceDirectory>
    </inputSourceDirectories>
    <outputFormat>FramedHTML</outputFormat>
    <outputDirectory>src/main/database/technical-docs</outputDirectory>
    <projectDirectory>src/main/database/technical-docs/settings</projectDirectory>
    <!-- dir must exist before generating natural docs -->
    <rebuild>true</rebuild>
  </configuration>
</execution>
```

The following is a short explanation on the parameters used in the `configuration` element:

- `naturalDocsHome`: The path to the folder containing the Natural Docs executable.

- `inputSourceDirectories`: Natural Docs will build the documentation from the files in these directories and all its subdirectories. It is possible to specify multiple directories.

- `outputFormat`: The output format. The supported formats are `HTML` and `FramedHTML`.

- `outputDirectory`: The folder in which Natural Docs will generate the technical documentation.

- `projectDirectory`: Natural Docs needs a place to store the project's specific configuration and data files.

■ **Note**   You need Perl 5.8 or newer installed on your machine to run Natural Docs. Mac and Linux users have Perl installed by default. If you are using Windows and have not installed it yet, you can get ActiveState's ActivePerl for free at `www.activestate.com/activeperl`.

Running the `mvn compile` command will now generate technical documentation. Listing 9-28 shows the part of the Maven build log generated by the `run-natural-docs` goal.

Listing 9-28.   The Build Log Generated by the run-natural-docs Goal

```
...
[INFO] --- orclapex-maven-plugin:1.0:run-natural-docs (generate-natural-docs) @ orclapex-
maven-demo ---
[INFO] Finding files and detecting changes...
[INFO] Parsing 21 files...
[INFO] Building 5 files...
[INFO] Building 3 indexes...
[INFO] Updating menu...
[INFO] Updating CSS file...
[INFO] Done.
...
```

The resulting HTML files are generated in the `outputDirectory` specified in the plugin's configuration section. Figure 9-9 shows the technical documentation for the `BL_USER_REGISTRATION` package.

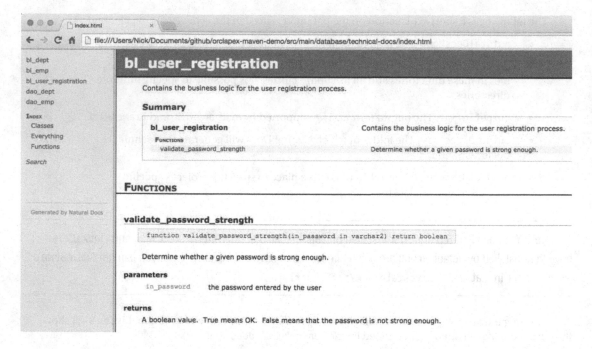

Figure 9-9. *The technical documentation for the BL_USER_REGISTRATION package*

Deploying Static Files

By now, the Maven build successfully covers two of the three parts for the deployment of a basic APEX application. Liquibase tackles the task of migrating database changes, and the APEX application import is taken care of by the import goal of the Oracle APEX Maven plugin. The last part you have to deal with is the deployment of static files. As already mentioned, APEX 5.0 includes several serious improvements that simplified static file deployment. The APEX development team could not have made it any easier for you by automatically exporting the static files as part of the application export.

You can safely skip this section if you decide to take advantage of the enhanced Files section under Shared Components. In that case, the Maven build as described in the previous sections is capable of deploying a basic APEX application with just a single command. For those who prefer to upload their static files to the server's file system, there is just one more task left.

■ **Note** Storing static files on the server's file system makes it possible to automate repetitive tasks related to static files. A CSS preprocessor, for example, can be used to enhance the writing of CSS. You can also add utilities to your workflow that validate and minify CSS and JavaScript files.

The steps required to perform the task of copying static files to the web server are in essence fairly simple:

1. Access the server's file system with a privileged OS user.

2. Remove any existing static files.

3. Copy the static files from the code repository to the web server.

The AntRun Plugin

The AntRun plugin provides the ability to execute Ant tasks from within a Maven build. Apache Ant is also a build automation tool and is considered a predecessor of Maven. I will spare you any further details on this matter, but it turns out that Ant is better suited for the task of copying files to a server's file system. Simply append the code fragment from Listing 9-29 to the plugins element in the pom.xml file.

Listing 9-29. The AntRun Plugin

```
<plugin>
  <groupId>org.apache.maven.plugins</groupId>
  <artifactId>maven-antrun-plugin</artifactId>
  <version>1.7</version>

  <dependencies>
    <dependency>
      <groupId>org.apache.ant</groupId>
      <artifactId>ant-jsch</artifactId>
      <version>1.9.4</version>
    </dependency>
  </dependencies>

  <executions>
    <execution>
      <id>file-copy</id>
      <phase>compile</phase>
      <goals>
        <goal>run</goal>
      </goals>

      <configuration>
        <target>
          <sshexec host="apex.contribute.be"
                   username="i"
                   password="secret"
                   trust="true"
                   verbose="false"
                   command="rm -rf /opt/apex/images/apex_custom/tst_demo &amp;&amp;
                            mkdir -p /opt/apex/images/apex_custom/tst_demo" />

          <scp todir="i:secret@apex.contribute.be:/opt/apex/images/apex_custom/tst_demo"
               trust="true"
               verbose="false">
            <fileset dir="src/main/web-files" />
          </scp>
        </target>
      </configuration>
    </execution>
  </executions>
</plugin>
```

The AntRun plugin requires the ant-jsch dependency because it includes the sshexec and scp tasks, which you need to successfully copy the static files. You do not need to manually install the Maven AntRun plugin or its dependencies because these are publicly available from the Maven repository.

The target element in the configuration section includes two tasks that will be executed by Ant. The sshexec task connects to a remote host with a specified user and executes two OS commands to clean up the existing static files directory. Files removed from the code repository this way will also be removed from the server's file system after the copy.

The scp task is responsible for the actual copy of the src/main/web-files folder content to the server's file system. The target location in the previous example is /opt/apex/images/apex_custom/tst_demo. Running the Maven build with the mvn compile command will now perform the file copy. Listing 9-30 shows the build log generated by the AntRun plugin.

■ **Note**   Secure Copy (SCP) is a protocol that securely transfers computer files between two hosts. It is based on the Secure Shell (SSH) protocol. Other protocols, such as FTP, are also supported by the Maven AntRun plugin. Please refer to the plugin documentation for more information on other protocols.

Listing 9-30. The Build Log Generated by the AntRun Plugin

```
...
[INFO] --- maven-antrun-plugin:1.7:run (file-copy) @ orclapex-maven-demo ---
[INFO] Executing tasks

main:
  [sshexec] Connecting to apex.contribute.be:22
  [sshexec] cmd : rm -rf /opt/apex/images/apex_custom/tst_demo &&
mkdir -p /opt/apex/images/apex_custom/tst_demo
      [scp] Connecting to apex.contribute.be:22
      [scp] done.
[INFO] Executed tasks
...
```

Multi-environment Setup

So far in this chapter, you have constantly been building to the same environment when executing the mvn compile command. That is because the pom.xml file includes the build and configuration details only for the test environment. However, a project setup should count at least three separate environments before being able to support an application's development and deployment lifecycle in a proper way. Figure 9-10 shows these three environments.

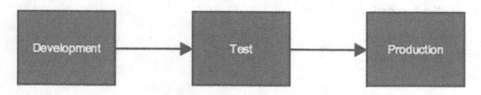

Figure 9-10. A basic build environment setup

- The development environment is where the actual development takes place. This environment always contains the latest version of the application because it is the place where new features and improvements are being implemented by the development team.

- In the test environment, the complete code base is merged together into a single product. This allows the development team to verify whether deployment has been successful and whether the application works as expected.

- The production environment contains the actual live application. It is recommended to install the runtime-only configuration of APEX in this environment. This will prohibit developers from accessing the application builder and SQL workshop, making it impossible to directly modify the live application.

More environments can be added to the previous setup, depending on the demands of the project. An acceptance environment, for example, is often introduced when business users are required to test the application before it gets deployed to production. In this way, business users are more involved because they can verify whether newly developed features or improvements meet the proposed business requirements. This approach separates user acceptance testing from the test environment, which is typically the subject of more technical tests. Figure 9-11 shows the environments within a DTAP street.

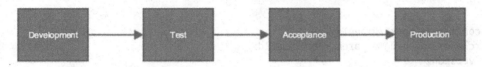

Figure 9-11. A DTAP cycle or street

The concept of an environment in terms of APEX development usually consists of three parts.

- An APEX workspace in which one or more applications will be imported

- A database schema to hold the database objects on which the APEX applications depend

- Optionally, a location on the server's file system to store the application's static files

As you have probably noticed, a clear mapping can be made between the Maven build tasks and the environment you have to deploy to.

- The import goal of the Oracle APEX Maven plugin is capable of importing an application export file into a target APEX workspace.

- The Liquibase Maven plugin takes care of database script execution.

- The AntRun plugin is able to copy local files to a location on the server's file system. You do not need this task during the build process in case you are using the Files section under Shared Components.

Building with Maven to Multiple Environments

The introduction of the multi-environment setup requires you to rethink the POM file in a way that it is capable of building to different environments in an organized way. Luckily, Maven includes several helpful features that allow you to come up with an elegant solution for this requirement. The two main elements on which the solution is built are inheritance and build profiles.

Inheritance

POM files in Maven have the ability to inherit from a parent POM, which defines global-level elements that can be shared across its child POMs. When associating a child with its parent, all parent elements become automatically part of the child. The demo project applies inheritance and includes a parent and child POM in the project's root folder: parent_pom.xml and multi_env_pom.xml. Creating a parent POM is easily achieved by assigning the value pom to the packaging coordinate element, as shown in Listing 9-31.

Listing 9-31. The packaging Coordinate Element

```
<groupId>com.contribute.apex</groupId>
<artifactId>orclapex-maven-demo-parent</artifactId>
<version>1.0</version>
<packaging>pom</packaging>
```

The child POM multi_env_pom.xml inherits parent_pom.xml by referencing the file in the parent element. All three coordinate elements must have the same value as defined in the parent POM. Listing 9-32 shows an example parent element.

Listing 9-32. Referencing the Parent POM with the parent Element in the Child POM

```
<parent>
  <groupId>com.contribute.apex</groupId>
  <artifactId>orclapex-maven-demo-parent</artifactId>
  <version>1.0</version>
  <relativePath>parent_pom.xml</relativePath>
</parent>
```

The goal of inheritance here is to standardize the build configuration across multiple environments. All Maven plugin definitions are moved to a central place in the parent POM under the pluginManagement element. The child POM will then be able to determine what and how plugins should be executed for each environment. This approach prevents the duplication of plugin definitions and improves reusability and maintainability. Take, for example, the Liquibase plugin definition, shown in Listing 9-33, which includes the same configuration properties as in the pom.xml file. The only difference is that most property values now contain variable substitution strings.

Listing 9-33. Substitution Strings in a Plugin's Configuration Section

```
<configuration>
  <driver>oracle.jdbc.driver.OracleDriver</driver>
  <url>${database.url}</url>
  <username>${database.username}</username>
  <password>${database.password}</password>
  <changeLogFile>src/main/database/changelog/master.xml</changeLogFile>
  <promptOnNonLocalDatabase>false</promptOnNonLocalDatabase>
  <verbose>false</verbose>
</configuration>
```

The ${property.name} syntax is a reference to a property defined in the child POM. These properties make it possible to dynamically reference plugins with different configuration settings. The technique of replacing substitution strings at runtime is called *interpolation* in Maven terms.

Build Profiles

The child POM includes a build profile for each environment in the project setup you have to build to. Build profiles divide a POM in distinct parts, making it possible to specify environment-specific properties and references to plugins defined in the parent POM. The technique of build profiles allows you to build the project to different environments from a single POM file. Listing 9-34 shows the definition of the dev build profile.

Listing 9-34. The dev Build Profile

```
<profile>
  <id>dev</id>
  <activation>
    <activeByDefault>true</activeByDefault>
  </activation>

  <properties>
    <database.url>jdbc:oracle:thin:@localhost:8202/pdbdb01</database.url>
    <database.username>dev_apex_maven_demo</database.username>
    <database.password>secret</database.password>
    <webserver.host>apex.contribute.be</webserver.host>
    <webserver.username>i</webserver.username>
    <webserver.password>secret</webserver.password>
    <webserver.directory>/opt/apex/images/apex_custom/dev_apex_maven_demo</webserver.
directory>
  </properties>

  <build>
    <plugins>
      <plugin>
        <groupId>org.apache.maven.plugins</groupId>
        <artifactId>maven-antrun-plugin</artifactId>
      </plugin>

      <plugin>
        <groupId>com.contribute</groupId>
        <artifactId>orclapex-maven-plugin</artifactId>

        <executions>
          <execution>
            <id>generate-natural-docs</id>
            <phase>compile</phase>
          </execution>
        </executions>
      </plugin>
    </plugins>
  </build>
</profile>
```

Every build profile gets an ID assigned, which is typically named after the environment it represents. You will use these IDs in combination with the –P command-line option. As an example, consider the following Maven command:

```
mvn -f multi_env_pom.xml -P tst compile
```

This command will activate the tst build profile in the multi_env_pom.xml POM file and will execute all plugin goals that fall under the compile phase. Entering a comma-delimited list of IDs can activate multiple build profiles. Setting the activeByDefault element to true within a build profile automatically activates the profile when the –P option is not provided.

The properties section defines the substitution strings that you have already seen in the parent POM's pluginManagement section. The plugin configuration properties in the parent POM will be replaced at runtime by the property values defined in the activated build profile.

The build element references the plugins from the parent POM based on groupId and artifactId. These references avoid duplication and keep plugin definitions centralized in one place. Build profiles do not have to execute the same plugins. Table 9-2 shows what build tasks are being executed per environment.

Table 9-2. *An Overview of What Build Tasks Are Being Executed per Environment*

Environment	Liquibase	AntRun Plugin	Application Import	Natural Docs
Development	x	x	x	x
Test	x	x	x	
Production	x	x	x	

The Liquibase Maven plugin is not being referenced in one of the build profiles in the multi_env_pom.xml file. Instead, it gets referenced in the build element of the child POM itself. Plugins defined at this level will be executed before the plugins from the build profiles that belong to the same phase. Thus, Liquibase will always be executed first, followed by any of the plugins defined in the build profiles. Listing 9-35 shows how to reference the parent POM's Liquibase Maven plugin.

Listing 9-35. A Reference to the Parent POM's Liquibase Maven Plugin

```
<build>
  <plugins>
    <plugin>
      <groupId>org.liquibase</groupId>
      <artifactId>liquibase-maven-plugin</artifactId>
    </plugin>
  </plugins>
</build>
```

One Code Base to Rule Them All

All environments are being provisioned from a central code repository. It is the single source of truth for the development team and contains, at a minimum, all the artifacts required to completely build and deploy the software product. The code repository concept enables you to take advantage of version control, something that should be part of every software development project, even if you are working all by yourself. Source control products include several essential features that are of great help for any developer.

- Track file changes and history

- Revert to an earlier version

- File merging capabilities

- The ability to branch and tag versions of the software product

- Backup and restore

- Easy to share the project's source code and configuration with other developers

Even though the APEX application export file is not source control friendly, it is still worth the investment to keep your projects under version control for other types of files. The thick database approach, for example, will inevitably lead to a significant amount of SQL files, which you will want to keep track of. It is also a good idea to put your static files under source control, especially when they are stored on the web server.

The most popular version control system these days is Git. It is a free and open source product designed to handle everything from small to large projects. The basic usage of Git is pretty straightforward, and some online services such as GitHub or BitBucket make it easy accessible and understandable. The demo project, for example, is hosted on GitHub, a web-based Git repository hosting service that makes it really simple to get started with Git thanks to a user-friendly graphical interface. Figure 9-12 shows the desktop version of GitHub for Mac.

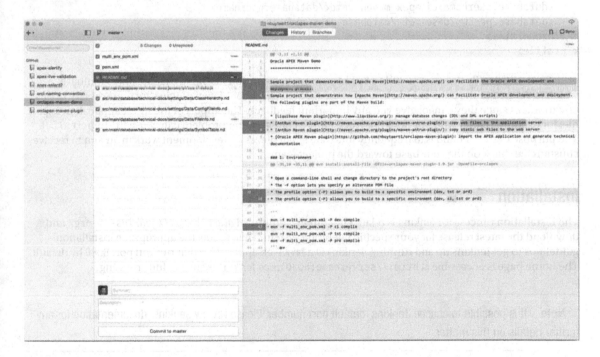

Figure 9-12. *The desktop version of GitHub for Mac*

It is also a good idea to directly work on the files in the code repository. Komodo Edit, Atom, or SublimeText are examples of advanced text editors that can boost your development productivity.

Jenkins

Jenkins is an open source continuous integration (CI) tool in which you can define and monitor repeated jobs, such as building a software product. *Continuous integration* refers to the practice of frequently pushing small amounts of development effort to the main development line, resulting in a fully automated and self-testing software build. This technique helps the development team to quickly identify problems with the code base because every commit to version control triggers a build that verifies that nothing has been broken. CI is broadly adopted in most mainstream development technologies, but it has never been fully explored in Oracle APEX development.

Before starting with Jenkins, you need to create an isolated environment where you can build the project an unlimited amount of times without any limitations. That is why you will introduce the CI environment to the project's environment setup. The multi_env_pom.xml file includes the ci build profile, shown in Listing 9-36, which will be activated when building to the CI environment.

Listing 9-36. The ci Build Profile

```
<profile>
  <id>ci</id>
  <properties>
    <database.url>jdbc:oracle:thin:@localhost:8202/pdbdb01</database.url>
    <database.username>ci_apex_maven_demo</database.username>
    <database.password>secret</database.password>
  </properties>
</profile>
```

The build profile does not include a build element because you intend to execute only Liquibase, which is defined in the main build element of the POM itself. Other Maven plugins are unnecessary in this environment since they cannot give you any important feedback. The import of the APEX application export file, for example, either works or does not work. Only a configuration problem can cause the import to fail. The purpose of the CI build is to frequently integrate small pieces of development work in an aim to receive constant feedback on the code base toward the project team.

Installation

The installation process for Jenkins is relatively simple. Simply navigate to http://jenkins-ci.org/ and download the latest release for your specific operating system. Then follow the appropriate installation guidelines to get Jenkins up and running. Jenkins is a Java web application that runs on port 8080 by default. The home page is accessible at http://servername:8080 once Jenkins is successfully running.

■ **Note**   It is possible to change Jenkins' default port number. Please review Jenkins' documentation for any further details on this matter.

If you are using Git as version control system, you will need to install the Git Plugin for Jenkins. Follow these steps to do so:

1. Open the Manage Jenkins section via the Jenkins' home page.

2. Select Manage Plugins.

3. Click on the Available tab.

4. Enter the search term **git plugin** in the Filter field.

5. Install the Git Plugin.

Creating a Build

In Jenkins, you will create a build for every environment in your project's setup. The configuration of such a Jenkins build is just a matter of correctly setting a series of properties. To get a better view on what sort of properties you have to set, it is important to understand what happens behind the scenes of a Jenkins build.

1. The first step is to locate the project's source code. It is possible to point to a directory on the local file system if you are not using any version control system. For the demo project, however, you will connect each Jenkins build to the public GitHub repository.

2. The Jenkins build will then locally check out a specific branch from the version control system.

3. Jenkins executes Maven to start the build and lets you specify the appropriate POM file and options.

The following steps outline how to create the Jenkins build for the CI environment:

1. Click the New Item link on the Jenkins home page.

2. Enter a name for the build in the Item Name input field.

3. Select Maven project as project type.

4. Click the OK button, which will take you to the build's configuration page.

5. Select and configure the appropriate version control system under the Source Code Management section for your project. Select None if you have no source control applied. Here is an overview of the configuration properties for the demo project, which uses Git as VCS:

    a. *Repository URL*: `https://github.com/nbuytaert1/orclapex-maven-demo`

    b. *Credentials*: `nickbuytaert/******`

    c. *Branch Specifier*: `*/master`

6. Under the Build Triggers section, select the Poll SCM option and enter ***/2 * * * ***
    in the Schedule item to check for changes every two minutes.

7. Under the Build section, enter the Root POM by pointing to the `multi_env_pom.xml`
    file, and specify the following Goals and Options: `-P ci compile`.

8. Optionally, enable E-mail Notification under Build Settings.

The SCM polling setting will cause the CI build to automatically run whenever new commits have been pushed to the version control system. The build executes Maven and activates the `ci` build profile in the `multi_env_pom.xml` file. This results in Liquibase being executed in order to verify whether anything has broken the build. Figure 9-13 shows the Jenkins home page after creating a build for every environment.

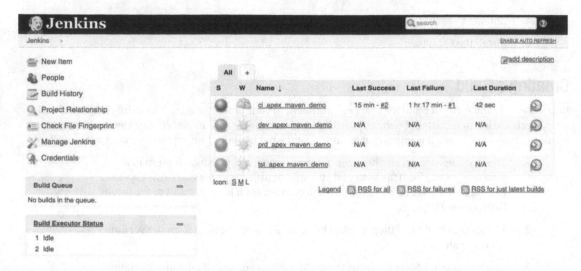

Figure 9-13. *The Jenkins home page with an overview of all builds*

The build configuration for the other environments is similar to the CI build configuration. There are just three differences you have to keep in mind.

- The Branch Specifier under Source Code Management for the production build will not be the master branch. You typically specify a branch or tag that has been declared production-ready.

- Do not define a build trigger since all other builds will be executed manually in Jenkins.

- Change the build profile in the Goals and Options setting according to the environment you want to build.

Summary

Lifecycle management in Oracle Application Express is definitely a challenging exercise. This chapter has introduced a solution that combines a number of open source products in an aim to gain more control over the development and deployment lifecycle. You have to take into account some limitations, but I do believe that the described solution can boost the quality and efficiency in APEX projects.

Keep in mind that this chapter has covered the build automation tasks for only a basic APEX application. Additional build tasks can quickly make their way into a project's build flow. Including automated tests, for example, is an excellent way to catch bugs faster and more efficiently. Luckily, you can take advantage of the central Maven repository to easily integrate new tasks in the build process.

CHAPTER 10

■ ■ ■

Plugins

by Dan McGhan

APEX has long been extensible. It was built in such a way that developers could add custom content to just about any part of a page constructed by the framework. The problem, however, was twofold. First, you had to be familiar enough with the related technologies to work outside the declarative environment that APEX provides. Second, even if you had enough knowledge to do a customization, repeating it on another page or in another application altogether was often quite cumbersome.

The APEX plugin architecture, introduced with APEX 4.0, solves the latter of those problems. You still need to have sufficient knowledge of the related technologies, which most often include SQL, PL/SQL, HTML, CSS, and JavaScript. But, provided you possess this knowledge, you can integrate customizations to APEX in a self-contained, easily reusable, and sharable way—as a plugin.

The plugin architecture has evolved quite a bit since APEX 4.0, with enhancements having been added in versions 4.1, 4.2, and most recently 5.0. There are currently six types of plugins, all of which extend native APEX component types, including regions, items, processes, dynamic actions, authentication schemes, and authorization schemes.

There are two main audiences for plugins: those who will build plugins and those who will use what others build. This chapter is written for the former—for APEX developers interested in learning how to create plugins for themselves and others to use. I will not cover plugin installation or configuration because I assume you already possess this knowledge.

The target audience for this chapter is one that is comfortable working with SQL and PL/SQL and has at least some working knowledge of HTML, CSS, and JavaScript. If you feel this doesn't describe you perfectly, don't be too worried. The tutorial in this chapter was written in such a way that you should be able to follow along, even if you don't quite understand everything you're doing.

Developing a plugin is a unique and rewarding experience. You may find yourself challenged at times as you constantly move between client-side and server-side programming languages while developing a reusable piece of an APEX application. But if you stick to it, eventually your efforts will pay off and you (and ideally the entire APEX community) will be able to enjoy the fruits of your labor.

The APEX Plugin Architecture

The pieces of the APEX plugin architecture that plugin developers work with include pages in the shared components of an application and PL/SQL APIs. The pages in the shared components are used to create and modify plugins, while the PL/SQL APIs provide required constructs as well as utility functions that minimize the amount of "plumbing" you might otherwise need to code. This section of the chapter will provide an introduction to these new components.

Create/Edit Page for Plugins

The Create/Edit plugin page is the main page used while developing plugins, so it's important to become acquainted with it. To navigate to the page, first go to the Plug-ins page by clicking the Plug-ins option in the Shared Components area (under Other Components). Once there, you can either drill down on an existing plugin or click the Create button and complete the Create Plug-in Wizard to create a new plugin.

The Create/Edit plugin page contains 13 regions in total. You may notice subtle differences when viewing this page at different times. Your mind is not playing tricks on you; the page changes depending on a number of factors. For example, not all regions are available at all times or for all plugin types. Also, the items in a region, as well as the times at which those items can be edited, can vary. All of this will be explained in the sections that follow.

Name

The Name region (see Figure 10-1) contains items that allow plugin developers to identify a plugin as well as the plugin type.

Figure 10-1. *The Name region of the Create/Edit page*

You can think of the Name attribute as the display name for plugin users. Plugin users will see and select this name to use the plugin via the declarative interface provided by the Application Builder. Exactly where they see the name will depend on the plugin type; for example, if you create an item plugin, the Name value will be displayed in the Type attribute of items in the application (see Figure 10-2).

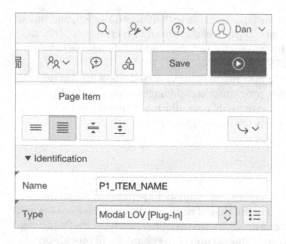

Figure 10-2. *An item plugin's name displayed in the Type attribute of a page item*

The Internal Name attribute serves as a unique identifier for the plugin within an application. The Internal Name attribute should be uppercase; lower- or mixed-case values will be converted to uppercase when creating or updating the plugin. Note that this attribute cannot be modified if the plugin is being used in the application.

When importing a plugin into an application, the value of the Internal Name attribute will be checked against other plugins in the application. If a plugin with the same Internal Name attribute already exists, users will need to confirm that they want to replace the existing plugin. For this reason, uniqueness of the Internal Name attribute is much more important than uniqueness of the Name attribute.

■ **Note**   See the "Plugin Best Practices" section later in this chapter for tips on naming and other topics.

The Type attribute, as I'm sure you've already guessed, defines the type of plugin you are working with. The Type attribute is obviously a major attribute of a plugin, and as such its value drives some of the other regions and items that are visible on the page. This attribute, like the Internal Name attribute, cannot be modified if the plugin is being used in the application.

The Category attribute (not visible in Figure 10-2) is available only for dynamic action plugins. This attribute is used to group similar dynamic actions together, which makes selection a little easier for plugin users; it has no other impact.

Subscription

The Subscription region (see Figure 10-3) is the same as it is throughout APEX. The Reference Master Plug-in From item allows you to link to a "master" copy of the plug-in. The master copy often resides in a centralized application used only for this purpose. Once established, the link between master and child allows for updates to be performed on a one-off basis from the child or in bulk from the master to all children.

Figure 10-3. The Subscription region of the Create/Edit page

Source

Plugin developers must write one or more PL/SQL functions for their plugin to work. The PL/SQL Code attribute in a region (see Figure 10-4) is where the code for these functions typically resides; however, it is possible to use code compiled in the database instead. The number and type of functions required vary depending on the plugin type—see the "Callbacks" section for more details.

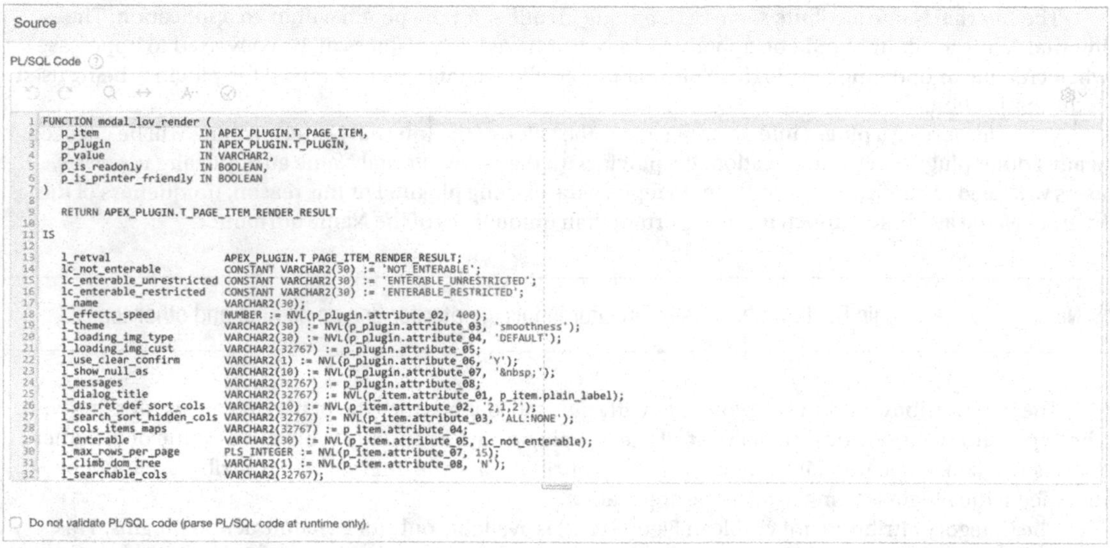

```
Source

PL/SQL Code ⓘ

⤵ ⤴ Q ⟷ A⁻ ⊘                                                                    ⚙⌄

1  FUNCTION modal_lov_render (
2      p_item               IN APEX_PLUGIN.T_PAGE_ITEM,
3      p_plugin             IN APEX_PLUGIN.T_PLUGIN,
4      p_value              IN VARCHAR2,
5      p_is_readonly        IN BOOLEAN,
6      p_is_printer_friendly IN BOOLEAN
7  )
8
9      RETURN APEX_PLUGIN.T_PAGE_ITEM_RENDER_RESULT
10
11 IS
12
13     l_retval              APEX_PLUGIN.T_PAGE_ITEM_RENDER_RESULT;
14     lc_not_enterable      CONSTANT VARCHAR2(30) := 'NOT_ENTERABLE';
15     lc_enterable_unrestricted CONSTANT VARCHAR2(30) := 'ENTERABLE_UNRESTRICTED';
16     lc_enterable_restricted   CONSTANT VARCHAR2(30) := 'ENTERABLE_RESTRICTED';
17     l_name                VARCHAR2(30);
18     l_effects_speed       NUMBER := NVL(p_plugin.attribute_02, 400);
19     l_theme               VARCHAR2(30) := NVL(p_plugin.attribute_03, 'smoothness');
20     l_loading_img_type    VARCHAR2(30) := NVL(p_plugin.attribute_04, 'DEFAULT');
21     l_loading_img_cust    VARCHAR2(32767) := p_plugin.attribute_05;
22     l_use_clear_confirm   VARCHAR2(1) := NVL(p_plugin.attribute_06, 'Y');
23     l_show_null_as        VARCHAR2(10) := NVL(p_plugin.attribute_07, ' ');
24     l_messages            VARCHAR2(32767) := p_plugin.attribute_08;
25     l_dialog_title        VARCHAR2(32767) := NVL(p_item.attribute_01, p_item.plain_label);
26     l_dis_ret_def_sort_cols VARCHAR2(10) := NVL(p_item.attribute_02, '2,1,2');
27     l_search_sort_hidden_cols VARCHAR2(32767) := NVL(p_item.attribute_03, 'ALL:NONE');
28     l_cols_items_maps     VARCHAR2(32767) := p_item.attribute_04;
29     l_enterable           VARCHAR2(30) := NVL(p_item.attribute_05, lc_not_enterable);
30     l_max_rows_per_page   PLS_INTEGER := NVL(p_item.attribute_07, 15);
31     l_climb_dom_tree      VARCHAR2(1) := NVL(p_item.attribute_08, 'N');
32     l_searchable_cols     VARCHAR2(32767);
```

☐ Do not validate PL/SQL code (parse PL/SQL code at runtime only).

Figure 10-4. *The Source region of the Create/Edit page*

Callbacks

The Callbacks region (see Figure 10-5) is used to register the PL/SQL functions you have defined (see the earlier "Source" section) with what is expected by the framework for the given plugin type. Simply add the function name, and the framework will invoke the function at the appropriate time (except the AJAX function, which is manually invoked when needed via JavaScript).

```
Callbacks

           Render Function Name   modal_lov_render                              ⓘ

            AJAX Function Name     modal_lov_ajax                               ⓘ

       Validation Function Name    modal_lov_validation                         ⓘ
```

Figure 10-5. *The Callbacks region of the Create/Edit page*

You can use any valid Oracle name for the functions, but the signature must match that which is expected for a given function type. Exactly which functions are available, required, or optional will vary based the plugin type. The easiest way to look up the expected signature is to click the help button (question mark on the right) for the function name. If the function is compiled in a package, simply prefix the function name with the package name followed by a period.

The number and types of functions available will vary depending on the plugin type. The most common functions include the render function, which is used to render the plugin on the page; the AJAX function, which is used to make asynchronous calls from the plugin to the server for additional data and processing; and the execution function (not displayed), which is used to perform some type of processing.

User Interfaces

The "Supported for" attribute of the User Interfaces region (see Figure 10-6) is used to specify which user interfaces your plugin will work with. Keep in mind that desktop and mobile UIs can be quite different. APEX uses jQuery Mobile for its mobile UI, so plugin developers who want to add support for that UI may need to learn about how jQuery Mobile expects its markup, what events are available and how they work, and so on.

Figure 10-6. *The "Supported for" attribute of the User Interfaces region*

Standard Attributes

Plugin developers can use two main types of attributes in plugins: *standard* (covered here) and *custom* (covered in the next section). Both standard and custom attributes are a plugin developer's means to provide declarative options to plugin users who can change the characteristics or behavior of a plugin.

In APEX, many attributes for a given component type are the same. For example, the Select List and Check Box items both have a List of Values definition. Likewise, both the Interactive and Classic Report regions have a Source attribute that requires a SQL query. Standard attributes give plugin developers the ability to add these types of common attributes to their plugins. Enabling standard attributes in plugins will simply present those options to plugin users when creating a new instance of the plugin. The values entered or selected by the developer will be passed to the plugin logic via parameters in the callback functions. It is the responsibility of plugin developers to check the values of these attributes and code the plugin to respond appropriately.

Always try to use standard attributes before creating custom equivalents. This will save you time and reduce the number of custom attributes used by your plugins. More importantly, standard attributes will be displayed where APEX developers are already familiar with them and in a way that's consistent with other instances of a particular component type.

The standard attributes available vary by plugin type. Figures 10-7 through 10-11 show the standard attributes available to item, region, dynamic action, process, and authentication scheme plugins. Authorization scheme plugins do not have any standard attributes.

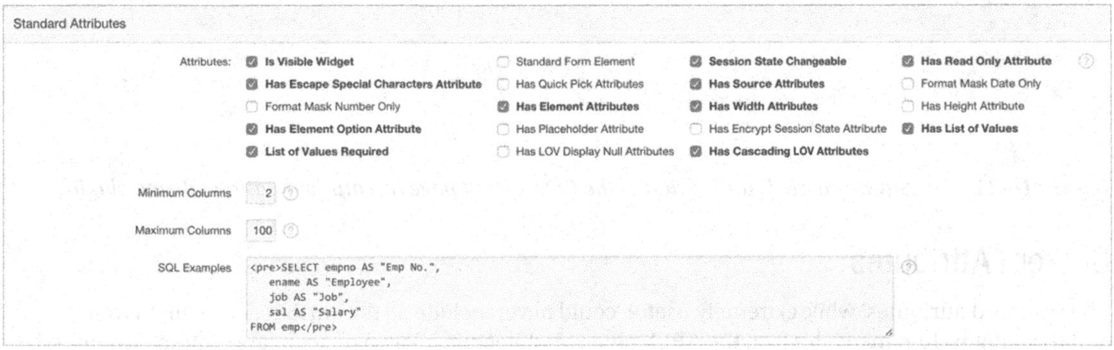

Figure 10-7. *The Standard Attributes region of the Create/Edit page for the Modal LOV plugin (an item plugin)*

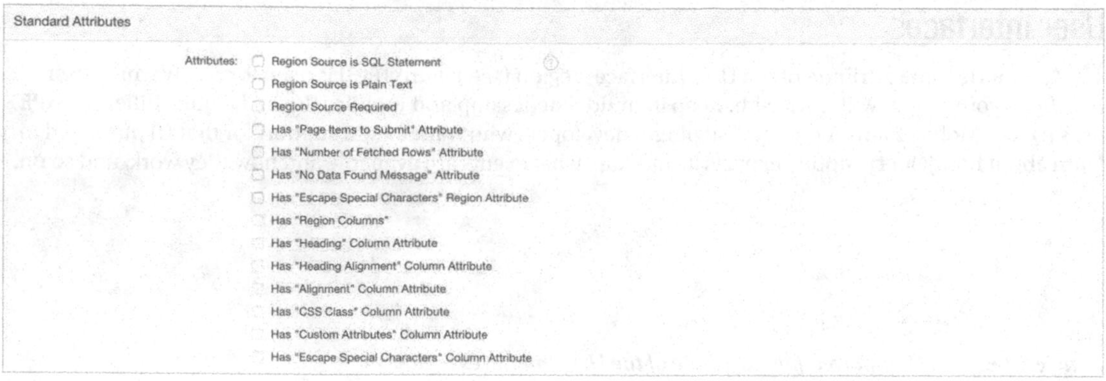

Figure 10-8. *The Standard Attributes region of the Create/Edit page (a region plugin)*

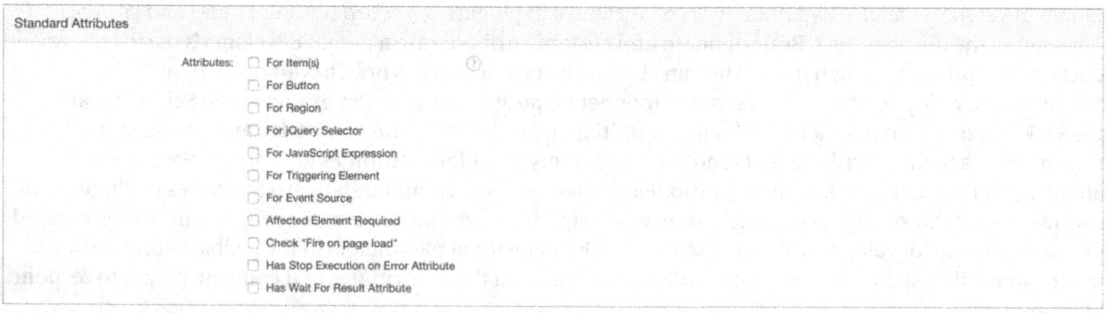

Figure 10-9. *The Standard Attributes region of the Create/Edit page (a dynamic action plugin)*

Figure 10-10. *The Standard Attributes region of the Create/Edit page (a process plugin)*

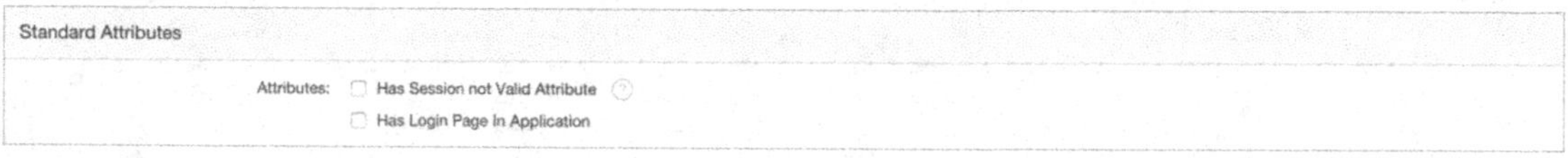

Figure 10-11. *The Standard Attributes region of the Create/Edit page (an authentication scheme plugin)*

Custom Attributes

The standard attributes, while extremely useful, could never include all the attributes you might want to add to a plugin. To remedy this fact, the APEX plugin architecture allows you to create custom attributes (see Figure 10-12) that are exposed to plugin users as *settings*.

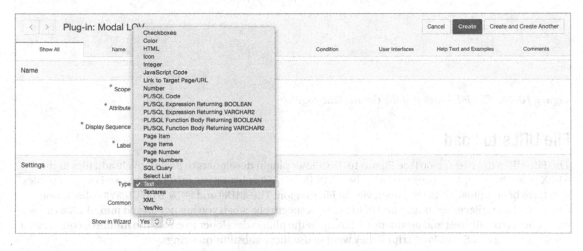

Label	Scope ↕	Attribute	Sequence	Type	Required	Default Value	Depending on
Search Type	Application	1	10	Text	Yes	INSTR(UPPER(#COLUMN_NAME#), UPPER(:ML_SEARCH)) > 0	
Enable Clear Confirm	Application	2	20	Yes/No	No	N	
Show Null Values As	Application	3	30	Text	Yes		
Messages	Application	4	40	Textarea	Yes	{ "openLabel": "Show Values", "clearLabel": "Clear", "searchLabel": "Search"}	
Dialog Title	Component	1	10	Text	No		
Display Column	Component	2	20	Integer	Yes	2	
Return Column	Component	3	30	Integer	Yes	1	
Enable Column Sorting	Component	4	40	Yes/No	No	Y	
Default Sort Column	Component	5	50	Integer	No		Enable Column Sorting
Map Columns (from)	Component	6	60	Text	No		
Map Items (to)	Component	7	70	Page Items	No		
Enterable	Component	8	80	Select List	Yes	NOT_ENTERABLE	
Use Value Validation	Component	9	90	Yes/No	No	Y	Enterable
Max Rows Per Page	Component	10	100	Integer	Yes	15	

Custom Attributes · Substitute Attribute Values Yes · Add Attribute

Figure 10-12. *The Custom Attributes region of the Create/Edit page for the Modal LOV plugin*

To add an attribute to a plugin, simply click the Add Attribute button. This will redirect you to the Edit Attribute page where the attribute can be configured. When creating a new custom attribute, you will need to specify the type. There are 23 different types of custom attributes that can be added to a plugin (see Figure 10-13).

Plug-in: Modal LOV

Checkboxes
Color
HTML
Icon
Integer
JavaScript Code
Link to Target Page/URL
Number
PL/SQL Code
PL/SQL Expression Returning BOOLEAN
PL/SQL Expression Returning VARCHAR2
PL/SQL Function Body Returning BOOLEAN
PL/SQL Function Body Returning VARCHAR2
Page Item
Page Items
Page Number
Page Numbers
SQL Query
Select List
✓ Text
Textarea
XML
Yes/No

Figure 10-13. *The Type options available when creating a custom attribute*

The type is used to determine how the attribute should be displayed to plugin users and in some cases can allow the plugin framework to ensure that valid values have been entered. Custom attributes can be made to display conditionally (based on the value of other custom attributes). You can create up to 25 custom attributes at the application level and another 25 custom attributes at the component level.

Placing attributes at the application level of a plugin is a good way to reduce the number of decisions that plugin users face each time they use a plugin, and it's a good way to enforce consistency. For example, an attribute that changes the color scheme of a plugin may be best at the application level so that the plugin is displayed the same way on different pages. Plugin users will set application-level attributes via Component Settings in the Shared Components page.

On the other hand, not all attributes are suited for the application level. An attribute used to identify a page-level item may be better off as a component-level attribute. This would allow the plugin to be used more than once in an application without different instances of the plugin interfering with each other. Plugin users will set component-level settings from a Settings region, displayed with the standard attributes, where the component is usually configured.

The Custom Attributes region of the Create/Edit plugin page is available only after the plugin is created. Also, certain parts of custom attributes, such as the scope, attribute (number), and LOV return values, cannot be modified if the plugin is being used in the application.

Files

Plugins often require the use of external files for various functionality. The most common types of files used in plugins include CSS, JavaScript, and image files (see Figure 10-14). Files uploaded here are stored in the database and directly associated with the plugin. It is possible to upload entire ZIP files that include directories. Directory structures will be preserved, so it's safe to use relative paths within files. Files uploaded to a plugin are not automatically added to the APEX page at runtime—see the "File URLs to Load" section to see how to accomplish that task.

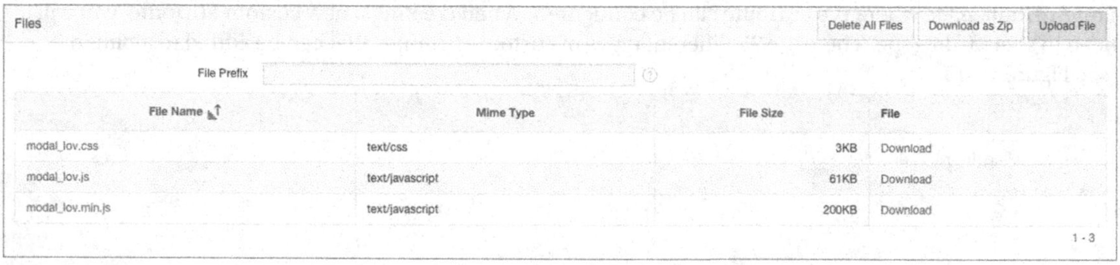

Files					Delete All Files	Download as Zip	Upload File
File Prefix							
File Name		Mime Type		File Size	**File**		
modal_lov.css		text/css		3KB	Download		
modal_lov.js		text/javascript		61KB	Download		
modal_lov.min.js		text/javascript		200KB	Download		
					1 - 3		

Figure 10-14. The Files region of the Create/Edit page

File URLs to Load

The File URLs to Load region (see Figure 10-15) allows plugin developers to declaratively add files to the APEX page that the plugin depends on. The #PLUGIN_FILES# substitution string can be used to point to files that have been uploaded to the plugin via the Files region. The #MIN# and #MIN_DIRECTORY# substitution strings will be replaced with .min and minified/, respectively, when you are not logged into APEX as a developer (typically test and production). It is up to the plugin developer to create the minified/compressed versions of their CSS and JavaScript if they want to use these substitution strings.

File URLs to Load

Cascading Style Sheet
```
#PLUGIN_FILES#modal_lov.css
```

JavaScript
```
#PLUGIN_FILES#modal_lov#MIN#.js
```

Figure 10-15. *The File URLs to Load region of the Create/Edit page*

CSS files will be added to the APEX page where the `#APEX_CSS#` substitution string is included in the page template header (the header of the HTML document). JavaScript files, on the other hand, will be added to the APEX page where the `#GENERATED_JAVASCRIPT#` substitution string in the page template footer (the bottom of the body of the HTML document). These locations follow best practices for adding CSS and JavaScript to web pages.

Events

The Events region (see Figure 10-16) allows plugin developers to add custom events to dynamic actions in an application. This ability would be useful only for plugins that trigger custom events. For example, if you created a countdown timer plugin, creating a "timeout" event would allow plugin users to create dynamic actions that react to the event. It's up to plugin developers to trigger custom events at the appropriate times. The Events region is visible only after the plugin is created.

Figure 10-16. *The Events region of the Create/Edit page*

Information

The Information region (see Figure 10-17) allows you to add the version number of the plugin as well as specify an About URL. The About URL should point to a location on the Web where plugin users can learn more about the plugin.

Figure 10-17. *The Information region of the Create/Edit page*

Help Text

The Help Text region (see Figure 10-18) allows plugin developers to add built-in documentation for plugin users. Any documentation added by plugin developers will be visible to plugin users via the same region.

Figure 10-18. *The Help Text region of the Create/Edit page*

Comments

The Comments region (see Figure 10-19) is similar to how it is with other components throughout APEX. The main difference here is that there are two types of users who may use the comments: plugin developers and plugin users (APEX developers). Plugin developers need to be aware that comments added to a plugin are exported with the plugin and are visible when it's later imported.

Figure 10-19. *The Comments region of the Create/Edit page*

PL/SQL APIs

Many tasks involved with developing plugins are somewhat common. Here are some examples:

- Reading plugin settings and altering the behavior of the plugin

- Querying data and processing the results

- Performing AJAX calls

A number of PL/SQL APIs have been developed to help make these tasks easier to complete than they would otherwise be. Learning about these APIs is important, even if only at the most basic level, because it could save you from reinventing the wheel when you really only want to build a plugin. This section provides an introduction to the PL/SQL APIs most commonly used for plugin development in APEX.

APEX_PLUGIN

The APEX_PLUGIN package contains a number of core types and functions that are used specifically for plugins. The record types are used in the callback functions of a plugin and provide context and setting values. Here's an example of a region render function's signature:

```
function some_item_render (
    p_item              in apex_plugin.t_page_item,
    p_plugin            in apex_plugin.t_plugin,
    p_value             in varchar2,
    p_is_readonly       in boolean,
    p_is_printer_friendly in boolean
)

    return apex_plugin.t_page_item_render_result
```

The T_PLUGIN record type, shown previously as the data type for the formal parameter p_plugin, is included as a parameter in every callback function. It provides developers with access to the application-level attributes of a plugin such as the name, file prefix, and any custom attributes added at that level.

Each type of plugin also has a number of dedicated record types defined in the APEX_PLUGIN package that are used in the callback functions: one used as a formal parameter and a number of others used as result types. The record type used as a formal parameter, T_PAGE_ITEM in this example, provides developers with access to the component-level attributes such as the name, standard attributes, and any custom attributes added at that level.

There is one result type defined for each of the callback functions a given plugin type can use. The example shows part of the render function of an item plugin, which uses the corresponding T_PAGE_ITEM_RENDER_RESULT record type as the result type. These result types allow developers to pass information back to the plugin framework such as whether a plugin is navigable.

In addition to the record types, there are two functions defined in the APEX_PLUGIN package as well: GET_INPUT_NAME_FOR_PAGE_ITEM and GET_AJAX_IDENTIFIER. The GET_INPUT_NAME_FOR_PAGE_ITEM function is used only for item plugins. It returns the value plugin developers should assign to the name attribute of the element that contains the correct value for the plugin. APEX uses the name attribute of elements to map an element's value on the page to the corresponding item's session state when a page is submitted. Here is an example from an item render function that demonstrates its use:

```
sys.htp.p(
    '<input type="password" name="' ||
    apex_plugin.get_input_name_for_page_item(p_is_multi_value => false) ||
    '" id="' || p_item.name ||
    '" size="' || p_item.element_width ||
    '" maxlength="' || p_item.element_max_length ||
    '" ' || p_item.element_attributes || '/>');
```

If you plan to take advantage of AJAX technology in your plugin, you'll need a means to call the AJAX callback function from JavaScript. To get around various issues related to calling the function by name, the plugin architecture requires you to call the function via a unique identifier, which is obtained from the GET_AJAX_IDENTIFIER function.

The function will work only in the context of the render function and only if an AJAX callback function has been defined. The result of the function call needs to be mapped through to the plugin's JavaScript code so that it can be used when needed. Here is an example from a region render function that demonstrates how the function is used (see the tutorial section for a complete example):

```
l_onload_code :=
  'apex.jQuery("div#' || p_region.static_id || '").calendar({'
  || apex_javascript.add_attribute(
         p_name => 'ajaxIdentifier',
         p_value => apex_plugin.get_ajax_identifier(),
         p_omit_null => FALSE,
         p_add_comma => FALSE)
  || '});';

apex_javascript.add_onload_code (
   p_code => l_onload_code
);
```

APEX_PLUGIN_UTIL

APEX_PLUGIN_UTIL is a utility package that eases the burden of developing plugins by providing production-ready code for many common plugin-related tasks. The package has many functions and procedures related to debugging, SQL and PL/SQL processing, and more.

Depending on their scope and complexity, debugging plugins can be a difficult task. Thankfully, the APEX_PLUGIN_UTIL package comes with a number of debug procedures—at least one for each plugin type. The debug procedures write data about the plugin to the APEX debug log when it is enabled. The name of the plugin and its attribute values are included with the output. Here's an example from a region render function that demonstrates how the procedure is used:

```
if apex_application.g_debug
then
  apex_plugin_util.debug_region (
     p_plugin => p_plugin,
     p_region => p_region
  );
end if;
```

In addition to this basic level of logging, it can be useful to instrument your code using the APEX_DEBUG package. With this package it's possible to separate logging messages according to levels such as error, warn, and trace, which minimizes the impact of the instrumentation when not needed.

APEX_CSS and APEX_JAVASCRIPT

The APEX_CSS and APEX_JAVASCRIPT packages consist of functions and procedures that allow you to add CSS and JavaScript to your HTML output. Prior to APEX 5.0, these packages were the best options for adding CSS and JavaScript needed in plugins. However, the declarative File URLs to Load region (see "File URLs to Load" earlier) is much easier to use and will satisfy the majority of use cases. Use these packages only when you require more programmatic control over whether or how CSS and JavaScript are added to the page.

APEX_WEB_SERVICE

The APEX_WEB_SERVICE package provides procedures and functions—too many to list here—that allow you to interact with both SOAP- and REST-based web services from PL/SQL. Prior to the introduction of this package, developers could have consumed web services from PL/SQL using other packages such as UTL_HTTP. However, the APEX_WEB_SERVICE package has greatly simplified and standardized how this type of code is written.

APEX_JSON

The APEX_JSON package provides procedures and functions related to creating, parsing, and stringifying JSON. APEX_JSON is a welcome package because JSON has quickly become the standard format by which data is transferred between client and server via AJAX. This package complements the JSON capabilities added to the SQL engine of Oracle Database 12.1.0.2, which allow users to query but not generate JSON data.

Other Packages

In addition to the packages covered in this chapter, there are a number of others that are frequently used while developing plugins in APEX. The Oracle Database PL/SQL Packages and Types Reference document now includes almost 300 packages. At a minimum, I recommend you explore the other APIs outlined in the Oracle Application Express API Reference as well as the packages that comprise the PL/SQL Web toolkit. A small amount of time spent here learning from these documents could save many hours of needless development.

Other Tools of the Trade

As you have seen, the APEX plugin architecture provides a wealth of useful functionality that allows you to create plugins. However, there are some other "tools of the trade" you may find useful. These tools can help you produce well-structured JavaScript code and attractive user interfaces.

jQuery and jQuery UI

jQuery is a JavaScript DOM (think "web page") manipulation library. jQuery provides simple methods for selecting elements, traversing and manipulating the DOM, executing AJAX calls, and much more. jQuery was created nearly ten years ago, when the DOM API was tedious and inconsistently implemented by various browser manufacturers. Things are much better today, but jQuery continues to be quite popular, especially when support for older browsers is important.

jQuery UI is a collection of lower-level user interface widgets. Some of the widgets included with the library include a date picker, dialog, and slider. jQuery UI can help plugin developers focus on the functionality of the plugins they want to build rather than the lower-level widgets needed to build them. Although jQuery UI includes its own set of icons, it may be worth exploring Font Awesome icons as an alternative because they can be styled better by the Theme Roller that customizes the Universal theme.

APEX includes the "base" jQuery UI theme, which is a neutral-colored theme. Many of the newer APEX themes include CSS that modifies the base theme to give the jQuery UI widgets a more integrated look. If your plugin has a visual component to it, you'll need to take this into account because the plugin should look as though it's a native part of the application. Using jQuery UI widgets and classes should go a long way to ensure your plugin looks great with any theme.

A quick Google search will reveal many different sources for learning more about jQuery and jQuery UI, many of which are free. The time spent learning these technologies should easily pay you back time and time again when you develop plugins in APEX.

jQuery UI Widget Factory

If you're creating a region, item, or dynamic action plugin, then JavaScript will likely be an important part of your plugin. If you come from an Oracle background, you may be comfortable working with PL/SQL but a little apprehensive about JavaScript. Newcomers to JavaScript can spend a lot of time just figuring out a good way to organize their code. The jQuery UI Widget Factory provides just that: a systematic approach to writing JavaScript that provides organization as well as a number of other features.

Because this chapter is about writing plugins for APEX, I will use the term *widget* in place of *plugin* when referring to the jQuery UI Widget Factory—although the terms are typically interchangeable. The jQuery UI Widget Factory allows you to create stateful jQuery widgets with minimal effort. *Stateful* means that the widget keeps track of its attribute values and even allows attribute updates and method calls after the widget has been initialized. One of the best ways to learn about the jQuery UI Widget Factory is to see an example of how it is used. The following tutorial will walk you through the steps needed to build a widget.

This tutorial will create a widget named `lengthLimit`. The `lengthLimit` widget will be used to enhance standard input elements so that they warn users when the number of characters entered approaches a defined maximum length. The widget will set the text color to a warning color when the text reaches 80 percent of the maximum length and then to an error color when the limit is reached. The widget will also trim any characters entered in the input that exceed the maximum length.

■ **Note** This is intended as a "read-along" tutorial. I'll use the concepts covered here in the "code-along" tutorial in the "Building a Region Plugin" section of this chapter.

The `$.widget` function is called to create the widget. The first parameter passed to the function consists of the namespace and name of the widget, which are separated by a period. The `ui` namespace is used by all the widgets in the jQuery UI library. The second parameter (currently just an empty object) is the prototype to be associated with the widget.

```
apex.jQuery.widget("ui.lengthLimit", {
    //widget code here
});
```

Before continuing to build the widget, it is important to take care of one important issue: $. Most people who use jQuery are familiar with using the dollar sign as a shorthand reference to the jQuery object rather than spelling out `jQuery`, or as it's been exposed in APEX, `apex.jQuery`. While it's possible to use the dollar sign in your widget code, it's best to protect references to the dollar sign from collisions with other JavaScript libraries. The technique used to do this is to wrap your code in an immediately invoked function expression, or IIFE (pronounced "ify"), that passes the jQuery object as an actual parameter to itself as a formal parameter, which uses the dollar sign for its name. If this concept sounds complex and confusing, don't worry—it requires only two lines of code (the first and last in the following example). Note that the previous reference to `apex.jQuery` has been replaced by the dollar sign now that it is safe to do so.

```
(function($){
$.widget("ui.lengthLimit", {
    //widget code here
});
})(apex.jQuery);
```

Let's continue building the widget by adding the `options` object. The `options` object is used to set default values for configuration options used by the widget.

```
(function($){
$.widget("ui.lengthLimit", {
    options: {
        warningColor: "yellow",
        errorColor: "red",
        maxLength: 50
    }
});
})(apex.jQuery);
```

Next you'll add a function named create that will be invoked automatically when the widget is first instantiated.

```
(function($){
$.widget("ui.lengthLimit", {
    options: {
        warningColor: "orange",
        errorColor: "red",
        maxLength: 50
    },
    _create: function() {
        var uiw = this;

        uiw.element.change(function() {
            var $textElmt = $(this);
            var currLength = $textElmt.val().length;
            var currPercent = currLength/uiw.options.maxLength;

            if (currPercent >= .9) {
                $textElmt
                    .val($textElmt.val().substr(0, uiw.options.maxLength))
                    .css('color', uiw.options.errorColor);
            } else if (currPercent >= .8) {
                $textElmt.css('color', uiw.options.warningColor);
            } else {
                $textElmt.css('color', 'black');
            }
        });
    }
});
})(apex.jQuery);
```

At this point you have a fully functioning widget. You could add this code to the Function and Global Variable Declaration section of an APEX page and then instantiate the widget on a page item by adding the following code to the Execute when Page Loads section. Notice that default option values can be overridden during instantiation.

```
$('#P1_FIRST_NAME').lengthLimit({
    maxLength: 10
});
```

After a little testing, you may notice two issues. First, the main logic, which sets the color and trims the text, is not executed when the page loads and the widget is initialized. Also, that same logic is wrapped up in an event handler that was bound to the change event of the element. As a consequence, developers have no way to execute that code without manually triggering the change event on the item, which may be undesirable. With a little refactoring, you can solve both issues while keeping the code maintainable.

```
(function($){
$.widget("ui.lengthLimit", {
   options: {
      warningColor: "orange",
      errorColor: "red",
      maxLength: 50
   },
   _create: function() {
      var uiw = this;

      uiw.element.change(function() {
         uiw.checkLength();
      });

      uiw.checkLength();
   },
   checkLength: function() {
      var uiw = this;
      var $textElmt = uiw.element;
      var currLength = $textElmt.val().length;
      var currPercent = currLength/uiw.options.maxLength;

      if (currPercent >= .9) {
         $textElmt
            .val($textElmt.val().substr(0, uiw.options.maxLength))
            .css('color', uiw.options.errorColor);
      } else if (currPercent >= .8) {
         $textElmt.css('color', uiw.options.warningColor);
      } else {
         $textElmt.css('color', 'black');
      }
   }
});
})(apex.jQuery);
```

The majority of the logic has been moved to a new function named checkLength. This function is used twice in the _create function: once in the change event handler on the element and then later at the end of the function.

You may have noticed that the new checkLength function didn't have the same leading underscore that the _create function did. This is an important distinction. The underscore is used to create "private" functions within a widget. They can help modularize your code but cannot be invoked from outside the widget (at least not as easily as public functions). Because the checkLength function name doesn't start with an underscore, it's registered as a public function and can be called at any time as follows:

```
$('#P1_FIRST_NAME').lengthLimit('checkLength');
```

Also note the subtle yet important change in reference to this. With the majority of code in a widget, this will refer to the widget instance. But in the original _create function, an anonymous function was bound to the change event of the element. When that function is executed, this will refer to the element that changed. After the refactoring, the element property of the widget instance (available automatically as part of the factory) was needed to access the same element—the element on which the widget was instantiated. Additionally, a local variable is declared in each function to hold a reference to this. This technique is optional but can help to avoid confusion and to take advantage of closure in JavaScript.

This introduction to the jQuery UI Widget Factory is by no means complete, but you should now have a basic understanding of how it can be utilized to write well-structured JavaScript with minimal plumbing. To learn more about the Widget Factory, find the "official" documentation available on the jQuery and jQuery UI web sites as well as the many tutorials found elsewhere on the Web.

Font Awesome

Font Awesome is an iconic font and CSS toolkit that is included with APEX. The latest version of Font Awesome as of this writing, 4.3, includes 519 icons! The icons were designed to scale from very small to very large without losing clarity or becoming distorted. While jQuery UI includes its own icons, they are image based and cannot be styled as easily as the font-based icons included with Font Awesome.

Font Awesome is easy to use; just create an icon tag with the right classes. Here's a simple example of the markup needed to create a font awesome icon: `<i class="fa fa-smile-o"></i>`. When rendered in APEX, users will see a happy face. Want to make it twice as big? Just add the `fa-2x` class. Want to spin it in circles? Just add the `fa-spin` class. You get the idea: it's easy to use Font Awesome!

To learn more about Font Awesome icons and view the library, visit `http://fortawesome.github.io/Font-Awesome`. Keep in mind that while developers are able to update the version of Font Awesome that is being used in their APEX applications, you should not make any assumptions about this. Only use icons that are available in the version of Font Awesome that is included by default with the version APEX for which you wrote the plugin.

Building a Region Plugin

In the first two sections of this chapter, you explored the APEX plugin architecture and other tools of the trade that can help when building plugins. Now you'll put all you've learned to use as you build a region plugin that allows developers to show data in a grid with some columns frozen on the left. The APEX plugin will really be a wrapper for the jqGrid plugin, which itself is a jQuery UI Widget; it's the plugin version of Inception.

■ **Note**   You can download the code listings in this section of the chapter from Apress.

The Base Plugin

You'll start by creating a new application to house the plugin. You may skip this part if you already have an application in which you'd like to create the plugin. Navigate to the Application Builder and complete these steps:

1. Click Create.

2. Click Next.

3. Set Name to **APEX jqGrid Plug-in.**

4. Click Create Application.

5. Click Create Application (on the confirmation page).

Now that the application in place, let's create the plugin. Navigate to the Shared Components ➤ Plug-ins and follow these steps, as shown in Figure 10-20:

1. Click Create.

2. Click Next .

3. Set Name to **APEX jqGrid**.

4. Set Internal Name to **COM_CORP_APEX_JQGRID**.

5. Set Type to Region.

6. Click Create Plug-in.

Figure 10-20. *Creating the APEX jqGrid plugin*

Woo-hoo! You've created a plugin, so let's use it! Navigate to the Page Designer for page 1 and do the following, as shown in Figure 10-21:

1. Drag and drop the APEX jqGrid [Plug-In] option into the CONTENT BODY area.

2. Click Save.

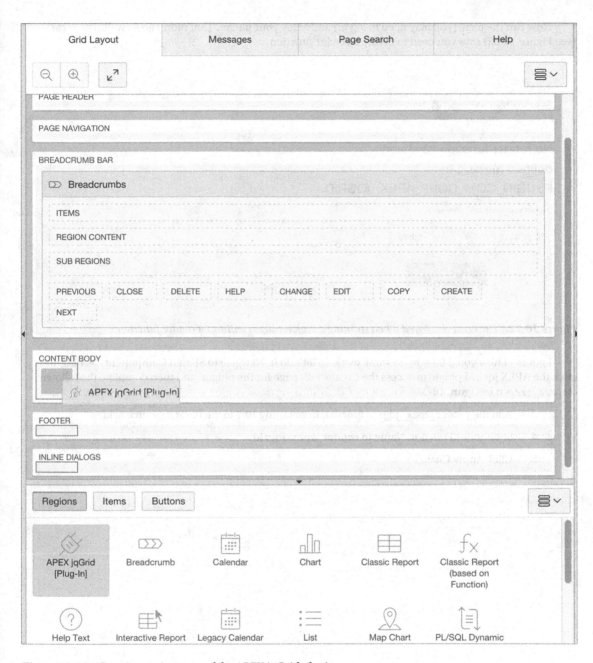

Figure 10-21. Creating an instance of the APEX jqGrid plugin

Now run the page (you may need to log in) and enjoy your plugin. That didn't go so well! The error (see Figure 10-22) says you need to define a render function.

Figure 10-22. *The error displayed when running a region plugin without a render function*

I guess I knew you'd have to do some work, so let's do it. Navigate to Shared Components ➤ Plug-ins, click the APEX jqGrid plugin to access the Create/Edit page for the plugin, and then complete the following steps, as shown in Figure 10-23:

3.   Add the render_apex_jqgrid function from Listing 10-1 to the PL/SQL Source field.

4.   Set Render Function Name to **render_apex_jqgrid**.

5.   Click Apply Changes.

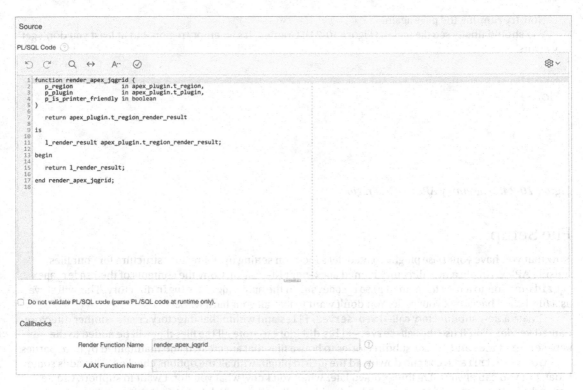

Figure 10-23. *The Source and Callbacks regions of the APEX jqGrid plugin*

■ **Note** Remember to click the help icon on the right of the function name to get the signature expected.

Listing 10-1. PL/SQL Code for the APEX jqGrid Plugin

```
function render_apex_jqgrid (
    p_region             in apex_plugin.t_region,
    p_plugin             in apex_plugin.t_plugin,
    p_is_printer_friendly in boolean
)

    return apex_plugin.t_region_render_result

is

    l_render_result apex_plugin.t_region_render_result;

begin

    return l_render_result;

end render_apex_jqgrid;
```

Now try running the page again.

You should finally see the region (Figure 10-24)! Granted, it's an empty region, but at least you don't get any errors.

Home
New

Figure 10-24. *The empty APEX jqGrid region*

File Setup

Now that you have your base plugin created, let's focus on setting up a directory structure for your files outside APEX. Create a new directory named apex-jqgrid-plugin. Copy the contents of the render_apex_ jqgrid function to a new file named plsql_code.sql in the apex-jqgrid-plugin directory. This will serve as a file-based backup of your code. You don't want to lose all your hard work!

Create a new subdirectory called web-server-files and within that directory create another directory named vendor. You'll use the web-server-files directory to store all the files that will be added to the web-server-files and vendor subdirectories to house files that are created and maintained by third parties.

Go to www.trirand.com and download the jqGrid plugin with all the options checked. This adds some bloat, but you can always slim things down later when you know what you don't want to support. Create a new subdirectory named jqgrid-4.8.2 (update the version as needed throughout this tutorial) in vendor and then unzip the contents of the jqGrid plugin you downloaded into that directory. At this point, the directory structure should look like Figure 10-25.

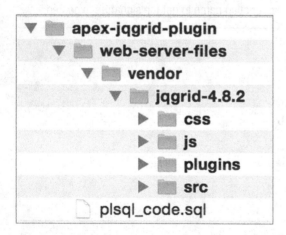

Figure 10-25. *The file structure for the APEX jqGrid plugin*

Now you need to make the jqGrid files available to your plugin in APEX and start using them. Zip up the contents of the `web-server-files` directory (the child directories, not the `web-server-files` directory itself) to a zip file named `web-server-files.zip`. Navigate to the plugin Create/Edit page for APEX jqGrid and complete the following steps:

1. Click Upload File.

2. Use File to select the `web-server-files.zip` file.

3. Click Upload.

This operation may take a little time because there are quite a lot of files to be loaded within the zip file. Once complete, the Files region of the plugin should look like Figure 10-26. Note that the top-level directory visible is `vendor`, not `web-server-files`.

Files				Upload File
File Prefix				
File Name	Mime Type	File Size	File	
vendor/jqgrid-4.8.2/css/ui.jqgrid-bootstarp.css	text/css	662	Download	
vendor/jqgrid-4.8.2/css/ui.jqgrid.css	text/css	14KB	Download	
vendor/jqgrid-4.8.2/js/Changes.txt	text/plain	44KB	Download	
vendor/jqgrid-4.8.2/js/i18n/grid.locale-ar.js	application/javascript	6KB	Download	
vendor/jqgrid-4.8.2/js/i18n/grid.locale-bg.js	application/javascript	6KB	Download	
vendor/jqgrid-4.8.2/js/i18n/grid.locale-ca.js	application/javascript	5KB	Download	

Figure 10-26. *The Files region (showing only six of many files) after uploading the web-server-files.zip*

Initial Grid Render

With the web server files uploaded, you are now ready to use them. Now let's try getting the jqGrid plugin to render in the most basic way possible. You won't even worry about the plugin user specifying a query for now. After exploring the jqGrid documentation, you'll learn the basics of how the jQuery plugin is used and find that it's possible to populate the grid with local data. You'll also learn that jqGrid needs some targets in the DOM for placing the grid and the pagination components. Let's make some changes to get things working. Navigate to the plugin Create/Edit page for APEX jqGrid and follow these steps:

1. Update the `render_apex_jqgrid` function in the PL/SQL Source field to the code from Listing 10-2. Don't forget to update your `plsql_code.sql` file too.

2. Create a new JavaScript file named `apex-jqgrid-plugin.js` with the contents in Listing 10-3. Save the file in the `web-server-files` directory created earlier.

3. Return to APEX and click Upload File.

4. Use File to select the `apex-jqgrid-plugin.js` file.

5. Click Upload.

6. Set Cascading Style Sheet in File URLs to Load to the following:

```
#PLUGIN_FILES#vendor/jqgrid-4.8.2/css/ui.jqgrid.css
```

7. Set JavaScript in File URLs to Load to the following:

```
#PLUGIN_FILES#vendor/jqgrid-4.8.2/js/i18n/grid.locale-en.js
#PLUGIN_FILES#vendor/jqgrid-4.8.2/js/jquery.jqGrid.min.js
#PLUGIN_FILES#apex-jqgrid-plugin.js
```

8. Click Apply Changes.

Listing 10-2. Updated render Function for the APEX jqGrid Plug-in

```
function render_apex_jqgrid (
    p_region             in apex_plugin.t_region,
    p_plugin             in apex_plugin.t_plugin,
    p_is_printer_friendly in boolean
)

    return apex_plugin.t_region_render_result

is

    l_render_result apex_plugin.t_region_render_result;

begin

    sys.htp.p('<table id="jqGrid"></table>');
    sys.htp.p('<div id="jqGridPager"></div>');

    return l_render_result;

end render_apex_jqgrid;
```

As you can see, you added two lines of code to the render function that use sys.htp.p to write to the HTTP buffer; that's how plugins write out their HTML.

Listing 10-3. Contents of apex-jqgrid-plugin.js

```
$(document).ready(function () {
    var data = [{
        "ProductName":"Steeleye Stout",
        "CategoryName":"Beverages",
        "Country":"UK",
        "Quantity":"65",
        "Price":"1008.0000"
    },
    {
        "ProductName":"Laughing Lumberjack Lager",
        "CategoryName":"Beverages",
        "Country":"USA",
        "Quantity":"10",
        "Price":"140.0000",
    }];
```

```
    var grid = $("#jqGrid").jqGrid({
        datatype: "local",
        colModel: [
            {label: 'Category Name', name: 'CategoryName', width: 75},
            {label: 'Product Name', name: 'ProductName', width: 90},
            {label: 'Country', name: 'Country', width: 100},
            {label: 'Price', name: 'Price', width: 80},
            {label: 'Quantity', name: 'Quantity', width: 80}
        ],
        viewrecords: true,
        width: 780,
        height: 200,
        rowNum: 30,
        loadonce: true,
        pager: "#jqGridPager"
    });

    data.forEach(function(row, idx) {
        grid.jqGrid('addRowData', idx + 1, row);
    });
});
```

The `apex-jqgrid-plugin.js` file starts by declaring an array named `data` that has two elements. The elements represent rows of data that should be displayed in the grid. The next part invokes the jqGrid plugin on the element you added to the DOM via the PL/SQL `render` function. Finally, you loop over the rows of data you want to show in the grid and invoke the `addRowData` method of `jqGrid` to add them.

Run the page and take a look! You should see something like Figure 10-27.

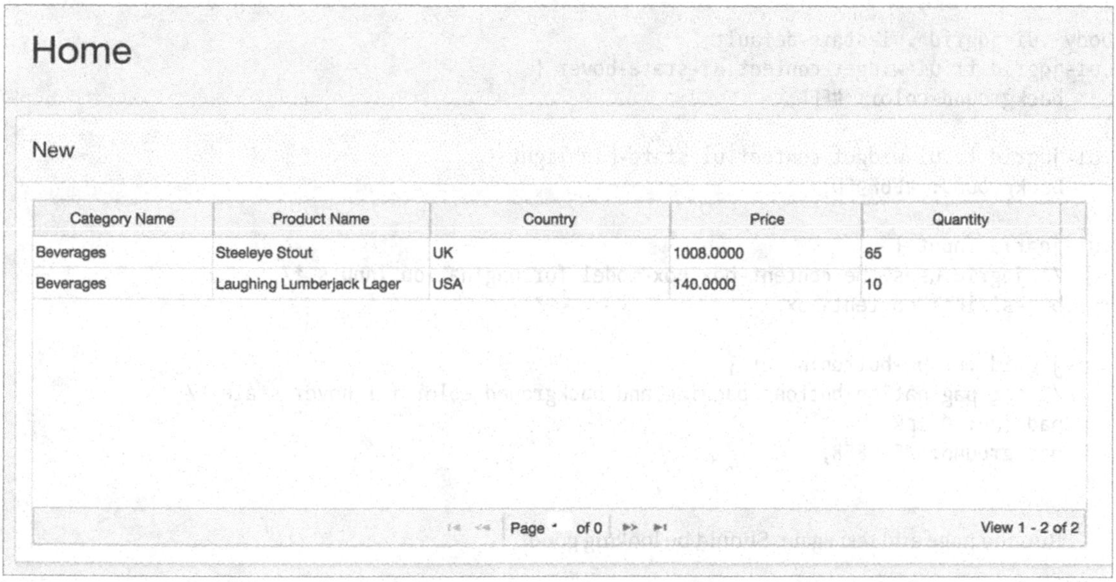
Home
New
Category Name
Product Name
Country
Price
Quantity
Beverages
Steeleye Stout
UK
1008.0000
65
Beverages
Laughing Lumberjack Lager
USA
140.0000
10
Page
of 0
View 1 - 2 of 2

***Figure 10-27.** The initial render of the APEX jqGrid plugin*

Adjusting the UI for APEX

Great, you can finally see the grid! However, upon closer inspection, you may notice some things don't look quite right. For example, hovering over rows shows strange border colors, and the pagination at the bottom doesn't display the current page correctly. Let's take a moment to fix those issues now. Navigate to the plugin Create/Edit page for APEX jqGrid and complete the following steps:

1. Create a new CSS file named apex-jqgrid-plugin.css with the contents in Listing 10-4. Save the file in the web-server-files directory created earlier.

2. Return to APEX and click Upload File.

3. Use File to select the apex-jqgrid-plugin.css file.

4. Click Upload.

5. Update Cascading Style Sheets in File URLs to Load to include the following:

   #PLUGIN_FILES#apex-jqgrid-plugin.css

6. Click Apply Changes.

Listing 10-4. Contents of apex-jqgrid-plugin.css

```
body .ui-jqgrid,
.ui-jqgrid tr.ui-widget-content {
    background: #F8F8F8;
}
.ui-jqgrid tr.jqgrow td {
    /* First set a border color for table cells to be a transparent black */
    border-color: rgba(0,0,0,.1);
}
body .ui-jqgrid .ui-state-default,
.ui-jqgrid tr.ui-widget-content.ui-state-hover {
    background-color: #FFF;
}
.ui-jqgrid tr.ui-widget-content.ui-state-highlight {
    background: #F6F9FD;
}
.ui-jqgrid input {
    /* jqgrid uses the content-box box-model for pagination inputs */
    box-sizing: content-box;
}
.ui-jqgrid .ui-pg-button:hover {
    /* set pagination buttons padding and background color for hover state */
    padding: 0 1px;
    background: #F8F8F8;
}
```

Run the page and test again. Should be looking good!

Getting Set Up for Success

With the styling issues addressed, it's pretty safe to assume that this jqGrid plugin will meet your needs. Before you continue building out the plugin, let's take a moment to refactor the code a little so that it's easier to maintain over time. The first thing you'll address is the PL/SQL code. Navigate to the plugin Create/Edit page for APEX jqGrid and follow these steps:

1. Update the render_apex_jqgrid function in the PL/SQL Source field to the code from Listing 10-5. Don't forget to update your plsql_code.sql file too.

2. Click Apply Changes.

Listing 10-5. Updated render Function for the APEX jqGrid Plugin

```
function render_apex_jqgrid (
    p_region              in apex_plugin.t_region,
    p_plugin              in apex_plugin.t_plugin,
    p_is_printer_friendly in boolean
)

    return apex_plugin.t_region_render_result

is

    l_render_result apex_plugin.t_region_render_result;
    l_onload_code   varchar2(4000);

begin

    if apex_application.g_debug
    then
        apex_plugin_util.debug_region (
            p_plugin => p_plugin,
            p_region => p_region
        );
    end if;

    sys.htp.p('<table id="' || p_region.static_id || '_APEX_JQ_GRID"></table>');
    sys.htp.p('<div id="' || p_region.static_id || '_APEX_JQ_GRID_PAGER"></div>');

    l_onload_code := 'apex.jQuery("#' || p_region.static_id || '").apex_jqgrid();';

    apex_javascript.add_onload_code (
        p_code => l_onload_code
    );

    return l_render_result;

end render_apex_jqgrid;
```

First you added some basic debug code to the render function. Next you updated the calls that output the HTML to ensure that the elements have unique id attributes. For this you used the region's static ID with some additional characters to differentiate them. This is the first time you start to make use of the parameters that are passed to you in the PL/SQL functions. Finally, in anticipation of making the plugin a jQuery UI widget, you added just enough JavaScript to load the widget (which will be created next).

If you run the application now, you'll see that it doesn't work anymore. This is because the current JavaScript code doesn't work with the new PL/SQL code. You need to update your JavaScript code so that it creates a jQuery UI widget. Return to the plugin Create/Edit page for APEX jqGrid and do the following:

1. Update the apex-jqgrid-plugin.js file to the code from Listing 10-6.

2. Click Upload File.

3. Use File to select the apex-jqgrid-plugin.js file.

4. Click Upload.

Listing 10-6. Updated apex-jqgrid-plugin.js

```
(function($){
    $.widget("ui.apex_jqgrid", {
        options: {},
        _create: function() {
            var uiw = this;
            var data = [{
                "ProductName":"Steeleye Stout",
                "CategoryName":"Beverages",
                "Country":"UK",
                "Quantity":"65",
                "Price":"1008.0000"
            },
            {
                "ProductName":"Laughing Lumberjack Lager",
                "CategoryName":"Beverages",
                "Country":"USA",
                "Quantity":"10",
                "Price":"140.0000"
            }];

            var grid = $('#' + uiw.element.attr('id') + '_APEX_JQ_GRID').jqGrid({
                datatype: "local",
                colModel: [
                    {label: 'Category Name', name: 'CategoryName', width: 75},
                    {label: 'Product Name', name: 'ProductName', width: 90},
                    {label: 'Country', name: 'Country', width: 100},
                    {label: 'Price', name: 'Price', width: 80},
                    {label: 'Quantity', name: 'Quantity', width: 80}
                ],
                viewrecords: true,
                width: 780,
                height: 200,
```

```
        rowNum: 30,
        loadonce: true,
        pager: '#' + uiw.element.attr('id') + '_APEX_JQ_GRID_PAGER'
    });

    data.forEach(function(row, idx) {
        grid.jqGrid('addRowData', idx + 1, row);
    });
    }
  });
})(apex.jQuery);
```

As you can see, the bulk of the previous code was moved to the _create function of the new widget. Also, the code was modified slightly to accommodate the unique element IDs. Rerun the page and ensure that the plugin works just as it did before.

Bringing on the AJAX

Now that the code has been made a bit more maintainable, let's set out to do something big: bring in data via AJAX! This is actually a pretty tall order to do all at once, so you'll break it up into a couple of steps. Let's start off by creating a baseline AJAX function and call it from your widget in the front end. You know the drill: navigate to the Create/Edit page for APEX jqGrid and complete these steps:

1. Update the code in the PL/SQL Source field with the code from Listing 10-7. Don't forget to update your plsql_code.sql file too.

2. Set AJAX Function Name to **ajax_apex_jqgrid**.

3. Click Apply Changes.

Listing 10-7. PL/SQL Code Updated for Basic AJAX Functionality

```
function render_apex_jqgrid (
    p_region            in apex_plugin.t_region,
    p_plugin            in apex_plugin.t_plugin,
    p_is_printer_friendly in boolean
)

    return apex_plugin.t_region_render_result

is

    l_render_result apex_plugin.t_region_render_result;
    l_onload_code   varchar2(4000);
    l_crlf          char(2) := chr(13)||chr(10);

begin
```

```
    if apex_application.g_debug
    then
        apex_plugin_util.debug_region (
            p_plugin => p_plugin,
            p_region => p_region
        );
    end if;

    sys.htp.p('<table id="' || p_region.static_id || '_APEX_JQ_GRID"></table>');
    sys.htp.p('<div id="' || p_region.static_id || '_APEX_JQ_GRID_PAGER"></div>');

    l_onload_code := 'apex.jQuery("#' || p_region.static_id || '").apex_jqgrid({' || l_crlf ||
        '   ' || apex_javascript.add_attribute('ajaxIdentifier',
        apex_plugin.get_ajax_identifier(), false, false) || l_crlf ||
        '});';

    apex_javascript.add_onload_code (
        p_code => l_onload_code
    );

    return l_render_result;

end render_apex_jqgrid;

function ajax_apex_jqgrid (
    p_region in apex_plugin.t_region,
    p_plugin in apex_plugin.t_plugin
)
    return apex_plugin.t_region_ajax_result
is

    l_ajax_result apex_plugin.t_region_ajax_result;

begin

    sys.htp.p('{"message": "Hello AJAX!"}');

    return l_ajax_result;

end ajax_apex_jqgrid;
```

The AJAX function just writes a simple JSON object to the HTTP buffer. But to call the function from the front end, you needed to pass the value returned from apex_plugin.get_ajax_identifier to your JavaScript code. The render function was updated to do this via the option object.

Now that the PL/SQL code has been updated, let's update the JavaScript code to get it in sync. Return to the Create/Edit page for APEX jqGrid and do the following:

1. Update the apex-jqgrid-plugin.js file to the code from Listing 10-8.

2. Click Upload File.

3. Use File to select the apex-jqgrid-plugin.js file.

4. Click Upload.

Listing 10-8. apex-jqgrid-plugin.js Updated for Basic AJAX Functionality

```
(function($){
    $.widget("ui.apex_jqgrid", {
        options: {
            ajaxIdentifier: null
        },
        _create: function() {
            var uiw = this;
            var data = [{
                "ProductName":"Steeleye Stout",
                "CategoryName":"Beverages",
                "Country":"UK",
                "Quantity":"65",
                "Price":"1008.0000"
            },
            {
                "ProductName":"Laughing Lumberjack Lager",
                "CategoryName":"Beverages",
                "Country":"USA",
                "Quantity":"10",
                "Price":"140.0000"
            }];

            var grid = $('#' + uiw.element.attr('id') + '_APEX_JQ_GRID').jqGrid({
                datatype: "local",
                colModel: [
                    {label: 'Category Name', name: 'CategoryName', width: 75},
                    {label: 'Product Name', name: 'ProductName', width: 90},
                    {label: 'Country', name: 'Country', width: 100},
                    {label: 'Price', name: 'Price', width: 80},
                    {label: 'Quantity', name: 'Quantity', width: 80}
                ],
                viewrecords: true,
                width: 780,
                height: 200,
                rowNum: 30,
                loadonce: true,
                pager: '#' + uiw.element.attr('id') + '_APEX_JQ_GRID_PAGER'
            });

            data.forEach(function(row, idx) {
                grid.jqGrid('addRowData', idx + 1, row);
            });
```

```
            apex.server.plugin(
                uiw.options.ajaxIdentifier,
                {},
                {
                    success: function(data) {
                        console.log(data);
                    }
                }
            );
        }
    });
})(apex.jQuery);
```

You've added an ajaxIdentifier property to the options object at the top and set its value to null. This is really just for documentation purposes because the value will be coming from the initialization code in the PL/SQL render function. Also, an AJAX request was made using apex.server.plugin, which is one of the JavaScript APIs that ships with APEX. If the request is successful, then the data returned will be logged to the browser's console.

Make sure you have the browser's developer tools open so you can see the console and run the page. If everything worked, you should see the JSON message in the console.

Now that you have a means to send data from the server to the client via AJAX, let's see whether you can send some dynamic data via a query! Navigate to the Create/Edit page for APEX jqGrid and complete these steps:

1. Update the ajax_apex_jqgrid function in the PL/SQL Source field with the code from Listing 10-9. Don't forget to update your plsql_code.sql file too.

2. Click Apply Changes.

Listing 10-9. AJAX Function Updated for Dynamic Data

```
function ajax_apex_jqgrid (
    p_region in apex_plugin.t_region,
    p_plugin in apex_plugin.t_plugin
)
    return apex_plugin.t_region_ajax_result
is

    l_ajax_result        apex_plugin.t_region_ajax_result;
    l_column_value_list apex_plugin_util.t_column_value_list;

begin

    l_column_value_list :=
        apex_plugin_util.get_data(
            p_sql_statement     => 'select cust_first_name, cust_last_name, cust_state from
            demo_customers',
            p_min_columns       => 2,
            p_max_columns       => 50,
            p_component_name    => p_region.name
    );
```

```
apex_json.open_array;

for row_idx in 1 .. l_column_value_list(1).count
loop
   apex_json.open_array;

   for column_idx in 1 .. l_column_value_list.count
   loop
      apex_json.write(l_column_value_list(column_idx)(row_idx));
   end loop;

   apex_json.close_array;
end loop;

apex_json.close_array;

return l_ajax_result;

end ajax_apex_jqgrid;
```

Now you're using apex_plugin_util to execute a query and apex_json to convert the resultset to JSON. Now when you run the page and view the console, you should see customer data coming across. That's cool, but how can you get that to display in the grid? After reviewing the demos of the jqGrid online, you'll learn enough to tackle the JavaScript. Return to the Create/Edit page for the plugin and do the following:

1. Update the apex-jqgrid-plugin.js file to the code from Listing 10-10.

2. Click Upload File.

3. Use File to select the apex-jqgrid-plugin.js file.

4. Click Upload.

Listing 10-10. apex-jqgrid-plugin.js Updated for Dynamic Data

```
(function($){
    $.widget("ui.apex_jqgrid", {
        options: {
            ajaxIdentifier: null
        },
        _create: function() {
            var uiw = this;

            var grid = $('#' + uiw.element.attr('id') + '_APEX_JQ_GRID').jqGrid({
                datatype: "local",
                colModel: [
                    { label: 'First Name', name: 'col0', width: 75 },
                    { label: 'Last Name', name: 'col1', width: 90 },
                    { label: 'State', name: 'col2', width: 100 }
                ],
                viewrecords: true,
                width: 780,
                height: 200,
```

```
                rowNum: 30,
                loadonce: true,
                pager: "#" + uiw.element.attr('id') + "_APEX_JQ_GRID_PAGER"
            });

            apex.server.plugin(
                uiw.options.ajaxIdentifier,
                {},
                {
                    success: function(data) {
                        var gridData = [];

                        data.forEach(function(row, rowIdx) {
                            var obj = {};

                            row.forEach(function(col, colIdx) {
                                obj['col' + colIdx] = col;
                            });

                            gridData.push(obj);
                        });

                        grid.jqGrid('setGridParam', { data: gridData});

                        grid.trigger('reloadGrid');
                    }
                }
            );
        }
    });
})(apex.jQuery);
```

Rather than log the data returned from the server, you now use it to populate the grid. Now when you run the page to test the plugin, you should see data coming from the table, as shown in Figure 10-28.

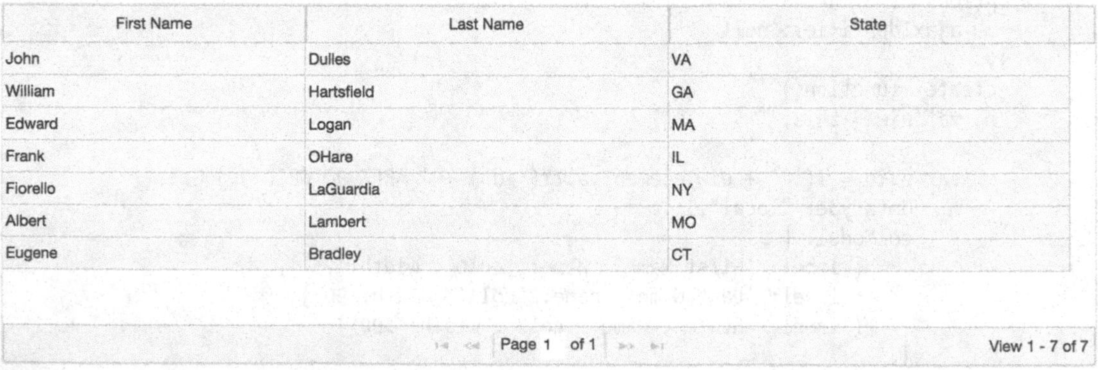

First Name	Last Name	State
John	Dulles	VA
William	Hartsfield	GA
Edward	Logan	MA
Frank	OHare	IL
Fiorello	LaGuardia	NY
Albert	Lambert	MO
Eugene	Bradley	CT

|◄ ◄◄ Page 1 of 1 ►► ►| View 1 - 7 of 7

Figure 10-28. *Dynamic data loaded in the grid*

Using User-Specified Queries

Excellent, you are now loading dynamic data into the grid! Of course, what you really want is to allow the developer using the plugin to specify the query. Let's start by updating the ajax_apex_jqgrid function to use the query specified in the region's source. Go to the plugin Create/Edit page for APEX jqGrid and make the following changes:

1. Update the ajax_apex_jqgrid function in the PL/SQL Source field with the code from Listing 10-11. Don't forget to update your plsql_code.sql file too.

2. Check the Region Source is SQL Statement check box in the Standard Attributes region.

3. Check the Region Source Required check box.

4. Set Maximum Columns to 50.

5. Click Apply Changes.

Listing 10-11. ajax_apex_jqgrid Updated for Dynamic Queries

```
function ajax_apex_jqgrid (
  p_region in apex_plugin.t_region,
  p_plugin in apex_plugin.t_plugin
)

  return apex_plugin.t_region_ajax_result

is

  l_ajax_result        apex_plugin.t_region_ajax_result;
  l_column_value_list  apex_plugin_util.t_column_value_list;

begin

  l_column_value_list :=
    apex_plugin_util.get_data(
      p_sql_statement    => p_region.source,
      p_min_columns      => 2,
      p_max_columns      => 50,
      p_component_name   => p_region.name
  );

  apex_json.open_array;

  for row_idx in 1 .. l_column_value_list(1).count
  loop
    apex_json.open_array;

    for column_idx in 1 .. l_column_value_list.count
    loop
      apex_json.write(l_column_value_list(column_idx)(row_idx));
    end loop;
```

```
    apex_json.close_array;
  end loop;

  apex_json.close_array;

  return l_ajax_result;

end ajax_apex_jqgrid;
```

Now you need to move the SQL Query to the region level. Navigate to the Page Designer for page 1 and do the following:

1. Click the plugin region in the Grid Layout.

2. Set SQL Query to select cust_first_name, cust_last_name, cust_state from demo_customers.

3. Click Save.

If you test the page now, it should be working as it was before only now the query is coming from the region, which is dynamic. However, you still have a problem with the column headings because they are still static in the JavaScript. If you were to change the query, things would break. The column model that jqGrid accepts could be created dynamically; you just need a way to get dynamic information related to the columns. This is where the Has "Region Columns" option in the standard attributes comes in. Return to the plugin Create/Edit page for APEX jqGrid and complete these steps:

1. Check the Has "Region Columns" check box in the Standard Attributes.

2. Check the Has "Heading" Column Attribute.

3. Click Apply Changes.

With those attributes enabled, let's update the region. Go back to the Page Designer for page 1 and do the following:

1. Click the plugin region in the Grid Layout.

2. Using the Component Selector (left column), expand the Columns node for the plugin region. If the node cannot be expanded, delete the region and re-create it now that the new options have been added to the plugin. This bug will be fixed in a future version of APEX, and it will not affect users of the plugin.

3. Select the CUST_FIRST_NAME column.

4. Using the Property Editor (right column), set Heading to First Name.

5. Select the CUST_LAST_NAME column.

6. Set Heading to Last Name.

7. Select the CUST_STATE column.

8. Set Heading to State.

9. Click Save.

Now that the headings for the columns are set with the correct values, you need to pass the values to your jQuery UI plugin. You've done this before with the AJAX identifier, so you just need to expand that code to do this the same way, only rather than pass a simple string through for the header, you'll pass an object that can be extended later. Go to the plugin Create/Edit page for APEX jqGrid and make the following changes:

1. Update the render_apex_jqgrid function in the PL/SQL Source field with the code from Listing 10-12. Don't forget to update your plsql_code.sql file too.

2. Click Save.

Listing 10-12. render_apex_jqgrid Updated for Dynamic Columns

```
function render_apex_jqgrid (
   p_region              in apex_plugin.t_region,
   p_plugin              in apex_plugin.t_plugin,
   p_is_printer_friendly in boolean
)

   return apex_plugin.t_region_render_result

is

   l_render_result apex_plugin.t_region_render_result;
   l_onload_code    varchar2(4000);
   l_crlf           char(2) := chr(13)||chr(10);

begin

   if apex_application.g_debug
   then
      apex_plugin_util.debug_region (
         p_plugin => p_plugin,
         p_region => p_region
      );
   end if;

   sys.htp.p('<table id="' || p_region.static_id || '_APEX_JQ_GRID"></table>');
   sys.htp.p('<div id="' || p_region.static_id || '_APEX_JQ_GRID_PAGER"></div>');

   l_onload_code := 'apex.jQuery("#' || p_region.static_id || '").apex_jqgrid({' || l_crlf ||
      '    ' || apex_javascript.add_attribute('ajaxIdentifier',
      apex_plugin.get_ajax_identifier(), false, true) || l_crlf ||
      '   columns: [' || l_crlf;

   for x in 1 .. p_region.region_columns.count
   loop
      if x > 1
      then
         l_onload_code := l_onload_code || ',' || l_crlf;
      end if;
```

```
        l_onload_code := l_onload_code ||
            '        {' || l_crlf ||
            '            ' || apex_javascript.add_attribute('heading',
            p_region.region_columns(x).heading, false, false) || l_crlf ||
            '        }';
    end loop;

    l_onload_code := l_onload_code || l_crlf ||
        '    ]' || l_crlf ||
        '});';

    apex_javascript.add_onload_code (
        p_code => l_onload_code
    );

    return l_render_result;

end render_apex_jqgrid;
```

That will send the headings through to your jQuery UI widget, but you need to make use of the heading values within that code. Let's update the apex-jqgrid-plugins.js to do just that. Return to the Create/Edit page for the plugin and do the following:

1. Update the apex-jqgrid-plugin.js file to the code from Listing 10-13.

2. Click Upload File.

3. Use File to select the apex-jqgrid-plugin.js file.

4. Click Upload.

Listing 10-13. apex-jqgrid-plugin.js Updated for Dynamic Columns

```
(function($){
    $.widget("ui.apex_jqgrid", {
        options: {
            ajaxIdentifier: null
        },
        _create: function() {
            var uiw = this;
            var colModel = [];

            uiw.options.columns.forEach(function(column, colIdx) {
                colModel.push({
                    label: column.heading,
                    name: 'col' + colIdx
                });
            });

            var grid = $('#' + uiw.element.attr('id') + '_APEX_JQ_GRID').jqGrid({
                datatype: "local",
                colModel: colModel,
                viewrecords: true,
```

```
            width: 780,
            height: 200,
            rowNum: 30,
            loadonce: true,
            pager: "#" + uiw.element.attr('id') + "_APEX_JQ_GRID_PAGER"
        });

        apex.server.plugin(
            uiw.options.ajaxIdentifier,
            {},
            {
                success: function(data) {
                    var gridData = [];

                    data.forEach(function(row, rowIdx) {
                        var obj = {};

                        row.forEach(function(col, colIdx) {
                            obj['col' + colIdx] = col;
                        });

                        gridData.push(obj);
                    });

                    grid.jqGrid('setGridParam', { data: gridData});

                    grid.trigger('reloadGrid');
                }
            }
        );
    }
});
})(apex.jQuery);
```

Notice the column model is now created using the columns array that's passed in via the options. Now the plugin is completely dynamic! Feel free to modify the query to ensure that it's working correctly.

Enabling Frozen Columns

Going back to the main feature of the plugin, you need to make it so that some columns can be frozen. Of course, there's no such standard attribute for this; that's where custom attributes come in. Let's add a custom attribute. Navigate to the plugin Create/Edit page for APEX jqGrid and follow these steps, as shown in Figure 10-29:

1. Click Add Attribute in the Custom Attributes region.

2. Set Scope to Region Column.

3. Set Label to Frozen.

4. Set Type to Yes/No.

441

5. Set Default Value to N.

6. Click Create.

< > Plug-in: APEX jqGrid					Cancel	**Create**	Create and Create Another
Show All	Name	Settings	Default Value	Condition	User Interfaces	Help Text and Exam...	Comments

Name

* Scope	Region Column	⌄ ⓘ
* Attribute	1	ⓘ
* Display Sequence	10	ⓘ
* Label	Frozen	ⓘ

Settings

Type	Yes/No	⌄ ⓘ
Common	Yes ⌄	ⓘ
Show in Wizard	Yes ⌄	ⓘ

Default Value

Default Value	N	ⓘ

Figure 10-29. *Creating a Frozen attribute*

Now navigate to the Page Designer for page 1 and click one of the columns for the plugin region. You should see the new Frozen attribute under Settings in the property editor (see Figure 10-30).

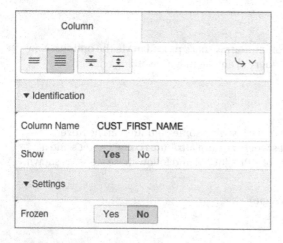

Figure 10-30. *New Frozen attribute in the column properties*

Set that to Yes for one or two columns and then click Save. You know what's next: you have to map the value through from the PL/SQL render function to the JavaScript widget and then utilize the value in the widget. Navigate to the Create/Edit page of the plugin and update the PL/SQL.

1. Update the render_apex_jqgrid function in the PL/SQL Source field with the code from Listing 10-14. Don't forget to update your plsql_code.sql file too.

2. Click Apply Changes.

Listing 10-14. render_apex_jqgrid Function Updated for Frozen Columns

```
function render_apex_jqgrid (
    p_region            in apex_plugin.t_region,
    p_plugin            in apex_plugin.t_plugin,
    p_is_printer_friendly in boolean
)

    return apex_plugin.t_region_render_result

is

    l_render_result apex_plugin.t_region_render_result;
    l_onload_code    varchar2(4000);
    l_crlf           char(2) := chr(13)||chr(10);

begin

    if apex_application.g_debug
    then
        apex_plugin_util.debug_region (
            p_plugin => p_plugin,
            p_region => p_region
        );
    end if;

    sys.htp.p('<table id="' || p_region.static_id || '_APEX_JQ_GRID"></table>');
    sys.htp.p('<div id="' || p_region.static_id || '_APEX_JQ_GRID_PAGER"></div>');

    l_onload_code := 'apex.jQuery("#' || p_region.static_id || '").apex_jqgrid({' || l_crlf ||
        '    ' || apex_javascript.add_attribute('ajaxIdentifier',
        apex_plugin.get_ajax_identifier(), false, true) || l_crlf ||
        '    columns: [' || l_crlf;

    for x in 1 .. p_region.region_columns.count
    loop
        if x > 1
        then
            l_onload_code := l_onload_code || ',' || l_crlf;
        end if;
```

```
    l_onload_code := l_onload_code ||
    '          {' || l_crlf ||
    '               ' || apex_javascript.add_attribute('heading', p_region.region_columns(x).
    heading, false, true) || l_crlf ||
    '               ' || apex_javascript.add_attribute('frozen', p_region.region_columns(x).
    attribute_01, false, false) || l_crlf ||
    '          }';
  end loop;

  l_onload_code := l_onload_code || l_crlf ||
  '     ]' || l_crlf ||
  '});';

  apex_javascript.add_onload_code (
    p_code => l_onload_code
  );

  return l_render_result;

end render_apex_jqgrid;
```

Now that the column's frozen Y/N value is being passed through to the JavaScript widget, let's adjust the JavaScript code to make use of the new attribute. Return to the Create/Edit page for the plugin and complete the following steps:

1. Update the apex-jqgrid-plugin.js file to the code from Listing 10-15.

2. Click Upload File.

3. Use File to select the apex-jqgrid-plugin.js file.

4. Click Upload.

Listing 10-15. apex-jqgrid-plugin.js Updated for Frozen Columns

```
(function($){
    $.widget("ui.apex_jqgrid", {
        options: {
            ajaxIdentifier: null
        },
        _create: function() {
            var uiw = this;
            var colModel = [];
            var frozenCols = [];
            var notFrozenCols = [];

            uiw.options.columns.forEach(function(column, colIdx) {
                var obj = {
                        label: column.heading,
                        name: 'col' + colIdx,
                        width: 150
                };
```

```
                if (column.frozen === 'Y') {
                    obj.frozen = true;
                    frozenCols.push(obj);
                } else {
                    obj.frozen = false;
                    notFrozenCols.push(obj);
                }

                colModel = frozenCols.concat(notFrozenCols);
        });

        var grid = $('#' + uiw.element.attr('id') + '_APEX_JQ_GRID').jqGrid({
            datatype: 'local',
            shrinkToFit: false,
            colModel: colModel,
            viewrecords: true,
            width: 780,
            height: 200,
            rowNum: 30,
            loadonce: true,
            pager: "#" + uiw.element.attr('id') + "_APEX_JQ_GRID_PAGER"
        });

        apex.server.plugin(
            uiw.options.ajaxIdentifier,
            {},
            {
                success: function(data) {
                    var gridData = [];

                    data.forEach(function(row, rowIdx) {
                        var obj = {};

                        row.forEach(function(col, colIdx) {
                            obj['col' + colIdx] = col;
                        });

                        gridData.push(obj);
                    });

                    grid.jqGrid('setGridParam', { data: gridData});

                    grid.trigger('reloadGrid');

                    if (frozenCols) {
                        grid.jqGrid("setFrozenColumns");
                    }
                }
            }
        );
    }
    });
})(apex.jQuery);
```

As you can see, you first declare two arrays to hold and separate out the frozen columns from those that are not frozen. This is done so that you can concatenate them back together later, placing the frozen columns first, as is required by jqGrid. Later, the frozenCols array is also used to determine whether a call to setFrozenColumns should be made on the grid.

Now run the page to give it a shot. Keep in mind that you'll need to have a lot of columns to see the full effect. Try changing the query for the region to select * from demo_customers for an easy way to test this.

With that code in place, you have achieved the major goal of this plugin. But as you can imagine, there is still much work to be done. There are still many attributes that must be mapped through, both at the grid/region level as well as at the column level. You're not going to do them all here because that would be the perfect exercise for you to get some practical experience. Here's a list of some of the more obvious mappings that should be done.

Standard attributes:

- Has "Heading Alignment" column attribute

- Has "Alignment" column attribute

Custom region attributes:

- Rows Per Page

Custom column attributes:

- Width

- Height

- Shrink Columns to Fit (Yes/No)

Another enhancement worth considering is "true" pagination. Currently all the rows are fetched from the query specified for the region, and pagination is done on the client side. This works well when there aren't too many rows (maybe a few thousand at most), but for larger datasets this will not perform so well. True pagination would be tricky because it would have to be customized, as APEX doesn't support the type of URLs that jqGrid expects. You will not implement true pagination in this chapter because it would focus less on the plugin architecture and more on jqGrid customization.

Securing the Plugin

Another issue to consider, and one that I will address because of its importance, is security. Currently your plugin is vulnerable to XSS attacks because you are not escaping the content returned from the queries. Also, you are not paying any attention to the is_displayed property of the columns that lets you know whether a column should be suppressed because of conditions or authorization schemes used on the column.

Let's start by addressing the XSS vulnerability. Navigate to the plugin Create/Edit page for APEX jqGrid and do the following:

1. Check the Has "Escape Special Characters" column attribute check box.

2. Update the ajax_apex_jqgrid function in the PL/SQL source field with the code from Listing 10-16. Don't forget to update your plsql_code.sql file too.

3. Click Apply Changes.

Listing 10-16. ajax_apex_jqgrid Function Updated to Escape Special Characters

```
function ajax_apex_jqgrid (
    p_region in apex_plugin.t_region,
    p_plugin in apex_plugin.t_plugin
)
    return apex_plugin.t_region_ajax_result
is

    l_ajax_result           apex_plugin.t_region_ajax_result;
    l_column_value_list apex_plugin_util.t_column_value_list;

begin

    l_column_value_list :=
        apex_plugin_util.get_data(
            p_sql_statement    => p_region.source,
            p_min_columns      => 2,
            p_max_columns      => 50,
            p_component_name   => p_region.name
    );

    apex_json.open_array;

    for row_idx in 1 .. l_column_value_list(1).count
    loop
        apex_json.open_array;

        for column_idx in 1 .. l_column_value_list.count
        loop
            if p_region.region_columns(column_idx).escape_output
            then
                apex_json.write(apex_escape.html(l_column_value_list(column_idx)(row_idx)));
            else
                apex_json.write(l_column_value_list(column_idx)(row_idx));
            end if;
        end loop;

        apex_json.close_array;
    end loop;

    apex_json.close_array;

    return l_ajax_result;
end ajax_apex_jqgrid;
```

447

You check the escape_output property of each column, and if it's true, you use apex_escape.html to escape the HTML output. The default value for this attribute will be true, which is part of the "secure by default" approach that APEX provides. If developers want to allow HTML markup through for some reason, then they'll have to manually set that attribute to No.

Now you should be able to run the page, and if there's any HTML markup in the grid data, it should be escaped automatically. If the escaping doesn't work for you, delete the region and re-create it now that the new attribute has been added. This bug will be fixed in a future version of APEX, and it will not affect users of the plugin.

Next you'll leverage the is_displayed property of the columns to prevent them from showing when they shouldn't. To do this correctly, you'll need to update both the render and AJAX functions in the PL/SQL. One last time, navigate to the Create/Edit page of the plugin and complete the following steps:

1. Update the PL/SQL Source with the code from Listing 10-17. Don't forget to update your plsql_code.sql file too.

2. Click Apply Changes.

Listing 10-17. render_apex_jqgrid and ajax_apex_jqgrid Functions Updated to Support is_displayed

```
function render_apex_jqgrid (
    p_region              in apex_plugin.t_region,
    p_plugin              in apex_plugin.t_plugin,
    p_is_printer_friendly in boolean
)

    return apex_plugin.t_region_render_result

is

    l_render_result apex_plugin.t_region_render_result;
    l_onload_code   varchar2(4000);
    l_crlf          char(2) := chr(13)||chr(10);
    l_col_idx       pls_integer := 0;

begin

    if apex_application.g_debug
    then
        apex_plugin_util.debug_region (
            p_plugin => p_plugin,
            p_region => p_region
        );
    end if;

    sys.htp.p('<table id="' || p_region.static_id || '_APEX_JQ_GRID"></table>');
    sys.htp.p('<div id="' || p_region.static_id || '_APEX_JQ_GRID_PAGER"></div>');

    l_onload_code := 'apex.jQuery("#' || p_region.static_id || '").apex_jqgrid({' || l_crlf ||
        '   ' || apex_javascript.add_attribute('ajaxIdentifier',
        apex_plugin.get_ajax_identifier(), false, true) || l_crlf ||
        '   columns: [' || l_crlf;
```

```
   for x in 1 .. p_region.region_columns.count
   loop
      if p_region.region_columns(x).is_displayed
      then
         l_col_idx := l_col_idx + 1;

         if l_col_idx > 1
         then
            l_onload_code := l_onload_code || ',' || l_crlf;
         end if;

         l_onload_code := l_onload_code ||
            '        {' || l_crlf ||
            '            ' || apex_javascript.add_attribute('heading', p_region.region_
            columns(l_col_idx).heading, false, true) || l_crlf ||
            '            ' || apex_javascript.add_attribute('frozen', p_region.region_
            columns(l_col_idx).attribute_01, false, false) || l_crlf ||
            '        }';
      end if;
   end loop;

   l_onload_code := l_onload_code || l_crlf ||
      '    ]' || l_crlf ||
      '});';

   apex_javascript.add_onload_code (
      p_code => l_onload_code
   );

   return l_render_result;

end render_apex_jqgrid;

function ajax_apex_jqgrid (
   p_region in apex_plugin.t_region,
   p_plugin in apex_plugin.t_plugin
)
   return apex_plugin.t_region_ajax_result

is

   l_ajax_result         apex_plugin.t_region_ajax_result;
   l_column_value_list apex_plugin_util.t_column_value_list;

begin
```

```
    l_column_value_list :=
      apex_plugin_util.get_data(
          p_sql_statement      => p_region.source,
          p_min_columns        => 2,
          p_max_columns        => 50,
          p_component_name     => p_region.name
    );

    apex_json.open_array;

    for row_idx in 1 .. l_column_value_list(1).count
    loop
      apex_json.open_array;

      for column_idx in 1 .. l_column_value_list.count
      loop
        if p_region.region_columns(column_idx).is_displayed
        then
          if p_region.region_columns(column_idx).escape_output
          then
            apex_json.write(apex_escape.html(l_column_value_list(column_idx)(row_idx)));
          else
            apex_json.write(l_column_value_list(column_idx)(row_idx));
          end if;
        end if;
      end loop;

      apex_json.close_array;
    end loop;

    apex_json.close_array;

    return l_ajax_result;

end ajax_apex_jqgrid;
```

As you can see, both functions are now referencing the is_displayed property of the columns to conditionally display them. It may have been tempting to just update the render function because that could have prevented the column data from having been displayed in the grid. However, to be truly secure, the data that should never be transferred to the client. That's why the ajax_apex_jqgrid function was updated too.

That's it; you've created a region plugin! Ideally this tutorial has demonstrated the iterative approach that one typically uses when building a plugin. At this point, you could export your plugin and share it with the world.

I recommend adding the plugin export file to the top level of your plugin files (in apex-jqgrid-plugin). Then you can zip up the entire directory structure and put it somewhere others can find it. If possible, put your source code on GitHub. Ideally others will not only use your hard work but help you make it better as well!

Best Practices for Developing Plugins

The best practices covered in this section have been compiled from a variety of sources. Some are evangelized by the same people who wrote the APEX plugin framework—they know their stuff. Others are based on well-established "best practices" from related technologies such as the Oracle Database and web development. I've even added a few practices I've learned while developing and maintaining several successful plugins over the past few years. While intended to help, "best practices" may not always be the best solution for every situation, so always test!

These are some best practices for plugins in general:

- Follow APEX standards when possible. Over the years the APEX team has implemented a number of standards used for native components. For example, items that render multiple elements on the page follow a standard naming convention. Learning about and adopting these standards in your own plugins will help maintain a level of constancy in APEX and help to ensure that your plugins work correctly.

- Choose the Name value wisely. Choosing a "good" name for your plugin is important. Your plugin should be easily distinguishable from others. Some plugin developers have adopted the practice of including their company name to help ensure uniqueness (and add a shameless plug, of course).

- Choose the Internal Name setting wisely. The Internal Name setting is used to determine whether a new plugin is being installed or an existing plugin is being replaced. For this reason, uniqueness of the Internal Name setting is even more important than the Name setting. A good convention that helps to ensure uniqueness is to base the Internal Name setting on your company name/URL, as is often done in Java class naming. An example would be `COM_CORP_CALENDAR`. Also, if you make changes to a plugin that are not compatible with previous versions, changing the Internal Name setting will allow plugin users to "migrate" to the new plugin without breaking existing instances. Consider appending a letter to the end of the Internal Name setting that is incremented each time there is a compatibility issue with the new release, as in `COM_CORP_CALENDAR_B`.

- Document, document, document. Having developed your own plugin, everything about it will be second nature to you. But it will not be as intuitive to others. The only solution is good documentation. Documentation should not be considered optional if you want heavy adoption. If you're more comfortable writing code than documentation, reach out to someone for help. Consider adding help in the following areas: the Help section of the plugin, the Help section of custom attributes, and a complete help file bundled with the plugin (TXT, RTF, HTML, and PDF all work well).

These are some best practices for JavaScript and CSS:

- Use the APEX JavaScript APIs when appropriate. Because jQuery is now included with APEX, it may be tempting to use the `val()` function to set the value of an element on the page. However, the `$v` and `$s` functions, part of the JavaScript APIs included with APEX, were created to work with APEX items specifically so they handle things like LOVs correctly. Newer, properly namespaced APIs are available as well. For example, `apex.item('PX_ITEM').getValue()` can be used in place of `$v('PX_ITEM')`. It's a bit more verbose, but by using only the functions in the APEX namespace, you can prevent issues that could result from collisions with other JavaScript libraries.

- Trigger events when appropriate. A number of events were introduced with APEX 4.0, such as apexbeforerefresh and apexafterrefresh. Ensuring that your plugins trigger these events when they apply allows plugin users to create dynamic actions on top of them. Also, depending on the plugin, you may want to consider triggering custom events and registering them with the plugin so that they are available via dynamic actions.

- Compress your JavaScript and CSS code. The JavaScript and CSS code used in your plugins will add to the overall page weight in APEX. To minimize the impact on performance, make sure to compress the code before deploying the plugin. There are many open source libraries available for compressing JavaScript and CSS; many are made to work with task runners such as Grunt or Gulp, which can help automate the process. Make sure to keep the original files safe for future development because compressed files are not very usable.

- Use files accessible via the file system of the web server. The APEX plugin framework makes it easy to "bundle" files with plugins by uploading them directly as part of the plugin. This is convenient for both installation and deployments because the files go with the plugin. However, the files are stored in the database, which adds a little overhead when the browsers go to retrieve them. Using files on the file system avoids this overhead but requires additional installation and deployment steps. Try to design your plugins in such a way that plugin files are bundled by default, but switching to file system files requires little effort.

- Protect references to the $ object for jQuery. Now that jQuery and jQuery UI are included with APEX, you may want to take advantage of them in your plugins. Many people who already use jQuery are familiar with referring to the jQuery object as $. While convenient, this practice can cause problems if another JavaScript library is using the $ as well. See the "jQuery UI Widget Factory" section for a working example of how to protect references to the $ object.

- Use debug/logging code in your code. Debug code is code that is added to code to provide insight into how the code is (or is not) working. Debug code can be useful to plugin developers as well as plugin users. For JavaScript code, APEX now includes the apex.debug namespace, which has different methods for logging based on log levels such as trace, warn, and error.

For PL/SQL, use these best practices:

- Use compiled code when appropriate. When the source code of a plugin is embedded in its PL/SQL code attribute, it is treated as an anonymous block and must all be compiled each time any one of the callback functions is executed. Using compiled code—code that has been placed in a PL/SQL package, for example—can avoid this overhead. This is especially important for plugins that use a lot of PL/SQL. However, plugin developers must keep in mind that this technique requires additional installation steps for plugin users. Try to design your plugins in such a way that plugin users can conveniently start using the plugin but can easily move to more performant code if needed.

- Escape user input when appropriate. Plugins will often display data that is maintained by end users. If the data is not properly escaped, the plugin could introduce cross-site scripting (XSS) vulnerabilities in an application. Using APEX_ESCAPE.HTML to escape special characters whenever working with user-maintained data is the best way to protect against XSS. However, because this may not always be the desired functionality, you may want to make it optional. See the "Creating a Region Tutorial" section for a working example of using APEX_ESCAPE.

- Use debug/logging code. Debug code can be useful to plugin developers as well as plugin users when it comes to hunting down and fixing bugs. See the "Creating a Region Tutorial" section for a working example of using `APEX_PLUGIN_UTIL` to output some basic debug information when the application was running in debug mode. Consider using the `APEX_DEBUG` package to add additional debug information in your plugins where appropriate.

- Use named notation as much as possible. In PL/SQL, parameters can be passed using positional notation, named notation, or a combination of both. While it may not make sense to always use named notation, using it as much as possible will help to self-document your code and possibly prevent repeated readings of the API documentation.

Summary

In the first part of this chapter, you learned about the various parts of the plugin architecture in APEX as well as some other tools that can help with plugin development, such as the jQuery UI Widget Factory. In the second part of the chapter, you put what you learned in the first part to use as you built a jqGrid region plugin. Many techniques, from creating custom attributes to fetching data via AJAX, were touched on along the way. Finally, some "best practices" were covered to help you create high-quality plugins. At this point, you should be armed with enough knowledge to begin development on your own plugins.

■ ■ ■

jQuery with APEX

by Tom Petrus

What is jQuery, and what does it mean for you in APEX? Basically, jQuery is a JavaScript library that was made with cross-browser compatibility in mind. It is meant to enhance the life of web developers who use JavaScript by making them able to actually develop more instead of spending time on implementing all sorts of hacks and tricks to make said developments work. This is especially true for several Internet Explorer (IE) iterations; specifically, IE 6, IE 7, and IE 8 are all dreadful in this regard because those versions especially often did not adhere to web standards, made own implementations, or just did something special like compatibility view.

jQuery makes an effort to implement various fixes and workarounds when problematic implementations are present in a browser (or its implementation). But more so than providing cross-browser safety, it is just as much a tool of convenience and improves the quality of life of web developers seeking to enhance their JavaScript tool set. Selecting elements, for example, has been made easy, manipulations of the DOM are done just as quick, and it has a solid AJAX interface.

The importance of jQuery in APEX has been increasing ever since it was bundled with APEX. It is not always visible, but many libraries, functions, and widgets have been making the move to jQuery implementations as APEX has progressed. Interactive reports are one example. In releases prior to 5, you were limited to one report, but now you can have multiple reports on one page. With that change came a shift in the JavaScript code used for interactive reports because the JavaScript code until then was targeted at only one interactive report, and it is now a jQuery UI widget. This goes to show that jQuery has been here for a while, and it is set to be with us for quite a while longer.

This chapter will take you through some of the basics of what jQuery is and how to employ it. While some of the coverage is general, many examples are seated in the Application Express atmosphere, selecting elements and performing manipulations on them. You'll see how to traverse the DOM starting from an element and how to deal with assigning and listening to events. Finally, you'll learn how AJAX calls are performed through jQuery and how this can be employed through APEX's API.

JavaScript and jQuery

There can be no chapter on jQuery without acknowledging JavaScript. After all, jQuery is a JavaScript library, and thus it remains important to have at least some basic knowledge of JavaScript. Having said that, this will not be an introductory course on JavaScript. But if you are serious about gaining some jQuery skills and want to interact more and more with your pages through JavaScript or jQuery, it is a good idea to learn about everything JavaScript offers.

Basic JavaScript knowledge encompasses things such as the following:

- The data types

- Equality and type coercion (== and ===)

- Scopes (functions)

- Closures

- Prototypes

Enhancing your proficiency with JavaScript will automatically enhance your jQuery proficiency because ultimately they're one and the same.

Basics of jQuery

This section will cover some of the more basic functionality of jQuery, including what it is and how it can be employed. You'll learn how to select elements and how to manipulate their attributes and properties.

The jQuery Object

To use jQuery in APEX, you do not need to do anything special. There is no additional JavaScript file you need to load somewhere. Since jQuery is so much at the core of APEX, this library is always present and thus allows you to use jQuery right from the start. Plainly put, jQuery exists on the page as two objects: the variables $ and jQuery. The $ variable is just a convenience shorthand reference to jQuery, which is a function that will return something when passed something such as a selector (though it is important to mention that selectors are not the only thing it can do something with).

Selecting Elements

Learning the basis of working with jQuery starts with selecting elements on the page to interact with. In short, jQuery utilizes CSS selectors and has extended that functionality with some of its own (pseudo) selectors. Selectors are passed in as the first argument in the jQuery function. Listing 11-1 shows a couple of selectors, and if you've written or seen CSS classes before, you'll be quickly familiar with how jQuery selects.

Listing 11-1. CSS Selectors

```
#P6_ENAME
.myClass
#emp-report td[headers=ENAME]
```

If these selectors are alien to you, I'll explain some of the more common ones here.

Selecting by ID

First is the ID selector #, which is used to target an element on the page through its id property. IDs are expected to be unique throughout a page, and thus an ID selector (usually) means you will expect a single item. In APEX, each page item you define will have its id attribute set with the item's name. Listing 11-2 shows a condensed version of the P6_ENAME page item's generated HTML. Knowing the name and the selector syntax results in the selector #P6_ENAME.

Listing 11-2. A Simple Input Element with an ID

```
<input type="text" id="P6_ENAME" value="Tom" />
```

Compare this easy-to-use selector for jQuery's method of selecting an element through an ID with the usual way of doing so in standard JavaScript with the DOM API, shown here:

```
document.getElementById("P6_ENAME")
```

Selecting by Class

The second selector you will encounter a lot is the class selector `.` (a dot, yes). The class selector will search elements through the class assigned to them. Elements can have no, one, or more classes assigned to them, and thus a class selector usually means you expect to select a collection of elements. Listing 11-3 has two input elements in it that have different IDs, and each has two classes assigned. But they both share a class, myClass.

Listing 11-3. Input Elements with Classes Assigned

```
<input type="text" id="P6_ENAME" class="myClass anotherClass" value="Tom" />
<input type="text" id="P6_EMPNO" class="myClass simpleClass" value="8456" />
```

Both elements can be selected simply by using this class name and the class selector, with a resulting selector of .myClass.

Another example is where you assign a class to a column link so you can intercept it for a dynamic action

Selecting by Attribute

Another important selector is the attribute selector [ ], by which you can select elements through a specific attribute and even a value. This selector is often used in APEX to select a collection of elements in classic reports or tabular forms since APEX assigns the header attribute with the column's alias from the query to each element. Listing 11-4 shows a simplified version of this structure generated in classic reports and tabular forms.

Listing 11-4. HTML Table Cells with an Attribute

```
<table>
<tr>
<td headers="ENAME">Tom</td><td headers="DEPT">Development</td>
<td headers="ENAME">Denes</td><td headers="DEPT">Development</td>
</tr>
</table>
```

The reason for applying this headers attribute to cells is that while selecting rows in tables is rather trivial, there are no methods to select columns. For example, say you have a classic report based on table EMP, which has among its columns the column ENAME. Selecting all the elements for this column would be achieved by using [headers="ENAME"] as a selector. Note that quotes are not necessary as long as the value is a valid identifier. It is also important to remember that selectors are also wrapped in quotes, and thus quotes will have to be stacked or escaped correctly when using them.

Hierarchy

Sometimes it is necessary to define a certain path to reach a certain selection. For example, an APEX page is defined with two regions on it, and each region contains two page items, which all have a same class assigned. Selecting the page items in the second region by only using the class selector requires the ability to narrow down the selection's path. And this can be achieved (and again, I'd like to iterate that this is the same as for defining CSS classes!) by specifying additional selectors in the same string. Listing 11-5 shows a simplified example of two regions with two input elements each. Both div elements have a different ID, and both are part of the body element. The input elements all have the class myClass assigned to them.

Listing 11-5. Input Elements with the Same Class over Multiple Regions

```
<body>
  <div id="region1">
    <input type="text" id="PAGE_ITEM_1" class="myClass" />
    <input type="text" id="PAGE_ITEM_2" class="myClass" />
  </div>
  <div id="region2">
    <input type="text" id="PAGE_ITEM_3" class="myClass" />
    <input type="text" id="PAGE_ITEM_4" class="myClass" />
  </div>
</body>
```

Selectors go from left to right, and this compares to narrowing down the search in the DOM from wide to narrow. It is easy to get all the input elements by simply using the node name as a selector $("input"), or in this specific example they can also be retrieved by using their assigned class $(".myClass"). It's important to note that if, for example, the div elements also had the myClass class, it would be possible to combine the previous statements to only target input elements with the assigned class $("input.myClass"). This is specifying on one level of selection but wouldn't solve targeting only the items in the second region.

And thus a path has to be made. This can be done by selecting the correct region first and then provide further selectors, and this can be read as first selecting one element and then within that element's context look for the existence of elements with further selectors. Selecting the second region is easy enough since the ID is plain to see: $("#region2") would return that div element. To get to the input elements within that element, I add a further selector, $("#region2 input.myClass"), and now only those two input elements would be retrieved. Note the space between both selectors and how there is no space between input and .myClass.

This sort of selection is especially handy to target elements in different regions or reports.

■ **Note**   Selectors as an argument to the jQuery function are to be passed as a string. This means you will have to put the selector in quotes as you pass it along!

DOM Nodes and jQuery Objects

When working with jQuery and making selections and alterations, you're actually manipulating the Document Object Model (DOM). This model is an API to interact with the page in the browser and has been built to resemble the page's HTML structure.

The DOM API is what you use when you, for example, use `document.getElementById`. This will return a DOM node, such as the input element with the ID P6_ENAME. This node can then be further altered by the functionality provided by the DOM API on this particular type of node. However, some problems start to arise when different browsers have different implementations or levels of support for certain features. For example, the property `.innerHTML` on nodes may not work properly across browsers.

This is where jQuery alleviates some of these more problematic implementations. When selecting elements through jQuery, there is of course also a DOM node, but it is held in a jQuery object. You can still easily access that DOM node and manipulate it with the API provided in the DOM, though that is not really the point because you really want to use the functionality jQuery layers over that direct access.

Too often selections between DOM nodes and jQuery objects are mixed up or not used with enough thought. It might be fine to use the DOM API without fear, but this really does require you to know what browsers you have to support and whether they support it correctly. As a rule of thumb, I simply always use jQuery to do what I want simply out of convenience and uniformity. It is up to you as a developer to have a critic's eye on this when you write or copy JavaScript code from anywhere!

Determining and Testing Selectors

Now that some basics have been established, it is time to look at how to employ this knowledge. To do this, you'll use the browser's developer tools. Personally, I strongly prefer using Chrome's or Firefox with the Firebug plugin over IE's tools. The developer tools offer a view on the document's elements, all loaded sources, network traffic, a console command interface, and others. By using these tools to inspect elements and what they are made up of and running commands from the console, you can determine and test all your code before having to save it somewhere in an APEX page or other location. This is a huge boon to developers, and you should check your selectors and code before placing that code into a component. Oftentimes I too need to fine-tune my selections or double-check selectors I've set up.

The developer tools can usually be opened in a Windows-based browser by pressing the F12 key, but are also accessible by going through the options menus. Figure 11-1 shows the developer tools opened in Chrome, with the elements panel opened. The page is a form page on the EMP table.

Figure 11-1. *Chrome's developer tools opened with the elements panel active*

Usually at the top of the elements panel you can find a magnifying-glass icon. This icon will allow you inspect the elements on the page itself. Clicking it will activate it, and you can see element specifics as you hover over them on the page, while the selection will be highlighted in the elements panel once the element has actually been clicked. Figure 11-2 shows what happens in the elements panel once element P7_ENAME has been selected because it will open the structure to that element.

```
▼<div class="row">
    ::before
  ▼<div class="col col-12 ">
    ▼<div class="t-Form-fieldContainer rel-col  " id="P7_ENAME_CONTAINER">
      ▶<div class="t-Form-labelContainer col col-3">…</div>
      ▼<div class="t-Form-inputContainer col col-9">
          <input type="hidden" name="p_arg_names" value="5405207687912020531">
          <input type="text" id="P7_ENAME" name="p_t02" class="text_field" value size="32" maxlength="10">
        </div>
      </div>
    </div>
    ::after
  </div>
```

Figure 11-2. *P7_ENAME selected in the elements panel*

Selecting elements on the page and navigating through the elements panel is a great help when needing to determine selectors. While usually it is logical to determine a specific item's name because it has also been defined in the Page Designer, it becomes a bit harder when selecting generic regions or collections of items.

So now I've determined the selector for item P7_ENAME, namely, #P7_ENAME, and I can test this selector by using jQuery in the developer tools' console window. In this console window JavaScript can be run on the current page, which is extremely helpful and powerful. Since jQuery is also present on the page, it is possible to use jQuery statements here as well. Again, you don't need any special initialization for using jQuery on your pages!

In Figure 11-3, the console panel has been opened, and I've entered and run my JavaScript statement. The console shows the output too: the return value of the code that has been run. jQuery returns the elements it has retrieved from the selector you gave as an argument.

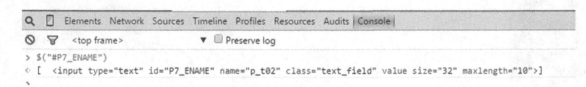

Figure 11-3. *The console window opened with the selector executed in jQuery*

Only one element was selected, and that is the input element you needed. So, now you have verified your selector and see that it works.

Basic Manipulations

Now that you understand selectors and how to execute them, it is time to explore what you can do with this selection. I mentioned before that jQuery's power lays in cross-browser implementations and how it is better to use it over that of the DOM's API, and here you'll see some examples.

The most basic form of accessing attributes is, as you will usually see, through the DOM API. This can be the value, an onclick attribute, a class, a custom property, and so on. Most actions can be performed on the nodes themselves, but once again, it is important to note how some of those API implementation may differ between browsers. In modern browsers, the value property (mostly) works as you'd expect, but there may be slight differences, and in older browsers it may simply not do exactly what you'd expect.

Elements can have a whole realm of possible attributes, and some attributes are really just that, attributes, while others can be more special. An example is the class attribute, which actually holds a list of classes, or the style attribute, which defines inline CSS rules. Not each attribute is accessed in the same way, nor do they all have a similar meaning. This is reflected in jQuery, where different functions to access these various attributes are used.

```
<input type="text" id="P6_ENAME" class="myClass" value="Tom" />
```

value and text

Even though value is a property, it is different because of how it behaves. jQuery has a dedicated function for getting and setting the value of items: .val(). To retrieve the value of an item, just val() can be called: $("#P6_ENAME").val(). To set the value, an argument can be passed to this function: $("#P6_ENAME").val("Not Tom"). You should always use .val() to do this and not use the DOM's .value API call. Even better would be to use APEX's apex_item API, but I'll cover more about that later.

Note that this function is used for input elements. Select lists are a different kind of element, and retrieving the value from a select list is completely different, and the same holds true for radio buttons. Also, be aware that APEX will generate HTML differently for check boxes in that it will not simply create an input element with the provided item name. This is why it is always important to double-check the HTML that has been generated so that you know what you need to select.

Don't try to use .val on elements such as span or div. It has no use since they have no actual value. Sure, you see text in them, but that does not mean they have an actual value attribute. And this is a common mix-up when first starting out. When looking at the actual HTML of, for instance, a span element, it is easy to spot the difference with an input element: <span id="myText">This is text to be displayed!</span>. It should further be noted that this text is actually a child node of the span tag in the form of a text node, and even in the DOM API there is no direct access to the text from this element without descending the tree one step further. Thankfully, jQuery saves the day by providing the .text() function. This function once again allows you to get and set the text of a node: $("#myText").text("This text has been altered").

Attributes

Attributes are generally all the actual attributes you can see on an element and always consist of a key and a value. For example, Listing 11-6 shows a really basic input element with just two attributes, id and value, put in a table cell with an attribute of headers. That is the representation in HTML, however, and in that plain form all the attributes are plain attributes. In the DOM, however, many attributes behave differently from just being plain getters and setters.

Listing 11-6. An input Element in a Table Cell with Some Basic Attributes

```
<td headers="SELECTION"><input id="P6_CHECKBOX_0" value="Tom" /></td>
```

In jQuery you can access all attributes on an element by using the `.attr()` function, providing the attribute's name as an argument to the function. This is in contrast with directly accessing the node's attributes through the DOM API. To retrieve the value of the headers attribute in Listing 11-6 or the value of id on the input element, `attr` can be used just like this:

```
$("td").attr("headers")
$("input").attr("id")
```

Boolean Properties

Some attributes on elements behave as properties in that they indicate a binary state. This is something that follows the HTML specification but has seen problematic implementation cross-browser for a long time. Some examples of these properties are as follows:

- `readonly`: Indicating whether the element should not be editable but still post its value when the form is submitted

- `disabled`: Indicating whether the element should not be editable and not post its value when the form is submitted

- `checked`: Indicating the state of the check box on a check box input item

Often you'll see these attributes added on elements in a manner that actually doesn't conform with the HTML specification. For example, the simple presence of the `readonly` attribute is enough to indicate that the input element is in a readonly state. It doesn't need further specifications such as is often seen.

- `readonly="readonly"`

- `readonly="true"`

These states exist because of how different browser used to react to these properties. Nowadays these problems don't exist as much anymore, but they still linger on a bit. In jQuery these properties can easily be checked by using the `.prop()` function, which will return a `true` or `false` value.

Listing 11-7 shows an example of using the prop function. An element is selected, and then the readonly property is tested.

Listing 11-7. Testing the prop Function

```
if ( $("#P6_ENAME").prop("readonly") ) {
  alert("Ename is readonly!");
} else {
  Alert("Ename is not readonly. You can simply edit it.");
};
```

To actually set a Boolean property on an element, `prop` has to be used with two arguments: the name of the property and a Boolean value. The correct syntax will be put on the element.

prop doesn't see much use overall. Plenty of people are still using `.attr()` to get and set the values of these properties, much in the way described earlier. But prop can be much more interesting when writing code since it will return a Boolean value, possibly reducing your code by not having to double-check the value of the attribute. For example, constructs like this end up being used: if (`$("#P6_ENAME").attr("readonly") === "readonly"`). Compare this with the ease of use of prop, and it should be easy to spot the difference. But be consistent in your use! Don't use prop one time and readonly another time. Take care when adding HTML in the various places you can in APEX. You may very well have used readonly="false" somewhere, and even though that is wrong, browsers are forgiving. This will mess with prop, however, because the simple existence of the readonly attribute counts as true.

Classes

Classes on elements are again a different type of property. A more apt naming for this attribute is classlist because this attribute holds a list of currently assigned classes to the element. It could be one, and it could be more. Using classes has multiple uses: they are used to assign style rules on them through CSS classes, and in JavaScript they are used to make selection easy, group elements, and track certain changes.

A common example of using a class to group a set of elements to make their selection easier is assigning a class to the column link of a report. Doing so will make all the generated links easily identifiable from JavaScript to assign, for example, a dynamic action to them.

The other common use in JavaScript is to toggle classes on elements to reflect a certain change done on them. A class could be assigned to items affected by a piece of code, which in turn makes identifying these changed items easy because they can easily be selected again.

And because classes behave more like an array of assigned classes than just a singular value, it has been reflected in jQuery as such. Adding, removing, or toggling a class has been made easy.

- addClass: Adds a class (or classes!) to an element and will not generate a duplicate entry. Here's an example: $("#P6_ENAME").addClass("trackingClass").

- removeClass: Removes the specified class(es) from the elements. Here's an example: $("#P6_ENAME").addClass("trackingClass").

- toggleClass: Adds or removes a class as necessary. For example, $("#P6_ENAME").toggleClass("trackingClass") will add trackingClass when it isn't present or remove it when it is.

Iterating Over a Selection of Elements

Oftentimes a selector will not target just one element on the page but rather a collection of them. This is especially the case when working with broader selections such as classes or node types. And often enough these elements have to be dealt with in an individual manner instead of with one sweeping all-altering statement. jQuery has several ways to deal with this, such as filtering a selection further down or allowing you to iterate over each element selected.

An iteration can be achieved by using the .each() function, which will execute a JavaScript function for each element in the selection and provide the current element in the set as the context.

In Listing 11-8, an HTML snippet holds a table with two rows. Both rows have two cells; one holds the ENAME, and the other holds the SAL value of an employee (employee name and salary, respectively). It is a condensed example of a tabular form. To target and manipulate the elements containing the salary, you'll employ the techniques shown so far and combine it in each statement.

Listing 11-8. A Simple Tabular Form HTML Representation

```
<table id="emp-tabular">
<tr><td headers="ENAME">King</td><td headers="SAL"><input type="text" name="f02"
value="5000" /></td></tr>
<tr><td headers="ENAME">>Tom</td><td headers="SAL"><input type="text" name="f02"
value="3500" /></td></tr>
</table>
```

Keep in mind this is a simplified example, and it is perfectly possible just to select input elements. In practice, you will quickly see this dashed; on an APEX page, there are plenty and plenty of input elements! So, the goal here is to show a selector that makes sense.

■ **Tip** If you'd like to follow the example selectors and code throughout, creating an APEX page with a tabular form on the EMP table will work absolutely fine! Provide a static ID to the region with the ID emp-tabular. The ENAME column is a display-only column.

To get those input elements, one way would be to go through the cells since they have a headers attribute. $("td[headers=SAL]") would achieve targeting the cells, while with the addition of the input selector, the input elements in those cells can be targeted with $("td[headers=SAL] input"). Running this statement will return an array with two elements, namely, those two input elements.

The code in Listing 11-9 will select those elements and apply the each function on this selection. The statement will print out the value of each element as it processes them. The each function takes a function as an argument, and thus an anonymous function is passed in. This function is then executed for each element, and jQuery will set the value of the context, the this object, to the DOM element of the current element in the each loop. This allows easy access to that node and thus allows an easy way to fetch the value each time.

The console.log function is a function that will print out lines to the developer tools' console window and thus allows for easy debugging. This is once again a great way to test and prototype code.

Listing 11-9. The Finished each Statement

```
$("td[headers=SAL] input").each(function(){
  console.log( $(this).val() );
});
```

■ **Tip** Take note that the this object is the DOM object and not a jQuery element. To leverage jQuery's value-accessing function, you need to create a jQuery object of this DOM element.

Advanced Uses of jQuery

This section will go a little deeper into some jQuery functionality than simply selecting elements and making basic manipulations. Most important, you will learn how to deal with events in various ways and how to travel up and down the DOM starting from a selection. You can then use chaining to make your code more concise, and finally you will see how to employ the power of AJAX calls.

Handling Events

Another common practice made easy with jQuery is attaching event handlers on elements. Examples of events are mouse clicks, cursor events such as entering and exiting an element, key presses, browser events such as a window resize, or even custom events. Handlers are attached to elements, and when the event triggers, the handler (or handlers) is resolved. This "metadata" way of handling events through events and listeners has been good practice for a while now. However, still a lot of code can be found that incorporates assigning handlers directly to the DOM nodes' attributes or in HTML.

Assigning Through Attributes

One such attribute is the onclick attribute, which is commonly found in forum posts or examples. I'm not a fan of it, and here is why: it's inconsistent, and it clashes with the event-handling system. Furthermore, adding this onclick attribute adds JavaScript code in what is supposed to be just HTML. It's usually good form to try to separate concerns: HTML represents the data, CSS applies style, and JavaScript applies dynamism. A reason frequently seen to use this attribute is for the sake of convenience or ease. It's tempting to provide this attribute in a property on an APEX item or a column link or adding it along in an apex_item call because it's easy to add some value to the function called. But nowadays this way is simply not regarded as being clean.

Assigning Through Convenience Functions

In jQuery, events are generally pretty easy to handle, especially basic ones such as a mouse click or acting on the change of an item's value. For instance, dealing with a change event is as easy as calling the change() function on a jQuery object.

```
$("#P7_SAL").change( function() {
  console.log( "My value has changed to " + $(this).val() );
} );
```

Calling the change() function requires one argument: a function to be used as a callback for the event. And once again, just like with each, the object this has been set to the element that triggered the event.

Just like the previous change event, there are many other convenience functions to quickly bind handlers to selections: click, focus, mouseover, and so on.

Assigning with on

The convenience functions are shorthand for commonly used handlers and actually call one of the core event-handling functions in jQuery. The two core functions are the .on() and .off() functions. Attaching the same change handler as done earlier with .change() can be done with on().

```
$("#P7_SAL").on("change", function() {
  console.log( "My value has changed to " + $(this).val() );
} );
```

Note that with this event handling, multiple handlers can be bound to the same element and to the same event. Running the previous two commands will simply double up the output in the console log.

Think back to the code in Listing 11-8 with the tabular form example. Selecting the input elements in it and applying an event handler to this selection will bind a handler to each element in that selection. In Listing 11-10, a change handler is assigned to each input element, and in the handler, the changed value is shown, as well as the current context. Note how an object can be passed to the console output, which is also shown in Figure 11-4. Providing an object as an argument to the console will make the console put out that object and allows inspecting its properties. If a DOM node is provided, it is even possible to see this element in the web page or jump to the elements panel, which is again a wonderful tool to help out with developing code.

Listing 11-10. Assign a Change Handler to All Input Elements

```
$("td[headers=SAL] input").on("change", function() {
  console.log( "Change event on: " );
  console.log( this );
  console.log( "My value has changed to " + $(this).val() );
} );
```

```
Q  🗋  Elements  Network  Sources  Timeline  Profiles  Resources  Audits | Console |
Ⓞ  ▽  <top frame>  ▼ ☐ Preserve log
  Change event on:
    <input type="text" name="f04" size="16" maxlength="2000" value="12" class="u-TF-item u-TF-item--text " id="f04_0001" autocomplete="off">
  My value has changed to 548
  >
```

Figure 11-4. *Console output for an object*

■ **Note**   When putting out an object in the console, take care not to concatenate it with text. This will implicitly call the `toString()` function of said object, resulting in an output you can't do anything with.

Dealing with Events on Dynamic Elements

There is a caveat, though. Assigning handlers through the shorthand or in the way shown earlier will create *static* handlers. These handlers are attached to the elements that were in the selection at the time of assignment. If elements that match the selector at a later point in time are added to the page (actually, the DOM), it is normal that no handler is assigned automatically (that's why it's called *static*). An example is the change event on elements in a tabular form, where the tabular form has pagination. When pagination occurs, the current elements are discarded from the DOM, and a new set is entered. Thus, new elements are added to the DOM; these are elements that were not there when the event handlers were first assigned. Another example is the column link on an interactive report with a class defined in its attributes. If a handler is assigned on those eligible elements on the initial page load, those handlers would be gone when the report refreshes or is paginated because those handler's elements are then removed from the DOM.

There is, of course, a way to have more *dynamic* handling of events. First, it is necessary to understand just a bit more of exactly how an event behaves. Events happen all the time; they don't just occur when a handler has been bound. They're also not stuck in the location they are fired from. Events will travel from the element they are fired from all the way to the top of the DOM tree. This behavior is called *bubbling* or *propagation.*

Thinking back once again to the tabular form example code and the change handler assigned on its input elements, this means that if a change handler is also assigned to the enclosing table, the output in the console will reflect this.

```
$("#emp-tabular, td[headers=SAL] input").on("change", function() {
  console.log( "Change event on: " );
  console.log( this );
} );
```

When changing an input element of the salary inputs, four lines of output will be produced. The two objects logged will be the element the change has taken place on and the table. This is to illustrate how the event has actually traveled up the tree and how it doesn't simply stop at the element it fired on!

■ **Tip** I've combined two selectors previously to expand the selection made by using a comma. Selectors separated by commas will simply expand the selection and not influence each other.

Now consider how once again static handlers have been assigned. But this time, if the tabular form were to be paginated and new input elements were added, the handler on the table would still be there, and it would still be triggered when one of the new input elements is changed (not just salary!) because the event bubbles up.

This event propagation can thus be used to account for changes in the DOM after a handler has been bound to a certain element. Certainly, a handler will have to be static at some element in the DOM to be able to intercept an event, but it is not limited to just those target elements.

Here is where the on() function offers the required functionality. Not only does it allow binding to one static set of elements, it allows binding to an element to listen for an event specifically fired on a set of children matching a selector. For example, it is possible to bind the change handler on the table but listen only for change events on the input elements for cells in the salary column.

```
$("#emp-tabular").on("change", "td[headers=SAL] input", function(e){
  console.log(this);
});
```

The second argument to the on function is another selector here. In the handler, the current object is once again logged to the console. And now the change event will always be able to be handled even when the report is paginated.

Removing Handlers

Adding handlers is pretty easy, and so is removing them. But do note that only handlers that have been added by using .on() can be removed. Simply use .off() to remove a handler, but pay attention that the specifications have to match those used for adding it through on().

Stopping Events

Stopping events is not the same as removing handlers. In APEX there is a dynamic action that will cancel an event, and this stops the event from being handled. You'll often see the statement return false; in online resources about APEX.

The difference is subtle but important. When you know how events work and that they bubble up in the DOM, you have different ways to stop an event. It is possible to handle the event and stop the event from bubbling further up the DOM or to handle the event and even stop other handlers on the same event from firing. Interacting with the event in an event handler is not hard. In the handlers shown in the previous example, a function was always passed in as an argument. jQuery actually passes in arguments to this function so that they can be interacted with if required. The first argument is the event object, which is a jQuery object containing information and interaction on the current event. Taking the change handler that is assigned to both the table and the input elements again, it is possible to make this event stop from bubbling up after the change event handlers have been executed on the input element.

```
$("#emp-tabular, td[headers=SAL] input").on("change", function(event) {
  console.log( "Change event on: " );
  console.log( this );
  event.stopPropagation();
} );
```

So, even though a change handler is bound to the table, no change event will be allowed to bubble up from the salary input elements to any elements above it. And in this example, no change event will propagate further up from any element in the table above the table since this event is once again stopped from bubbling there.

Another thing of note are *default events*. For example, the anchor tags <a href="#> have a default click handler because when the element is clicked, the browser will redirect to the URL specified in the href attribute. So, usually in examples on APEX that involve setting up column links and attaching an event handler to these elements, be it through dynamic actions or through handlers in jQuery, this default event is not dealt with correctly. The dynamic action "Cancel event" is correct; returning false in code is not. Assigning onclick="return false;" to the link element is also incorrect!

The correct method to stop a default event from executing its default action is by using preventDefault.

```
$("a.myColumnLinkClass").click(function(){
  alert("you clicked this link!");
  event.preventDefault();
});
```

Reacting on the Page Load Event

There is one specific event I'd like to highlight, and that is the *page load event*. This event is triggered when the page has finished loading. All content and scripts have been loaded, parsed, and rendered. Oftentimes it is necessary to wait for all this to happen before executing a block of code. For example, selecting a range of elements may not return the full set of expected elements when run before the page has finished loading since more elements may still be added to the DOM afterward depending on where the code is being ran. Another example is a script not having been loaded yet. Nowadays the trend is to place scripts near the bottom of the page simply because this is a better user experience. The DOM will first load the data structure and render this and then get to the script tags, loading those. Certain libraries or scripts added may thus end up getting loaded later.

Much depends on using page templates and just exactly where you will want to add code. But overall the load event will be something you want to wait for. In APEX there are several ways already to do this. Using dynamic actions, there is the page load event, an action itself can be set to trigger on page load, and not least of all the "Execute on page load" section on a page. These are all good places to put code, if not the best.

It may be, however, that some dynamic code is required to interact with this event or required simply because code has been put in a JavaScript file. This load event has a specific handler in jQuery that can be used: the ready() function. This function will wait for the DOM to be ready before executing the code here. There is also a load function, but the differences are subtle. This ready() function is also the function used by APEX in the various places mentioned earlier.

The ready() function has to always be bound to the document element and takes a function as an argument.

```
$( document ).ready(function(){
  //here comes the code you wish to perform on page load
  console.log("Page is ready!");
})
```

APEX's Refresh

As an example for custom events, APEX has the perfect example. Whenever APEX refreshes an element, it will fire two events at specific times, for example when an interactive report is refreshed.

Right before the region is refreshed, an event apexbeforerefresh is triggered on the region, and when the refreshing has finished the event, apexafterrefresh is triggered. Binding to a region is easiest when providing the region with a static ID since this makes selecting it through jQuery easier. For example, with an interactive report region with a static ID set to myStaticRegionId, it is possible to bind to the afterrefresh event.

```
$("#myStaticRegionId").on("apexafterrefresh", function(){
  console.log("Report has finished refreshing!");
});
```

Traversing the DOM

The DOM can be seen as a big tree, with the document as the root and all other nodes under it. Selecting elements will then return matching nodes from this tree. But sometimes it is necessary to retrieve information from nodes that are children, siblings, or parents.

Note again how selecting elements with selectors is not hard at all. This is always top to bottom, from the root to a set of elements. It is even possible to select elements within a given context. This goes to show how it is relatively easy to narrow down a set from parent to children.

However, the same can't be done from bottom to top. Selectors don't do this. Fortunately, jQuery has many handy functions that allow traversing the tree structure of the DOM.

Going Up

Look back at the code in Listing 11-8 with its tabular form structure and the selector used to fetch the salary inputs. It's possible in that listing to retrieve the row element for each input element. There are several methods to do this, though usually the requirement would be to have as flexible code as possible to deal with markup. For instance, it is obvious from the snippet that the input element is nested in a td element, and this element in turn is nested in a tr element. For direct traversal upward, parent() could be used, and this will return the direct parent node of the selected elements. Thus, it could be argued that calling this function twice on the selected input elements will return the row element, and this would be correct. However, a simple template change could completely destroy this kind of code. Therefore, it is more interesting to use the closest() function. This function will traverse up the tree, starting at the origin element, until it found an element matching the selector provided as an argument. This is great because it allows a lookup otherwise not possible.

In Listing 11-11. each input element is retrieved, and for each element the parent row is retrieved and put out in the console. This combines several of the techniques already shown.

Listing 11-11. Printing Each Element's Parent Row

```
$("td[headers=SAL] input").each(function(){
  var myRow = $(this).closest("tr") ;
  console.log( myRow );
});
```

Going Down

It is also possible to easily descend a node's structure, which can be regarded as searching in a certain context. The function `find()` accepts a selector as an argument and will look for elements matching this selector within the context of the given jQuery object.

So, going further with the example from Listing 11-11, which finds the given parent node for the current element, it is possible to once again search for a certain node within the context of this given row. This opens up so many possibilities when working with reports or tabular forms in APEX! In Listing 11-12 the code from the previous listing has been expanded to not only retrieve the parent row but also find the cell with ENAME in it and print its text.

Listing 11-12. Finding the ENAME Cell in the Same Row

```
$("td[headers=SAL] input").each(function(){
  var myRow = $(this).closest("tr") ;
  var enameCell = myRow.find("td[headers=ENAME]");
  var ename = enameCell.text();
  console.log( "The salary $"+ $(this).val() + " belongs to " + ename );
});
```

Note how the word *context* has already been used in several places, especially with `find()`. So far, I've always used jQuery's invocation with one argument, a selector or a DOM node. It is, however, possible to provide a second argument, which when combined with a selector or DOM node will represent the *context* for the first argument. So, instead of using `find()` to get the matching nodes within myRow, it is the same as using myRow as the second argument in a call to jQuery with the selector as the first argument.

```
var enameCell = $("td[headers=ENAME]", myRow);
```

Keeping It Level

Traversing doesn't always mean traveling up or down the tree. It may mean finding elements on the same level as the current element. To this end, there is the `siblings()` function. This function also accepts a selector as an argument to filter the set of sibling nodes. So, instead of traveling up from the salary input element, it is possible to go up to the cell element and then filter that cell's siblings to find the ENAME cell.

```
$("td[headers=SAL] input").each(function(){
  var myCell = $(this).closest("td") ;
  var enameCell = myCell.siblings("td[headers=ENAME]");
  var ename = enameCell.text();
  console.log( "The salary $"+ $(this).val() + " belongs to " + ename );
});
```

Chaining Functions

With all functionality available on jQuery objects, it can be troublesome to always store the output in a variable and then do something with that output. As discussed earlier with traversing, a jQuery function is called three times, and the output is always stored. This isn't really necessary because jQuery allows chaining functions.

What this really means is that when a call is made to a jQuery function that returns a jQuery object, another function can immediately be called on that returned object; this is called *chaining*.

With this, it is possible to rewrite the code in Listing 11-12 instead of assigning to variables to chain the functions together.

```
$("td[headers=SAL] input").each(function(){
  var ename = $(this).closest("tr").find("td[headers=ENAME]").text();
  console.log( "The salary $"+ $(this).val() + " belongs to " + ename );
});
```

This can really help in keeping code concise and having to assign to variables all the time.

Chaining can go pretty far. The following snippet illustrates how chaining can be used and how the end() function can be used to return to the original selector:

```
$("#emp-tabular")
  .find("td[headers=ENAME] input")
  .each(function(){ console.log('Ename:' + $(this).val()); })
.end()
  .find("td[headers=SAL] input")
  .each(function(){ console.log('Sal:' + $(this).val()); })
.end()
```

This code will first select the element with the ID emp-tabular. The find() function is then used to find elements within that selection. Next, these elements are iterated over by using each(), and in which the value of the element is sent to the console output. Then end() is called, which will cause the next chained function to start again from the original selection, namely, the emp-tabular element. Again, a selection is made with find(), and each is used to loop and written to the console. A final end() call will cause the final returned element to be the emp-tabular element.

APEX JavaScript APIs

APEX has an own extensive set of JavaScript functions to deal with APEX-specific functionality on its pages. Over the years of APEX development and releases, much functionality has changed and been added. Most notable is the shift from working with DOM nodes to working with jQuery selectors and objects.

Overall, my advice is to use APEX functionality whenever possible. An example of this would be retrieving values in JavaScript from the different sorts of page items. The API apex.item() implements value retrieval from normal text items, select lists, check boxes, radio groups, and so on. Even though .val() has been explained here, .val() just does not hold the same value as apex.item.getValue() because the latter will work on any type of item. And similarly for setting values, apex.item.setValue() is a better option.

It is important to take note of the API documentation, though. Many functions of the API have the ability to take different sorts of input (similar to jQuery), though usually it is limited to a string, which may or may not be a selector or a DOM node. For example, apex.item() will take an ID for an item but not a selector. Creating an apex_item object for P7_ENAME will be in the form of apex.item("P7_ENAME") and *not* like apex.item("#P7_ENAME"). The reason here is likely to be that apex_item implicitly expects to target one and just one element and thus assumes the #.

AJAX Calls and AJAX Callback Processes

Another area jQuery has a strong implementation for is performing AJAX calls. The interface it provides is extensive and will safely work in all browsers. Furthermore, APEX has implemented an interface to call on-demand processes from JavaScript based on the jQuery AJAX suite, which means it's interesting to look at. The documentation for the APEX implementation also mentions this; there are some presets and extensions, but all settings can still be provided and overridden.

First, the important thing to understand is what the first *A* in AJAX stands for: asynchronous. What it comes down to in short is that a function is called but will not return an answer right away. This has a big benefit for users because the browser is not locked up while waiting for the function to return a result.

As an example, think of APEX's interactive report pagination. The next set of records will be fetched through an AJAX call and will then be added to the DOM, replacing the current set. A spinning icon will be shown throughout to indicate this process is occurring. Imagine this form of code:

```
function(){
  start_the_spinner;
  refresh_report;
  stop_the_spinner;
};
```

This is the most common mistake when first dealing with asynchronicity. It assumes that `refresh_report` is called and fully resolved before stopping the spinner. However, consider that `refresh_report` will actually initiate an AJAX call, asking the server for a reply (the new set of records), and when the server has returned these records, it replaces the nodes. If this happened synchronously and fetching the new rows took five seconds, the user would look at a locked-up screen, with a nonspinning spinner since the thread has no time to make it spin. But everything would occur "inline."

With AJAX calls, you can provide a function to a success handler, which will execute the function when the call has completed. Thus, `stop_the_spinner` should be put in a success handler of the call to `refresh_report`.

On to jQuery's AJAX implementation: if ever the need is there to get some data from an on-demand process, this can do it.

Setting Up an AJAX Callback Process

Listing 11-13 has some simple PL/SQL code to be used as an on-demand process. This code creates a new process named `MY_CALLBACK` on an APEX page under the AJAX Callback point.

Listing 11-13. An Example AJAX Callback Process

```
DECLARE
  lReturn VARCHAR2(1000);
BEGIN
  lReturn := 'Value of x01: ' || apex_application.g_x01 ||', value of x02: '|| apex_
application.g_x02;
  htp.p(lReturn);
END;
```

This is a simplistic piece of code. It will concatenate the value of two variables and then return that string. The X01 and X02 variables are variables usable in requests made in APEX. They go from 1 to 10, and there are also global arrays, F##.

Using jQuery to Call a Process

Listing 11-14 shows how to call this process from JavaScript using jQuery's ajax() function. Starting with the actual jQuery call, which is the last-to-previous line, jQuery's ajax() function takes one argument, which is an object with all settings for the AJAX request to be made. This object is the variable ajaxSettings, which contains these properties:

- url: wwv_flow.show is APEX's show page procedure.

- data: The data that needs to get sent in this request. This is another object and is configured before the ajaxSettings object.

- type: The type of request to make. There are, for example, also GET requests, but I want to use a POST request here because I don't want the server to cache the results of this call.

- dataType: This defines the data type of the callback's return.

- success: This is the handler that will be executed when the call has completed. The function's first argument is the return from the callback parsed according to the defined data type. In this code, the return is then logged to the console.

These settings are pretty usual and will cover most cases. The data type will usually differ, though, and usually this may be of the data type JSON because this is a common and universal data type used to exchange information and is natively accessible from JavaScript.

Passing data to a callback is done through the data property. This property is filled out through the ajaxData object.

- p_request: This defines what has to be called. Here the application process MY_CALLBACK is to be called; this is the callback process defined earlier.

- p_flow_id: This is the application ID. The value is retrievable from the page and is fetched through a shorthand for the apex.item().getValue() function.

- p_flow_step_id: This is the page ID and is retrieved similar to p_flow_id. This parameter is required when a process is to be called that is defined on the page concerned. If left out, an application process can be used.

- p_instance: This is the session ID and is retrieved similar to p_flow_id.

- x01, x02,...: These represent a series of singular value parameters usable in these kind of calls. They're great because this way no additional page items have to be created to use a callback process!

- f01, f02,...: These accept an array with values (not used in this example).

- p_arg_names, p_arg_values: There are two properties that accept an array of values. The former holds an array with page item names, while the latter holds an array with values for the specified items. Note that the matching of items with their values is done on position within the arrays. (This is not used in this example).

Listing 11-14. Calling an AJAX Callback Process with jQuery

```
(function(){
var ajaxData = {"p_request"      : "APPLICATION_PROCESS=MY_CALLBACK",
                "p_flow_id"      : $v('pFlowId'),
                "p_flow_step_id" : $v('pFlowStepId'),
                "p_instance"     : $v('pInstance'),
                "x01"            : "Tom",
                "x02"            : "King"
               };

var ajaxSettings = {
  url: "wwv_flow.show"
, data: ajaxData
, type: "POST"
, dataType: "text"
, success: function(data){
        //handle the successful return -> data
        console.log(data);
    }
}

$.ajax(ajaxSettings);
})()
```

■ **Tip**   The code to perform the call has been wrapped in a function, and this is wrapped in parentheses, followed by (). This will execute the function anonymously, preventing variables from polluting the global scope.

Using APEX's AJAX Functionality

APEX also has a strong implementation for making AJAX calls from JavaScript, implementing everything shown in the previous example and expanding on it with APEX-specific functionality, since it is nothing but a wrapper for jQuery.ajax(). In Listing 11-15, a call is made to the same callback process as in Listing 11-14. It's much more concise since APEX implicitly adds some settings by itself. Most evident is the setting of the application, page, and session IDs. It requires just the process name. The second argument is the actual data object, with data that needs to be sent for use in the callback process. Instead of having to use the p_arg_names and p_arg_values arrays for items, APEX has provided the pageItems property, which allows you to specify selectors for items to retrieve their name and value from and which automatically adds these to the request.

The third argument is the settings object that will be passed to ajax(). Additionally, it allows you to easily show a waiting indicator.

Listing 11-15. Performing an AJAX Call with apex.server.process

```
(function(){
apex.server.process( 'MY_CALLBACK'
                , {x01: "Tom", x02: "King"}
                , { dataType: "text"
                , success: function(data){ console.log(data); }
                }
                );
})()
```

jQuery Versions

Important to mention is the jQuery version that comes bundled with APEX. APEX versions 4.0 through 4.2 have been with use for quite a while, but unlike many improvements on the APEX side, the jQuery version has been the same for much of this time. This meant that the jQuery API has become quite outdated for a while now, and this began to show as more industrious members of the community started seeking out new and advanced functions, which brought along plenty other problems. So, the jump being made with APEX 5 is rather significant.

```
jQuery has been updated from version 1.7.1 to version 2.1.3.
jQueryUI has been updated from version 1.8.14 to version 1.10.4.
```

This is a big jump from versions 1.7 to 2.1...very big. Version 2.0 was a major release and cut out much of what was considered legacy functionality; examples were workarounds for browsers like IE 6. This shouldn't be a surprise. Technology does not stand still, and at a certain point this kind of cleanup is necessary to keep the library as clean and lean as possible and provide a starting point for future implementations.

Be aware that if you have or had custom implementations in applications for versions previous to APEX 5, you may need to update the jQuery library! Or if you previously loaded an updated jQuery library version, it may not be necessary to do so anymore, speeding up your page.

apex.jQuery

Throughout this chapter I've been using $ and jQuery as the objects I perform jQuery actions with. However, there is also the apex.jQuery object. As shown earlier, APEX comes bundled with a certain version of jQuery, and as we progress in time, so will jQuery and APEX. At one point in the future we may end up at the same situation as we had with APEX 4.2 and its outdated jQuery library. It may become increasingly interesting to use another jQuery version than the bundled one, and then apex.jQuery comes in handy. Just as the global-scoped jQuery object will reference a certain jQuery version, so will apex.jQuery reference the jQuery version that APEX uses. After all, updating the library does not mean that all functionality will remain the same, and thus APEX always needs its own version.

This means that when you decide to use apex.jQuery instead of $ or jQuery, you will protect yourself from any adventures with other jQuery libraries loaded on the page. This may or may not be interesting depending on the situation, but generally it is a better idea to use apex.jQuery.

Pitfalls

Even though many things are easily resolved by using jQuery, don't become complacent. Technology never stands still, and it is part of your job to keep up. Even though jQuery keeps evolving and has extended functionality does not mean you have to use it for every single thing.

An example is the native support of several functions on arrays in JavaScript, such as forEach. These native functions are usually inherently faster than jQuery's implementation. There are even polyfills available to provide this functionality in browsers that do not support it yet.

In other words, it is wise to keep up with how JavaScript evolves.

Resources

- *jQuery API*: http://api.jquery.com/

- *jQuery Learning Center*: http://learn.jquery.com/

- *MDN JavaScript tutorials*: https://developer.mozilla.org/en-US/Learn/JavaScript

- *APEX JavaScript APIs*: http://api.oracleapex.com

- *DOM*: www.w3.org/TR/WD-DOM/introduction.html

Summary

With what you've learned in this chapter, you should be able to deal with at least some of the basic jQuery interactions on your APEX pages. There is, of course, much more you can do with jQuery, and this chapter was a primer to tickle your sense of adventure. By now, though, you should have a grasp of some of these basics, such as to be able to select a set of elements and perform an action on them like a manipulation, binding an event handler, or using it as a starting point for a DOM travel trip. With a short foray into AJAX, you should now have a lot of power in your hands once you begin to see the possibilities created by combining all these techniques. Anything is possible on your APEX page with the power of JavaScript and jQuery, though it will take mastering to temper oneself. Never forget to utilize the power of APEX too!

■ ■ ■

Map Integration

by Christoph Ruepprich

Any database application that contains location data, such as addresses or geographic coordinates, may benefit from displaying this data on a map. It may be of further benefit to allow users to interact with this data by associating it with other data or even performing geometric calculations against it.

In this chapter, you will explore some options to free the geographic data from its confines of the database tables and render it in useful ways on interactive maps. To accomplish this, you will look at a number of tools and techniques available to you in APEX, the Oracle Database, and some publicly available APIs.

You will learn how to turn address data into geographic coordinates and how to use these coordinates to display addresses on a map. Further, you will take a look at various mapping APIs and how to use Oracle's powerful spatial features to find relationships between geographic data points.

Geocoding

Geocoding is the process of turning addresses from plain text into coordinates. To do this, you will make use of some publicly available web services that do the heavy lifting for you. You can simply call such a web service with an address, and the service will return a cleaned-up version of this address, along with other data elements, including coordinates. You can then store these coordinates in the database and visualize them on a map.

■ **Note**   Reverse geocoding takes a pair of coordinates as input and attempts to return the address associated with them.

Coordinates

The coordinates used for mapping are simply numeric values for latitude and longitude. There are a number of ways of expressing coordinates. Two notations are worth noting.

> DMS: Degree Minutes Seconds

> DD: Decimal Degrees

Oracle's APIs use DD notation. Latitude values range from -90 to 90, and longitude values range from -180 to 180; both can go up to 15 decimal places. A four-decimal coordinate is accurate to about 11 meters, and a five-decimal coordinate is accurate to about 1 meter. The accuracy can vary with the position on the globe and the coordinate system being used (see "SDO_GEOMETRY" later in the chapter).

Web Services

There are a number of available web services that provide geographic data. They can take various types of queries as input and return detailed geographic data in the form of XML or JSON. Depending on which service is being used, the input can range from a simple address or location to an actual SQL query, as in the case of Yahoo. Let's take a look at some of these services.

■ **Note**   Make sure to check the terms and conditions for using these web services because they are subject to change.

Yahoo Web Services

Yahoo provides a public web service for geocoding. As input, the user provides a query against one of the available Yahoo tables. The geocoding table at Yahoo is called geo.placefinder. The following URL calls the Yahoo web service and passes it the query against the geo.placefinder table. The web service then responds with the query results in XML format.

```
https://query.yahooapis.com/v1/public/yql?q=select * from geo.placefinder where text="1400
6th Ave, Seattle, WA 98101"
```

The default output is XML. Here's an example:

```
<query xmlns:yahoo="http://www.yahooapis.com/v1/base.rng" yahoo:count="1" yahoo:lang="en-US">
    <results>
        <Result>
    <quality>87</quality>
    <addressMatchType>POINT_ADDRESS</addressMatchType>
    <latitude>47.610378</latitude>
    <longitude>-122.333832</longitude>
    <offsetlat>47.610512</offsetlat>
    <offsetlon>-122.333511</offsetlon>
    <radius>400</radius>
    <name/>
    <line1>1400 6th Ave</line1>
    <line2>Seattle, WA 98101-2318</line2>
    <line3/>
    <line4>United States</line4>
    <house>1400</house>
    <street>6th Ave</street>
```

To receive a JSON result, add the format parameter.

```
https://query.yahooapis.com/v1/public/yql?format=json&q=select * from geo.placefinder where
text="1400 6th Ave, Seattle, WA 98101"
```

For further usage details, see the following:

```
https://developer.yahoo.com/yql/guide/usage_info_limits.html
```

Yahoo also provides a developer console that you can use to test and explore the available services. You can find that console at `https://developer.yahoo.com/yql/console`.

Google Web Services

Google's geocoding web service works similarly to that of Yahoo, except that it doesn't use a query syntax. For example, here is a URL invoking the web service on an address in Seattle:

```
http://maps.googleapis.com/maps/api/geocode/xml?sensor=false&address=1400 6th Ave,
Seattle, WA 98101
```

As you can see by the URL path, the result would be returned in XML. To get a JSON result, simply substitute json for xml in the path.

The web service call responded with the following XML:

```
<GeocodeResponse>
<status>OK</status>
        <result>
    <type>street_address</type>
    <formatted_address>1400 6th Avenue, Seattle, WA 98101, USA</formatted_address>
    <address_component>
    <long_name>1400</long_name>
    <short_name>1400</short_name>
    <type>street_number</type>
    </address_component>
    <address_component>
    <long_name>6th Avenue</long_name>
    <short_name>6th Ave</short_name>
    <type>route</type>
    </address_component>
    <address_component>
    <long_name>Pike Pine Retail Core</long_name>
    <short_name>Pike Pine Retail Core</short_name>
    <type>neighborhood</type>
    <type>political</type>
    </address_component>
    <address_component>
    <long_name>Seattle</long_name>
    <short_name>Seattle</short_name>
    <type>locality</type>
    <type>political</type>
    </address_component>
```

A reverse geocoding URL may look like this. Only the `latlng` parameter is needed.

```
http://maps.googleapis.com/maps/api/geocode/xml?latlng= 48.858012, 2.294746
```

The reverse geocoding call responded with a complete address in XML format.

```
<GeocodeResponse>
<status>OK</status>
      <result>
    <type>street_address</type>
    <formatted_address>8 Avenue Gustave Eiffel, 75007 Paris, France</formatted_address>
    <address_component>
```

What Are XML and JSON?

Extensible Markup Language (XML) is a plain-text markup language to describe data. It looks a lot like HTML, but the tags describe data field names, which you get to define yourself. The actual data exists between the opening and closing tags, as in `<first_name>Christoph</first_name>`.

JavaScript Object Notation (JSON) is a lightweight, plain-text data format, similar to XML. It is a way of organizing data in plain text so that JavaScript can easily process it and so that humans can still easily read it. JSON consists of objects, which are mainly name-value pairs enclosed by curly brackets (`{ }`), and lists of values, which function as arrays and are enclosed with square brackets (`[ ]`). JSON can get pretty complex when you start nesting objects and arrays. But for these purposes, JSON is quite simple.

The following example is a list of gas stations, each with a number of attributes (ID, brand, latitude, longitude). A representation of this in JSON looks something like this:

```
{
    "stations":[
       {
          "id":"1",
          "brand":"Shell",
          "lat":32.343214,
          "lng":-97.398834
       },
       {
          "id":"2",
          "brand":"Valero",
          "lat":32.15534,
          "lng":-97.19984
       },
       {
          "id":"3",
          "brand":"Exxon",
          "lat":33.92234,
          "lng":-94.88223
       }
    ]
}
```

Here you have an object named `stations`, containing an array of name-value pairs. You are going to generate this JSON string with PL/SQL in your AJAX callback and then pass it to your JavaScript function so that it can be parsed and the results rendered on the map.

Processing XML/JSON Results

Once you have geocoded results, you can process those results in a number of ways. If you receive XML or JSON results, you may want to parse the data and store it. If you use the Oracle Elocation Geocoder APEX plugin, from the Sample Geolocation Showcase sample application, you can simply work off the collection returned by that plugin. The data contained in the collection is already parsed into the address components (for example, street, city, state, and so on).

To decide whether you want to process XML or JSON, you should consider first where the data will primarily be used. If you plan to directly display it on a map, you may want to consider JSON since the map APIs are written in JavaScript, where JSON is easily processed.

If you plan to work with the results in PL/SQL and you are working in Oracle 11g or older, XML may be the better choice because JSON processing requires the help of a third-party package. To find out more, see https://ruepprich.wordpress.com/2013/09/17/geocoding-with-pljson/.

Oracle 12c provides native JSON processing and makes this the clear choice because you can easily use the results in JavaScript and PL/SQL.

If you do not need to process the geocoding results in JavaScript, the Oracle Elocation Geocoder plugin is a good choice since it directly populates an APEX collection, which allows for easy PL/SQL processing.

Oracle Web Services

Oracle also provides geocoding web services. Using them with Application Express is quite easy because Oracle already has a geocoding plugin. That plugin is the Elocation Geocoder plugin used in the sample application Geolocation Showcase of APEX version 4.2.5 and higher. This plugin uses Oracle's own geocoding service. To use this and other plugins, simply export it from the sample application and import it into your own.

The plugin provides a text field for input and a submit button. On submit, the plugin calls Oracle's web services and populates a collection with the results, which can then be easily displayed and processed in APEX.

The following is the process for creating a geocoding page with the Oracle plugin:

1. Create a page with a static region (HTML region in versions 4 and earlier).

2. Create search and country text fields.

3. Create a search button.

4. Add a classic report region.

5. Add a dynamic action to call the geolocation service.

6. Add a dynamic action to respond to the completed service call.

The following subsections describe each step in more detail.

Creating a Page

The first step is to create a page with a static region. This is just a basic page, and the static region should be empty at this point in the process.

Creating Search and Country Fields

Create a basic text field called Pn_SEARCH with a source type of Null. The country field (Pn_COUNTRY) is required by the plugin and contains the country abbreviation. For this example, you will just use the hard-coded value of USA, but you can always add an LOV with a list of countries and their respective codes.

Adding a Classic Report

Create a classic report region named Results using a query based on the collection that will be populated by the geolocation dynamic action. The following query maps the generic collection columns to recognizable column names. The values of the columns are determined by the plugin.

```
select
    nvl(c001, 'N/A') as street,
    c002 as house_number,
    c003 as postal_code,
    c004 as settlement,
    c005 as builtup_area,
    nvl(c006,c005) as municipality,
    case
      when c011  = 'US' then c007
      else initcap(c007)
    end as order1_area,
    c008 as side,
    c009 as error_message,
    c010 as match_vector,
    n001 as sequence,
    n002 as longitude,
    n003 as latitude,
    n004 as edge_id
from apex_collections where collection_name = 'GEOCODER_RESULTS'
and n002 is not null and n003 is not null
order by seq_id;
```

Creating a Search Button

You also need a button called GEOCODE that executes the search. The button uses the action Defined by Dynamic Action. This action fires on a click of this button and executes Oracle's geocoding services. Be sure to specify a collection name matching that in the query from the preceding section. In this case, that collection name should be specified as GEOCODER_RESULTS. Figure 12-1 shows the definition of the dynamic action invoking Oracle's geocoding service.

▾ Identification
Name
When Geocode Button Clicked
▾ Execution Options
Sequence
10
▾ When
Event
Click
Selection Type
Button
Button
geocode

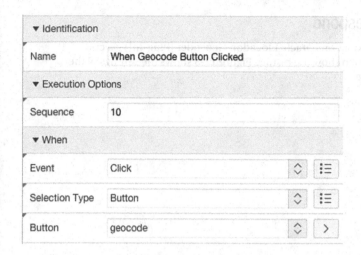

Figure 12-1. *Definition of the dynamic action invoking Oracle's geocoding service*

Add a True action that passes the search criteria to the plugin, as shown in Figure 12-2.

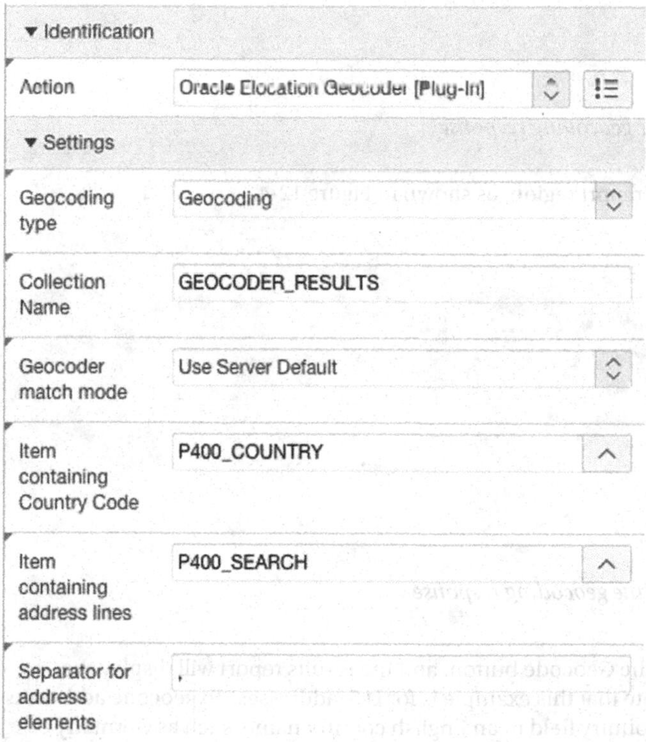

▾ Identification
Action
Oracle Elocation Geocoder [Plug-In]
▾ Settings
Geocoding type
Geocoding
Collection Name
GEOCODER_RESULTS
Geocoder match mode
Use Server Default
Item containing Country Code
P400_COUNTRY
Item containing address lines
P400_SEARCH
Separator for address elements
,

Figure 12-2. *Settings for the True action of the dynamic action*

Adding a Dynamic Action to Respond

This action fires after the previous dynamic action (Oracle Elocation Geocoder [Plug-In]) executes successfully and refreshes the report region to show the results. Figure 12-3 shows the settings of the dynamic action for the geocoding response.

Figure 12-3. *Settings of the dynamic action for geocoding response*

Now you add a True action to refresh the report region, as shown in Figure 12-4.

Figure 12-4. *The settings of the True action of the geocoding response*

Now you can enter an address and click the Geocode button, and the results report will display the geocoding results as shown in Figure 12-5. Note that this example is for U.S. addresses. To geocode addresses in other countries, make sure to change the Country field to an English country name, such as Germany or Canada.

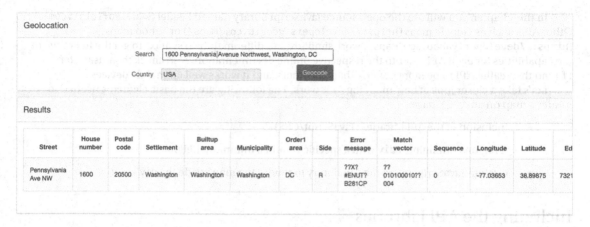

Figure 12-5. *The sample page and the search results*

Choosing a Geocoding Service

Of course, there are more web services available, but which one should you choose? I have compared the results of Yahoo, Google, and Oracle and have found that each one returns almost the same results as far as latitude and longitude are concerned.

The main differences are in the additional data provided, such as cleaned-up addresses, and the way address elements are split up. Of course, you will have to review the terms and conditions of each service to make sure you are in compliance. You may also test the response times of each service because they may differ depending on your location, as well as the accuracy of some of your sample data.

The Mapping API

You can take the coordinates from your geocoding efforts and plot them onto a map. A map consists of map tiles and layers. Map tiles are images that show the geographic features on a map, such as roads, rivers, land, and water masses. Most mapping APIs will allow you to choose from different map tiles, such as road maps, satellite imagery, topographical features, and so on. These map tiles are provided by a tile server web service. This web service can be a proprietary one, as in the case of Google and Yahoo, or it can be a third-party provider, as in the case of Leaflet maps. When passing a coordinate pair and a zoom factor to the API, the map tiles for that location, and the surrounding area, will be provided by the tile server.

To draw something onto a map, you use layers. Layers contain elements such as pins, polygons, text (other than that included on the map tiles), and so on. Through the use of JavaScript calls, you can tell the map where and how to draw a layer. Layers typically allow further formatting, such as colors and size, and even can be extended with event handlers to allow them to react to mouse clicks and hovers.

You can display single coordinate pairs, which I will call *points* from here on, with a map marker or pin. You can also use these points and draw a circle around them. More complex shapes, such as lines and polygons, require multiple points.

Any marker or shape you draw on top of a map exists on a separate layer that the mapping APIs render. These layers can then be shown, hidden, altered, or removed. Depending on the API used, these shapes can also have additional attributes. Markers, for example, can use image files as their representations. Lines and polygons can have attributes such as line thickness, color, and opacity. The layers can also have JavaScript listeners attached to them that respond to clicks and hovers.

In this chapter, you will use the open source JavaScript library named Leaflet (`www.leafletjs.com`). Other APIs such as Google maps (`https://developers.google.com/maps/`) or Yahoo maps (`https://developer.yahoo.com/maps/`) work similarly and differ mainly in syntax. To get the full range of the capabilities for each API, refer to the respective online documentation. Also check their usage terms. I found the Leaflet API to be more concise than the others, and it works well on mobile devices.

Let's take a closer look at how mapping APIs work. The following are the basic elements needed to render a map on an APEX page:

- Inclusion of the API libraries (JavaScript/CSS)

- A region containing a `div` with a specific ID and a minimum height

- Custom JavaScript using the API library to render the map inside the `div`

Including the API Libraries

First you must include these libraries in your application. You can download these libraries and store them in the application's static files or on your server, or you can refer to their URLs on the Web. When choosing the latter, keep in mind that the libraries may change over time and affect your application in unexpected ways.

In the example shown in Figure 12-6, I downloaded the Leaflet JavaScript library and saved it to the static files of the application, and then I included it by making a URL reference to it in the page's JavaScript attribute.

Figure 12-6. *Including the Leaflet JavaScript library in the page's JavaScript attribute*

Note that APEX 5 now allows you to save static files under different directories. To keep my static files organized, I saved my JavaScript files in the `js` directory and the CSS files in the `css` directory.

This particular API also requires a CSS library, which I obtained from its website and stored in the application static files. I then included the CSS library by adding the URL into the CSS File URL attribute of the page, as shown in Figure 12-7.

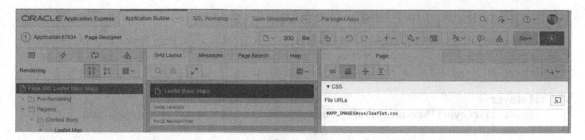

Figure 12-7. Including the leaflet.css CSS library in the page's CSS attribute

Creating a div to Hold the Map

APEX regions of type Static Content are similar to blank HTML pages and allow you to add HTML to the region source. You will create such a region to simply hold a `div` container with a unique ID. The map JavaScript will then use this ID to render the map inside the `div` tags. Add the following syntax to the region's source:

```
<div id="mapRegion" style="width:100%;height:430px;"></div>
```

Figure 12-8 shows the region's definition in APEX. You can see the preceding code in the Region Source field at the very bottom of the image.

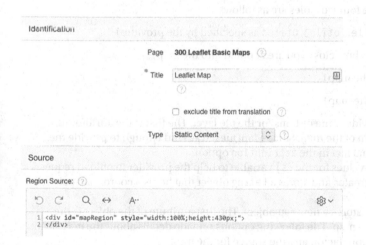

Figure 12-8. The static region with the div container

Writing JavaScript to Render the Map

Let's add the following JavaScript code to the page's JavaScript Execute when Page Loads attribute. When the page runs, the JavaScript will automatically be executed to render the map in the div created in the previous section.

```
var tileLayer =
        new L.tileLayer('http://otile{s}.mqcdn.com/tiles/1.0.0/map/{z}/{x}/{y}.jpeg'
            , {
                attribution: 'Tiles Courtesy of MapQuest'
                ,subdomains: '1234'
                });

var latlng = new L.LatLng(47.610871,-122.333451);

var map = new L.Map('mapRegion'
                , { center: latlng
                  ,zoom: 8
                  ,layers: [tileLayer]
                  });
```

With a few lines of code, you are able to draw the map. First you declare the variable tileLayer, which tells the API from where to pull the map tiles. In this case, you get the tiles from MapQuest, as specified in the URL. The URL contains four variables. The included JavaScript library will provide their values from the data you provide when you invoke to map. The four variables are as follows:

- {s}: Subdomain (otile1, otile2, otile3, otile4 as specified by the provider)

- {z}: Zoom factor (determines how close you are zoomed into the map)

- {x}: X coordinate (center of the map)

- {y}: Y coordinate (center of the map)

The curly brackets after the URL provide some options for the tile layer. The first is the attribution, which prints some text on the bottom right of the map. Since MapQuest was kind enough to provide the service for obtaining tiles, you attribute that fact in the attribution option.

The subdomains option provides the values for the {s} variable to help the provider to offload requests to different servers. The latlng variable creates and stores a LatLng object that holds a coordinate pair (x and y).

Finally, the map variable creates and stores a new Map object. The first attribute of the object is the ID of the div where you want to render the map. The following options provide details about the map itself: its center with X and Y coordinates, the zoom factor, and the source for the tiles.

By simply declaring the map variable, the map is then rendered inside the div on the page. See Figure 12-9 for an example of how the map appears.

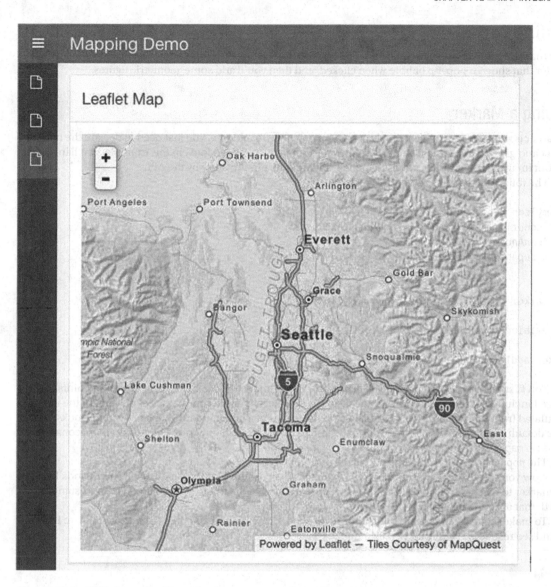

Figure 12-9. *With just a few lines of code, you can easily render a map in APEX*

Adding Layers

Now that you have a basic map, let's make it a bit more interesting by adding some layers. First you'll add a marker that shows a pop-up bubble when clicked, and then you'll add some geometric figures.

Adding a Marker

A marker is a special layer object that represents a map pin. To add one, you just need to declare the marker object and give it a coordinate pair and some data about how it should look. In this example, you'll include a custom image for the marker, rather than the standard blue pin provided by the API.

The following is the JavaScript to add a marker:

```
var myIcon = L.icon({
    iconUrl: '#APP_IMAGES#img/marina-2-red.png',
    iconAnchor: [22, 94],
    popupAnchor: [-6, -85]
});

var marker = L.marker(latlng,{icon: myIcon});

marker.bindPopup('Welcome to Seattle!');

marker.addTo(map);
```

You first create an icon that you will use as the custom marker image. The iconUrl option points to an image I included in the application's static files. The iconAnchor is the coordinates of the "tip" of the icon calculated from the top left. This is useful in case the icon is of a nonstandard shape or it simply looks odd in its default position. You may have to tweak these numbers by trial and error. For custom map icons, see https://mapicons.mapsmarker.com/.

The popupAnchor gives the position of the pop-up bubble.

Now you create the actual marker, where you tell it its position (latlng) and what it should look like. For the marker to react to a click, you add the bindPopup method to the marker. The method accepts standard HTML that allows further styling.

To make the marker appear on the map, invoke the addTo method and pass the map variable to it. You should see results like in Figure 12-10.

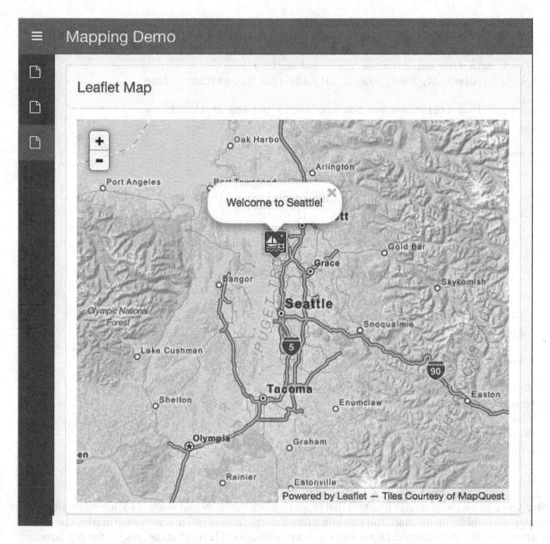

Figure 12-10. A map marker with a custom icon image and a pop-up bubble

Adding Many Markers

If you have a large number of markers to add to the map, you can make use of JSON. You can store all the coordinates for the markers in a JSON string. Then you can use JavaScript to loop through the JSON object and render each marker.

You first fetch the data from the database and store it in a hidden page item (P320_JSON). You do that using a Before Header PL/SQL page process. Here is what the code looks like:

```
declare
    l_json VARCHAR2(32000);
    l_i PLS_INTEGER;
begin
    -- Begin the JSON string
    l_json := '{"stations": [';
```

```
    -- Start a counter to help with formatting
    l_i := 0;

    -- Fetch data from our database table and begin a loop
    for c1 in (select id, name, brand, lat, lng from gas_stations) loop

        -- For loop iterations > 0 add a comma to the end of the string
        if l_i > 0 then
            l_json := l_json || ',';
        end if;

        -- Build the JSON string
        -- Use apex_escape.html() to escape special characters
        l_json := l_json || '{"id": "'        || c1.ID
                         || '", "name": "'   || apex_escape.html(c1.NAME)
                         || '", "brand": "'  || apex_escape.html(c1.BRAND)
                         || '", "lat": '     || c1.LAT
                         || ', "lng": '      || c1.LNG
                         || '}';

        -- Increment the counter
        l_i := l_i + 1;

    end loop;

    -- Finalize the JSON string
    l_json := l_json || ']}';

    -- Store the JSON string in a page item
    :P320_JSON := l_json;

end;
```

Next you add a new JavaScript function that loops through the JSON and renders each marker, along with its pop-up bubble, on the map. You also add a function that allows you to remove the markers by clicking a button. For this example, I have also saved a new image (fillingstation.png) to the img directory in the static files. I also created a hidden page item (P320_JSON) to store the JSON from the JavaScript. The complete code now looks as follows:

```
//Tile source
var tileLayer =
    new L.tileLayer('http://otile{s}.mqcdn.com/tiles/1.0.0/map/{z}/{x}/{y}.jpeg'
        , {
            attribution: 'Tiles Courtesy of MapQuest'
            ,subdomains: '1234'
        });

//Initial map center
var latlng = new L.LatLng(32.935217,-97.084862);
```

```
//Map definition
var map = new L.Map('mapRegion'
        , { center: latlng
            ,zoom: 11
            ,layers: [tileLayer]
          });

//Create a custom icon
var gasIcon = new L.icon({iconUrl: '#APP_IMAGES#img/fillingstation.png'
                         ,iconAnchor: [12,41]
                        });

//Create an offset for the popup bubble, 3 points to the right
//and 25 points up.
var popupOptions = {
  offset:  new L.Point(3, -25)
};

//Load the JSON from the page item into a json variable
var json = JSON.parse($v('P320_JSON'));

//Parse out the stations array and save it in gs (gas stations)
var gs = json.stations;

//Add additional variables
var marker, name, text, id, lat, lng;
var Markers = [];

//Loop through gs array
for (var i = 0; i < gs.length; i++) {

    //Set ID (primary key of gas stations)
    id   = gs[i].id;

    //Set latituted and longitude
    lat  = Number(gs[i].lat);
    lng  = Number(gs[i].lng);

    //Set name and format text for popup
    name = gs[i].name;
    text = '<span class="gasStationName">' + "Station " + gs[i].id + "<hr>" + name + '</
span>';

    //Create a marker and bind popup bubble
    marker = L.marker([lat,lng],{icon: gasIcon});
    marker.bindPopup(text,popupOptions);

    //Attach custom properties:
    marker.id = id;
    marker.name = name;
```

```
        //Add marker to global array so we can remove it later
        Markers.push(marker);
        //Add marker to the map
        marker.addTo(map);
}

//Create function to remove markers
window.removeMarkers = function() {
        //Loop through markers
        Markers.forEach (function(e) {
            map.removeLayer(e);
        });
        Markers = [];
}
```

The function removeMarkers() is created in the windows namespace so that it can be called from a button on your page. Create a button labeled Remove Markers and define its behavior to redirect to a URL that executes a JavaScript function call, as shown in Figure 12-11.

Figure 12-11. *The Remove Markers button behavior attributes*

Note that you are using a trick here to remove the markers from the map. To know which layer to remove, you simply store each marker in an array called Markers. In the removeMarkers() function, you simply loop through the array and delete it. There's one more thing: Notice how you use the gas station ID as the array index (Markers[gs[i].id] = marker;). This means that if the first gas station ID is 10, the array will not have anything in it for indexes 0 to 9. Therefore, as you loop through the array from zero to Markers.length, you need to check whether an array element is defined (Markers[idx] !== undefined) before you remove the marker from the map.

Figure 12-12 shows the multiple markers, with their custom icons and pop-up bubble. The data for the marker coordinates and gas station names came from the JSON object, which was generated with PL/SQL.

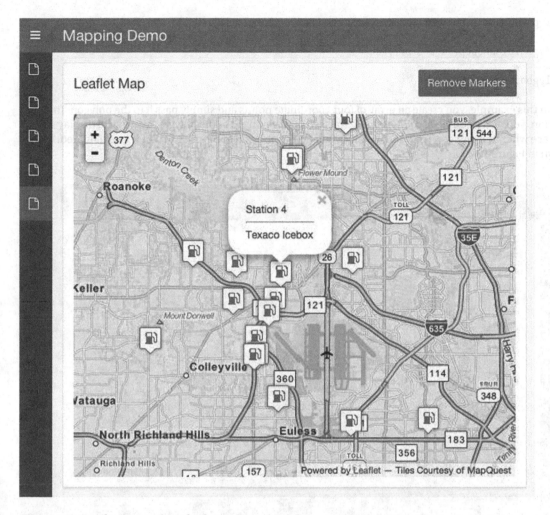

Figure 12-12. *The map with multiple markers whose data came from a JSON object*

Adding a Polygon

Rendering polygons on a map is similar to rendering markers. The main difference is that multiple points are specified for a polygon rather than a single point for a marker. The mapping API will take care of the rest by connecting the points with lines and optionally filling the resulting shape with a color. A polygon can also be bound to a listener that can react to clicks and hovers.

Let's add a polygon to the map. Like the previous marker object, Leaflet also provides a polygon object, which accepts an array of points. Leaflet will then connect the points with straight lines to draw the polygon. The following JavaScript code demonstrates how to create a polygon. Place it after the map definition.

```
var corners = [ [48.108239, -123.326049]
           ,[48.108239, -121.848388]
           ,[47.227851, -121.870360]
           ,[47.227851, -123.326049]
         ];
```

```
var polygon = L.polygon(corners,{color: 'red',fillColor: 'red'});

polygon.bindPopup("I'm a polygon!");

polygon.addTo(map);
```

In this example, you create an array of four coordinate points and simply pass it to the polygon. In addition, you add a couple of color options. You also bind a pop-up to the polygon, which will display a message when the polygon is clicked. Finally, you add the polygon to the map so that it gets rendered, as shown in Figure 12-13.

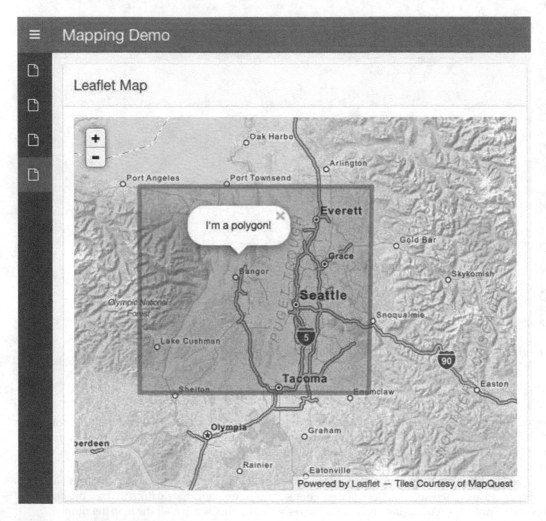

Figure 12-13. *Map with polygon*

Since the polygon is drawn in order of the point array, it is important to make sure that the order is correct; otherwise, the polygon may render in unexpected ways. Figure 12-14 shows what can happen if you get the ordering wrong.

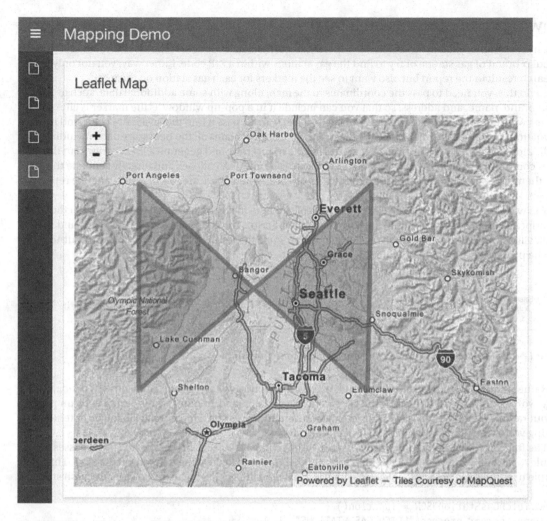

Figure 12-14. *The map wth jumbled polygon points*

Interacting with the Database

Displaying geographic data on maps in APEX is powerful stuff. But let's kick it up a notch and see how you can dynamically interact with the database. You may dynamically show markers on a map depending on report results, update page elements, or fetch data as map items are clicked. To get this level of interactivity, you'll make use of the on-demand processes (AJAX calls).

■ **Note** Asynchronous JavaScript and XML (AJAX) allows data to be sent to a web page without having to reload the page.

Showing Query Results on a Map

In the next example, you have a searchable report that returns data about gas stations. You could search for a particular brand of gas station or try to find the gas stations within a ZIP code. Either way, you not only want the search result in the report but also want to see the markers for each gas station on the map.

To do this, you need to pass the coordinates to the map, along with some additional data, such as gas station brand, name, and address, so that you can include it in a pop-up window as the marker is clicked. The best way to do this is to capture the data inside a JSON array, pass it into the JavaScript code, and run the functions to render the map. Since the GAS_STATIONS table contains all the necessary data, including the coordinates, you could use a dynamic action to read the report rows and generate a JSON array from them. Or you could simply rerun the query in the background with an AJAX callback and directly generate the JSON there. The second option may be better for those cases where there are lots of results and the report will consist of multiple pages.

You will store the JSON in a CLOB column of a collection to make use of a convenient feature in the APEX JavaScript API that allows you to read the collection in JavaScript. The code calls the AJAX callback and then uses a callback function to render the results on the map, once the results have been completely returned.

The process flow looks like Figure 12-15.

Figure 12-15. *Process flow for displaying query output onto a map*

Rather than laying out the entire example here, you'll look at some of the trickier elements needed to do the work. Let's begin with fetching the gas station data on demand, in other words, not directly on page load but rather when a button is clicked. Fetching on demand gives you a bit more flexibility by potentially allowing you to include user input in your data fetch process.

The following JavaScript function invokes the AJAX callback PL/SQL process on the page, passes a variable to it, waits for the results, and then calls another function to draw the markers on the map. This example uses the page item P115_SEARCH, which is a text field into which the user can enter a search string.

```
window.fetchGasStationJSON = function() {
    apex.server.process("FETCH GAS STATIONS", {
        pageItems: "#P115_SEARCH"
    }, {
        success: function(a) {
            var b = new apex.ajax.clob(function() {
                var a = p.readyState;
                if (a == 1 || a == 2 || a == 2) ; else if (a == 4) {
                    gJSON = p.responseText;
                    showGasStations();
                } else return false
            });
            b._get();
        },
        dataType: "text",
        loadingIndicator: "#P115_SEARCH"
    });
};
```

This function, like any of the previous JavaScript functions, is placed in the JavaScript Function and Global Variable Declaration of the APEX page attributes. You define this function in the window scope so it can be called from the APEX page, for example from a button. The function calls the build APEX JavaScript API apex.server.process, which in turn calls the AJAX callback PL/SQL process named in the first parameter (FETCH GAS STATIONS). Following this parameter is a number of options. The first, pageItems, sets the specified items in session state. This allows the AJAX callback to read its value. The next option consists of three suboptions: success, dataType, and loadingIndicator. The success option specifies what to do after the AJAX callback call succeeds. Here you specify a callback function, which reads the CLOB value from the collection in the AJAX callback into a JavaScript variable (gJSON). This function has another callback function, which waits until the CLOB has been completely read, assigns the CLOB to the gJSON variable, and then calls the function (showGasStations()) to draw the markers on the map. The dataType option simply specifies the data type for the call, and the loadingIndicator specifies the page item next to which to display a spinner graphic while the function is executing.

■ **Note**   In this example, gJSON is a globally defined variable. Using globally defined variables can help in debugging with the browser's JavaScript console. To define a JavaScript variable globally, place it in the Function and Global Variable Declaration of the page attributes.

Next you create the AJAX callback process in the page, as shown in Figure 12-16.

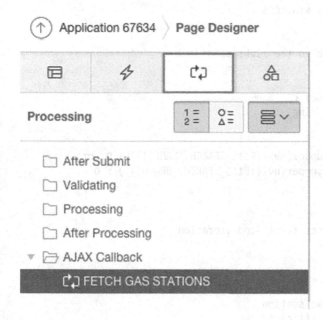

Figure 12-16. *AJAX callback*

The following is the PL/SQL code for the FETCH GAS STATIONS AJAX callback. It creates a collection for the JSON result. It uses a cursor-for-loop to retrieve data from the GAS_STATIONS table where either the name or the brand matches the search term in P115_SEARCH and then stores the result in the collection.

```
declare
    l_json clob;
    l_idx PLS_INTEGER;
    l_station clob;
begin

    -- Set up collection:
    -- If it exists, delete it.
    if apex_collection.collection_exists(p_collection_name=>'CLOB_CONTENT')
    then
      apex_collection.delete_collection(p_collection_name=>'CLOB_CONTENT');
    end if;

    -- Create a new collection.
    apex_collection.create_or_truncate_collection(p_collection_name=>'CLOB_CONTENT');

    -- Create a temporary CLOB
    dbms_lob.createtemporary( l_json, false, dbms_lob.SESSION );

    -- Setup JSON beginning with the object stations
    l_json := '{"stations": [';

    -- l_idx is used to put the first comma in the right place
    l_idx := 0;

    -- Fetch the gas station data into cursor c1
    for c1 in (select id, name, brand, lat, lng
                 from gas_stations
               where (
                     instr(upper("NAME"),upper(nvl(:P115_SEARCH,"NAME"))) > 0  or
                     instr(upper("BRAND"),upper(nvl(:P115_SEARCH,"BRAND"))) > 0
                     )
           ) loop

        -- Add a trailing comma to JSON after first loop iteration
        if l_idx > 0 then
            l_json := l_json || ',';
        end if;

        -- Create array element for each gas station
        l_station :=        '{"id": "'        || c1.id
                     || '", "name": "'  || c1.name
                     || '", "brand": "' || c1.brand
                     || '", "lat": "'   || c1.lat
                     || '", "lng": "'   || c1.lng;
        l_json := l_json || l_station || '"}';
        l_idx := l_idx + 1;
    end loop;
```

```
    -- Terminate the JSON
    l_json := l_json || ']}';

    -- Send JSON to clob
    apex_collection.add_member(p_collection_name => 'CLOB_CONTENT'
                                           ,p_clob001                    => l_json);

    -- Pass a success message back to the calling JavaScript function
    htp.p('Success. JSON length: ' || length(l_json));
end;
```

In this example, you use yet another trick: since the generated JSON can be quite large, you store it inside a CLOB. To pass this CLOB back to your JavaScript function, you store the CLOB in a collection, where the built-in apex.ajax.clob function can pick it up.

To build the JSON string, you use a cursor-for-loop to iterate through the wanted rows in the table and simply build the JSON string, with its brackets, commas, and quotes. The htp.p call at the end sends a success message to the calling JavaScript and is mainly used for debugging.

■ **Tip**   As you are working with JSON, you may find that you get some errors because it is malformed. By using a globally defined JavaScript variable (gJSON in this example), you can use the browser's JavaScript console to see its value. Free online JSON validation tools like http://jsonformatter.curiousconcept.com/ let you verify your JSON to find any errors in it.

At this point, you have all the basic elements you need to display a map with all the gas stations that were queried in the report. You know how to do the following:

- Draw a map on the page

- Put a marker on the map

- Call a PL/SQL procedure from JavaScript

- Create a JSON object in PL/SQL

- Process JSON and draw the markers

Once the JSON is generated and passed to the APEX collection, the callback function in JavaScript can now parse the JSON and render the markers for each station on the map. The pseudocode looks something like this:

```
Loop through JSON
    Create a map marker.
    Assign  a popup to the marker with data from a gas station.
    Add the marker to an array, so that we can later remove it.
    Add the marker to the map
End loop
```

Here is the complete JavaScript source:

```javascript
var tileLayer =
    new L.tileLayer('http://otile{s}.mqcdn.com/tiles/1.0.0/map/{z}/{x}/{y}.jpeg'
        , {
            attribution: 'Tiles Courtesy of MapQuest'
            ,subdomains: '1234'
        });

var latlng = new L.LatLng(32.935217,-97.084862);

var map = new L.Map('mapRegion'
        , { center: latlng
          ,zoom: 11
          ,layers: [tileLayer]
        });

//Create a custom icon
var gasIcon = new L.icon({iconUrl: '#APP_IMAGES#img/fillingstation.png'
                        ,iconAnchor: [12,41]
                    });

//Create an offset for the popup bubble, 3 points to the right and 25 points up.
var popupOptions = {
  offset:  new L.Point(3, -25)
};

function showGasStations() {
    //Parse JSON string in gJSON into json variable
    var json = JSON.parse(gJSON);

    //Parse out the stations array and save it in gs (gas stations)
    var gs = json.stations;

    //Add additional variables
    var marker, name, text, id, lat, lng;
    var Markers = [];

    //Loop through gs array
    for (var i = 0; i < gs.length; i++) {

        //Set ID (primary key of gas stations)
        id   = gs[i].id;

        //Set latituted and longitude
        lat  = Number(gs[i].lat);
        lng  = Number(gs[i].lng);

        //Set name and format text for popup
        name = gs[i].name;
        text = '<span class="gasStationName">' + "Station " + gs[i].id + "<hr>" + name + '</span>';
```

```
        //Create a marker and bind popup bubble
        marker = L.marker([lat,lng],{icon: gasIcon});
        marker.bindPopup(text,popupOptions);

        //Attach custom properties:
        marker.id = id;
        marker.name = name;

        //Add marker to global array so we can remove it later
        Markers[gs[i].id] = marker;

        //Add marker to the map
        marker.addTo(map);
    }
}

//Create function to remove markers
window.removeMarkers = function() {

    //Loop through markers
    for (idx = 0; idx < Markers.length; idx++) {

        //If marker index exists remove that marker's layer from the map
        if (Markers[idx] !== undefined ){

          //Remove marker from the map
          map.removeLayer(Markers[idx]);

          //Remove marker from array
          Markers[idx] = 0;
        }
    }
}

window.fetchGasStationJSON = function() {
    apex.server.process("FETCH GAS STATIONS", {
        pageItems: "#P330_SEARCH"
    }, {
        success: function(a) {
            var b = new apex.ajax.clob(function() {
                var a = p.readyState;
                if (a == 1 || a == 2 || a == 2) ; else if (a == 4) {
                    gJSON = p.responseText;
                    showGasStations();
                } else return false
            });
            b._get();
        },
        dataType: "text",
        loadingIndicator: "#P330_SEARCH"
    });
};
```

Now define the global variable gJSON in the page attributes, as shown in Figure 12-17.

Figure and Global Variable Declaration

```
var gJSON;
```

Figure 12-17. A JavaScript variable declared globally can also be accessed by the browser's inspector

Then add a region button to call the fetchGasStations function. See Figure 12-18 for an example.

Figure 12-18. Button to call JavaScript procedure

This should give you a good example of how to dynamically fetch geographic data from the database and display it on the map.

Spatial Math

Being able to display geographic data on a map is quite powerful; being able to analyze the relationships between geographic points is even more so. The Oracle Locator feature provides a number of features and services to make geographic calculations such as finding the distance between two points or calculating the area of a polygon.

Oracle Locator is a no-cost feature of Oracle Database 11*g* and 12*c* and is a subset of the for-cost option Oracle Spatial. Some of the capabilities that were available only in 11*g* Spatial at additional cost have been included in 12*c* at no additional cost.

You already encountered the geographic data type sdo_geometry earlier in the chapter. To do any of the spatial calculations, you not only need that data type but also a special spatial index and some spatial metadata.

SDO_GEOMETRY

The SDO_GEOMETRY data type contains various parameters that allow Oracle to make the right kind of spatial calculations. These calculations take into account the type of geometry (point, line, polygon) and the type of coordinate system that's being used. When comparing geometries, you should always use the same coordinate system. Coordinate systems are identified by a spatial reference ID (SRID). In the examples, you will use SRID 4326, which is based on the World Geodetic System WGS84, a global coordinate system. The SDO_GEOMETRY is a built-in Oracle object type that stores the particulars for a geometric object.

This example creates an SDO_GEOMETRY of a single coordinate point:

```
SDO_GEOMETRY(
          2001  -- SDO_GTYPE: point
         ,4326  -- SDO_SRID (coordinate system)
         ,MDSYS.SDO_POINT_TYPE(lon, lat, NULL) -- POINT_TYPE
         ,NULL  -- SDO_ELEM_INFO_ARRAY
         ,NULL  -- SDO_ORDINATE_ARRAY
)
```

The SDO_GTYPE value defines the type of geometry (point, line, polygon). It is a "smart" number where the first digit represents the number of dimensions, the second the linear referencing system, and the last two the geometry type (line, polygon, and so on; see Oracle documentation http://bit.ly/1Dau4st. SRID is the coordinate system identifier as mentioned earlier. POINT_TYPE further defines the point's location. SDO_ELEM_INFO_ARRAY and SDO_ORDINATE_ARRAY are used for geometries that consist of multiple points, such as lines or polygons.

SDO Metadata

Before being able to create a spatial index, you need to tell the database a few details about the table and column you want to index. The data dictionary table user_sdo_geom_metadata holds that information. Along with the table and column name, you need to specify an sdo_dim_array, which basically stores the minimum and maximum latitude and longitude you want to work with. Also, the SRID needs to be specified. The following example creates an entry in user_sdo_geom_metadata for the geom column in the gas_stations table. It further specifies that you want to use SRID 4326. The SDO_DIM_ARRAY specifies the size of the geometry grid you want to work with. In this case, that is the entire earth, which spans from -180 to 180 longitude and -90 to 90 latitude.

```
INSERT INTO user_sdo_geom_metadata
    (TABLE_NAME,
     COLUMN_NAME,
     DIMINFO,
     SRID)
  VALUES (
  'GAS_STATIONS',
  'GEOM',
  SDO_DIM_ARRAY(
       SDO_DIM_ELEMENT('X', -180, 180, 1),
       SDO_DIM_ELEMENT('Y',  -90,  90, 1)
     ),
  4326
);
```

Spatial Indexes

Once the spatial metadata is defined for the table and column, you can then create the index. Create it using the following statement:

```
CREATE INDEX gas_stations_geom_idx
  ON gas_stations(geom)
  INDEXTYPE IS MDSYS.SPATIAL_INDEX;
```

APEX_SPATIAL Package

The APEX_SPATIAL package provides you with an easy utility to create the metadata and the index in a single PL/SQL call. It is necessary when creating user_sdo_geom_meatadata records from within APEX. This example also creates a row in user_sdo_geom_metadata for the geom column in the gas_stations table.

```
begin
    apex_spatial.insert_geom_metadata (
            p_table_name          => 'GAS_STATIONS'
            ,p_column_name   => 'GEOM'
            ,p_diminfo             => SDO_DIM_ARRAY (
                                          SDO_DIM_ELEMENT('X', -180, 180, 1),
                                          SDO_DIM_ELEMENT('Y',  -90,  90, 1)
                                      )
            ,p_srid                => 4326
            ,p_create_index_name => 'GAS_STATIONS_GEOM_IDX'
    );
end;
```

■ **Note**   If you want to build spatial indexes through the SQL Workshop in APEX, you will need to use the APEX_SPATIAL package.

Now that all three pieces are in place (the sdo_geometry column, metadata, and index), you can do your spatial math. Let's take a look at a few functions to make geographic calculations.

Calculating Distance

To calculate the distance between two points, use the SDO_GEOM.SDO_DISTANCE function. The function simply takes two points in the form of the sdo_geometry data type and returns the distance in the desired unit (miles, meters, kilometers, and so on). The following query shows how to calculate the distance in miles between gas stations with IDs 1 and 2:

```
SELECT ROUND(SDO_GEOM.SDO_DISTANCE (
                            a.geom
                           ,b.geom
                           ,1
                           ,'unit=mile'
                           )
                     ,2) as miles
  FROM gas_stations a
            ,gas_stations b
 WHERE a.id = 1
     AND b.id = 2;
```

Search Within Distance

Another useful example is to show which gas stations are within 3 kilometers of a particular point. The following query compares the sdo_geometry attributes of all the gas stations to the given point (- 97.078686, 32.939251). If the distance from the given point is 3 km or less, the query returns the string TRUE.

```
SELECT *
  FROM gas_stations g
 WHERE
  SDO_WITHIN_DISTANCE(
                 g.geom
               , MDSYS.SDO_GEOMETRY(
                       2001
                     , 4326
                     , MDSYS.SDO_POINT_TYPE(- 97.078686, 32.939251, NULL)
                     , NULL
                     , NULL
                 )
               ,'distance = 3 unit=km'
  ) = 'TRUE'
```

Calculate Area

The SDO_AREA function can be used to calculate the area of a polygon. It takes an SDO_GEOMETRY object as its argument. The SDO_GEOMETRY object should be set as a two-dimensional object with an SDO_ORDINATE_ARRAY of coordinate points that describe the outer points of the polygon.

```
select SDO_GEOM.SDO_AREA(
            SDO_GEOMETRY(
                    2003  -- GTYPE: two-dimensional polygon
                   ,4326  -- SRID
                   ,NULL  -- POINT TYPE
                   ,SDO_ELEM_INFO_ARRAY(1,1003,1)
                   ,SDO_ORDINATE_ARRAY(3,3, 6,3, 6,5, 4,5, 3,3)
               )
        ,1) AREA
  from dual;
```

Third-Party Data

At some point you may want to consider receiving more complex geographic data, such as ZIP code, census, or neighborhood boundaries from a third-party provider. These data sets can be quite large because they may consist of tens of thousands of coordinate points. For example, a ZIP code boundary would be displayed as a polygon layer on top of a map as shown in Figure 12-19. Since ZIP code boundaries may be intricate, they can contain a large number of points.

Figure 12-19. *A ZIP code polygon can consist of a large number of coordinate points that define its perimeter*

While there are multiple formats in which geometry data can be communicated, one that is fairly easy to deal with in the Oracle Database is Well Known Text (WKT).

WKT is a plain-text markup language for representing vector geometries, such as points, lines, and polygons. The example in Figure 12-20 shows how multiple coordinate pairs make up polygons and multipolygons.

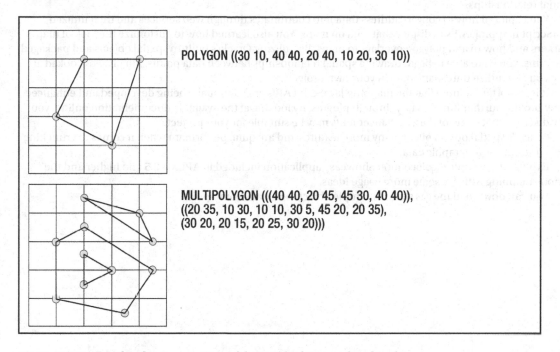

POLYGON ((30 10, 40 40, 20 40, 10 20, 30 10))

MULTIPOLYGON (((40 40, 20 45, 45 30, 40 40)),
((20 35, 10 30, 10 10, 30 5, 45 20, 20 35),
(30 20, 20 15, 20 25, 30 20)))

Figure 12-20. Graphical representations of the WKT polygon and multipolygons

What makes WKT easy to deal with in Oracle is the fact that Oracle already has a built-in function to parse WKT and convert it into the sdo_geometry data type. The function SDO_UTIL.FROM_WKTGEOMETRY will take the WKT string and convert it into a SDO_GEOMTERY data type.

A simple conversion technique would be to build a table with a WKT column (CLOB) and a SDO_GEOMETRY column. Then simply run an update statement to make the conversion. Here's an example:

```
UPDATE zip_code_table
      SET geom = sdo_util.from_wktgeometry(wkt_column);
```

It is important to then update the sdo_geometry column and specify its spatial reference ID:

```
UPDATE zip_code_table a
      SET a.geom.sdo_srid = 4326;
```

Now the table is ready for spatial calculations.

Oracle also contains conversion functions for WKB and GML. WKB is the binary format of WKT. GMS is the Geography Markup Language. When dealing with third-party data, using any of these three data formats will serve you well because the data conversion can be made with Oracle's built-in functionality.

Summary

Including interactive maps and perfoming spatial calculations on geographic data in an APEX application can be quite powerful. Just like charts and graphs allow a user to comprehend numeric data more efficiently, maps remove the abstraction of addresses and coordinate points and allow the user to better understand spatial relationships.

You explored how to convert address data into coordinates through web services and then utilized JavaScript mapping APIs to display that data on maps. You also learned how to customize the look of map markers and how to add polygon overlays to maps. By utilizing Oracle's built-in spatial objects and packaged programs, you were able to begin drawing spatial relationships between data points. Finally, you looked at how you can utilize third-party data in your own projects.

It is important to note that the mapping JavaScript APIs are continually being developed and enhanced. Many provide further functionality through plugins. By looking at the available documentation online, you may discover that some of these enhancements may be suitable for your projects.

Oracle's spatial option offers many more features and are quite performant when it comes to crunching large amounts of geographic data.

Explore the Sample Geolocoation Showcase application included in APEX 4.2.5 and higher and the various mapping APIs for some more usage ideas.

You can download the gas stations sample objects and data from Apress.

CHAPTER 13

∎ ∎ ∎

Themes and Templates

by Jorge Rimblas

Everything you see on an APEX page is the result of some template. Let that sink in for a moment.

We often decide on a template without giving it much thought. I say, that's just fine. That is the elegance and beauty of APEX. You're able to start building functional, responsive, and even (sometimes) beautiful web applications with little effort and not much concern for how all the HTML makes it into the page. However, if you've ever been asked to change the look of an element on your page, want to learn about other UI elements, take your applications to the next level, or simply understand what makes an application tick, this chapter is for you. (If you're just learning about APEX, you should probably wait before reading this chapter, at least until you have a solid application or two under your belt.)

Themes and templates allow APEX to separate the application logic from the visual look and feel. This is why you're able to start building web applications so fast without the need to get bogged down in color, fonts, and layout decisions. A *theme* is the all-encompassing collection of HTML, CSS, and JavaScript that gives your application a consistent look. Templates are part of a theme. *Templates* are the building blocks of all visual elements in an application. Everything you see on the screen is the result of a template.

Before APEX 5, if you didn't know CSS, you were not going to get too far changing the font or colors of your application and making a lot of style changes. With the introduction of the new Universal theme and the Theme Roller, APEX 5 changes all that. APEX 5 goes as far as designating Theme 42 as the *only* standard theme. All the other 26 themes that came previously are now the "other" themes or legacy themes.

Don't get me wrong. In previous versions of APEX, you could still control a lot of the layout on a page. I will attempt to show some techniques that can be used with all versions of APEX and any theme.

What Is a Template?

Within APEX you will see the following information about how templates are used:

> *The Application Express engine constructs the appearance of each page in an application using Templates. Templates define how pages, page controls, and page components display.*

Based on that information and since you know that web pages are made of basically three elements (HTML, CSS, and JavaScript), you can infer that templates are nothing more than a combination of these elements. I like to think of HTML as the structure, the scaffold, or the bones of a web page. The veneer and paint you apply to this structure will be the CSS. The pages, regions, labels, buttons, reports, lists, breadcrumbs, and so on, are the result of some data being applied and merged with a template or, at the least, content from a template.

■ **Note**   Items themselves are not based on templates. However, you can still affect them with the CSS on the page. That CSS may be part of the theme or perhaps part of your own additions. An item's name becomes its unique ID on the page. In CSS, you can target an item with the #Pn_ITEM_NAME notation.

What Is a Theme?

Themes are the skin of your application. They attempt to give your applications, as a whole, a consistent and uniform appearance. I will call this the *look and feel* of an application. I also like the definition that Application Express uses, shown here:

> *A theme is a named collection of templates used to define the user interface of an application.*

In addition to grouping templates under one umbrella, a theme also gives you a set of attributes that will drive the behavior of the theme as a whole. One of the many ways themes do this is by allowing you to define default choices within your applications. They will also have information about which templates will be the default. You can find these by going to Shared Components ➤ Themes and clicking your current theme. These attributes are as follows:

- Component Defaults
- Region Defaults
- Dialog Defaults

Component Defaults

Component Defaults is the section where you tell APEX which template to use by default for each of the possible elements. For example, in Figure 13-1, you can see that Page is set to Standard. Other options are Left Side Column, Left and Right Side Columns, Login, and so on.

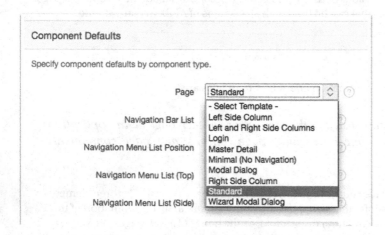

Figure 13-1. Theme attributes: Component Defaults

■ **Note** In the case of pages, it is recommended that you do not choose a page template every time you create a new page unless you want to override this default. You would choose the appropriate default here. All your pages will use the default value, and only those that require a different type of page layout would specify a template.

In a different example, scrolling further down the list of component defaults, buttons can have a default too. You can see that Text is the default value, and the other possible values are Icon, Text, and Text with Icon. Text in this case means that the button will contain readable text (such as Save, Add, and Delete). This will probably be your most used button template. (See Figure 13-2)

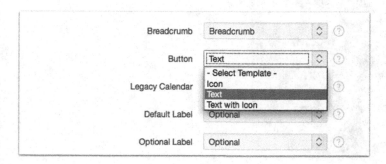

Figure 13-2. Component Defaults: button templates

Region Defaults

The Region Defaults settings are similar to the Component Defaults settings, but these apply to regions on the page. The distinction is subtle but still important. Many components in the Component Defaults section are elements that can be used only inside a region. That means that these regions apply an extra layer of styling to them. As a case in point, lists are both a region type and a component element. This is because you cannot display a list without a container for it, in other words, the region. The component is the list itself, and the region will contain the component. The List default setting for the component is Links List, and the default for List Region is 42. Standard. Translation, the component default for a list, will be Linked Lists, and it will be placed inside a 42. Standard region.

Dialog Defaults

APEX 5 introduced a new way of displaying pages, the Dialog page. In the past, I've called this type of UI element a *modal page*. A modal dialog, by definition, stops interaction with the calling page until it is dismissed. Dialogs, on the other hand, can be modal or nonmodal. The Dialog Defaults settings define the default type of template you want to use when you create new dialogs in your applications.

Out of the box, the Universal theme contains just a little over 50 templates. This number may be different as new releases come out. Regardless, this is a dramatic reduction from previous Application Express themes that would usually contain close to and upward of 100 (109 on Theme 26, for example).

All the magic from a theme happens in the templates. Template themselves have a powerful muscle to get things done called *substitution strings*.

The Substitution Strings

Have you ever seen the Russian dolls that fit one inside the other? Figure 13-3 shows a couple of sets of these dolls, and you can see how the different dolls in each set are sized in stepwise fashion.

Figure 13-3. *Templates work similar to Russian dolls*

Templates are somewhat similar to those dolls in that many of them go inside one another. Often, templates cannot be used without placing them inside another template. For example, as shown in Figure 13-4, you may have a button, inside a region, inside a page. All those three elements are templates. When you declare a button, you specify, at least, a label and usually an action. APEX will use that information, via substitution strings, to create the button. Then the completed button becomes a unit of information that will be placed inside a region. In this example, items are also part of that region. Once the region is generated, it also becomes a unit of information, and it becomes the substitution strings themselves that will be placed on a page.

```
←  →  C    Q http://apex.domain.com/apex/f?p=app          ≡

┌─ Login ──────────────────────────────────────────┐
│                                                   │
│    Username   [                    ]              │
│                                                   │
│    Password   [                    ]   [ Login ]  │
│                                                   │
└───────────────────────────────────────────────────┘
```

Figure 13-4. *Button inside a region inside a page*

Even more to the point, some elements, like regions, can also have subregions. The level of nesting can be even higher in these situations. I'll talk more about subregions later in the chapter. Figure 13-5 graphically shows how elements get to be part of other elements. It starts to become clear why the Russian doll analogy makes sense.

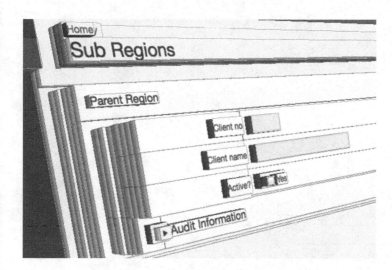

Figure 13-5. *3D representation of how components fit inside other components*

You can see how APEX places some content inside more content and yet again inside even other content. That nested placement is accomplished via substitution strings. Substitution strings are like programming variables that take a value, and whenever they are referenced, their value becomes what is used. You'll recognize them in a template because they are in uppercase and have hash signs at the beginning and end, for example #BODY#. #BODY# is one of the most popular substitution strings. It's popular mainly because it's often mandatory in many templates and because it corresponds to the Source section for many components. In Figure 13-6, you can see the Text field inside the Source section that will be used by the #BODY# substitution string.

Figure 13-6. *Source region attribute for a Standard region template*

Let's turn some HTML into a template. Say you have the following HTML:

```
<div>Hello</div>
```

To turn this into a template, you can do this:

```
<div>#BODY#</div>
```

There, you've built your first template! The substitution string #BODY# will now take many different values, and the template doesn't have to change. All the divs in Listing 13-1 can be outputs from the first template.

Listing 13-1.

```
<div>Hello World!</div>

<div><ul><li>List 1</li><li>List 2</li></ul></div>

<div>
  <button onclick="apex.submit('SAVE');">Apply Changes</button>
</div>
```

Since APEX provides a mechanism for you to pass CSS classes to a template, you may want to add the #REGION_CSS_CLASSES# substitution string to accomplish that. The CSS Classes field shown in Figure 13-7 corresponds to this substitution string.

```
<div class="#REGION_CSS_CLASSES#">#BODY#</div>
```

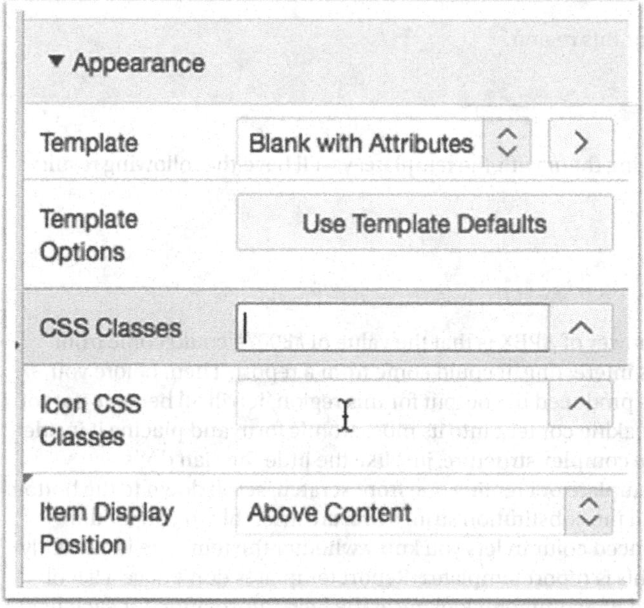

Figure 13-7. *The CSS Classes attribute in the builder maps to #REGION_CSS_CLASSES# in the template*

Next, sometimes you want to reference a region by name within CSS or JavaScript. In a region's attributes, in the Advanced section, you'll see Static ID. The value entered here goes straight into #REGION_STATIC_ID#; let's add that too.

```
<div id="#REGION_STATIC_ID#" class="#REGION_CSS_CLASSES#">
#BODY#
</div>
```

Finally, let's add a handful more substitution strings to the first template: #REGION_ATTRIBUTES# and #SUB_REGIONS#.

```
<div id="#REGION_STATIC_ID#" #REGION_ATTRIBUTES# class="#REGION_CSS_CLASSES#">
#BODY##SUB_REGIONS#
</div>
```

Save for some other small changes, you have just replicated the Blank with Attributes region template. In previous APEX releases and in certain themes, you've known this template as DIV Region with ID. It's an incredibly simple construct, with not a lot of visual footprint on the page, and yet, as you will see later, it's a powerful tool for placing content.

Table 13-1. *Values to Use for Building a Region*

Substitution String	Value
REGION_STATIC_ID	clientRegion
REGION_CSS_CLASSES	
REGION_ATTRIBUTES	
BODY	This is the content for this region.
SUB_REGIONS	

Given the values in Table 13-1, after merging them with the template, you'll have the following result:

```
<div id="clientRegion" class="">
This is the content for this region.
</div>
```

This example may seem simple, but the power of APEX is that the value of #BODY# could come from another completely different region. Or just as interesting, it could come from a report. Then, before you can see any of it on the screen, once APEX has produced the output for this region, it will all become part of the #BODY# attribute on a page. You end up breaking content into its most atomic form and placing it inside other elements in order to create a much more complex structure, just like the little Russian dolls.

Whenever you're looking at an existing template or creating one from scratch, scroll down to the bottom of the definition page. You'll see a table with all the substitution strings that are available to you for the specific type of template you're in. The Referenced column lets you know whether the template is currently using the substitution. The one exception to this is report templates. Report templates don't have a list of available and used substitution strings. Instead, I recommend looking at the help information for each field to learn what is available.

Finding Substitution Strings in the Application

Many components and application attributes have a clear relationship to certain substitution strings. Let's point out some that are important or frequently used.

The substitution strings #THEME_JAVASCRIPT# and #THEME_CSS# are accessible when you edit your theme attributes. They correspond to a list of files that will be added to every page in your application. You should enter one file per line, with a fully qualified path, and you don't need to use the <script> or <link> tag. If you reference a file uploaded to your application or workspace files, you can use #APP_IMAGES# or #WORKSPACE_IMAGES#, respectively, in the name. In the case of CSS files, you can optionally prefix each file with a condition like [if IE] or a media query. These substitution strings should be kept specific to making the theme function correctly as opposed to specific to the application. Put another way, this will be code that will be required across and used in all the applications that use this same theme.

The substitution strings #APPLICATION_JAVASCRIPT# and #APPLICATION_CSS# are similar to the previous two, but, as their name suggests, these are application specific. I find their placement, within APEX, hard to find at first. They are under User Interface Details. This means that if you're using a desktop and a mobile user interface, there will be two places where you can enter application-specific CSS and JavaScript. Go to Shared Components ➤ User Interface Attributes. Then edit the Desktop user interface. At the bottom of the page, as shown in Figure 13-9, you'll see a JavaScript and a Cascading Style Sheets section.

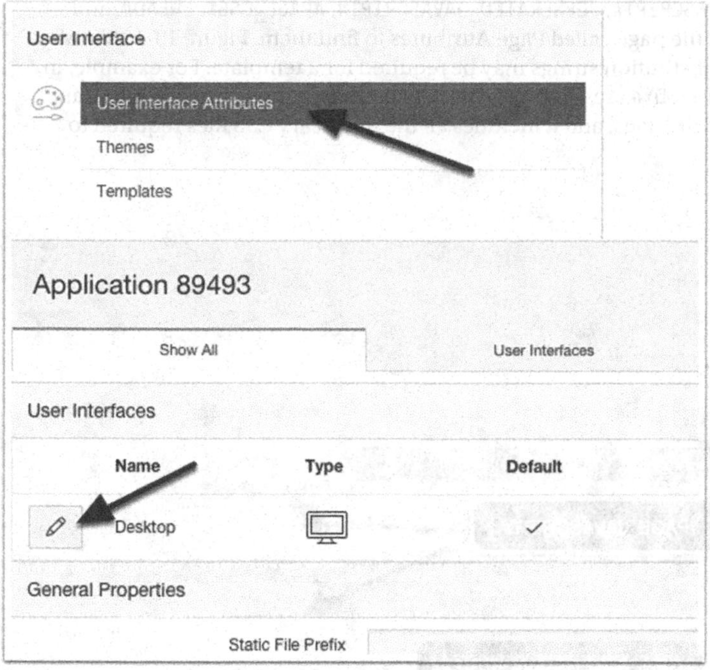

Figure 13-8. User Interface Attributes option

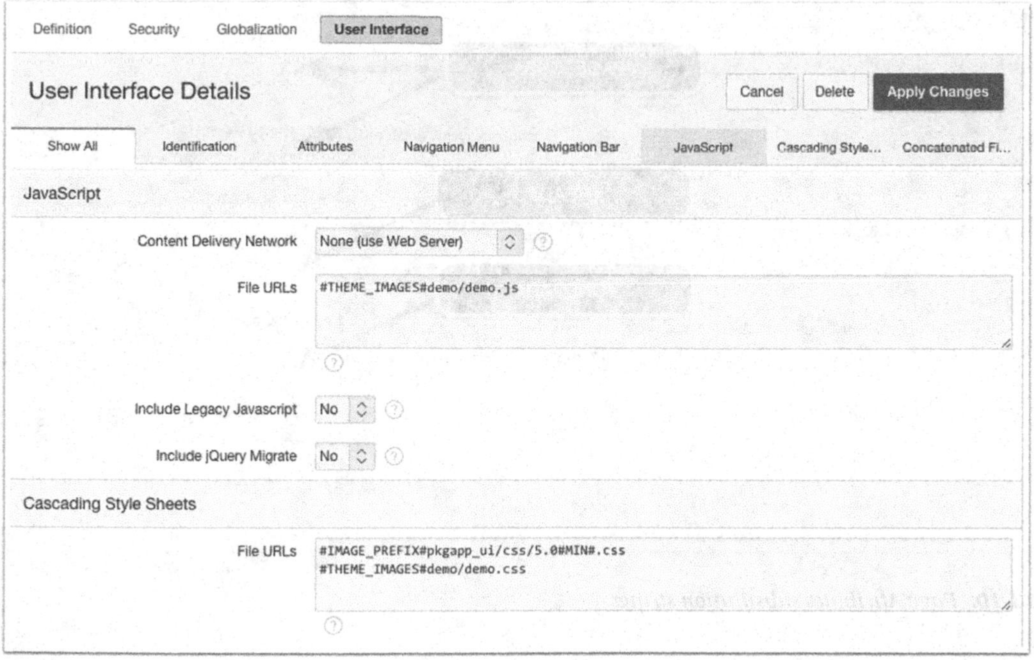

Figure 13-9. User Interface Details page

The substitution strings #PAGE_JAVASCRIPT#, #GENERATED_JAVASCRIPT#, #PAGE_CSS#, #HEAD#, and #ONLOAD# are specific to each page. Edit the page called Page Attributes to find them. Figure 13-10 shows which is which. Be aware that certain substitution strings may be required for a template. For example, in the case of a page template, #HEAD# and #BODY# are required. The #HEAD# substitution string is important because it will include certain meta and link tags, and it includes all the necessary CSS files required to correctly render the page.

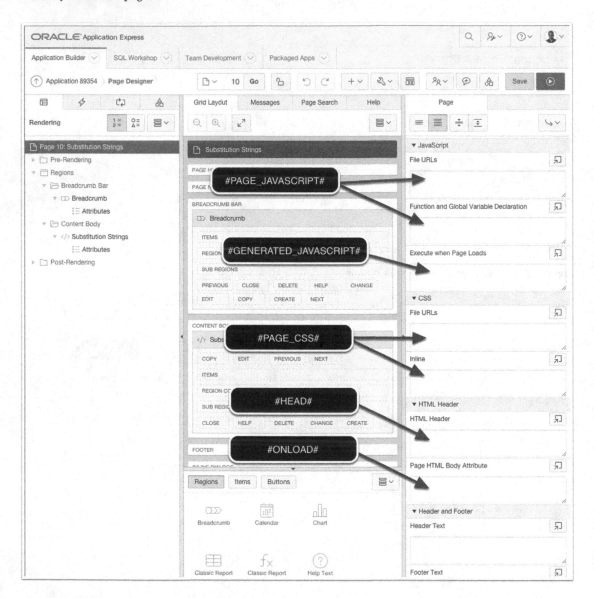

Figure 13-10. *Page Attributes substitution strings*

There are placeholder fields for substitution strings all throughout APEX. Keep an eye out for them. Recognizing them and identifying their use in a template will go a long way in helping you understand and maximize their uses. I'm going to finish this section identifying those used in a list template. Lists are a powerful tool while building APEX applications, and they have almost unlimited applications.

The following SQL sample, for a dynamic list, shows which values are mapped to which substitution strings. If you were using a static list, you would find the same fields and mappings.

```
--      column                   alias                       substitution string
----------------------------------------------------------------------------
select level,
       labelValue              label,                      #TEXT#
       [targetValue]           target,                     #LINK#
       [is_current]            is_current_list_entry,
       [imageValue]            image,                      #IMAGE#
       [imageAttributeValue]   image_attribute,            #IMAGE_ATTR#
       [imageAltValue]         image_alt_attribute,
       [attribute1]            attribute1,                 #A01#
       [attribute2]            attribute2,                 #A02#
       [attribute3]            attribute3,                 #A03#
       [attribute4]            attribute4,                 ...
       [attribute5]            attribute5
       ...
from ...
where ...
order by ...
```

In the case of a Linked List template, #IMAGE# is used to optionally define a class name to specify an icon. #A01# is used as the badge value. This badge can be anything, but it's often a count. Take a look at the following SQL:

```
select 1              lvl
     , 'Clients'      label
     , apex_util.prepare_url(
       'f?p=' || :APP_ID || ':CLIENTS:' || :APP_SESSION) target
     , 'NO'           is_current_list_entry
     , 'fa-user'      image
     , null           image_attribute
     , null           image_alt_attribute
     , null           attribute1
  from dual
union all
select 1              lvl
     , 'Providers'    label
     , apex_util.prepare_url(
       'f?p=' || :APP_ID || ':PROVIDERS:' || :APP_SESSION) target
     , 'NO'           is_current_list_entry
     , 'fa-building'  image
     , null           image_attribute
     , null           image_alt_attribute
     , 7              attribute1
  from dual
```

You can see, on Figure 13-11, how clients will have an icon defined by `fa-user` and providers will have an icon defined by `fa-building` and a badge value of 7.

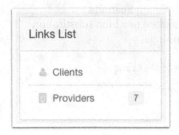

Figure 13-11. List with icons and badges

The following is the actual HTML template of the list that is creating the previous list. As you can see, there are substitution strings for the #LINK#, #TEXT#, #A01#, and so on.

```
<li class="t-LinksList-item is-current #A03#">
  <a href="#LINK#" class="t-LinksList-link" #A02#>
   <span class="t-LinksList-icon">
     <span class="t-Icon #IMAGE#"></span>
   </span>
   <span class="t-LinksList-label">#TEXT#</span>
   <span class="t-LinksList-badge">#A01#</span>
  </a>
</li>
```

■ **Note**   By default, the Linked List template does not display icons or badges. You need to enable them via the Template Options settings. The Template Options settings are explained in more detail later in the chapter.

Theme Styles

Theme styles provide an easy way to change the look of an app without changing the theme or template. They define a set of CSS styles that your application will use. Applications can have any number of theme styles defined; however, only one can be current at a time. Different from themes, theme styles can be changed at runtime. Calling the following API from within your application will change the theme style at runtime and make a different, previously created theme style current:

```
apex_util.set_current_theme_style (
  , p_theme_number    => l_theme_number
  , p_theme_style_id => l_theme_style_id
);
```

You can obtain the two parameter values from `apex_application_themes.theme_number`, where `is_current ='Yes'`, and from `apex_application_theme_styles.theme_style_id` dictionary objects.

■ **Note**   Calling `apex_util.set_current_theme_style` means that your application is going to modify itself. APEX 5 has a security setting to allow or deny such activities. Go to Application Attributes ➤ Security and under Runtime API Usage select the appropriate option.

This is a powerful feature because you could even let your users change the look of the application. Imagine giving your end users the ability to switch the theme style of an application they use day-in and day-out. All of a sudden, they will have a renewed excitement using an application that has a new skin but whose functionality has not been compromised by them changing the style. This activity can be as simple as changing the wallpaper on their desktop.

In the initial release of APEX 5, the Universal theme has two predefined theme styles: Vita, which uses a blue color scheme, and Vita – Slate, which is a gray to dark gray color scheme. It is easy for developers to create new ones via a powerful new tool in APEX 5, the Theme Roller.

"Style is the way you say who you are without having to speak."

—Rachel Zoe

The Theme Roller

Another amazing new feature of APEX 5 is the Theme Roller. The Theme Roller is a tool that allows developers to customize many aspects of certain application components. It allows developers to pick styles and colors and see their effect on the application via an interactive tool. Figure 13-12 shows the Theme Roller button you will use to invoke it via the Developer Toolbar. Figure 13-13 demonstrates the Style select list available from within the Theme Roller. Finally, Figure 13-14 shows the end result of switching from the Vita style to the Vita – Slate style.

Figure 13-12.   *Theme Roller option on the Developer Toolbar*

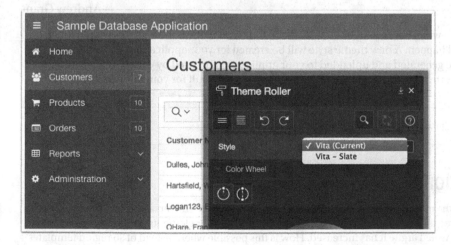

Figure 13-13.   *Switching theme styles from within the Theme Roller*

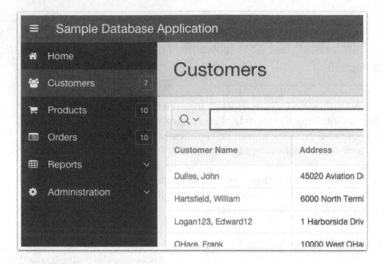

Figure 13-14. *Sample Database Application page after switching to Vita – Slate theme style*

To create a new theme style from the Theme Roller, all you have to do is pick your starting style and start modifying attributes and colors. In addition to colors, some of the attributes that can be changed with the Theme Roller are border radius for several components, navigation tree width, actions and left-side column widths, and the maximum width of the body container. There's also a Custom CSS field where you can enter any other CSS classes and attributes you need to override or reference.

When it comes to picking colors, however, I strongly recommend you seek the assistance of a graphic designer or at least use a tool to help you select colors that complement each other or provide a cohesive tonal range across all components of your application. Your favorite sport team's colors will most likely not work well for an application (unless the application is for said team). Nothing damages the trust of your users on an application faster than a bad-looking UI.

> ""*You never get a second change to make a first impression.*"

—Andrew Grant

Once you're pleased with your new style, click the Save As button at the bottom of the Theme Roller. At this time, two things will happen. A new theme style will be created for your application, and a new CSS file with your choices will be generated and uploaded to your application and used by your new style. After this is done, use the Set as Current button to make your new creation the default for your application.

───

■ **Note**   The Theme Roller is an APEX 5 and Universal theme feature only.

───

Template Options

I mentioned before that the number of templates is drastically reduced in the Universal theme (Theme 42) from previous themes. However, the flexibility and number of options to style your elements on the screen did not go down. On the contrary, I would argue it has increased. How is this possible when instead of 36 region templates (on Theme 25) you now have 13 (on the new Theme 42)? How is this possible when in the case of buttons the number has gone from 10 templates to now 3 in the Universal theme? The answer is Template Options settings.

Template Options settings add an extra degree of configuration (or styling) to just about any template. It's an elegant, simple, and yet powerful approach to styling templates with developer-defined options. Take, for example, Figure 13-15. All variations from the default view were achieved by simply selecting the options Accent, Item Size Large, and Remove Borders. Figure 13-16 shows the dialog where the Template Options settings can be selected.

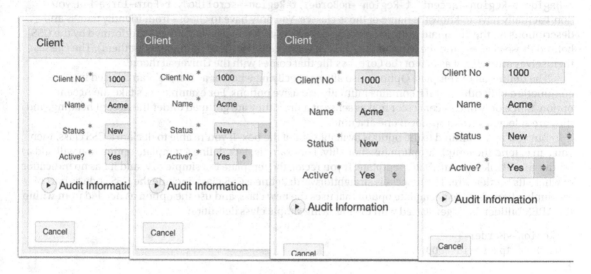

Figure 13-15. *Using Accent 5, Item Size Large, and Remove Borders*

Figure 13-16. *Available Template Options settings for the standard template*

This was only a small portion of all the default Template Options settings available to the standard template used by this region.

At their core, think of a template option as a value pair, meaning a name and assigned value. The name is what you will see when you select the option, and the value is a CSS class (or list of CSS classes). In the previous example, the following CSS classes were added by APEX to the region as the options were selected: t-Region, t-Region--accent5, t-Region--noBorder, t-Region--scrollBody, t-Form—large. But, you don't actually have to know the name of those classes. You only have to choose from friendly names and descriptions on the Template Options selection page. The actual magic, of course, is performed by the CSS behind those classes (and the effort of the APEX development team that thought about them). The classes themselves are defined as part of the Core.css file that comes with the Universal theme.

The definition of Template Options also allows specifying whether a "feature" can be used in conjunction with others or if it contains mutually exclusive options. For example, let's take the Accent option. Since only one Accent color makes sense at a time, they are grouped under the Accent heading, and they are selected via a drop-down one at a time.

But you're not limited to the options available out of the box. If you're able to declare a CSS class, then you can extend the template option functionality. For example, let's define a template option that will add a border to a Blank with Attributes template. If you recall, the template is a simple div, and it has no indication of where its borders are. The process is straightforward: define a CSS class, include the CSS code as part of the application, declare a template option that uses the new class, and use the option as needed from within the APEX builder. Let's get started with the following simple class definition:

```
.c-Region--Border {
  border: 1px solid #DDD;
}
```

You can then define a With Border template option that will add a 1-pixel solid line all around in a light gray color. You'll add this to the Blank with Attributes template. Go to Shared Components ➤ Templates ➤ Find and edit the Blank with Attributes template. In the Template Options section, click Add Template Option and use the values shown in Figure 13-17.

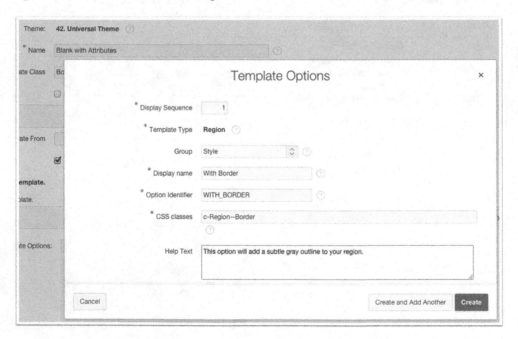

Figure 13-17. *Define a template option*

With the template option defined, you are ready to apply the new With Border Template Option setting to any of the Blank with Attributes regions. Select the region in the Page Designer, under Appearance find Template Options, and click it. Figure 13-18 shows where you can find this. Once you click the Template Options button, you'll see a modal dialog, as shown in Figure 13-19.

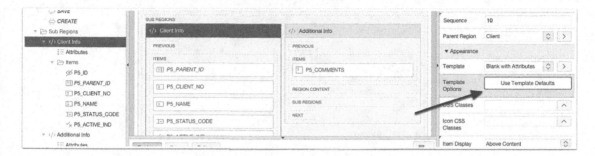

Figure 13-18. *Editing a region's template options*

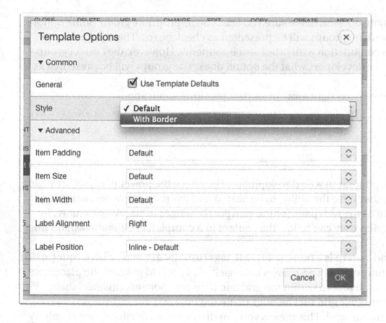

Figure 13-19. *Finding the new Style option With Border*

You are almost ready to test your handy work, except for one important step. You need to add the CSS Class definition to your application. Normally, best practice would be to place it in a file and register the file as part of the user interface under "Cascading Style Sheets." APEX will then add it as part of the #APPLICATION_CSS# mentioned earlier in the chapter. However, for this example, placing the CSS on the Page Attributes Inline CSS setting will do just fine.

Figure 13-20 shows the before and after effect of adding the new template option to a Blank with Attributes subregion.

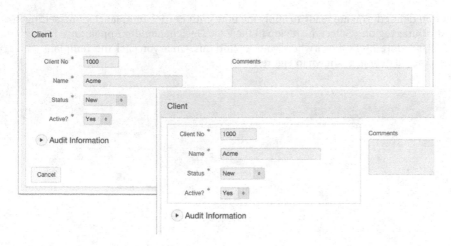

Figure 13-20. *Subregion Blank with Attributes with new With Border option applied (before and after)*

When you create your own template options, make sure you select an appropriate group. Some options will not need one. Template options with no groups will be presented as check boxes. These are elements that can be compounded and used in conjunction with other visual elements. However, the correct group will go a long way in explaining to future developers what the option does. The groups will be presented as a select list.

As a bonus, template options can be used right away in all your previous applications and themes, not just with the Universal theme.

The Grid

Grid systems have become incredibly popular in web development. They have the power of neatly arranging and uniformly spacing elements. Yet, they have the ability to be nested and the property of becoming fluid and changing in size and arrangement as the web page (or the viewport) changes in size. What's more, in small screens, like that of a mobile device, they can reflow the content in a completely different fashion from a desktop layout.

To put it simply and bluntly, a grid system is a bunch of HTML tags (usually div tags) where your (main) web content is placed and some carefully crafted CSS classes arrange it all. This grid governs the placement of the main content on a page. Regions are placed within the grid and then components (mainly labels, items, and buttons) are placed inside another grid that belongs to the region.

The Universal theme uses a 12-column grid. This means you can divide your available space evenly by 12. I think it helps to think of the screen as having 12 units or buckets, of equal size, to place your content on. First, you start by placing elements on the first row. Then, as you're done placing elements on that row, you can move to the next one and so on. On every row, you once again have 12 columns to work with. As elements are placed, you need to make sure always to use (or account for) all 12 columns. When you need more control or your layout is complex, it's also possible to nest one grid within another. If you were building web sites with a text editor or some other tool or framework other than APEX, I would now start talking about the row class, column class, first and last column classes, spans, offsets, nesting, and so on. However, APEX makes all this declarative and simple for you to use. (See Figure 13-21.)

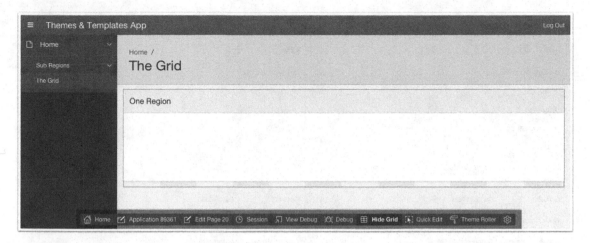

Figure 13-21. *Twelve-column grid visible behind the region thanks to the Show/Hide Grid option*

The APEX Developer Toolbar provides a useful toggle button to show or hide the grid. In Figure 13-21, you can see the grid overlay just peeking behind the One Region area. You can count 12 columns, all exactly the same size. If you resize the browser, there will still be 12 columns of exactly the same size, only smaller in width.

In Figure 13-22 you can see the grid attributes that you can use to control the placement of regions and items (or elements within a region). As you can see, they are identical. This is because whether you're placing a region or placing an item, you have the same rules to play with. Keep this in mind as I discuss each attribute. Start New Row means that the previous row in the grid, if present, will be closed, and a new grid row will start. This is important because the new row will once again allow for 12 columns for a layout. If you were working on the first row in your layout, then Start New Row would have no bearing. However, it is still a good practice to decide whether you want the Star New Row attribute to be Yes if you added a row above. In general, I think you want to start your first row with a Yes in this attribute to avoid future layout surprises. The Column option indicates in which of the 12 columns of the grid this element or component will be placed. The Automatic option allows APEX to calculate the column where the next element will be placed; of course, APEX will start from the left with column 1. When the Column calculation is changed from Automatic to a specific value, Column Span becomes available. Column Span indicates how many columns the element will use. When left as Automatic, APEX will simply fill out the rest of the row.

Figure 13-22. *On the left, Grid options for a region. On the right, Grid options for an item*

The Grid options shown in Figure 13-22 depend on specific values defined in the grid section of the page template. This means that each page could potentially use a different type of grid. However, unless you're creating your templates, this will be of no concern for most users.

APEX will make every effort to avoid invalid grid value combinations that violate the limit of a 12-column grid. If your current column position plus the column span is greater than 12, APEX will generate an error because the placement will not be possible. For example, see Figure 13-23. If you specify placement on column 4 but indicate a column span of 10 (10 + 4 > 12), you will see an error.

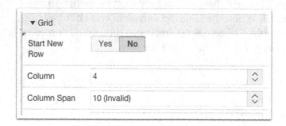

Figure 13-23. *Invalid grid value combination*

You may already have noticed that APEX 5 by default will display either "common" component attributes or the most used attributes. When placing items there are three more attributes that you should know about and they are visible only when you click the Show All selector: Label Column Span, Column CSS Classes, and Column Attributes. Figure 13-24 shows what you're looking for.

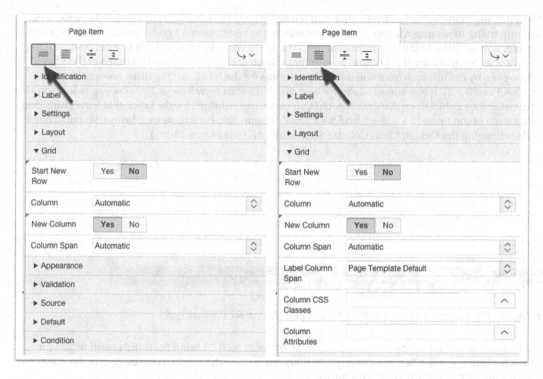

Figure 13-24. Extra attributes available when you click the Show All selector

Label Column Span is a new APEX 5 attribute and a welcome enhancement. Its default value is specified at the page template level, and it can be modified for specific items. To edit the default, you simply edit the page template you're using, go to the Grid Layout section, and find the Default Label Column Span attribute. The default value for the Standard page template is three. This means that every item placed on a row will require three columns for the label alone. Then nine columns are available for the rest of the item. (See Figure 13-25.)

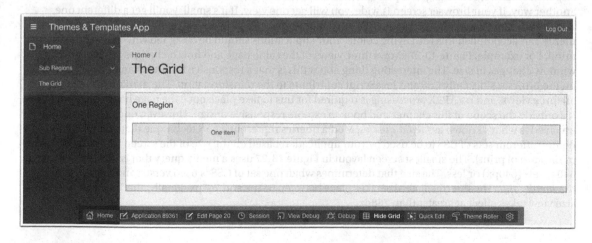

Figure 13-25. Using the Developer Toolbar to visualize the default three-column label span

When placing items in front of each other, you'll want to keep the label span in mind. Otherwise, it can be frustrating trying to arrange a layout and not understanding where your 12 grid columns are being used. For example, if in addition to the One Item item in Figure 13-25 you add another item in front by specifying Start New Row as No and leave the Column as Automatic, then each item will use 6 columns of the 12-grid layout. However, by default each item will use three columns for the label, leaving three more columns for the item (3 + 3 and 3 + 3). If you added one more item also with Start New Row as No, now you're looking at each item using four columns on the grid. If each item uses three columns for the label, that leaves only one column for each of the items (3 + 1, 3 + 1, and 3 + 1). At this point, depending on your layout, you may need to consider changing the Default Label Column Span attribute. (See Figure 13-26.)

Figure 13-26. *Three items: three column labels and one column for the item*

The Default Label Column Span attribute can also be set to zero. This is a powerful layout technique when the label is not needed. Setting it to zero will place the item in the column exactly next to the previous item (or column 1 if this is the first item on the row).

When using Start New Row as No and New Column as No also, APEX will now place two items inside the same grid cell. However, in many layouts, as a default behavior, they will be placed below each other unless some extra CSS attributes (or custom template option) are applied to them.

Responsive Layout

The other powerful feature of the Universal theme's grid layout is responsiveness. You call a layout *responsive* when it can change the placement of elements on the screen based on the space available. Put another way, if your browser screen is wide, you will get one view. If it's small, you'll get a different one, and if you're on the smallest of screens, like on a mobile device, you'll see yet another view. The Universal theme can accomplish this with flying colors. Your applications should be designed with this feature in mind. For example, Figure 13-27 shows three views of the same page and how it changes as the browser window changes in size. The interesting thing about this is that a responsive layout is handled exclusively on the browser side. Only CSS and JavaScript contribute to the transformation. The markup is the same for all three views, and no APEX processing is required for this to take place once the page has been rendered. It's outside the scope of this chapter and book to explore responsive design. However, one of the techniques involved is what's known as *media queries*. Media queries represent a CSS technique that allows you to define different sets of CSS to be used by your application based on the size of the screen (or the media like in the case of print). The smallest screen layout in Figure 13-27 uses a media query that is used on screens of 640 pixels (640px) or less. The size that determines when one set of CSS is used versus another is known as the *breakpoint*. The intermediate size takes place between 641px and 767px. Finally, the "normal" desktop size view takes effect at greater than 768px.

Figure 13-27. *Effects of different screen sizes on a responsive design*

Subregions

It's common to have several regions on one page, certainly more than one. If you've ever had to place more than a dozen items on one page or some items and a report, you probably placed multiple regions on a page already. However, did you know APEX supports regions within regions? Any time you place some region inside another one, I'll call it a *subregion*. See Figure 13-28 for an example of placing several subregions inside each other. This example may not seem that useful, but it demonstrates the powerful ability to nest one region within another. This goes back to the substitution strings and the Russian dolls analogy I made before. You can always break down a layout into the smallest parts you can and then place them inside another to create much more complex designs.

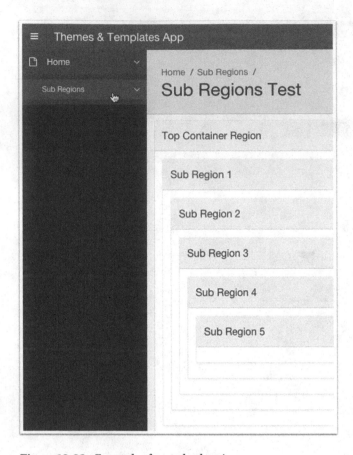

***Figure 13-28.** Example of nested subregions*

I think subregions are usually an underutilized feature for placing content on the page. Consider the following standard layout from the APEX wizard, as shown in Figure 13-29.

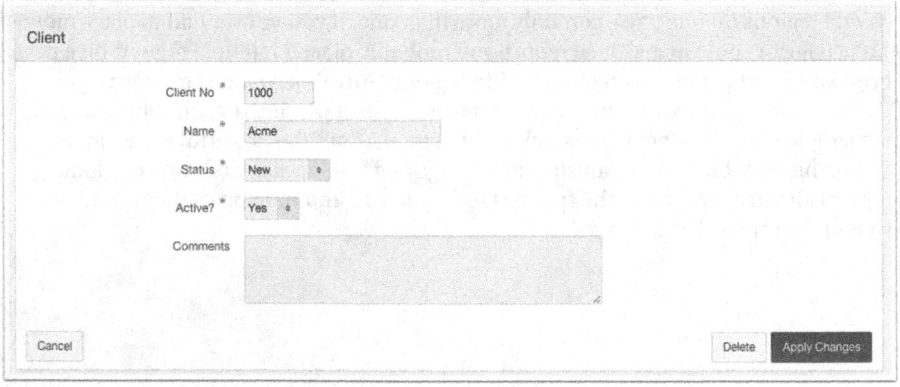

***Figure 13-29.** Standard wizard layout*

If you ask me, it seems like this layout could better utilize space on the right side. Turn on the template option in the region called Stretch Form Fields to get the effect shown in Figure 13-30.

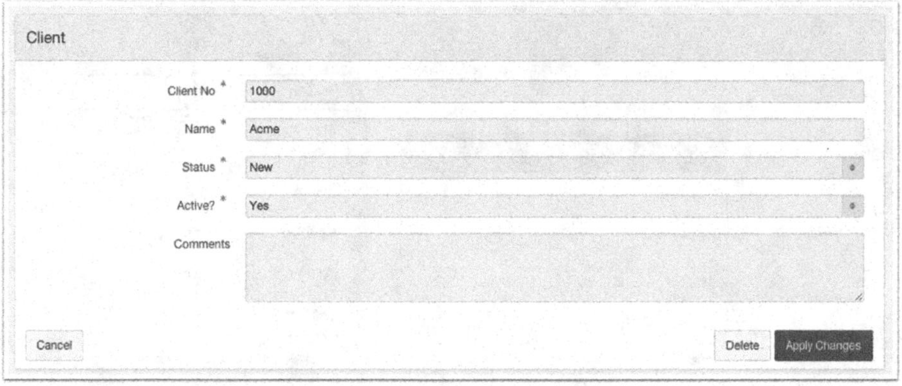

Figure 13-30. *Stretch Form Fields template option applied*

However, I think that sometimes a subregion could give you a nice end result. I left the Client region as a standard template. Then I added a new region, Client Info, as a subregion of Clients using the Blank with Attributes template and moved all the items except the comments to it. Then I added another subregion to Clients, also with a Blank with Attributes template, and called it Additional Info. I changed the grid attributes for this one, setting Star New Row to No and New Column to Yes. This way, both Client Info and Additional Info are side by side. You already know APEX would use six columns for one and six for the other (if you leave everything as Automatic). However, depending on your layout, you could try different settings with the Column and Column Span attributes. The Comments item gets moved to the new Additional Info region, and its label is changed to Above. Figure 13-31 shows the result.

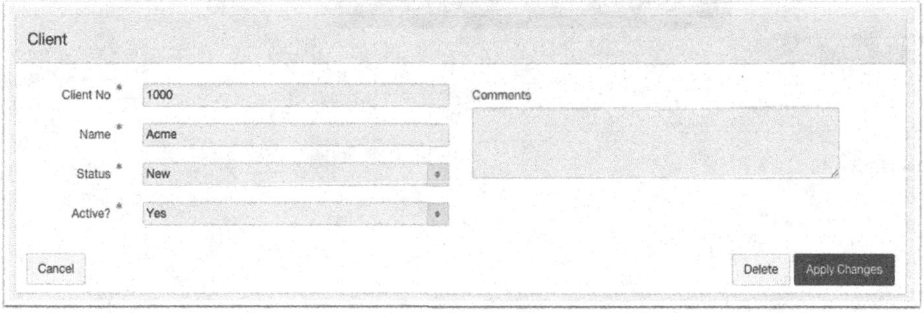

Figure 13-31. *Layout using two subregions for item placement side by side*

Remember that inside each of the subregions (Client Info and Additional Info), you still get 12 columns inside each to work out a layout. Keep this in mind that these 12 columns will be significantly smaller than the 12 columns available to the parent Client region (roughly half the size to be exact). Optionally, you could also apply the With Border template option you defined earlier in the chapter to the Client Info subregion. This effect will give you a nice grouping of items, which something is important to draw the viewer's eyes to a set of elements on the screen.

Figure 13-32. *Page Designer with Client region and subregions*

Let's look at the new Tabs Container template. This new template in the Universal theme couldn't be easier to use. You add a static region and select Tabs Container as the template. Then add regions inside it as subregions. Figure 13-33 shows the tab region with the following interactive reports that will be displayed as tabs: Orders, Contacts, Statements, and Batches. Finally, Figure 13-34 shows the end result of the Contacts tab selected. As the tabs are selected, the other tabs are hidden.

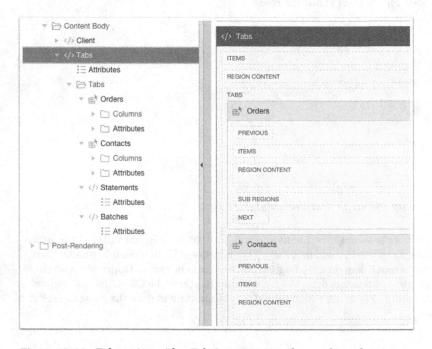

Figure 13-33. *Tabs region with a Tab Container template and its subregions*

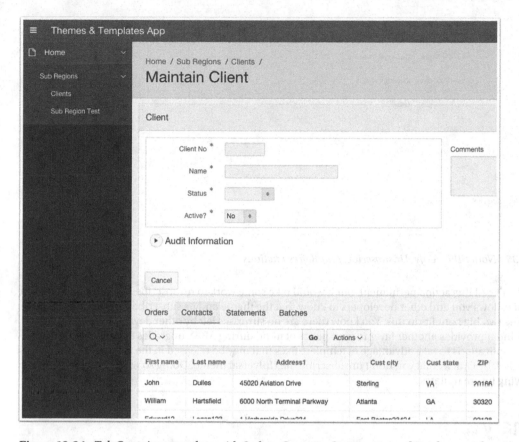

Figure 13-34. *Tab Container template with Orders, Contacts, Statements, and Batches as subregions*

Theme Subscriptions

Theme subscriptions are a powerful feature that allow organizations to create applications that share a theme with a single application. This application becomes the keeper or the master for the theme. Said another way, if you want to change a template on a subscribed theme, you would need to either break the subscription or, better yet, change the master and refresh the subscription. By refreshing subscriptions, you ensure consistency across all applications.

In APEX 5, when you create a new application based on any theme, the theme will be subscribed to the master in the theme repository. Effectively, this means your application theme and all the templates within are locked from modifications.

However, don't worry. If required, you can still add new templates to the theme, and these will be fully editable. Now, to make the whole theme fully editable, you can unsubscribe from the theme repository. When you attempt to unsubscribe a theme, you will see the following verbiage.

Note that subscribed themes can be extended by adding templates, styles, and files that are local to the theme, for example by creating a new template or copying a subscribed template. Templates, styles, and files added to a subscribed theme will be editable. However, subscribed components are read-only.

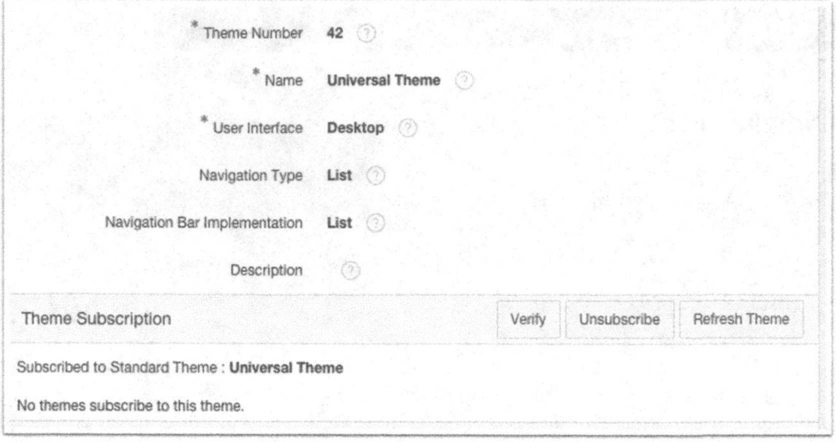

* Theme Number	42 ⑦	
* Name	**Universal Theme** ⑦	
* User Interface	**Desktop** ⑦	
Navigation Type	**List** ⑦	
Navigation Bar Implementation	**List** ⑦	
Description	⑦	

Theme Subscription	Verify	Unsubscribe	Refresh Theme

Subscribed to Standard Theme : **Universal Theme**

No themes subscribe to this theme.

Figure 13-35. *Notice the Verify, Unsubscribe, and Refresh actions*

I wouldn't call this action permanent, but it would take some work to resubscribe. There's a good reason for this. This allows you and other developers to know that the theme and its subscribed templates are still pristine. I see two big benefits to this. You know there are no surprises left by other developers hidden in the templates, and it provides another layer to your peace of mind during APEX upgrades and patches. It will allow your applications to take advantage of template fixes that may be released in the future. It is strongly recommended, by Oracle, that you don't unsubscribe the Universal theme. Doing so will prevent your theme from receiving future updates.

Summary

Themes and templates in APEX are a vast topic. There are many areas still left to uncover. However, it was my goal to demystify some core aspects and give you the foundation and tools that to give you the confidence to venture deeper on your own. I find the whole architecture and functionality of themes and templates within APEX fascinating and incredibly powerful.

For your next steps, I recommend investing time learning and understanding HTML and CSS. The more you know about CSS, the more you will understand the capabilities and tools at your disposal. The more you understand HTML, the better you can build creative and functional layouts.

Now go forth and make your applications your own; make them sing!

CHAPTER 14

■ ■ ■

Report Printing

by Karen Cannell

Report printing in APEX is a wide topic, with perhaps as many solutions as there are organizations looking to address the problem. This chapter focuses on the APEX-supplied standard report printing solution for producing Portable Document Format (PDF) output. This option uses the built-in generic XSL Formatting Objects (XSL-FO) templates for classic and interactive reports and uses APEX report queries and customized report layouts for more specialized report configurations.

Introduction

Report printing gets a bad rap in APEX. Some simply say APEX has none and that APEX report printing is achieved only through other Oracle or third-party tools or plugins. Some maintain the report printing features APEX does include are insufficient. The negative messages steer people away from the report printing options that APEX does have. But they deserve a closer look.

The naysayers are partially correct: APEX does not have a declarative what-you-see-is-what-you-get (WYSIWYG) report printing solution. Why not? Well, report printing means many things to many organizations. What to build? At the cost of what other features? Report printing is often addressed though an external reporting tool, one specifically designed to address a specific set of enterprise report generation and report printing use cases.

Those who say APEX report printing features are insufficient are also partially correct. APEX offers report printing features in two configurations: standard and advanced. Standard configuration is through the Apache Formatted Objects Processor (FOP) PDF print processor. The FOP processor is supplied with APEX installation material or can be accessed through Oracle Rest Data Services (ORDS) when APEX is deployed via ORDS. Advanced configuration is through Oracle Business Intelligence Publisher (BI Publisher) at an added cost. The advanced report printing configuration offers a wider variety of formats and layout options with significantly less effort, at a significantly higher price tag. Because of the added license, you could rightly argue the advanced report printing is not really an APEX option; it is an add-on.

Neither the standard nor advanced report printing option covers all printing use cases. Neither of these options is declarative WYSIWYG, and neither is effortless in producing a given set of possible results. In that light, both options could be deemed insufficient. These options do cover many simple report printing options, however, and are, in my opinion, overlooked and underused.

This chapter focuses on the standard configuration: producing PDF output solutions in APEX using the built-in generic XSL-FO templates for classic and interactive reports and using report queries and customized report layouts for more customized report layouts.

I'll focus on the standard report printing features because

- Standard report printing may be configured at no additional cost in all APEX instances.

- Many APEX developers do not take the time to understand report layouts to make practical use of them.

The goal is to demonstrate the extent of report printing options possible with standard APEX report printing.

Report Printing

For the scope of this chapter, *report printing* is the generation of a formatted, printable representation of a given APEX report, in other words, the ability to produce a report as PDF output.

Report printing is distinct from generating an HTML page, where the purpose of the output is display; a Microsoft Excel spreadsheet, where the purpose of the output is display and manipulation; or an export format suitable for database inserts or imports, where the purpose of the output is transport or consumption by another tool.

Printable formats usually take the form of a Word document, a Rich Text Format (RTF) document, or a PDF document. The use of APEX standard report printing limits your output type to PDF.

■ **Note**   If RTF or Excel output is required, these formats can be achieved using similar methods with the advanced report printing option using BI Publisher. With BI Publisher, generating report layouts is much simpler. This chapter assumes that you do not have access to BI Publisher and explains the long way of building XSL-FO report layouts. If you are lucky enough to have BI Publisher, you may not need the rest of this chapter except for reference.

APEX Standard Report Printing

APEX is great at declaratively generating reports, classic and interactive. APEX is less great at *declaratively* generating PDF output representations of those classic and interactive reports, but it still does a commendable job with most configurations, with little effort and no added cost.

APEX standard report printing is available in all APEX installations but needs to be implemented with Apache FOP or another XSL-FO print engine, either through the use of ORDS (which includes Apache FOP 1.1) or through the deployment of FOP on Glassfish, WebLogic, or a similar Java runtime environment (such as Tomcat).

Advanced printing refers to the set of features available when APEX is configured with BI Publisher. Using BI Publisher requires a valid license from Oracle. BI Publisher brings significantly improved report configuration features at a significant price tag that may be prohibitive for some organizations. Perhaps the biggest advantage of using BI Publisher is the ability to build and use RTF templates that make it easier to produce more complex report formats and embed graphics and charts. For more information on BI Publisher, see the Oracle BI Publisher page at `https://go.oracle.com/LP=4639?elqCampaignId=7916&src1 =ad:pas:go:dg:bi&src2=wwmk14056808mpp010&SC=sckw=WWMK14056808MPP010`.

The chapter aims to dispel the myths surrounding APEX standard report printing options. Yes, XSL-FO layouts used in APEX report layouts are difficult to build. They are downright painful to build manually, and XSL-FO WYSIWYG editors can be expensive. In fact, the perhaps best report layout editor for APEX reports, BI Publisher, can be expensive if you have not already invested in an Oracle Business Intelligence license. The combination of complex XSL-FO syntax and expensive editors means that many organizations dismiss using the APEX report templates before giving them an honest try.

Prerequisites

The examples in this chapter assume you have a working APEX 5 installation configured for PDF printing or have an `apex.oracle.com` workspace. Specifically, you need the following:

- Oracle Database 11.2 or newer

- APEX 4.2 or newer (though all the screenshots and examples are based on APEX 5.0)

- Oracle Rest Data Services 3.0 configured as a web listener for APEX (though APEX Listener 2.0.6 or newer will suffice)

For the XSL-FO examples, it is recommended that you have at least an editor that provides XML syntax highlighting. An XSL-FO WYSIWYG editor is not required, though using one will help you learn XSL-FO faster and will likely help you build XSL-FO templates faster. Consider using a trial version of a third-party XSL-FO tool or one of the following:

- Altova StyleVision

- Stylus Studio

- Java4Less FO Designer

For general PL/SQL editing, an PL/SQL IDE is recommended. The examples in this chapter were created using SQL Developer 4.1. SQL Developer does have syntax highlighting for XML documents, including XSL and XSL-FO documents. If all you are doing is editing existing XSL-FO documents, SQL Developer will suffice. To learn more about XSL-FO, try one of the recommended editors.

Standard Report Printing Configuration

Standard APEX report printing requires configuration. It is not enabled by default as part of the APEX installation process. Standard report printing configuration for an APEX instance entails two steps:

1. Install and configure an FOP print processor.

2. Set the APEX instance's report printing attributes.

For APEX standard print processing, there are three main options for an FOP print processor.

- Use the Apache FOP print engine included in ORDS.

- Use the `fop.war` file supplied with the APEX installation.

- Use an external XSL-FO print processor.

The overall architecture and flow of APEX standard FOP print processing is slightly different depending on which of the previous options you use. Figure 14-1 illustrates the standard APEX report printing architecture using an external FOP processor.

When using the FOP processor embedded in ORDS, the flow is similar except that the PDF output is rendered in the ORDS listener and then returned to the client; there is no need to pass the PDF output back to the database. Because of this, when using the FOP in ORDS, the APEX print APIs are not supported.

When a user clicks a report's Print link or an interactive report's Download PDF option, APEX generates and sends an XML version of the report data to the FOP print engine, along with an XSL-FO report template (either the generic template or a named-column report template defined in a report layout). The FOP processor generates PDF output from the XML data and the XSL-FO template. The PDF output is displayed to the end user (when using ORDS) or passed back to the database and then to the end user (when using an external FOP processor), as shown in Figure 14-1.

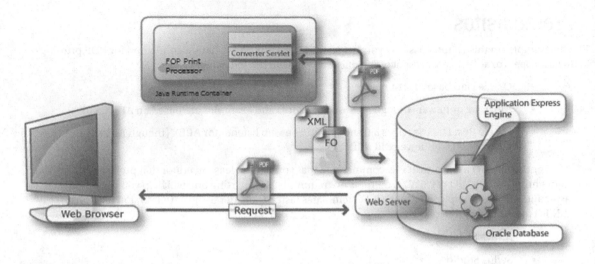

Figure 14-1. *APEX standard report printing architecture with external FOP*

FOP Processor in ORDS

If the APEX instance is deployed using ORDS 3 or newer, the instance can be configured to use the Apache FOP 1.1 engine included in ORDS. The FOP processor is not enabled by default in ORDS 3.0 and newer, like it was in earlier versions of ORDS. If you are using ORDS earlier than version 2.2, you may not need to specifically enable FOP as described in the remainder of this section.

To enable the FOP Print Server in ORDS 3.0 or newer, ensure the following line exists in the defaults.xml ORDS configuration file:

```
<entry key="misc.enableOldFOP">true</entry>
```

■ **Note**   While not essential, it is nice to keep like entries in defaults.xml together because it makes it easier for you or the next person to find a particular entry in the future. I recommend placing the misc.enableOldFOP entry with the other misc entries.

To enable FOP in ORDS 3.0 or newer, follow these steps:

1. Locate the defaults.xml file in the ORDS deployment directory. This will be at the top level of the ORDS configuration directory you specified when ORDS was configured.

2. Edit defaults.xml. Locate the misc entries. Add the following line:

```
<entry key="misc.enableOldFOP">true</entry>
```

Save and exit the file.

3. Restart ORDS for the changed FOP setting to take effect.

4. Set the APEX instance Report Printing attributes to use ORDS, as shown in Figure 14-2.

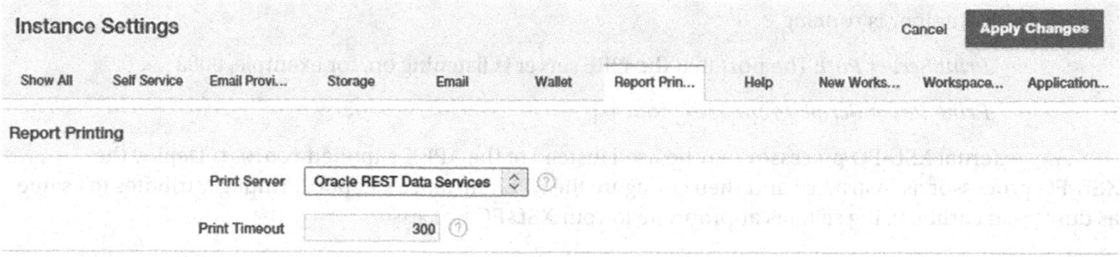

Figure 14-2. *APEX instance's Report Printing settings for ORDS*

External FOP Processor

If not configured with ORDS, the `fop.war` file supplied in the APEX installation media may be deployed on Glassfish, WebLogic, or a similar Java runtime server such as Apache Tomcat or IBM JBoss.

See the Oracle APEX document "PDF Printing in Application Express" at the following location for instructions on deploying Apache FOP:

www.oracle.com/technetwork/developer-tools/apex/application-express/configure-printing-093060.html

While much of this document describes BI Publisher configuration, section 5 addresses installing and configuring Apache FOP, and section 6 addresses configuring other XSL-FO processing engines. Once `fop.war` is deployed, the APEX instance Report Printing attributes need to be set as shown in Figure 14-3.

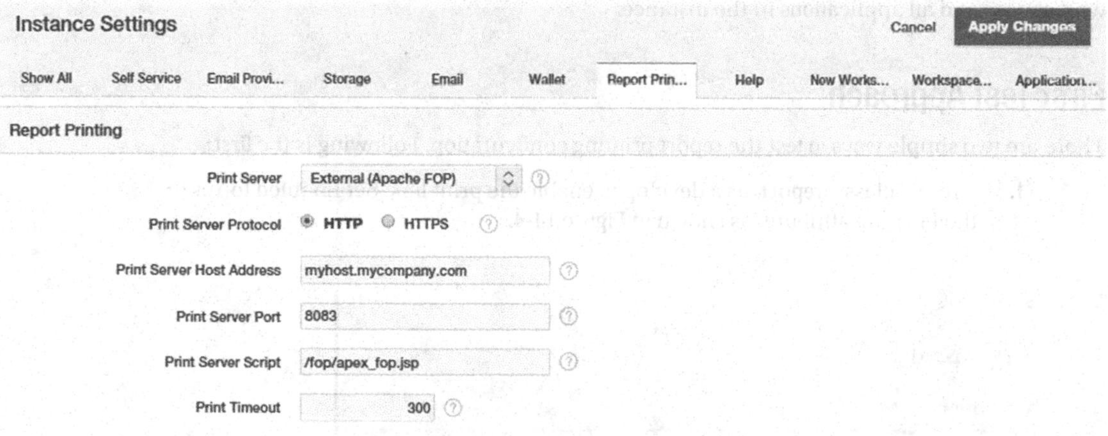

Figure 14-3. *APEX Report Printing attributes with external Apache FOP*

The attributes are as follows:

Print Server Protocol: HTTP or HTTPS depending on your configuration

Print Server Host Address: The hostname for the machine where the Java container is running

Print Server Port: The port that the J2EE server is listening on, for example, 8083

Print Server Script: /fop/apex_fop.jsp

Any external XSL-FO processor may be used instead of the APEX-supplied fop.war. Deploy the XSL-FO processor as instructed and then configure the APEX instance's Report Printing attributes the same as described earlier, using settings appropriate to your XSL-FO processor.

Enable Network Services

For Oracle Database 11.1 and newer, database network services are disabled by default. If network services for printing, e-mail, or any other purposes were not needed previously, network services may still be disabled. Using any XSL-FO processing engine requires network services for the database to communicate with the XSL-FO processor. Enabling network services is usually done as a post-installation step of the APEX installation process but is not essential until features needing network services are in place. To enable network services, follow the instructions in the Oracle Application Express Installation Guide's "Enabling Network Services in Oracle 11g" section.

Attempting to produce PDF output when network services are not enabled will produce this error:

```
ORA-20001: The printing engine could not be reached because either
the URL specified is incorrect or a proxy URL needs to be specified.
```

Note that this error will also be produced when the reference URL in the APEX instance's Report Printing attributes is incorrect. That setting should be validated as well.

Once the APEX instance Report Printing attributes are configured, PDF output is enabled for all workspaces and all applications in the instance.

First Test Approach

There are two simple ways to test the report printing configuration. Following is the first:

1. From a classic report, as a developer, enable the print link. Set Enabled to Yes in the Printing attribute, as shown in Figure 14-4.

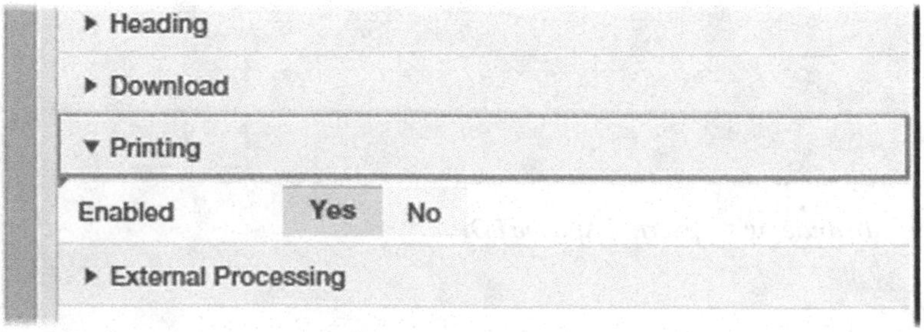

Figure 14-4. Setting Printing Enabled to Yes in the classic report attributes

2. Then, in the Printing Attributes panel's the Output section, enter some text, such as **Print**, in the Link Text property, as shown in Figure 14-5.

Printing
▾ Output
Link Text
Print
Format
PDF
Layout
Default Report Layout
Response Header
Custom
View File As
Attachment
File Name
Classic_Report

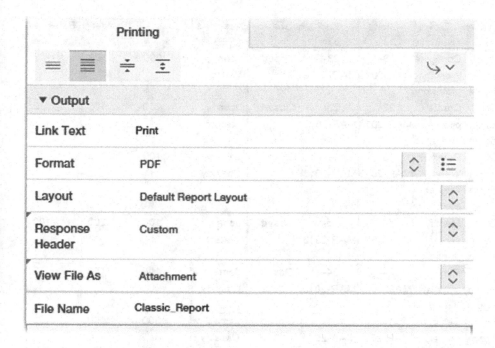

***Figure 14-5.** Setting printing link text*

3. When printing is enabled for a classic report, by default the Print link appears at the bottom left of the report, next to the Download to CSV link, if one is enabled, as shown in Figure 14-6.

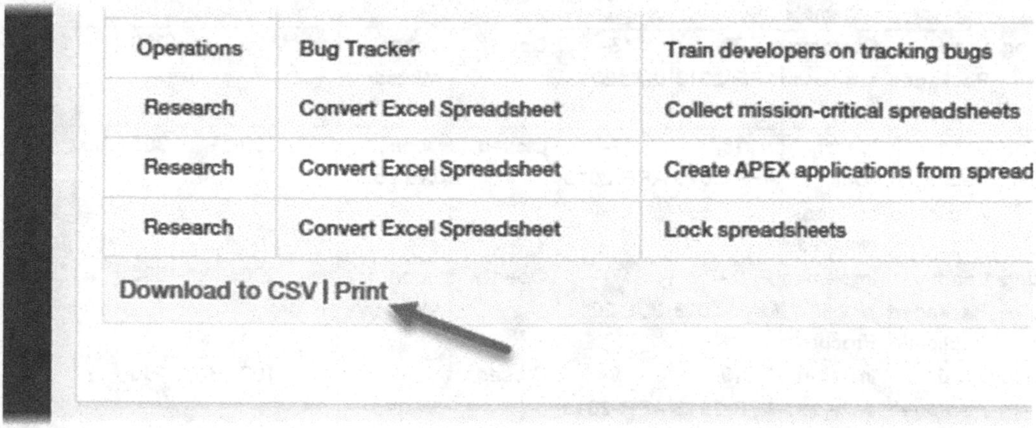

Operations
Bug Tracker
Train developers on tracking bugs
Research
Convert Excel Spreadsheet
Collect mission-critical spreadsheets
Research
Convert Excel Spreadsheet
Create APEX applications from spread
Research
Convert Excel Spreadsheet
Lock spreadsheets
Download to CSV | Print

***Figure 14-6.** Classic report Print link*

4. Then, as an end user, run the report and click the Print link. Report output using the generic format similar in appearance to the output shown in Figure 14-7 should appear.

Departmen	Project	Task Name	Start Date	End Date	Status	Assigned To	Cost	Budget	Balance
Accounting	APEX Environme Configura	Configure Workspac provisioni	23-MAR-2013	23-MAR-2013	Closed	John Watson	200	100	-100
Accounting	APEX Environme Configura	Create pilot workspac	23-MAR-2013	23-MAR-2013	Closed	John Watson	100	100	0
Accounting	APEX Environme Configura	Determine Web listener configurat	15-MAR-2013	15-MAR-2013	Closed	James Cassidy	100	100	0
Accounting	APEX Environme Configura	Identify server requireme	14-MAR-2013	15-MAR-2013	Closed	John Watson	100	200	100
Accounting	APEX Environme Configura	Run installatio	24-MAR-2013	24-MAR-2013	Closed	James Cassidy	100	100	0
Accounting	APEX Environme Configura	Select servers for Developm Test, Productio	16-MAR-2013	21-MAR-2013	Closed	James Cassidy	200	600	400
Accounting	APEX Environme Configura	Specify security authentic scheme(s	16-MAR-2013	18-MAR-2013	Closed	John Watson	200	300	100
Accounting	Load Packaged Applicatio	Customiz solutions	20-APR-2013	13-JUL-2013	Open	John Watson	1500	4000	2500
Accounting	Load Packaged Applicatio	Identify point solutions required	15-APR-2013	17-APR-2013	Closed	John Watson	200	300	100
Accounting	Load Packaged Applicatio	Implemen in Productio	09-MAY-2013	17-JUL-2013	Open	John Watson	200	1500	1300
Accounting	Load Packaged Applicatio	Install in developm	19-APR-2013	19-APR-2013	Closed	John Watson	100	100	0

Figure 14-7. *Default classic report sample output*

Second Test Approach

Alternatively, you can test using the following approach:

1. From an interactive report, as a developer, in the interactive report's Attributes panel, ensure the Download option is enabled and the PDF download option is checked, as shown in Figure 14-8.

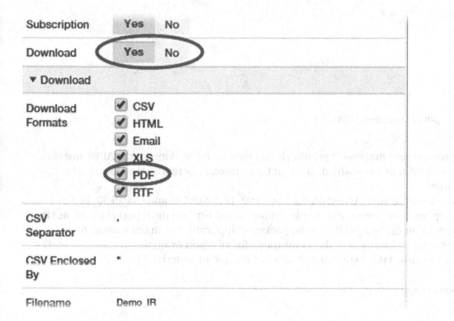

Figure 14-8. *Interactive report's download option enabled*

2. As an interactive report user, select the Download option from the Action menu and then select the PDF button in the Download dialog, as in Figure 14-9. Notice in Figure 14-9 that the RTF download option does not appear, even though it is selected in the Download attributes shown in Figure 14-8. This is because the sample instance is not configured with Oracle BI Publisher; therefore, the RTF download option is not configured.

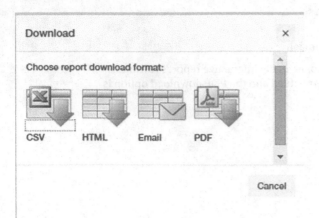

Figure 14-9. *Interactive report's Download dialog*

The rest of this chapter assumes that report printing is configured and working for the APEX instance and that for a classic report, a Print link is enabled, and that for an interactive report, the Download action's PDF output option is enabled.

All report samples use a simple query based on the EBA_DEMO_IR.PROJECTS and EBA_DEMO_IR.DEPT tables. The data in these reports is irrelevant; the simple example is focusing on the report printing, not the data. These tables are included in the Sample Reporting packaged application, with one change to add a DEPTNO table to the Projects table. Listing 14-1 shows the query for all report examples in this chapter. The scripts to create and populate these tables are in the Chapter 14 download material.

Listing 14-1. Sample Report Query

```
select p.ID,
       p.ROW_VERSION_NUMBER,
       p.PROJECT,
       p.TASK_NAME,
       p.DEPTNO,
       INITCAP(d.DNAME) Department,
       p.START_DATE,
       p.END_DATE,
       p.STATUS,
       p.ASSIGNED_TO,
       p.COST,
       p.BUDGET,
       (p.BUDGET - p.COST) Balance
  from EBA_DEMO_IR_PROJECTS P,
       EBA_DEMO_IR_DEPT D
 where p.deptno = d.deptno;
```

APEX Standard Report Printing

Once an APEX instance is configured for standard report printing, PDF output is enabled for all workspaces and all applications on classic reports, interactive reports, and report queries set to use the generic report layout.

For classic reports, the developer can use the default, generic, XSL-FO layout; can declaratively set report header, footer, column heading, data appearance, and relative column widths; and can define a report query and report layout pair for custom layouts of the same report data.

For interactive reports, the developer can use the default, generic, XLS-FO layout; can declaratively set report header, footer, column heading, and data appearance; and can elect to define one or more sets of report query/report layout pairs for custom layouts of specific sets of the report data. Using the generic XSL-FO template with interactive reports captures current column orders, filters, and sorts. It does not honor group by, chart, or pivot views, and it does not include aggregates or highlighting. When any of these conditions apply, either the Download option is disabled or the tabular view of the data is downloaded.

The following sections address classic report print options and interactive report print options and then introduce report queries and report layouts for more customized report output.

Classic Report Printing

For classic reports, APEX provides declarative PDF output using the built-in, generic XSL-FO printing template. By default, when the report printing option is turned on by setting the Printing attribute to Yes, a Print link appears at the bottom of the report. If no other print attributes are changed, APEX uses the generic XSL-FO template with the default settings. Figure 14-10 shows the sample classic report. Notice that on the web page, the Project and Task Name columns naturally display wider on the HTML page relative to the other columns. Most modern browsers automatically handle the width adjustment without any additional CSS settings. That's not the case with printed output.

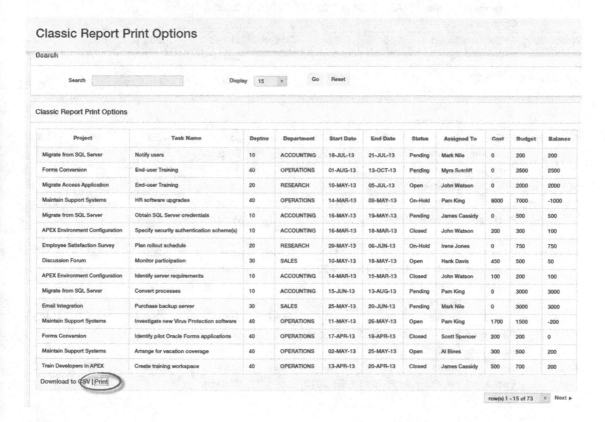

Classic Report Print Options

Project	Task Name	Deptno	Department	Start Date	End Date	Status	Assigned To	Cost	Budget	Balance
Migrate from SQL Server	Notify users	10	ACCOUNTING	18-JUL-13	21-JUL-13	Pending	Mark Nile	0	200	200
Forms Conversion	End-user Training	40	OPERATIONS	01-AUG-13	13-OCT-13	Pending	Myra Sutcliff	0	2500	2500
Migrate Access Application	End-user Training	20	RESEARCH	10-MAY-13	05-JUL-13	Open	John Watson	0	2000	2000
Maintain Support Systems	HR software upgrades	40	OPERATIONS	14-MAR-13	09-MAY-13	On-Hold	Pam King	8000	7000	-1000
Migrate from SQL Server	Obtain SQL Server credentials	10	ACCOUNTING	16-MAY-13	19-MAY-13	Pending	James Cassidy	0	500	500
APEX Environment Configuration	Specify security authentication scheme(s)	10	ACCOUNTING	16-MAR-13	18-MAR-13	Closed	John Watson	200	300	100
Employee Satisfaction Survey	Plan rollout schedule	20	RESEARCH	29-MAY-13	06-JUN-13	On-Hold	Irene Jones	0	750	750
Discussion Forum	Monitor participation	30	SALES	10-MAY-13	18-MAY-13	Open	Hank Davis	450	500	50
APEX Environment Configuration	Identify server requirements	10	ACCOUNTING	14-MAR-13	15-MAR-13	Closed	John Watson	100	200	100
Migrate from SQL Server	Convert processes	10	ACCOUNTING	15-JUN-13	13-AUG-13	Pending	Pam King	0	3000	3000
Email Integration	Purchase backup server	30	SALES	25-MAY-13	20-JUN-13	Pending	Mark Nile	0	3000	3000
Maintain Support Systems	Investigate new Virus Protection software	40	OPERATIONS	11-MAY-13	26-MAY-13	Open	Pam King	1700	1500	-200
Forms Conversion	Identify pilot Oracle Forms applications	40	OPERATIONS	17-APR-13	18-APR-13	Closed	Scott Spencer	200	200	0
Maintain Support Systems	Arrange for vacation coverage	40	OPERATIONS	02-MAY-13	25-MAY-13	Open	Al Bines	300	500	200
Train Developers in APEX	Create training workspace	40	OPERATIONS	13-APR-13	20-APR-13	Closed	James Cassidy	500	700	200

Download to CSV | Print

row(s) 1 - 15 of 73   Next ▶

Figure 14-10. Classic report with printing enabled

Beyond enabling printing, no additional settings are required. The generic XSL-FO template will be applied with all the default settings. Figure 14-11 shows the PDF output produced by clicking the Print option at the bottom of the report with no Print attributes set.

Department	Project	Task Name	Start Date	End Date	Status	Assigned To	Cost	Budget	Balance
Accounting	APEX Environm Configura	Configure Workspac provisioni	23-MAR-2013	23-MAR-2013	Closed	John Watson	200	100	-100
Accounting	APEX Environm Configura	Create pilot workspac	23-MAR-2013	23-MAR-2013	Closed	John Watson	100	100	0
Accounting	APEX Environm Configura	Determine Web listener configurat	15-MAR-2013	15-MAR-2013	Closed	James Cassidy	100	100	0
Accounting	APEX Environm Configura	Identify server requireme	14-MAR-2013	15-MAR-2013	Closed	John Watson	100	200	100
Accounting	APEX Environm Configura	Run installatio	24-MAR-2013	24-MAR-2013	Closed	James Cassidy	100	100	0
Accounting	APEX Environm Configura	Select servers for Developm Test, Productio	16-MAR-2013	21-MAR-2013	Closed	James Cassidy	200	600	400
Accounting	APEX Environm Configura	Specify security authentica scheme(s	16-MAR-2013	18-MAR-2013	Closed	John Watson	200	300	100
Accounting	Load Packaged Applicatio	Customize solutions	20-APR-2013	13-JUL-2013	Open	John Watson	1500	4000	2500
Accounting	Load Packaged Applicatio	Identify point solutions required	15-APR-2013	17-APR-2013	Closed	John Watson	200	300	100
Accounting	Load Packaged Applicatio	Implemen in Productio	09-MAY-2013	17-JUL-2013	Open	John Watson	200	1500	1300
Accounting	Load Packaged Applicatio	Install in developm	19-APR-2013	19-APR-2013	Closed	John Watson	100	100	0

Figure 14-11. *Classic report default output from generic XSL-FO template*

Observe that the default layout is portrait, the font is Helvetica, there is no Page Header or Footer text, the column headers are blue background, the columns are gray background, all text is the same size, and all columns are equal width. The print processor rightly wraps words in cells at natural word breaks, but when a word is too wide for a column, it is truncated. These default settings may work for some simple reports, but clearly they do not for the sample classic report (which is also quite simple). The Department, Project, Task, Start Date and End Date columns are scrunched and have truncated data. The alignment of values in the Cost, Budget, and Balance columns is not ideal. The color scheme leaves a lot to be desired, and there is no header or footer text.

To address these shortcomings in a classic report, an APEX developer can declaratively set page header, footer, column header, column format, and page layout properties. In a classic report, a developer can also set relative column widths, using percentages or points. To access these settings, open the printing attributes in the rightmost panel by clicking the Printing element under the classic report in the Rendering panel, as shown in Figure 14-12.

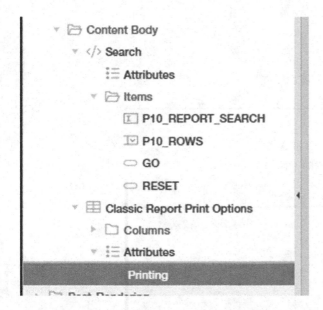

Figure 14-12. *Page Designer access to classic report print attributes*

The Printing properties panel contains regions for declaratively setting options; they include Output, Page , Page Header, Column Headings, Columns, Page Footer, and a print server override. Figures 14-13 to 14-19 show the settings for each of these sections of the Printing properties. These figures show the values in the sample report to produce the PDF output shown in Figure 14-21. It's much better! But let's describe these printing properties first.

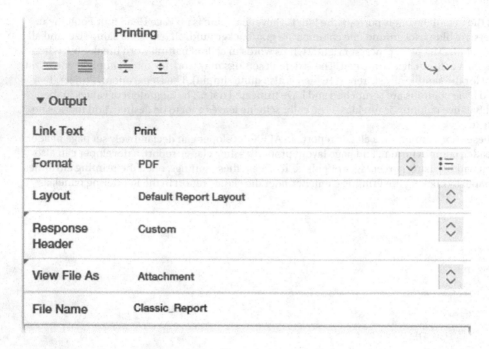

Figure 14-13. *Output properties*

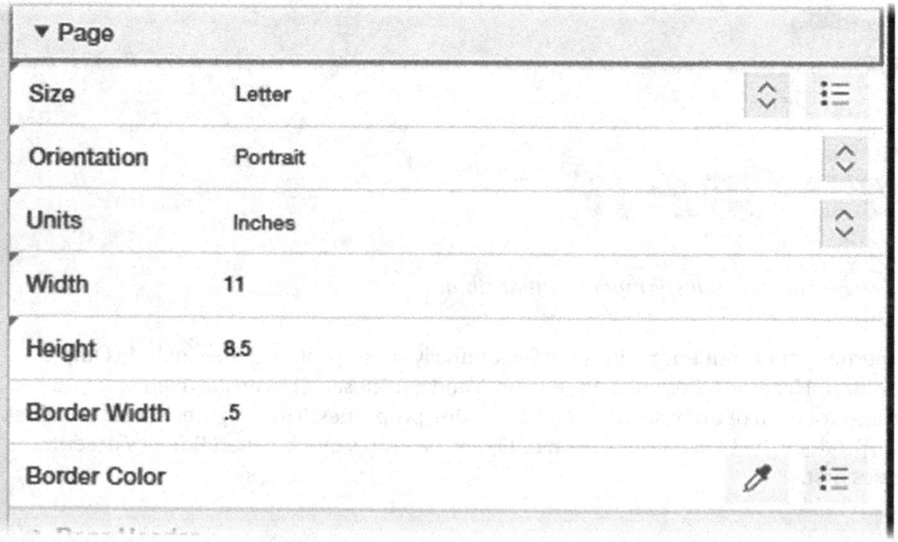

▼ Page

Size	Letter	◇	≔
Orientation	Portrait	◇	
Units	Inches	◇	
Width	11		
Height	8.5		
Border Width	.5		
Border Color		✎	≔

Figure 14-14. *Page properties*

Page Header
Font
Helvetica
Font Weight
Bold
Font Size
12
Font Color
#000000
Alignment
center
Text
APress Expert Oracle Application Express
Classic Report Print Options

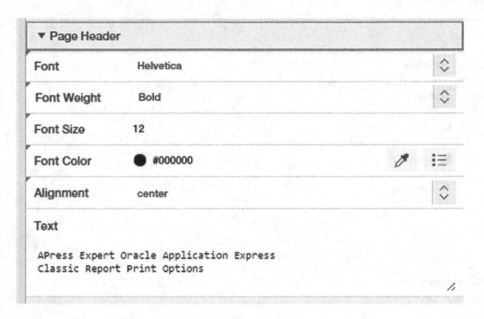

Figure 14-15. Page Header properties

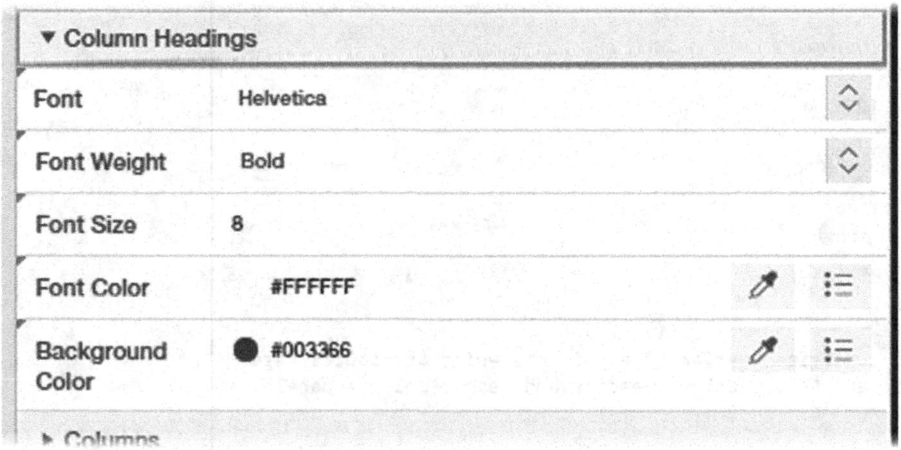

Column Headings
Font
Helvetica
Font Weight
Bold
Font Size
8
Font Color
#FFFFFF
Background Color
#003366
Columns

Figure 14-16. Column Headings properties

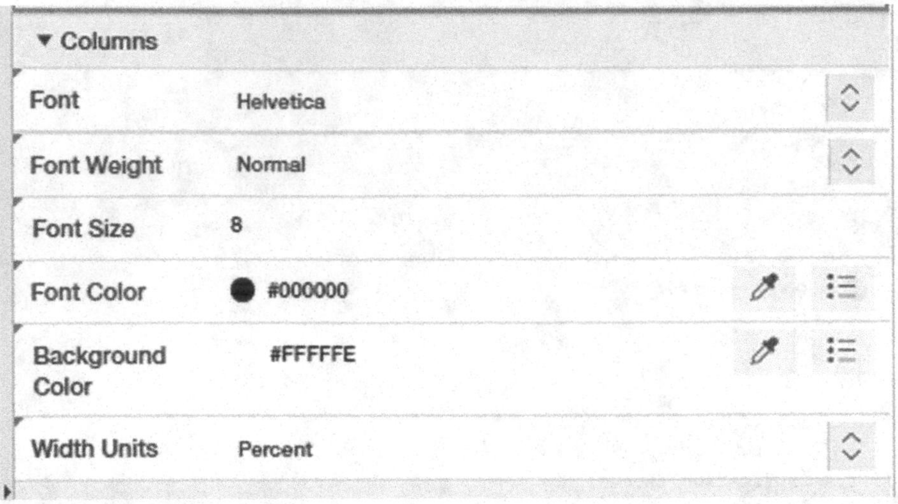

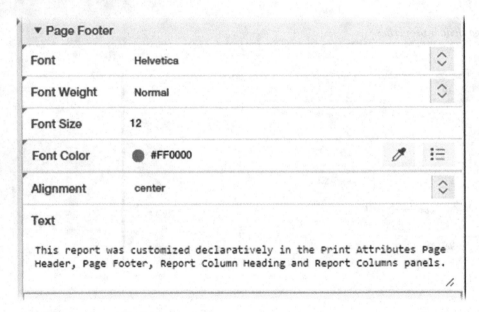

Figure 14-17. *Columns properties*

Figure 14-18. *Page Footer properties*

Figure 14-19. *Advanced properties*

In this example on the classic report, you did not set a print server override, but this setting allows a developer to set an alternate print processor. This is helpful for large reports, for example, to divert large reports to a server configured to handle larger volume output or, during development, to use a print processor for which the server logs are available for debugging. Debugging XSL-FO output is discussed in the "Debugging XSL-FO" section.

The classic report's printing options shown in the earlier figures are defined as follows:

Output

- *Link Text*: This is the text to display on the print link. Usually this is Print but can be any text.

- *Format:* This is the output format. For this purpose, this is set to PDF. The options are as follows:

  - *Derive From Item*: The output format will be defined by the value of an item, usually a select list. Using this option allows end users to select their output format. Be sure to limit your select list to options that are configured for your APEX instance and that make sense for your data.

  - *Format Item*: The page item that contains the format.

  - *PDF*: This is the PDF output via the FOP processor.

  - *Word*: This is Microsoft Word. This actually produces an RTF document.

  - *Excel*: This is a Microsoft Excel document, in XLS format.

  - *HTML*: This is a searchable HTML document.

  - *XML*: This is am XML representation of the data.

- *Layout*: This sets the report layout used to generate the output. By default, this is Default Report Layout. Any valid report layout can be used. All valid report layouts will *appear in the select list.*

- *Response Header: This is either Custom or Print Server; this sets whether the response header generated is based on the report settings or the print server. The response header contains the date, size, and type of file the server is sending back to the client. When View File As is set, the response header attribute must be Custom.*

- *View File As: This is Attachment or Inline. The Attachment option will open in a new window or a new tab according to the end user's browser settings. The Inline option replaces the current page with the output document.*

- *Link Example: This field contains the URL to use when building a custom button for an end user to access the report.*

Page

- *Size, Orientation, Units, Width, Height, and Border Width*: These attributes are exactly what they say they are.

Page Header: This collection of attributes defines the report page header.

- *Font*: Set this to Helvetica, Times, or Courier.

- *Font Weight*: Set this to Normal or Bold.

- *Font Size*: Enter a value, usually 8 through 48.

- *Font Color*: Enter or select a hex value for the desired font color.

- *Alignment*: Set this to Center, Left, or Right.

- *Text*: Enter the report heading text.

Column Headings: These are the same Font, Font Weight, Font Size, Font Color settings as for Page Header, plus the following:

- *Background Color*: This is a hexadecimal format (#FFFFFF) color for column background color.

Columns: These are the same Font, Font Weight, Font Size, Font Color, Background Color settings as for Column Header, plus the following:

- *Width Units*: These are the units for column widths, either Percent or Point.

Page Footer: These are the same Font, Font Weight, Font Sze, Font Color, Alignment, and Text attributes as in Page Header, except these define the page footer.

Advanced: This section contains one property, Print Server Override.

- *Print Server Overwrite*: Use this option to specify an optional print server. This option is often used to direct output to a locally deployed print server for access to the server log file for debugging.

Column Width Settings

In the Page Designer, the column width settings are on the individual column attribute's panels. When setting all column widths, it may be easier to switch to Component View and then navigate to the Print Attributes tab. Figure 14-20 shows the Report Columns attributes as shown in Component View.

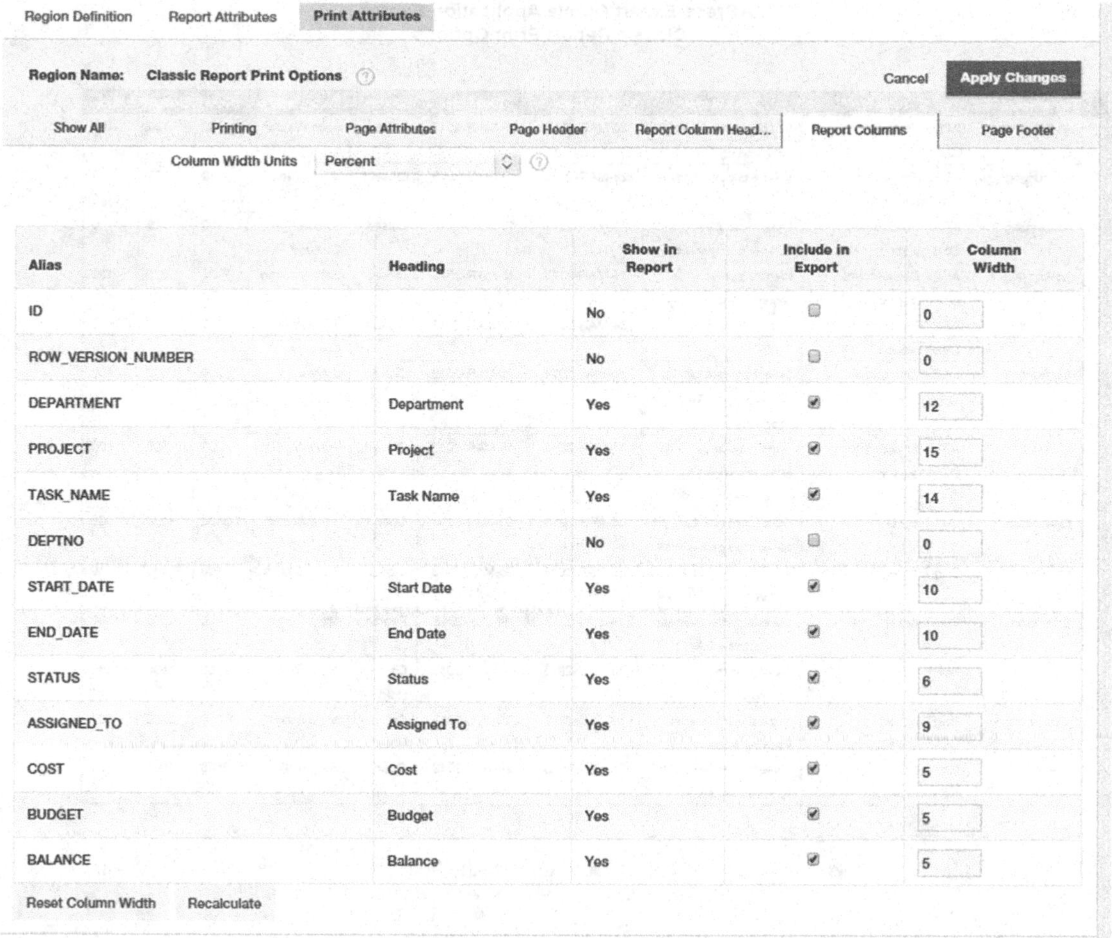

| Region Definition | Report Attributes | **Print Attributes** | | | | | |

Region Name: **Classic Report Print Options** (?)   Cancel   **Apply Changes**

| Show All | Printing | Page Attributes | Page Header | Report Column Head... | Report Columns | Page Footer |

Column Width Units | Percent   ⬍ | (?)

Alias	Heading	Show in Report	Include in Export	Column Width
ID		No	☐	0
ROW_VERSION_NUMBER		No	☐	0
DEPARTMENT	Department	Yes	☑	12
PROJECT	Project	Yes	☑	15
TASK_NAME	Task Name	Yes	☑	14
DEPTNO		No	☐	0
START_DATE	Start Date	Yes	☑	10
END_DATE	End Date	Yes	☑	10
STATUS	Status	Yes	☑	6
ASSIGNED_TO	Assigned To	Yes	☑	9
COST	Cost	Yes	☑	5
BUDGET	Budget	Yes	☑	5
BALANCE	Balance	Yes	☑	5

Reset Column Width   Recalculate

Figure 14-20. Classic report column attributes in Component View

Column attributes can be set in points or percentages. Using Percent is often easier since column widths should add up to (and cannot exceed) 100. Points may give you finer-grained control, depending on the number of columns. When using Percent, try not to exceed 100 because an error occurs and all your entries are cleared.

For the sample classic report, you can set the Project, Task Name, Department, Start Date, and End Date columns wider and shorten the Deptno, Cost, Budget, and Balance columns. Hidden columns are automatically set to not show in the output report.

In the example, swap the page layout orientation, lower the font size, and set font and background color values for the Page Header, Page Footer, Column Headings, and Column attributes. The resulting PDF output version of the classic report is much improved, as shown in Figure 14-21.

APress Expert Oracle Application Express
Classic Report Print Options

Department	Project	Task Name	Start Date	End Date	Status	Assigned To	Cost	Budget	Balance
Accounting	APEX Environment Configuration	Configure Workspace provisioning	23-MAR-2013	23-MAR-2013	Closed	John Watson	200	100	-100
Accounting	APEX Environment Configuration	Create pilot workspace	23-MAR-2013	23-MAR-2013	Closed	John Watson	100	100	0
Accounting	APEX Environment Configuration	Determine Web listener configuration(s)	15-MAR-2013	15-MAR-2013	Closed	James Cassidy	100	100	0
Accounting	APEX Environment Configuration	Identify server requirements	14-MAR-2013	15-MAR-2013	Closed	John Watson	100	200	100
Accounting	APEX Environment Configuration	Run installation	24-MAR-2013	24-MAR-2013	Closed	James Cassidy	100	100	0
Accounting	APEX Environment Configuration	Select servers for Development, Test, Production	16-MAR-2013	21-MAR-2013	Closed	James Cassidy	200	600	400
Accounting	APEX Environment Configuration	Specify security authentication scheme(s)	16-MAR-2013	18-MAR-2013	Closed	John Watson	200	300	100
Operations	Bug Tracker	Document quality assurance procedures	28-APR-2013	01-JUN-2013	Open	Myra Sutcliff	3500	4000	500
Operations	Bug Tracker	Implement bug tracking software	28-MAR-2013	28-MAR-2013	Closed	Myra Sutcliff	100	100	0
Operations	Bug Tracker	Measure effectiveness of improved QA	14-JUN-2013	14-JUL-2013	Pending	Myra Sutcliff	0	1500	1500
Operations	Bug Tracker	Review automated testing tools	29-MAR-2013	27-APR-2013	On-Hold	Myra Sutcliff	2750	1500	-1250
Operations	Bug Tracker	Train developers on tracking bugs	02-JUN-2013	22-JUL-2013	On-Hold	Myra Sutcliff	0	2000	2000
Research	Convert Excel Spreadsheet	Collect mission-critical spreadsheets	27-APR-2013	28-JUN-2013	Open	Pam King	2500	4000	1500

This report was customized declaratively in the Print Attributes Page
Header, Page Footer, Report Column Heading and Report Columns panels.

Figure 14-21. Classic report, generic template with declarative settings

---

■ **Tip** In APEX 5.0.0.00.31, it appears the Portrait and Landscape Orientation options' Width and Height values are swapped from what they should be. Go by the desired Width and Height settings to get what you want, not the Portrait or Landscape label. No doubt this will be corrected in a future release.

The new, declaratively adjusted report output is much better and accomplished entirely with the generic XSL-FO layout. This quality of output is likely acceptable for internal organization output, and the level of effort (minutes of developer time to set the Print attributes) makes it practical for a large number of reports.

For cases where you need more customization, such as multiple font colors, font weights, background shading, a nontabular format, or a corporate logo in the header, you need to create a custom, named-column report layout. Then, the developer needs to assign the custom report layout to the classic report in the Layout print attribute. Report layouts are discussed in greater detail in the "Report Layout" section.

Interactive Report PDF Output

For interactive reports, APEX provides declarative PDF output using the built-in, generic XSL-FO printing template, much the same as for classic reports; however, for interactive reports, there is no option to specify column widths. All interactive report columns are equal width in the PDF output. This is likely not what you want because words that cannot wrap and do not fit are truncated. You have the same output format problems as observed for the default-setting classic report PDF output in Figure 14-10.

However, APEX does pick up the current interactive report column order, sorts, filters, and computed columns in the generated PDF output. This is great because you want end users to have a PDF output option for whatever column arrangement and report configuration they devise. But (of course, there is a "but") there are significant limitations. While APEX standard printing honors columns, column orders, sorts, and filters, it ignores aggregates and highlighting and does not recognize group by, chart, or pivot views.

For break views of an interactive report (when one or more break columns are specified), the Download PDF output is the same as for the tabular view of the data. For group by and pivot views, the Download PDF option does not exist at all.

For the chart view, the Download PDF option again is the standard tabular view of the data, not a chart at all. In an interactive report's chart view, there is no AnyChart right-click Print option like there is for regular APEX AnyChart charts.

These behaviors regarding the alternate views of an interactive report may not be exactly what you are looking for, but for simple tabular reports, these options cover the basic need to output the as-displayed data in PDF format for the majority of cases.

The declarative Printing attributes for interactive reports are similar to those of classic reports, omitting the proportional column section. To access the Printing attributes of an interactive report, click the Attributes section in the interactive report's Attributes element in the Rendering panel, as shown in Figure 14-22. The Printing option is the last of the Attributes elements. This is similar to the Printing attribute's location for a classic report.

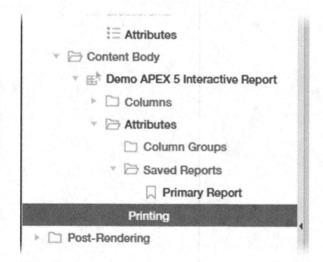

Figure 14-22. Accessing an interactive report's Printing attributes

The Printing attributes are organized the same as for classic reports, including Output, Page, Page Header, Column Headings, Columns, Page Footer, and Advanced sections to declaratively customize the appearance of the PDF output. Figure 14-23 shows the interactive report's Printing attributes panel with the Columns and Page Footer elements expanded. Notice there is no Column Width element under the Columns grouping. This is the only significant difference between the classic report Printing attributes and the interactive report Printing attributes.

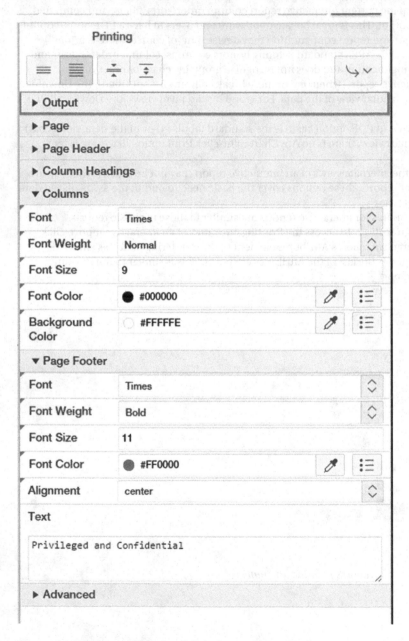

Figure 14-23. *Interactive report's Printing attributes*

By default, the PDF output for the interactive report with no print attribute settings is similar to that of the classic report's default PDF output, shown earlier in Figure 14-10. Figure 14-24 shows the PDF output generated for the sample interactive report using the same declarative settings used for the classic report (except for the column width settings, which do not exist for interactive reports). Notice this version of PDF output is better than the default, but the wrapping and unwanted truncation problems may persist, as shown in the circled area. Reducing the font size eliminates some of the wrapping issues in the sample report, but no doubt this will not cover all cases, especially when there are many columns.

**APress Expert Oracle Application Express
Interactive Report Printing**

Department	Project	Task Name	Start Date	End Date	Status	Assigned To	Cost	Budget	Balance
Accounting	APEX Environment Configuration	Configure Workspace provisioning	23-MAR-13	23-MAR-13	Closed	John Watson	200	100	-100
Accounting	APEX Environment Configuration	Create pilot workspace	23-MAR-13	23-MAR-13	Closed	John Watson	100	100	0
Accounting	APEX Environment Configuration	Determine Web listener configuration(s	15-MAR-13	15-MAR-13	Closed	James Cassidy	100	100	0
Accounting	APEX Environment Configuration	Identify server requirements	14-MAR-13	15-MAR-13	Closed	John Watson	100	200	100
Accounting	APEX Environment Configuration	Run installation	24-MAR-13	24-MAR-13	Closed	James Cassidy	100	100	0
Accounting	APEX Environment Configuration	Select servers for Development, Test, Production	16-MAR-13	21-MAR-13	Closed	James Cassidy	200	600	400
Accounting	APEX Environment Configuration	Specify security authentication scheme(s)	16-MAR-13	18-MAR-13	Closed	John Watson	200	300	100
Accounting	Load Packaged Applications	Customize solutions	20-APR-13	13-JUL-13	Open	John Watson	1500	4000	2500

1

This report was formatted by declarative Printing Attributes. The formatting works for the default view, honors sorts and filters, but does not honor Group By, Chart and Pivot views. and does not include Aggregates or Highlighting.

Figure 14-24. *Interactive report with declarative Printing attributes*

The advantage of the interactive report's declarative PDF output is that for many interactive report configurations, there is, essentially, an out-of-the-box report printing solution. It needs to be enabled for each report (by default it is not enabled), and there is minimal developer time involved to declaratively set display properties. The downside is that for cases where equal-width columns are not enough, this output is not acceptable for production reports. The more displayed columns in the report, the more likely the declarative PDF output options will not suffice to produce an acceptable document.

When more tailored PDF output is required, you need to advance to using report queries and report layouts to achieve the desired results. The report queries will work off the base interactive report query, as obtained using variations of the APEX_IR API. The report layout will be a named-column XSL-FO template that defines the table columns and their widths, at minimum. Report queries and report layouts are discussed in the following section. Then I will return to the interactive report topic to discuss a custom PDF output solution.

Report Queries and Report Layouts

For situations where formatted, printable output is required and the output provided by APEX classic reports and interactive reports does not suffice, APEX provides report queries and report layouts. *Report queries* are a set of one or more SQL queries that define the complete set of data to be formatted for printing. The report query defines the set of XML data sent to the FOP print processor. *Report layouts* are XLS-FO templates that contain formatting instructions for the XML dataset defined in the report query. All data elements referenced by the report layout must exist in the report query. However, not all the report query elements need to be used by the report layout.

The two work as a pair to generate report output. The report query defines the dataset. The report layout defines the layout. For the standard APEX reporting purposes, the report layout is always either the generic XSL-FO template or a named-column XSL-FO template.

On request, the report query generates an XML representation of the SQL query result set. The XML dataset is sent along with the XSL-FO template defined by the report layout to the FOP print engine. The FOP print engine formats the data using the XSL-FO template to produce PDF output.

Note that this is the same flow as used for default classic and interactive report PDF output options. In the default cases, APEX generates the XML for the report (the equivalent of the report query) and uses the built-in generic XSL-FO template (the report layout).

A report query is associated with exactly one report layout. If a report layout is not specified, the default generic XSL-FO template applies by default.

A report layout may be used in multiple report queries, as long as the data elements referenced in the report layout exist in the report query. If a report layout is not referenced by at least one report query, it just sits there, defined but unused.

A report query may include any number of queries. The corresponding report layout references the elements of each query, using the full XML path to the elements to distinguish references to the row sets and individual data elements.

Report queries may be edited within APEX. Report queries may, and most often do, incorporate session state values, specified as parameters to the SQL queries.

Report layouts can be uploaded and downloaded but not edited within APEX. The XSL-FO templates are created outside of APEX, with or without an XSL-FO editor, and then uploaded into APEX. This is where minor adjustments to XSL-FO templates can be easily edited with SQL Developer. For more complex edits, such as layout adjustments, a specialized XSL-FO editor will often make the editing process easier.

Report Query

To build a report query, go to Shared Components, choose Report Query, and click Create. See the APEX documentation for complete details on building a report query. Figure 14-25 shows the basic report query interface. Note the Print URL element. This URL is the code to use in the button URL field when creating a custom print button. The custom print button may be anywhere your APEX application, as long as any required session state values are set; it need not be alongside the web version of the report.

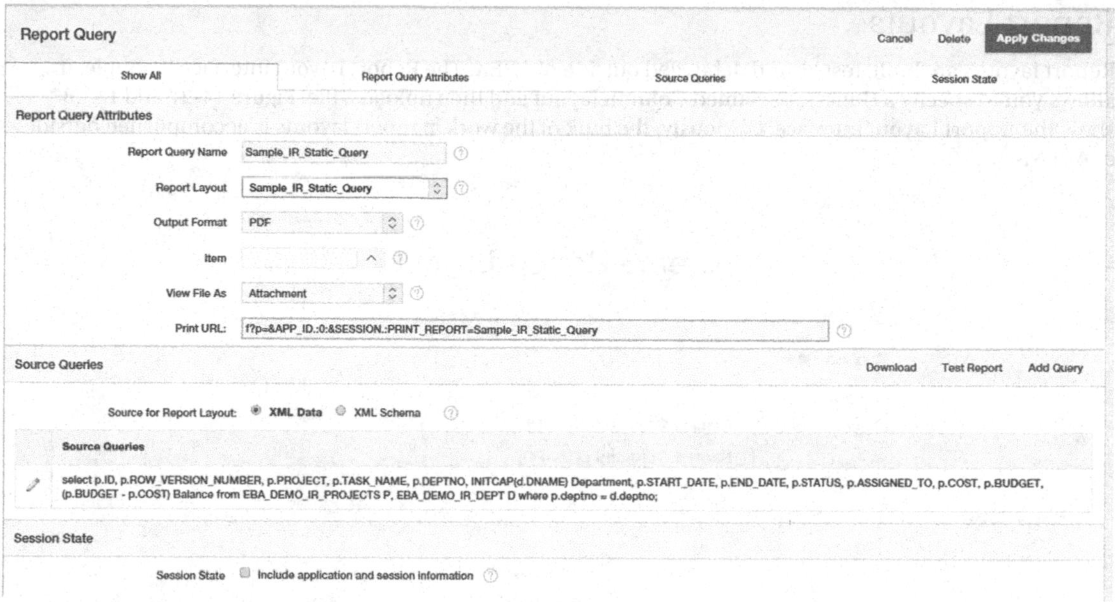

Figure 14-25. *Report Query interface*

To add session state values, select the Session State check box and then type in the items to the list. Doing so tells APEX to include the current session state values in your report query's XML dataset when generating the XML and passing it to the FOP processor. Including session state values is the key to capturing as-displayed values in your output reports.

Use the options for downloading the XML and XML schema, as shown in Figure 14-26. These two files are most helpful in building your report layout and in fact are essential in some XSL-FO editors.

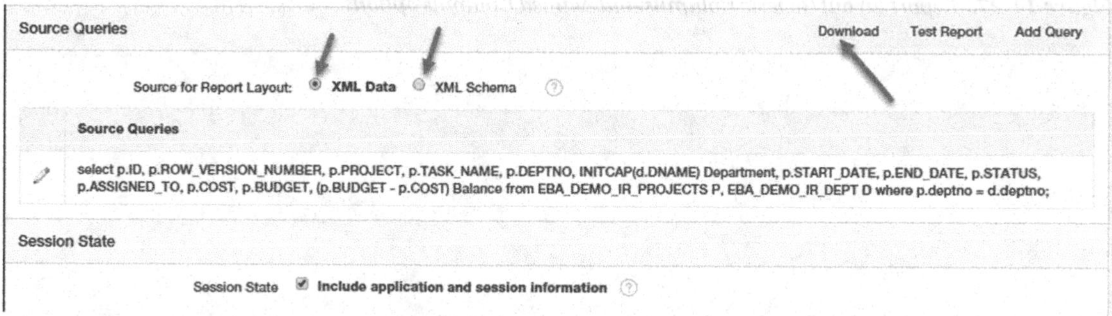

Figure 14-26. *XML data and XML schema download options*

The XML Data option generates the XML representation of the report query results. The XML Schema option generates just the schema. If you have session state variables in your query, to generate XML data, you will need to edit the query and use the Set Bind Variables option to set test values for your session state variables.

Report Layouts

Report layouts are built, tested, and debugged outside of APEX. The Report Layout interface is simple; it allows you to specify a Generic or Named Column layout and then upload a file. Figure 14-27 and 14-28 show the Report Layout interface. Obviously, the bulk of the work in report layouts is accomplished outside of APEX.

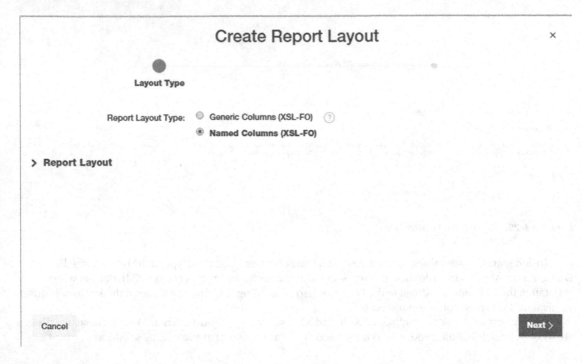

Figure 14-27. *Report layout Generic Columns and Named Columns options*

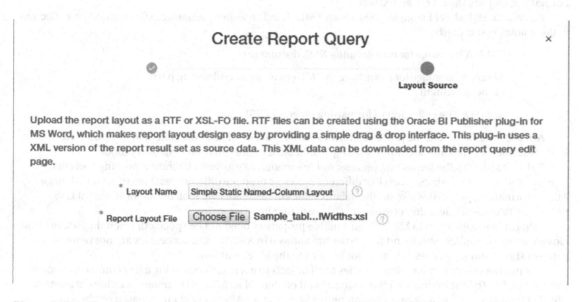

Figure 14-28. Report layout upload

Once the report layout is uploaded, the developer needs to return to the report query and select the new report layout as the layout for the report query. If a report layout is deleted and reloaded, as one does in testing, the report query reverts to the generic template. The developer needs to return to the report query to reset the report layout each time the report layout is re-created. This is a tedious, but that is the process; there is no report layout update option.

XSL-FO 101

Before delving deeper into how to build report layouts, it is helpful to know some basics about XSL-FO. First, understand that you do not need to learn everything about XSL-FO to output formatted documents; you do need to know enough to produce the formatted output results you need. Most of what you need will be covered here. Most likely you will learn more FO elements and how to use them as the requirements to use them present themselves. There are many references online, and each XSL-FO editing tool has its own set of reference documentation.

The following are the best references I have found for working with XSL-FO templates in APEX:

Apache FOP: https://xmlgraphics.apache.org/fop/

Practical Formatting Using XSL-FO (Extensible Stylesheet Language Formatting Objects), Crane Softwrights, Ltd.: www.CraneSoftwrights.com

XSL-FO

XSL-FO is one member of the Extensible Stylesheet Language (XSL) family, which consists of XSLT, XSL Formatting Objects (XSL-FO), and XPath.

Extensible Stylesheet Language (XSL) is an XML-based stylesheet language. XSL is actually a collection of the following standards:

> *XSLT*: A language for transforming XML documents
>
> *XPath*: A language for navigating in XML documents, addressing parts of the document
>
> *XSL-FO*: The collection of formatting objects of XSL

An XSL style sheet tells the processor how to format data in an XML document for output. Note that XML describes the data hierarchy but nothing at all related to presentation or delivery mode.

XSL-FO specifies the formatting process, not the rendering process. Different rendering tools may produce different renderings, much like different browsers produce different versions of an HTML page. Absent formatting properties take on the default values of the rendering tool, the same as absent CSS properties take on the defaults according to the particular browser.

Inheritance does apply in XSL-FO. Inheritable properties need not be specified; when they are not, the closest ancestor applies. Shorthand properties are allowed in XSL-FO, but processors are not required to support shorthand properties. When in doubt, stick to the longhand form.

It is not necessary to know all properties of all objects to get results. Knowing a few common elements can get you far. To best understand the structure and content of an XSL-FO template, let's look at a simple XSL-FO template used as a named-column report layout for an APEX report query based on the sample query in Listing 14-1.

The XML

Prior to building an XSL-FO formatting template, you need to know and understand the structure of the XML, which is the data to be formatted. The Report Query interface gives you options for obtaining that XML.

To view the XML associated with a report query, use the XML Data and XML Schema download options in the Report Query interface. You will need both: the schema, an .xsd file, to view the architecture of the XML document, and the data, an .xml file, to view the data. The structure is convenient for locating the XML elements in the hierarchy. Listing 14-2 shows the XSD for the sample report query.

Listing 14-2. Sample Report Query XSD Schema Definition

```
<?xml version="1.0" encoding="UTF-8"?>
<xs:schema xmlns:xs="http://www.w3.org/2001/XMLSchema">
  <xs:element name="DOCUMENT">
    <xs:complexType>
      <xs:sequence>
        <xs:element ref="DATE"/>
        <xs:element ref="USER_NAME"/>
        <xs:element ref="APP_ID"/>
        <xs:element ref="APP_NAME"/>
        <xs:element ref="TITLE"/>
        <xs:element ref="REGION"/>
      </xs:sequence>
    </xs:complexType>
  </xs:element>
```

```xml
<xs:element name="DATE">
  <xs:simpleType>
    <xs:restriction base="xs:string"/>
  </xs:simpleType>
</xs:element>
<xs:element name="USER_NAME">
  <xs:simpleType>
    <xs:restriction base="xs:string"/>
  </xs:simpleType>
</xs:element>
<xs:element name="APP_ID">
  <xs:simpleType>
    <xs:restriction base="xs:string"/>
  </xs:simpleType>
</xs:element>
<xs:element name="APP_NAME">
  <xs:simpleType>
    <xs:restriction base="xs:string"/>
  </xs:simpleType>
</xs:element>
<xs:element name="TITLE">
  <xs:simpleType>
    <xs:restriction base="xs:string"/>
  </xs:simpleType>
</xs:element>
<xs:element name="REGION">
  <xs:complexType>
    <xs:sequence>
      <xs:element ref="ROWSET"/>
    </xs:sequence>
    <xs:attribute name="ID" use="required">
      <xs:simpleType>
        <xs:restriction base="xs:byte">
          <xs:enumeration value="0"/>
        </xs:restriction>
      </xs:simpleType>
    </xs:attribute>
  </xs:complexType>
</xs:element>
<xs:element name="ROWSET">
  <xs:complexType>
    <xs:sequence>
      <xs:element ref="ROW"/>
    </xs:sequence>
  </xs:complexType>
</xs:element>
<xs:element name="ROW">
  <xs:complexType>
    <xs:sequence>
      <xs:element name="ID">
        <xs:simpleType>
```

```
        <xs:restriction base="xs:string"/>
      </xs:simpleType>
    </xs:element>
    <xs:element name="ROW_VERSION_NUMBER">
      <xs:simpleType>
        <xs:restriction base="xs:string"/>
      </xs:simpleType>
    </xs:element>
    <xs:element name="PROJECT">
      <xs:simpleType>
        <xs:restriction base="xs:string"/>
      </xs:simpleType>
    </xs:element>
    <xs:element name="TASK_NAME">
      <xs:simpleType>
        <xs:restriction base="xs:string"/>
      </xs:simpleType>
    </xs:element>
    <xs:element name="DEPTNO">
      <xs:simpleType>
        <xs:restriction base="xs:string"/>
      </xs:simpleType>
    </xs:element>
    <xs:element name="DEPARTMENT">
      <xs:simpleType>
        <xs:restriction base="xs:string"/>
      </xs:simpleType>
    </xs:element>
    <xs:element name="START_DATE">
      <xs:simpleType>
        <xs:restriction base="xs:string"/>
      </xs:simpleType>
    </xs:element>
    <xs:element name="END_DATE">
      <xs:simpleType>
        <xs:restriction base="xs:string"/>
      </xs:simpleType>
    </xs:element>
    <xs:element name="STATUS">
      <xs:simpleType>
        <xs:restriction base="xs:string"/>
      </xs:simpleType>
    </xs:element>
    <xs:element name="ASSIGNED_TO">
      <xs:simpleType>
        <xs:restriction base="xs:string"/>
      </xs:simpleType>
    </xs:element>
    <xs:element name="COST">
      <xs:simpleType>
        <xs:restriction base="xs:string"/>
```

```
        </xs:simpleType>
      </xs:element>
      <xs:element name="BUDGET">
        <xs:simpleType>
          <xs:restriction base="xs:string"/>
        </xs:simpleType>
      </xs:element>
      <xs:element name="BALANCE">
        <xs:simpleType>
          <xs:restriction base="xs:string"/>
        </xs:simpleType>
      </xs:element>
    </xs:sequence>
  </xs:complexType>
  </xs:element>
</xs:schema>
```

The XML data is needed for testing and validating. Listing 14-3 shows a portion of the XML file for the sample report query.

Listing 14-3. Portion of Sample Report Query XML Representation

```
<?xml version="1.0" encoding="UTF-8"?>
<DOCUMENT>
<ROWSET>
  <ROW>
    <ID>2717586985605873663377800068796288561218</ID>
    <ROW_VERSION_NUMBER>2</ROW_VERSION_NUMBER>
    <PROJECT>Migrate from SQL Server</PROJECT>
    <TASK_NAME>Decommission SQL Server</TASK_NAME>
    <DEPTNO>10</DEPTNO>
    <DEPARTMENT>Accounting</DEPARTMENT>
    <START_DATE>06/14/2013</START_DATE>
    <END_DATE>09/11/2013</END_DATE>
    <STATUS>Pending</STATUS>
    <ASSIGNED_TO>Al Bines</ASSIGNED_TO>
    <COST>0</COST>
    <BUDGET>500</BUDGET>
    <BALANCE>500</BALANCE>
  </ROW>
  <ROW>
    <ID>1567488874192989750311953724714716l0893</ID>
    <ROW_VERSION_NUMBER>2</ROW_VERSION_NUMBER>
    <PROJECT>Migrate from SQL Server</PROJECT>
    <TASK_NAME>Map data usage</TASK_NAME>
    <DEPTNO>10</DEPTNO>
    <DEPARTMENT>Accounting</DEPARTMENT>
    <START_DATE>06/02/2013</START_DATE>
    <END_DATE>07/15/2013</END_DATE>
    <STATUS>Pending</STATUS>
```

```
        <ASSIGNED_TO>Mark Nile</ASSIGNED_TO>
        <COST>0</COST>
        <BUDGET>8000</BUDGET>
        <BALANCE>8000</BALANCE>
    </ROW>
    <ROW>
        <ID>23540522987111510131118311120175048355</ID>
...
```

FO Document Structure

XSL-FO style sheets look similar to XSL documents, with sets of <fo:...> directives dispersed throughout. Listing 14-4 shows the complete XSL-FO stylesheet used for this section. This listing will be broken down into logical parts to describe the main components of the simple XSL-FO stylesheet. This stylesheet produces the PDF output shown in Figure 14-29.

Listing 14-4. XSL-FO for Sample Report Layout

```
<?xml version='1.0' ?>
<xsl:stylesheet version="1.0" xmlns:xsl="http://www.w3.org/1999/XSL/Transform">
 <xsl:template match="/">
  <fo:root xmlns:fo="http://www.w3.org/1999/XSL/Format">
   <fo:layout-master-set>
    <fo:simple-page-master master-name="default-page" page-height="8.5in"
                           page-width="11in" margin-left="0.5in"
                           margin-right="0.5in" margin-top="0.25in"
                           margin-bottom="0.25in">
     <fo:region-body margin-top="0.25in" margin-bottom="0.5in"/>
     <fo:region-before extent="1.0in"/>
     <fo:region-after extent="0.3in"/>
    </fo:simple-page-master>
   </fo:layout-master-set>
   <fo:page-sequence master-reference="default-page">
    <fo:static-content flow-name="xsl-region-before" font-size="8pt"
                       font-family="times,serif" color="red"
                       text-align="center">
     <fo:table>
      <fo:table-column column-width="5in"/>
      <fo:table-column column-width="5in"/>
      <fo:table-body>
       <fo:table-row>
        <fo:table-cell>
         <fo:block text-align="start" color="#006633" font-size="12pt"
                   font-family="times,serif" font-weight="bold">
          <fo:block>
           <xsl:text>APress Expert Oracle Application Express - Chapter 14
                     Report Printing</xsl:text>
          </fo:block>
         </fo:block>
        </fo:table-cell>
        <fo:table-cell>
```

```
      <fo:block text-align="end" color="black">
        <xsl:value-of select="DOCUMENT/DATE"/>
      </fo:block>
    </fo:table-cell>
  </fo:table-row>
 </fo:table-body>
</fo:table>
</fo:static-content>
<fo:static-content flow-name="xsl-region-after" font-size="8pt"
                   font-family="times,serif" color="red"
                   text-align="center">
<fo:block>This report was made using a Report Query and a customized XSL-FO
          Repory Layout</fo:block>
<fo:table>
 <fo:table-column column-width="5in"/>
 <fo:table-column column-width="5in"/>
 <fo:table-body>
  <fo:table-row>
   <fo:table-cell>
    <fo:block text-align="start" color="black">
     <xsl:value-of select="DOCUMENT/USER_NAME"/>
    </fo:block>
   </fo:table-cell>
   <fo:table-cell>
    <fo:block text-align="right" color="black">
     Page
     <fo:page-number/>
     of
     <fo:page-number-citation ref-id="EndOfDocument"/>
    </fo:block>
   </fo:table-cell>
  </fo:table-row>
 </fo:table-body>
</fo:table>
</fo:static-content>
<fo:flow flow-name="xsl-region-body">
 <fo:block>
  <fo:block text-align="center">
   <fo:block>
    <fo:inline font-family="times,serif">Sample Interactive Report XSL-FO
                              Demo Simple Table</fo:inline>
   </fo:block>
   <fo:block>
    <fo:table width="10in" border-style="solid" border-width="thin"
            background-repeat="repeat">
     <fo:table-column column-width="1.0in"/>
     <fo:table-column column-width="1.5in"/>
     <fo:table-column column-width="2.0in"/>
     <fo:table-column column-width="1.0in"/>
     <fo:table-column column-width="1.0in"/>
     <fo:table-column column-width="1.0in"/>
```

571

```
            <fo:table-column column-width="1.0in"/>
            <fo:table-column column-width="0.5in"/>
            <fo:table-column column-width="0.5in"/>
            <fo:table-column column-width="0.5in"/>
            <fo:table-header>
             <fo:table-row background-color="green" border-style="solid"
                        border-width="thin" border-color="green">
              <fo:table-cell border-style="solid" border-width="1pt"
                        border-color="gray" padding="2pt"
                        background-repeat="repeat" display-align="center">
               <fo:block font-family="times,serif" font-size="9pt" color="#FFFFFF"
                     background-color="#008000">
                <fo:block>
                 <xsl:text>Department</xsl:text>
                </fo:block>
               </fo:block>
              </fo:table-cell>
              <fo:table-cell border-style="solid" border-width="1pt"
                        border-color="gray" padding="2pt"
                        background-repeat="repeat" display-align="center">
               <fo:block font-family="times,serif" font-size="9pt"
                     text-align="center" color="#FFFFFF"
                     background-color="#008000">
                <fo:block>
                 <xsl:text>Project</xsl:text>
                </fo:block>
               </fo:block>
              </fo:table-cell>
              <fo:table-cell border-style="solid" border-width="1pt"
                        border-color="gray" padding="2pt"
                        background-repeat="repeat" display-align="center">
               <fo:block font-family="times,serif" font-size="9pt" color="#FFFFFF"
                     background-color="#008000">
                <fo:block>
                 <xsl:text>Task</xsl:text>
                </fo:block>
               </fo:block>
              </fo:table-cell>
              <fo:table-cell border-style="solid" border-width="1pt"
                        border-color="gray" padding="2pt"
                        background-repeat="repeat" display-align="center">
               <fo:block font-family="times,serif" font-size="9pt" color="#FFFFFF"
                     background-color="#008000">
                <fo:block>
                 <xsl:text>Start Date</xsl:text>
                </fo:block>
               </fo:block>
              </fo:table-cell>
              <fo:table-cell border-style="solid" border-width="1pt"
                        border-color="gray" padding="2pt"
                        background-repeat="repeat" display-align="center">
```

```
      <fo:block font-family="times,serif" font-size="9pt" color="#FFFFFF"
              background-color="#008000">
        <fo:block>
          <xsl:text>End Date</xsl:text>
        </fo:block>
      </fo:block>
    </fo:table-cell>
    <fo:table-cell border-style="solid" border-width="1pt"
                  border-color="gray" padding="2pt"
                  background-repeat="repeat" display-align="center">
      <fo:block font-family="times,serif" font-size="9pt" color="#FFFFFF"
              background-color="#008000">
        <fo:block>
          <xsl:text>Status</xsl:text>
        </fo:block>
      </fo:block>
    </fo:table-cell>
    <fo:table-cell border-style="solid" border-width="1pt"
                  border-color="gray" padding="2pt"
                  background-repeat="repeat" display-align="center">
      <fo:block font-family="times,serif" font-size="9pt" color="#FFFFFF"
              background-color="#008000">
        <fo:block>
          <xsl:text>Assigned</xsl:text>
        </fo:block>
      </fo:block>
    </fo:table-cell>
    <fo:table-cell border-style="solid" border-width="1pt"
                  border-color="gray" padding="2pt"
                  background-repeat="repeat" display-align="center">
      <fo:block font-family="times,serif" font-size="9pt" color="#FFFFFF"
              background-color="#008000">
        <fo:block>
          <xsl:text>Cost</xsl:text>
        </fo:block>
      </fo:block>
    </fo:table-cell>
    <fo:table-cell border-style="solid" border-width="1pt"
                  border-color="gray" padding="2pt"
                  background-repeat="repeat" display-align="center">
      <fo:block font-family="times,serif" font-size="9pt" color="#FFFFFF"
              background-color="#008000">
        <fo:block>
          <xsl:text>Budget</xsl:text>
        </fo:block>
      </fo:block>
    </fo:table-cell>
    <fo:table-cell border-style="solid" border-width="0.5pt"
                  border-color="gray" padding="2pt"
                  background-repeat="repeat" display-align="center">
```

```
          <fo:block font-family="times,serif" font-size="8pt" color="#FFFFFF"
                    background-color="#008000">
           <fo:block>
            <xsl:text>Balance</xsl:text>
           </fo:block>
          </fo:block>
         </fo:table-cell>
        </fo:table-row>
       </fo:table-header>
       <fo:table-body>
        <xsl:for-each select="DOCUMENT/REGION/ROWSET/ROW">
         <fo:table-row>
          <fo:table-cell border-style="solid" border-width="0.5pt"
                    border-color="gray" padding="2pt"
                    background-repeat="repeat" display-align="center">
           <fo:block font-family="times,serif" font-size="8pt">
            <fo:block>
             <xsl:value-of select="DEPARTMENT"/>
            </fo:block>
           </fo:block>
          </fo:table-cell>
          <fo:table-cell border-style="solid" border-width="0.5pt"
                    border-color="gray" padding="2pt"
                    background-repeat="repeat" display-align="center">
           <fo:block font-family="times,serif" font-size="8pt">
            <fo:block>
             <xsl:value-of select="PROJECT"/>
            </fo:block>
           </fo:block>
          </fo:table-cell>
          <fo:table-cell border-style="solid" border-width="0.5pt"
                    border-color="gray" padding="2pt"
                    background-repeat="repeat" display-align="center">
           <fo:block font-family="times,serif" font-size="8pt">
            <fo:block>
             <xsl:value-of select="TASK_NAME"/>
            </fo:block>
           </fo:block>
          </fo:table-cell>
          <fo:table-cell border-style="solid" border-width="0.5pt"
                    border-color="gray" padding="2pt"
                    background-repeat="repeat" display-align="center">
           <fo:block font-family="times,serif" font-size="8pt">
            <fo:block>
             <xsl:value-of select="START_DATE"/>
            </fo:block>
           </fo:block>
          </fo:table-cell>
          <fo:table-cell border-style="solid" border-width="0.5pt"
                    border-color="gray" padding="2pt"
                    background-repeat="repeat" display-align="center">
```

```
<fo:block font-family="times,serif" font-size="8pt">
 <fo:block>
  <xsl:value-of select="END_DATE"/>
 </fo:block>
</fo:block>
</fo:table-cell>
<fo:table-cell border-style="solid" border-width="0.5pt"
               border-color="gray" padding="2pt"
               background-repeat="repeat" display-align="center">
 <fo:block font-family="times,serif" font-size="8pt">
  <fo:block>
   <xsl:value-of select="STATUS"/>
  </fo:block>
 </fo:block>
</fo:table-cell>
<fo:table-cell border-style="solid" border-width="0.5pt"
               border-color="gray" padding="2pt"
               background-repeat="repeat" display-align="center">
 <fo:block font-family="times,serif" font-size="8pt">
  <fo:block>
   <xsl:value-of select="ASSIGNED_TO"/>
  </fo:block>
 </fo:block>
</fo:table-cell>
<fo:table-cell border-style="solid" border-width="0.5pt"
               border-color="gray" padding="2pt"
               background-repeat="repeat" display-align="center">
 <fo:block font-family="times,serif" font-size="8pt">
  <fo:block>
   <xsl:value-of select="COST"/>
  </fo:block>
 </fo:block>
</fo:table-cell>
<fo:table-cell border-style="solid" border-width="0.5pt"
               border-color="gray" padding="2pt"
               background-repeat="repeat" display-align="center">
 <fo:block font-family="times,serif" font-size="8pt">
  <fo:block>
   <xsl:value-of select="BUDGET"/>
  </fo:block>
 </fo:block>
</fo:table-cell>
<fo:table-cell border-style="solid" border-width="0.5pt"
               border-color="gray" padding="2pt"
               background-repeat="repeat" display-align="center">
 <fo:block font-family="times,serif" font-size="8pt">
  <fo:block>
   <xsl:value-of select="BALANCE"/>
  </fo:block>
 </fo:block>
</fo:table-cell>
```

```
          </fo:table-row>
         </xsl:for-each>
        </fo:table-body>
       </fo:table>
      </fo:block>
     </fo:block>
    </fo:block>
    <fo:block id="EndOfDocument"></fo:block>
   </fo:flow>
  </fo:page-sequence>
 </fo:root>
 </xsl:template>
</xsl:stylesheet>
```

All XSL-FO stylesheets have a common header and footer that generally take on the same or similar format.

```
<?xml version="1.0"?>
<xsl:stylesheet version="1.0" xmlns:xsl=="http://www.w3.org/1999/XSL/Transform">
  <xsl:template match="/">
    <fo:root xmlns:fo="http://www.w3.org/1999/XSL/Format">
...
```

The first line identifies the document as XML. The second line identifies the XSL namespace. Additional namespace listings in this line are optional. If you use a commercial XSL-FO editor, that editor may insert an additional namespace for you. For example, style sheets built with Stylus Studio automatically insert this namespace:

```
xmlns:s="http://www.stylusstudio.com/xquery"
```

This directive tells the processor to include the Stylus Studio XQuery library.

Beware that the use of external namespaces is great when they are recognized in the scope of your processing environment and all your output processing is done there. Most of these will not work with the FOP processor delivered with APEX, nor will they work with the FOP processor in ORDS.

The third line tells the processor to apply the template to the root of the XML document, in this case, the whole XML data set.

The fourth line identifies the XSL/Format (XSL/FO) namespace. All XSL-FO stylesheets must have an <fo:root ... > formatting object. This is the document element.

Combined, these first four lines identify this document as an XSL-FO document.

Extension objects and properties are allowed, and non-XSL-FO namespaces are allowed for embedded graphic images. For most APEX purposes, extension and non-XSL-FO namespaces will not be required. And as mentioned, for most APEX FOP installations, extension namespaces will not be recognized by the APEX-provided FOP processor.

When writing fo object and property directives, these rules apply:

- All characters are lowercase.

- A hyphen separates multiple words in an object name.

- A dot separates object or property names from compound elements.

Here's an example:

```
space-before="12pt"
space-before.conditionality="retain"
```

The next lines in the sample XSL-FO template, shown in Listing 14-5, are for page layout.

Listing 14-5. XSL-FO Layout Master Set

```
<fo:layout-master-set>
  <fo:simple-page-master master-name="default-page"
      page-height="8.5in" page-width="11in" margin-left="0.5in"
      margin-right="0.5in" margin-top="0.25in" margin-bottom="0.25in">
    <fo:region-body margin-top="0.25in" margin-bottom="0.25in"/>
    <fo:region-before extent="1.0in"/>
    <fo:region-after extent="0.3in"/>
  </fo:simple-page-master>
</fo:layout-master-set>
```

All XSL-FO style sheets must have a <layout-master-set> formatting object. The <layout-master-set> object defines the collection of page regions available for page layout and sequences. The <layout-master-set> object will include a <simple-page-master> or <page-sequence-master> object.

The <simple-page-master> object used in the sample describes a page and standard regions within the page. A typical <simple-page-master> object sets the page height, width, and margins, and it defines properties for the standard region-body, region-before (header), and region-after (footer) regions on the page. This <simple-page-master> defines an 8.5 by 11-inch landscape orientation page with 1/2-inch left and right margins and 1/4-inch top and bottom margins. The page header, the region-before area, is 1 inch, and the footer, which is called region-after, is 0.3 inch. The body, called region-body, has an additional top margin of 1/4 inch and a 1/2-inch bottom margin. These settings apply to all pages since there is no other page definition.

All XSL-FO structures must have a page sequence, and each <page-sequence> must have at least one flow object. The <page-sequence> defines the content that goes in the regions listed in the page master. In the sample report layout, there is one page sequence. All pages have the same format. The page sequence includes three tables. Two of these are static content for the header and footer regions. The third is a flow object that contains the rows of the sample report query, flowing for as many pages as required.

The header table is a simple two-column table that holds the heading text, placed at the top right on the page; the document date, which is at the top right of the page; and the title of the report, which is centered on the page in a separate line. Listing 14-6 shows the XSL-FO template excerpt that describes the report header table.

Listing 14-6. XSL-FO for Report Heading Table

```
<fo:static-content flow-name="xsl-region-before" font-size="8pt" font-family="times,serif"
text-align="center">
 <fo:table>
  <fo:table-column column-width="5in"/>
  <fo:table-column column-width="5in"/>
  <fo:table-body>
   <fo:table-row>
    <fo:table-cell>
     <fo:block text-align="start" color="#006633" font-size="12pt"
       font-family="times,serif" font-weight="bold">
```

```
      <fo:block>
       <xsl:text> APress Expert APEX - Ch 18 Report Printing</xsl:text>
      </fo:block>
     </fo:block>
    </fo:table-cell>
    <fo:table-cell>
     <fo:block text-align="end" color="black">
      <xsl:value-of select="DOCUMENT/DATE"/>
     </fo:block>
    </fo:table-cell>
   </fo:table-row>
  </fo:table-body>
 </fo:table>
</fo:static-content>
```

Since this is a simple little table, it is practical to describe the FO table format directives here. The `<fo:table...>` directive opens a fo table. The next step is to define columns for the table and then the body. The table body has table rows and table cells. The first row may be a section that defines the table heading row. In this case, the heading row is omitted. The table row directive wraps a set of table cell directives, one for each of the table columns.

The `<fo:block>` directive marks an element output, which is a chunk of text, if you will. Formatting attributes most often are applied to the `<fo:block ...>` element. Here's an example:

```
text-align="start" color="#006633" font-size="12pt" font-family="times,serif" font-weight="bold"
```

While these attributes are not exactly the same as for HTML, they are so similar as to be easily recognized by most web developers as describing text that is left-aligned (the start for English left-to-right lines), blue (#006633 is a hexadecimal for a medium blue color), 12 point, Times-Serif, bold text. Pretty simple and intuitive. These same directives could have been applied at the `table-row` or `table-cell` level, where they would have applied to all inner elements unless overridden by a directive at a lower level. This concept of inheritance is similar to how attributes are inherited in HTML tables.

The `<xsl:text>` directive signals plain text for the contents of the table cell, ended by the `</xsl:text>` end tag.

The `<xsl:value-of SELECT="DOCUMENT/DATE">` directive tells the XSL-FO processor to use a value, the DOCUMENT/DATE value from the XML data, as the text in this table cell. This element, as are all elements, is ended by that analogous end tag `</xsl:value>`.

Each `<fo:block>` is ended by a closing `</fo:block>`.

At the end of the table, the ending `</fo:table-cell></fo:table-row></fo:table>` directives close the table. The table structure overall is similar to that of an HTML table, with fo directives instead.

By now you are getting the idea that writing XSL-FO templates is similar to writing HTML documents, with different directives. You've got it! The trick is using the correct series of fo directives to tell the FO processor how to format your output.

To continue describing the sample XSL-FO template, the next `fo:static` directive describes the page footer. There is one block of text, the page footer text, followed by a two-column, no-header, one-row table for displaying the username in the bottom-left corner and the page number in the bottom-right corner. Refer to Listing 14-1, the full XSL-FO template, to pick out the footer region. Notice that the footer, a static region, is defined before the flow, the table body.

The next section starts the first flow object and describes how to format the data in the simple report query. The `<fo:flow ...>` directive tells the processor that this starts a region of output that flows page to page until the data is exhausted. In this case, the flow includes a single table, indicated by the `<fo:table ...>` directive. For this table, the table column directives define the table column widths, in order, as shown in Listing 14-7. Note the columns in the table definition are not named; just the widths are defined.

Listing 14-7. fo:table-column Definitions

```
<fo:table width="100%" border-style="outset" border-width="2pt" background-repeat="repeat">
 <fo:table-column column-width="1.0in"/>
 <fo:table-column column-width="1.5in"/>
 <fo:table-column column-width="2.0in"/>
 <fo:table-column column-width="1.0in"/>
 <fo:table-column column-width="1.0in"/>
 <fo:table-column column-width="1.0in"/>
 <fo:table-column column-width="1.0in"/>
 <fo:table-column column-width="0.5in"/>
 <fo:table-column column-width="0.5in"/>
 <fo:table-column column-width="0.5in"/>
```

Next comes the table header definition; this table does have static table headings. Listing 14-8 shows part of the table heading XSL-FO definition.

Listing 14-8. fo:table-heading Definitions (Partial)

```
<fo:table-column column-width="0.5in"/>
 <fo:table-header>
  <fo:table-row background-color="green" border-style="solid" border-"
    border-color="green">
   <fo:table-cell border-style="solid" border-width="1pt" border-color="gray"
     padding="2pt" background-repeat="repeat" display-align="center">
    <fo:block font-family="times,serif" font-size="9pt" color="#FFFFFF"
      background-color="#008000">
     <fo:block>
      <xsl:text>Department</xsl:text>
     </fo:block>
    </fo:block>
   </fo:table-cell>
 <fo:table-cell border-style="solid" border-width="1pt" border-color="gray" padding="2pt"
background-repeat="repeat" display-align="center">
    <fo:block font-family="times,serif" font-size="9pt" text-align="center" color="#FFFFFF"
background-color="#008000">
     <fo:block>
      <xsl:text>Project</xsl:text>
     </fo:block>
    </fo:block>
 </fo:table-cell>
 <fo:table-cell border-style="solid" border-width="1pt" border-color="gray" padding="2pt"
background-repeat="repeat" display-align="center">
   <fo:block font-family="times,serif" font-size="9pt" color="#FFFFFF" background-
color="#008000">
    <fo:block>
     <xsl:text>Task </xsl:text>
    </fo:block>
   </fo:block>
 </fo:table-cell>
...
```

The table body definition follows the table header row. The interesting features to note here are the `<xsl:for-each ...>` element and the ROW element.

Listing 14-9 shows the table body.

Listing 14-9. fo:table-body Definition (Partial)

```
<fo:table-body>
<xsl:for-each select="/DOCUMENT/ROWSET/ROW">
 <xsl:variable name="ROW" select="."/>
 <fo:table-row font-family="times,serif" font-size="8pt">
  <fo:table-cell border-style="inset" border-width="2pt" padding="2pt"
   background-repeat="repeat" display-align="center">
   <fo:block>
    <xsl:value-of select="DEPARTMENT"/>
   </fo:block>
  </fo:table-cell>
  <fo:table-cell border-style="inset" border-width="2pt" padding="2pt"
   background-repeat="repeat" display-align="center">
   <fo:block>
    <xsl:value-of select="PROJECT"/>
   </fo:block>
  </fo:table-cell>
  <fo:table-cell border-style="inset" border-width="2pt" padding="2pt"
   background-repeat="repeat" display-align="center">
   <fo:block>
    <xsl:value-of select="TASK_NAME"/>
   </fo:block>
  </fo:table-cell>
...
```

The `<xsl:for-each ...>` directive tells the processor to apply the following formatting for each set of the DOCUMENT/ROWSET/ROW elements in the incoming XML. That means write this output row this way for each of the rows in the XML input.

Each cell of the table includes an `<xsl:value-of ...>` directive to pull in the corresponding element of the XML tree. Each cell is wrapped in an `<fo:block ...>` so that formatting can be applied. This extra `<fo:block ...>` wrapper is not required, but it is routinely added by some tools to hold formatting applied at the lowest level.

The table-row, xsl:for-each, table-body, and table elements all end with the appropriate closing tags.

The EndofDocument block deserves special mention. This is a dummy, named, no-content block that is used to mark the end of the flow for pagination purposes. The `<fo:block ...>` processor needs to know where the end of the flow is in order to calculate the total pages. The `<fo:page-number-citation ref-id="EndOfDocument"/>` directive in the page-number directive (back up in the static content region-after section) references the EndofDocument ID.

```
<fo:block text-align="right" color="black">
                        Page
 <fo:page-number/> of
 <fo:page-number-citation ref-id="EndOfDocument"/>
</fo:block>
```

So, now you know all there is to know to build a basic table, with header, footer, formatted column headings, and column text. From here, you can build more features on your simple report output while learning more XSL-FO formatting features.

Now you will put that simple XSL-FO template to use in APEX. First, you upload the XSL-FO code as a report layout. Next, you assign that report layout to a static report query. For this example, the report query is the same as the sample query for the classic and interactive reports. Figure 14-29 shows the output of that report query/report layout set.

APress Expert Oracle APEX - Chapter 14 Report Printing   07/14/2015

Sample Interactive Report XSL-FO Demo Simple Table

Department	Project	Task	Start Date	End Date	Status	Assigned	Cost	Budget	Balance
Accounting	Migrate from SQL Server	Decommission SQL Server	06/14/2013	09/11/2013	Pending	Al Bines	0	500	500
Accounting	Migrate from SQL Server	Map data usage	06/02/2013	07/15/2013	Pending	Mark Nile	0	8000	8000
Accounting	Migrate from SQL Server	Implement integration using Oracle	06/16/2013	07/16/2013	Pending	Mark Nile	0	1500	1500
Accounting	Migrate from SQL Server	Migrate table structures	07/07/2013	08/01/2013	Pending	John Watson	0	2500	2500
Accounting	Migrate from SQL Server	Import data	07/08/2013	08/04/2013	Pending	John Watson	0	1000	1000
Accounting	Migrate from SQL Server	Notify users	07/18/2013	07/21/2013	Pending	Mark Nile	0	200	200
Accounting	Software Projects Tracking	Customize Software Projects software	04/27/2013	06/02/2013	Open	Tom Suess	600	1000	400
Accounting	APEX Environment Configuration	Identify server requirements	03/14/2013	03/15/2013	Closed	John Watson	100	200	100
Accounting	APEX Environment Configuration	Determine Web listener configuration(s)	03/15/2013	03/15/2013	Closed	James Cassidy	100	100	0
Accounting	APEX Environment Configuration	Specify security authentication scheme(s)	03/16/2013	03/18/2013	Closed	John Watson	200	300	100
Accounting	APEX Environment Configuration	Select servers for Development, Test, Production	03/16/2013	03/21/2013	Closed	James Cassidy	200	600	400
Accounting	APEX Environment Configuration	Configure Workspace provisioning	03/23/2013	03/23/2013	Closed	John Watson	200	100	-100
Accounting	APEX Environment Configuration	Create pilot workspace	03/23/2013	03/23/2013	Closed	John Watson	100	100	0
Accounting	APEX Environment Configuration	Run installation	03/24/2013	03/24/2013	Closed	James Cassidy	100	100	0
Accounting	Load Packaged Applications	Identify point solutions required	04/15/2013	04/17/2013	Closed	John Watson	200	300	100
Accounting	Software Projects Tracking	Conduct project kickoff meeting	04/17/2013	04/17/2013	Closed	Pam King	100	100	0
Accounting	Load Packaged Applications	Install in development	04/19/2013	04/19/2013	Closed	John Watson	100	100	0
Accounting	Load Packaged Applications	Customize solutions	04/20/2013	07/13/2013	Open	John Watson	1500	4000	2500
Accounting	Software Projects Tracking	Enter base data (Projects, Milestones, etc.)	04/22/2013	04/23/2013	Closed	Tom Suess	200	200	0
Accounting	Software Projects Tracking	Load current tasks and enhancements	04/24/2013	04/28/2013	Closed	Tom Suess	400	500	100
Accounting	Load Packaged Applications	Implement in Production	05/09/2013	07/17/2013	Open	John Watson	200	1500	1300
Accounting	Migrate from SQL Server	Obtain SQL Server credentials	05/16/2013	05/19/2013	Pending	James Cassidy	0	500	500
Accounting	Migrate from SQL Server	Create DB Connection to Oracle	05/21/2013	05/21/2013	Pending	Scott Spencer	0	100	100
Accounting	Migrate from SQL Server	Identify integration points	05/21/2013	06/10/2013	Pending	Mark Nile	0	2000	2000
Accounting	Load Packaged Applications	Train developers / users	05/23/2013	08/06/2013	Pending	John Watson	0	8000	8000
Accounting	Migrate from SQL Server	Convert processes	06/15/2013	08/13/2013	Pending	Pam King	0	3000	3000
Research	Migrate Access Application	Identify pilot Access applications	04/22/2013	04/27/2013	Closed	Mark Nile	300	500	200
Research	Migrate Access Application	Migrate pilot applications to APEX	04/29/2013	05/04/2013	Closed	Mark Nile	500	500	0
Research	Migrate Access Application	Post-migration review	05/06/2013	05/06/2013	Closed	Mark Nile	100	100	0
Research	Migrate Access Application	Plan migration schedule	05/08/2013	05/08/2013	Closed	Mark Nile	600	200	-400

APRESS   This report was made using a Report Query and a customized XSL-FO Report Layout   Page 1 of 3

Figure 14-29. Static report query and simple report layout

This is a bit better than using the generic XSL-FO output because you have more control over column widths and a full set of appearance attributes to work with. Still, you have not done much work, just some basic XSL-FO table and static object (header and footer) formatting.

The next section describes how to use a simple XSL-FO template in a report layout to generate PDF output for an interactive report query. The sections after that describe adding additional formatting features to the report query and the report layout. The intent is to demonstrate some simple conditions, providing enough information to build on to develop more complex output layouts.

Customized PDF Output for Interactive Reports

For interactive reports, you really want to capture the sorts and filters applied by the end user and apply a custom template. That gives you PDF output that more closely matches what the user is seeing in the online interactive report. To do so, the report query must be dynamic to capture the as-displayed sorts and filters currently applied. For the report layout, you want to use your own XSL-FO template to override the default, generic XSL-FO template. Ideally, you want WYSIWYG PDF output for your interactive reports. To achieve this, you would need a report layout generator, one that captures the current interactive report query and then generates an appropriate report layout depending on the current display format.

■ **Note** The ALGEN project by ApexNinjas started along that path, but that was several APEX versions back. The concepts used by ApexNinjas for capturing the report filters are still sound. See the ApexNinjas blog for more information on ALGEN.

My compromise approach is to produce a static-column report layout and capture the sorts and filters of the current report. In some situations, a series of such reports may be required to cover all essential views of the data where PDF output is required.

To capture the SQL for the as-displayed interactive report, the best APEX 5 (actually APEX 4.2 or newer) option is to use the Get IR Query plugin by Denes Kubiceck, combined with a table function.

First, define a SQL object type for the report query contents and a table type of that object type. This is the type of row set the function will return. Listing 14-10 shows the declarations for the types required for the new, to-be-constructed report query. You can use the same tables and columns as in the sample query, but here, the order and data types of the columns in your type and in your report query are critical. The column order and column data type must match, and the query result set must match the output object type; otherwise, you will get a data type mismatch error.

Listing 14-10. Type and Table Type for the Dynamic Report Query

```
CREATE OR REPLACE TYPE "IR_RPT_TYPE"
AS OBJECT
( /*  IR Demo Report data elements */
ID      NUMBER,
ROW_VERSION_NUMBER    NUMBER,
PROJECT     VARCHAR2(30),
TASK_NAME    VARCHAR2(255),
START_DATE     DATE,
END_DATE     DATE,
STATUS     VARCHAR2(30),
ASSIGNED_TO     VARCHAR2(30),
COST     NUMBER,
BUDGET     NUMBER,
DEPTNO     NUMBER(10,0),
DEPARTMENT VARCHAR2(255),
BALANCE NUMBER
);

CREATE OR REPLACE TYPE IR_RPT_TABTYPE AS TABLE OF IR_RPT_TYPE;
```

Listing 14-11 shows the GET_IR_QUERY function that returns data as IR_RPT_TABTYPE. Exception handling has been removed from the listing, for brevity.

Listing 14-11. GET_IR_QRY Function

```
create or replace FUNCTION GET_IR_QRY (P_QUERY IN VARCHAR2)
RETURN IR_RPT_TABTYPE AS
  v_sql VARCHAR2(4000);
  v_ir_report_tab IR_RPT_TABTYPE;
BEGIN
  v_sql := 'SELECT CAST(MULTISET( '||p_query||') AS IR_RPT_TABTYPE) FROM DUAL';
  EXECUTE IMMEDIATE v_sql INTO v_ir_report_tab;
  RETURN v_ir_report_tab;

END GET_IR_QRY;
```

The single parameter in the function is the output of the GET_IR_QRY plugin. For complete documentation and installation instructions for the GET_IR_QRY plugin, see http://deneskubicek. blogspot.com/2014/03/apex-ir-query-plugin.html. The plugin gets applied as a dynamic action called After Refresh of the Interactive Report region. The result is stored in a page item (usually hidden). The value of this page item—the SQL for the as-displayed interactive report—is passed into the GET_IR_QRY function. The function slightly modifies the query to cast the output as type IR_RPT_TABTYPE. Then the function performs an EXECUTE IMMEDIATE and returns.

Listing 14-12 shows the SQL for the new report query that consumes the GET_IR_QRY function. This report query gets paired with the same report layout as used to produce the static content PDF output. The same layout is fine; the goal is to adjust the SQL query to reflect the current sorts and filters.

Listing 14-12. Dynamic Report Query for Interactive Report Use

```
select p.ID,
       p.ROW_VERSION_NUMBER,
       p.PROJECT,
       p.TASK_NAME,
       p.DEPTNO,
       p.Department,
       p.START_DATE,
       p.END_DATE,
       p.STATUS,
       p.ASSIGNED_TO,
       p.COST,
       p.BUDGET,
       p.Balance,
       CASE WHEN p.balance < 0 THEN
         'yellow'
       ELSE
         'white'
       END rowbg
  from TABLE( GET_IR_QRY( :P20_IR_QUERY)) p;
```

583

Figure 14-30 displays the resulting PDF output when the dynamic report query is combined with the advanced report layout. I will address how to add background shading and colors on the Status column font in the next section. For now, let's focus on the filtered data. Note that in this output the data set is filtered to show just the Operations department, the same filter the user applied in the interactive report.

APress Expert Oracle APEX - Chapter 14 Report Printing   14-JUL-15

Sample Interactive Report XSL-FO Demo Simple Table

Department	Project	Task	Start Date	End Date	Status	Assigned	Cost	Budget	Balance
Operations	Bug Tracker	Document quality assurance procedures	28-APR-13	01-JUN-13	Open	Myra Sutcliff	3500	4000	500
Operations	Bug Tracker	Implement bug tracking software	28-MAR-13	28-MAR-13	Closed	Myra Sutcliff	100	100	0
Operations	Bug Tracker	Measure effectiveness of improved QA	14-JUN-13	14-JUL-13	Pending	Myra Sutcliff	0	1500	1500
Operations	Bug Tracker	Review automated testing tools	29-MAR-13	27-APR-13	On-Hold	Myra Sutcliff	2750	1500	-1250
Operations	Bug Tracker	Train developers on tracking bugs	02-JUN-13	22-JUL-13	On-Hold	Myra Sutcliff	0	2000	2000
Operations	Forms Conversion	End-user Training	01-AUG-13	13-OCT-13	Pending	Myra Sutcliff	0	2500	2500
Operations	Forms Conversion	Identify pilot Oracle Forms applications	17-APR-13	18-APR-13	Closed	Scott Spencer	200	200	0
Operations	Forms Conversion	Migrate Oracle Forms	08-MAY-13	15-SEP-13	Open	Pam King	300	12000	11700
Operations	Forms Conversion	Migrate pilot Forms to APEX	19-APR-13	02-MAY-13	Closed	Scott Spencer	400	500	100
Operations	Forms Conversion	Plan migration schedule	04-MAY-13	04-MAY-13	Closed	Pam King	100	100	0
Operations	Forms Conversion	Post-migration review	03-MAY-13	03-MAY-13	Closed	Pam King	100	100	0
Operations	Forms Conversion	Rollout migrated Forms in APEX	04-OCT-13	15-OCT-13	Pending	Pam King	0	500	500
Operations	Forms Conversion	Test migrated applications	14-JUN-13	06-OCT-13	Pending	Russ Saunders	0	6000	6000
Operations	Forms Conversion	User acceptance testing	29-JUN-13	01-OCT-13	Pending	Russ Saunders	0	2500	2500
Operations	Maintain Support Systems	Apply Billing System updates	14-MAR-13	13-MAY-13	On-Hold	Russ Sanders	9500	7000	-2500
Operations	Maintain Support Systems	Arrange for vacation coverage	02-MAY-13	25-MAY-13	Open	Al Bines	300	500	200
Operations	Maintain Support Systems	HR software upgrades	14-MAR-13	09-MAY-13	On-Hold	Pam King	8000	7000	-1000
Operations	Maintain Support Systems	Investigate new Virus Protection software	11-MAY-13	26-MAY-13	Open	Pam King	1700	1500	-200
Operations	Train Developers in APEX	Create training workspace	13-APR-13	20-APR-13	Closed	James Cassidy	500	700	200
Operations	Train Developers in APEX	Publish development standards	10-APR-13	16-JUN-13	On-Hold	John Watson	1000	2000	1000
Operations	Train Developers in APEX	Publish links to self-study courses	13-APR-13	13-APR-13	Closed	John Watson	100	100	0

Figure 14-30. *Filtered, sorted custom IR report query and report layout*

In this option, you lose the interactivity of letting the user control the columns and column order—the template is a fixed-column format—but you gain the ability to control column width and apply other formatting features not possible in the generic layout. A developer may need to build multiple report query/report layout sets—one to cover the main tabular view, one for the Group By view, and another for the pivot view, depending on business requirements.

The dynamic report query strategy is to utilize the GET_IR_QRY plugin or to use the APEX_IR package directly to return the SQL query for the as-filtered, as-displayed report.

The report layout strategy is to build a custom XSL-FO template that specifically sets named-column widths and conditionally applies other formatting features to meet business requirements. The next sections cover some more advanced (but still simple) XSL-FO options for applying custom formatting.

Advanced XSL-FO Examples

The basics of XSL-FO templates described earlier give you a start. The custom interactive report example demonstrates how to use a basic XSL-FO template that formats a tabular no-frills view of the data.

No doubt you will need more. As illustrated in the output shown in Figure 14-30, it is possible to add highlighting and color-coded text. In fact, most any type of formatting you require can be achieved with an XSL-FO template. The trick is to know the right directives to apply to achieve your desired layout and coloring. Note that XSL-FO templates may be used for static or dynamic report queries. FOP does not care where the XML data comes from; it sees only the XML dataset and applies the corresponding report layout.

The examples in this section show you how to apply a simple condition to your template and how to define a variable and use that variable for conditional formatting. These examples are simple on purpose; they are meant to hint at the formatting possibilities when introducing variables and conditions.

The following paragraphs detail two of the most common condition types found in XSL-FO templates:

- Customizing an XSL-FO template for color coding using a simple value condition

- Using a column as a variable in a condition, for conditional backgrounds and other simple report formatting

Both of these techniques are applied to the report layout, producing the results in Figure 14-31. Notice that rows where the balance is negative are highlighted in yellow, and the Status column font color changes based on the Status value: red for Closed, orange for Pending, blue for On-Hold, and green for Open.

Listing 14-13 shows the XSL-FO template—Report Layout—to produce the PDF output shown in Figure 14-31.

Listing 14-13. XSL-FO to Produce PDF Output Shown in Figure 14-31

```
<?xml version='1.0' ?>
<xsl:stylesheet version="1.0" xmlns:xsl="http://www.w3.org/1999/XSL/Transform">
 <xsl:template match="/">
  <fo:root xmlns:fo="http://www.w3.org/1999/XSL/Format">
   <fo:layout-master-set>
    <fo:simple-page-master master-name="default-page" page-height="8.5in"
                           page-width="11in" margin-left="0.5in"
                           margin-right="0.5in" margin-top="0.25in"
                           margin-bottom="0.25in">
     <fo:region-body margin-top="0.25in" margin-bottom="0.5in"/>
     <fo:region-before extent="1.0in"/>
     <fo:region-after extent="0.3in"/>
    </fo:simple-page-master>
   </fo:layout-master-set>
   <fo:page-sequence master-reference="default-page">
    <fo:static-content flow-name="xsl-region-before" font-size="8pt"
                       font-family="times,serif" color="red"
                       text-align="center">
     <fo:table>
      <fo:table-column column-width="5in"/>
      <fo:table-column column-width="5in"/>
      <fo:table-body>
       <fo:table-row>
        <fo:table-cell>
```

```
          <fo:block text-align="start" color="#006633" font-size="12pt"
                    font-family="times,serif" font-weight="bold">
           <fo:block>
            <xsl:text>APress Expert Oracle APEX - Chapter 14 Report Printing</xsl:text>
           </fo:block>
          </fo:block>
        </fo:table-cell>
        <fo:table-cell>
         <fo:block text-align="end" color="black">
          <xsl:value-of select="DOCUMENT/DATE"/>
         </fo:block>
        </fo:table-cell>
       </fo:table-row>
      </fo:table-body>
     </fo:table>
    </fo:static-content>
    <fo:static-content flow-name="xsl-region-after" font-size="8pt"
                       font-family="times,serif" color="red"
                       text-align="center">
     <fo:block>This report was made using a Report Query and a customized XSL-FO
              Report Layout</fo:block>
     <fo:table>
      <fo:table-column column-width="5in"/>
      <fo:table-column column-width="5in"/>
      <fo:table-body>
       <fo:table-row>
        <fo:table-cell>
         <fo:block text-align="start" color="black">
          <xsl:value-of select="DOCUMENT/USER_NAME"/>
         </fo:block>
        </fo:table-cell>
        <fo:table-cell>
         <fo:block text-align="right" color="black">
          Page
          <fo:page-number/>
          of
          <fo:page-number-citation ref-id="EndOfDocument"/>
         </fo:block>
        </fo:table-cell>
       </fo:table-row>
      </fo:table-body>
     </fo:table>
    </fo:static-content>
    <fo:flow flow-name="xsl-region-body">
     <fo:block>
      <fo:block text-align="center">
       <fo:block>
        <fo:inline font-family="times,serif">Sample Interactive Report XSL-FO
                                 Demo Simple Table</fo:inline>
       </fo:block>
       <fo:block>
```

```
<fo:table width="10in" border-style="solid" border-width="thin"
          background-repeat="repeat">
 <fo:table-column column-width="1.0in"/>
 <fo:table-column column-width="1.5in"/>
 <fo:table-column column-width="2.0in"/>
 <fo:table-column column-width="1.0in"/>
 <fo:table-column column-width="1.0in"/>
 <fo:table-column column-width="1.0in"/>
 <fo:table-column column-width="1.0in"/>
 <fo:table-column column-width="0.5in"/>
 <fo:table-column column-width="0.5in"/>
 <fo:table-column column-width="0.5in"/>
 <fo:table-header>
  <fo:table-row background-color="green" border-style="solid"
                border-width="thin" border-color="green">
   <fo:table-cell border-style="solid" border-width="1pt"
                  border-color="gray" padding="2pt"
                  background-repeat="repeat" display-align="center">
    <fo:block font-family="times,serif" font-size="9pt" color="#FFFFFF"
              background-color="#008000">
     <fo:block>
      <xsl:text>Department</xsl:text>
     </fo:block>
    </fo:block>
   </fo:table-cell>
   <fo:table-cell border-style="solid" border-width="1pt"
                  border-color="gray" padding="2pt"
                  background-repeat="repeat" display-align="center">
    <fo:block font-family="times,serif" font-size="9pt"
              text-align="center" color="#FFFFFF"
              background-color="#008000">
     <fo:block>
      <xsl:text>Project</xsl:text>
     </fo:block>
    </fo:block>
   </fo:table-cell>
   <fo:table-cell border-style="solid" border-width="1pt"
                  border-color="gray" padding="2pt"
                  background-repeat="repeat" display-align="center">
    <fo:block font-family="times,serif" font-size="9pt" color="#FFFFFF"
              background-color="#008000">
     <fo:block>
      <xsl:text>Task</xsl:text>
     </fo:block>
    </fo:block>
   </fo:table-cell>
   <fo:table-cell border-style="solid" border-width="1pt"
                  border-color="gray" padding="2pt"
                  background-repeat="repeat" display-align="center">
```

```
    <fo:block font-family="times,serif" font-size="9pt" color="#FFFFFF"
            background-color="#008000">
     <fo:block>
      <xsl:text>Start Date</xsl:text>
     </fo:block>
    </fo:block>
   </fo:table-cell>
   <fo:table-cell border-style="solid" border-width="1pt"
                  border-color="gray" padding="2pt"
                  background-repeat="repeat" display-align="center">
    <fo:block font-family="times,serif" font-size="9pt" color="#FFFFFF"
            background-color="#008000">
     <fo:block>
      <xsl:text>End Date</xsl:text>
     </fo:block>
    </fo:block>
   </fo:table-cell>
   <fo:table-cell border-style="solid" border-width="1pt"
                  border-color="gray" padding="2pt"
                  background-repeat="repeat" display-align="center">
    <fo:block font-family="times,serif" font-size="9pt" color="#FFFFFF"
            background-color="#008000">
     <fo:block>
      <xsl:text>Status</xsl:text>
     </fo:block>
    </fo:block>
   </fo:table-cell>
   <fo:table-cell border-style="solid" border-width="1pt"
                  border-color="gray" padding="2pt"
                  background-repeat="repeat" display-align="center">
    <fo:block font-family="times,serif" font-size="9pt" color="#FFFFFF"
            background-color="#008000">
     <fo:block>
      <xsl:text>Assigned</xsl:text>
     </fo:block>
    </fo:block>
   </fo:table-cell>
   <fo:table-cell border-style="solid" border-width="1pt"
                  border-color="gray" padding="2pt"
                  background-repeat="repeat" display-align="center">
    <fo:block font-family="times,serif" font-size="9pt" color="#FFFFFF"
            background-color="#008000">
     <fo:block>
      <xsl:text>Cost</xsl:text>
     </fo:block>
    </fo:block>
   </fo:table-cell>
   <fo:table-cell border-style="solid" border-width="1pt"
                  border-color="gray" padding="2pt"
                  background-repeat="repeat" display-align="center">
```

```
    <fo:block font-family="times,serif" font-size="9pt" color="#FFFFFF"
            background-color="#008000">
    <fo:block>
     <xsl:text>Budget</xsl:text>
    </fo:block>
   </fo:block>
  </fo:table-cell>
  <fo:table-cell border-style="solid" border-width="0.5pt"
              border-color="gray" padding="2pt"
              background-repeat="repeat" display-align="center">
    <fo:block font-family="times,serif" font-size="8pt" color="#FFFFFF"
            background-color="#008000">
    <fo:block>
     <xsl:text>Balance</xsl:text>
    </fo:block>
   </fo:block>
  </fo:table-cell>
 </fo:table-row>
</fo:table-header>
<fo:table-body>
 <xsl:for-each select="DOCUMENT/REGION/ROWSET/ROW">
  <xsl:variable name="rowbg">
   <xsl:value-of select="ROWBG"/>
  </xsl:variable>
  <fo:table-row background-color="{$rowbg}">
   <fo:table-cell border-style="solid" border-width="0.5pt"
               border-color="gray" padding="2pt"
               background-repeat="repeat" display-align="center">
    <fo:block font-family="times,serif" font-size="8pt">
     <fo:block>
      <xsl:value-of select="DEPARTMENT"/>
     </fo:block>
    </fo:block>
   </fo:table-cell>
   <fo:table-cell border-style="solid" border-width="0.5pt"
               border-color="gray" padding="2pt"
               background-repeat="repeat" display-align="center">
    <fo:block font-family="times,serif" font-size="8pt">
     <fo:block>
      <xsl:value-of select="PROJECT"/>
     </fo:block>
    </fo:block>
   </fo:table-cell>
   <fo:table-cell border-style="solid" border-width="0.5pt"
               border-color="gray" padding="2pt"
               background-repeat="repeat" display-align="center">
```

```
    <fo:block font-family="times,serif" font-size="8pt">
     <fo:block>
      <xsl:value-of select="TASK_NAME"/>
     </fo:block>
    </fo:block>
   </fo:table-cell>
   <fo:table-cell border-style="solid" border-width="0.5pt"
                  border-color="gray" padding="2pt"
                  background-repeat="repeat" display-align="center">
    <fo:block font-family="times,serif" font-size="8pt">
     <fo:block>
      <xsl:value-of select="START_DATE"/>
     </fo:block>
    </fo:block>
   </fo:table-cell>
   <fo:table-cell border-style="solid" border-width="0.5pt"
                  border-color="gray" padding="2pt"
                  background-repeat="repeat" display-align="center">
    <fo:block font-family="times,serif" font-size="8pt">
     <fo:block>
      <xsl:value-of select="END_DATE"/>
     </fo:block>
    </fo:block>
   </fo:table-cell>
   <fo:table-cell border-style="solid" border-width="0.5pt"
                  border-color="gray" padding="2pt"
                  background-repeat="repeat" display-align="center">
    <fo:block font-family="times,serif" font-size="8pt">
     <xsl:variable name="statcolor">
      <xsl:choose>
       <xsl:when test="STATUS='Pending'">orange</xsl:when>
       <xsl:when test="STATUS='Closed'">red</xsl:when>
       <xsl:when test="STATUS='On-Hold'">blue</xsl:when>
       <xsl:when test="STATUS='Open'">green</xsl:when>
       <xsl:otherwise>black</xsl:otherwise>
      </xsl:choose>
     </xsl:variable>
     <fo:inline color="{$statcolor}">
      <xsl:value-of select="STATUS"/>
     </fo:inline>
    </fo:block>
   </fo:table-cell>
   <fo:table-cell border-style="solid" border-width="0.5pt"
                  border-color="gray" padding="2pt"
                  background-repeat="repeat" display-align="center">
    <fo:block font-family="times,serif" font-size="8pt">
     <fo:block>
      <xsl:value-of select="ASSIGNED_TO"/>
     </fo:block>
    </fo:block>
   </fo:table-cell>
```

```
            <fo:table-cell border-style="solid" border-width="0.5pt"
                          border-color="gray" padding="2pt"
                          background-repeat="repeat" display-align="center">
              <fo:block font-family="times,serif" font-size="8pt">
               <fo:block>
                <xsl:value-of select="COST"/>
               </fo:block>
              </fo:block>
            </fo:table-cell>
            <fo:table-cell border-style="solid" border-width="0.5pt"
                          border-color="gray" padding="2pt"
                          background-repeat="repeat" display-align="center">
              <fo:block font-family="times,serif" font-size="8pt">
               <fo:block>
                <xsl:value-of select="BUDGET"/>
               </fo:block>
              </fo:block>
            </fo:table-cell>
            <fo:table-cell border-style="solid" border-width="0.5pt"
                          border-color="gray" padding="2pt"
                          background-repeat="repeat" display-align="center">
              <fo:block font-family="times,serif" font-size="8pt">
               <fo:block>
                <xsl:value-of select="BALANCE"/>
               </fo:block>
              </fo:block>
            </fo:table-cell>
           </fo:table-row>
          </xsl:for-each>
         </fo:table-body>
        </fo:table>
       </fo:block>
      </fo:block>
     </fo:block>
     <fo:block id="EndOfDocument"></fo:block>
    </fo:flow>
   </fo:page-sequence>
  </fo:root>
 </xsl:template>
</xsl:stylesheet>
```

APress Expert Oracle APEX - Chapter 18 Report Printing   05/03/2015

Department	Project	Task	Start Date	End Date	Status	Assigned	Cost	Budget	Balance
Research	Convert Excel Spreadsheet	Collect mission-critical spreadsheets	04/27/2013	06/28/2013	Open	Pam King	2,500.00	4,000.00	1,500.00
Research	Migrate Access Application	Migrate Access applications	05/10/2013	07/03/2013	Open	Mark Nile	1,000.00	8,000.00	7,000.00
Research	Convert Excel Spreadsheet	Create APEX applications from spreadsheets	04/27/2013	10/11/2013	Open	Pam King	10,000.00	6,000.00	-4,000.00
Research	Convert Excel Spreadsheet	Lock spreadsheets	04/27/2013	10/11/2013	Open	Pam King	1,000.00	800.00	-200.00
Research	Convert Excel Spreadsheet	Send links to previous spreadsheet owners	04/28/2013	10/13/2013	Open	Pam King	1,000.00	1,500.00	500.00
Research	Employee Satisfaction Survey	Complete questionnaire	04/30/2013	05/14/2013	On-Hold	Irene Jones	1,200.00	800.00	-400.00
Research	Migrate Access Application	User acceptance testing	05/14/2013	07/13/2013	Open	Mark Nile	1,500.00	6,000.00	4,500.00
Research	Migrate Access Application	End-user Training	05/10/2013	07/05/2013	Open	John Watson	.00	2,000.00	2,000.00
Research	Employee Satisfaction Survey	Review with legal	05/22/2013	05/28/2013	On-Hold	Irene Jones	200.00	400.00	200.00
Research	Employee Satisfaction Survey	Plan rollout schedule	05/29/2013	06/06/2013	On-Hold	Irene Jones	.00	750.00	750.00
Sales	Public Website	Develop web pages	05/23/2013	06/28/2013	On-Hold	Tiger Scott	800.00	2,000.00	1,200.00
Sales	Discussion Forum	Identify owners	05/01/2013	05/04/2013	Closed	Hank Davis	250.00	300.00	50.00
Sales	Email Integration	Complete plan	03/21/2013	04/26/2013	Closed	Mark Nile	3,000.00	1,500.00	-1,500.00
Sales	Public Website	Plan rollout schedule	06/30/2013	06/30/2013	On-Hold	Tom Suess	.00	100.00	100.00
Sales	Email Integration	Purchase backup server	05/25/2013	06/20/2013	Pending	Mark Nile	.00	3,000.00	3,000.00
Sales	Public Website	Determine host server	04/18/2013	04/19/2013	Closed	Tiger Scott	200.00	200.00	.00
Sales	Email Integration	Get RFPs for new server	04/25/2013	05/16/2013	Open	Mark Nile	2,000.00	1,000.00	-1,000.00
Sales	Email Integration	Check software licenses	04/24/2013	04/25/2013	Closed	Mark Nile	200.00	200.00	.00
Sales	Public Website	Purchase additional software licenses, if needed	04/22/2013	05/15/2013	On-Hold	Al Bines	300.00	1,000.00	700.00
Sales	Discussion Forum	Install APEX application on internet server	05/09/2013	05/09/2013	Closed	Hank Davis	100.00	100.00	.00
Sales	Public Website	Check software licenses	04/19/2013	04/19/2013	Closed	Tom Suess	100.00	100.00	.00
Sales	Discussion Forum	Monitor participation	05/10/2013	05/18/2013	Open	Hank Davis	450.00	500.00	50.00
Operations	Train Developers in APEX	Create training workspace	04/13/2013	04/20/2013	Closed	James Cassidy	500.00	700.00	200.00
Operations	Forms Conversion	Identify pilot Oracle Forms applications	04/17/2013	04/18/2013	Closed	Scott Spencer	200.00	200.00	.00
Operations	Forms Conversion	Migrate pilot Forms to APEX	04/19/2013	05/02/2013	Closed	Scott Spencer	400.00	500.00	100.00
Operations	Bug Tracker	Document quality assurance procedures	04/28/2013	06/01/2013	Open	Myrn Sutcliff	3,500.00	4,000.00	500.00
Operations	Forms Conversion	Post-migration review	05/03/2013	05/03/2013	Closed	Pam King	100.00	100.00	.00
Operations	Forms Conversion	Plan migration schedule	05/04/2013	05/04/2013	Closed	Pam King	100.00	100.00	.00
Operations	Forms Conversion	Migrate Oracle Forms	05/08/2013	09/15/2013	Open	Pam King	300.00	12,000.00	11,700.00
Operations	Maintain Support Systems	Investigate new Virus Protection software	05/11/2013	05/26/2013	Open	Pam King	1,700.00	1,500.00	-200.00
Operations	Train Developers in APEX	Publish links to self-study courses	04/13/2013	04/13/2013	Closed	John Watson	100.00	100.00	.00
Operations	Train Developers in APEX	Publish development standards	04/10/2013	06/16/2013	On-Hold	John Watson	1,000.00	2,000.00	1,000.00
Operations	Bug Tracker	Review automated testing tools	03/29/2013	04/27/2013	On-Hold	Myrn Sutcliff	2,750.00	1,500.00	-1,250.00
Operations	Bug Tracker	Implement bug tracking software	03/28/2013	03/28/2013	Closed	Myrn Sutcliff	100.00	100.00	.00

APRESS   This report was made using a Report Query and a customized XSL-FO Report Layout   Page 2 of 3

Figure 14-31. *Report layout with conditional formatting*

Now the PDF output report is starting to look like something useful. Colors and formatting make this output much more useful for your users. The following sections describe the XSL-FO additions to add conditional row highlighting and font coloring to the PDF output. The techniques will be familiar to most programmers: you define a variable and then use that variable in a logical condition.

<xsl:value-of select=...> Conditional Formatting

The <xsl:value of select=...> construct allows you to set a variable name based on a value. There are many options for xsl:value of. This example uses the simplest form, select = "XML COLUMN", where XML COLUMN is a column in the XML dataset.

The yellow row background highlight is achieved by applying a simple <xsl-value-of ...> test (read "condition") to each of your table rows. You create an XSL variable, set its value using <xsl:value of select=...>, and use that variable to set the row background color.

In this example, I used a SQL CASE statement in the report query to create a ROWBG column in the output dataset. Listing 14-14 shows the full report query. This gives you the row background color you want for that row: the value. The value could also be created using XSL logic or any XSL variable, but I opted for simple in this example. Note that ROWBG is not defined in the report layout table, so it does not appear in the output report. The ROWBG value is still passed as part of the XML dataset, however, and in this example you use it for your <xsl:value of ...> test to set your rowbg variable.

Listing 14-14. Report Query with ROWBG Value

```
select p.ID,
       p.ROW_VERSION_NUMBER,
       p.PROJECT,
       p.TASK_NAME,
       p.DEPTNO,
       INITCAP(d.DNAME) Department,
       p.START_DATE,
       p.END_DATE,
       p.STATUS,
       p.ASSIGNED_TO,
       TO_CHAR(p.COST,'999G999D00') cost,
       TO_CHAR(p.BUDGET,'999G999D00') budget,
       TO_CHAR((p.BUDGET - p.COST),'999G999D00') Balance,
       CASE WHEN (p.BUDGET - p.COST) < 0 THEN
          'yellow'
       ELSE
          'white'
       END rowbg
  from EBA_DEMO_IR_PROJECTS P,
       EBA_DEMO_IR_DEPT D
 where p.deptno = d.deptno;
```

One other technique to note in Listing 14-14 is the use of TO_CHAR to explicitly format your numbers to the desired output format. With PDF output, you do not care if the value is a number or a character; it is just a value on a printed page. Formatting numeric format in the SQL query is the simplest technique for achieving the desired numeric output format. You are not asking XSL-FO to do your number formatting for you; you are delivering the values to FOP exactly as you want them formatted. The caveat is in the use of special characters, percent signs, and ampersands in particular. When essential, these will need to be escaped or delivered in Unicode because the FOP processor may interpret them as directives, with unexpected, nonreadable results.

Listing 14-15 shows the simple <xsl-value-of ...> test. First you define a variable, using <xsl:variable name="rowbg">; then you set it using the <xsl:value-of select="ROWBG"/> line. Then you use the variable to set the row background color in the <fo:table-row ...> directive.

Listing 14-15. Our simple test

```
<xsl:variable name="rowbg">
  <xsl:value-of select="ROWBG"/>
</xsl:variable>
<fo:table-row background-color="{$rowbg}">
```

The resulting output highlights rows with a negative balance in yellow, as in Figure 14-31. The technique of using an additional value in a report for conditional formatting is also recommended within APEX for declarative online formatting with interactive reports, so many times such columns may already be available for use as variables. Note that the xsl variable name does not need to correspond to the XML column name; I did so here simply for convenience.

Now that you know how to define variables, let's see what else you can do with them. The next section introduces <xsl:choose...>, the XSL-FO version of IF-THEN-ELSE logic.

<xsl:choose ...> Conditional Formatting

For times when more than a simple variable selection is required, the <xsl:choose...> element offers IF-THEN-ELSE-style conditional formatting options. Listing 14-16 shows the general format of an <xsl:choose...> element.

Listing 14-16. <xsl:choose...> Format

```
<xsl:choose>
  <xsl:when test="expression">
  ... some output ...
  </xsl:when>
  <xsl:otherwise>
  ... some output ....
  </xsl:otherwise>
</xsl:choose>
```

The format is similar to familiar PL/SQL IF-THEN-ELSE statements or SQL CASE statements.

Listing 14-17 shows the report layout excerpt that uses <xsl:choose ...>to set the Status column font color. The example <xsl:choose...> element is contained within an <fo:block ...> element. This is a common good practice; the variable is defined close to where it is used. This is not essential, but it sure makes things easier to follow.

Reading through Listing 14-17, you open the table cell and then open a formatting block. You next define a variable using <xsl:variable name = "statcolor">. Then comes <xsl:choose ...>.

Listing 14-17. XLS-FO for Status Column Font Color Coding

```
<fo:table-cell border-style="solid" border-width="0.5pt" border-color="gray" padding="2pt"
background-repeat="repeat" display-align="center">
  <fo:block font-family="times,serif" font-size="8pt">
   <xsl:variable name="statcolor">
   <xsl:choose>
   <xsl:when test="STATUS='Pending'">orange</xsl:when>
   <xsl:when test="STATUS='Closed'">red</xsl:when>
   <xsl:when test="STATUS='Open'">green</xsl:when>
    <xsl:otherwise>blue</xsl:otherwise>
   </xsl:choose>
   </xsl:variable>
   <fo:inline color="{$statcolor}">
     <xsl:value-of select="STATUS"/>
   </fo:INLINE>
   </fo:block>
</fo:table-cell>
```

This <xsl:choose...> element with its inner <xsl:when ...> directives sets a variable statcolor depending on the value of the STATUS column in the current row. Statcolor is then used to set the color of the STATUS text for that table-cell, color="{$statcolor}". The resulting PDF output is color-coded text based on the value of the STATUS column.

These simple examples scratch the surface of what can be achieved with XSL and XSL-FO. The xsl directives handle the transformation and logic applied to the incoming XML. The fo directives handle the formatting.

XSL-FO Editors

Commercial XSL-FO editors certainly make developing XSL-FO templates easier and facilitate learning XSL-FO object and property syntax. Syntax highlighting and WYSIWYG editing make the template-building process bearable. Beware that these editors are also likely to include extra or excess markup and may include directives that are recognized by that tool's built-in FOP processor but are not recognized by the APEX-supplied Apache FOP 1.1 processor. When developing an XSL-FO template for use in APEX, remember to stick with Apache FOP 1.1 objects and properties.

■ **Tip** My first venture into building a complex XSL-FO template was using Stylus Studio. I built and tested my template including XQuery conditions for required color coding and background shading and was quite pleased with my result. When I moved the template to APEX, nothing worked. Nothing. One by one I debugged, and removed, all of my nice XQuery conditions. Apparently they were a nicety of the Stylus Studio parsers and processors but not recognized by the stricter Apache FOP 1.0. I learned to build the same conditions the long way using standard XSL and XPath; it was the same results, just a different syntax. And I learned to stay close to my deployment tool stack, using the Apache FOP web site as my reference for object and property syntax.

Here are some recommendations for choosing an XSL-FO editor:

Set a budget: XSL-FO editors come in several flavors and in a wide range of price tags, from "free" to $100 to more than $1,000 per seat. Some vendors offer periodic sales that cut the price by up to 25 percent. Decide how important an XSL-FO editor is to your organization and how many licenses are needed. Base your budget on how important building XSL-FO templates quickly is to your organization. How many XSL-FO templates are needed? How often will new XSL-FO templates be developed? How many licenses are required? It may make sense to have one XSL-FO editor seat and have the developer specialize in building templates for the rest of the team. Compare the costs to how long it takes to develop comparable XSL-FO templates manually.

Try before you buy: My experience is none of these tools is truly intuitive. I found that none of the tools was as simple as point, click, and *voila*—out pops an XSL-FO template. Plan on using the 30-day trials, and plan for a learning curve. Make sure you can use one of the trial templates in an APEX report layout. Some tools will be easier to learn for you than others. Download and work on the trial versions and then decide whether to buy and which tool to buy.

Beware the free options: A web search for *XSL-FO editor free* lists several options, but most of them are free trials or products where the XSL-FO features are not included in the free version. XSL-FO editors are most often included as a for-cost option in XML-editor families. The XSL-FO editing or transformation may not be included in the core product; you may need to purchase an upgraded option to obtain XSL-FO features.

Check the features: Make sure the XSL-FO editor is included in the version of the tool you purchase. XSL-FO editors are also usually part of an XML/XSLT editor family of tools. Licensing may be in several tiers. Where this happens, the XSL-FO features are often bundled into the enterprise or most expensive licensing option, which may or may not be in your budget.

Consider that the tool may include its own flavor of parsers for preprocessing and the FOP processor. APEX deployed via ORDS uses FOP 1.1. XSL-FO templates generated in a tool that uses a different XSL parser and/or a different FOP processor may not work the same, or at all, on Apache FOP 1.1. A clue that this might happen is the list of extensions in the template heading. The way you will know this is happening is that the fo template that works fine in the XSL-FO tool fails in your APEX deployment. Most often this is because of an object or property directive that is not recognized or not supported by Apache FOP 1.1. To be safe, use the Apache FOP site as a reference. To validate your "plain" XSL-FO, remove the extra namespace declarations and test without them. Adjust as needed. Be easy on yourself; others have been as frustrated before you.

When this occurs, the output PDF document—if one is produced—is invalid. To troubleshoot, read the messages in the app server logs or read the contents of the "bad" PDF output file. For more information on troubleshooting failed PDF output, see the "Debugging XSL-FO" section.

My experience is that the more features, the more expensive the XSL-FO tool. Features such as syntax highlighting, code completion, and integrated PDF preview and WYSIWYG editing are essential for any XSL-FO editor investment. Ensure that the version of tool purchased includes the XSL-FO editor, not just an FOP processor. Weigh the cost of the tool with the productivity gain in using it over time.

Debugging XSL-FO

As you may have guessed by now, building XSL-FO templates is tedious at best and downright frustrating in general. To make matters worse, debugging failed PDF output is a matter of being methodical, patient, and in part a sleuth.

PDF output generation failures come in two categories:

- No output at all

- Invalid PDF output

The debugging approach is the same for both cases.

First, if you do not have enough patience to call to your cable company about a service outage, do not even start debugging your XSL-FO. Take a break, gather your wits, borrow some from your neighbor, and come back later. The obtuse nature of XSL-FO error messages and the tedious nature of finding the errors in a sea of fo directives, even with syntax highlighting, make debugging XSL-FO a task for the well fortified.

The best source of messages is the server logs on which the FOP is deployed. The location of the server logs depends on the APEX instance's report printing configuration and on where ORDS or FOP is deployed. If running on a stand-alone ORDS, the FOP processing output messages are written to the console window in which ORDS was launched. If ORDS is deployed on Glassfish, WebLogic, or another J2EE server, the server logs are in the location specific to that application server.

Your system administrator may not allow direct read access to the server logs. If not, ask your database administrator for read-only access through an external table setup. The following describes the steps to create external table access to the server logs for a Windows-based Glassfish server. As a privileged database user, follow these steps:

1. Create an Oracle directory that points to the file server location of the server logs.

```
CREATE DIRECTORY GF_LOG_DIR AS 'C:\glassfish41\domains\domain1\logs';
GRANT READ ON GF_LOG_DIR TO <user>;
```

2. Create an external table that points to the server log.

```
CREATE TABLE "THTECH"."GF_LOG_TBL"
  (
    "MESSAGE" VARCHAR2( 4000 )
  )
  ORGANIZATION EXTERNAL
  (
    TYPE ORACLE_LOADER DEFAULT DIRECTORY "GF_LOG_DIR" ACCESS PARAMETERS
    ( RECORDS DELIMITED BY NEWLINE
    NOBADFILE
    NOLOGFILE
    FIELDS TERMINATED BY '|'
    MISSING FIELD VALUES ARE NULL
    REJECT ROWS
WITH ALL NULL FIELDS( MESSAGE ) ) LOCATION( 'server.log' )
  ) REJECT LIMIT UNLIMITED
```

3. Create a view of the external table.

```
CREATE VIEW GF_LOGS_VW AS SELECT * FROM <user>.GF_LOG_TBL;
```

4. Grant access to the database view to the developers who need access to review
    FOP messages.

```
GRANT SELECT ON <user>.GF_LOG_TBL to <Developer User>
```

The developer could build an APEX interactive report on the server log view, for ease of viewing server log contents.

This access should be granted only in development environments for FOP debugging purposes. Ideally such access will not be required at all in production; everything will be working perfectly by then!

Now that you have access to the server logs, what are you looking for? You are looking for anything that looks like an FOP message. These are usually quite obvious. There are warning messages and error messages. Listing 14-18 shows a typical FOP WARNING error message. This particular set of warning messages is output from a run of the generic XLS-FO template against a simple interactive report where some of the columns are wider than the generic template expected. The PDF output completed fine, with some overlap in many of the columns.

Listing 14-18. FOP WARNING Error Messages in Stand-Alone Console

```
...
WARNING: Line 2 of a paragraph overflows the available area by 6810 millipoints.
(See position 1:593228)
May 03, 2015 12:10:30 AM org.apache.fop.events.LoggingEventListener processEvent
WARNING: Line 4 of a paragraph overflows the available area by 700 millipoints.
(See position 1:599723)
May 03, 2015 12:10:30 AM org.apache.fop.events.LoggingEventListener processEvent
WARNING: Line 2 of a paragraph overflows the available area by 4600 millipoints.
(See position 1:599723)
May 03, 2015 12:10:30 AM org.apache.fop.events.LoggingEventListener processEvent
WARNING: Line 1 of a paragraph overflows the available area by 4040 millipoints.
(See position 1:599723)
...
```

Listing 14-19 displays another common but innocuous WARNING message. This message tells you that table-layout="auto" has not been implemented by Apache FOP yet. table-layout="auto" is the default when no table layout option is specified. Even though you specifically set column widths for all three of the tables, the tables still defaults to table-layout="auto" according to the standard. This message highlights the fact that when using the FOP supplied with APEX or using ORDS, you are dealing with Apache FOP 1.1 and are limited to those features implemented therein. This is why the Apache FOP Project web site (https://xmlgraphics.apache.org/fop/fo.html) is an excellent reference for writing and debugging XSL-FO. Relying on the Apache FOP minimizes the likelihood of trying to implement a feature that is described in the XSL-FO standard but not yet implemented in Apache FOP.

Listing 14-19. Apache FOP table-layout="auto" WARNING Message

```
May 02, 2015 2:53:09 PM org.apache.fop.events.LoggingEventListener processEvent
WARNING: The following feature isn't implemented by Apache FOP, yet: table-layout
="auto" (on fo:table) (See position 1:689)
May 02, 2015 2:53:09 PM org.apache.fop.events.LoggingEventListener processEvent
WARNING: The following feature isn't implemented by Apache FOP, yet: table-layout
="auto" (on fo:table) (See position 2:28)
May 02, 2015 2:53:09 PM org.apache.fop.events.LoggingEventListener processEvent
WARNING: The following feature isn't implemented by Apache FOP, yet: table-layout
="auto" (on fo:table) (See position 7:136)
```

The messages shown previously are all WARNING messages that did not interrupt completion of FOP processing. When an error occurs that does abort processing, that error message will be the last in the set of FOP messages for that FOP output request. Note that it may not be the last message in the server log, nor the last FOP output set in the log, because the server log includes messages from other modules as well.

Often when an error aborts processing, the same error is written to the PDF output file and is readily readable there. In these cases, outfile.PDF is invalid as a PDF file, but when read in a plain-text editor, it gives clues about what went wrong. Figure 14-32 shows a typical nonhelpful XSL-FO output message.

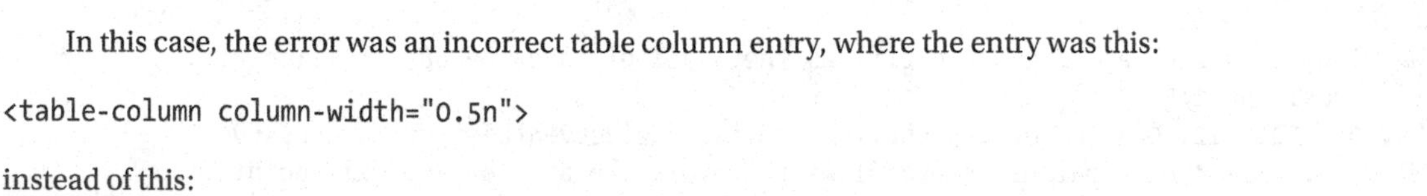

Figure 14-32. XSL-FO ERROR message in failed -file PDF

In this case, the error was an incorrect table column entry, where the entry was this:

```
<table-column column-width="0.5n">
```

instead of this:

```
<table-column column-width="0.5in">
```

It took a long time to find that missing *I*. The error message told me to inspect the table elements but not much else. I have yet to find any error that can translate or navigate to position 8:3545. This is where the sleuthing comes in. Another time this same error message occurred was when I tested my report without including session state values. I found that problem by trial and error. Be prepared for such messages, and be fastidious in writing and testing your code.

Have no fear, not all messages are that vague. For example, the cause and correction for this message is obvious:

```
The element type "xsl:textw" must be terminated by the matching end-tag "</xsl:textw>".
```

Since there is no xsl:textw element, simply search for *textw*, correct it to text, save, upload the revised XSL-FO file to a report layout, reassign the report query to the report layout, and retest. Yes, it is that many steps per change. And it is still worth it to be methodical, make small changes, and retest.

For this error message, the fix is again obvious but may be harder to find:

```
The element type "fo:block" must be terminated by the matching end-tag "</fo:block>".
```

Somewhere in your template is a missing or misspelled </fo:block> tag. If you have been editing in small increments, locating the error will be easier.

Start small and clean. Get a basic template working and then add features one at a time. Add, test, add, test. That way, when an error occurs, the source of that error is easier to find in the last changes you made.

Above all, debugging FOP output takes a lot of patience. There are few how-to examples out there other than the most basic examples. It is likely what you are looking for is not out there, and you will need to think, be clever, do some sleuthing, and be prepared to learn by trial and error to achieve customized features.

Third-Party Report Printing Solutions

Now back to the overall "report printing" solution. APEX offers standard printing, which was just covered, and advanced printing with Oracle BI Publisher. Beyond that, there are a number of third-party tools that can be integrated with APEX to provide more sophisticated reporting solutions.

The tools and products listed here each have their strengths and weaknesses. Some cost money; some are open source. Some require specific configuration to integrate with APEX. Others are as simple as building PL/SQL procedures or adding a plugin.

The right reporting tool for your organization depends on your reporting requirements, including staff, monetary, and time resources.

General Report Printing Solutions

Here are the 30-second elevator pitches for some commonly used reporting printing solutions for APEX instances:

> *BI Publisher*: An excellent Oracle-owned solution with a high price tag, unless already licensed for Oracle Business Intelligence products. Read the fine print for licensing combinations and costs.

> *PL/PDF*: A relatively low-code PL/SQL-based product for writing PL/SQL programs to generate PDF output. This is a popular option because no FOP processor is required. The downside is every report must be coded.

> *BIRT*: A Java Eclipse-based open source web reporting solution. There are two components, a Java-based Report Designer and a runtime component to deploy a J2EE application server. For organizations with Eclipse resources, this may be a good fit. For information on integrating BIRT and APEX, see https://emoracle. wordpress.com/2012/05/02/using-birt-with-apex-for-pdf-reports/.

> *Jasper Reports*: Perhaps the most popular APEX report printing option. Jasper Reports is another Java-based open source high-fidelity reporting tool for producing reports in various formats including PDF, RTF, and XLS. The best source for Jasper Reports and APEX information is by Dietmar Aust, at www.opal-consulting.de/apex/f?p=20090928:4:0.

Plugins: There are several solid plugins for providing PDF output for all or part of reports on a page. These provide no to limited formatting options and generally capture most interactive report configurations. See www.apexplugins.com for more information.

Crystal Reports: A SAP business intelligence reporting tool. Crystal Reports can also be configured to work with APEX. Those already invested in this tool may want to integrate with APEX.

Oracle Reports: May be integrated with APEX. Organizations with legacy Oracle Reports and an existing license may want to use this option.

Each of these solutions serves a different purpose. Each requires configuration of the report data and the report layout and configuring (or not) printing options. All of these can be integrated into APEX pages. None of these is perfect for every set of "report printing" requirements. If a more complete reporting solution is required for your organization, beyond what is offered by APEX standard printing and beyond what is practical with XSL-FO, investigate the previous option for possible solutions.

The Future

APEX 5.0 has no new standard printing features, other than the updated FOP processor (to FOP 1.1), which is arguably not APEX 5 but more ORDS and the external FOP processor. There are no significant new features for standard printing planned for APEX 5.1, though the APEX 5.1 Statement of Direction used to include the following statement:

> *"PDF Printing – Improve the printing capabilities utilizing the Oracle REST Data Services FOP Support."*

As of the release of APEX 5.0, the APEX 5.1 Statement of Direction was shortened, and the reference to PDF printing was removed. So, plan on no significant new features for a while. And plan on getting comfortable with XSL-FO for customized report layouts.

Summary

No, APEX does not have an out-of-the-box, WYSIWYG PDF output capability. APEX does *not* have an all-encompassing point-and-click report printing solution. And it never will; it is just too broad a feature to build. What APEX *does* have for standard report printing is basic output generation for classic and interactive reports and customized PDF output through the use of report queries and XSL-FO report templates.

The recommendation is to use APEX standard report printing options for as much as possible for cases where end users desire PDF output and specialized formatted output is not essential. Where equal-spaced columns are acceptable, embedded charts and graphs are not required, and where declarative settings can account for most report output configurations, APEX standard report printing is a viable no-cost minimal configuration option. When specific nontabular formats are involved, when graphics or charts are required, or when highlighted and color coding are required, use report queries and report layouts to achieve the desired report configuration.

Building XSL-FO templates is not as difficult as it seems. Though there is a learning curve involved, most configurations can be readily constructed with an investment in learning XSL-FO syntax and layout basics, plus time, patience, some sleuthing, and a bit of ingenuity. Good luck!

CHAPTER 15

■ ■ ■

Working with APEX Collections

by Raj Mattamal

When writing applications, developers often need a way to store an unknown number of items in a temporary structure. The most pervasive example of this is the online shopping cart. When a user browses an online store, developers don't know the number of items the user intends to purchase. To address this, application developers use collections to store these variable pieces of data.

The term *collections* itself is a rather general one. Many, if not most, programming techniques offer some method of storing variable collection–type data, and terms such as *arrays*, *sets*, and *lists* are common across them. In Oracle PL/SQL, the need to store collection data is most commonly met using constructs such as nested tables, varrays, and associative arrays. Unfortunately, these constructs aren't generally useful across pages of Oracle APEX applications because they tend to persist for the life of the given database session, whereas APEX page views can span multiple database sessions.

To address this need to temporarily manage an unknown number of items in an application user session that might span multiple database sessions, Oracle APEX offers APEX collections. Much in the same way that APEX manages the session-related information stored into page- and application-level items, APEX collections allow developers to temporarily store variable amounts of data within a user session without burdening the developer with the mechanics of session state management. What follows is an exploration of the need for collections, some common use cases, and tips and tricks that use collections.

When to Use APEX Collections

As already mentioned, APEX collections provide application developers an easy way to store variable amounts of data. When discussing this in the context of database applications, people often ask why the information shouldn't be stored in temporary tables. The answer to this is simple: APEX web applications are ultimately stateless, and each page view is generally a distinct database session. As temporary tables do not persist beyond the current database session, the data gathered from one page view or process in an APEX application won't be readily available in subsequent ones. It is logical then to consider using regular database tables to store collection data. In fact, APEX collections are stored in regular database tables, but the developer does not need to be aware of this. You will take a closer look at the back-end mechanics of collections later; for now, you can think of APEX collections almost as regular tables that are associated with the session of the user currently logged into the application. What makes collections an excellent choice for storing temporary data in APEX applications is that APEX manages the session state of the collections as users click through multiple page views, and by extension multiple database sessions, without the developer having to mind the underlying concepts. To appreciate this, it is worthwhile to take a quick look into this extra overhead that APEX manages behind the scenes.

Session State Management: A Quick Overview

Most conventional web application architectures are inherently stateless. Simply put, this means that the data is not retained between subsequent executions. To allow for more complex applications, though, many web architectures have mechanisms to retain or rejoin to session data so that processing can occur across page views in what amounts to a single application session or user session.

Oracle APEX approaches this by using a session cookie stored on the user's browser. When a user first instantiates a session in an APEX application, a session cookie is placed on the user's computer. When that user attempts to access the same application again with a valid cookie, APEX recognizes the returning user and makes that user's session data available. A simple example of how this would be useful is a multiple page survey that collects information from a user.

Imagine a user, John, is entering information into a web survey written in APEX. When John enters his name into an item on the first page, P1_NAME, and then clicks to the next, his name appears at the top of the second page in the form of static text, for example, "John's Survey Responses, Page 2." APEX was aware that it was John accessing the second page and not some random user because, behind the scenes, it recognized the valid session cookie and made that session's value of P1_NAME available to the application. It is certainly possible to manage this nontrivial logic on your own, but APEX does this incredibly efficiently and seamlessly for you. Later, when the user's session has been inactive for a significant period of time, APEX even purges the older data so that unnecessary values like P1_NAME aren't store beyond their usefulness.

Session State–Managed Tables

Similar to the way APEX handles session data for page- and application-level items, APEX collections allow developers an easy way to share data across page views without having to check for cookies and rejoin session data. In this sense, APEX collections can be thought of as tables that automatically provide session state management. With this concept in mind, you can take a deeper look into the logical workings of the traditional shopping cart example that so often is associated with APEX collections.

Logically Walking Through a Web Shopping Cart Implementation

If you built an APEX application to serve as a store for online purchases, you would need a way to track some basic information about the items being purchased by users as they browse your store. To have this data available at checkout time, you need to tie the data to the users' session in some way. Earlier, I walked through the example of a single APEX item, P1_NAME, whose data persists across user session page views, and this might meet your needs if your customers were allowed to buy only one book per store visit—however, that's an unlikely rule. To store information about the unknown number of items your customers might buy, you would want to create a collection storing information such as the product description, price, and quantity purchased. This way, as the user clicked between pages of your online store, APEX would automatically recognize returning users and make their shopping cart available each time. At checkout, you could take the information gathered in the collection, process it as necessary, and store the relevant details in some sort of Orders table. To avoid clutter, you could then drop the collection—but if you overlooked this advisable course, APEX would handle the purging for you at a later time.

A Look Under the Covers

Before actually discussing APEX collection use cases and techniques, it is worthwhile to take a quick peek into the APEX engine to see how collection data is stored and made available to developers. As mentioned earlier, APEX collections are in fact stored in regular database tables. Once this data is stored, users can then access it via the publically available APEX_COLLECTIONS synonym, which in turn points to the

WWV_FLOW_COLLECTIONS view in the APEX engine schema. Ultimately, it is only the APEX_COLLECTIONS view and the associated APEX_COLLECTION API that developers need to familiarize themselves with. Still, in the interest of thoroughness, let's take a deeper dive.

Private Collections Objects Inside the APEX Engine

The APEX engine is effectively a single schema in the database with some helper schemas to serve specific purposes. It is within this main schema that APEX stores all its session data. Collection data is no exception to this. Specifically, APEX collections are stored entirely in two tables: WWV_FLOW_COLLECTIONS$ and WWV_FLOW_COLLECTION_MEMBERS$. A quick glance at the column names in Listing 15-1 shows you that the WWV_FLOW_COLLECTIONS$ table doesn't store application data. Instead, it stores the information APEX needs to handle the session state management functionality discussed earlier.

Listing 15-1. Description of the WWV_FLOW_COLLECTIONS$ Table

```
SQL> desc WWV_FLOW_COLLECTIONS$
```

Name	Null?	Type
ID	NOT NULL	NUMBER
SESSION_ID	NOT NULL	NUMBER
USER_ID	NOT NULL	VARCHAR2(255)
FLOW_ID	NOT NULL	NUMBER
COLLECTION_NAME	NOT NULL	VARCHAR2(255)
COLLECTION_CHANGED	NOT NULL	VARCHAR2(10)
CREATED_ON	NOT NULL	DATE
SECURITY_GROUP_ID	NOT NULL	NUMBER

When you take a look at the second collections table's description in Listing 15-2, you immediately see what appear to be placeholder columns for data such as C001 and C002 for text, N001 for numbers, and D001 for dates. It is into this table that APEX stores its collection data, but, again, it uses WWV_FLOW_COLLECTIONS$ to expose the right collected data to the right sessions in the right applications.

Listing 15-2. Description of the WWV_FLOW_COLLECTION_MEMBERS$ Table

```
SQL> desc WWV_FLOW_COLLECTION_MEMBERS$
```

Name	Null?	Type
COLLECTION_ID	NOT NULL	NUMBER
SEQ_ID	NOT NULL	NUMBER
C001		VARCHAR2(4000)
C002		VARCHAR2(4000)
C003		VARCHAR2(4000)
C004		VARCHAR2(4000)
C005		VARCHAR2(4000)
C006		VARCHAR2(4000)
C007		VARCHAR2(4000)
C008		VARCHAR2(4000)
C009		VARCHAR2(4000)
C010		VARCHAR2(4000)

C011	VARCHAR2(4000)
C012	VARCHAR2(4000)
C013	VARCHAR2(4000)
C014	VARCHAR2(4000)
C015	VARCHAR2(4000)
C016	VARCHAR2(4000)
C017	VARCHAR2(4000)
C018	VARCHAR2(4000)
C019	VARCHAR2(4000)
C020	VARCHAR2(4000)
C021	VARCHAR2(4000)
C022	VARCHAR2(4000)
C023	VARCHAR2(4000)
C024	VARCHAR2(4000)
C025	VARCHAR2(4000)
C026	VARCHAR2(4000)
C027	VARCHAR2(4000)
C028	VARCHAR2(4000)
C029	VARCHAR2(4000)
C030	VARCHAR2(4000)
C031	VARCHAR2(4000)
C032	VARCHAR2(4000)
C033	VARCHAR2(4000)
C034	VARCHAR2(4000)
C035	VARCHAR2(4000)
C036	VARCHAR2(4000)
C037	VARCHAR2(4000)
C038	VARCHAR2(4000)
C039	VARCHAR2(4000)
C040	VARCHAR2(4000)
C041	VARCHAR2(4000)
C042	VARCHAR2(4000)
C043	VARCHAR2(4000)
C044	VARCHAR2(4000)
C045	VARCHAR2(4000)
C046	VARCHAR2(4000)
C047	VARCHAR2(4000)
C048	VARCHAR2(4000)
C049	VARCHAR2(4000)
C050	VARCHAR2(4000)
N001	NUMBER
N002	NUMBER
N003	NUMBER
N004	NUMBER
N005	NUMBER
D001	DATE
D002	DATE
D003	DATE
D004	DATE
D005	DATE
CLOB001	CLOB
BLOB001	BLOB

```
MD5_ORIGINAL                               VARCHAR2(4000)
SECURITY_GROUP_ID              NOT NULL NUMBER
XMLTYPE001                                 SYS.XMLTYPE STORAGE BINARY
```

Public Collections Objects Inside the APEX Engine

As already said, APEX exposes its collection data to developers in the form of the APEX_COLLECTIONS public synonym. A quick glance at Listing 15-3 shows that the view associated with APEX_COLLECTIONS, WWV_FLOW_ COLLECTIONS, closely mirrors the columns in the WWV_FLOW_COLLECTION_MEMBERS$ table.

Listing 15-3. Description of the APEX_COLLECTIONS View

```
SQL> desc APEX_COLLECTIONS

Name                                       Null?    Type
------------------------------------------ -------- ---------------------------
COLLECTION_NAME                            NOT NULL VARCHAR2(255)
SEQ_ID                                     NOT NULL NUMBER
C001                                                VARCHAR2(4000)
C002                                                VARCHAR2(4000)
C003                                                VARCHAR2(4000)
C004                                                VARCHAR2(4000)
C005                                                VARCHAR2(4000)
C006                                                VARCHAR2(4000)
C007                                                VARCHAR2(4000)
C008                                                VARCHAR2(4000)
C009                                                VARCHAR2(4000)
C010                                                VARCHAR2(4000)
C011                                                VARCHAR2(4000)
C012                                                VARCHAR2(4000)
C013                                                VARCHAR2(4000)
C014                                                VARCHAR2(4000)
C015                                                VARCHAR2(4000)
C016                                                VARCHAR2(4000)
C017                                                VARCHAR2(4000)
C018                                                VARCHAR2(4000)
C019                                                VARCHAR2(4000)
C020                                                VARCHAR2(4000)
C021                                                VARCHAR2(4000)
C022                                                VARCHAR2(4000)
C023                                                VARCHAR2(4000)
C024                                                VARCHAR2(4000)
C025                                                VARCHAR2(4000)
C026                                                VARCHAR2(4000)
C027                                                VARCHAR2(4000)
C028                                                VARCHAR2(4000)
C029                                                VARCHAR2(4000)
C030                                                VARCHAR2(4000)
C031                                                VARCHAR2(4000)
C032                                                VARCHAR2(4000)
C033                                                VARCHAR2(4000)
C034                                                VARCHAR2(4000)
```

CO35	VARCHAR2(4000)
CO36	VARCHAR2(4000)
CO37	VARCHAR2(4000)
CO38	VARCHAR2(4000)
CO39	VARCHAR2(4000)
CO40	VARCHAR2(4000)
CO41	VARCHAR2(4000)
CO42	VARCHAR2(4000)
CO43	VARCHAR2(4000)
CO44	VARCHAR2(4000)
CO45	VARCHAR2(4000)
CO46	VARCHAR2(4000)
CO47	VARCHAR2(4000)
CO48	VARCHAR2(4000)
CO49	VARCHAR2(4000)
CO50	VARCHAR2(4000)
CLOB001	CLOB
BLOB001	BLOB
XMLTYPE001	SYS.XMLTYPE STORAGE BINARY
N001	NUMBER
N002	NUMBER
N003	NUMBER
N004	NUMBER
N005	NUMBER
D001	DATE
D002	DATE
D003	DATE
D004	DATE
D005	DATE
MD5_ORIGINAL	VARCHAR2(4000)

So, although APEX developers do not need to be aware of the underlying tables in the main APEX engine schema, familiarizing yourself with the structure of the exposed APEX_COLLECTIONS view is helpful when developing. The most important points to glean from this are

- The data in APEX_COLLECTIONS is effectively keyed off by the COLLECTION_NAME and SEQ_ID columns.

- The remaining columns of the APEX collections infrastructure allows for the storing of multiple data types.

  - Varchar2

  - BLOBs

  - CLOBs

  - XMLTYPEs

  - Numbers

  - Dates

  - The number of values that can be stored per row is limited to the number of columns exposed in the view. (Workarounds for this will be discussed later in the chapter.)

The other publically accessible part of the APEX collections infrastructure is the PL/SQL API, APEX_COLLECTION, which you will explore in the next section.

Getting Started with Collections

With a basic understanding of the APEX collections infrastructure, you are now ready to start using them. To do so, let's use the example that comes available with every APEX instance, the sample database application demonstration.

■ **Note** If the sample database application isn't already available in your APEX workspace, it can quickly be installed by clicking the Create icon atop the Application Builder home, clicking Packaged Applications, and then selecting the sample database application.

Much like the shopping cart example, the sample database application allows users to create an order form for a variable number of products. Once the desired number of products has been selected, the user can place the order, which effectively moves the collection data to the more permanent tables stored in the application schema. To achieve this, a few key APEX_COLLECTION API calls are used, and these are the first methods to understand when using collections. The application actually performs these functions in both its desktop and mobile interfaces, so I will walk you through these methods in the application's mobile interface next.

Initializing a Collection

Before using a collection, it is necessary to define it in the context of the current application session. This can be thought of as initialization. To access the mobile page in the sample database application where the collection is first referenced, log in, click the Mobile option in the top navigation bar, and then click the Monthly Orders option in the panel menu. Once there, clicking the Create button takes the user to page 216 of the application, and this is where your collection is first referenced. Specifically, a new collection is initialized in a PL/SQL Anonymous Block process that fires Before Header when the user first comes to page 11 (see Listing 15-4).

Listing 15-4. Initializing a Collection called ORDER

```
apex_collection.create_or_truncate_collection
  (p_collection_name => 'ORDER');
```

As shown in Listing 15-4, this initial call to the APEX_COLLECTION API offers developers a means from one API call to either clear out any collection called ORDER or, if one does not yet exist, to create it. It is important to note here that the APEX_COLLECTION API indeed offers separate procedures to create and truncate collections, but most APEX developers tend to use the create_or_truncate call to eliminate the need to check for the collection's existence before resetting it. Listing 15-5 shows the somewhat more cumbersome way to achieve the same collection initialization as in Listing 15-4.

Listing 15-5. Initializing a Collection Called ORDER Using More Granular Methods

```
begin
    if not apex_collection.collection_exists('ORDER') then
        apex_collection.create_collection('ORDER');
    else
        apex_collection.truncate_collection('ORDER');
    end if;
end;
```

The important points to note from this longer example are

- Collection names must be unique within an application session. Because of this requirement, the best practice is to check for the existence of the ORDERS collection before attempting to create it.

- Attempting to manipulate a collection that does not exist returns an error. To avoid this, the best practice before performing operations such as truncating the collection is to check for its existence first.

Again, though, more often than not, developers tend to use the simpler call shown in Listing 15-4 over the more granular ones shown in Listing 15-5 unless there is a compelling need for the finer control.

Adding and Removing Data from Collections

Once the collection is initialized within an application session, the APEX_COLLECTION API offers numerous ways to manipulate its contents. You will explore the two simple methods from the sample database application in this section, and then you will explore some more advanced techniques.

After selecting a customer name from page 216 of the sample database application and clicking the Next button, the user is taken to page 217. From this page, clicking links on the right side of the screen adds or removes members from the current ORDER ollection. Before examining these actions, it is important to understand what exactly a collection member is.

As mentioned earlier, APEX collections are effectively session-based tables. When examining the APEX_ COLLECTIONS view in Listing 15-4, you saw that collection rows have a specific format with the VARCHARs first, large object types next, and so on. A collection member is simply a row in the APEX_COLLECTIONS view, and it will always conform to the structure of the APEX_COLLECTIONS view. The needs of the sample database application are simple, and so it suffices to store the collected data into the first few member columns of the collection even though those columns are VARCHAR2s and some of those member attributes are actually numbers. The sample database application uses the Before Header PL/SQL process from page 217, Add Product to the ORDER Collection, shown in Listing 15-6.

Listing 15-6. Adding a Member to the ORDER Collection

```
declare
  l_count number := 0;
begin
for x in (select p.rowid, p.* from demo_product_info p where product_id = :P217_PRODUCT_ID)
loop
  ...
  apex_collection.add_member(
    p_collection_name => 'ORDER',
    p_c001 => x.product_id,
    p_c002 => x.product_name,
    p_c003 => x.list_price,
```

```
    p_c004 => 1,
    p_c010 => x.rowid);
end loop;
end;
```

However, if you wanted, for example, to later perform aggregate functions on the number values stored, it would be better to store the numeric values into the NUMBER columns. This is done by simply passing the numeric value into the ADD_MEMBER numeric input parameters rather than the VARCHAR2 ones, as shown in Listing 15-7.

Listing 15-7. Adding a Member to the ORDER Collection

```
for x in (select * from demo_product_info where product_id = :P217_PRODUCT_ID)
loop
  apex_collection.add_member(
    p_collection_name => 'ORDER',
    p_c001 => x.product_id,
    p_c002 => x.product_name,
    p_c010 => x.rowid,
    p_n001 => x.list_price,
    p_n002 => 1);
end loop;
end;
```

Upon further examining this PL/SQL block, you can see that your collection will end up storing one row for every item added to the order, regardless of quantity. Again, although this suffices for the needs of the sample database application, there might be cases where you would want to update the quantity column for repeated product selections rather than simply inserting a new collection row each time. Doing so affords you the opportunity to use the UPDATE_MEMBER method, as shown in Listing 15-8.

Listing 15-8. Updating an Existing Member When Available

```
declare
    l_product_already_added boolean := false;
begin
    -- check if product was already selected and update member if so
    for x1 in (select seq_id, n002
                 from apex_collections
                where collection_name = 'ORDER'
                  and c001 = :P217_PRODUCT_ID)
    loop
        l_product_already_added := true;
        apex_collection.update_member_attribute (
          p_collection_name => 'ORDER',
          p_seq => x1.seq_id,
          p_attr_number => 2
          p_number_value => x1.noo2 + 1);
    end loop;

    -- insert new collection row if product wasn't previously selected
    if not l_product_already_added then
        for x2 in (select * from demo_product_info where product_id = :P217_PRODUCT_ID)
        loop
```

```
        apex_collection.add_member(
          p_collection_name => 'ORDER',
          p_c001 => x2.product_id,
          p_c002 => x2.product_name,
          p_c010 => x2.rowid,
          p_n001 => x2.list_price,
          p_n002 => 1);
      end loop;
    end if;
end;
```

This approach offers a cleaner way to store the data in your scenario, of course, but it also highlights one of the overloaded `UPDATE_MEMBER_ATTRIBUTE` procedures available in the `APEX_COLLECTION` API. More specifically, `UPDATE_MEMBER_ATTRIBUTE` comes in six overloaded varieties—one for each of the support APEX collection datatypes. Listing 15-8 calls the one that's intended for the numeric columns, and because you're updating the second numeric column, `APEX_COLLECTIONS.N002`, you pass in a `p_attr_number` value of 2.

■ **Note**   APEX versions prior to 4.x did not support numeric, date, BLOB, or XMLTYPE data. Therefore, the equivalent overloaded update procedures are not available in those versions.

Deleting an attribute member is a simple matter of calling the `DELETE_MEMBER` procedure in `APEX_COLLECTION`. You can see this in action in the sample database application when users click the X link next to an item selected in their shopping carts. Also defined on page 217 of the application, the call just requires the two values that effectively key your collections view, the collection name, and the sequence ID of the member to be removed, as shown in Listing 15-9.

Listing 15-9. Removing a Member from the ORDER Collection

```
for x in
  (select seq_id, c001 from apex_collections
    where collection_name = 'ORDER' and c001 = :P217_PRODUCT_ID)
loop
  apex_collection.delete_member(
    p_collection_name => 'ORDER',
    p_seq => x.seq_id);
end loop;
```

This simple `DELETE_MEMBER` procedure works fine for the default implementation within the sample database application, but it would not suffice for the more advanced implementation suggested when using `UPDATE_MEMBER`. In that case, your collection can store multiple instances of a selected product per row, so you need to adjust your code to update it accordingly. As shown in Listing 15-10, this is accomplished with the same procedure call used in the more advanced implementation of the addition of new members.

Listing 15-10. Removing a Product from the ORDER Collection

```
begin
    -- get seq_id of member containing product to be removed
    for x1 in (select seq_id, n002
                 from apex_collections
```

```
              where collection_name = 'ORDER'
                and c001 = :P217_PRODUCT_ID)
   loop
       -- reduce quantity of collection member by 1
       apex_collection.update_member_attribute (
          p_collection_name => 'ORDER',
          p_seq => x1.seq_id,
          p_attr_number => 2
          p_number_value => x1.noo2 - 1);
   end loop;
end;
```

Using the Collection Contents

After a user is done selecting products and clicks the Place Order button on that screen, a page-level PL/SQL
process is executed that does the two final pieces of the initial collections walk-through: it makes use of the
collected information and deletes the APEX collection to free up resources. You have already seen examples
of querying the collection contents in both of the more advanced order management code sections earlier,
and, as you can see in Listing 15-11, this final use of the ORDERS collection is no different. With the
collection contents stored more permanently in a table in your schema, DEMO_ORDER_ITEMS, you are able to
clear out the contents using the TRUNCATE_COLLECTION call.

Listing 15-11. Using and Then Emptying the Collection Contents

```
-- Loop through the ORDER collection and insert rows into the Order Line Item table
for x in (select c001, c003, sum(c004) c004 from apex_collections
  where collection_name = 'ORDER' group by c001, c003)
loop
   insert into demo_order_items values
      (null, l_order_id, to_number(x.c001), to_number(x.c003),to_number(x.c004));
end loop;
...
-- Truncate the collection after the order has been placed
apex_collection.truncate_collection(p_collection_name => 'ORDER');
```

A final detail to observe from the walk-through is the simple validation that is executed when the user
clicks the Place Order button. Specifically, note the validation a function from the APEX_COLLECTION API
called COLLECTION_MEMBER_COUNT, as shown in Listing 15-12. As the name suggests, this function returns the
number of items (rows) stored in a given collection.

Listing 15-12. Counting Collection Members via the APEX_COLLECTION API

```
apex_collection.collection_member_count('ORDER') >= 1;
```

The validation could have equivalently queried the count of relevant rows from the APEX_COLLECTIONS
view, but using the provided API function keeps the code short and tidy.

Exploring Another Use Case

Another common scenario in which APEX developers use collections in their applications is to store check box values that are checked in paginated reports. The reason for this is that check boxes rendered inline in a report are generally created using the APEX_ITEM API. Form elements rendered using this API do not support the same notion of session state as regular APEX page- and application-level items. Instead, the elements are rendered, and the developer is required to programmatically store the submitted values. Given this, when report rows are paginated, APEX won't automatically remember which rows were checked on a prior screen if the user has navigated away. In the case where a user is presented with check boxes in each row of a long report, the checked values will be forgotten each time the user clicks the report's Previous and Forward navigation options. Put simply, if the user checks a row on the first page of the result set, clicks Next to view the next set of records, and then clicks Back to return to the beginning, the user will find that the originally checked rows are no longer checked. For this reason, developers save checked values in a collection so that APEX has the values available to it when the user navigates back to prior pages. It is this association between the user's session and the user's checked values that makes APEX collections ideally suited to this purpose.

Expanding the Example

To better understand how to save check box values implemented using collections, let's modify the sample database application to allow users to delete orders in bulk directly from the main Orders page. Specifically, you will add check boxes to each row of the Orders listing as well as a new Delete Checked button to page 4 of the application, which will allow users to delete the rows checked. As the user clicks each check box, you'll store the associated values to a collection to be processed upon the user clicking the Delete Checked button.

Setting Up the Example

Before getting into collection processing, let's set up the UI for this expanded example. Start by adding a new button to page 4 of the application within the Breadcrumbs [Global Page] region. When creating the new button, accept all the default values except for the attributes shown in Listing 15-13. Doing so will make the new button match the Enter New Order button already on that page.

Listing 15-13. Attributes for New Delete Checked Orders Button

```
Button Name: DELETE_CHECKED
Label: Delete Checked Rows
Region: Breadcrumbs [Global Page]
Button Position: Create
Button Template: Text with Icon
```

Shortly, you'll modify the query in the Orders region to render the check boxes, but let's first add some of the supporting pieces to manage the new collection. Start by adding three application-level processes to perform the PL/SQL used to manage the checked values. To create the first process, navigate to the Application Processes section within the Shared Components section of the sample database application. Next click the Create button, enter a Name of **store_checked_order**, select "On Demand: Run this application process when requested by a page process" for Point, and click Next. Enter the code shown in Listing 15-14, click Next, and then click Create Process.

Listing 15-14. PL/SQL to Be Called Upon Check Box Clicks

```
declare
    l_collection_name    varchar2(1000) := 'CHECKED_ORDERS';
    l_order_id           number := wwv_flow.g_x01;
    l_value_unchecked    boolean := false;
begin
    --
    -- create the collection in case it's not already there
    --
    if not apex_collection.collection_exists(l_collection_name) then
        apex_collection.create_collection(l_collection_name);
    end if;
    --
    -- check collection contents to see if order is already stored
    --    if so, this row was UNchecked as opposed to checked
    --
    for c1 in (select seq_id
                 from apex_collections c
                where c.collection_name = l_collection_name
                  and c.c001 = l_order_id)
    loop
        --
        -- remove order row from collection
        --
        apex_collection.delete_member(
            p_collection_name => l_collection_name
           ,p_seq => c1.seq_id);
        --
        -- note that the value was unchecked
        --
        l_value_unchecked := true;
    end loop;
    --
    -- add order to collection if it wasn't unchecked
    --
    if not l_value_unchecked then
        apex_collection.add_member(
            p_collection_name => l_collection_name
           ,p_c001            => l_order_id);
    end if;
end;
```

The PL/SQL in the new process will be called from JavaScript when users check or uncheck orders on page 4. Although this code uses many of the same APEX_COLLECTION calls you've already reviewed, it brings them together into one block to intelligently add or remove ORDER_ID values into the new collection. Reviewing the comments within the code, you can also see that the process will create the collection if it's not already there. This logic is included so that you're guaranteed to have a place to store the ORDER_ID even on the first click. As an additional note, it would be slightly more performant to have the calls to apex_collection.add_member use the numeric p_n001 parameter instead of the varchar2 p_c001 parameter that's shown because values passed into p_n001 are stored in the numeric collections column, N001, saving you from having to rely on implicit conversions later. For simplicity later in the example, however, you'll have the code use the first available collection column, C001. (Please see Listing 15-3 for a description of these columns in the APEX_COLLECTIONS view.)

Beyond allowing users to check individual check boxes, the example will include a check box at the top of the report to allow users to check or uncheck all the rows of the report. The two remaining application processes you will create support the "uncheck all" and "check all" functionalities, respectively.

Create a new application process exactly as you did for store_checked_order, but call this one unstore_all and have it use the PL/SQL, as shown in Listing 15-15.

Listing 15-15. Source for unstore_all Application Process

```
begin
    --
    -- remove any stored values in collection
    --
    apex_collection.create_or_truncate_collection ('CHECKED_ORDERS');
end;
```

Notice here that even though the purpose of this process is to clear out any values stored in the CHECKED_ORDERS collection, you are using the create_or_truncate API call. This is a common technique used by APEX developers because it accomplishes the goal of clearing out the collection while not having to check first for its existence. If you had used the more intuitive delete_collection procedure, there's a risk that APEX would return an error if for some reason the collection hadn't already been created. To get around this possible error, a lengthier way to code the unstore_all process is shown in Listing 15-16.

Listing 15-16. Alternate Source for unstore_all Application Process

```
begin
    --
    -- first check to see a collection was instantiated
    --
    if apex_collection.collection_exists('CHECKED_ORDERS') then
        --
        -- delete the collection (and its members)
        --
        apex_collection.delete_collection('CHECKED_ORDERS');
    end if;
end;
```

The last application process you need to create effectively replaces the collection contents with all available ORDER_IDs when the user checks the Check All check box. Create the new application process the same way you did for the prior two processes, but call this one store_all and have it use the PL/SQL shown in Listing 15-17. (Please note that this process calls the APEX_IR API to fetch the last version of the report shown on page 4. This is done in case the user has filtered the rows displayed before checking the Check All check box. By calling the APEX_IR API, you will know exactly what order numbers were presented on the screen when the user clicked Check All.)

Listing 15-17. PL/SQL Source for store_all Application Process

```
declare
    l_collection_name    varchar2(1000) := 'CHECKED_ORDERS';
    l_report             apex_ir.t_report;
    l_ir_query           varchar2(32767) default null;
```

```
    l_collection_query  varchar2(32767) default null;
    l_names             wwv_flow_global.vc_arr2;
    l_values            wwv_flow_global.vc_arr2;
begin
    --
    -- query the apex interactive reports view to find the
    --   region_id of the "Orders" Interactive Report
    --
    for c1 in (select region_id
                  from apex_application_page_ir
                 where application_id = :APP_ID
                   and page_id = 4)
    loop
        --
        -- use the region_id value to fetch the last viewed
        --   version of the Orders report
        --
        l_report := apex_ir.get_report (
                        p_page_id => 4,
                        p_region_id => c1.region_id);
        l_ir_query := l_report.sql_query;
    end loop;
    --
    -- apex interactive report query will contain bind variables
    --      internal to apex, so use the bind information fetched
    --      into the l_report variable to separate the respective
    --      names and values
    --
    for i in 1..l_report.binds.count loop
        l_names(l_names.count + 1) := l_report.binds(i).name;
        l_values(l_values.count + 1) := l_report.binds(i).value;
    end loop;
    --
    -- wrap the fetched query with one that just
    --   selects the order_id values
    --
    l_collection_query := 'select order_id from ('||l_ir_query ||')';
    --
    -- delete the collection if one already exists
    --
    if apex_collection.collection_exists(l_collection_name) then
        apex_collection.delete_collection(l_collection_name);
    end if;
    --
    -- (re)create the CHECKED_ORDERS collection using
    -- the new query which will store all shown order_ids
    -- from page 4.
    --
```

```
    apex_collection.create_collection_from_query_b (
        p_collection_name => l_collection_name,
        p_query => l_collection_query,
        p_names => l_names,
        p_values => l_values);
end;
```

This final application process introduces a powerful APEX_COLLECTION procedure, create_collection_ from _query_b. As the name suggests, the procedure takes in a query and stores its result set into a new collection. It's worth mentioning that the APEX_COLLECTION API also offers a simpler CREATE_COLLECTION_ FROM_QUERY procedure, but it is advisable to call CREATE_COLLECTION_FROM_QUERY_B whenever possible because it takes advantage of bulk SQL operations for better performance.

With the three application processes created, you need to put some logic on page 4 directly and add the check boxes to the report to complete the expanded example. The logic needed on page 4 comes in the form of two JavaScript snippets to call your application processes and one PL/SQL process that actually deletes the checked orders. You'll start by adding the JavaScript snippets to the page header. Within the APEX builder, navigate to the definition of page 4, and enter the text shown in Listing 15-18 in the Function and Global Variable Declaration field with the JavaScript region of the page-level attributes.

Listing 15-18. JavaScript to Call the New Application Processes

```
function storeCheckedOrder(pOrderId){
    //  use apex.server javascript api to call our app-level
    //  process, store_checked_order, passing in the order_id  to be stored.
    apex.server.process("store_checked_order", {x01: pOrderId}, {dataType: 'text'});
}


$(document).ready(function(){
    $('#selectAllCheckboxes').on('click',function(){
    // if the check all checkbox was checked,
    // mark all checkboxes in the report as checked and
    // call the store_all application process
        if ($(this).is(':checked')) {
            $("input:checkbox[id^='del_']").each(function(){
                this.checked = true;
            });
    apex.server.process("store_all", {x01: null}, {dataType: 'text'});
    // if the check all checkbox was UNchecked,
    // mark all checkboxes in the report as unchecked and
    // call the unstore_all application process to clear the collection
        }else{
            $("input:checkbox[id^='del_']").each(function(){
                this.checked = false;
            });
    apex.server.process("unstore_all", {x01: null}, {dataType: 'text'});
        }
    })
});
```

Reviewing the script in Listing 15-18, you can see that it contains two pieces: the JavaScript function, storeCheckedOrder, which calls the store_checked_order application process via an XMLHttpRequest, and a jQuery-based JavaScript snippet that calls the other two application-level processes you added depending on whether the user has checked or unchecked the Check All check box. Please note that many APEX developers prefer to handle the JavaScript logic over using APEX dynamic actions. You're using regular JavaScript in this example so as to reduce the number of steps.

Now you are ready to add the final piece of logic to page 4, which is the process that actually deletes the selected orders. This logic will be implemented in the form of a PL/SQL process that fires when the user clicks the DELETE_CHECKED button you added earlier. To add the process, enter the PL/SQL shown in Listing 15-19 into the source of a new process on page 4 that has the attributes shown in Listing 15-20.

Listing 15-19. PL/SQL Source for Delete Checked Orders Page Process

```
declare
    l_collection_name    varchar2(100) := 'CHECKED_ORDERS';
begin
    --
    -- loop through collection of order_id's
    --      and delete associated order rows
    --
    for c1 in (select c.c001 order_id
                    from apex_collections c
                where collection_name = l_collection_name)
    loop
        delete from demo_orders where order_id = c1.order_id;
    end loop;
    --
    -- drop the collection now that we're done
    --
    apex_collection.delete_collection (l_collection_name);
end;
```

Listing 15-20. Attributes for Delete Checked Orders Page Process

```
Process Name: Delete Checked Orders
Type:  PL/SQL Code
Point: Processing
Success Message: Successfully Deleted Checked Orders
Error Message: Failed to Delete Checked Orders
When Button Pressed: DELETE_CHECKED
```

Next, let's add check boxes to the report. To do so, you'll simply add a new column to the query used in the Orders region. As mentioned earlier, check boxes to be rendered within reports are best added using the APEX_ITEM API. In this case, you'll use the CHECKBOX2 function and indicate that it should call our storeCheckedOrder JavaScript with each click. Beyond calling storeCheckedOrder, the other consideration for the check boxes is to have them remember previously checked values. This is actually the heart of the example in that you need to refer to your collection for those saved checked values in case the user has navigated off the page after making selections and comes back. As collection values are easily accessible from the apex_collections view, you simply need to join it into your query and refer to its stored ORDER_IDs when calling CHECKBOX2. Both of these changes are reflected in Listing 15-21, so replace the current source of the Orders report region with the query shown in the listing.

Listing 15-21. New Query Source for Orders Report

```
select lpad(to_char(o.order_id),4,'0000') order_number,
    o.order_id,
    to_char(o.order_timestamp,'Month YYYY') order_month,
    trunc(o.order_timestamp) order_date,
    o.user_name sales_rep,
    o.order_total,
    c.cust_last_name||', '||c.cust_first_name customer_name,
    (   select count(*)
        from demo_order_items oi
        where oi.order_id = o.order_id
            and oi.quantity != 0 ) order_items,
    o.tags tags,
    --new column below renders checkboxes
    APEX_ITEM.CHECKBOX2(
        p_idx => 1,
        p_value => o.order_id,
        -- attribute parameter is used here to have checkboxes
        -- call storeCheckedOrder passing in the order_id
        -- with each click
        p_attributes => ' onclick="javascript:storeCheckedOrder('||o.order_id||');" '
            --attribute parm is being used to conditionally set the checkbox to Checked
            --when the order_id is one of the ones in our collection.
            || DECODE(col.order_id,o.order_id,'CHECKED',null),
        p_item_id => 'del_'||o.order_id ) delete_chk
from demo_orders o,
    demo_customers c,
    (select c.c001 order_id
        from apex_collections c
        where collection_name = 'CHECKED_ORDERS') col
where o.customer_id = c.customer_id
  -- use an outter join to join in the collection as
  -- it might only contain a subset of all order_id's
  and o.order_id = col.order_id  (+)
```

The last detail necessary to complete the example is to adjust the column header for the new checkbox column so that it cleanly renders a Check All check box. To do so, navigate to the column attributes screen for the new DELETE_CHK column and replace the Heading attribute with the text shown in Listing 15-22.

Listing 15-22. New Column Heading for Check Box Column

```
Delete<BR /><input type="checkbox" ID="selectAllCheckboxes">
```

Disable all the Enable Users To options presented on the DELETE_CHK column header attributes screen. Specifically, this entails toggling the selectors for Hide, Sort, Filter, Highlight Control Break, Aggregate, Compute, Chart, Group By, and Pivot to No. Additionally, set the Escape Special Characters attribute to No. Disabling these extra features allows the column header to cleanly render without advanced interactive report functionality interfering.

Finally, set the "Escape special characters" option to No.

With the setup complete, your page 4 should resemble Figure 15-1. Your sample database application now uses a collection called CHECKED_ORDERS to store ORDER_IDs and delete them in bulk. After adding a few orders, try checking some values on one page of the result set, navigate to the next, and notice your values are still checked when you return to the prior page. Notice, too, that if you check the Check All check box on one page of the resultset and navigate to the next, those order are checked as well. All of this is made possible by using an APEX collection to remember which orders were checked.

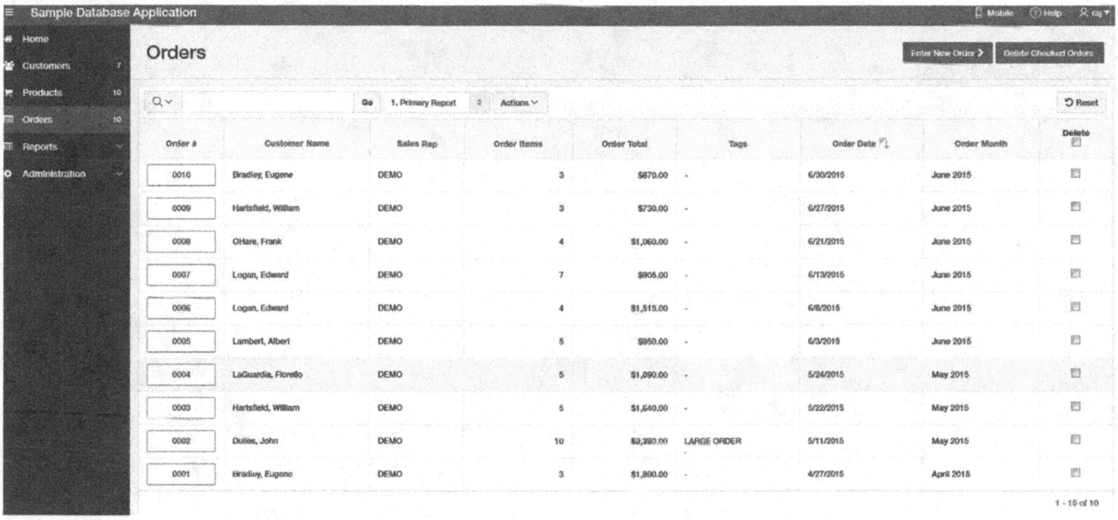

Figure 15-1. Adjusted order form

Summary

Offering the ability to extend APEX's native session state management functionality into session-based tables, APEX collections still tend to be surprisingly underused among beginner and even intermediate APEX developers. Using the techniques described in this chapter, I hope that more developers will take advantage of this powerful functionality available within APEX applications. Although I have covered only the most conventional uses of APEX collections here, a quick search on the Web will reveal developers thinking outside of the proverbial box to use collections to bring new and even unforeseen power to their APEX applications.

Index

■ L

■ M

■ N

■ O

〈IOUG〉 independent oracle users group · *For the Complete Technology & Database Professional*

IOUG represents the **voice of Oracle technology and database professionals** - empowering you to be **more productive in your business** and career by **delivering education,** sharing **best practices** and providing technology direction and **networking opportunities.**

Context, Not Just Content

IOUG is dedicated to helping our members become an #IOUGenius by staying on the cutting-edge of Oracle technologies and industry issues through practical content, user-focused education, and invaluable networking and leadership opportunities:

- *SELECT Journal* is our quarterly publication that provides in-depth, peer-reviewed articles on industry news and best practices in Oracle technology

- Our #IOUGenius blog highlights a featured weekly topic and provides **content driven by Oracle professionals and the IOUG community**

- Special Interest Groups provide you the chance to collaborate with peers on the specific issues that matter to you and even take on leadership roles outside of your organization

- COLLABORATE is our once-a-year opportunity to connect with the members of not one, but three, Oracle users groups (IOUG, OAUG and Quest) as well as with the top names and faces in the Oracle community.

Who we are...

... **more than 20,000** database professionals, developers, application and infrastructure architects, business intelligence specialists and IT managers

... **a community of users** that share experiences and knowledge on issues and technologies that matter to you and your organization

Interested? Join IOUG's community of Oracle technology and database professionals at www.ioug.org/Join.

Independent Oracle Users Group | phone: (312) 245-1579 | email: membership@ioug.org
330 N. Wabash Ave., Suite 2000, Chicago, IL 60611

Printed in the United States
by Bookmasters

Printed in the United States
By Bookmasters